THE

HISTORICAL GEOGRAPHY OF EUROPE

THE HISTORICAL GEOGRAPHY OF EUROPE

BY

EDWARD A. FREEMAN, D.C.L., LL D.

FORMERLY REGIUS PROF. OF MODERN HISTORY IN THE UNIVERSITY OF OXFORD

THIRD EDITION WITH A PREFACE AND EDITED BY

J. B. BURY, M.A., D.Litt., LL.D.

REGIUS PROFESSOR OF MODERN HISTORY IN THE UNIVERSITY OF CAMBRIDGE

ARES PUBLISHERS INC.
CHICAGO MCMLXXIV

Unchanged Reprint of the Edition:
London, 1903.
ARES PUBLISHERS INC.
150 E. Huron Street
Chicago, Illinois 60611
Printed in the United States of America
International Standard Book Number:
0-89005-045-7
Library of Congress Catalog Card Number:
74-82062

PREFATORY NOTE

TO

THE THIRD EDITION

While this book does not rank with the most important of Mr. Freeman's historical works, it is not too much to say that none of them is more original. It is remarkable for the novelty of its conception, and for the perfectly amazing skill with which he has marshalled and set forth numerous arrays of dry facts, which become through his masterly arrangement easy to understand and survey. It has an artistic construction depending on the central idea, which groups the geographical vicissitudes of Europe in relation to the Roman Empire; and, though every sentence is thronged with names, it is not a mere book of reference like the meritorious text to the Spruner-Menke Atlas; it can be read consecutively. It is a book, too, which need never become antiquated. It may be predicted that it will be as fresh and as useful to students a hundred years hence as it is to-day; and it can always be easily brought up to date by brief additions, without the necessity of any change in its texture.

Such brief additions have been made in the present edition; the few shiftings in political geography of the past twenty years have been noticed at the appropriate places. In editing a manual of this kind, it does not seem incumbent or convenient to treat the text as sacrosanct, as one would treat Gibbon or the author's own *Norman Conquest.* The practical purpose of the work suggests, and its arrangement invites, insertions in the text rather than an appendix. Besides insertions of this kind, with the very slight changes which they sometimes necessitated, few alterations have been made. Some footnotes have been modified, some omitted, one or two added; and a few trifling errors have been corrected.

There is one point on which I venture to think that if Mr. Freeman were here to edit this book himself he might have been induced to modify his language. It is his use of the word Aryan. Though 'Aryanism' was, if I may say so, one of the pillars of his construction of history, I think he might have been induced to substitute the phrase 'of Aryan speech' in many cases when he committed himself to 'Aryan.' For the truth is that, in designating a people as Aryan, speech was his criterion, and the inference from Aryan speech to Aryan stock is invalid. How the Indo-Germanic tongue spread is still an unsolved problem, but it is certain that all the European peoples who spoke or speak tongues of this family are not of common race, and many of them probably have very little 'Aryan' blood. In studying Section 3 of Chapter I., on the 'Geographical Distribution of Races,' the reader will do well to bear this caution in mind.

J. B. B.

PREFACE

TO

THE FIRST EDITION.

It is now several years since this book was begun. It has been delayed by a crowd of causes, by a temporary loss of strength, by enforced absence from England, by other occupations and interruptions of various kinds. I mention this only because of the effect which I fear it has had on the book itself. It has been impossible to make it, what a book should, if possible, be, the result of one continuous effort. The mere fact that the kindness of the publishers allowed the early part to be printed some years back has, I fear, led to some repetition and even contradiction. A certain change of plan was found unavoidable. It proved impossible to go through the whole volume according to the method of the earlier chapters. Instead of treating Europe as a whole, I found it needful to divide it into several large geographical groups. The result is that each of the later chapters has had to go over again some small amount of ground which had been already gone over in the earlier chapters. In some cases later lights have led to some changes of view or expression. I have marked these, as far as I could, in the Additions and Corrections. If in any case I have failed to do so, the later statement is the one which should be relied on.

I hope that I have made the object of the work clear in the Introductory Chapter. It is really a very humble one. It aims at little more than tracing out the extent of various states at different times, and at attempting to place the various changes in their due relation to one another and to their causes. I am not, strictly speaking, writing history. I have little to do with the internal affairs of any country. I have looked at events mainly with reference to their effect on the European map. This has led to a reversal of what to many will seem the natural order of things. In a constitutional history of Europe, our own island would claim the very first place. In my strictly geographical point of view, I believe I am right in giving it the last.

I of course assume in the reader a certain elementary knowledge of European history, at least as much as may be learned from my own General Sketch. Names and things which have been explained there I have not thought it needful to explain again. I need hardly say that I found myself far more competent to deal with some parts of the work than with others. No one can take an equal interest in, or have an equal knowledge of, all branches of so wide a subject.

Some parts of the book will represent real original research; others must be dealt with in a far less thorough way, and will represent only knowledge got up for the occasion. In such cases the reader will doubtless find out the difference for himself. But I have felt my own deficiencies most keenly in the German part. No part of European history is to me more attractive than the early history of the German kingdom as such. No part is to me less attractive than the endless family divisions and unions of the smaller German states.

In the Slavonic part I have found great difficulty in following any uniform system of spelling. I consulted several Slavonic scholars. Each gave me advice, and each supported his own advice by arguments which I should have thought unanswerable, if I had not seen the arguments in support of the wholly different advice given me by the others. When the teachers differ so widely, the learner will, I hope, be forgiven, if the result is sometimes a little chaotic. I have tried to write Slavonic names so as to give some approach to the sound, as far as I know it. But I fear that I have succeeded very imperfectly.

In such a crowd of names, dates, and the like, there must be many small inaccuracies. In the case of the smaller dates, those which do not mark the great epochs of history, nothing is easier than to get wrong by a year or so. Sometimes there is an actual difference of statement in different authorities. Sometimes there is a difference in the reckoning of the year. For instance, In what year was Calais lost to England? We should say 1558. A writer at the time would say 1557. Then again there is no slip of either pen or press so easy as putting a wrong figure, and, except in the case of great and obvious dates, or again when the mistake is very far wrong indeed, there is no slip of pen or press so likely to be passed by in revision. And again there is often room for question as to the date which should be marked. In recording a transfer of territory from one power to another, what should be the date given? The actual military occupation and the formal diplomatic cession are often several years apart. Which of these dates should be chosen? I have found it hard to follow any fixed rule in such matters. Sometimes the military occupation seems the most important point, sometimes the diplomatic cession. I believe that in each case where a question of this sort might arise, I could give a reason for the date which has been chosen; but here there has been no room to enter into discussions. I can only say that I shall be deeply thankful to any one who will point out to me any mistakes or seeming mistakes in these or any other matters.

The maps have been a matter of great difficulty. I somewhat regret that it has been found needful to bind them separately from the text, because this looks as if they made some pretensions to the character of an historical atlas. To this they lay no claim. They are meant simply to illustrate the text, and in no way enter into competition either with such an elaborate collection as that of Spruner-Menke, or even with collections much less elaborate than that. Those maps are meant to be companions in studying the history of the several periods. Mine do not pretend to do more than to illustrate changes of boundary in a general way. It was found, as the work went on, that it was better on the whole to increase the number of maps, even at the expense of making each map smaller. There are disadvantages both ways. In the maps of South-Eastern Europe, for instance, it was found impossible to show the small states which arose in Greece after the Latin conquest at all clearly. But this evil seemed to be counterbalanced by giving as many pictures as might be of the shifting frontier of the Eastern Empire towards the Bulgarian, the Frank, and the Ottoman.

In one or two instances I have taken some small liberties with my dates. Thus, for instance, the map of the greatest extent of the Saracen dominion shows all the countries which were at any time under the Saracen power. But there was no one moment when the Saracen power took in the whole extent shown in the map. Sind and Septimania were lost before Crete and Sicily were won. But such a view as I have given seemed on the whole more instructive than it would have been to substitute two or three maps showing the various losses and gains at a few years' distance from one another.

I have to thank a crowd of friends, including some whom I have never seen, for many hints, and for much help given in various ways. Such are Professor Pauli of Göttingen, Professor Steenstrup of Copenhagen, Professor Romanos of Corfu, M. J-B. Galiffe of Geneva, Dr. Paul Turner of Budapest, Professor A. W. Ward of Manchester, the Rev. H. F. Tozer, Mr. Ralston, Mr. Morfill, Mrs. Humphry Ward, and my son-in-law Arthur John Evans, whose praise is in all South-Slavonic lands.

Somerleaze, Wells:
December 16, 1880.

PREFACE

TO

THE SECOND EDITION.

THE reception which has been given to the first edition of this book may be taken as showing that it supplied a real want, and that, notwithstanding some manifest defects, it has been found to be useful. The speedy demand for a second edition has led to a revision, as thorough as the very short time which circumstances allowed for it has made possible. And I trust that I have made considerable improvements, especially in the early part. I believe that I have done something to lessen the faults which followed almost necessarily from the circumstances under which it was first written. But I fear that they may still be too clearly seen, even in the present form of the work. I could see also that many improvements might have been made in the maps, especially the earlier ones. But a thorough revision of them would have needed a far longer time than could just now be given to the work. I have therefore done nothing more than adapt the last map in the South-Eastern series to the latest arrangements of 1880–1881. It shows how unstable a thing political geography is that changes of this kind have already been needed, both in the map and in the text. And I may perhaps be forgiven if I hope that my work in this way may not yet be over.

SOMERLEAZE, WELLS:
September 20, 1881.

CONTENTS.

CHAPTER I.

INTRODUCTION.

CHAPTER II.

GREECE AND THE GREEK COLONIES.

§ 1. *The Eastern or Greek Peninsula.*

§ 2. *Insular and Asiatic Greece.*

§ 3. *Ethnology of the Eastern Peninsula.*

§ 4. *Earliest Geography of Greece and the Neighbouring Lands.*

§ 5. *Change from Homeric to Historic Greece.*

§ 6. *The Greek Colonies.*

§ 7. *Growth of Macedonia and Epeiros.*

§ 8. *Later Geography of Independent Greece.*

CHAPTER III.

FORMATION OF THE ROMAN EMPIRE.

§ 1. *The Inhabitants of Italy and Sicily.*

§ 5. *Conquests under the Empire.*

CHAPTER IV.

THE DISMEMBERMENT OF THE EMPIRE.

§ 1. *The Later Geography of the Empire.*

§ 2. *The Division of the Empire.*

§ 3. *The Teutonic Settlements within the Empire.*

§ 4. *Settlement of the English in Britain.*

§ 5. *The Eastern Empire.*

CHAPTER V.

THE FINAL DIVISION OF THE EMPIRE.

§ 1. *The Reunion of the Empire.*

§ 2. *Settlement of the Lombards in Italy.*

§ 3. *Rise of the Saracens.*

§ 4. *Settlements of the Slavonic Nations.*

§ 5. *The Transfer of the Western Empire to the Franks.*

§ 6. *Northern Europe.*

CHAPTER VI.

THE BEGINNING OF THE MODERN EUROPEAN STATES.

§ 1. *The Division of the Frankish Empire.*

§ 2. *The Eastern Empire.*

§ 3. *Origin of the Spanish Kingdoms.*

§ 4. *Origin of the Slavonic States.*

§ 5. *Northern Europe.*

CHAPTER VII.

THE ECCLESIASTICAL GEOGRAPHY OF WESTERN EUROPE.

§ 6. *The Ecclesiastical Divisions of Northern and Eastern Europe.*

CHAPTER VIII.

THE IMPERIAL KINGDOMS.

§ 1. *The Kingdom of Germany.*

§ 4. *The Later Geography of Italy.*

§ 5. *The Kingdom of Burgundy.*

§ 6. *The Swiss Confederation.*

§ 7. *The State of Savoy.*

§ 9. *The Dominions of Austria.*

CHAPTER IX.

THE KINGDOM OF FRANCE.

§ 3. *The Colonial Dominion of France.*

§ 4. *Acquisitions of France during the Revolutionary Wars.*

CHAPTER X.

THE EASTERN EMPIRE.

§ 1. *Changes in the Frontier of the Empire.*

§ 2. *The Kingdom of Sicily.*

§ 3. *The Crusading States.*

§ 4. *The Eastern Dominion of Venice and Genoa.*

§ 5. *The Principalities of the Greek Mainland.*

§ 6. *The Slavonic States.*

§ 7. *The Kingdom of Hungary.*

§ 8. *The Ottoman Power.*

§ 9. *The Liberated States.*

CHAPTER XI.

THE BALTIC LANDS.

§ 1. *The Scandinavian Lands after the Separation of the Empires.*

§ 2. *The Lands East and South of the Baltic at the Separation of the Empires.*

§ 3. *German Dominion on the Baltic.*

§ 4. *The Growth of Russia and Sweden.*

§ 5. *The Decline of Sweden and Poland.*

§ 6. *The Modern Geography of the Baltic Lands.*

CHAPTER XII.

THE SPANISH PENINSULA AND ITS COLONIES.

§ 1. *The Foundation of the Spanish Kingdoms.*

§ 2. *Growth and Partition of the Great Spanish Monarchy.*

§ 3. *The Colonial Dominion of Spain and Portugal.*

CHAPTER XIII.

THE BRITISH ISLANDS AND COLONIES.

§ 1. *The Kingdom of Scotland.*

§ 2. *The Kingdom of England.*

§ 3. *Ireland.*

§ 4. *Outlying European Possessions of England.*

§ 5. *The American Colonies of England.*

§ 6. *Other Colonies and Possessions of England.*

HISTORICAL GEOGRAPHY OF EUROPE.

CHAPTER I.

INTRODUCTION.

CHAP. I.

Definition of Historical Geography.

THE WORK which we have now before us is to trace out the extent of territory which the different states and nations of Europe and the neighbouring lands have held at different times in the world's history, to mark the different boundaries which the same country has had, and the different meanings in which the same name has been used. It is of great importance carefully to make these distinctions, because great mistakes as to the facts of history are often caused through men thinking and speaking as if the names of different countries, say for instance England, France, Burgundy, Austria, have always meant exactly the same extent of territory. Historical geography, in this sense, differs from physical geography, which regards the natural features of the earth's surface. It differs also from studies like ethnology and comparative philology, which have to do directly with the differences between one nation and another, with their movements from one part of the world to another, and with the relations to be found among the languages spoken by them. But, though historical geography is

CHAP. I.

distinct from these studies, it makes much use of them. For the physical geography of a country always has a great effect upon its political history, and the dispersions and movements of different nations are exactly those parts of history which have most to do with fixing the names and the boundaries of different countries at different times. *England*, for instance, is, in strictness, the land of the English wherever they may settle, whether in their old home on the European continent, or in the isle of Britain, or in New England beyond the Ocean. But the extent of territory which was in this way to become England was largely determined by the physical circumstances of the countries in which the English settled. And the history of the English nation has been influenced, above all things, by the fact that the great English settlement which has made the English name famous was made in an island. But, when England had become the name of a distinct political dominion, its meaning was liable to change as that dominion advanced or went back. Thus the borders of England and Scotland have greatly changed at different times, and forgetfulness of this fact has led to many misunderstandings in reading the history of the two countries. And so with all other cases of the kind; the physical nature of the country, and the settlements of the different nations which have occupied it, have always been the determining causes of its political divisions. But it is with the political divisions that historical geography has to deal in the first place. With the nature of the land, and with the people who occupy it, it has to deal only so far as they have influenced the political divisions. Our present business in short is, first to draw the map of the countries with which we are concerned as it appeared after each of the different changes which they have gone through, and then to point out the historical causes which have led to the changes on the map. In this way we shall always see what was the meaning of any geographical name at any particular time, and we shall thus avoid mistakes, some of which have often led to really important practical consequences.

Distinction of Geographical and Political Names.

From this it follows that, in looking at the geography of Europe for our present purpose, we must look first at the land itself, and then at the nations which occupy it. And, in so doing, it may be well first of all to distinguish between two kinds of names which we shall have to use. Some names of countries are strictly geographical; they really mean a certain part of the earth's surface marked out by boundaries which cannot well be changed. Others simply mean the extent of country which is occupied at any time by a particular nation, an extent whose boundaries may easily be changed. Thus *Britain* is a strictly geographical name, meaning an island whose shape and boundaries must always be nearly the same. *England*, *Scotland*, *Wales*, are names of parts of that island, called after different nations which have settled in it, and the boundaries of all of which have differed greatly at different times. *Spain* again is the geographical name of a peninsula which is almost as well marked out by nature as the island of Britain. *Castile*, *Aragon*, *Portugal*, are political names of parts of the peninsula of Spain. They are the names of states whose boundaries have greatly varied, and which have sometimes formed separate governments and sometimes have been joined together.[1] *Gaul*

[1] In modern use we speak of *Spain* as only one part, though

CHAP. I.

again is the geographical name of a country which is not so clearly marked out all round by nature as the island of Britain and the peninsula of Spain, but which is well marked on three sides, to the north, south, and west. Within the limits of Gaul, names like *France*, *Flanders*, *Britanny*, *Burgundy*, and *Aquitaine*, are political names of parts of the country, whose limits have varied as much at different times as those of the different parts of Britain and Spain. This is the difference between strictly geographical names which do not alter and political names which do alter. No doubt *Gaul* and *Britain* were in the beginning political names, names given to the land from those who occupied it, just as much as the names *France* and *England*. But the settlements from which those lands took the names of Gaul and Britain took place long before the beginning of trustworthy history, while the settlements from which parts of those lands took the names of France and England happened in times long after trustworthy history began, and for which we are therefore ready with dates and names. Thus Gaul and Britain are the oldest received names of those lands; they are the names which those lands bore when we first hear of them. It is therefore convenient to keep them in use as strictly geographical names, as always meaning that part of the earth's surface which they meant when we first hear of them. In this book therefore, *Gaul*, *Britain*, *Spain*, and other names of the same kind,

much the larger part, of the peninsula, and of *Portugal* as another part. But this simply comes from the accident that, for some centuries past, all the other Spanish kingdoms have been joined under one government, while Portugal has remained separate. In speaking of any time till near the end of the fifteenth century of our æra, the word *Spain* must always be used in the geographical sense, as the name of the whole peninsula.

will always be used to mean a certain space on the map, whoever may be its inhabitants, or whatever may be its government, at any particular time. But names like *France*, *England*, *Castile*, will be used to mean the territory to which they were politically applied at the time of which we may be speaking, a territory which has been greater and less at different times. Thus, the cities of Carlisle and Edinburgh have always been in *Britain* since they were built. They have sometimes been in *England* and sometimes not. The cities of Marseilles, Geneva, Strassburg, and Arras, have always been in *Gaul* ever since they were built. They have sometimes been in *France* and sometimes not, according to political changes.

§ 1. *Geographical Aspect of Europe.*

Our present business is with the Historical Geography of Europe, and with that of other parts of the world only so far as they concern the geography of Europe. But we shall have to speak of all the three divisions of the Old World, Europe, Asia, and Africa, in those parts of the three which come nearest to one another, and in which the real history of the world begins. These are those parts of all three which lie round the Mediterranean sea, the lands which gradually came to form the Empire of Rome. In these lands the boundaries between the three great divisions are very easily marked. Modern maps do not all place the boundary between Europe and Asia at the same point; some make the river Don the boundary and some the Volga. But this question is of little importance for history. In the earliest historical times, when we have to do only with the countries round the Mediterranean sea, there can

The Mediterranean Lands.

CHAP. I.

be no doubt how much is Europe and how much is Asia and Africa. Europe is the land to the north of the Mediterranean sea and of the great gulfs which run out of it. If an exact boundary is needed in the barbarous lands north of the Euxine, the mouth of Tanais or Don is clearly the boundary which should be taken. In all these lands the Mediterranean and its gulfs divide Europe from Asia. But the northern parts of the two continents really form one geographical whole, the boundary between them being one merely of convenience. A vast central mass of land, stretching right across the inland parts of the two continents, sends forth a system of peninsulas and islands, to the north and south. And it is in the peninsular lands of Europe that European history begins.

The peninsulas of Europe and Asia.

Alike in Europe and in Asia, the southern or peninsular part of the continent is cut off from the central mass by a mountain chain, which in Europe is nearly unbroken. Thus the southern part of Europe consists of the three great peninsulas of *Spain*, *Italy*, and what we may, in a wide sense, call *Greece*. These answer in some sort to the three great Oceanic peninsulas of Asia, those of *Arabia*, *India*, and *India* beyond the *Ganges*. But the part of Asia which has historically had most to do with Europe is its Mediterranean peninsula, the land known as *Asia Minor*. In the northern part of each continent we find another system of great gulfs or inland seas; but those in Asia have been hindered by the cold from ever being of any importance, while in Europe the Baltic sea and the gulfs which run out of it may be looked on as forming a kind of secondary Mediterranean. We may thus say that Europe consists of two insular and peninsular regions, north and south, with a great unbroken mass of land between them. But there are some parts of Europe which seem as it were connecting links between the three main divisions of the continent. Thus we said that the three great peninsulas are cut off from the central mass by a nearly unbroken mountain chain. But the connexion of the central peninsula, that of Italy, with the eastern one or Greece, is far closer than its connexion with the western one, or Spain. Italy and Spain are much further apart than Italy and Greece, and between the Alps and the Pyrenees the mountain chain is nearly lost. We might almost say that a piece of central Europe breaks through at this point and comes down to the Mediterranean. This is the south-eastern part of Gaul; and Gaul may in this way be looked on as a land which joins together the central and the southern parts of Europe. But this is not all; in the north-western corner of Europe lies that great group of islands, two large ones and many small, of which our own Britain is the greatest. The British Islands are closely connected in their geography and history with Gaul on one side, and with the islands and peninsulas of the North on the other. In this way we may say that all the three divisions of Europe are brought closely together on the western side of the continent, and that the lands of Gaul and Britain are the connecting links which bind them together.

§ 2. *Effect of Geography on History.*

Beginning of history in the European peninsulas.

Now this geographical aspect of the chief lands of Europe has had its direct effect on their history. We might almost take for granted that the history of Europe should begin in the two more eastern among the three great southern peninsulas. Of these two, Italy and

CHAP. I.

Greece, each has its own character. Greece, though it is the part of Europe which lies nearest to Asia, is in a certain sense the most European of European lands. The characteristic of Europe is to be more full of peninsulas and islands and inland seas than the rest of the Old World. And Greece, the peninsula itself and the neighbouring lands, are fuller of islands and promontories and inland seas than any other part of Europe. On the other hand, Italy is the central land of all southern Europe, and indeed of all the land round the Mediterranean. It was therefore only natural that Greece should be the part of Europe in which all that is most distinctively European first grew up and influenced other lands. And so, if any one land or city among the Mediterranean lands was to rule over all the rest, it is in Italy, as the central land, that we should naturally look for the place of dominion. The destinies of the two peninsulas and their relations to the rest of the world were thus impressed on them by their geographical position.

Characteristics of Greece; of Italy.

If we turn to recorded history, we find that it is a working out of the consequences of these physical facts. Greece was the first part of Europe to become civilized and to play a part in history; but it was Italy, and in Italy it was the most central city, Rome, which came to have the dominion over the civilized world of early times—that is, over the lands around the Mediterranean. These two peninsulas have, each in its own way, ruled and influenced the rest of Europe as no other parts have done. All the other parts have been, in one way or another, their subjects or disciples. The effect of the geographical position of these countries is also marked in the stages by which Rome advanced to the general dominion of the Mediterranean lands.

Advance of the Roman dominion.

She first subdued Italy; then she had to strive for the mastery with her great rival Carthage, a city which held nearly the same central position on the southern coast of the Mediterranean which she herself did on the northern. Then she subdued, step by step, the peninsulas on each side of her and the other coast lands of the Mediterranean—European, Asiatic, and African. Into the central division of Europe she did not press far, never having any firm or lasting dominion beyond the Rhine and the Danube. Into Northern Europe, properly so called, her power never reached at all. But she subdued the lands which we have seen act as a kind of connecting link between the different parts of Europe, namely Gaul and the greater part of Britain. Thus the Roman Empire, at its greatest extent, consisted of the lands round the Mediterranean, together with Gaul and Britain. For the possession of the Mediterranean lands would have been imperfect without the possession of Gaul, and the possession of Gaul naturally led to the possession of Britain.

Effect of the geographical position of

In this way the early history of Greece and Italy, and the formation of the Roman Empire, were affected by the geographical character of the countries themselves. The same was the case with the other European lands, when they came to share in that importance which once belonged to Greece and Italy only. Thus Germany, as being the most central part of Europe, came at one time to fill something like the same position which Italy had once held. It came to be the country which had to do with all parts of Europe, east, west, north, and south, and even to be a ruling power over some of them. So, as France became the chief state of Gaul, it took upon it something like the old position of Gaul as

Germany,

France,

CHAP. I.

a means of communication between the different parts of Western Europe. Meanwhile, as the Scandinavian and Spanish peninsulas are both cut off in a marked way from the mainland of Europe, each of them has often formed a kind of world of its own, having much less to do with other countries than Germany, France, and Italy had. The same was for a long time the case with our own island. Britain was looked on as lying outside the world.

Spain and Scandinavia.

Thus the geographical position of the European lands influenced their history while their history was still purely European. And when Europe began to send forth colonies to other continents, the working of geographical causes came out no less strongly. Thus the position of Spain on the Ocean led Portugal and Castile to be foremost among the colonizing nations of Europe. For the same reason, our own country was one of the chief in following their example, and so was France also for a long time. Holland too, when it rose into importance, became a great colonizing power, and so did Denmark and Sweden to some extent. But an Italian colony beyond the Ocean was never heard of, nor has there ever been a German colony in the same sense in which there have been Spanish and English colonies. Meanwhile, the north-eastern part of Europe, which in early times was not known at all, has always lagged behind the rest, and has become of importance only in later times. This is mainly because its geographical position has almost wholly cut it off both from the Mediterranean and from the Ocean.

The colonizing powers.

Thus we see how, in all these ways, both in earlier and in later times, the history of every country has been influenced by its geography. No doubt

CHAP. I.

the history of each country has also been largely influenced by the disposition of the people who have settled in it, by what is called the national character. But then the geographical position itself has often had something directly to do with forming the national character, and in all cases it has had an influence upon it, by giving it a better or a worse field for working and showing itself. Thus it has been well said that neither the Greeks in any other country nor any other people in Greece could have been what the Greeks in Greece really were. The nature of the country and the nature of the people helped one another, and caused Greece to become all that it was in the early times of Europe. It is always useful to mark the points both of likeness and unlikeness of the different nations whose history we study. And of this likeness and unlikeness we shall always find that the geographical character, though only one cause out of several, is always one of the chief causes.

Influence of national character.

§ 3. *Geographical Distribution of Races.*

Our present business then is with geography as influenced by history, and with history as influenced by geography. With ethnology, with the relations of nations and races to one another, we have to deal only so far as they form one of the agents in history. And it will be well to avoid, as far as may be, all obscure or controverted points of this kind. But the great results of comparative philology may now be taken for granted, and a general view of the geographical disposition of the great European races is needful as an introduction to the changes which historical causes have wrought in the geography of the several parts of Europe.

CHAP. I.

In European ethnology one main feature is that the population of Europe is, and from the very beginnings of history has been, more nearly homogeneous, at least more palpably homogeneous, than that of any other great division of the world. Whether we look at Europe now, or whether we look at it at the earliest times of which we have any glimmerings, it is pre-eminently an Aryan continent. Everything non-Aryan is at once marked as exceptional. We cannot say this of Asia, where, among several great ethnical elements, none is so clearly predominant as the Aryan element is in Europe. There are in Europe non-Aryan elements, both earlier and later than the Aryan settlement; but they have, as a rule, been assimilated to the prevailing Aryan mass. The earlier non-Aryan element consists of the remnants which still remain of the races which the Aryan settlers found in Europe, and which they either exterminated or assimilated to themselves. The later elements consist of non-Aryan races which have made their way into Europe within historical times, and in their case the work of assimilation has been much less complete. It follows almost naturally from the position of Europe that the primæval non-Aryan element has survived in the west and in the north, while the later or intrusive non-Aryan element has made its way into the east and the south. In the mountains of the western peninsula, in the border lands of Spain and Gaul, the non-Aryan tongue of the *Basque* still survives. In the extreme north of Europe the non-Aryan tongue of the *Fins* and *Laps* still survives. The possible relations of these tongues either to one another or to other non-Aryan tongues beyond the bounds of Europe is a question of purely

Europe an Aryan continent.

Non-Aryan remnants.

philological concern, and does not touch historical geography. But historical geography is touched by the probability, rising almost to moral certainty, that the isolated populations by whom these primitive tongues are still spoken are mere remnants of the primitive races which formed the population of Europe at the time when the Aryans first made their way into that continent. Everything tends to show that the *Basques* are but the remnant of a great people whom we may set down with certainty as the præ-Aryan inhabitants of Spain and a large part of Gaul, and whose range we may, with great probability, extend over Sicily, over part at least of Italy, and perhaps as far north as our own island. Their possible connexion with the early inhabitants of northern Africa hardly concerns us. The probability that they were themselves preceded by an earlier and far lower race concerns us not at all. The earliest historical inhabitants of south-western Europe are those of whom the Basques are the surviving remnant, those who, under the names of *Iberians* and *Ligurians*, fill a not unimportant place in European history.

Extent of the Basques.

When we come to the Aryan settlements, we cannot positively determine which among the Aryan races of Europe were the earliest settlers in point of time. The members of the great race which, in its many subdivisions, contains the *Greeks*, the *Italians*, and the nations more immediately akin to them, are the first among the European Aryans to show themselves in the light of history; but it does not necessarily follow that they were actually the first in point of settlement. It may be that, while they were pressing through the Mediterranean peninsulas and islands, the *Celts*

Order of the Aryan settlements.

Greeks and Italians.

Celts.

CHAP. I.

were pushing their way through the solid central land of Europe. The Celts were clearly the vanguard of the Aryan migration within their own range, the first swarm which made its way to the shores of the Ocean. Partially in Spain, more thoroughly in Gaul and the British Islands, they displaced or assimilated the earlier inhabitants, who, under their pressure and that of later conquerors, have been gradually shut up in the small mountainous region which they still keep. Of the Celtic migration we have no historical accounts, but all probability would lead us to think that the Celts whom in historic times we find on the Danube and south of the Alps were not emigrants who had followed a backward course from the great settlement in Transalpine Gaul, but rather detachments which had been left behind on the westward journey. Without attempting to settle questions as to the traces of Celtic occupancy to be found in other lands, it is enough for our purpose that, at the beginnings of their history, we find the Celts the chief inhabitants of a region stretching from the Æsis to the furthest known points of Britain. Gaul, Cisalpine and Transalpine, is their great central land, though even here they are not exclusive possessors ; they share the land with a non-Aryan remnant to the south-west, and with the next wave of Aryan new-comers to the north-east.

The settlements of these two great Aryan races come before authentic history. After them came the *Teutonic* races, which pressed on the Celts from the east ; and in their wake, to judge from their place on the map, must have come the vast family of the *Slavonic*

Teutons and Slaves.

nations. But the migrations of the Teutons and

Slaves come, for the most part, within the range of recorded history. Our first glimpse of the Teutons shows them in their central German land, already occupying both sides of the Rhine, though seemingly not very old settlers on its left bank. The long wanderings of the various Teutonic and Slavonic tribes over all parts of central Europe, their settlements in the southern and western lands, are all matters of history. So is the great Teutonic settlement in the British Islands, which partly exterminated, partly assimilated, their Celtic inhabitants, so as to leave them as a mere remnant, though a greater remnant, as they themselves had made the Basques. And, as the process which made the north-western islands of Europe Teutonic is a matter of history, so also are the later stages of the process which made the northern peninsulas Teutonic. But it is only the later stages which are historical; we know that in the strictly Scandinavian peninsula the Teutonic invaders displaced non-Aryan Fins; we have only to guess that in the Cimbric Chersonêsos they displaced Aryan Celts. But beyond the Teutons and Slaves lies yet another Aryan settlement, one which, in a purely philological view, is the most interesting of all, the small and fast vanishing group which still survives in *Lithuania* and the neighbouring lands. Of these there is historically really nothing to be said. On the eastern shores of the Baltic we find people whose tongue comes nearer than any other European tongue to the common Aryan model; but we can only guess either at the date when they came thither or at the road by which they came.

Lithuanians.

These races then, Aryan and non-Aryan, make up the immemorial population of Europe. The remnants of the older non-Aryan races, and the successive waves of Aryan settlement, are all immemorial facts which we must accept as the groundwork of our history and our geography. They must be distinguished from other movements which are strictly matters of written history, both movements among the Aryan nations themselves and later intrusions of non-Aryan nations. Thus the Greek colonies and the conquests of the hellenized Macedonians hellenized large districts of Europe, Asia, and Africa, partly by displacement, partly by assimilation. The conquests of Rome, and the Teutonic settlements within the Roman Empire, brought about but little in the way of displacement, but a great deal in the way of assimilation. The process indeed was opposite in the two cases. The Roman conqueror assimilated the conquered to himself; the Teutonic conqueror was himself assimilated by those whom he conquered. Britain and the Rhenish and Danubian lands stand out as marked exceptions. The Slavonic settlements in the East wrought far more of displacement than the Teutonic settlements in the West. Vast regions, once Illyrian or Thracian—that is, most likely, more or less nearly akin to the Greeks—are now wholly Slavonic. Lastly come the incursions on European lands made by non-Aryan settlers in historic times. Their results have been widely different in different cases. The Semitic *Saracens* settled in Spain and Sicily, bringing with them and after them their African converts, men possibly of originally kindred race with the first inhabitants both of the peninsula and of the island. These non-Aryan settlers have vanished. The displacement of large bodies of them is a fact of comparatively recent history, but it can hardly fail that

Movements among the Aryan races.

Later intrusion of Non-Aryan races.

Semitic.

some degree of assimilation must also have taken place. Then come the settlements, chiefly in eastern Europe, of those nations which we may group together as *Turanian*. We need not discuss the abstract propriety of that name; for our purposes it is a convenient negative name for whatever in European and Western Asiatic history is neither Aryan nor Semitic. Among Turanian invaders in this sense, the *Huns* of Attila have left only a name. The more lasting settlement of the *Avars* has vanished, how far by displacement, how far by assimilation, it might be hard to say. *Chazars*, *Patzinaks*, a crowd of other barbarian races, have left no sign of their presence. The *Bulgarians*, originally Turanian conquerors, have been assimilated by their Slavonic subjects. The Finnish *Magyars* have received a political and religious assimilation; their kingdom became a member of the commonwealth of Christian Europe, though they still keep their old Turanian language. The latest intruders of all, the *Ottoman Turks*, still remain as they were when they first came, aliens on Aryan and Christian ground. But here again is a case of assimilation the other way; the Ottoman Turks are an artificial nation which has been kept up by the constant incorporation of European renegades who have thrown aside the speech, the creed, and the civilization, of Europe.

Turanian.

CHAPTER II.

GREECE AND THE GREEK COLONIES.

§ 1. *The Eastern or Greek Peninsula.*

CHAP. II.

Characteristics of the Eastern peninsula.

THE Historical Geography of Europe, if looked at in chronological order, must begin with the most eastern of the three peninsulas of Southern Europe. Here the history of Europe, and the truest history of the world, began. It was in the insular and peninsular lands between the Ionian and Ægæan seas that the first steps towards European civilization were taken; it is there that we see the first beginnings of art, science, and political life. But Greece or *Hellas*, in the strict sense of the name, forms only a part of the great Eastern peninsula, though it is its leading and characteristic part. As the whole peninsular land gradually tapers southwards from the great mass of central Europe, it becomes at each stage more and more peninsular, and it also becomes at each stage more and more Greek. Greece indeed and the neighbouring lands form, as was long ago remarked by Strabo,[1] a series of peninsulas within peninsulas. It is not easy to find

[1] See the first chapter of his eighth book (vol. ii. p. 139 of the Tauchnitz edition). He makes four peninsulas within peninsulas, beginning from the south with Peloponnêsos, and he enlarges on the general character of the country as made up of gulfs and promontories.

a name for the whole region, as it stretches far beyond any limits which can be given to Greece in any age of the world or according to any use of the name. But the whole land seems to have been occupied by nations more or less akin to the Greeks. The history of those nations chiefly consists of their relations to the Greeks, and all of them were brought more or less within the range of Greek influences. We may therefore not improperly call the whole land, as opposed to Italy and Spain, the *Greek* peninsula. Latterly it has more commonly been called the *Balkan* peninsula, from the great chain of mountains, the continuation of the Alps of Western Europe, which spans it from sea to sea. It has also been called the *Byzantine peninsula*, as nearly answering to the European part of the Eastern division of the Roman Empire, when its seat of government was at Byzantion, Constantinople, or New Rome.

Its chief divisions.

Taking the great range of mountains which divides southern from central Europe as the northern boundary of the eastern or Greek peninsula, it may be said to take in the lands which are cut off from the central mass by the *Dalmatian Alps* and the range of *Haimos* or *Balkan*. It is washed to the east, west, and south, by various parts of the Mediterranean and its great gulf the Euxine. But the northern part of this region, all that lies north of the Ægæan sea, taking in therefore the whole of the Euxine coast, still keeps much of the character of the great central mass of Europe; it forms a land intermediate between that and the more strictly peninsular lands to the south. Still the boundary is a real one, for all the lands south of this range have come more or less within Greek influences, and have played their part in Greek history.

CHAP. II.

But when we get beyond the mountains, into the valley of the Danube, we find ourselves in lands which, excepting a few colonies on the coast, have hardly come at all under Greek influences till quite modern times. This region between Haimos and the more strictly Greek lands takes in *Thrace*, *Paionia*, and *Illyria* in the narrower sense. Of these, Thrace and Illyria, having a sea coast, received many Greek colonies, especially on the northern coast of the Ægæan and on the *Propontis* or Sea of Marmora. The Thracian part of this region, as bordering on these more distinctly Grecian seas, became more truly a part of the Grecian world than the other lands to the west of it. Yet geographically

Thrace and Illyria.

Thrace is more widely cut off from Greece than Illyria is. For there is no such great break on the western shore of the great peninsula as that which, on the eastern side, marks the point where we must draw the line between Greece and its immediate neighbours and the lands to the north of them. This is at the point where a peninsula within a peninsula breaks off to the south, comprising *Greece*, *Macedonia*, and *Epeiros*. There is here no very marked break on the Illyrian coast, but the Ægæan coast of Thrace is fenced in as it were at its two ends, to the east by the long narrow peninsula known specially as the *Chersonêsos*, and to the west by the group of peninsulas called *Chalkidikê*. These have nothing answering to them on the Illyrian side unless we reckon the mere bend in the coast above Epidamnos. This last point however marks the extent of the earlier Greek colonization in those regions, and it has become a still more important boundary in later times.

Beyond Chalkidikê to the west, the specially Greek peninsula projects to the south, being itself

Greece proper and its peninsulas.

again composed of peninsulas within peninsulas. The *Ambrakian Gulf* on the west and the *Pagasaian* on the east fence off a peninsula to the south, by which the more purely Greek lands are fenced off from *Macedonia*, *Epeiros*, and *Thessaly*. Within this peninsula again another may be marked off by a line drawn from *Thermopylai* to the *Corinthian* gulf near Delphoi. This again shuts out to the west *Akarnania*, *Aitolia*, and some other of the more backward divisions of the Greek name. Thus *Phôkis*, *Boiôtia*, and *Attica* form a great promontory, from which Attica projects as a further promontory to the south-east, while the great peninsula of *Peloponnêsos*—itself made up on its eastern and southern sides of smaller peninsulas—is joined on by the narrow isthmus of Corinth. In this way, from Haimos to *Tainaros*, the land is ever becoming more and more broken up by greater or smaller inlets of the sea. And in proportion as the land becomes more strictly peninsular, it also becomes more strictly Greek, till in Peloponnêsos we reach the innermost citadel of the Greek nation.

Peloponnêsos.

§ 2. *Insular and Asiatic Greece.*

Continuous Hellas.

Greece Proper then, what the ancient geographers called *Continuous Hellas* as distinguished from the Greek colonies planted on barbarian shores, is, so far as it is part of the mainland, made up of a system of peninsulas stretching south from the general mass of eastern Europe. But the neighbouring islands equally form a part of continuous Greece; and the other coasts of the Ægæan, Asiatic as well as Thracian, were so thickly strewed with Greek colonies as to form, if not part of continuous

CHAP. II.

Greece, yet part of the immediate Greek world. The western coast, as it is less peninsular, is also less insular, and the islands on the western side of Greece did not reach the same importance as those on the eastern side. Still they too, the Ionian islands of modern geography, form in every sense a part of Greece. To the north of *Korkyra* or *Corfu* there are only detached Greek colonies, whether on the mainland or in the islands; but all the islands of the Ægæan are, during historical times, as much part of Greece as the mainland. One island on each side, *Leukas* on the west and the greater island of *Euboia* on the east, might almost be counted as parts of the mainland, as peninsulas rather than islands. To the south the long narrow island of *Crete* forms a sort of barrier between Greek and barbarian seas. It is the most southern of the purely Greek lands. *Sicily* to the west and *Cyprus* to the east received many Greek colonies, but they never became purely Greek in the same way as Crete and the islands to the north of it.

The Islands.

Asiatic Greece.

But, besides the European peninsulas and the islands, part of Asia must be looked on as forming part of the immediate Greek world, though not strictly of continuous Greece. The peninsula known as *Asia Minor* cannot be separated from Europe either in its geography or in its history. With its central mass we have little or nothing to do; but its coasts form a part of the Greek world, and its Ægæan coast was only less thoroughly Greek than Greece itself and the Greek islands. It would seem that the whole western coast of Asia Minor was inhabited by nations which, like the European neighbours of Greece, were more or less nearly akin to the Greeks. And the Ægæan coast of Asia is almost as full of inlets of the sea, of peninsulas and promontories and islands near to the shore, as European Greece itself. All these shores therefore received Greek colonies. The islands and the most tempting spots on the mainland were occupied by Greek settlers, and became the sites of Greek cities. But Greek influence never spread very far inland, and even the coast itself did not become so purely Greek as the islands. When we pass from the Ægæan coast of Asia to the other two sides of the peninsula, to its northern coast washed by the Euxine and its southern coast washed by the Mediterranean, we have passed out of the immediate Greek world. Greek colonies are found on favourable spots here and there; but the land, even the coast, as a whole, is barbarian.

§ 3. *Ethnology of the Eastern Peninsula.*

The Greeks and the kindred races.

The immediate Greek world then, as opposed to the outlying Greek colonies, consists of the shores of the Ægæan sea and of the peninsulas lying between it and the Ionian sea. Of this region a great part was exclusively inhabited by the Greek nation, while Greek influences were more or less dominant throughout the whole. But it would further seem that the whole, or nearly the whole, of these lands were inhabited by races more or less akin to the Greeks, races which had a good deal in common with the Greeks, and of whom the Greeks were simply the foremost and most fortunate. Their higher developement was doubtless greatly favoured by the geographical nature of the country which they occupied. But a distinction must be drawn between the nearer and the more remote neighbours of Greece.

It is hardly necessary for our present purpose to determine whether the Greeks had or had not any connexion with Thracians, European or Asiatic, with Phrygians and Lydians, and other neighbouring nations. All these were in Greek eyes simply Barbarians, but

Nations more remote, but probably kindred.

modern scholarship has seen in them signs of a kindred with the Greek nation nearer than the share which both have in the common Aryan stock. We need not settle here whether all the inhabitants of the geographical district which we have marked out were, or were not, kinsmen in this sense; but with some among them the question assumes a deeper interest and a nearer approach

Illyrians

to certainty. The great Illyrian race, of whom the Albanians or *Skipetar* are the modern representatives, a race which has been so largely displaced by Slaves at one end and assimilated by Greeks at the other, can hardly fail to have had a nearer kindred with the Greeks than that which they both share with Celts and Teutons. When we come to the lands which are yet more closely connected with Greece, both in geographical position and in their history, the case becomes clearer still. We can hardly doubt as to the close connexion between the Greeks and the nations which bordered on Greece immediately to the north in

Epeiros, Macedonia, Sicily, and Italy.

Edeiros and Macedonia, as well as with some at least of those which they found occupying the opposite coasts of the Ægæan, as well as in Sicily and Italy. The Greeks and Italians, with the nations immediately connected with them, clearly belong to one, and that a well marked, division of the Aryan family. Their kindred is shown alike by the evidence of language and by the remarkable ease with which in all ages they received Greek civilization.

Into more minute inquiries as to these matters it is hardly our province to go here. It is perhaps enough to say that the *Pelasgian* name, which has given rise to so much speculation, seems to have been used by the Greeks themselves in a very vague way, much as the word *Saxon* is used among ourselves.[1] It is therefore dangerous to form any theories about the matter. Sometimes the Pelasgians seem to be spoken of simply as *Old-Hellênes*, sometimes as a people distinct from the Hellênes. Whether the Hellênes, on their entering into Greece, found the land held by earlier inhabitants, whether Aryan or non-Aryan, is a curious and interesting speculation, but one which does not concern us. It is enough for our purpose that, as far back as history or even legend can carry us, we find the land in the occupation of a branch of the Aryan family, consisting, like all other nations, of various kindred tribes. It is a nation which is as well defined as any other nation, and yet it shades off, as it were, into the other nations of the kindred stock. Clearly marked as Greek and barbarian are from the beginning, there still are frontier tribes in Epeiros and Macedonia which must be looked on as forming an intermediate stage between the two classes, and which are accordingly placed by different Greek writers sometimes in one class and sometimes in the other.

Pelasgians.

The Greek nation.

[1] [There is evidence which connects the *Pelasgians* in a stricter sense with (1) Thessaly, where their name is preserved in the division of *Pelasgiôtis*, (2) Attica, (3) Crete.]

CHAP. II.

§ 4. *The Earliest Geography of Greece and the Neighbouring Lands.*

The Homeric map of Greece.

Our first picture of Greek geography comes from the Homeric catalogue.[1] Whatever may be the historic value of the Homeric poems in general, it is clear that the catalogue in the second book of the Iliad must represent a real state of things. It gives us a map of Greece so different from the map of Greece at any later time that it is inconceivable that it can have been invented at any later time. We have in fact a map of Greece at a time earlier than any time to which we can assign certain names and dates. Within the range of Greece itself the various Greek races often changed their settlements, displacing or conquering earlier Greek settlers; and the different states which they formed often changed their boundaries by bringing other states into subjection or depriving them of parts of their territory. The Homeric catalogue gives us a wholly different arrangement of the various branches of the nation from any that we find in the Greece of historic times. The *Dorian* and *Ionian* names, which were afterwards so famous, are hardly known; the name of *Hellênes* itself belongs only to a small district.

Tribal divisions of Homeric Greece.

The names for the whole people are *Achaians*, *Argeians* (*Argos* seeming to mean all Peloponnêsos), and *Danaoi*, the last a name which goes quite out of use in historic times. The boundary of Greece to the west is narrower than it was in later times. The land called *Akarnania* has not yet got that name, if indeed it was then a Greek land at all. It is spoken of vaguely as

[1] [For Homeric geography see further Mr. Monro's article in *English Historical Review*, i. 43 *sqq.*]

Epeiros or the mainland,[1] and it appears as part of the possessions of the king of the neighbouring islands, *Kephallênia* and *Ithakê*. The islands to the north, *Leukas* and *Korkyra*, were not yet Greek. The *Thesprotians* in Epeiros are spoken of as a neighbouring and friendly people, but they form no part of the Greek nation. The *Aitolians* appear as a Greek people, and so do most of the other divisions of the Greek nation; only their position and relative importance is often different from what it was afterwards. Thus, to mention a few examples out of many, the *Lokrians*, who, in historic times, appear both on the sea of Euboia and on the Corinthian gulf, appear in the catalogue in their northern seats only.

Groupings of cities.

When we turn from tribes to cities, the difference is still greater. The cities which held the first place in historic times are not always those which are greatest in the earlier time, and their grouping in federations or principalities is wholly unlike anything in later history. Thus in the historic *Boiôtia* we find *Orchomenos* as the second city of a confederation of which *Thebes* is the first. In the catalogue Orchomenos and the neighbouring city *Asplêdôn* form a separate division, distinct from Boiôtia. Euboia forms a whole; and, what is specially to be noticed, *Attica*, as a land, is not mentioned, but only the single city of *Athens*, with Salamis as a kind of dependency. Peloponnêsos again is divided in a manner quite different from

[1] Ἤπειρος is simply the mainland, and came only gradually to mean a particular country. We may compare the use of 'terra firma' in South America. In the catalogue (*Iliad*, ii. 620–635), after the island subjects of Odysseus have been reckoned up, we read: *οἵ τ' Ἤπειρον ἔχον, ἠδ' ἀντιπέραι' ἐνέμοντο.* This must mean the land afterwards called Akarnania. It was remarked at a later time that the Akarnanians were the only people of Greece who did not appear in the catalogue.

anything in later times. The ruling city is *Mykênê*, whose king holds also a general superiority over all Hellas, while his immediate dominion takes in *Corinth*, *Kleônai*, *Sikyôn*, and the whole south coast of the Corinthian gulf, the *Achaia* of later times. The rest of the cities of the Argolic peninsula are grouped round *Argos*. Northern Greece again is divided into groups of cities which answer to nothing in later times. And its relative importance in the Greek world is clearly far greater than it was in the historic period.

Extent of Greek colonization.

The catalogue also helps us to our earliest picture of the Ægæan islands and of the northern and eastern coasts of the Ægæan sea. We see the extent which Greek colonization had already reached. It had as yet taken in only the southern islands of the Ægæan. *Crete* was already Greek; so were *Rhodes*, *Kôs*, and the neighbouring islands; but these last are distinctly marked as new settlements. The coast of Asia and the northern islands are still untouched, except through the events of the Trojan war itself, in which the Greek conquest of *Lesbos* is distinctly marked. In Asia, besides *Trojans* and *Dardanians*, we find *Pelasgians* as a distinct people, as also *Paphlagonians*, *Mysians*, *Phrygians*, *Maionians*, *Karians*, and *Lykians*. We find in short the nations which fringe the whole Ægæan coast of Asia and the south-western coast of the Euxine. In Europe again we have Thracians and Paionians, names familiar in historic times, and whose bearers seemingly occupied nearly the same lands which they do in later times. The presence of Thracians in Asia is implied rather than asserted. The *Macedonian* name is not found. The northern islands of the Ægæan are mentioned only incidentally. Everything leads us to believe

The Asiatic Catalogue.

that the whole region, European and Asiatic, with which we are now concerned, was, at this earliest time of which we have any glimpses, occupied by various races more or less closely allied to each other. The islands were largely Karian,[1] but the *Phœnicians*, a Semitic people from the eastern coast of the Mediterranean, had planted colonies in several of them. But Karians and Phœnicians had now begun to give way to Greek settlements. The same rivalry in short between Greeks and Phœnicians must have gone on in the earliest times in the islands of the Ægæan which went on in historic times in the greater islands of Cyprus and Sicily.

Phœnician and Greek settlements in the islands.

§ 5. *Change from Homeric to Historic Greece.*

The state of things which is set before us in the catalogue was altogether broken up by later changes, changes which still come before the beginnings of contemporary history, and which we understand chiefly by comparing the geography of the catalogue with the geography of later times. According to received tradition, a number of *Dorian* colonies from Northern Greece were gradually planted in the chief cities of Peloponnêsos, and drove out or reduced to subjection their older *Achaian* inhabitants. Mykênê from this time loses its importance; Argos, Sparta, Corinth, and Sikyôn, become Dorian cities; Sparta gradually wins the dominion over all the towns, whether Dorian or Achaian, within her immediate dominion of Lakonia. To the west of Lakonia arises the Dorian state of *Messênê*, which is the name only of a district, as there was as yet no city so called. As part of the same movement, an

Changes in Peloponnêsos.

[1] [Note that Milêtos, the only one of the Ionian cities which is mentioned in the catalogue, appears there as a Karian town.]

CHAP. II.

Aitolian colony is said to have occupied *Êlis* on the west coast of Peloponnêsos. Êlis again was at this time the name of a district only; the cities both of Messênê and Êlis are of much later date. First Argos, and then Sparta, rises to a supremacy over their fellow-Dorians and over the whole of Peloponnêsos. Historical Peloponnêsos thus consists (i) of the cities, chiefly Dorian, of the Argolic *Aktê* or peninsula, together with *Corinth* on the Isthmus and *Megara*, a Dorian outpost beyond the Isthmus; (ii) of *Lakonikê*, the district immediately subject to Sparta, with a boundary towards Argos which shifted as Sparta advanced and Argos went back; (iii) of *Messênê*, which was conquered by Sparta before the age of contemporary history, and was again separated in the fourth century B.C.; (iv) of *Êlis*, with the border-districts between it and Messênê; (v) of the *Achaian* cities on the coast of the Corinthian gulf; (vi) of the inland country of *Arkadia*. The relations among these districts and the several cities within them often fluctuated, but the general aspect of the map of Peloponnêsos did not greatly change from the beginning of the fifth century till the later days of the third.

Changes in Northern Greece.

According to the received traditions, migrations of the same kind took place in Northern Greece also between the time of the catalogue and the beginning of contemporary history. Thus Thessaly, whose different divisions form a most important part of the catalogue,[1] is said to have suffered an invasion at the hands of the half Hellenic *Thesprotians*. They are said to have become the ruling people in Thessaly itself, and to have held a supremacy over the neighbouring lands, including the

[1] [But the name *Thessaly* is not found in Homer, though Thessalos, its eponymous hero, is mentioned in *Iliad* ii. 679.]

peninsula of *Magnêsia* and the Phthiôtic *Achaia*. It is certain that in the historical period Thessaly lags in the background, and that the true Hellenic spirit is much less developed there than in other parts of Greece. There is less reason to accept the legend of a migration out of Thessaly into Boiôtia; but in historic times Orchomenos no longer appears as a separate state; it becomes the second city of the Boiotian confederacy, yielding the first place to Thebes with great unwillingness. The Lokrians also now appear on the Corinthian gulf as well as on the sea of Euboia. And the land to the west of Aitôlia, so vaguely spoken of in the catalogue, has become the seat of a Greek people under the name of *Akarnania*. The Corinthian colonies along this coast, the city of *Ambrakia*, the island or peninsula of *Leukas*, the great island of *Korkyra*, colonies whose foundation is placed in the eighth century B.C., come almost within the time of trustworthy history. They are not Greek in the catalogue; they are Greek when we first hear of them in history. Ambrakia forms the last outpost of continuous Hellas on the mainland, as Korkyra was long the most northern Greek island. Beyond these are only outlying Greek settlements, mostly of much later date, on the Illyrian coasts and islands.

These changes in the geography of continental Greece, both within and without Peloponnêsos, make the main differences between the Greece of the Homeric catalogue and the Greece of the Persian and Peloponnesian wars. During the sixth, fifth, and fourth, centuries before Christ there were constant changes in political relations of the Greek states to one another; but there were not many changes which greatly affected the geography. Cities were constantly brought in subjection to one another, and were again relieved from

Changes in later times.

CHAP. II.

B.C. 370–369.

the yoke. In the course of the fourth century two new Peloponnesian cities, *Messênê* and *Megalopolis*, were founded. In Boiôtia again, *Plataia* and *Orchomenos* were destroyed by the Thebans, and Thebes itself was destroyed by Alexander; but these cities were afterwards rebuilt. In Peloponnêsos Mykênê was destroyed

B.C. 468.

by the Argeians at an earlier time, and was never rebuilt. But most of these changes do not affect geography, as they did not involve any change in the seats of the great divisions of the Greek name. The only exception is that of the foundation of *Messênê*, which was accompanied by the separation of the old Messenian territory from Sparta, and the consequent establishment of a new or restored division of the Greek nation.

§ 6. *The Greek Colonies.*

The Ægæan colonies.

It must have been in the time between the days represented by the catalogue and the beginnings of contemporary history, that most of the islands of the Ægæan became Greek, and that Greek colonies were planted on the Ægæan coast of Asia. We have seen that the southern islands were already Greek at the time of the catalogue, while some of the northern ones, *Thasos*, *Lêmnos*, and others, did not become Greek till times to which we can give approximate dates, from the eighth to the fifth centuries. During this period, at some time before the eighth century, the whole Ægæan coast of

Colonies in Asia.

Asia had become fringed with Greek cities, *Dorian* to the south, *Aiolian* to the north, *Ionian* between the two. The story of the Trojan war itself is most likely a legendary account of the beginning of these settlements; and this may make us think that the Greek colonization of this coast began in the north, in the lands bordering on the Hellespont. At all events, by the eighth century these settlements had made the Asiatic coast and the islands adjoining it a part, and a most important part, not only of the Greek world, but we may almost say of Greece itself. The Ionian cities, above all, *Smyrna*, *Ephesos*, *Milêtos*, and the islands of *Chios* and *Samos*,[1] were among the greatest of Greek cities, more flourishing certainly than any in European Greece. Milêtos, above all, was famous for the number of colonies which it sent forth in its own turn. But, if the day of greatness of the Asiatic colonies came before that of the European Greeks, they were also the first to come under the power of the Barbarians. In the course of the fifth century the Greek cities on the continent of Asia came under the power, first of the *Lydian* kings and then of their *Persian* conquerors, who subdued several of the islands also. It was this subjection of the Asiatic Greeks to the Barbarians which led to the Persian war, with which the most brilliant time in the history of European Greece begins. We thus know the Asiatic cities only in the days of their decline. The coasts of Thrace and Macedonia were also sprinkled with Greek cities, but they did not lie so thick together as those on the Asiatic coast, except only in the three-fingered peninsula of *Chalkidikê*, which became a thoroughly Greek land. Some of these colonies in Thrace, as *Olynthos* and *Potidaia*, play an important part in Greek history, and two among them fill a place in the history of the world. *Thermê*, under its later name of *Thessalonikê*, has kept on its importance under all changes down to our own time. And *Byzantion*, on the Thracian Bosporus,

Their early greatness.

Lydian and Persian conquests.

Colonies in Thrace.

Thermê and Byzantion.

[1] [In the *Iliad* Samos means Samothrace, in the *Odyssey* it means Kephallênia.]

CHAP. II.

rose higher still, becoming, under the form of *Constantinople*, the transplanted seat of the Empire of Rome.

The settlements which have been thus far spoken of can hardly be counted as parts of continuous Hellas, but they may be all counted as coming within the immediate Greek world. They were planted in lands so near to the mother-country, and they lay so near to one another, that the whole region round the Ægæan may be looked on as more or less thoroughly Greek. Some parts were wholly Greek, and everywhere Greek influences were predominant. But, during this same period of distant enterprise, between the time of the Homeric catalogue and the time of the Persian War, many Greek settlements were made in far more distant lands. All of course came within the range of the Mediterranean world; no Greek ever passed through the Straits of Hêraklês to found settlements on the Ocean. But a large part of the coast both of the Mediterranean itself and of the Euxine was gradually dotted with Greek colonies. These outposts of Greece, unless they were actually conquered by Barbarians, almost always remained Greek; they kept their Greek language and manners, and they often spread them to some extent among their Barbarian neighbours. But it was not often that any large tract of country in these more distant lands became so thoroughly Greek as the Ægæan coast of Asia became. We may say however that such was the case with the coasts of Sicily and Southern Italy, where many Greek colonies were planted, which will be spoken of more fully in another chapter. All Sicily indeed did in the end really become a Greek land, though not till after its conquest by the Romans. But in Northern and Central Italy, the Latins, Etruscans, and other nations of Italy, were too

More distant colonies.

strong for any Greek colonies to be made in those parts. On the other side of the Hadriatic, Greek colonies had spread before the Peloponnesian war as far north as *Epidamnos*. The more northern colonies on the coast and among the islands of Dalmatia, the Illyrian *Epidauros*, *Pharos*, *Black Korkyra*, and others, were among the latest efforts of Greek colonization in the strict sense.

Colonies in the Hadriatic.

Fourth century B.C.

In other parts of the Mediterranean coasts the Greek settlements lay further apart from each other. But we may say that they were spread here and there over the whole coast, except where there was some special hindrance to keep the Greeks from settling. Thus, in a great part of the Mediterranean the Phœnicians had got the start of the Greeks, both in their own country on the coast of Syria, and in the colonies sent forth by their great cities of Sidon and Tyre. The Phœnician colonists occupied a large part of the western half of the southern coast of the Mediterranean, where lay the great Phœnician cities of *Carthage*, *Utica*, and others. They had also settlements in southern Spain, and one at least outside the straits and on the Ocean. This is *Gades* or *Cadiz*, which has kept its name and its unbroken position as a great city from an earlier time than any other city in Europe. The Greeks therefore could not colonize in these parts. In the great islands of Sicily and Cyprus there were both Phœnician and Greek colonies, and there was a long struggle between the settlers of the two nations. In Egypt again, though there were some Greek settlers, yet there were no Greek colonies in the strict sense. That is, there were no independent Greek commonwealths. Thus the only part of the southern coast of the Mediterranean which lay open to Greek colonization

Phœnician colonies.

CHAP. II.

Greek colonies in Africa, Gaul, and Spain.

was the land between Egypt and the dominions of Carthage. In that land accordingly several Greek cities were planted, of which the chief was the famous *Kyrênê*. On the southern coast of Gaul arose the great Ionian city of *Massalia* or *Marseilles*, which, like the Phœnician Gades, has kept its name and its prosperity down to our own time. Massalia became the centre of a group of Greek cities on the south coast of Gaul and the east coast of Spain, which were the means of spreading a certain amount of Greek civilization in those parts.

Massalia.

Colonies on the Euxine.

Besides these settlements in the Mediterranean itself, there were also a good many Greek colonies on the western, northern, and southern coasts of the Euxine, of which those best worth remembering are the city of *Chersonêsos* in the peninsula called the *Tauric Chersonêsos*, now Crimea, and those of *Sinôpê* and *Trapezous* on the southern coast. Chersonêsos and Trapezous above all deserve notice as being two specially abiding seats of Greek influence. Chersonêsos, under the name of *Chersôn*, remained an independent Greek commonwealth longer than any other, and Trapezous or *Trebizond* became the seat of Greek-speaking Emperors, who outlived those of Constantinople. Speaking generally then, we may say that, in the most famous times of European Greece, in the time of the Persian and Peloponnesian wars, the whole coast of the Ægæan was part of the immediate Greek world, while in Sicily and Cyprus Greek colonies were contending with the Phœnicians, and in Italy with the native Italians. Massalia was the centre of a group of Greek states in the north-west, and Kyrênê in the south, while the greater part of the coast of the Euxine was also dotted with Greek cities here and there. In most of these colonies the

Greeks mixed to some extent with the natives, and the natives to some extent learned the Greek language and manners. We thus get the beginning of what we may call an artificial Greek nation, a nation Greek in speech, feeling, and culture, but not purely Greek in blood, which has held its place in the world ever since.

Beginning of the artificial Greek nation.

§ 7. *Growth of Macedonia and Epeiros.*

But while the spread of the Greek language and civilization, and therewith the growth of the artificial Greek nation, was brought about in a great degree by the planting of independent Greek colonies, it was brought about still more fully by events which went far to destroy the political independence of Greece itself. This came of the growth of the kindred nations to the north of Greece, in Macedonia and Epeiros. The Macedonians were for a long time hemmed in by the Barbarians to the north and west of them and by the Greek cities on the coast, and they were also weakened by divisions among themselves. But when the whole nation was united under its great King Philip, Macedonia soon became the chief power in Greece and the neighbouring lands. Philip greatly increased his dominions at the expense of both Greeks and Barbarians, especially by adding the peninsulas of Chalkidikê to his kingdom. But in Greece itself, though he took to himself the chief power, he did not actually annex any of the Greek states to Macedonia, so that his victories there do not affect the map. His yet more famous son Alexander, and the Macedonian kings after him, in like manner held garrisons in particular Greek cities, and brought some parts of Greece, as Thessaly and Euboia, under a degree of Macedonian influence which hardly

Growth of Macedonia.

Reign of Philip, B.C. 360–336.

Conquests of Alexander, 336–323.

CHAP. II.

differed from dominion; but they did not formally annex them. The conquests of Alexander in Asia brought most of the Greek cities and islands under Macedonian dominion, but some, as Crete, Rhodes, Byzantion, and *Hêrakleia* on the Euxine, kept their independence. Meanwhile Epeiros became united under the Greek kings of *Molossis*, and under Pyrrhos, who made Ambrakia his capital, it became a powerful state. And a little kingdom called *Athamania*, thrust in between Epeiros, Macedonia, and Thessaly, now begins to be heard of.

Epeiros under Pyrrhos, B.C. 295–272.

The Macedonian kingdoms in Asia.

The conquests of Alexander in Asia concern us only so far as they called into being a class of states in Western Asia, all of which received a greater or less share of Hellenic culture, and some of which may claim a place in the actual Greek world. By the division of the empire of Alexander after the battle of Ipsos, *Egypt* became the kingdom of Ptolemy, with whose descendants it remained down to the Roman conquest. The civilization of the Egyptian court was Greek, and Alexandria became one of the greatest of Greek cities. Moreover the earlier kings of the Ptolemaic dynasty held various islands in the Ægæan, and points on the coast of Asia and even of Thrace, which made them almost entitled to rank as a power in Greece itself. The great Asiatic power of Alexander passed to *Seleukos* and his descendants. The early kings of his house ruled from the Ægæan to the Hyphasis; but this great dominion was at all times fringed and broken in upon by the dominions of native princes, by independent Greek cities, and by the dominions of other Macedonian kings. And in the third century their dominion was altogether cut short in the east by the revolt of the *Parthians* in northern Persia, by whom the eastern provinces of the Seleukid kingdom were lopped

B.C. 301.

Egypt under the Ptolemies.

The Seleukid dynasty.

Circa B.C. 256.

CHAP. II.

away. And when Antiochos the Great provoked a war with Rome, his dominion was cut short to the west also. The Seleukid power now shrank up into a local kingdom of *Syria*, with Tauros for its north-western frontier.

B.C. 191–181.

Growth of independent states in Asia Minor. B.C. 283. Pergamos.

By the cutting short of the Seleukid kingdom, room was given for the growth of the independent states which had already sprung up in Asia Minor. The kingdom of *Pergamos* had already begun, and the dominions of its kings were largely increased by the Romans at the expense of Antiochos. Pergamos might count as a Greek state, alongside of Macedonia and Epeiros. But the other kingdoms of Asia Minor, *Bithynia*, *Kappadokia*, *Paphlagonia*, and *Pontos*, the kingdom of the famous Mithridates, must be counted as Asiatic. The Greek influence indeed spread itself far to the east. Even the Parthian kings affected a certain amount of Greek culture, and in all the more western kingdoms there was a greater or less Greek element, and several of their kings fixed their capitals in Greek cities. Still in all of them the Asiatic element prevailed in a way in which it did not prevail at Pergamos. Meanwhile other states, either originally Greek or largely hellenized, still remained east of the Ægæan. Thus, at the south-western corner of Asia Minor, *Lykia*, though seemingly less thoroughly hellenized than some of its neighbours, became a federal state after the Greek model. Far to the east, *Seleukeia* on the Tigris, whether under Syrian or Parthian overlordship, kept its character as a Greek colony, and its position as what may be called a free imperial city. Further to the west other more purely Greek states survived. The Pontic *Hêrakleia* long remained an independent Greek city, sometimes a commonwealth, sometimes under

Spread of Hellenic culture.

Seleukeia

Hêrakleia.

CHAP. II.

B.C. 188.

tyrants; and *Sinôpê* remained a Greek city till it became the capital of the kings of Pontos. On the north of the Euxine, *Bosporos* still remained a Greek kingdom.

§ 8. *The later Geography of Independent Greece.*

Later political divisions of Greece.

The political divisions of independent Greece, in the days when it gradually came under the power of Rome, differ almost as much from those to which we are used during the Persian and Peloponnesian wars, as these last differ from the earlier divisions in the Homeric catalogue. The chief feature of these times was the power which was held, as we have already seen, by the Macedonian kings, and the alliances made by the different Greek states in order to escape or to throw off their yoke. The result was that the greater part of Greece was gradually mapped out among large confederations, much larger at least than Greece had ever seen before.

The Achaian League, B.C. 280.

The most famous of these, the League of *Achaia*, began among the old Achaian cities on the south of the Corinthian gulf. It gradually spread, till it took in the whole of Peloponnêsos, together with Megara

B.C. 191.

and one or two outlying cities. Thus Sikyôn, Corinth, Argos, Elis, and even Sparta, instead of being distinct states as of old, with a greater or less dominion over other cities, were now simply members of one federal

The Aitolian League.

body. In Northern Greece the League of *Aitôlia* now became very powerful, and extended itself far beyond its old borders. Akarnania, Phôkis, Lokris, and Boiôtia formed federal states of less power, and so did *Epeiros*, where the kings had been got rid of, and which was now reckoned as a thoroughly Greek state. The Macedonian kings held different points at different times: Corinth itself for a good while, and Thessaly and Euboia for longer periods, might be almost counted as parts of their kingdom

This was the state of things in Greece at the time when the Romans began to meddle in Greek and Macedonian affairs, and gradually to bring all the Greek and Macedonian lands, like the rest of the Mediterranean world, under their power. But it should be remarked that this was done, as the conquests of the Romans always were done, very gradually. First the island of Korkyra and the cities of Epidamnos and Apollônia on the Illyrian coast became Roman allies, which was always a step to becoming Roman subjects. The Romans first appeared in Greece itself as allies of the Aitolians, but by the *Peace of Epeiros* Rome obtained no dominion in Greece itself, merely some increase of her Illyrian territory. The second Macedonian war made Macedonia dependent on Rome, and all those parts of Greece which had been under the Macedonian power were declared free at its close. As the Aitolians joined Antiochos of Syria against Rome, they were made a Roman dependency. From that time Rome was always meddling in the affairs of the Greek states, and they may be counted as really, though not formally, dependent on Rome. After the third Macedonian war, Macedonia was cut up into four separate commonwealths; and at last, after the fourth, it became a Roman province. About the same time the Leagues of Epeiros and Boiôtia were dissolved; the Achaian League also became formally dependent on Rome, and was dissolved for a time also. It is not certain when Achaia formally became a Roman province; but, from this time, all Greece was practically subject to Rome. Athens remained nominally independent, as did Rhodes, Byzantion, and several other islands and outlying cities. Some of these were not formally incorporated with the Roman dominion till the time of the Emperor Vespasian.

Roman interference in Greece.

B.C. 229.

B.C. 205.

B.C. 200–197.

Progress of Roman conquests.

B.C. 196.

B.C. 189.

B.C. 169.

B.C. 149.

B.C. 146.

Free states incorporated by Vespasian.

CHAP. II.

Nominal freedom of Athens and other cities.

Of some, Athens for one, it may be doubted whether they were ever formally incorporated at all. Surrounded by the Empire, subject to it in every practical sense of the word, these once sovereign commonwealths sank into mere municipalities without any one moment of formal change, and lived and died the life and the death of the other municipalities of the Roman world.

As we go on with the geography of other lands which came under the Roman dominion, we shall learn more of the way in which Rome thus enlarged her territories bit by bit. But it seemed right to begin with the geography of Greece, and this could not be carried down to the time when Greece passed under Roman dominion without saying something of the Roman conquest. From B.C. 146 we must look upon Greece and the neighbouring lands as being, some of them formally and all of them practically, part of the Roman dominion. And we shall not have to speak of them again as separate states or countries till many ages later, when the Roman dominion began to fall in pieces. Having thus traced the geography of the most eastern of the three great European peninsulas down to the time when it became part of the dominion which took in all the lands around the Mediterranean, we will now go on to speak of the middle peninsula which became the centre of that dominion, namely the peninsula of Italy.

Special character of Greek history.

Greece and the neighbouring lands are the only parts of Europe which can be said to have a history quite independent of Rome, and beginning earlier than the Roman history. Of the other countries therefore which became part of the Roman Empire it will be best to speak in their relation to Italy, and, as nearly as possible, in the order in which they came under the Roman power.

CHAPTER III.

FORMATION OF THE ROMAN EMPIRE.

CHAP. III.

Different meanings of the name *Italy*.

THE second of the three great peninsulas of southern Europe, that which lies between the other two, is that of Italy. The name of *Italy* has been used in several meanings at different times, but it has always meant either the whole or a part of the land which we now call Italy. The name gradually spread itself from the extreme south to the north.[1] At the time when our survey begins, the name did not go beyond the long narrow peninsula itself; and indeed it hardly took in the whole of that. During the time of the Roman commonwealth, Italy, in its greatest extent, did not reach beyond the little rivers *Macra* on one side, near *Luna*, and *Rubico* on the other side, near *Ariminum*. The land to the north, as far as the Alps, was not counted for Italy till after the time of Cæsar. But the Alps are the natural boundary which fence off the peninsular land from the great mass of central Europe; so that, looking at the matter as a piece of geography, we may count the whole land within the Alps as Italy. It will be at once seen that the Italian peninsula, though so long and narrow, is by no means cut up into promontories and

Its meaning under the Roman commonwealth.

Geography of Italy.

[1] We shall come as we go on to two uses of the name in which Italy, oddly enough, meant only the northern part of the land commonly so called. But in both these cases the name had a purely political and technical meaning, and it never came into common use in this sense.

CHAP. III.

smaller peninsulas in the way that the Greek peninsula is. Nor is it surrounded by so many islands. It is only quite in the south, where the long narrow peninsula splits off into two smaller ones, that the coast has at all the character of the Greek coast, and there only in a much slighter degree. Close by this end of Italy lies the great island of *Sicily*, whose history has always been closely connected with that of Italy. Further off lie the two other great islands of *Corsica* and *Sardinia*, which in old times were not reckoned to belong to Italy at all. Besides these there are several smaller islands, *Elba* and others, along the Italian coast; but they lie a good way from each other, and do not form any marked feature in the geography. There is nothing at all like even the group of islands off western Greece, much less like the endless multitude, great and small, in the Ægæan. Through the whole length of the peninsula, like a backbone, runs the long chain of the *Apennines*. These branch off from the Alps in north-western Italy near the sea, and they run through the whole length of the country to the very toe of the boot, as the Italian peninsula has been called from its shape. From all this it follows that, though Italy was the land which was destined in the end to have the rule over all the rest, yet the people of Italy were not likely to begin to make themselves a name so early as the Greeks did. Least of all were they likely to take in the same way to a sea-faring life, and to plant colonies in far-off lands.

The Italian islands.

§ 1. *The Inhabitants of Italy and Sicily.*

Non-Aryans in Italy.

We seem to have somewhat clearer signs in Italy than we have in Greece of the men who dwelled in the land

Ligurians.

before the Aryans who appear as its historical inhabitants. On the coast of *Liguria*, the land on each side of the city of Genoa, a land which was not reckoned Italian in early times, we find people who seem not to have been Aryan. And these Ligurians seem to have been part of a race which was spread through Italy and Sicily before the Aryan settlements, and to have been akin to the non-Aryan inhabitants of Spain and southern Gaul, of whom the Basques on each side of the Pyrenees remain as a remnant. And in historical times a large part of Italy was held by the Etruscans, who had in earlier times held a much greater dominion. These are a people about whose origin and language there have been many theories, but nothing can as yet be said to be certainly known. The Etruscans, in historical times, formed a confederacy of twelve cities in the land west of the Apennines, between the Macra and the Tiber; and in earlier times they had settlements both more to the north, on the Po, and more to the south, in Campania. If they were a non-Aryan race, the part of the non-Aryans in the geography and history of Italy becomes greater than it has been in any part of Western Europe except Spain.

Etruscans.

But whatever we make of the Etruscans, the rest of Italy in the older sense was held by various branches of an Aryan race nearly allied to the Greeks, whom we may call the *Italians*. Of this race there were two great branches. One of them, under various names, seems to have held all the southern part of the western coast of Italy, and to have spread into Sicily. Some of the tribes of this branch seem to have been almost as nearly akin to the Greeks as the Epeirots and other kindred nations on the east side of the Hadriatic. Of this branch of the

The Italians.

Latins.

Italian race, the most famous people were the *Latins*; and it was the greatest of Latin cities, the border city of the Latins against the Etruscans, the city of *Rome* on the Tiber, which became, step by step, the mistress of Latium, of Italy, and of the Mediterranean world. The other branch, which held a much larger part of the peninsula, taking in the *Sabines*, *Æquians*, *Volscians*, *Samnites*, *Lucanians*, and other peoples who play a great part in the Roman history, may perhaps, notwithstanding considerable differences among themselves, be classed together for our purpose as *Opicans* or *Oscans*, in distinction from the Latins, and the other tribes allied to them. These tribes seem to have pressed from the eastern, the Hadriatic, coast of Italy, down upon the nations to the south-west of them, and to have largely extended their borders at their expense.

Opicans.

But part of ancient Italy, and a still larger part of Italy in the modern sense, was inhabited by nations other than the Italians. In the heel of the boot were the *Iapygians*, a people of uncertain origin, but who seem to have had a special gift of receiving the Greek language and manners. And in the northern part, in the lands which were not then counted as part of Italy, were the *Gauls*, a Celtic people, akin to the Gauls beyond the Alps, and whose country was therefore called *Cisalpine Gaul* or Gaul on this side of the Alps. They were found on both sides of the Po, and on the Hadriatic coast they stretched in early times as far south as the Æsis near *Ancona*. In the north-east corner of Italy were yet another people, the *Veneti*, perhaps of Illyrian origin, whose name was long after taken by the city of *Venice*. But during the whole time with which we have now to do, there

Iapygians.

Gauls.

Veneti.

was no city so called, and the name of *Venetia* is always the name of a country.

Greek colonies in Italy.

All these nations we may look on as original inhabitants of Italy; that is, all were there before anything like contemporary history begins.[1] But besides these original nations, there were in one part of Italy many Greek colonies, and also in the island of Sicily. Some cities of Italy claimed to be Greek colonies, without any clear proof that they were so. But there seems no reason to doubt that *Kymê* or *Cumæ* on the western coast of Italy, and *Ankôn* or *Ancona* on the Hadriatic, were solitary Greek colonies far away from any other Greek settlements. Cumæ, though so far off, is said to have been the earliest Greek colony in Italy. But where the Greeks mainly settled was in the two lesser peninsulas, the heel and the toe of the boot, into which the great peninsula of Italy divides at its southern end. Here, as was before said, there is a nearer approach to the kind of coast to which the Greeks were used at home. Here then arose a number of Greek cities, stretching from the extreme south almost up to Cumæ. As in the case of the Greek cities in Asia, the time of greatness of the Italian Greeks came earlier than that of the Greeks in Greece itself. In the sixth century B.C. some of these Greek colonies in Italy, as *Taras* or *Tarentum*, *Krotôn* or *Crotona*, *Sybaris*, and others, were among the greatest cities of the Greek name. But, as the Italian nations grew stronger, the Greek cities lost

[1] Some may think that the Cisalpine Gauls ought to be excepted, as the common Roman story represents them as having crossed the Alps from Transalpine Gaul at a time which almost comes within the range of contemporary history. But this is a point about which there is no real certainty; and it seems quite as likely that the Gaulish settlements on the Italian side of the Alps were as old as those on the other side.

CHAP. III.

their power, and many of them, Cumæ among them, fell into the hands of Italian conquerors, and lost their Greek character more or less thoroughly. Others remained Greek till they became subject to Rome, and the Greek speech and manners did not wholly die out of southern Italy till ages after the Christian æra.

Inhabitants of Sicily.

The geography and history of the great island of Sicily, which lies so near to the toe of the boot, cannot be kept apart from those of Italy. The mainland and the island were, to a great extent, inhabited by the same nations. The *Sikanians* in the western part of the island may not unlikely have been akin to the Ligurians and Basques; but the *Sikels*, who gave their name to the island, and who are the people with whom the Greeks had most to do, were clearly of the Italian stock, and were nearly allied to the Latins.[1] The Phœnicians of Carthage planted some colonies in the western and northern parts of the island, the chief of which was the city which the Greeks called *Panormos*, the modern capital *Palermo*. But the eastern and southern sides of the triangle were full of Greek cities, which are said to have been founded from the eighth century B.C. to the sixth, the earliest point occupied being *Naxos* on the east coast. Several of these, especially *Syracuse* on the east coast, and *Akragas* or *Agrigentum* on the south, were among the chief of Greek cities; and from them the Greek speech and manners gradually spread themselves over the natives, till in the end Sicily was reckoned as altogether a Greek land. But for some centuries Sicilian history is chiefly made up of struggles for

Phœnician and Greek colonies.

[1] [This view is improbable. The names Sikan and Sikel can hardly be separated; both peoples probably belonged to the same stock, and the Sikel language was probably non-Aryan.]

the mastery between Carthage and the Greek cities. This was in truth a struggle between the Aryan and the Semitic race, and we shall see that, many ages after, the same battle was again fought on the same ground.

§ 2. *Growth of the Roman power in Italy.*

Gradual conquest of Italy.

The history of ancient Italy, as far as we know it, is the history of the gradual conquest of the whole land by one of its own cities; and the changes in its political geography are mainly the changes which followed the gradual bringing of the whole peninsula under the Roman dominion. But the form which the conquests of Rome took hindered those conquests from having so great an effect on the map as they otherwise might have had. The cities and districts of Italy, as they were one by one conquered by Rome, were commonly left as separate states, in the relation of dependent alliance, from which most of them were step by step promoted to the rights of Roman citizenship.

Different positions of the Italian cities.

An Italian city might be a dependent ally of Rome; it might be a Roman colony with the full franchise, or a colony holding the inferior Latin franchise; it might have been completely incorporated with Rome by being made part of a Roman tribe. All these were very important political differences; but they do not make much difference in the look of things on the map. The most important of the changes which can be called strictly geographical belong to the early days of Rome, when there were important national movements among the various races of Italy.

Origin of Rome.

Rome arose at the point of the union of the three races, Latin, Oscan, and Etruscan, and it arose from an union between the Latin and Oscan races. Two Latin and one Sabine settlements seem to have joined together to form the

CHAP. III.

Rome a Latin city.

city of Rome; but the Sabine element must have been thoroughly latinized, and Rome must be counted a Latin city, the greatest, though very likely the youngest, among the cities of Latium.

Her early Latin dominion.

Rome, planted on a march, rose, in the way in which marchlands often do rise, to supremacy among her fellows. Our first authentic record of the early commonwealth sets Rome before us as bearing rule over the whole of Latium. This dominion she seems to have lost soon after the driving out of the kings, and some of her territory right of the Tiber seems to have become Etruscan. Presently Rome appears, no longer as mistress of Latium, but as forming one member of a triple league concluded on equal terms with the Latins as a body, and with the *Hernicans*.

Wars with her neighbours.

This league was engaged in constant wars with its neighbours of the Oscan race, the *Æquians* and *Volscians*, by whom many of the Latin cities were taken.

More distant wars.

But the first great advance of Rome's actual dominion was made on the right bank of the Tiber, by the
B.C. 396. taking of the Etruscan city of *Veii*. Fifty years later
B.C. 343. Rome began to engage in more distant wars; and we may say generally that the conquest of Italy was going
B.C. 296. on bit by bit for eighty years more. By the end of that time, all Italy, in the older sense, was brought in one shape or another under the Roman dominion. The neighbouring districts, both Latin and of other races, had been admitted to citizenship. Roman and Latin colonies were planted in various parts of the country; elsewhere the old cities, Etruscan, Samnite, Greek, or any other, still remained as dependent allies of Rome.

Incorporation of the Italian states.

Presently Rome went on to win dominion out of Italy; but the Italian states still remained in their old relation to Rome, till the allies received the Roman franchise after the *Social* or *Marsian* war. The *Samnites* alone held out, and they may be said to have been altogether exterminated in the wars of Sulla. The rest of Italy was Roman.

B.C. 89.

§ 3. *The Western Provinces.*

The great change in Roman policy, and in European geography as affected by it, took place when Rome began to win territory out of Italy. The relation of these foreign possessions to the ruling city was quite different from that of the Italian states. The foreign conquests of Rome were made into *provinces*. A province was a district which was subject to Rome, and which was put under the rule of a Roman governor, which was not done with the dependent allies in Italy. But it must be borne in mind that, though we speak of a province as having a certain geographical extent, yet there might be cities within its limits whose formal relation to Rome was that of dependent, or even of equal, alliance. There might also be Roman and Latin colonies, either colonies really planted or cities which had been raised to the Roman or Latin franchise. All these were important distinctions as regarded the internal government of the different states; still practically all alike formed part of the Roman dominion. In a geographical survey it will therefore be enough to mark the extent of the different provinces, without attending to their political, or more truly municipal, distinctions, except in a few cases where they are of special importance.

Nature of the Roman Provinces.

The provinces then are the foreign dominions of Rome, and they fall naturally into two, or rather three,

CHAP. III.

Eastern and Western Provinces.

divisions. There are the provinces of the West, in which the Romans had chiefly to contend with nations much less civilized than themselves, and in which therefore the provincials gradually adopted the language and manners of their conquerors. But in the provinces to the east of the Hadriatic, the Greek language and Greek manners had become the standard of civilized life, and their supremacy was not supplanted by those of Rome in any land where they were fully established. But in those parts of the Eastern peninsula where Greek culture had not established itself, the Latin language seems to have spread much as it did in the West. In the further East, in Syria and Egypt, such Greek civilization as there was did not go beyond a mere varnish ; the mass of the people still kept to their old manners and languages as they were before the Macedonian conquests. In these lands therefore the Latin tongue and Roman civilization made but little progress. The Roman conquests went on on both sides of the Hadriatic at the same time, but it was to the west that they began. The first Roman province however forms a sort of intermediate class by itself, standing between the eastern and the western.

Sicily.

This first Roman province was formed in the great island of *Sicily*, which, by its geographical position, belongs to the western part of Europe, while the fact that Greek became the prevailing language in it, as well as its long retention by the Eastern Empire in later times, rather connects it with the eastern part. The Roman dominion in Sicily began when the Carthaginian possessions in the island were given up to Rome, as the result of the first Punic war. But, as Hierôn of *Syracuse* had helped Rome against Carthage, his kingdom remained in alliance with Rome, and was not dealt with

First Roman possessions in the island. B.C. 241.

as a conquered land. It was only when Syracuse turned against Rome in the second Punic war that it was, on its conquest, formally made a Roman possession. Eighty years later the condition of Sicily under the Roman government was finally settled, and the settlement may be taken as a type of the endless variety of relations in which the different districts and cities throughout the Roman dominions stood to the ruling commonwealth. The greater part of the island became altogether subject; the land was held to be forfeited to the Roman People, and the former inhabitants held it simply as tenants on the payment of a tithe. But some cities were called free, and kept their land; others remained in name independent allies of the Roman People. Other cities were afterwards raised to the Latin franchise; in others Latin or Roman colonies were planted, and one Sicilian city, that of *Messana*, received the full citizenship of Rome. Sicily, by the time of the conquest, was looked on as a thoroughly Greek land. The Greek language and manners had now spread themselves everywhere among the Sikels and the other inhabitants of the island. And Sicily remained a thoroughly Greek land, till, ages afterwards, it again became, as it had been in the days of the Greek and Phœnician colonies, a battle-field of the Aryan and Semitic races in the days of the Mahometan conquests.

CHAP. III.

Conquest of Syracuse. B.C. 212.

B.C. 132.

State of Sicily.

Greek civilization of Sicily.

The two great islands of *Sardinia* and *Corsica* seem almost as natural appendages to Italy as Sicily itself; but their history is very different. They have played no important part in the history of the world. The original stock of their inhabitants seems to have been akin to the non-Aryan element in Spain and Sicily. The attempts at Greek colonization in them were but

Sardinia and Corsica.

CHAP. III.

feeble, and they passed under the dominion, first of Carthage and then of Rome, without any important change in their condition. These two islands became a Roman province, one which was always reckoned among the most worthless of provinces, in the interval between the first and second Punic wars.

B.C. 238.

Cisalpine Gaul.

Thus far the Roman dominion did not reach beyond what we should look upon as the natural extent of the dominion of an Italian power. Indeed, as long as Italy did not reach to the Alps, we should say that it had not reached the natural extent of an Italian dominion. But the conquest of Cisalpine Gaul cannot be separated from the general conquest of Western Europe. The Roman conquest of Gaul and Spain, by gradually spreading the Latin language and Roman civilization over those countries, created two of the chief nations and languages of modern Europe. But the process was simply the continuation of a process which began within the borders of what we now call Italy. Gaul within the Alps was as strictly a foreign conquest as Spain or as Gaul beyond the Alps. Only the geographical position of Cisalpine Gaul allowed it to be easily and speedily incorporated with Italy in a way in which the lands beyond the Alps could not be. The beginnings of conquest in this direction took place after the end of the Samnite wars. Then the colony of *Sena Gallica*, now *Sinigaglia*, was founded on Gaulish soil, and it was presently followed by the foundation of *Ariminum* or *Rimini*. The Roman arms were carried beyond the Po in the time between the first and the second Punic war; after the second Punic war, Cisalpine Gaul was thoroughly conquered, and was secured by the foundation of many

Foundation of Sena Gallica. B.C. 282.

Conquest of Cisalpine Gaul B.C. 201–191.

Roman and Latin colonies. The Roman and Latin franchises were gradually extended to most parts of the country, and at last Cisalpine Gaul was formally incorporated with Italy.

B.C. 43.

Conquest of Liguria and Venetia.

Closely connected with the conquest of Cisalpine Gaul was the conquest of the other non-Italian lands within the boundaries of modern Italy. These were *Liguria* to the south-west of Cisalpine Gaul and *Venetia* to the north-east. Both these lands held out longer than Cisalpine Gaul; but by the time of Augustus they were all, together with the peninsula of *Istria*, counted as part of Italy. The dominion of Rome in this region was secured at an early stage of the conquest by the foundation of the great colony of *Aquileia*. We thus see that, not only Venice, but Milan, Pavia, Verona, Ravenna, and Genoa, cities which played so great a part in the after history of Italy, arose in lands which were not originally Italian. But we also see that Italy, with the boundaries given to it by Augustus, took in a somewhat larger territory to the north-east than the kingdom of Italy does now.

Foundation of Aquileia, B.C. 183.

The lands within the Alps may be fairly said to have been conquered by Rome in self-defence, and we are tempted to look on the three great islands as natural parts of an Italian dominion. The conquests of the Romans in lands altogether beyond their own borders began in Western Europe with the conquest of *Spain*, which began before that of Transalpine Gaul. Spain and Gaul, using the names in the geographical sense, have much which binds them together. On the borders of the two countries traces are still left of the old non-Aryan inhabitants who still speak the Basque language. These represent the old *Iberian* inhabitants of

Spain.

Connexion of Spain and Gaul.

Iberians in Spain.

CHAP. III.

Spain and Gaul, who, when our history begins, stretched
Celts. into Gaul as far as the Garonne. But the *Celts*, the
first wave of the Aryan migration in Europe, had
pressed into both Gaul and Spain; in Gaul they had,
when trustworthy history begins, already occupied by
far the greater part of the country. The Mediterranean
coasts of Gaul and Spain were also connected together
Greek and by the sprinkling of Greek colonies along those shores,
of which *Massalia* was the head. And, beside the
primitive non-Aryan element, there was an intrusive
non-Aryan element also. In southern Spain several
Phœnician settlements. Phœnician settlements had been made, the chief of
which was *Gades* or *Cadiz*, beyond the straits, the one
great Phœnician city on the Ocean. And, between the
first and second Punic wars, Carthage obtained a large
Spanish dominion, of which *New Carthage* or *Carthagena* was the capital.

It was the presence of these last settlements which
First Roman province in Spain. first brought Spain under the Roman dominion. *Saguntum* was an ally of Rome, and its taking by Hannibal was the beginning of the second Punic war.
The campaigns of the Scipios during that war led to
B.C. 218–206. the gradual conquest of the whole country. The Carthaginian possessions first became a Roman province,
B.C. 49. while Gades became a favoured ally of Rome, and at
last was admitted to the full Roman franchise. Meanwhile the gradual conquest of the rest of Spain went
B.C. 133. on, till, after the taking of *Numantia*, the whole
peninsula, except the remote tribes in the north-west,
Final conquest. had become a Roman possession. These tribes, the
B.C. 19. *Cantabrians* and their neighbours, were not fully subdued till the time of Augustus. But, long before
that time, the Latin language and Roman manners

spread fast through the country, and in Augustus' time southern Spain was altogether romanized. It was only in a small district close to the Pyrenees that the ancient language held out, as it has done ever since.

Romanization of Spain.

The conquest of Spain, owing to the connexion of the country with Carthage, thus began while a large part even of Cisalpine Gaul was still unsubdued. And the Roman arms were not carried into Gaul beyond the Alps till the conquest of Spain was pretty well assured. The foundation of the first Roman colony at *Aquæ Sextiæ*, the modern *Aix*, was only eleven years later than the fall of Numantia. The Romans stepped in as allies of the Greek city of Massalia, and, as usual, from helping their allies they took to conquering on their own account. A Roman province, including the colonies of *Narbonne* and *Toulouse*, was thus formed in the south-eastern part of Transalpine Gaul. The advance of Rome in this direction seems to have been checked by the invasion of the Cimbri and Teutones, but through that long delay Roman influences were able to establish themselves more firmly. This part of Gaul was early and thoroughly romanized, and part of it still keeps, in its name of *Provence*, the memory of its having been the first Roman province beyond the Alps. The rest of Gaul was left untouched till the great campaigns of Cæsar.

Transalpine Gaul. B.C. 122. The Transalpine Province. B.C. 125–105.

It is from Cæsar, ethnologer as well as conqueror, that we get our chief knowledge of the country as it was in his day. Transalpine Gaul, as a geographical division, has well-marked boundaries in the Mediterranean, the Alps, the Rhine, the Ocean, and the Pyrenees. But this geographical division has never answered to any divisions of blood and language. Gaul in Cæsar's

Conquests of Cæsar. B.C. 58–51. Boundaries of Transalpine Gaul.

CHAP. III.

Its three divisions, and their inhabitants, Iberian, Celtic, and German.

day, that is Gaul beyond the Roman province, formed three divisions—*Aquitaine* to the south-west, *Celtic Gaul* in the middle, and *Belgic Gaul* to the north-east. Aquitaine, stretching to the Garonne—the name was under Augustus extended to the Loire—was Iberian, akin to the people on the other side of the Pyrenees: a trace of its old speech remains in the small Basque district north of the Pyrenees. Celtic Gaul, from the Loire to the Seine and Marne, was the most truly Celtic land, and it was in this part of Gaul that the modern French nation took its rise. In the third division, Belgic Gaul, the tribes to the east, nearer to the Rhine, were some of them purely German, and others had been to a great extent brought under German influences or mixed with German elements. There was, in fact, no unity in Gaul beyond that which the Romans brought with them. In seven years Cæsar subdued the whole land, and the work of assimilation began. The Roman language gradually displaced all the native languages, except where Basque and Breton survive in two corners; but in a large part of Belgic Gaul the events of later times brought the German tongue back again. There is no Roman province in which, among all changes, the ancient geography has had so much effect upon that of all later times. In southern Gaul most of the cities still keep their old names with very little change. But in northern Gaul the cities have mostly taken the names of the tribes of which they were the heads. Thus *Tolosa* is still *Toulouse*; but *Lutetia Parisiorum* has become *Paris*.

Romanization of Gaul.

Permanence of the ancient geography.

Roman Africa.

The lands which we have thus gone through, Cisalpine Gaul with Liguria and Venetia, Spain, and Transalpine Gaul, form a marked division in historical geography. They are those parts of Western Europe which Rome conquered during the time of her Commonwealth, and they are those parts which have mainly kept their Roman speech to this day. But these did not make up the whole of the lands where Rome planted her Latin speech, at least for a while. The conquest of Britain belongs to the days of the Empire; but Rome, during the Commonwealth, made another conquest, which, though not in Europe, may be counted as belonging to the Western or Latin-speaking half of her dominion. This is that part of *Africa* which Rome won as the result of her wars with Carthage. The only African possession won by Rome during the days of the Commonwealth was *Africa* in the strictest sense, the immediate dominion of Carthage. This became a province when the Punic wars were ended by the destruction of Carthage. The neighbouring state of *Numidia*, after passing, like Carthage itself, through the intermediate state of a dependency, was made a province by Cæsar, being called *New Africa*, the former African province becoming the *Old*. Cæsar also restored the city of Carthage as a Roman colony, and it became the chief of the Latin speaking cities of the Empire, second only to Rome herself. But in Africa, just as in Britain, the land never was thoroughly romanized like Gaul and Spain. The Roman tongue and laws therefore died out in both lands at the first touch of an invader, the English in one case and the Saracens in the other. The strip of fertile land between the sea on one side and the mountains and the Great Desert on the other received, first Phœnician and then Roman civilization. But neither of them could really take root

Province of Africa, B.C. 146; of New Africa, B.C. 49. Restoration and greatness of Carthage.

there in the way that the Roman civilization took root in Gaul and Spain.

§ 4. *The Eastern Provinces.*

Contrast between the Eastern and Western provinces.

The Hadriatic sea may be roughly taken as the boundary between the Eastern and Western parts of the Roman dominion. In the West, the Romans carried with them, not only their arms, but their tongue, their laws, and their manners. They were not only conquerors but civilizers. The native Iberians and Celts adopted Roman fashions, and the isolated Greek and Phœnician cities, like Massalia and Gades, gradually became Roman also. East of the Hadriatic the state of things was quite different. Here the language and civilization of Greece had, through the conquests of the Macedonian kings, become everywhere predominant. Greek was everywhere the polite and literary language, and a certain varnish of Greek manners had been everywhere spread. In some parts indeed it was the merest varnish; still it was everywhere strong enough to withstand the influence of Latin. Sicily and southern Italy are the only lands which have altogether thrown away the Greek tongue, and have taken to Latin or any of the languages formed out of Latin. East of the Hadriatic Latin nowhere displaced Greek, unless in a few isolated colonies. But in those parts of the Eastern peninsula into which Greek culture had not spread itself, that is, in a large part of the Illyrian and Thracian lands, Latin undoubtedly displaced the native languages, just as it did in the West. The *Rouman* people, keeping their Latin name and speech to this day, are the witness of that fact. Still no part of the eastern half of the Roman dominion ever became

Greek civilization in the East.

thoroughly Roman in the same way as Gaul and Spain.

Distinctions among the Eastern provinces.

With these exceptions, the whole of the lands east of the Hadriatic may, as opposed to the Latin-speaking lands of the west, be called, in different degrees, Greek-speaking lands. There are some wide distinctions to be drawn among them. First, there was old Greece itself and the Greek colonies, and lands like *Epeiros*, which had become thoroughly Greek. Secondly, there were the kingdoms, like *Macedonia* in Europe and *Pergamos* in Asia, which had adopted the Greek speech and manners, but which did not, like Epeiros, become Greek in any political sense. Thirdly, there were a number of native states, *Bithynia* and others, whose kings also tried to imitate Greek ways, but naturally could not do so as thoroughly as the kings of Macedonia and Pergamos. Fourthly, beyond Mount Tauros lay the kingdoms of *Syria* and *Egypt*, which were ruled by Macedonian kings, which contained great Greek or Macedonian cities like *Antioch* and *Alexandria*, but where there were native languages, and an old native civilization, which neither Greek nor Roman influences could ever root out. We shall see as we go on that Tauros makes a great historical boundary. The lands on this side of it really came, though very gradually, under the dominion of the Greek speech and the Roman law, and remained under them till the Turkish invasions. Beyond Mount Tauros both the Greek and the Roman element lay merely on the surface, and therefore those lands easily fell away when they were attacked by the Saracens. We must now go through such of the lands east of the Hadriatic as were formed into Roman provinces during the time of the Roman Commonwealth.

Lands beyond Tauros.

CHAP. III.

The Illyrian Provinces.

But again, between the Latin and the Greek parts of the Roman dominion there was a border land, namely, the lands held by the great *Illyrian* race. The southern parts of Illyria came within the reach of Greek influences, and it was through the affairs of Illyria that Rome was first led to meddle in the affairs of Greece. The use of the name *Illyria* is at all times very vague; but it has a more definite meaning as the name of a kingdom whose capital was *Skodra*, and which, in the second half of the third century, was a dangerous neighbour to the Greek cities and islands on that coast. This kingdom was involved in the third Macedonian war, and it came to an end at the same time. As usual, it is not easy to distinguish how much, if any, of the country actually became a Roman province, and how much was left for a while in the intermediate state of dependent alliance. But, for all practical purposes, the Illyrian kingdom of Skodra formed from this time a part of the Roman dominion. With the fall of Skodra, the parts of Illyria which lay further to the north, beyond the bounds of the Greek world, first came into notice. The Greek colonies in Dalmatia had played their part in the first Illyrian war; but the land itself, whose cities were to become an outlying fringe of Italy lying east of the Hadriatic, is now first heard of as a distinct country formed by a separation from the kingdom of Skodra. The first Dalmatian war soon followed; but it was not till after several wars that Dalmatia became a province, and even after that time there were several revolts. Before long, Dalmatia was settled with several Roman colonies, as *Jadera* or *Zara*, and, above all, *Salona*, which became one of the chief cities of the Roman dominion. The neighbouring lands of *Liburnia*, *Istria*, and the land of the

The kingdom of Skodra.

B.C. 168.

Dalmatian wars.

B.C. 156.

B.C. 34.

Roman colonies in Dalmatia.

Iapodes, were gradually reduced during the same period. Istria, like the neighbouring land of Venetia, was actually incorporated with Italy, and *Pola*, under the name of *Pietas Julia*, became a Roman colony.

Istria incorporated with Italy.

The outlying Greek lands.

We have already traced the process by which old Greece and the neighbouring lands of Macedonia and Epeiros gradually sank, first practically, and then formally, into parts of the Roman dominion. We have seen how hard it is to say at what particular moment many of the Greek cities and islands sank from the relation of obedient allies into that of acknowledged subjects, while we may doubt if some of them were formally annexed at all. Thus the Greek cities on the Euxine do not seem to have been formally annexed till a late period of the Eastern Empire. Other outlying Greek lands and cities became so mixed up with the history of the Asiatic kingdoms that they will come in for a mention along with them. *Crete* kept its independence to become a nest of pirates, and to be specially conquered. It then formed one province with the then recent conquest of *Kyrênê*, the one great Greek settlement in Africa, which had become an appanage of the Macedonian kings of Egypt. The same had been the fate of *Cyprus*, an island which had always been partly Greek, and which had been further hellenized under its Macedonian kings. Cyprus too became a province. Thus, before Rome lost her own freedom, she had become the formal or practical mistress of all the earlier abodes of freedom. Men could not yet foresee that a time would come when *Greek* and *Roman* should be words having the same meaning, and when the place and name of Rome herself should be transferred to one of the Greek cities which Vespasian reduced from formal alliance to bondage.

Their late formal annexation.

Conquest of Crete, B.C. 67,

of Cyprus, B.C. 58.

CHAP. III.

The Asiatic Provinces.

B.C. 191–188.

In Roman history one war and one conquest always led to another, and, as the affairs of Illyria had led to Roman interference in Greece, so the affairs of Greece led to Roman interference in *Asia*. The first war which Rome waged with *Antiochos* of Syria led to no immediate increase of the Roman territory, but all the Seleukid possessions on this side Tauros were divided among the allies of Rome. This, as usual, was the first step towards the conquest of Asia, and it was quite according to the usual course of things that the first Roman province beyond the Ægæan, the province of *Asia*, should be formed of the dominions of Rome's first and most useful allies, the kings of Pergamos. The mission of Alexander and his successors, as the representatives of Western civilization against the East, now passed into the hands of Rome. Step by step, the other lands west of Tauros came under the formal or practical dominion of Rome. *Bithynia* was the first to be annexed, and this acquisition was one of the causes which led to the second war between Rome and the famous *Mithridates* of *Pontos*. His final overthrow brought a number of other lands under Roman dominion or influence. The Greek cities of *Sinôpê* and *Hêrakleia* obtained a nominal freedom, and vassal kings went on reigning in part of Pontos itself, and in the distant Greek kingdom of *Bosporos*. Rome was now mistress of Asia Minor. The land was divided among her provinces and her vassal kings, save that the wise federal commonwealth of *Lykia* still kept the highest amount of freedom that was consistent with the practical supremacy of Rome.

Province of Asia, B.C. 133–129.

Bithynia. B.C. 74.

Overthrow of Mithridates. B.C. 64.

Lykia.

The Mithridatic war, which made Rome mistress of Asia in the narrower sense, at once involved her in the affairs of the further East. Tigranes of *Armenia* had been the chief ally of Mithridates; but, though his power was utterly broken, no Armenian province was added to the Roman dominion for a long time to come. But the remnant of the Seleukid monarchy became the Roman province of *Syria*. As usual, several cities and principalities were allowed to remain in various relations of alliance and dependence on the ruling commonwealth. Among these we find *Judæa* and the rest of *Palestine*, sometimes under a Roman procurator, sometimes united under a single vassal king, sometimes parted out among various kings and tetrarchs, as suited the momentary caprice or policy of Rome. In all these various relations between the native states and the ruling city we have a lively foreshadowing of the relations between England and her subject and dependent lands in India. The conquests of Rome in these regions made her more distinctly than ever the representative of the West against the East, and these conquests presently brought her into collision with the one power in the known world which could meet her on at all equal terms. She had stepped into the place of Alexander and Seleukos so far as that all those parts of Alexander's Asiatic conquests which had received even a varnish of Hellenic culture had become parts of her dominion. The further East beyond the Euphrates was again under the command of a great barbarian power, that of *Parthia*, which had stepped into the place of Persia, as Rome had stepped into the place of Greece and Macedonia. Rome had now again a rival, in a sense in which she had not had a rival since the overthrow of Carthage and Macedonia.

Province of Syria. B.C. 64.

Palestine.

Comparison with British India.

Rome the champion of the West.

Her rivalry with Parthia.

CHAP. III.

Conquest of Egypt. B.C. 31.

One only of the Macedonian kingdoms now remained to be gathered in. The annexation of *Egypt*, an annexation made famous by the names of Kleopatra, Antonius, the elder and the younger Cæsar, completed the work. Rome was now fully mistress of her own civilized world. Her dominion took in all the lands round the great inland sea. If, here and there, her formal dominion was broken by a city or principality whose nominal relation was that of alliance, the distinction concerned only the local affairs of that city or principality. Within the whole historic world of the three ancient continents, the Roman Peace had begun. Rome had still to wage wars, and even to annex provinces; but those wars and annexations were now done rather to round off and to strengthen the territory which had been already gained, than in the strictest sense to extend it.

Pax Romana.

§ 5. *Conquests under the Empire.*

At the same moment when the Roman commonwealth was practically changed into a monarchy, the Roman dominion was thus brought, not indeed to its greatest extent, but to an extent of which its further extension was only a natural completion. There seems a certain inconsistency when we find Augustus laying down a rule against the enlargement of the Empire, while the Empire was, during his reign and that of his successor, extended in every direction. But the conquests of this time were mainly conquests for the purpose of strengthening the frontier; the occasional changes of this and that city or district from the dependent to the provincial relation, or sometimes from the provincial to the

Conquests under Augustus and Tiberius.

CHAP. III.

dependent, are now hardly worth mentioning. Between Augustus and Nero, or, at all events, between Augustus and Vespasian, all the dependent lands in Asia and Africa, such as *Mauritania*, *Kappadokia*, *Lykia*, and others, were finally incorporated with the Empire to which they had long been practically subject. These annexations can hardly be called conquests. And when the small corner of Spain which still kept its independence was brought under the Roman power, it was merely finishing a work which had been begun two hundred years before. The real conquests of this time consisted in the strengthening of the European frontier. No frontier nearer than the Rhine and the Danube could be looked on as safe. This lesson was easily learned; but it had also to be accompanied by another lesson which taught that the Rhine and the Danube, and not any more distant points, were to be the real frontiers of Rome.

Incorporation of the dependent kingdoms.

Strengthening of the frontier.

This brings us both to the lands which were then our own and to the lands which became our own in after times. During the reign of Augustus two conquests which most nearly concern our own history were planned, and one of them was attempted. The annexation of the land which was to become England was talked of; the annexation of the land which then was England, along with the rest of the German lands, was seriously attempted. But the conquest of Britain was put off from the days of Augustus to the days of Claudius. The attempt at the conquest of Germany, which was deemed to have been already carried out, was shivered when Arminius overthrew the legions of Varus. The expeditions of Drusus and Germanicus into northern Germany must have brought

Attempted conquest of Germany. B.C. 11–A.D. 9.

A.D. 19.

CHAP. III.

the Roman armies into contact with our own forefathers, for the first time, and, for several ages, for the last time. But from this time the relations between Rome and southern Germany begin, and constantly increase in importance. The two great rivers were fixed as a real frontier. The lands between the Alps and the Danube, *Rœtia*, *Vindelicia*, *Noricum*, *Pannonia*, with *Mœsia* on the lower Danube, were all added to the Empire during the reign of Augustus. These were strictly defensive annexations, annexations made in order to remove the dangerous frontier further from Italy. Beyond the Rhine and the Danube the Roman possessions were mere outposts held for the defence of the land between the two great streams.

Conquests on the Danube.

Meanwhile, while the attempt of the conquest of Germany came to so little, an attempt at conquest at the other end of the world, in the *Arabian* peninsula, came to even less. It marks the policy of Rome and the gradual nature of her advance that, while these more distant conquests were made or attempted, *Thrace* still retained her dependent princes, the only land of any extent within the European dominions of Rome which did so. But Thrace, surrounded by Roman provinces, was in no way dangerous; it might remain a dependency while more distant lands were incorporated. It was not till uniformity was more sought after, till, under Vespasian, the nominal freedom of so many cities and principalities came to an end, that Thrace became a province. Such parts both of Thrace and of the neighbouring lands as had not adopted Greek culture, learned the Latin tongue, and gradually came to take the Roman name which some of their inhabitants still bear. And it was then too that, among

Attempt on Arabia. B.C. 24.

Thrace.

her latest formal acquisitions in Europe, Rome annexed the city which was, in the course of ages, to take her own place and name in a truer sense.

Annexation of Byzantion.

Thus, in the days between Augustus and Trajan, the conquests which Rome actually made were mainly of a defensive and strengthening character. To this rule there is one, and only one, exception of any importance. This is the annexation to the Roman world of the land which was looked on as another world, the conquest of the greater part of the Isle of *Britain*. But the annexation of Britain, though it did not come under the same law as the defensive annexations of Rætia and Pannonia, was naturally suggested by the annexation of Gaul and by the visits of the first Cæsar to the island. No actual conquest however took place till the reign of Claudius. Forty years later, the Roman conquests in Britain were pushed by *Agricola* as far as the isthmus between the friths of Forth and Clyde, the boundary marked by the later rampart of *Antoninus*. But the lasting boundary of the Roman dominion in Britain cannot be looked on as reaching beyond the line of the southern wall of *Hadrian*, *Severus*, and *Stilicho*, between the Solway and the mouth of the Tyne. The northern part of Britain remained unconquered, and the conquest of Ireland was not even attempted. For us the conquest of the land which afterwards became our own has an interest above all the other conquests of Rome. But it is a purely geographical interest. The British victories of Cæsar and Agricola were won, not over our own forefathers, but over those Celtic Britons whom our forefathers more thoroughly swept away. The history of our own nation is still for some ages to be looked for by the banks of the Elbe

Conquest of Britain.

Claudius. B.C. 43.

Agricola. B.C. 84.

CHAP. III.

and the Weser, not by those of the Severn and the Thames.

The Eastern conquests of Trajan.

Britain was the last to be won of the Western provinces of Rome, and the first to be lost. Still it was, for more than three hundred years, thoroughly incorporated with the Empire, and its loss did not happen till that general break-up of the Empire of which its loss was the first stage. But between the conquest of Britain and its loss there was a short time in which Rome again extended her dominion in the old fashion, both in Europe and Asia. This was during the reign of Trajan, when the Roman borders were again widely extended in both Europe and Asia. Under him the Danube ceased to be a boundary stream in one continent and the Euphrates in the other. But a marked distinction must be drawn between his Asiatic and his European warfare. Trajan's Asiatic conquests were strictly momentary; they were at once given up by his successor; and they will be better dealt with when we speak in another chapter of the long strife between Rome and her Eastern rival, first Parthian and then Persian. The only lasting Asiatic conquest of Trajan's reign was not made by Trajan himself, namely the small Roman province in Northern *Arabia*.

Conquests of Trajan. A.D. 98–117.

His Asiatic and European conquests.

Conquest of Arabia Petræa. A.D. 106.

The European conquests of Trajan stand on another ground. If not strictly defensive, like those of Augustus, they might easily seem to be so. The *Dacians*, to the north of the lower Danube, were really threatening to the Roman power in those regions, and they had dealt Rome more than one severe blow in the days of Domitian. Trajan now formed the lands which are now known as Transylvania and Little Walachia into the Roman province of *Dacia*. Thus this province did

Dacia.

A.D. 106.

CHAP. III.

not include the present kingdom of Roumania; it only took in that part of it which lies west of the river Aluta.[1] The last province to be won was the first to be given up; for Aurelian withdrew from it, and transferred its name to the Mœsian land immediately south of the Danube. For four hundred years more that great river remained the northern boundary of the Empire in this region, marking, it may be, that the wisdom of the Illyrian who withdrew within the elder frontier was greater than that of the Spaniard who advanced beyond it.

A.D. 270.

Summary.

The Roman Empire was thus gradually formed by bringing, first Italy and then the whole of the Mediterranean lands, under the dominion of the one Roman city. In every part of that dominion the process of conquest was gradual. The lands which became Roman provinces passed through various stages of alliance and dependence before they were fully incorporated. But, in the end, all the civilized world of those times became Roman. Speaking roughly, three great rivers, Rhine, Danube, and Euphrates, formed the European and Asiatic boundaries of the Empire. In Africa the Roman dominion consisted only of the strip of fertile land between the Mediterranean and the mountains and deserts. Britain and Dacia, the only two great provinces lying beyond this range, were the last conquered and the first given up. In Western

[1] [Great Walachia, east of the Aluta, was committed to the supervision of the military commanders in Lower Mœsia. The western boundary of the Dacian province did not coincide with the Theiss, but with an irregular line drawn from Orsova to Kis Sebes. The plain of the Temes was joined to Upper Mœsia. See Domaszewski's article in *Arch.-Epigr. Mittheilungen*, xiii.]

CHAP. III.

Europe and in Africa Rome carried her language and her civilization with her, and in those lands the Roman speech still remains, except where it has been swept away by Teutonic and Saracen conquests. In all those lands, from the Hadriatic to Mount Tauros, which had been brought more or less under Greek influences, the Greek speech and civilization stood their ground, and in those lands Greek still survives wherever it has not been swept away by Slavonic and Turkish conquests. In the further east, in Syria and Egypt, where there was an old native civilization, neither Greek nor Roman influences took real root. The differences between these three parts of the Roman Empire, the really Roman, the Greek, and the Oriental, will be clearly seen as we go on.

CHAPTER IV.

THE DISMEMBERMENT OF THE EMPIRE.

§ 1. *The Later Geography of the Empire.*

CHAP. IV.

THE Roman dominion, as we have seen, grew up by the successive annexation of endless kingdoms, districts, and cities, each of which, after its annexation, still retained, whether as an allied province or a subject state, much of the separate being which it had while it was independent. The allies and subjects of Rome remained in a variety of different relations to the ruling city, and the old names and the old geographical boundaries were largely preserved. But, as the old ideas of the commonwealth gradually died out, and as the power of the Emperors gradually grew into an avowed monarchy, the political change naturally led to a geographical change. The Roman dominion ceased to be a collection of allied and subject states under a single ruling city; it changed into a single Empire, all whose parts, all whose inhabitants, were equally subject to its Imperial head. The old distinctions of Latins, Italians, and provincials, died out when all free inhabitants of the Empire became alike Romans. Italy had no longer any privilege; it was simply part of the Empire, like any other part. The geographical divisions which had been, first independent, then dependent states, sank into purely administrative divisions, which might be mapped out afresh at any time when it was found convenient to

Wiping out of old divisions under the Empire.

CHAP. IV.

do so. Italy itself, in the extended sense which the word Italy had then come to bear, was mapped out afresh into *regions* as early as the time of Augustus. These divisions, eleven in number, mark an epoch in the process by which the detached elements out of which the Roman Empire had grown were fused together into one whole. As long as Italy was a collection of separate commonwealths, standing in various relations to the ruling city, there could not be any systematic division of the country for administrative purposes. Now that the whole of Italy stood on one level of citizenship or of subjection, the land might be mapped out in whatever way was most convenient. But the eleven regions of Augustus did not work any violent change. Old names and old boundaries largely remained. The famous names of *Etruria*, *Latium*, *Samnium*, *Umbria*, *Picenum*, *Lucania*, *Apulia* and *Calabria*—these two last forming a single region—still lived on, though not always with their ancient boundaries. And, though all the land as far as the Alps was now Italy, two of the divisions of Italy kept their ancient names of *Gaul on this side the Po* and *Gaul beyond the Po*. *Liguria* and *Venetia*, now Italian lands, make up the remainder of Northern Italy.

New division of Italy under Augustus.

The eleven Regions.

Italy had thus been mapped out afresh; what was done with Italy in the time of Augustus was done with the whole Empire in the time of Constantine. What Italy was in the earlier time the whole Empire was in the later; the old distinctions had been wiped out, and the whole of the Roman world stood ready to be parted out into fresh divisions. Under Diocletian, the Empire was divided into four parts, forming the realms of the four Imperial colleagues of his system, the two

Divisions under Constantine.

Division of the Empire under Diocletian. A.D. 292.

Augusti and their subordinate Cæsars. Diocletian's system of government involved a practical degradation of Rome from the headship of the Empire. Augusti and Cæsars now dwelled at points where their presence was more needed to ward off Persian and German attacks from the frontiers; Rome was forsaken for Nikomêdeia and Milan, for Antioch, York, and Trier. The division between the four Imperial colleagues lasted under another form after the Empire was reunited under Constantine, and it formed the groundwork of the more lasting division of the Empire into East and West between the sons of Theodosius.

Reunion under Constantine. A.D. 323.

Division between the sons of Theodosius. A.D. 395.

The whole Empire was now mapped out according to a scheme in which ancient geographical names were largely preserved, but in which they were for the most part used in new or, at least, extended meanings.

The four Prætorian Prefectures.

The Empire was divided into four great divisions called Prætorian *Prefectures*. These were divided into *Dioceses*—a name whose use in this nomenclature must be kept quite apart from the ecclesiastical sense which was borrowed from it—and the dioceses again into *Provinces*. The four great prefectures of the *East*, *Illyricum*, *Italy*, and *Gaul*, answer nearly to the fourfold division under Diocletian; and we may say that, in the final division, Illyricum and the East formed the Eastern Empire, and Italy and Gaul formed the Western. But it is only roughly that either the prefectures or their smaller divisions answer to any of the great national or geographical landmarks of earlier times.

Prefecture of the East.

The Prefecture of the *East* is that one among the four which least answers to anything in earlier geography, natural or historical. Its boundaries do not answer to those of any earlier dominion, nor yet to any great

CHAP. IV.

division of race or language. It stretched into all the three continents of the old world, and took in all those parts of the Empire which were never fully brought under either Greek or Roman influences. But it also took in large tracts which we have learned to look on as part of the Hellenic world—not only lands which had been, to a great extent, hellenized in later times, but even some of the earliest Greek colonies. The four dioceses into which the Prefecture was divided formed far more natural divisions than the Prefecture itself.

Dioceses of the East,

Three of these were Asiatic. The first, specially called the *East*, took in all the possessions of Rome beyond Mount Tauros, together with Isauria, Kilikia, and the island of Cyprus. Its eastern boundaries naturally fluctuated according as Rome or Persia prevailed on the Euphrates and the Tigris, fluctuations of which we shall have again to speak more specially. The diocese

Egypt,

of *Egypt*, besides Egypt in the elder sense, took in, under the name of *Libya*, the old Greek land of the

Asia.

Kyrenaic Pentapolis. The diocese of *Asia*, a reminder of the elder province of that name and of the kingdom of Pergamos out of which it grew, took in the Asiatic coasts of the Ægæan, together with Pamphylia, Lykia, and the Ægæan Islands. The diocese of *Pontos*, preserving the name of the kingdom of Mithridates, took in the lands of the Euxine, with the fluctuating Armenian possessions of Rome.

Diocese of Thrace.

Besides these Asiatic lands, the Eastern Prefecture contained one European diocese, that of *Thrace*, which took in the lands stretching from the Propontis to the Lower Danube. The names of two of its provinces are remarkable. Rome now boasts of a province of *Scythia*. But, among the varied uses of that name, it has now shrunk up to mean the land immediately south of the mouths of the Danube. The other name is *Europa*, a name which, as a Roman province, means the district immediately round the New Rome. Constantine had now fixed his capital on the site of the old Byzantion, the site from which the city on the Bosporos might seem to bear rule over two worlds. With whatever motive, the name of Europe was specially given to that corner of the Western continent where it comes nearest to the Eastern. Nor was the name ill-chosen for the district surrounding the city which was so long to be the bulwark of Europe against invading Asia.

Province *Europa*.

And, besides the New Rome, this Prefecture, as containing those parts of the Empire which had belonged to the great Macedonian kingdoms, contained an unusual proportion of the great cities of the world. Besides a crowd of less famous places, it took in the two great Eastern seats of Grecian culture, the most renowned Alexandria and the most renowned Antioch, themselves only the chief among many other cities bearing the same names. All these, it should be remarked, were comparatively recent creations, bearing the names of individual men. That cities thus artificially called into being should have kept the position which still belonged to the great Macedonian capitals is one of the most speaking signs of the effect which the dominion of Alexander and his successors had on the history of the world.

Great cities of the Eastern Prefecture.

The nomenclature of the second Prefecture marks how utterly Greece, as a country and nation, had died out of all reckoning. The Prefecture of the Eastern *Illyricum* answered roughly to European Greece and its immediate neighbours. It took in the lands stretching from the Danube to the southern point of Peloponnêsos.

Prefecture of Illyricum.

CHAP. IV.

Greece, as part of the Roman Empire, was included under the name of the barbarian land through which Rome was first brought into contact with Greek affairs. She was further included under the name of the half-barbarian neighbour who had become Greek through the process of conquering Greece. In the system of Prefectures, Greece formed part of Macedonia, and Macedonia formed part of Illyricum. So low had Greece, as a land, fallen at the very moment when her tongue was making the greatest of all its conquests, when a Greek city was raised to the rank of another Rome. The Illyrian Prefecture contained the two dioceses of *Macedonia* and *Dacia*. This last name, it will be remembered, had, since the days of Aurelian, withdrawn to the south of the Danube. The Macedonian diocese contained six provinces, among which, besides the familiar and venerable names of Macedonia and Epeiros, we find the names, still more venerable and familiar, of *Thessaly* and *Crete*. And one yet greater name lives on with them. *Hellas* and *Græcia* have alike vanished from the map; but the most abiding name in Grecian history, the theme of Homer and the theme of Polybios, has not perished. Among all changes, *Achaia* is there still.

Dioceses of Macedonia and Dacia.

Province of Achaia.

Prefecture of Italy.

In the new system Italy and Rome herself were in no way privileged over the rest of the Empire. The *Italian* Prefecture took in Italy itself and the lands which might be looked on as necessary for the defence and maintenance of Italy. It took in the defensive conquests of the early Empire on the Upper Danube, and it took in the granary of Italy, Africa. Its three dioceses were *Italy*, *Illyricum*, and *Africa*. Here Illyricum strangely gave its name both to a distinct Prefecture and to one diocese of the Prefecture of Italy. The

Dioceses of Italy,

special Italian diocese stretches as far beyond the bounds of the Italy of Augustus, as the Italy of Augustus stretched beyond the bounds of the Italy of the old Commonwealth. The Gaulish name has now wholly vanished from the lands south of the Alps. The new Italy has spread beyond the Alps, and reaches to the Danube. Two Ræetian provinces, *Prima* and *Secunda*, form part of it. Three other provinces are formed by the three great islands, Sicily, Sardinia, and Corsica, which are now reckoned as Italian. Twelve Provinces are left for Italy in the more usual sense of the name. In the new division the name of *Liguria* withdrew to the north into the old Gaul beyond the Po, a change which accounts for the often puzzling use of the Ligurian name in after times. The former Liguria became the province of the *Cottian Alps*. Venetia remained in its corner. Three provinces, *Æmilia* and *Flaminia* south of the Po, *Valeria* in central Italy, took their names from the great Roman roads, as the roads themselves took their names from Roman magistrates. The ancient names of *Tuscia*—the newer form of Etruria—*Picenum*, *Campania*, *Apulia* with *Calabria*—*Calabria* still keeping its older meaning—still survive, but often with changed boundaries. *Campania* specially has spread into Latium, the district to which the name still cleaves in modern usage. The diocese of the *Western Illyricum* took in *Pannonia*, *Dalmatia*, and *Noricum*. The third diocese, that of *Africa*, took in the old *Africa*, *Numidia*, and western *Mauritania*. The union of these lands with Italy may seem less strange when we remember that the colony of the first Cæsar, the restored Carthage, was the greatest of Latin-speaking cities after Rome herself.

Illyricum,

Africa.

Greatness of Carthage.

Prefecture of Gaul.

The fourth Prefecture took in the Roman dominions

CHAP. IV.

Diocese of Spain; its African territory.

in Western Europe, the great Latin-speaking provinces beyond the Alps. Among the seven provinces of *Spain* are reckoned, not only the Balearic islands, a natural appendage to the Spanish peninsula, but a small part of the African continent, the province of *Tingitana*, stretching from the now Italian Africa to the Ocean. This was according to the general law by which, in almost all periods of history, either the masters of Spain have borne rule in Africa or the masters of Africa have borne rule in Spain. The diocese of *Gaul*, with its seventeen provinces, keeps, at least in name, the boundaries of the old Transalpine land. It still numbers the two Germanies west of the Rhine among its provinces. The five provinces of the diocese of *Britain* took in, at the moment when the Empire was beginning to fall asunder, a wider territory than Rome had held in the island in the days of her greatest power. The exploits of the elder Theodosius, who drove back the Pict by land and the Saxon by sea, for a moment added to the Empire a province beyond the wall of Hadrian, which received the name of *Valentia*.

Diocese of Gaul;

of Britain.

Province of Valentia. A.D. 367.

§ 2. *The Division of the Empire.*

Change in the position of Rome.

The mapping out of the Empire into Prefectures, and its division between two or more Imperial colleagues, led naturally to its more lasting division into what were practically two Empires. The old state of things had altogether passed away. Rome was no longer the city ruling over subject states. From the Ocean to the Euphrates all was alike, if not Rome, at least *Romania*; all its inhabitants were equally Romans. But to be a Roman now meant, no longer to be a citizen of a commonwealth, but to be the subject of an

CHAP. IV.

Emperor. The unity of the Empire was not broken by the division of its administration between several Imperial colleagues; but Rome ceased to be the only Imperial dwelling-place, and, from the latter years of the third century, it ceased to be an Imperial dwelling-place at all. As long as Rome held her old place, no lasting division, nothing more than an administrative partition among colleagues, could be thought of. There could be no division to mark on the map. But, when the new system had fully taken root at the end of the fourth century, we come to a division which was comparatively lasting, one which fills an important place in history, and which is capable of being marked on the map. On the death of Theodosius the Great, the Empire was divided between his two sons, Arcadius taking the Eastern provinces, answering nearly to the Prefectures of the East and of Illyricum, while Honorius took the Western provinces, the Prefectures of Italy and Gaul. Through the greater part of the fifth century, the successors of Arcadius and of Honorius formed two distinct lines of Emperors, of whom the Eastern reigned at Constantinople, the Western most commonly at Ravenna. But as the dominions of each prince were alike Roman, the Eastern and Western Emperors were still looked on in theory as Imperial colleagues charged with the administration of a common Roman dominion. Practically however the dominions of the two Emperors may be looked on as two distinct Empires, the Eastern having its seat at the New Rome or Constantinople, while the Western had its seat more commonly at Ravenna than at the Old Rome.

Division of the Empire between the sons of Theodosius. A.D. 395.

Practically two Empires.

This division of the Empire is the great political feature of the fifth century; but the fate of the two

CHAP. IV.

Enemies of Rome.

Empires was widely different. From the very beginning of the Empire, Rome had had to struggle with two chief enemies, in the East and in the West, in Europe and in Asia, the nature of whose warfare was widely different. In the East she had, first the Parthian and then the regenerate Persian, as strictly a rival power on equal terms. This rivalry went on from the moment when Rome stepped into the place of the Seleukids till the time when Rome was cut short, and Persia overthrown, by the Saracenic invasions. But, except during the momentary conquests of Trajan and during the equally momentary alternate conquests of Rome and Persia in the seventh century, the whole strife was a mere border warfare which did not threaten the serious dismemberment of either power. This and that fortress was taken and retaken; this and that province was ceded and ceded back again; but except under Trajan and again under Chosroes and Heraclius, neither power ever saw its existence and dominion seriously threatened. The Eastern Empire naturally inherited this part of the calling of the undivided Empire, the long strife with Persia.

Rivalry with Parthia and Persia.

Rivalry with Persia passes on to the Eastern Empire.

At the other end of the Empire, the enemy was of quite another kind. The danger there came through the incursions of the various Teutonic nations. There was no one Teutonic power which could be a rival to Rome in the same sense in which Persia was in the East; but a crowd of independent Teutonic tribes were pressing into the Empire from all quarters, and were striving to make settlements within its borders. The task of resisting these incursions fell to the Western Empire. The Eastern Empire indeed was often traversed by wandering Teutonic nations; Teutonic powers

Teutonic incursions in the Western Empire.

No Teutonic settlements in the Eastern Empire.

arose for a while on its frontiers; but no permanent Teutonic settlement was ever made within its borders, no dismemberment of its provinces capable of being marked on the map was made, whether by Teutonic or by any other invaders, till a much later time. But the Western Empire was altogether dismembered and broken in pieces by the settlement of the Teutonic nations within it. The geographical aspects of the two Empires during the fifth century are thus strikingly unlike one another; but each continues one side of the history of the undivided Empire. It will therefore be well to trace those two characteristic aspects of the two Empires separately. We will first speak of the Teutonic incursions, through which in the end the Western Empire was split up and the states of modern Europe were founded. We will then trace the geographical aspect of the long rivalry between Rome and Persia in the East.

§ 3. *The Teutonic Settlements within the Empire.*

The Wandering of the Nations.

Our subject is historical geography, and neither ethnology nor political history, except so far as either national migrations or political changes produce a directly geographical effect. The great movement called the Wandering of the Nations, and its results in the settlement of various Teutonic nations within the bounds of the Roman Empire, concern us now only so far as they wrought a visible change on the map. The exact relations of the different tribes to one another, the exact course of the migrations which led to the final settlement of each, belong rather to another branch of inquiry. But there are certain marked stages in the relations of the Empire to the nations beyond

CHAP. IV.

its borders, certain marked stages in the growth and mutual relations of those nations, which must be borne in mind in order to explain their settlements within the Empire. It will be at once seen that the geography and nomenclature of the German nations in the third century is for the most part quite different from their geography and nomenclature as we find it in Cæsar and Tacitus. New names have come to the front, names all of which play a part in history, many of which remain to this day. Meanwhile, with one or two exceptions, the older names sink into the background. It is therefore hardly needful to go through the ethnology and geography of Tacitus, or to deal with any of the controverted points which are suggested thereby. We have to look at the German nations purely in their relations to Rome.

Changes in the nomenclature of the Teutonic nations.

We have seen that the history of Rome in her western provinces was, from an early stage of the Empire, a struggle with the Teutonic nations on the Rhine and the Danube. We have seen that all attempts at serious conquest beyond those boundaries came to nothing. The Roman possessions beyond the two great rivers were mere outposts for the better security of the land within the rivers. The district beyond them, fenced in by a wall and known as the *Agri Decumates*, was hardly more than such an outlying post on a great scale. The struggle along the border was, almost from the beginning, a defensive struggle on the part of Rome. We hear of Roman conquests from the second century to the fifth; but they are strictly defensive conquests, the mere recovery of lost possessions, or at most the establishment of fresh outposts. From the moment of the first appear-

Warfare on the Rhine and the Danube.

Roman possessions beyond those rivers.

ance of Rome on the two rivers, the Teutonic nations were really threatening to Rome, and the warfare of Rome became really defensive. From the very beginning too a process seems to have been at work among the German nations themselves which greatly strengthened their power as enemies of Rome. New nations or confederacies, bearing, for the most part, names unknown to earlier times, begin to be far more dangerous than the smaller and more scattered tribes of the earlier times had been. These movements among the German nations themselves, hastened by pressure of other nations to the east of them, caused the Teutonic attacks on the Empire to become more and more formidable, and at last to grow into Teutonic settlements within the Empire. But, in the course of this process, several stages may be noticed. Thus the *Marcomanni* and the *Quadi* play a part in this history from the very beginning. The Marcomanni appear in Cæsar, and, from their name of *Markmen*, we may be sure that they were a confederacy of the same kind as the later confederacies of the Franks and Alemanni. In the first and second centuries the Marcomanni are dangerous neighbours, threatening the Empire and often penetrating beyond its borders, and their name appears in history as late as the fifth century. But they play no part in the Teutonic settlements within the Empire. They do not affect the later map; they had no share in bringing about the changes out of which modern Europe arose. Their importance ceases just at the time when a second stage begins, when, in the course of the third century, we begin to hear of those nations or confederacies whose movements really did affect later history and geography.

Formation of confederacies among the Germans.

Marcomanni and Quadi.

CHAP. IV.

Beginning of modern European history.

The new confederacies.

Defensive warfare of Rome.

In the third and fourth centuries the history of modern Europe begins. We now begin to hear names which have been heard ever since, *Franks*, *Alemans*, *Saxons*, all of them great confederacies of German tribes. Defence against German inroads now becomes the chief business of the rulers of Rome. The invaders were constantly driven back; but new invaders were as constantly found to renew their incursions. Men of Teutonic race pressed into the Empire in every conceivable character. Besides open enemies, who came with the hope either of plunder or of settlement, crowds of Germans served in the Roman armies and obtained lands held by military tenure as the reward of their services. Their chiefs were promoted to every rank and honour, military and civil, short of the Imperial dignity itself. These were changes of the utmost importance in other points of view; still they do not directly affect the map of the Empire. Lands and cities were won and lost over and over again; but such changes were merely momentary; the acknowledged boundaries of the Roman dominion were not yet altered; it is not till the next stage that geography begins to be directly concerned.

Germans within the Empire.

Beginning of national kingdoms.

This last stage begins with the early years of the fifth century, and thus nearly coincides with the division of the Empire into East and West. Gothic and other Teutonic kings could now march at pleasure at the head of their armies through every corner of the Empire, sometimes bearing the titles of Roman officers, sometimes dictating the choice of Roman Emperors, sometimes sacking the Old Rome or threatening the New. It was when these armies under their kings settled down and formed national kingdoms within the limits of the Empire, that the change comes to have an effect on the map. In the course of the fifth century the Western provinces of Rome were rent away from her. In most cases the loss was cloaked by some Imperial commission, some empty title bestowed on the victorious invader; but the Empire was none the less practically dismembered. Out of these dismemberments the modern states of Europe gradually grew. It will now be our business to give some account of those nations, Teutonic and otherwise, which had an immediate share in this work, passing lightly by all questions, and indeed all nations, which cannot be said to have had such an immediate share in it.

Teutonic Settlements in the West.

The nations which in the fourth and fifth centuries made settlements in the Western provinces of Rome fall under two chief heads; those who made their settlements by land, and those who made them by sea. This last class is pretty well co-extensive with the settlement of our own forefathers in Britain, which must be spoken of separately. Among the others, the nations which play an important part in the fourth and fifth centuries are the *Goths*, the *Vandals*, the *Burgundians*, the *Suevi*, and the *Franks*. And their settlements again fall into two classes, those which passed away within a century or two, and those which have had a lasting effect on European history. Thus it is plain at the first glance that the Franks and the Burgundians have left their names on the modern map. The Suevi have left their name also: but it is now found only in their older German land; it has vanished for ages from their western settlement. The name of the Goths has passed away from the kingdoms which they

Settlements within the Empire.

Franks, Burgundians, Suevi, Goths,

founded, but their presence has affected the history of both the Spanish and the Italian peninsulas. The Vandals alone, as a nation and kingdom, have left no traces whatever, though it may be that they have left their name to a part of one of the lands of their sojourn. All these nations founded kingdoms within the Western Empire, kingdoms which at first admitted a nominal superiority in the Empire, but which were practically independent from the beginning. But the history of the several kingdoms is very different. Some of them soon passed away altogether, while others became the beginnings of the great nations of modern Europe. Gaul and Spain fell off very gradually from the Empire. But, in the course of the fifth century, all the nations of which we have been speaking formed more or less lasting settlements within those provinces. Pre-eminent among them are the great settlements of the Goths and the Franks. Out of the settlement of the Franks arose the modern kingdoms of Germany and France, and out of the settlement of the Goths arose the various kingdoms of Spain. Those of the Burgundians, Vandals, and Suevi, were either smaller or less lasting. All of them however must be mentioned in their order.

(Vandals.) (Their kingdoms.) (Various circumstances of their history.)

(Migrations of the West-Goths.)

First and greatest come the *Goths.*[1] It is not needful for our purpose to examine all that history or legend has to tell us as to the origin of the Goths, or all the theories which ingenious men have formed on the subject. It is enough for our purpose that the Goths began to show themselves as dangerous enemies of the Empire in the second half of the third century. We then find them forming a great kingdom in the lands north of the Danube. The withdrawal of the

(Defeat of the Goths by Claudius. A.D. 269.)

[1] See the author's article 'Goths' in the *Encyclopædia Britannica.*

Roman power from the elder Dacia was in fact an acknowledgement of the Gothic possession of that land. A century later a large body of them was driven to seek shelter within the bounds of the Eastern Empire from the pressure of the invading *Huns*. These last were a Turanian people who had been driven from their own older settlements by movements in the further East which do not concern us, but who become an important element in the history of the fifth century. They affected the Empire, partly by actual invasions, partly by driving other nations before them; but they made no lasting settlements within it. Nor did the Goths themselves make any lasting settlement in the Eastern Empire. While one part of the Gothic nation became subject to the Huns, another part crossed the Danube; but they crossed it by Imperial licence, and if they took to arms, it was only to punish the treachery of the Roman officers. Presently we find Gothic chiefs marching at pleasure through the dominions of the Eastern Cæsar; but they simply march and ravage; it is not till they have got within the boundary of the West that they found any lasting kingdoms. In fact, the Goths, and the Teutonic tribes generally, had no real mission in the East; to them the East was a mere highway to the West. The movements of Alaric in Greece, Illyricum, and Italy, his sieges and his capture of Rome, are of the highest historical importance, but they do not touch geography. The Goths first win for themselves a local habitation and a place on the map when they left Italy to establish themselves in the further West.

Gothic kingdom on the Danube.

Goths driven onwards by the Huns.

They cross the Danube. A.D. 377.

Career of Alaric. A.D. 394-410.

Under Alaric's successor Athaulf, the first foundations were laid of that great West-Gothic kingdom which

Beginning of the West-Gothic kingdom under Athaulf. A.D. 412.

we are apt to look on as specially Spanish, but which in truth had its first firm establishment in Gaul, and which kept some Gaulish territory as long as it lasted. But the Goths passed into those lands, not in the character of avowed conquerors, not as founders of an avowed Gothic state, but as soldiers of the Empire,

Condition of Gaul and Spain.

sent to win back its lost provinces. Those provinces were now occupied or torn in pieces by a crowd of

The Alans.

invaders, *Suevi*, *Vandals*, and *Alans*. These last are a puzzling race, our accounts of whom are somewhat contradictory, but who may perhaps be most safely set down as a non-Aryan, or, at any rate, a non-Teutonic people, who had been largely brought under Gothic influences. But early in the fifth century they possessed a dominion in central Spain which stretched from sea to sea. Their dominion passed for a few

The Suevi in Spain.

years into the hands of the Suevi, who had already formed a settlement in north-western Spain, and who still kept a dominion in that corner long after the greater part of the peninsula had become Gothic. The Vandals occupied Bætica; but they presently passed into

The Vandals in Africa. A.D. 425.

Africa, and there founded the one Teutonic kingdom in that continent, with Carthage to its capital, a kingdom which took in also the great islands of the western

Independence of the Basques.

Mediterranean, including Sicily itself. Through all these changes the unconquerable people of the Basque and Cantabrian mountains seem never to have fully submitted to any conquerors; but the rest of Spain and south-western Gaul was, in the course of the second half of the fifth century, formed into the great West-Gothic kingdom. The appearance of Athaulf in Spain did not lead to the foundation of any Gothic power in the peninsula. The first West-Gothic kingdom arose in

Aquitaine between the Garonne and the Loire. Southern Gaul, *Novempopulana*—the later Gascony—and the province of Narbonne with the Tarraconese province in Spain, were won back by the Gothic sword for the Empire. But the Gothic kingdom grew on both sides of the Pyrenees. In the time of its greatest extent it stretched from the pillars of Hêraklês to the Loire and the Rhone, and its capital was placed, not on Spanish but on Gaulish ground, at the Gaulish Tolosa or *Toulouse*. It now took in the whole of Spain, except the independent districts in the north and the Suevian realm in the north west corner. The Gothic dominion in Gaul was doomed not to be lasting; all was lost to the Frank except the province of Narbonne or Septimania, which, as remaining to the Goth when the rest was lost, kept the name of *Gothia*. But the Gothic dominion in Spain lasted down to the Saracen conquest, and all the later Christian kingdoms of Spain may be looked on as fragments or revivals of it. Spain however never changed her name for that of her conquerors, and her rulers remained Kings of the Goths, but not Kings of Spain. The Vandals, on the other hand, though they passed altogether out of Spain, have left their name to this day in its southern part under the form of *Andalusia*, a name which, under the Saracen conquerors, spread itself over the whole peninsula.

Gothic kingdom of Toulouse.

Gothia.

Andalusia.

The other great Teutonic nations or confederacies of which we have to speak have had a far more lasting effect on the nomenclature of Europe. We have now to trace the steps by which the *Franks* gradually became the ruling people both of Germany and of Gaul. They have stamped their name on both countries. The dominions of the Franks got the name of *Francia*,

The Franks.

Uses of the word *Francia*.

a name whose meaning has constantly varied, according to the extent of the Frankish dominion at different times. In modern use it still cleaves to two parts of their dominions, to that part of Germany which is still called *Franken* or *Franconia*, and to that part of Gaul which is still called *France*. And the history of the Franks is closely mixed up with that of another nation or confederacy, that of the *Alemanni*, who again have, in the French tongue, given their name to the whole of Germany. Franks and Alemanni alike begin to be heard of in the third century, and the Alemanni even attempted an actual invasion of Italy; but the geographical importance of both confederacies does not begin till the fifth. All through the fourth century it was the chief business of the Emperors who ruled in Gaul to defend the frontier of the Rhine against their incursions, against the Alemanni along the upper part of its course, and against the Franks along its lower part. To the east of the Franks and Alemanni lay the *Thuringians*; to the north, along the coasts of the German Ocean, the Low-Dutch tribes, *Saxons* and *Frisians*. In the course of the fifth century their movements also began to affect the geography of the Empire.

The Alemanni.

A.D. 275.

Thuringians. The Low-Dutch tribes.

During the whole of that century the Franks were pressing into Gaul. The Imperial city of Trier was more than once taken, and the seat of the provincial government was removed to Arles. The union of the two chief divisions of the Frankish confederacy, and the overthrow of the Alemanni, made the Franks, under their first Christian king, Chlodwig or Clovis, the ruling people of northern Gaul and central Germany. Their territory thus took in both lands which had been part of the Empire, and lands which had

Reign of Chlodwig. A.D. 481–511.

never been such. This is a special characteristic of the Frankish settlement, and one which influences the whole of their later history. There was, from the very beginning, long before any such distinction was consciously drawn, a *Teutonic* and a *Latin Francia*. There were Frankish lands to the East which never had been Roman. There were lands in northern Gaul which remained practically Roman under the Frankish dominion. And between them lay, on the left bank of the Rhine, those Teutonic lands which had formed part of the Roman province of Gaul, but which now became Teutonic again. *Moguntiacum*, *Augusta Treverorum*, and *Colonia Agrippina*, cities founded on Teutonic soil, now again became German, ready to be in due time, by the names of *Mainz*, *Trier*, and *Köln*, the metropolitan and electoral cities of Germany. These lands, with the older German land of the Franks, formed the *Eastern* or *Teutonic Francia*, where the Franks, or their German allies and subjects, formed the real population of the country. In the *Western Francia*, between the Loire and the Channel, though the Franks largely settled and influenced the country in many ways, the mass of the population remained Roman. Over the western peninsula of *Armorica* the dominion of the Franks was always precarious and at most external. Here the ante-Roman population still kept its Celtic language, and it was further strengthened by colonies from Britain, from which the land took its later name of the *Lesser Britain* or *Britanny*. Thus, at the end of the fifth century, the Frankish dominion was firmly established over the whole of central Germany and northern Gaul. Their dominion was fated to be the most lasting of the Teutonic kingdoms formed on the

Character and divisions of the Frankish kingdom.

Roman Germany teutonized afresh.

Eastern and Western *Francia*.

Armorica or Britanny.

Extent of the Frankish dominion. A.D. 500.

CHAP. IV.

Roman mainland. The reason is obvious; while the Goths in Spain and the Vandals in Africa were isolated Teutonic settlers in a Roman land, the Franks in Gaul were strengthened by the unbroken Teutonic mainland at their back.

The Burgundians.

The greater part of Gaul was thus, at the end of the fifth century, divided between the Franks in the north and the West-Goths in the south. But, early in the fifth century, a third Teutonic power grew up in south-eastern Gaul. The *Burgundians*, a people who, in the course of the Wandering of the Nations, seem to have made their way from the shores of the Baltic, established themselves in the lands between the Rhone and the Alps, where they formed a kingdom which bore their name. Their dominion in Gaul may be said to have been more lasting than that of the Goths, less lasting than that of the Franks. *Burgundy* is still a recognized name; but no name in geography has so often shifted its place and meaning, and it has for some centuries settled itself on a very small part of the ancient kingdom of the Burgundians. At the end of the fifth century the Rhone was a Burgundian river; *Autun*, *Besançon*, *Lyons*, and *Vienne* were Burgundian cities; but the sea coast, the original Roman *Province*, the land which has so steadily kept that name, though it fell for a moment under the Burgundian power, followed at this time, as became the first Roman land beyond the Alps, the fortunes of Italy rather than those of Gaul.

Their kingdom.

Meaning of the word *Burgundy*.

Provence Burgundian. A.D. 500–510.

510–536.

Invasion of the Huns.

Among these various conquests and shiftings of dominion, all of which affected the map at the time, some of which have affected history and geography ever since, it may be well to mention, if only by way of contrast, an inroad which fills a great place in the history of the fifth century, but which had no direct effect on geography. This was the invasion of Italy and Gaul by the *Huns* under Attila, and their defeat at Châlons by the combined forces of Romans, West-Goths, and Franks. This battle is one of the events which are memorable, not for working change, but for hindering it. Had Attila succeeded, the greatest of all changes would have taken place throughout all Western Europe. As it was, the map of Gaul was not affected by his inroad. On the map of Italy it did have an indirect effect; he destroyed the city of Aquileia, and its inhabitants, fleeing to the Venetian islands, laid the foundation of one of the later powers of Europe in the form of the commonwealth of *Venice*.

Battle of Châlons. A.D. 451.

Destruction of Aquileia, and origin of Venice.

While Spain and Gaul were thus rent away from the Empire, Italy and Rome itself were practically rent away also, though the formal aspect of the event was different. A vote of the Senate reunited the Western Empire to the Eastern; the Eastern Emperor Zeno became sole Emperor, and the government of the diocese of Italy—that is, it will be remembered, of a large territory besides the Italian peninsula—was entrusted by his commission to Odoacer, a general of barbarian mercenaries, with the rank of Patrician. Odoacer was practically a barbarian king independent of the Empire; but the unity of the Empire was preserved in form, and no separate kingdom of Italy was set up. Presently Odoacer was overthrown by Theodoric King of the East-Goths, who, though king of his own people, reigned in Italy by an Imperial commission as Patrician. Practically he founded an East-Gothic kingdom, taking in Italy and the other lands which formed the dioceses of Italy and Western Illyricum. His dominion also took in the coast of

Reunion of the Empire.

Rule of Odoacer. B.C. 476–493.

The East-Goths in Italy.

Rule of Theodoric. A.D. 493–526.

CHAP. IV.

Extent of his dominion.

what we may now call *Provence*, and his influence was extended in various ways over most of the kingdoms of the West. The seat of the Gothic dominion, like that of the later Western Empire, was at Ravenna. Theodoric and his successors were in truth independent kings, and, as chiefs of their own people, they bore the kingly title. Hence, as Rome formed part of their dominions, it is practically true to say that under them Rome ceased to be part of the Roman Empire. Still in theory the Imperial supremacy went on. The King of the East-Goths who ruled in Italy was simply King of the East-Goths; *King of Italy* he never thought of calling himself. In this way it became much easier for Italy to be won back to the Empire at a somewhat later time.

Theory of the Empire.

§ 4. *Settlement of the English in Britain.*

Meanwhile, in another part of Europe, a Teutonic settlement of quite another character from those on the mainland was going on. Spain and Gaul fell away from the Empire by slow degrees; but the Roman dominion in Britain came to an end by a definite act at a definite moment. The Roman armies were withdrawn from the province, and its inhabitants were left to themselves. Presently, a new settlement took place in the island which was thus left undefended. It is specially important to mark the difference between the Teutonic settlements in Britain and the Teutonic conquests on the mainland. The Teutonic conquests in Gaul and Spain were made by Teutonic neighbours who had already learned to know and respect the Roman civilization, who were either Christians already or became Christians soon after they entered the Empire.

The Romans withdraw from Britain. A.D. 410.

Difference between the conquest of Britain and other Teutonic conquests.

They pressed in gradually by land; they left the Roman inhabitants to live after the Roman law, and they themselves gradually adopted the speech and much of the manners of Rome. The only exception to this rule on the continent is to be found in the lands immediately on the Rhine and the Danube, where the Teutonic settlement was complete, and where the Roman tongue and civilization were pretty well wiped out. This same process happened yet more completely in the Teutonic conquest of Britain. The great island possession of Rome had been virtually abandoned by Rome before the Teutonic settlements in it began. The invaders had therefore to struggle rather with native Britons than with Romans. Moreover they were invaders who came by sea, and who came from lands where little or nothing was known of the Roman law or religion. They therefore made a settlement of quite another kind from the settlement of the Goths, or even from that of the Franks. They met with a degree of strictly national resistance such as no other Teutonic conquerors met with; therefore in the end they swept away all traces of the earlier state of things in a way which took place nowhere else. As far as such a process is possible, they slew or drove out the older inhabitants; they kept their heathen religion and Teutonic language, and were thus able to grow up as a new Teutonic nation in their new home without any important intermixture with the earlier inhabitants, Roman or British.

Character of the English settlement; long struggle with the Britons.

The English remain Teutonic.

The conquerors who wrought this change were our own forefathers, the Low-Dutch inhabitants of the borderlands of Germany and Denmark, quite away from the Roman frontier; and among them three tribes, the *Angles*, the *Saxons*, and the *Jutes*, had the

The Low-Dutch settlements in Britain.

Saxons.

CHAP. IV.

chief share in the conquest of Britain. The Saxons had, as has already been said, attempted a settlement in the fourth century. They were therefore the tribe who were first known to the Roman and Celtic inhabitants of the island; the Celts of Britain and Ireland have therefore called all the Teutonic settlers *Saxons* to this day. But, as the Angles or *English* occupied in the end by far the greater part of the land, it was they who, when the Teutonic tribes in Britain began to form one nation, gave their name to that nation and its land. That nation was the *English*, and their land was *England*. While *Britain* therefore remains the proper geographical name of the whole island, *England* is the political name of that part of Britain which was step by step conquered by the English. Before the end of the fifth century several Teutonic kingdoms had begun in Britain. The Jutes began the conquest by their settlement in *Kent*, and presently the *Saxons* began to settle on the south coast and on a small part of the east coast, in *Sussex*, *Wessex*, and *Essex*. And along a great part of the eastern coast various *Anglian* settlements were made, which gradually grew into the kingdoms of *East-Anglia*, *Deira*, and *Bernicia*, which two last formed by their union the great kingdom of *Northhumberland*. But, at the end of the sixth century, the English had not got very far from the southern and eastern coasts. The Britons, whom the English called *Welsh* or strangers, held out in the West, and the Picts and Scots in the North. The *Scots* were properly the people of Ireland; but a colony of them had settled on the western coast of northern Britain, and, in the end, they gave the name of Scotland to the whole northern part of the island.

Origin of the name *English*.

Jutes in Kent. A.D. 449.

Saxon and Anglian settlements.

The Welsh and Scots.

§ 5. *The Eastern Empire.*

CHAP. IV.

Contrast between the Eastern and Western Empires.

We have already seen the differences between the position of the Eastern and Western Empires during this period. While in the West the provinces were gradually lopped away by the Teutonic settlements, the provinces of the East, though often traversed by Teutonic armies, or rather nations, did not become the seats of lasting Teutonic settlements. We can hardly count as an exception the settlement of the *Tetraxite Goths* in the Tauric Chersonêsos, a land which was rather in alliance with the Empire than actually part of it. The distinctive history of the Eastern Empire consists, as has been already said, in the long struggle between East and West, in which Rome had succeeded to the mission of Alexander and the Seleukids, as the representative of Western civilization. To this mission was afterwards added the championship of Christianity, first against the Fire-worshipper and then against the Moslem. In Eastern history no event is more important and more remarkable than the uprising of the regenerate *Persian* nation against its Parthian masters. But, as far as either the history or the geography of Rome is concerned, the Persian simply steps into the place of the Parthian as the representative of the East against the West. From our point of view, the long wars on the eastern frontier of Rome, and the frequent shiftings of that frontier, form one unbroken story, whether the enemy to be striven against was the successor of Arsakes or the successor of Artaxerxes. And besides the natural rivalry of two great powers in such a position, the border kingdom of *Armenia*, a name which has changed its meaning and its

The Tetraxite Goths.

Rivalry with Persia.

Revival of the Persian kingdom. A.D. 226.

Position of Armenia.

CHAP. IV.

frontiers almost as often as Burgundy or Austria, supplied constant ground for dispute between Rome and her Eastern rival, whether Parthian or Persian.

In the geographical aspect of this long struggle three special periods need to be pointed out. The first is that of the momentary conquests of Trajan. Under him *Armenia*, hitherto a vassal kingdom of Rome, was incorporated as a Roman province. *Albania* and *Iberia* took its place as the frontier vassal states. Beyond the Euphrates, even beyond the Tigris, the Roman dominion took in *Mesopotamia*, *Atropatênê*, and *Babylonia*. The Parthian capital of *Ktêsiphôn* and the outlying Greek free city of *Seleukeia* were included within the boundaries of a dominion which for a moment touched the Caspian and the Persian Gulf. Rome, as the champion of the West, seemed to have triumphed for ever over her Eastern rival, when the Parthian kingdom was thus shorn of the borderlands of the two worlds, and when its king was forced to become a Roman vassal for the dominions that were left to him. But this vast extension of the Roman power was only for a moment. What Trajan had conquered Hadrian at once gave back; the Empire was again bounded by the Euphrates, and Armenia was again left to form matter of dispute between its Eastern and its Western claimant. The second stage begins when, under Marcus, the Roman frontier again began to advance. Between the Euphrates and the Tigris *Osrhoênê* became a Roman dependency: under the house of Severus it became a Roman province; and the fortress of *Nisibis*, so famous in later wars, was planted as the eastern outpost of Rome against the Parthian. Ten years later the Parthian power was no more; but, as seen with Western eyes, the revived monarchy of Persia had simply stepped into its

Conquests of Trajan. A.D. 114–117.

Conquests of Trajan surrendered by Hadrian. A.D. 117.

Conquests of Marcus. A.D. 162–166.

Of Severus. A.D. 197–202.

place. The wars of Alexander Severus, the captivity of Valerian, the wasting march of Sapor through the Roman provinces, left no trace on the map. But under the mighty rule of Diocletian the glories of Trajan were renewed. Mesopotamia again became Roman; five provinces beyond the Tigris were added to the Empire; Armenia, again the vassal of Rome, was enlarged at the expense of Persia, and Iberia became once more a Roman dependency. In the third stage the Roman frontier again went back. The wars of the second Sapor did little but deprive Rome of two Mesopotamian fortresses. But after the fall of Julian, the lands beyond the Tigris were given back to Persia; even Nisibis was yielded, and the Persian frontier again reached the Euphrates. Armenia was now tossed to and fro, conquered and reconquered, till the kingdom was divided between the vassals of the two Empires, a division which was again confirmed by the hundred years' peace between Rome and Persia. This was the state of the Eastern frontier of Rome at the time when the West-Goths were laying the foundation of their dominion in Aquitaine and Spain, when Goth and Roman joined together to overthrow the mingled host of Attila at Châlons, and when the first English keels were on their way to the shores of Britain.

Conquests under Diocletian. A.D. 297.

Surrender of provinces by Jovian. A.D. 363.

Division of Armenia. 387.

The Hundred Years' Peace. 421.

Summary.

We may now draw the picture of the civilized world at the end of the fifth century. The whole of the Western dominions of Rome, including Italy and Rome herself, have practically, if not everywhere formally, fallen away from the Roman Empire. The whole West is under the rule of Teutonic kings. The Frank has become supreme in northern Gaul, without losing his ancient hold on western and central Germany.

CHAP. IV.

The West-Goth reigns in Spain and Aquitaine; the Burgundian reigns in the lands between the Rhone and the Alps. Italy and the lands to the north of the Alps and the Hadriatic have become, in substance though not in name, an East-Gothic kingdom. But the countries of the European mainland, though cut off from Roman political dominion, are far from being cut off from Roman influences. The Teutonic settlers, if conquerors, are also disciples. Their rulers are everywhere Christian; in northern Gaul they are even Orthodox. Africa, under the Arian Vandal, is far more utterly cut off from the traditions of Rome than the lands ruled either by the Catholic Frank or by the Arian Goth. To the north of the Franks lie the independent tribes of Germany, still untouched by any Roman influence. They are beginning to find themselves new homes in Britain, and, as the natural consequence of a purely barbarian and heathen conquest, to sever from the Empire all that they conquered yet more thoroughly than Africa itself was severed. Such is the state of the West. In the East the Roman power lives on in the New Rome, with a dominion constantly threatened and insulted by various enemies, but with a frontier which to the north has hardly changed since the time of Aurelian, which to the east has, after many changes, pretty well come back to what it was in the days of Hadrian. No lasting Teutonic settlement has been made within its borders. In its endless wars with Persia, its frontier sometimes advances and sometimes retreats. In our next chapter we shall see how much of life still clung to the majesty of the Roman name, and how large a part of the ancient dominion of Rome could still be won back again.

CHAPTER V.

THE FINAL DIVISION OF THE EMPIRE.

§ 1. *The Reunion of the Empire.*

CHAP. V.

Continuity of Roman rule.

THE main point to be always borne in mind in the history, and therefore in the historical geography, of the sixth, seventh, and eighth centuries, is the continued existence of the Roman Empire. It was still the Roman Empire, although the seat of its dominion was no longer at the Old Rome, although for a while the Old Rome was actually separated from the Roman dominion. Gaul, Spain, Africa, Italy itself, had been lopped away. Britain had fallen away by another process. But the Roman rule went on undisturbed in the Eastern part of the Empire, and even in the West the memory of that rule had by no means wholly died out. Teutonic kings ruled in all the lands of the West; but nowhere on the continent had they become national sovereigns in the eyes of the people of the land. They were still simply the chiefs of their own people reigning in the midst of a Roman population. The Romans meanwhile everywhere looked to the Cæsar of the New Rome as their lawful sovereign, from whose rule they had been unwillingly torn away. Both in Spain and in Italy the Gothic kings had settled in the country as Imperial lieutenants with an Imperial commission. The formal aspect of the event of 476 had been the

Position of the Teutonic kings.

reunion of the Western Empire with the Eastern. It was perfectly natural therefore that the sole Roman Emperor reigning in the New Rome should strive, whenever he had a chance, to win back territories which he had never formally surrendered, and that the Roman inhabitants of those territories should welcome him as a deliverer from barbarian masters. The geographical limits within which, at the beginning of the sixth century, the Roman power was practically confined, the phænomena of race and language within those limits, might have suggested another course. But considerations of that kind are seldom felt at the time; they are the reflexions of thoughtful men long after. The Roman dominion, at the accession of Justinian, was shut up within the Greek and Oriental provinces of the Empire; its enemies were already beginning to speak of its subjects as *Greeks*. Its truest policy would have been to have anticipated several centuries of history, to have taken up the position of a Greek state, defending its borders against the Persian, withstanding or inviting the settlement of the Slave, but leaving the now Teutonic West to develope itself undisturbed. But in such cases the known past is always more powerful than the unknown future, and it seemed the first duty of the Roman Emperor to restore the Roman Empire to its ancient extent.

Recovery of territory by the Empire.

Extent of the Roman dominion at the accession of Justinian, 527.

Conquests of Justinian.

It was during the reign of Justinian that this work was carried out through a large part of the Western Empire. Lost provinces were won back in two continents. The growth of independent Teutonic powers was for ever stopped in Africa, and it received no small check in Europe. The Emperor was enabled, through the weakness and internal dissensions of the Vandal and Gothic kingdoms, to win back Africa and Italy to the Empire.

The work was done by the swords of Belisarius and Narses—the Slave and the Persian were now used to win back the Old Rome to the dominion of the New. The short *Vandal* war restored Africa in the Roman sense, and a large part of Mauretania, to the Empire. The long *Gothic* war won back Illyricum, Italy, and the Old Rome. Italy and Africa were still ruled from Ravenna and from Carthage; but they were now ruled, not by Teutonic kings, but by Byzantine exarchs. Meanwhile, while the war with the East-Goths was going on in Italy, a large part of southern Spain was won back from the West-Goths. Two Teutonic kingdoms were thus wiped out; a third was weakened; and the acquisition of so great a line of sea-coast, together with the great islands, Sicily, Sardinia, Corsica, and the Balearic Islands, gave the Empire an undisputed supremacy by sea. In one corner only did the Imperial frontier even nominally go back, or any Teutonic power advance at its expense. The seaboard of Provence, which had long been practically lost to the Empire, was now formally ceded to the Franks. Yet the coins of the Provençal cities, down to a much later time, show that they clave at least to the memory of their old allegiances to Rome and Cæsar.

Vandal war. 533–535.

Gothic war. 537–554.

Conquest of southern Spain. 550.

Provence ceded to the Franks, 548.

In a geographical aspect the map of Europe has seldom been so completely changed within a single generation as it was during the reign of Justinian. At his accession his dominion was bounded to the west by the Hadriatic, and he was far from possessing the whole of the Hadriatic coast. Under his reign the power of the Roman arms and the Roman law was again extended to the Ocean. The Roman dominion was indeed no longer spread round the whole shore of the Mediterranean;

Geographical changes under Justinian.

CHAP. V.

the Imperial territories were no longer continuous as of old: but, if the Empire was not still, as it had once been, the only power in the Mediterranean lands, it had again become beyond all comparison the greatest power. Moreover, by the recovery of so large an extent of Latin-speaking territory, the tendency of the Empire to change into a Greek or Oriental state was checked for several centuries. We are here concerned only with the geographical, not with the political or moral aspect of the conquests of Justinian. Some of those conquests, like those of Trajan, were hardly more than momentary. But the changes which they made for the time were some of the most remarkable on record, and the effect of those changes remained, both in history and geography, long after their immediate results were again undone.

Effects of Justinian's conquests.

§ 2. *Settlement of the Lombards in Italy.*

The conquests of Justinian hindered the growth ot a national Teutonic kingdom in Italy, such as grew up in Gaul and Spain, and they practically made the cradle of the Empire, Rome herself, an outlying dependency of her great colony by the Bosporos. But the reunion of all Italy with the Empire lasted only for a moment. The conquest was only just over when a new set of Teutonic conquerors appeared in Italy. These were the *Lombards*, who, in the great wandering, had made their way into the ancient Pannonia about the time that the East-Goths passed into Italy. They were thus settled within the ancient boundaries of the Western Empire. But the Roman power had now quite passed away from those regions; the Lombard kingdom in Pannonia was practically altogether beyond the Imperial borders; it had not even that Roman tinge which

Pannonian kingdom of the Lombards.

affected the Frankish and Gothic kingdoms. To the east of the Lombards, in the ancient Dacia, another Teutonic kingdom had arisen, that of the *Gepidæ*, a people seemingly closely akin to the Goths. The process of wandering had brought the Turanian *Avars* into those parts, and their presence seriously affected all later history and geography. With the Gepidæ in Dacia and the Lombards in Pannonia, there was a chance of two Teutonic states growing up on the borders of East and West. These might possibly have played the same part in the East which the Franks and Goths played in the West, and they might thus have altogether changed the later course of history. But the Lombards allied themselves with the Avars. In partnership with their barbarian allies, they overthrew the kingdom of the Gepidæ, and they themselves passed into Italy. Thus the growth of Teutonic powers in those regions was stopped. A new and far more dangerous enemy was brought into the neighbourhood of the Empire, and the way was opened for the Slavonic races to play in some degree the same part in the East which the Teutons played in the West. But while the East lost this chance of renovation at Teutonic hands, the Lombard settlement in Italy was the beginning of a new Teutonic power in that country. But it was not a power which could possibly grow up into a national Teutonic kingdom of all Italy, as the dominion of the East-Goths might well have done. The Lombard conquest of Italy was at no time a complete conquest; part of the land was won by the Lombards; part was kept by the Emperors; and the Imperial and Lombard possessions intersected one another in a way which hindered the growth of any kind of national unity under either

Gepidæ.

Avars.

Teutonic powers on the Lower Danube.

The Gepidæ overthrown by the Lombards and Avars. 566.

The Lombards pass into Italy. 567.

Character of the Lombard kingdom.

Incomplete conquest of Italy.

CHAP. V.

power. The new settlers gradually founded the great Lombard kingdom in the North of Italy, which has kept the Lombard name to this day, and the smaller Lombard states of *Spoleto* and *Beneventum*. But a large part of Italy still remained to the Empire. Ravenna, the dwelling-place of the Exarchs, Rome itself, Naples, and the island city of Venice, were all centres of districts which still acknowledged the Imperial rule. The Emperors also kept the extreme southern points of both the peninsulas of southern Italy, and, for the present, the three great islands. The Lombard kings were constantly threatening Rome and Ravenna. Rome never fell into their hands, but in the middle of the eighth century Ravenna was taken, and with it the district specially known as the *Exarchate* was annexed to the Lombard dominion. But this greatest extent of the Lombard power caused its overthrow: for it led to a chain of events which, as we shall presently see, ended in transferring not only the Lombard kingdom, but the Imperial crown of the West, to the hands of the Franks.

Lombard duchies.

Imperial possessions in Italy.

Ravenna taken by the Lombards. c. 753.

§ 3. *Rise of the Saracens.*

But, before we give any account of the revolutions which took place among the already existing powers of Western Europe, it will be well to describe the geographical changes which were caused by the appearance of absolutely new actors on both sides of the Empire. One point however may be noticed here, as standing apart from the general course of events, namely, that the Roman province in Spain was won gradually back by the West-Goths. The inland cities, as Cordova, were hardly kept forty years, and the whole of the Imperial possessions in Spain were lost during the reign of

Roman province in Spain recovered by the Goths. 534–572, 616–624.

Heraclius. Thus the great dominion which Justinian had won back in the West, important as were its historical results, was itself of very short duration; a large part of Italy was lost almost as soon as it was won, and the recovered dominion in Spain did not abide longer than ninety years.

But meanwhile, in the course of the seventh century, nations which had hitherto been unknown or unimportant began to play a great part in history and greatly to change the face of the map. These new powers fall under two heads, those who appeared on the northern and those who appeared on the eastern frontier of the Empire. The nations which appeared on the north were, like the early Teutonic invaders of the Empire, ready to act, if partly as conquerors, partly also as disciples; those who appeared on the east were the champions of an utterly different system in religion and everything else. In short, the old rivalry of the East and West now takes a distinctly aggressive form on the part of the East. As long as the Sassanid dynasty lasted, Rome and Persia still continued their old rivalry on nearly equal terms. The long wars between the two Empires made little difference in their boundaries. In the last stage of their warfare, Chosroes took Jerusalem and Antioch, and encamped at Chalkêdôn. Heraclius pressed his eastern victories beyond the boundaries of the Empire under Trajan. But even these great campaigns made no lasting difference in the map, except so far as, by weakening Rome and Persia alike, they paved the way for the greatest change of all. More important for geography was a change which took place at somewhat earlier time when, during the reign of Justinian, the

Wars between Rome and Persia.

Wars of Chosroes and Heraclius, 603–628.

Extension of the Roman power on the Euxine.

CHAP. V.

Roman power was extended on the Eastern side of the Euxine in *Colchis* or *Lazica*. The southern borders of each Empire were to some extent protected by the dominion of dependent Arabian kings, the *Ghassanides* being vassals of Rome, and the *Lachmites* to the east of them being vassals of Persia. But a change came presently which altogether overthrew the Persian kingdom, which deprived the Roman Empire of its Eastern, Egyptian, and African provinces, and which gave both the Empire and the Teutonic kingdoms of the West an enemy of a kind altogether different from any against whom they hitherto had to strive.

The Arabian vassals of Rome and Persia.

The cause which wrought such abiding changes was the rise of the *Saracens* under Mahomet and his first followers. A new nation, that of the Arabs, now became dominant in a large part of the lands which had been part of the Roman Empire, as well as in lands far beyond its boundaries. The scattered tribes of Arabia were first gathered together into a single power by Mahomet himself, and under his successors they undertook to spread the Mahometan religion wherever their swords could carry it. And, with the Mahometan religion, they carried also the Arabic language, and what we may call Eastern civilization as opposed to Western. A strife, in short, now begins between Aryan and Semitic man. Rome and Persia, with all their differences, were both of them Aryan powers. The most amazing thing is the extraordinary speed with which the Saracens pressed their conquests at the expense of both Rome and Persia, forming a marked contrast to the slow advance both of Roman conquest and of Teutonic settlement. In the course of less than eighty years, the Mahometan conquerors formed

Rise of the Saracens.

Arabia united under Mahomet, 622–632.

Conquests of the Saracens.

a dominion greater than that of Rome, and, for a short time, the will of the Caliph of the Prophet was obeyed from the Ocean to lands beyond the Indus. In a few campaigns the Empire lost all its possessions beyond Mount Tauros; that is, it lost one of the three great divisions of the Empire, that namely in which neither Greek nor Roman civilization had ever thoroughly taken root.

Loss of the Eastern provinces of Rome. 632–639.

While the Roman Empire was thus dismembered, the rival power of Persia was not merely dismembered, but utterly overwhelmed. The Persian nationality was again, as in the days of the Parthians, held down under a foreign power, to revive yet again ages later. But the Saracen power was very far from merely taking the place of its Parthian and Persian predecessors. The mission of the followers of Mahomet was a mission of universal conquest, and that mission they so far carried out as altogether to overthrow the exclusive dominion of Rome in her own Mediterranean. Under Justinian, if the Imperial possession of the Mediterranean coast was not absolutely continuous, the small exceptions in Africa, Spain, and Gaul in no way interfered with the maritime supremacy of the Empire, and Gaul and Spain, even where they were not Roman, were at least Christian. But now a gradual advance of sixty-four years annexed the Roman dominions in Africa to the Mahometan dominion. Thence the Saracens passed into Spain, and found the West-Gothic kingdom an easier prey than the Roman provinces. Within three years after the final conquest of Africa, the whole peninsula was conquered, save where the Christian still held out in the inaccessible mountain fastnesses. The Saracen power was even carried beyond the Pyrenees

Saracen conquest of Persia. 632–651.

Saracen conquest of Africa. 647–711. Of Spain. 711–714.

CHAP. V.

Saracen provinces in Gaul, 713–755.

into the province of *Septimania*, the remnant of the Gaulish dominion of the West-Gothic kings. Narbonne, Arles, Nîmes, all became for a while Saracen cities.

Effects of Saracen conquest.

In this way, of the three continents round the Mediterranean, Rome lost all her possessions in Africa, while both in Europe and Asia she had now a neighbour and an enemy of quite another kind from any which she had had before. The Teutonic conquerors, if conquerors, had been also disciples; they became part of the Latin world. The Persian, though his rivalry was religious as well as political, was still merely a rival, fighting along a single line of frontier. But every province that was conquered by the Saracens was utterly lopped away; it became the possession of men altogether alien and hostile in race, language, manners, and religion. A large part of the Roman world passed from Aryan and Christian to Semitic and Mahometan dominion. But the essential differences among the three main parts of the Empire now showed themselves very clearly. The Eastern provinces, where either Roman or Greek life was always an exotic, fell away at the first touch. Africa, as being so greatly romanized, held out for sixty years. The provinces of Asia Minor, now thoroughly Greek, were often ravaged, but never conquered. Spain and Septimania were far more easily conquered than Africa—a sign perhaps that the West-Gothic rule was still felt as foreign by the Roman inhabitants.

Different fates of the Eastern, Latin, and Greek provinces.

647–709.

With the conquest of Spain the undivided Saracenic Empire, the dominion of the single Caliph, reached its greatest extent in the three continents. Detached conquests in Europe were made long after, but on the whole the Saracen power went back. Forty years

Greatest extent of Saracen provinces. 750.

later they lost *Sind*, their furthest possession to the East. Five years later Spain became the seat of a rival dynasty, which after a while grew into a rival Caliphate. In the same year the Saracen dominion for the first time went back in Europe. The battle of Tours answers to the repulse of Attila at Châlons; it did not make changes, but hindered them; but before long the one province which the Saracens held beyond the Pyrenees, that of *Septimania* or *Gothia*, was won from them by the Franks.

CHAP. V.

Separation of Spain. 755.

Battle of Tours. 732.

Frankish conquest of Septimania. 755.

§ 4. *Settlements of the Slavonic Nations.*

The movements of the sixth century began to bring into notice a branch of the Aryan family of nations which was to play an important part in the affairs both of the East and of the West. These were the various nations of the great *Slavonic* race. We are concerned with their history only so far as it affects that of the Empire, and for the present only of its Eastern provinces. They made their way into the Empire in the same diversity of character as the Goths at an earlier time; and it would seem that the march of Theodoric helped to open a way for their migrations. But their main importance began in the sixth century, when the movements of the *Avars* seem to have had much the same effect upon the Slaves which the movements of the Huns in the fourth century had upon the Teutons. The inroads of the Avars had, as we have seen, checked the growth of Teutonic powers on the Lower Danube, and had led to the Lombard settlement in Italy. But the Avars only formed the vanguard of a number of Turanian nations, some of them at least Turkish, which were now pressing westward. The Avars formed a great

Movements of the Slaves

CHAP. V.

Kingdom of the Avars.

Magyars, &c.

kingdom in the lands north of the Danube; to the east of these, along the northern coasts of the Euxine, bordering on the outlying possessions and allies of the Empire in those regions, lay *Magyars*, *Patzinaks*, and the greater dominion of the *Chazars*. All these play a part in Byzantine history; and the Avars were in the seventh century the most dangerous invaders and ravagers of the Roman territory. But south of the Danube they appeared mainly as ravagers; geography knows them only in their settled kingdom to the north of that river. Even that kingdom lasted no very great time; the real importance of all these migrations consists in the effect which they had on the great Aryan race which now begins to take its part in history. The Slaves seem to have been driven by the Turanian incursions in two directions, to the North-west and to the South-west. The North-western Slaves do not become of importance till a little later. But the South-western division plays a great part in the history of the sixth and seventh centuries. Their position with regard to the Eastern Empire is a kind of shadow of the position held by the Teutonic nations with regard to the Western Empire. The Slaves play in the East, though less thoroughly and less brilliantly, the same part, half conquerors, half disciples, which the Teutons played in the West. During the sixth century they appear only as ravagers; in the seventh they appear as settlers. There seems no doubt that Heraclius encouraged Slavonic settlements south of the Danube, doubtless with a view to defence against the more dangerous Avars. Much like the Teutonic settlers in the West, the Slaves came in at first as colonists under Imperial authority, and presently became practically independent. A number of Slavonic states

North-western and South-eastern Slaves.

Analogy between Teutons and Slaves.

Slavonic settlements under Heraclius. c. 620.

CHAP. V.

thus arose in the lands north and east of the Hadriatic, as *Servia*, *Chrobatia* or *Croatia*, and *Carinthia*, of which the first two are historically connected with the Eastern, and the third with the Western Empire. They pressed within the borders of the ancient, and even of the modern Italian kingdom; Istria and much of Venetia became largely Slavonic. So did *Dalmatia* yet more thoroughly, with the exception of the maritime cities, which, among many vicissitudes, clave to the Empire. And even among them considerable revolutions took place. Thus *Salona* was destroyed, and out of Diocletian's palace in its neighbourhood arose the new city of *Spalato*. The Dalmatian *Epidauros* was also destroyed, and *Ragusa* took its place. In many of these inroads Slaves and Avars were mixed up together; but the lasting settlements were all Slavonic. And the state of things which thus began has been lasting; the north-eastern coast of the Hadriatic is still a Slavonic land with an Italian fringe.

Settlements in Istria, Venetia, and Dalmatia.

Destruction of Salona, 639.

Origin of Spalato and Ragusa.

In these migrations the Slaves displaced whatever remnants were left of the old Illyrian race in the lands near the Danube. They have themselves to some extent taken the Illyrian name, a change which has sometimes led to confusion. But the movement for a while went much further south. The Slaves pressed on into a large part of Macedonia and Greece, and, during the seventh and eighth centuries, the whole of those lands, except the fortified cities and a fringe along the coast, were practically cut off from the Empire. The name of *Slavinia* reached from the Danube to Peloponnêsos, leaving to the Empire only islands and detached points of coast from Venice round to Thessalonica. Their settlements in these regions gave a new meaning to an ancient name,

Displacement of the Illyrians.

Extent of Slavonic settlement.

CHAP. V.

and the word *Macedonian* now began to mean *Slavonic*. The Slavonic occupation of Greece is a fact which must neither be forgotten nor exaggerated. It certainly did not amount to an extirpation of the Greek nation; but it certainly did amount to an occupation of a large part of the country, which was hellenized afresh from those cities and districts which remained Greek or Roman.

Nature of Slavonic settlement in Greece.

While these changes were going on in the Hadriatic and Ægæan lands, another immigration later in the seventh century took place in the lands south of the lower Danube, and drove back the Imperial frontier to Haimos. This was the incursion of the *Bulgarians*, another Turanian people, but one whose history has been different from that of most of the Turanian immigrants. By mixture with Slavonic subjects and neighbours they became practically Slavonic, and they still remain a people speaking a Slavonic language. Thus the Empire, though it still kept its possessions in Italy, together with the great Mediterranean islands—though its hold on Western Africa lasted on into the eighth century—though it still kept outlying possessions on the northern and eastern coasts of the Euxine—was cut short in that great peninsula which seems made to be the immediate possession of the New Rome.

Settlement of the Bulgarians. c. 679.

The Eastern Empire cut short in its own peninsula.

But, exactly as happened in the West, the loss of political dominion carried with it the growth of moral dominion. The nations which pressed into these provinces gradually accepted Christianity in its Eastern form, and they have always looked up to Constantinople with a feeling the same in kind, but less strong in degree, as that with which the West has looked up to the elder Rome. But, at the beginning of the eighth century, though the Imperial power still held posts here and

Moral influence of Constantinople.

Extent of the Eastern Empire.

there from the pillars of Hêraklês to the Kimmerian Bosporos, Saracens on the one side and Slaves on the other had cut short the continuous Roman dominion to a comparatively narrow space. The unbroken possessions of Cæsar were now confined to Thrace and that solid peninsula of Asia Minor which the Saracens constantly ravaged, but never conquered. Mountains had taken the place of rivers as the great boundaries of the Empire: instead of the Danube and the Euphrates, the Roman Terminus had fallen back to Haimos and Tauros.

§ 5. *The Transfer of the Western Empire to the Franks.*

Growth of the Franks.

Meanwhile we must go back to the West, and trace the growth of the great power which was there growing up, a power which, while the elder Empire was thus cut short in the East, was in the end to supplant it in the West by the creation of a rival Empire. For a while the *Franks* and the Empire had only occasional dealings with each other. Next to Britain, which had altogether ceased to be part of the Roman world, the part of the Western Empire which was least affected by the re-awakening of the Roman power in the East was the former province of Transalpine Gaul. The power of the Franks was fast spreading, both in their old home in Germany and in their new home in Gaul. The victory of Chlodwig over the *Alemanni* made the Franks the leading people of Germany. The two German powers which had so long been the chief enemies of the Roman power along the Rhine were now united. Throughout the sixth century the German dominion of the Franks was growing. The Frankish supremacy was extended over *Thuringia*, and later in the century loosely

Frankish conquest of the Alemanni, 496; of the Thuringians, c. 531;

CHAP. V.

of Bavaria.

over *Bavaria*. The Bavaria of this age, it must be remembered, has a much wider extent to the south than the Bavaria of modern geography, reaching to the northern borders of Italy. The Bavarians seem to have been themselves but recent settlers in the land between the Alps and the Danube; but their immigration and their reduction under Frankish supremacy, which became a real dominion in the eighth century, made the lands immediately south of the Danube thoroughly Teutonic, as the earlier Frankish conquests had done by the lands immediately west of the Rhine. Long before this time, the Franks had greatly extended their dominions in Gaul also. In the later years of Chlodwig the greater part of *Aquitaine* was won from the West-Goths. Further conquests at their expense were afterwards made, and about the same time Burgundy came under Frankish supremacy.

Conquest of Aquitaine [507–511] and Burgundy. 532–534. Novempopulana. 567.

The Franks now held, either in possession or dependence, the whole oceanic coast of Gaul; but they were still shut out from the Mediterranean. The West-Goths still kept the land from the Pyrenees to the Rhone, the land of *Septimania* or *Gothia*. The land which was specially *Provincia*, the first Roman possession in Transalpine Gaul, the coast from the Rhone to the Alps, formed part of the East-Gothic dominion of Theodoric. An invasion of Italy during the long wars between the Goths and Romans failed to establish a Frankish dominion on the Italian side of the Alps. But as the Franks, by their conquest of Burgundy, were now neighbours of Italy, it led to a further enlargement of their Gaulish dominions, and to their first acquisition of a Mediterranean seaboard. It was now that Massalia, Arelate, and the rest of the Province were, by an Imperial grant, one of the last exercises of Imperial

Cession of Provence. 536.

power in those regions, added to the kingdom of the Franks. By the time that the Roman reconquest of Italy was completed, the Frankish dominion, united for a moment under a single head, took in the whole of Gaul, except the small remaining West-Gothic territory, together with central Germany and a supremacy over the southern German lands. To the north lay the still independent tribes of the Low-Dutch stock, Frisian and Saxon.

Extent of the Frankish dominions.

As the Frankish dominion plays so great a part in European history and geography, a part in truth second only to that played by the Roman dominion, it will be needful to consider the historical position of the Franks. Their dominion was that of a German people who had made themselves dominant alike in Germany and in Gaul. But it was only in a small part of the Frankish territory that the Frankish people had actually settled. It was only in northern Gaul and central Germany, in the lands to which they have permanently given their name, that the Franks can be looked on as really occupying the land. In their German territory they of course remained German; in northern Gaul their position answered to that of the other Teutonic nations which had formed settlements within the Empire. They were a dominant Teutonic race in a Roman land. Gradually they adopted the speech of the conquered, while the conquered in the end adopted the name of the conquerors. But the fusion of German and Roman was slower in the Frankish part of Gaul than elsewhere, doubtless because elsewhere the Teutonic settlements were cut off from their older Teutonic homes, while the Franks in Gaul had their older Teutonic home as a back-

Position of the Franks.

Slow fusion of Franks and Romans.

CHAP. V.

German and Gaulish dependencies of the Franks.

ground. Beyond the bounds of these more strictly Frankish lands, German and Gaulish, the dominion of the Franks was at most a political supremacy, and in no sense a national settlement. In Germany Bavaria was ruled by its own vassal princes; in Gaul south of the Loire the Frank was at most an external ruler. Aquitaine had to be practically conquered over and over again, and new dynasties of native princes were constantly rising up. The Teutonic element in Southern Gaul, an element much slighter than the Teutonic element in Northern Gaul, is not Frankish, but Gothic and Burgundian. The native Romance speech of those lands is wholly different from the Romance speech of Northern Gaul. In short, there was really nothing in common between the two great parts of Gaul, the lands south and the lands north of the Loire, except their union, first under Roman and then under Frankish dominion. And in Armorica the old Celtic population, strengthened by settlers from Britain, formed another and a yet more distinct element.

Ethnology of Southern Gaul.

Divisions of the Frankish dominions.

Thus within the Frankish dominions there were wide national diversities, containing the germs of future divisions. It needed a strong hand even to keep the Teutonic and the Latin *Francia* together, much more to keep together all the dependent lands, German and Gaulish. During the ages when the Empire was being cut short by Lombards, Goths, Slaves, and Saracens, the Frankish dominion was never in the like sort cut short by foreign settlements; but its whole history under the Merowingian dynasty is a history of divisions and reunions. The tendencies to division which were inherent in the condition of the country were strengthened by endless partitions among the members of the reigning house. Speaking roughly, it may be said that the more strictly Frankish territory showed a tendency to divide itself into two parts, the Eastern or Teutonic land, *Austria* or *Austrasia*, and *Neustria*, the Western or Romance land. These were severally the germs which grew into the kingdoms of Germany and France. As for the mere name of *Francia*, it fared like other names of the kind; it shifted its geographical use according to the wanderings of the people from whom it was taken. After many such changes of meaning, it gradually settled down as the name of those parts of Germany and Gaul where it still abides. There are the Teutonic or Austrian *Francia*, part of which still keeps the name of *Franken* or *Franconia*, and the Romance or Neustrian *Francia*, which by various annexations has grown into modern *France*.

Austria and Neustria.

Use of the name *Francia*.

At last, after endless divisions, reconquests, and reunions, of the different parts of the Frankish territory, the whole Frankish dominion was again, in the second half of the eighth century, joined together under the Austrasian, the purely German, house of the *Karlings*. The Dukes and Kings of that house consolidated and extended the Frankish dominion in every direction. Under Pippin and Charles the Great, the power of the ruling race was more firmly established over the dependent states, such as Bavaria and Aquitaine. Under Pippin the conquest of the province of Septimania, once Gothic, in his day Saracen, extended the Frankish power over the whole of Gaul; and under Charles the Great, the Frankish dominion was extended by a series of conquests in every direction. Of these, his Italian conquests were rather the winning of a new crown for the Frankish king than the extension of the Frankish kingdom. But the

The Karlings. Dukes, 687–752; Kings, 752–987.

Pippin conquers Septimania. 752.

Conquests of Charles the Great. 768–814.

CHAP. V.

conquest of *Saxony* at the one end and of the *Spanish March* at the other, as well as the overthrow of the Pannonian kingdom of the Avars, were in the strictest sense extensions of the Frankish dominions. The Frankish power which now plays so great a part in the world was a power essentially German. The Franks and their kings, the kings who reigned from the Elbe to the Ebro, were German in blood, speech, and feeling; but they bore rule over other lands, German, Latin, and Celtic, in many various degrees of incorporation and subjection.

German character of the Frankish power.

The three great powers of the eighth century; Romans, Franks, Saracens.

Thus the effect of the Saracen conquests was to leave in Europe one purely European power, namely the kingdom of the Franks, one power both European and Asiatic, namely the Roman Empire with its seat at Constantinople, and one power at once Asiatic, African, and European, namely the Saracen Caliphate. Through the eighth century these three are the great powers of the world, to which the other nations of Europe and Asia form, as far as we are concerned, a mere background. But the Caliphate, as a Semitic and Mahometan power, could be European only in a geographical sense. Even after the establishment of the independent Saracen dominion in Spain, the new power still remained an exotic. A great country of Western Europe was no longer ruled from Damascus or Bagdad; but the emirate, afterwards Caliphate, of Cordova, and the kingdoms into which it afterwards broke up, still remained only geographically European. They were portions of Asia—in after times rather of Africa—thrusting themselves into Europe, like the Spanish dominion of Carthage in earlier times. The two great Christian powers, the two great really European powers, are the Roman and

Character of the Caliphate.

The Saracen dominion in Spain.

the Frankish. We now come to the process which for a while caused the Roman and Frankish names to have the same meaning within a large part of Europe, and by which the two seats of Roman dominion were again parted asunder, never to be reunited.

Relations of the Franks and the Empire.

The way by which the Roman and Frankish powers came to affect one another was through the affairs of Italy. The steps by which the Imperial power was, during the eighth century, weakened step by step in the territories which still remained to the Empire in central Italy are, either from an ecclesiastical or from a strictly historical point of view, of surpassing interest. But, as long as the authority of the Emperor was not openly thrown off, no change was made on the map. The events of those times which did make a change on the map were, first the conquest of the Exarchate by the Lombards, and secondly, the overthrow of the Lombard kingdom itself by the Frank king Charles the Great. The Frankish power was thus at last established on the Italian side of the Alps, but it must be remarked that the new conquest was not incorporated with the Frankish dominion. Charles held his Italian dominion as a separate dominion, and called himself King of the Franks and Lombards. He also bore the title of Patrician of the Romans; but, though the taking of that title was of great political significance, it did not affect geography. The title of Patrician of itself implied a commission from the Emperor, and, though it was bestowed by the Bishop and people of Rome without the Imperial consent, the very choice of the title showed that the Imperial authority was not formally thrown off. Charles, as Patrician, was virtually sovereign of Rome,

The Imperial possessions in Italy.

Lombard conquest of the Exarchate. Overthrow of the Lombards by Charles. 774.

Lombardy a separate kingdom.

Title of Patrician.

CHAP. V.

and his acquisition of the patriciate practically extended his dominion from the Ocean to the frontiers of Beneventum. But, down to his Imperial coronation in the last week of the eighth century, the Emperor who reigned in the New Rome was still the nominal sovereign of the Old. The event of the year 800, with all its weighty significance, did not practically either extend the territories of Charles or increase his powers.

Nominal authority of the Empire.

Effect of the Imperial coronation of Charles. 800.

Still the Imperial coronation of Charles is one of the great landmarks both of history and of historical geography. The whole political system of Europe was changed when the Old Rome cast off its formal allegiance to the New, and chose the King of the Franks and Lombards to be Emperor of the Romans. Though the powers of Charles were not increased nor his dominions extended, he held everything by a new title. The Roman Empire was divided, never to be joined together again. But its Western half now took in, not only the greatest of its lost provinces, but vast regions which had never formed part of the Empire in the days of Trajan himself. Again, the distinctive character of the older Roman Empire had been the absence of nationality. The whole civilized world had become Rome, and all its free inhabitants had become Romans. But from this time each of the two divisions of the Empire begins to assume something like a national character. East and West alike remained Roman in name and in political traditions. The Old Rome was the nominal centre of one; the New Rome was both the nominal and the real centre of the other. But there was a sense in which both alike from this time ceased to be Roman. The Western Empire passed to a German

Final division of the Empire.

Growing nationality of the two Empires, German and Greek.

king, and later changes tended to make his Empire more and more German. The Eastern Empire meanwhile, by the successive loss of the Eastern provinces, of Latin Africa, and of Latin Italy, became nearly co-extensive with those parts of Europe and Asia where the Greek speech and Greek civilization prevailed. From one point of view, both Empires are still Roman; from another point of view, one is fast becoming German, the other is fast becoming Greek. And the two powers into which the old Roman Empire is thus split are in the strictest sense two Empires. They are no longer mere divisions of an Empire which has been found to be too great for the rule of one man. The Emperors of the East and West are no longer Imperial colleagues dividing the administration of a single Empire between them. They are now rival potentates, each claiming to be exclusively the one true Roman Emperor, each boasting himself to be the one true representative of the common predecessors of both in the days when the Empire was still undivided.

Rivalry of the two Empires.

It is further to be noted that the same kind of change which now happened to the Christian Empire, had happened earlier in the century to the Mahometan Empire. The establishment of a rival dynasty at Cordova, even though the assumption of the actual title of Caliph did not follow at once, was exactly analogous to the establishment of a rival Empire in the Old Rome. The Mediterranean world has now four great powers, the two rival Christian Empires, and the two rival Mahometan Caliphates. Among these, it naturally follows that each is hostile to its neighbour of the opposite religion, and friendly to its neighbour's rival. The Western Emperor is the

The two Caliphates.

Rivalry of the Empires and Caliphates.

enemy of the Western Caliph, the friend of the Eastern. The Eastern Emperor is the enemy of the Eastern Caliph, the friend of the Western. Thus the four great powers stood at the beginning of the ninth century. And it was out of the dismemberments of the two great Christian and the two great Mahometan powers that the later states, Christian and Mahometan, of the Mediterranean world took their rise.

Extent of the Carolingian Empire.

It is a point of geographical as well as of historical importance that Charles the Great, after he was crowned Emperor, caused all those who had been hitherto bound by allegiance to him as King of the Franks to swear allegiance to him afresh as Roman Emperor. This marks that all his dominions, Frankish, Lombard, and strictly Roman, are to be looked on as forming part of the Western Empire. Thus the Western Empire now took in all those German lands which the old Roman Emperors never could conquer. Germany became part of the Roman Empire, not by Rome conquering Germany, but by Rome choosing the German king as her Emperor.

Contrast of its boundaries with those of the elder Empire.

The boundaries of the Empire thus became different from what they had ever been before. Of the provinces of the old Western Empire, Britain, Africa, and all Spain save one corner, remained foreign to the new Roman Empire of the Franks. But, on the other hand, the Empire now took in all those lands in Germany and beyond Germany over which the Frankish power now reached, but which had never formed part of the elder Empire. The long wars of Charles with the Saxons led to

Conquest of Saxony. 772–804.

their final conquest, to the incorporation of *Saxony* with the Frankish kingdom, and, after the Imperial coronation of the Frankish king, to its incorporation with the Western Empire.

The conquests of Charles had thus, among their other results, welded Germany into a single whole. For though the Franks had long been the greatest power in Germany, yet Germany could not be said to form a single whole as long as the Saxons, the greatest people of Northern Germany, remained independent. The conquest of Saxony brought the Frankish power for the first time in contact with the *Danes* and the other peoples of *Scandinavia.* The dominions of Charles took in what was then called Saxony beyond the Elbe, that is the modern Holstein, and the *Eider* was fixed as the northern boundary of the Empire. More than one Danish king did homage to Charles and to some of the Emperors after him ; but Denmark was never incorporated with the Empire or even made permanently dependent. To the east, the immediate dominions of Charles stretched but a little way beyond the Elbe ; but here the Western Empire came in contact, as the Eastern had done at an earlier time and by a different process, with the widely spread nations of the Slavonic race. The same movements which had driven one branch of that race to the south-west had driven another branch to the north-west, and the wars of Charles in those regions gave his Empire a fringe of Slavonic allies and dependents along both sides of the Elbe, forming a barrier between the immediate dominions of the Empire and the independent Slaves to the east. To the south Charles overthrew the kingdom of the *Avars* ; he thus extended his dominions on the side of south-eastern Germany, and here he came in contact with the southern branch of the Slaves, a portion of whom, in *Carinthia* and the neighbouring lands, became subjects of his Empire. In Spain he acquired the north-eastern corner

Boundary of the Eider.

Slavonic allies and neighbours.

Overthrow of the Avar kingdom. 796.

CHAP. V.

The Spanish March. 778.

as far as the Ebro, forming the *Spanish March* of his kingdom and Empire.

Divisions of the Empire.

Thus the new Western Empire took in all Gaul, all that was then Germany, the greater part of Italy, and a small part of Spain.[1] It thus took in both Teutonic and Romance lands, and contained in it the germs of the chief nations of modern Europe. It was a step towards the formation of those nations when Charles, following the example both of earlier Roman Emperors and of earlier Frankish kings, planned several divisions of his dominions among his sons. Owing to the deaths of all his sons but one, none of these divisions took effect. And it should be noticed that as yet none of these schemes of division agreed with any great natural or national boundary. They did not even foreshadow the division which afterwards took place, and out of which the chief states of Western Europe grew. In two cases only was anything like a national kingdom thought of. Charles's son Lewis reigned under him

Kingdom of Aquitaine.

as king in *Aquitaine*, a kingdom which took in all Southern Gaul and the Spanish March, answering pretty nearly to the lands of the Provençal tongue or

Death of Charles. 814.

tongue of *Oc*. And when Charles died, and was succeeded in the Empire by Lewis, Charles's grandson Bernard still went on reigning under his uncle as King

Kingdom of Italy.

of Italy. The *Kingdom of Italy* must be understood as taking in the Italian mainland, except the lands in the south which were held by the dependent princes of Beneventum and by the rival Emperors of the East.

Use of the name *Francia*.

During this period *Francia* commonly means the strictly

[1] The geographical extent of the Frankish dominion before and after the conquest of Charles is most fully marked by Einhard, Vita Karoli, c. 15.

Frankish kingdoms, Gaulish and German. The words *Gallia* and *Germania* are used in a strictly geographical sense.

§ 6. *Northern Europe.*

Scandinavians and English.

Meanwhile other nations were beginning to show themselves in those parts of Europe which lay beyond the Empire. In north-western Europe two branches of the Teutonic race were fast growing into importance; the one in lands which had never been part of the Empire, the other in a land which had been part of it, but which had been so utterly severed from it as to be as if it had never belonged to it. These were the *Scandinavian* nations in the two great peninsulas of Northern Europe, and the *English* in the isle of Britain. The history of these two races is closely connected, and it has an important bearing on the history of Europe in general.

Stages of the English conquest of Britain.

In Britain itself the progress of the English arms had been gradual. Sometimes conquests from the Britons were made with great speed: sometimes the English advance was checked by successes on the British side, by mere inaction, or by wars between the different English kingdoms. The fluctuations of victory, and consequently of boundaries, between the English kingdoms were quite as marked as the warfare between the English and the Britons. Among the many Teutonic settlements in Britain, small and great, seven kingdoms stand out as of special importance, and three of these, *Wessex*, *Mercia*, and *Northumberland*, again stand out as candidates for a general supremacy over the whole English name. At the end of the eighth century a large part of Britain remained, as it still

The English kingdoms.

Britain at the end of the eighth century.

remains, in the hands of the elder Celtic inhabitants; but the parts which they still kept were now cut off from each other.

Celtic states.

Cornwall or *West-Wales*, *North-Wales* (answering nearly to the modern principality), and *Strathclyde* or *Cumberland* (a much larger district than the modern county so called) were all the seats of separate, though fluctuating, British states. Beyond the Forth lay the independent kingdoms of the *Picts* and *Scots*, which, in the course of the ninth century, became one.

West Saxon supremacy under Ecgberht. 802–837.

It was the West-Saxon kingdom to which the supremacy over all the kingdoms of Britain, Teutonic and Celtic, came in the end. Ecgberht, its king, had been a friend and guest of Charles the Great, and he had most likely been stirred up by his example to do in his own island what Charles had done on the mainland. In the course of his reign, West-Wales was completely conquered; the other English kingdoms, together with North-Wales, were brought into a greater or less degree of dependence. But both in North-Wales and also in Mercia, Northumberland, and East-Anglia, the local kings went on reigning under the supremacy of the King of the West-Saxons, who now began sometimes to call himself *King of the English*. In the north both Scotland and Strathclyde remained quite independent.

The Scandinavian nations.

The Danes.

That part also of the Teutonic race which lay altogether beyond the bounds of the Empire now begins to be of importance. The *Danes* are heard of as early as the days of Justinian; but neither they nor the other Scandinavian nations play any part in history before the time of Charles the Great. A number of small states gradually settled down into three great kingdoms, which remain still, though their boundaries have greatly changed. The boundary between Denmark and the Empire was, as we have seen, fixed at the Eider. Besides the peninsula of Jutland and the islands which still belong to it, Denmark took in *Scania* and other lands in the south of the great peninsula that now forms *Sweden* and *Norway*. Norway, on the other hand, ran much further inland, and came down much further south than it does now. These points are of importance, because they show the causes of the later history of the three Scandinavian states. Both Denmark and Norway had a great front to the Ocean, while *Swithiod* and *Gauthiod*, the districts whose union formed the original kingdom of Sweden, had no opening that way, but were altogether turned towards the Baltic. It thus came about that for some centuries both Denmark and Norway played a much greater part in the general affairs of Europe than Sweden did. Denmark was an immediate neighbour of the Empire, and from both Denmark and Norway men went out to conquer and settle in various parts of Britain, Ireland and Gaul, besides colonizing the more distant and uninhabited lands of *Iceland* and *Greenland*. Meanwhile the Swedes pressed eastward on the Finnish and Slavonic peoples beyond the Baltic. In this last way they had a great effect on the history of the Eastern Empire; but in Western history Sweden counts for very little till a much later time.

Extent of Denmark and Norway.

Sweden.

Danish and Norwegian settlements.

Pressure of Sweden to the East.

During the period which has been dealt with in this chapter, taking in the sixth, seventh, and eighth centuries, we thus see, first of all the reunion of the greater part of the Roman Empire under Justinian—then the lopping away of the Eastern and African provinces by the conquests of the Saracens—then the

Summary.

CHAP. V.

gradual separation of all Italy except the south, ending in the re-establishment of a separate Western Empire under Charles the Great. We thus get two great Christian powers, the Eastern and Western Empires, balanced by two great Mahometan powers, the Eastern and Western Caliphates. All the older Teutonic kingdoms have either vanished or have grown into something wholly different. The Vandal kingdom of Africa and the East-Gothic kingdom have wholly vanished. The West-Gothic kingdom, cut short by Franks on one side and by Saracens on the other, survives only in the form of the small Christian principalities which still held their ground in Northern Spain. The Frankish kingdom, by swallowing up the Gothic and Burgundian dominions in Gaul, the independent nations of Germany, the Lombard kingdom, and the more part of the possessions of the Empire in Italy, has grown into a new Western Empire. The two Empires, both still politically Roman, are fast becoming, one German and the other Greek. Meanwhile, nations beyond the bounds of the Empire are growing into importance. The process has begun by which the many small Teutonic settlements in Britain grew in the end into the one kingdom of England. The three Scandinavian nations, Danes, Swedes, and Norwegians or Northmen, now begin to grow in importance. In a religious point of view, if Syria, Egypt, Africa, and the more part of Spain were lost to Christendom, the loss was in some degree made up by the conversion to Christianity of the Angles and Saxons in Britain, of the Old-Saxons in Germany, and of the other German tribes which at the beginning of the sixth century had still been heathen. At no time in the world's history did the map undergo greater changes. This period is the time of real transition from the older state of things represented by the undivided Roman Empire to the newer state of things in which Europe is made up of a great number of independent states. The modern kingdoms outside the Empire, in Britain and Scandinavia, were already forming. The great continental nations of Western Europe had as yet hardly begun to form. They were to grow out of the break-up of the Carolingian Empire, the Roman Empire of the Franks.

CHAPTER VI.

THE BEGINNING OF THE MODERN EUROPEAN STATES.

§ 1. *The Division of the Frankish Empire.*

CHAP. VI.

Dissolution of the Frankish dominion.

The chief states of modern Europe spring out of it.

National kingdoms not yet formed.

Extent of *Francia.*

THE great dominion of the Franks, the German kingdom which had so strangely grown into a new Western Roman Empire, did not last long. In the course of the ninth century it altogether fell to pieces. But the process by which it fell to pieces must be carefully traced, because it was out of its dismemberment that the chief states of Western Europe arose. Of all the possessions of the Carolingian Empire in Germany, Gaul, Italy, and Spain, it was only Italy, and sometimes Aquitaine, which showed any approach to the character of a separate or national kingdom. Northern Gaul and central Germany were still alike *Francia*; and, though the Romance speech prevailed in one, and the Teutonic speech in the other, no national distinction was drawn between them during the time of Charles the Great. Among the proposed divisions of his Empire, none proposed to separate *Neustria* and *Austria*, the Western and the Eastern *Francia*. But Italy did form a separate kingdom under the superiority of the Emperor; and so for a while there was an under-kingdom of Aquitaine, answering roughly to Gaul south of the Loire. This is the land of the *Provençal* tongue, the

Separate being of Italy and Aquitaine.

tongue of Oc, a tongue which, it must be remembered, reached to the Ebro. It is in the various divisions, contemplated and actual, among the sons of Lewis the Pious, the successor of Charles the Great, that we see the first approaches to a national division between Germany and Gaul, and the first glimmerings of a state answering in any way to *France* in the modern sense.

Division under Lewis the Pious. First glimpses of Modern France.

The earliest among those endless divisions that we need mention is the division of 817, by which two new subordinate kingdoms were founded within the Empire. Lewis and his immediate colleague Lothar kept in their own hands *Francia*, German and Gaulish, and the more part of Burgundy. South-western Gaul, Aquitaine in the wide sense, with some small parts of Septimania and Burgundy, formed the portion of one under-king; south-eastern Germany, Bavaria and the march-lands beyond it, formed the portion of another. Italy still remained the portion of a third. Here we have nothing in the least answering to modern France. The tendency is rather to leave the immediate Frankish kingdom, both in Gaul and Germany, as an undivided whole, and to part off its dependent lands, German, Gaulish, and Italian. But, in a much later division, Lewis granted Neustria to his son Charles, and in the next year, on the death of Pippin of Aquitaine, he added his kingdom to that of Charles. A state was thus formed which answers roughly to the later kingdom of France, as it stood before the long series of French encroachments on the German and Burgundian lands. The kingdom thus formed had no definite name, and it answered to no national division. It was indeed mainly a kingdom of the Romance speech, but it did not

Division of 817.

Union of Neustria and Aquitaine the first step to the creation of *France*. 838.

Character of the *Western Kingdom*.

CHAP. VI.

answer to any one of the great divisions of that speech. It was a kingdom formed by accident, because Lewis wished to increase the portion of his youngest son. Still there can be no doubt that we have here the first beginning of the kingdom of *France*, though it was not till after several other stages that the kingdom thus formed took that name. The final division of Verdun went a step further in the direction of the modern map. It left Charles in possession of a kingdom which still more nearly answered to France, as France stood before its Burgundian and German annexations. It also founded a kingdom which roughly answered to the later Germany before its great extension to the East at the expense of the Slavonic nations. And, as the Western kingdom was formed by the addition of Aquitaine to the Western *Francia*, so the Eastern kingdom was formed by the addition of the Eastern *Francia* to Bavaria. Lewis of Bavaria became king of a kingdom which we are tempted to call the kingdom of *Germany*. Still it would as yet be premature to speak of France at all, or even to speak of Germany, except in the geographical sense. The two kingdoms are severally the kingdoms of the *Eastern* and of the *Western Franks*. But between these two states the policy of the ninth century instinctively put a barrier. The Emperor Lothar, besides Italy, kept a long narrow strip of territory between the dominions of his Eastern and Western brothers. After him, Italy remained to his son the Emperor Lewis, while the borderlands of Germany and Gaul passed to the younger Lothar. This land, having thus been the dominion of two Lothars, took the name of *Lotharingia*, *Lothringen*, or *Lorraine*,

Division of Verdun. 843.

Kingdoms of the Eastern and Western Franks.

Kingdom of *Lotharingia*, Lothringen, Lorraine.

CHAP. VI.

a name which part of it has kept to this day. This kingdom, sometimes attached to the Eastern kingdom, sometimes to the Western, sometimes divided between the two, sometimes separated from both, always kept its character of a borderland. The kingdom to the west of it, in like manner took the name of *Karolingia*, which, according to the same analogy, should be *Karlingen* or *Charlaine*. It is only by a caprice of language that the name of Lotharingia has survived, while that of Karolingia has died out.

The Western Kingdom called *Karolingia.*

Meanwhile, in south-eastern Gaul, between the Rhone and the Alps, another kingdom arose, namely the kingdom of *Burgundy*. Under Charles the Third, commonly known as the Fat, all the Frankish dominions, except Burgundy, were again united for a moment. On his deposition they split asunder again. We have now four distinct kingdoms, those of the *Eastern* and *Western Franks*, the forerunners of Germany and France, the kingdom of *Italy*, and *Burgundy*, sometimes forming one kingdom and sometimes two. *Lotharingia* remained a borderland between the Eastern and Western kingdoms, attached sometimes to one, sometimes to the other. Out of these elements arose the great kingdoms and nations of Western Europe. The four can hardly be better described than they are by the Old-English Chronicler: 'Arnulf then dwelled in the land to the east of Rhine; and Rudolf took to the Middle kingdom; and Oda to the West deal; and Berengar and Guy to the Lombards' land, and to the lands on that side of the mountain.' But the geography of all the four kingdoms which now arose must be described at somewhat greater length.

Burgundy, or the Middle Kingdom.

Union under Charles the Fat. 884.

Division on his deposition. 887.

It must be borne in mind that all these divisions

CHAP. VI.

of the great Frankish dominion were, in theory, like the ancient divisions of the Empire, a mere parcelling out of a common possession among several royal colleagues. The kings had no special titles, and their dominions had no special names recognized in formal use. Every king who ruled over any part of the Frankish dominions was a King of the Franks, just as all among the many rulers of the Roman Empire in the days of Diocletian and Constantine were equally Roman Augusti or Cæsars. As the kings and their kingdoms had no formal titles specially set apart for them, the writers of the time had to describe them as they might.[1] The Eastern part of the Frankish dominions, the lot of Lewis the German and his successors, is thus called the *Eastern Kingdom*, the *Teutonic Kingdom*. Its king is the *King of the East-Franks*, sometimes simply the King of the *Eastern men*, sometimes the *King of Germany*. This last name is often found in the ninth century as a description, but it was not used as a formal title. For, though convenient in use, it was in strictness inaccurate, as the *Regnum Teutonicum* lay geographically partly in Germany, partly in Gaul.[2] To the men of the Western kingdom the Eastern king sometimes appeared as the *King beyond the Rhine*. He himself, like other kings, for the most part simply

No formal titles or names of the Frankish kingdoms.

Various names of the Eastern Kingdom or *Germany*.

[1] The best account of the various names by which the East-Frankish kings and their people are described is given by Waitz, *Deutsche Verfassungsgeschichte*, v. 121 et seqq.

[2] So Wippo (2) describes the gathering of the men of the kingdom: 'Cis et circa Rhenum castra locabant. Qui dum Galliam a Germanis dividat, ex parte *Germaniæ* Saxones cum sibi adjacentibus Sclavis, Franci orientales, Norici, Alamanni, convenere. De *Gallia* vero Franci qui super Rhenum habitant, Ribuarii, Liutharingi, coadunati sunt.' These two sets of Franks are again distinguished from the Latin or French 'Franci.'

calls himself *Rex*, till the time came when his rank as King of Germany or of the East-Franks became simply a step towards the higher title of Emperor of the Romans. But it must be remembered that the special connexion between the Roman Empire and the German kingdom did not begin at once on the division of 887. Arnulf indeed, the first German King after the division, made his way to Rome and was crowned Emperor; and it marks the position of the Eastern kingdom as the chief among the kingdoms of the Franks, that the West-Frankish king Odo did homage to Arnulf before his lord's Imperial coronation, when he was still simply German king. But the rule that whoever was chosen King of Germany had a right, without further election, to the kingdom of Italy and to the Roman Empire, began only with the coronation of Otto the Great. Up to that time, the German king is simply one among the kings of the Franks, though it is plain that he held the highest place among them.

Connexion between the Eastern Kingdom and the Empire.

Imperial coronation of Arnulf. 896.

Homage of Odo to Arnulf. 888.

Final union of Germany with the Empire under Otto the Great. 963.

This Eastern or German kingdom, as it came out of the division of 887, had, from north to south, nearly the same extent as the Germany of later times. It stretched from the Alps to the Eider. Its southern boundaries were somewhat fluctuating. *Verona* and *Aquileia* are sometimes counted as a German march, and the boundary between Germany and Burgundy, crossing the modern Switzerland, often changed. To the North-east the kingdom hardly stretched beyond the Elbe, except in the small Saxon land between the Elbe and the Eider. The great extension of the German power over the northern Slavonic lands beyond the Elbe had hardly yet begun. Towards

Extent of the German kingdom.

CHAP. VI.

The Carinthian marks. The great duchies.

the southern Slaves, at the south-east corner of the kingdom, lay the mark of *Kärnthen* or *Carinthia.* But the main part of the kingdom consisted of the great duchies of *Saxony*, *Eastern Francia*, *Alemannia*, and *Bavaria.* Of these the two names of Saxony and Bavaria must be carefully marked as having widely different meanings from those which they bear on the modern map. Ancient Saxony lies, speaking roughly, between the Eider, the Elbe, and the Rhine, though it never actually touches the last-named river. To the south of Saxony lies the Eastern *Francia*, the centre and kernel of the German kingdom. The Main and the Neckar both join the Rhine within its borders. To the south of Francia lie *Alemannia* and *Bavaria.* Bavaria reaches much further to the east and south than the kingdom now so called, and not nearly so far to the north and west. It borders on Italy, and has Botzen for its frontier town. Alemannia is the land in which both the Rhine and the Danube take their source; it stretches on both sides of the *Bodensee* or Lake of Constanz, with the Rætian Alps as its southern boundary. For several ages to come, there is no distinction, national or even provincial, between the lands north and south of the Bodensee.

Saxony. Eastern or Teutonic *Francia*. Bavaria. Alemannia.

Lotharingia.

These lands make up the undoubted Eastern or German territory. To the west of this lies the borderland of *Lotharingia*, which has a history of its own. For the first century after the division of 887, the possession of Lotharingia fluctuated several times between the Eastern and the Western kingdom, and for a few years formed a kingdom by itself. After the change of dynasty in the Western kingdom, Lotharingia became

Kingdom of Lotharingia. 896–900. 987.

definitely and undoubtedly German in allegiance, though it always kept up something of a distinct being, and its language was partly German and partly Romance. Lotharingia took in the two duchies of the *Ripuarian Lotharingia* and *Lotharingia on the Mosel.* The former contains a large part of the modern Belgium and the neighbouring lands on the Rhine, including the royal city of Aachen. Lotharingia on the Mosel answers roughly to the later duchy of that name, though its extent to the East is considerably larger.

The Western Kingdom.

The part of the Frankish dominions to which the Frankish name has stuck most lastingly has been the Western kingdom or *Karolingia,* which gradually got the special name of *France.* This came about through the events of the ninth and tenth centuries. The Western kingdom, as it was formed under Charles the Bald and as it remained after the division of 887, nominally took in a great part of modern France, namely all west of the Rhone and Saône. It took in nothing to the east of those rivers, and Lotharingia, as we have seen, was a borderland which at last settled down as part of the Eastern kingdom. Thus the extent of the old *Karolingia* to the east was very much smaller than the extent of modern France. But, on the other hand, the Western kingdom took in lands at three points which are not part of modern France. These are the march or county of *Flanders* in the north, the greater part of which forms part of the modern kingdom of Belgium; the *Spanish March,* which is now part of Spain; and the *Norman Islands,* which are now held by the sovereign of England. And it is hardly needful to say that, even within these

Its extent.

CHAP. VI.

boundaries, the whole land was not in the hands of the King of the West-Franks. He had only a supremacy, which was apt to become nearly nominal, over the vassal princes who held the great divisions of the kingdom. South of the Loire the chief of these vassal states were the duchy of *Aquitaine*, a name which now means the land between the Loire and the Garonne—the duchy of *Gascony* between the Garonne and the Pyrenees—the county of *Toulouse* to the east of it—the marches of *Septimania* and *Barcelona*. North of the Loire were *Britanny*, where native Celtic princes still reigned under a very doubtful supremacy on the part of the Frankish kings—the march of *Flanders* in the north—and the duchy of *Burgundy*, the duchy which had Dijon for its capital, and which must be carefully distinguished from other duchies and kingdoms of the same name. And, greatest of all, there was the duchy of *France*, that is *Western* or *Latin France*, *Francia Occidentalis* or *Latina*. Its capital was Paris, and its princes were called *Duces Francorum*, a title in which the word *Francus* is just beginning to change from its older meaning of *Frank* to its later meaning of *French*. From this great duchy of France several great fiefs, as *Anjou* and *Champagne*, were gradually cut off, and the part of France between the Seine and the Epte was granted to the Scandinavian chief Rolf, which, under him and his successors, grew into the great duchy of *Normandy*. Its capital was Rouen, and this settlement of the Normans had the effect of cutting off France and its capital Paris from the sea.

The great fiefs.

The Duchy of France.

Normandy cut off from France. 912.

The modern French kingdom gradually came into being during the century after the deposition of

Fluctuations between the Duchy of the French at Paris and the Karlings at Laon. 888–987.

Charles the Fat. During this time the crown of the Western kingdom passed to and fro more than once between the Dukes of the French at Paris and the princes of the house of Charles the Great, whose only immediate dominion was the city and district of *Laon* near the Lotharingian border. Thus, for a hundred years, the royal city of the Western kingdom was sometimes Laon and sometimes Paris, and the King of the West-Franks was sometimes the same person as the Duke of the French and sometimes not. But after the election of Hugh Capet, the kingdom and the duchy were never again separated. The Kings of *Karolingia* or the Western kingdom, and the Dukes of the *Western Francia*, were now the same persons. *France* then—the Western or Latin *Francia*, as distinguished from the German *Francia* or *Franken*—properly meant only the King's immediate dominions. Though Normandy, Aquitaine, and the Duchy of Burgundy, all owed homage to the French king, no one would have spoken of them as parts of France. But, as the French kings, step by step, got possession of the dominions of their vassals and other neighbours, the name of *France* gradually spread, till it took in, as it does now, by far the greater part of Gaul. On the other hand, Flanders, Barcelona, and the Norman Islands, though once under the homage of the French kings, fell away from all connexion with the kingdom without having ever been brought under the immediate sovereignty of its kings. They have therefore never been reckoned as parts of France. Thus the name of France supplanted the name of *Karolingia* as the name of the Western kingdom. And, as it happened

Union of the French Duchy with the West-Frankish kingdom. 987.

New meaning of the word *France*.

Advance of the French kingdom.

CHAP. VI.

Title of *Rex Francorum*.

that the Western kings kept on the title of *Rex Francorum* after it had been dropped in the Eastern kingdom, the title gradually came to mean, not King of the *Franks*, but King of the *French*, King of the new Romance-speaking nation which grew up under them. Thus it was that the modern kingdom and nation of France arose through the crown of the Western kingdom passing to the Dukes of the Western *Francia*. Paris is not only the capital of the kingdom; it is the kernel round which the kingdom and nation grew.

Origin of the French nation.

Paris the kernel of France.

The Middle Kingdom or Burgundy.

Various meanings of the name *Burgundy*.

Of all geographical names, that which has changed its meaning the greatest number of times is the name of *Burgundy*. It is specially needful to explain its different meanings at this stage, when there are always two, and sometimes more, distinct states bearing the Burgundian name. Of the older Burgundian kingdom, the north-western part, forming the land best known as the *Duchy of Burgundy*, was, in the divisions of the ninth century, a fief of Karolingia or the Western kingdom. This is the Burgundy which has Dijon for its capital, and which was held by more than one dynasty of dukes as vassals of the Western kings, first at Laon and then at Paris. This Burgundy, which, as the name of France came to bear its modern sense, may be distinguished as the *French Duchy*, must be carefully distinguished from the *Royal* Burgundy, the *Middle Kingdom* of our own chronicler. This is a state which arose out of the divisions of the ninth century, and which, sometimes as a single kingdom, sometimes as two, took in all that part of the old Burgundian kingdom which did not form part of the French duchy.

The French Duchy.

The Kingdom of Burgundy or Arles.

It may be roughly defined as the land between the Rhone and Saône and the Alps, though its somewhat fluctuating boundaries sometimes stretched west of the Rhone, and its eastern frontier towards Germany changed more than once. It thus took in the original Roman province in Gaul, which may be now spoken of as *Provence*, with its great cities, foremost among them *Arelate* or *Arles*, which was the capital of the kingdom, and from which the land was sometimes called the *Kingdom of Arles*. It also took in Lyons, the primatial city of Gaul, Geneva, Besançon, and other important Roman towns. In short, from its position, it contained a greater number of the former seats of Roman power than any of the new kingdoms except Italy itself. When Burgundy formed two kingdoms, the Northern one, known among other names as *Regnum Jurense*, took in, speaking roughly, the lands north of Lyons, and the Southern, the kingdom of *Provence*, took in the lands between Lyons and the sea. These last are now wholly French. The Northern Burgundian kingdom is in modern geography divided between France and Switzerland.

Cities of the Burgundian kingdom

Kingdom of Northern Burgundy, 888–933.

Southern Burgundy.

The history of this Burgundian kingdom differs in one respect from that of any other of the states which arose out of the break-up of the Frankish Empire. It parted off from the Carolingian dominion before the division of 887. It formed no part of the reunited Empire of Charles the Fat. It may therefore be looked on as having parted off altogether from the immediately Frankish rule, though it often appears as more or less dependent on the kings of the Eastern Francia. But its time of separate being was short. After about a century and a half from its foundation, the Burgundian kingdom was united under the same

Burgundy separated from the Frankish kingdoms.

Union of the kingdom with Germany, 933–4.

CHAP. VI.

Later history of Burgundy: mostly annexed by France.

kings as Germany, and its later history consists of the way in which the greater part of the old Middle Kingdom has been swallowed up bit by bit by the modern kingdom of France. The only part which has escaped is that which now forms the western cantons of Switzerland. In truth the Swiss Confederation may be looked on as having, in some slight degree, inherited the position of the Burgundian kingdom as a middle state. Otherwise, while the Eastern and Western kingdoms of the Franks have grown into two of the greatest powers and nations in modern Europe, the Burgundian kingdom has been altogether wiped out. Not only its independence, but its very name, has passed from it. The name of Burgundy has for a long time past meant the French duchy only.

Partly represented by Switzerland.

The Kingdom of Italy.

Italy, unlike Burgundy, formed part of the reunited dominion of Charles the Fat; but it altogether passed away from Frankish rule at the division of 887. It must be remembered that, though Lombardy was conquered by Charles the Great, yet it was not merged in the Frankish dominions, but was held as a separate kingdom by the King of the Franks and Lombards. Till the reunion under Charles the Fat, Italy, as a separate kingdom, was ruled by kings of the Carolingian house, some of whom were crowned at Rome as Emperors. After the final division, it had separate kings of its own, being not uncommonly disputed between two rival kings. Some of these kings even obtained the Imperial crown. The Italian kingdom, it must be remembered, was far from taking in the whole Italian peninsula. Its southern boundary was much the same as the old boundaries of Latium and Picenum,

Carolingian Kings of Italy.

Italian Emperors.

Extent of the Italian kingdom.

Separate principalities of Benevento and Salerno.

reaching somewhat further to the south on the Hadriatic coast. To the south were the separate principalities of *Benevento* and *Salerno*, and the lands which still clave to the Eastern Emperors. The kingdom thus took in Lombardy, Liguria, *Friuli* in the widest sense, taking in *Trent* and *Istria*, though these latter lands are sometimes counted as a German march, while the Venetian islands and the narrow coast of their *lagoons* still kept up their connexion with the Eastern Empire. It took in also *Tuscany*, *Romagna* or the former Exarchate of Ravenna, *Spoleto*, and *Rome* itself. The Italian kingdom thus represented the old Lombard kingdom, together with the provinces which were formally transferred from the Eastern to the Western Empire by the election of Charles the Great. But it may be looked on as essentially a continuation of the Lombard kingdom. The rank of capital of the Italian kingdom, as distinguished from the Roman Empire, passed away from the old Lombard capital of *Pavia* to the ecclesiastical metropolis of *Milan*, and Milan became the crowning-place of the Kings of Italy.

The Kingdom of Italy represents the Lombard Kingdom.

Milan its capital.

Abeyance of the Empire.

For nearly eighty years after the division of 887, the Roman Empire of the West may be looked on as having fallen into a kind of abeyance. One German and several Italian kings were crowned Emperors; but they never obtained any general acknowledgement throughout the West. There could not be said to be any Western Empire with definite geographical boundaries. A change in this respect took place in the second half of the tenth century under the German king Otto the Great. While he was still only German king, Berengar King of Italy became his man, as Odo of

Restoration of the Western Empire by Otto.

952.

CHAP. VI.

962, 963.

Paris had become the man of Arnulf. Afterwards Otto himself obtained the Italian kingdom, and was crowned Emperor at Rome. The rule was now fully established that the German king who was crowned at Aachen had a right to be crowned King of Italy at Milan and to be crowned Emperor at Rome. A geographical Western Empire was thus again founded, consisting of the two kingdoms of Germany and Italy, to which Burgundy was afterwards added. These three kingdoms now formed the Empire, which thus consisted of the whole dominions of Charles the Great—allowing for a different eastern frontier—except the part which formed the Western kingdom, *Karolingia*, afterwards *France*. This union of three of the four kingdoms gave a more distinct and antagonistic character to the fourth which remained separate. Karolingia looked like a part of the great Frankish dominion lopped off from the main body. On the other hand, now that the German kings, the Kings of the East-Franks, were also Kings of Italy and Burgundy and Emperors of the Romans, they gradually dropped their Frankish style. But, as that style was kept by the Western kings, and still more as the name of their duchy of France gradually spread over so large a part of Gaul, the kingdom of France had a superficial look of representing the old Frankish kingdom. The newly-constituted Empire had thus a distinctly rival power on its western side. And we shall find that a great part of our story will consist of the way in which, on this side, the Imperial frontier went back, and the French frontier advanced. On the other side, the Eastern frontier of the Empire was capable of any amount of advance at the cost of its Slavonic neighbours.

The three Imperial kingdoms.

Relations between the Empire and France.

§ 2. *The Eastern Empire.*

CHAP. VI.

The Eastern Empire.

The various changes of the seventh and eighth centuries, the rise of the Saracens, the settlement of the Slaves, the transfer of the Western Empire to the Franks, seem really to have had the effect of strengthening the Eastern Empire which they so terribly cut short. It began for the first time to put on something of a national character. As the Western Empire was fast becoming German, so the Eastern Empire was fast becoming Greek. And a religious distinction was soon added to the distinction of language. As the schism between the Churches came on, the Greek-speaking lands attached themselves to the Eastern, and not to the Western, form of Christianity. The Eastern Empire, keeping on all its Roman titles and traditions, thus became nearly identical with what may be called the artificial Greek nation. It continues the work of hellenization which was begun by the old Greek colonies and which went on under the Macedonian kings. No power gives more work for the geographer; through the alternate periods of decay and revival which make up nearly the whole of Byzantine history, provinces were always being lost and always being won back again. And it supplies also a geographical study of another kind, in the new divisions into which the Empire was now mapped out, divisions which, for the most part, have very little reference to the divisions of earlier times.

It takes a Greek character.

Rivalry of the Eastern and Western or Greek and Latin Churches.

Fluctuations in the extent of the Empire.

The *Themes* or provinces of the Eastern Empire, as they stood in the tenth century, have had the privilege of being elaborately described by an Imperial geographer in the person of Constantine Porphyrogennêtos.[1]

The *Themes* as described by Constantine Porphyrogennêtos.

[1] See the special treatise on the Themes in the third volume of

CHAP. VI.

He speaks of the division as comparatively recent, and of some themes as having been formed almost in his own time. The themes would certainly seem to have been mapped out after the Empire had been cut short both to the north and to the east. The nomenclature of the new divisions is singular and diversified. Some ancient national names are kept, while the titles of others seem fantastic enough. Thus in Asia *Paphlagonia* and *Kappadokia* remain names of themes with some approach to their ancient boundaries; but the *Armeniac* theme is thrust far to the west of any of the earlier uses of the name, so that the Halys flows through it. Between it and the still independent Armenia lay the theme of *Chaldia*, with Trapezous, the future seat of Emperors, for its capital. Along the Saracen frontier lie the themes of *Kolôneia*, *Mesopotamia*—a shadowy survival indeed of the Mesopotamia of Trajan, of which it was not even a part—*Sebasteia*, *Lykandos*, *Kappadokia*, and *Seleukeia*, called from the Isaurian or Kilikian city of that name. Along the south coast the city of *Kibyra* has given—in mockery, says Constantine—its name to the theme of the *Kibyrraiôtians*, which reaches as far as Milêtos. The isle of *Samos* gives its name to a theme reaching from Milêtos to Adramyttion, while the theme of the *Ægæan Sea*, besides most of the islands, stretches on to the mainland of the ancient Aiolis. The rest of the Propontis is bordered by themes bearing the strange names of *Opsikion* and *Optimatôn*, names of Latin origin, in the former of

Asiatic Themes.

the Bonn edition. The Treatise which follows, 'de Administrando Imperio,' is also full of geographical matter. [Two earlier lists are given in the 'De Cerimoniis' (in the first volume of the Bonn edition), book ii. chap. 52 (pp. 713–4 and 727–8), and chap. 50. The system of Themes originated in the seventh century.]

which the word *obsequium* is to be traced. To the east of them the no less strangely named *Thema Boukellariôn* takes in the Euxine Hêrakleia. Inland and away from the frontier are the themes *Thrakêsion* and *Anatolikon*, while another Asiatic theme is formed by the island of *Cyprus*.

The European Themes.

The nomenclature of the European themes is more intelligible. Most of them bear ancient names, and the districts which bear them are at least survivals of the lands which bore them of old. After a good deal of shifting, owing to the loss and recovery of so many districts, the Empire under Constantine Porphyrogennêtos numbered twelve European themes. *Thrace* had shrunk up into the land just round Constantinople and Hadrianople, the latter now a frontier city against the Bulgarian. *Macedonia* had been pushed to the east, leaving the more strictly Macedonian coast-districts which the Empire still kept to form the themes of *Strymôn* and *Thessalonikê*. Going further south, the name of *Hellas* has revived, and that with a singular accuracy of application. Hellas is now the eastern side of continental Greece, taking in the land of Achilleus. The abiding name of Achaia has vanished for a while, and the peninsula which had been won back from the Slave again bears its name of *Peloponnêsos*. But *Lakedaimonia* now appears on the list of its chief cities instead of Sparta. This and other instances in which one Greek name has been supplanted by another are witnesses of the Slavonic occupation of Hellas and its recovery by a Greek-speaking power. Off the west coast the realm of Odysseus seems to revive in the theme of *Kephallênia*, which takes in also the mythic isle of Alkinoos. Such parts of Êpeiros and Western

Use of the name Hellas.

CHAP. VI.

The Hadriatic lands.

Greece as clave to the Empire form the theme of *Nikopolis*. To the north, on the Hadriatic shore, was the theme of *Dyrrhachion*, and beyond that again, the Dalmatian and Venetian cities still counted as outlying portions of the Empire. Beyond the Hadriatic, southern Italy forms the theme of *Lombardy* and *Calabria*—the latter name has now moved from the heel to the toe—interrupted by the principality of *Salerno*, while Naples, Gaeta, and Amalfi were outlying posts like Venice and Ragusa. *Sicily* was still reckoned as a theme; but it was now wholly lost to the Saracen. And far away in the Tauric peninsula, the last of the Hellenic commonwealths, the furthest outpost of Hellenic civilization, had sunk in the ninth century into the Byzantine theme of *Chersôn*.

Possessions of the Empire in Italy.

Chersôn.

Seeming Asiatic character of the Empire.

The first impression conveyed by this geographical description is that the Eastern Empire had now become a power rather Asiatic than European. It is only in Asia that any solid mass of territory is kept. Elsewhere there are only islands and fringes of coast. But they were almost continuous fringes of coast, fringes which contained some of the greatest cities of Christendom, and which gave their masters an undisputed supremacy by sea. If the Mediterranean was not a Byzantine lake, it was only the presence of the Saracen, the occasional visits of the Northman, which hindered it from being so. Then again, the whole history of the Empire, if it is a history of losses, is also a history of recoveries, and before long the Roman arms again became terrible by land. The picture of Constantine Porphyrogennêtos shows us the Empire at a moment when neither process was actually going on; but the times before and after his reign were times, first of loss

Nature of its European possessions.

Maritime supremacy of the Empire.

and then of recovery. The details of these changes will come at a later period of our inquiry; their general result was that, while, at the time of the division of the two Empires, the Imperial power in Eastern Europe was almost wholly cut down to the coasts and islands, early in the eleventh century the Eastern Rome was again the head of a solid continental dominion which made it undoubtedly the greatest among Christian powers, a dominion greater than it had been at any time since the Saracenic and Slavonic inroads began.

The Eastern Empire under Basil the Second.

§ 3. *Origin of the Spanish Kingdoms.*

The historical geography of two of the three great Southern peninsulas is thus bound up with that of the Empires of which they were severally the centres. The case is quite different with the third great peninsula, that of Spain. There the Roman dominion, even the province which had been recovered by Justinian, had quite passed away, and it was only a small part of the land which was ever reincorporated, even in the most shadowy way, with either Empire. Spain was now conquered by the Saracens, as it had before been conquered by the Romans, with this difference, that it had been among the longest and hardest of the Roman conquests, while no part of the Saracen dominion was won in a shorter time. But, if the Roman conquest was slow, it was in the end complete. The swifter Saracen conquest was never quite complete; it left a remnant by which the land was in the end to be won back. But the part of the land which withstood the Saracen was, as could hardly fail to be the case, the same part as that which held out for the longest time against the Roman. The mountainous regions of the North

Position of Spain.

The Saracen conquest. 710–713.

CHAP. VI.

Asturia, 732, united with Cantabria, 751.

were never wholly conquered. *Cantabria* and *Asturia*, which had been so slow in submitting to the Roman, which had never fully submitted to the Goth, now again became the seat of resistance under princes who claimed to represent the Gothic kings. These independent territories grew to the south, and other Christian states arose to the east. The story of their growth will come in a later chapter. But early in the eleventh century the whole north-western part of Spain, and a considerable fringe of territory in the north-east, had been formed into Christian states. Among these had been laid the foundations of the two famous kingdoms of Castile and Aragon. Portugal did not arise till a later stage.

Beginnings of Castile and Aragon.

History of Castile and Aragon.

Of these three, Castile was fated to play the same part that was played by Wessex in England and by France in Gaul, to become the leading power of the peninsula. Aragon, when her growth had brought her to the Mediterranean, was to fill for a long time a greater place in general European politics than any other Spanish power. The union of Castile and Aragon was to form that great Spanish monarchy which became the terror of Europe. Meanwhile Portugal, lying on the Ocean, had first of all to extend her borders at the cost of the common enemy, and afterwards to become a beginner of European enterprise in distant lands, a path in which Castile and other powers did but follow in her steps.

Portugal.

Break-up of the Spanish Caliphate.

Meanwhile the advance of the Christians was helped by the division of the Saracenic power. The Caliphates of the East and of the West fell to pieces, exactly as the Christian Empires did. The undivided Mahometan dominion in Spain was at the height of its power in the tenth century. Yet even then, amid many fluctuations, the Christian frontier was on the whole advancing in the north-west. In the north-east Christian progress was slower. Early in the eleventh century, the Caliphate of Cordova broke in pieces. Out of its fragments arose a crowd of small Mahometan kingdoms, and it was only by renewed invasions from Africa that the Mahometan power in Spain was kept up.

1028.

§ 4. *Origin of the Slavonic States.*

Slavonic and Turanian invasions.

We left the borders of both the Eastern and the Western Empire beset by neighbours of Slavonic race, who, in the case of the Eastern Empire, were largely mingled with other neighbours of Turanian race. Of these last, *Avars*, *Patzinaks*, *Khazars*, have passed away; they have left no trace on the modern map of Europe. With two of the Turanian settlements the case is different. The settlement of the *Bulgarians*, the foundation of a kingdom of slavonized Turanians south of the Danube, has been already mentioned. Another Turanian settlement to the north of the Bulgarians has been of yet greater importance in European history. In the last years of the ninth century the Finnish *Magyars* or *Hungarians*, the *Turks* of the Byzantine writers, began to count as a power in Europe. From their seats between the mouths of the Dnieper and the Danube, they pressed eastward into the lands which had been Dacia and Pannonia. The Bulgarian power was thus confined to the lands south of the Danube, and *Great Moravia*, a name which then took in the western part of modern Hungary, fell wholly under Magyar dominion.

Bulgarians.

Settlement of the Magyars or Hungarians, 895.

Great Moravia.

Peculiar character of the Magyar settlement.

This settlement is one which stands altogether by itself. The Magyars and the Ottoman Turks are the only Turanian settlers in Europe who have grown into

CHAP. VI.

permanent Turanian powers on European ground. The Bulgarians have been lost in the mass of their Slavonic neighbours and subjects, whose language they have adopted. Magyars and Ottomans still remain, speaking a Turanian tongue on Aryan soil. But it is only the Magyars that have grown into a really European state. After appearing as momentary ravagers in Germany, Italy, and even Gaul, the Magyars settled down into a Christian kingdom, which, among many fluctuations of supremacy and dependence, has remained a distinct kingdom to this day. The Christianity of Hungary however came from the Western Church and not from the Eastern. And this fact has had a good deal of bearing upon the history of those regions. But for this almost incidental connexion with the Old Rome, Hungary, though settled by a Turanian people, would most naturally have taken its place among the Slavonic states which fringed the dominion of the New Rome. As it has turned out, difference of religion has stepped in to heighten difference of blood, and Hungary has formed a kingdom quite apart, closely connected in its history with Servia and Bulgaria, but running a course which has been in many things unlike theirs.

The Kingdom of Hungary.

Effect of its religious connexion with Rome.

The Magyars separate the Northern and Southern Slaves.

The geographical results of the Magyar settlement were to place a barrier between the Northern and the Southern Slaves. This it did both directly and indirectly. The *Patzinaks* pressed into what had been the former Magyar territory; they appear in the pages of the Imperial geographer as a nation with whom the Empire always strove to maintain peace, as they formed a barrier against both Hungarians and *Russians*. This last name begins to be of importance in the ninth

The Russians.

century. A part of the Eastern branch of the Slavonic race, united under Scandinavian rulers and bearing a Scandinavian name, the Russians were cut off from the Eastern Slaves south of the Danube by the new Turanian settlements. The Magyars again parted the South-eastern Slaves from the North-western, while the Russians were still neighbours of the North-western Slaves. The geographical position of these three divisions of the Slavonic race has had an important effect on European history. The South-eastern Slaves in Servia, Croatia, Dalmatia, and the neighbouring lands, formed a debateable ground between the two Empires, the Magyar kingdom, and the Venetian republic, as soon as Venice grew into a distinct and conquering state. These lands have, down to our own time, played an important, but commonly a secondary, part in history. In later times their history has chiefly consisted in successive changes of masters. But the power of Servia, among many shiftings of its boundaries and relations, must be looked on as forming an element in Europe down to the Ottoman conquest. The history of the North-western Slaves mainly consists in different degrees of vassalage or incorporation with the Western Empire. But, besides several considerable duchies, there grew up among them the momentary dominion of Great Moravia and the more lasting kingdoms of *Bohemia* and *Poland*. Of these two, Poland established its complete independence of the Empire, and became for a while one of the chief powers of Europe. Russia meanwhile, forming a third division, appears, in the ninth and tenth centuries, first as a formidable enemy, then as a spiritual conquest, of the Empire and Church of Constantinople. Russia had then already assumed the

Effects of the geographical position of the Slaves.

History of the South-eastern Slaves.

The North-western Slaves.

Bohemia, Poland.

Russia.

CHAP. VI.

character which it has again put on in later times, that of the one great European power at once Slavonic in race and Eastern in faith. Russia is now fully established as an European power. The variations of its territorial extent must be traced in a distinct chapter.

§ 5. *Northern Europe.*

The Scandinavian settlements.

The European importance of the Scandinavian nations at this time chiefly arises from their settlements in various parts of Europe, and specially in Britain and Gaul. The three great Scandinavian kingdoms were already formed. Sweden was doing its work towards the east; the Norwegians, specially known as Northmen, colonized the extreme north of Britain, the Scandinavian earldoms of Caithness and Sutherland, together with the islands to the north and west of Britain, Orkney, Shetland, Faroe, the so-called Hebrides, and Man. They also colonized the eastern coast of Ireland, where they were known as *Ostmen.* And it was from Norway also that the settlers came by which the coast of *France* in the strictest sense, the French duchy, was cut off from the dominion of Paris to form the Duchy of *Normandy.* But the chief field for the energy of Denmark properly so called lay within the limits of that part of Britain which we may now begin to call *England.* It was during this period that the united English kingdom grew up, that the many English settlements in Britain coalesced into one English nation. And this work was in a singular way promoted by the very cause, namely the Danish invasions, which seemed best suited to hinder it.

England and Denmark. 789–1017.

Up to this time the great island had been in truth,

as it was often called, another world. It had but little influence on any of the lands which formed part of either of the continental Empires, and it was but little influenced by them. The English history of these times, a history which is specially connected with geography, consists of two great facts. The first is the union of all the English states in Britain into one English kingdom under the West-Saxon kings. The other is the establishment of a vague supremacy on the part of those kings over the whole island. The dominion established by Ecgberht was in no sense a kingdom of England. It consisted simply in a supremacy on the part of the West-Saxon king over all the princes of Britain, Teutonic and Celtic, save only the Picts, Scots, and Welsh of Strathclyde or Cumberland. The smaller kingdoms of Kent, Sussex, and Essex, formed appanages for West-Saxon *æthelings*; but the superiority over East-Anglia, Mercia, Northumberland, and the Welsh princes was purely external. The change of this power into an united English kingdom holding a supremacy over the whole island was largely helped by the Danish incursions and settlements. These incursions began in the last years of the eighth century; they became more frequent and more dangerous in the middle of the ninth; and in the latter part of that century they grew from mere incursions into actual settlements. This was the result of the great struggle in the days of the first Æthelred and his more famous brother Ælfred. By Ælfred's treaty with the Danish Guthrum, the West-Saxon king kept his own West-Saxon kingdom and all the other lands south of the Thames, together with western Mercia. The rest of Mercia, with East-Anglia and *Deira* or southern Northumberland, passed under

Formation of the Kingdom of England.

West-Saxon supremacy under Ecgberht. 825–830.

The Danish invasions. 789.

Division between Ælfred and Guthrum. 878.

Bernicia not Danish.

Danish rule. *Bernicia*, or northern Northumberland from the Tees to the Forth, still kept its Anglian princes, seemingly under Danish supremacy. Over the lands which thus became Danish the West-Saxon king kept a mere nominal and precarious supremacy. In Scotland and Strathclyde the succession of the Celtic princes was not disturbed; but in part at least of Strathclyde, in the more modern Cumberland, a large Scandinavian population, though probably Norwegian rather than Danish, must have settled.

Scandinavian settlements in Cumberland.

Increase of the immediate kingdom of Wessex.

By these changes the power of the West-Saxon king as an overlord was greatly cut short, while his immediate kingdom was enlarged. The dynasty which had come so near to the supremacy of the whole island seemed to be again shut up in its own kingdom and the lands immediately bordering on it. But, by overthrowing the other English kingdoms, the Danes had prepared the way for the second West-Saxon advance in the tenth century. The West Saxon king was now the only English king, and he further became the English and Christian champion against intruders who largely remained heathen. The work of the first half of the tenth century was to enlarge the Kingdom of Wessex into the Kingdom of England. Eadward the Elder, King, not merely of the West-Saxons but of the English, extended his immediate frontier, the frontier of the one English kingdom, to the Humber. Wales, Northumberland, English and Danish, and now, for the first time, Scotland and Strathclyde, all acknowledged the English supremacy. Under Æthelstan Northumberland was for the first time incorporated with the kingdom, and after several revolts and reconquests, it finally became an integral part of England, form-

Second West-Saxon advance. 910–954.

Wessex grows into England.

First submission of Scotland and Strathclyde. 923.

926.

CHAP. VI.

ing sometimes one, sometimes two, English earldoms. Meanwhile Cumberland was subdued by Eadmund, and was given as a fief to the kings of Scots, who commonly granted it as an appanage to their sons. Meanwhile, partly, it would seem, by conquest, partly by cession, the Scottish kings became possessed of the northern part of Northumberland, under the name of the earldom of Lothian. Thus, in the second half of the tenth century, a single kingdom of England had been formed, of which the Welsh principalities, as well as Scotland, Strathclyde, and Lothian, were vassal states.

Cumberland granted as a fief to Scotland. 945.

Lothian granted to Scotland.

Thus the English kingdom was formed, and with it the English Empire. For the English kings in the tenth and eleventh centuries, acknowledging no superiority in the Cæsar either of East or West and holding within their own island a position analogous to that of the Emperors on the mainland, did not scruple to assume the Imperial title, and to speak of themselves as Emperors of the other world of Britain. The kingdom and Empire thus formed were transferred by the wars of Swegen and Cnut from a West-Saxon to a Danish king. Under Cnut England was for a moment the chief seat, and Winchester the Imperial city, of a Northern Empire which might fairly claim a place alongside of the Old and the New Rome. England, Denmark, Norway, had a single king, whose supremacy further extended over the rest of Britain, over Sweden and a large part of the Baltic coast. That Empire split in pieces on Cnut's death. The Scandinavian kingdoms were again separated; England itself was divided for a moment. The kingdom, again reunited, first passed back to the West-Saxon house, and then, by a second conquest, to the Norman. After this

The English Empire.

Use of the Imperial titles.

Northern Empire of Cnut. 1016–1035.

The Norman Conquest. 1066–70.

CHAP. VI.

England finally united by William.

last revolution a division of the kingdom was never more heard of. William the Conqueror put the finishing stroke to the work of Ecgberht, and made England for ever one. And, by uniting England under the same ruler as Normandy, and by thus leading her into the general current of continental affairs, he gave her an European position such as she had never held under her native kings.

Summary.

Thus gradually, out of the state of things that followed the final division of the Empire by the election of Charles the Great, the chief nations of Europe were formed. The Western Empire, after many shiftings, took a definite shape. The Imperial dignity and the two royal crowns of Italy and Burgundy were now attached to the German kingdom. The Empire, in short, though keeping its Roman titles and associations, and with them its influence over the minds of men, practically became a German power. Its history from this time mainly consists in the steps by which the German Emperors of Rome lost their hold on their Italian and Burgundian kingdoms, and of the steps by which the German dominion was extended over the Slaves to the East. To the West the Western Kingdom has altogether detached itself from the Empire; the union of its crown with the Duchy of France has created the French kingdom and nation, with its centre at Paris, and with a supremacy, as yet little more than nominal, over a large part of Gaul. As the Western Empire becomes German, the Eastern Empire becomes Greek; in the early years of the eleventh century it again forms a powerful and compact state, ruling from Naples to Antioch. Of the states to the north of it, Bulgaria,

The Western Empire and the Imperial Kingdoms.

France

The Eastern Empire.

Servia, Hungary, Russia, have taken their position among the Christian powers of Europe, though Servia, for a short time, and Bulgaria, for a much longer time, were actually reincorporated with the Empire. The powers of Poland and Bohemia have arisen on the borders of the Western Empire. Prussia, Lithuania, and the Finnish lands to the immediate north of them remain heathen. In Spain, the Christians have won back a large part of the peninsula. Castile and Navarre are already kingdoms; Aragon, though not yet a kingdom, has begun her history. In Northern Europe, the three Scandinavian nations are clearly distinguished and firmly established. Within the isle of Britain the kingdoms of England and Scotland were formed in the course of the ninth and tenth centuries, and the union of England and Normandy in the eleventh opened the way to altogether new relations between the continent and the great island. In short, at the time of the separation of the Empires, we can hardly say that any of the modern, or even mediæval, powers of Europe existed in anything like their later shape. By the end of the eleventh century all are in being, except Portugal, the Sicilian kingdoms, and the states which have come into being in much more recent times.

The Slavonic states.

Spain.

The Scandinavian kingdoms.

England and Normandy.

Having then reached a stage when most of the European powers have come into being, and when the two Roman Empires are fast becoming a German and a Greek power alongside of other powers, it will be well to change the form of our present inquiry. Thus far we have treated the historical geography of Europe as a whole, gathering round two centres at the Old and the New Rome. It will henceforth be more

CHAP. VI.

convenient to take the history of the great divisions of Europe separately, and to trace out in distinct chapters the later changes in the boundaries of each state down to our own time. But before we enter on the history of these geographical and political divisions, it will be well to take a view of the ecclesiastical divisions of Western Christendom, which are of great importance, and which are constantly referred to in the times with which we are now concerned.

Ecclesiastical geography.

CHAPTER VII.

THE ECCLESIASTICAL GEOGRAPHY OF WESTERN EUROPE.

CHAP. VII.

Character of ecclesiastical geography.

Permanence of the ecclesiastical divisions.

They represent older civil divisions.

THE ecclesiastical geography of Western Europe was by this time formed. The great ecclesiastical divisions were now almost everywhere mapped out, and from hence they are more permanent than the political divisions. The ecclesiastical geography in truth constantly preserves an earlier political geography. The ecclesiastical divisions were always mapped out according to the political divisions of the time when they were established, and they often remained unaltered while the political divisions went through many revolutions.

Illustrations from England and France.

Thus in France the dioceses represented the jurisdictions of the Roman cities; in England they represented the ancient English kingdoms and principalities. In both cases they outlived by many ages the political divisions which they represented. While the political map was altered over and over again, the ecclesiastical map lasted down to quite modern times, with hardly any change beyond the occasional division of a large diocese or the occasional union of two small dioceses. Thus the greater permanence of the ecclesiastical map often makes it useful as a standard for reference in describing political changes.

Lyons and Rheims.

To take an instance, the city of Lyons has been at different times under Burgundian and under Frankish

CHAP VII.

kings; it has been a free city of the Empire and a city of the modern kingdom of France. But, among all these changes, the Archbishop of Lyons has always remained Primate of all the Gauls, while the Archbishop of Rheims has held a wholly different position alongside of him as first prelate and first peer of the modern kingdom of France. Paris meanwhile, the political capital of the modern kingdom, remained till the seventeenth century the seat of a simple bishopric, a suffragan church of the province of *Sens*.

Patriarchates, Provinces, Dioceses.

In this way the ecclesiastical divisions will be found almost everywhere to keep up the remembrance of an earlier political state of things. As the Empire became Christian, it was mapped out into *Patriarchates* as well as into Prefectures. Under these were the metropolitan and episcopal districts, which in after-times borrowed, though in a reverse order of dignity, the civil titles of *provinces* and *dioceses*. As the Church carried her spiritual conquests beyond the bounds of the Empire, new ecclesiastical districts were of course formed in the newly converted countries. As a rule, every kingdom had at least one archbishopric; the smaller principalities, provinces, or other divisions, became the dioceses of bishops. But the different social conditions of southern and northern Europe caused a marked difference in the ecclesiastical arrangements of the two regions. In the South the bishop was bishop of a city; in the North he was bishop of a tribe or a district. Within the Empire each city had its bishop. Thus in Italy and Southern Gaul, where the cities were thickest on the ground, the bishops were most numerous and their dioceses were smallest. In Northern Gaul the cities are fewer and the dioceses larger, while outside the

Divisions within and without the Empire.

Bishops of cities and of tribes.

Empire, the dioceses which represented a tribe or principality were larger again. Also again, within the Empire the bishop, as bishop of a city, always took his title from the city; outside the Empire, especially in the British islands both Celtic and Teutonic, the bishop of a tribe or principality often bore a tribal or territorial title. Within the Empire the territorial titles were known only in the case of metropolitans. Prelates of that rank, besides their local title as archbishops of this or that city, often took a territorial title from the kingdom or principality within which they held metropolitan rank. This practice is found both within and without the Empire. Such titles as Primate of all the Gauls, Primate of all England, Primate of Normandy, Primate of Munster, borne by the archbishops of Lyons, Canterbury, Rouen, and Cashel, are familiar instances.

Territorial titles of metropolitans.

§ 1. *The Great Patriarchates.*

The highest ecclesiastical divisions, the Patriarchates, though they did not exactly answer to the Prefectures, were clearly suggested by them. And whenever the boundaries of the Patriarchates departed from the boundaries of the Prefectures, they came nearer to the great divisions of race and language. For our purpose, it is enough to take the Patriarchates, as they grew up, after the establishment of Christianity, in the course of the fourth and fifth centuries. The four older ones were seated at the *Old* and the *New Rome*, and at the two great Eastern cities of *Antioch* and *Alexandria*. Out of the patriarchate of Antioch the small patriarchate of *Jerusalem* was afterwards taken. This last seems a piece of sentimental geography; the other divisions were

The Patriarchates suggested by the Prefectures.

CHAP. VII.

Rome.

eminently practical. Whether we look on the original jurisdiction of the Bishop of the Old *Rome* as taking in the whole *prefecture* of Italy or only the *diocese* of Italy, it is certain that it was gradually extended over the two prefectures of Italy and Gaul. That is, it took in the Latin part of the Empire, and it thence spread over the Teutonic converts in the West, as well as over Hungary and the Western Slaves. The Patriarchate of *Constantinople* or New Rome took in the Prefecture of Illyricum, and three dioceses in the Prefecture of the East, those of Thrace, Asia, and Pontus. This territory pretty well answers to the extent of the Greek language and influence. But the two dioceses of the Illyrian prefecture, Dacia and Macedonia, were, possibly through some confusion arising out of the two meanings of the word *Illyricum*, claimed by the Popes of Old Rome. But, when the Empires and Churches parted asunder, Macedonia and Greece were not likely to cleave to the Western division. But the claims of the Popes over Dacia, in the form of the Bulgarian kingdom, led to many difficulties in later times. In course of time the Byzantine patriarchate became nearly coextensive with the Byzantine Empire, and it became the centre of conversion for the Slaves of the East, just as the patriarchate of Old Rome was for the Teutons of the West. The patriarchate of *Antioch*, before its dismemberment in favour of the tiny patriarchate of *Jerusalem*, took in the whole diocese of the East, and the churches beyond the limits of the Empire in that direction. The patriarchate of *Alexandria* answered to the diocese of Egypt, with the churches beyond the Empire on that side, specially the *Abyssinian* church, which has kept its nationality

Extended beyond the Empire.

Constantinople.

Its relation to the Eastern Empire and to the Slaves.

Antioch.

Jerusalem.

Alexandria.

to our own time. That these Eastern patriarchates have been for ages disputed by claimants belonging to different sects of Christianity is a fact which concerns both theology and history, but does not concern geography. Whether the see was in Orthodox or heretical —that is commonly innational—hands, the see and its diocese, the geographical extent on the map, remained the same.

Later nominal patriarchates.

These then are the five great patriarchates which formed the most ancient geographical divisions of the Church. In later times the name patriarchate has been more loosely applied. As the Roman bishop grew into something more than the Patriarch of the West, the title of Patriarch was given to several metropolitans, sometimes, as far as one can see, without any particular reason. The Metropolitans of *Aquileia* assumed the title during a time of separation from the Roman see in the sixth century. The distractions caused by this schism led in the end to the strange result of two almost adjoining towns, Aquileia and *Grado*, each having prelates bearing the patriarchal title. The patriarchate of Grado was in the fifteenth century removed to *Venice*. Almost more anomalous was the patriarchate of *Lisbon*, created in the eighteenth century, while the older, though still modern, archbishopric went on beside it. But nominal patriarchates of this kind must be carefully distinguished from the five great churches to which the name was anciently attached. In the East the name was never extended beyond its four original holders, till a new patriarchate of *Moscow* arose in Russia, to mark the greatest spiritual conquest of the Orthodox Church. Of the four original Eastern patriarchates it is only that of

Aquileia, Grado, Venice.

Lisbon, 1716.

Patriarchate of Moscow. 1589–170.

Constantinople which plays much part in later history. The seats of the other three fell into the hands of the Saracens in the very beginning of their conquests.

§ 2. *The Ecclesiastical Divisions of Italy.*

Great numbers of the Italian bishoprics.

In no part of Christendom do the bishoprics lie so thick upon the ground as in Italy, and especially in the southern part. But from that very fact it follows that the ecclesiastical divisions of Italy are of less historical importance than those of most other Western countries.

Small size of the provinces.

In southern Italy above all, the bishoprics were so numerous, and the dioceses therefore so small, that the archiepiscopal provinces were hardly so large as the episcopal dioceses in more northern lands. So it is in the islands; Sicily contained four provinces and Sardinia three.

Effect of the commonwealths on the position of the prelates.

The peculiar characteristics of Italian history also hindered ecclesiastical geography from being of the same importance as elsewhere. Where every city became an independent commonwealth, the bishops, and even the metropolitans, sank to a lower rank than they held in the lands where each prelate was a great feudal lord.

Relation to the Roman see.

It follows then that there are only a few of the archbishoprics and bishoprics of Italy which at all stand out in general history. The growth of the Roman see also more distinctly overshadowed the Italian bishops than it did those of other lands.

Rivals of Rome.

The bishoprics which have most historical importance are those which at one time or another stood out in rivalry or opposition to Rome.

Milan.

Such was the great see of *Milan*, whose province took in a crowd of Lombard bishoprics; such was the

Aquileia.

patriarchal see of *Aquileia*, whose metropolitan jurisdiction took in Como at one end and the Istrian Pola at the other. The patriarchs of Aquileia, standing as they did on the march of the Italian, Teutonic, and Slavonic lands, grew, unlike most of the Italian prelates, into powerful temporal princes. *Ravenna* was the head of a smaller province than either Milan or Aquileia; but Ravenna too stands out as one of the churches which kept up for a while an independent position in the face of the growing power of Rome. Milan and Ravenna, in short, never lost the memory of their Imperial days; and Aquileia took advantage, first of a theological difference, and secondly of its temporal position as the great border see.

Ravenna.

In the rest of Italy the case is different. Rome herself was the immediate head of a large province stretching from sea to sea. Within this the *suburbicarian* sees, those close around Rome, stood in a special and closer relation to the patriarchal see itself. Their holders formed the order of *Cardinal Bishops*. The famous cities of *Genoa*, *Bologna*, *Pisa*, *Florence*, and *Siena*, were also metropolitan sees, though their ecclesiastical dignity is quite overshadowed by their civic greatness. *Lucca* has been added to the same list in modern times. The provinces of Pisa and Genoa are notable as having been extended into the island of Corsica after its recovery from the Saracens. The history and extent of the Italian dioceses is, with these few exceptions, a matter almost wholly of local ecclesiastical concern. In the south the endless archiepiscopal sees preserve the names of some famous cities, as *Capua*—the later Capua on the site of Casilinum—*Taranto*, *Bari*, *Otranto*, and others. But some even of the metropolitan churches are fixed in places of quite secondary importance, and the simple bishoprics are endless.

The immediate Roman Province.

Metropolitan sees of central Italy.

Pisa and Genoa.

The southern provinces.

In Sicily.

CHAP. VII.

§ 3. *The Ecclesiastical Divisions of Gaul and Germany.*

By taking a single view of the ecclesiastical arrangements of the whole of the Western Empire on this side of the Alps and the Pyrenees, some instructive lessons may be learned. Such a way of looking at the map will bring out more strongly the differences between bishoprics of earlier and later foundation. And, if we take the name of Gaul in the old geographical sense, taking in the German lands west of the Rhine which formed part of the older Empire, we shall find that several ecclesiastical provinces may be called either Gaulish or German. With the boundaries of the French kingdom we have no concern, except so far as the boundary between the Eastern and Western kingdoms of the Franks did to some extent follow ecclesiastical lines. Modern annexations of course have had no regard to them.

Gaulish and German dioceses.

Province of South Gaul.

On first crossing the Alps from Italy, we find the ecclesiastical phænomena of Italy continued in the lands nearest to it. The two provinces of *Tarantaise* (answering to the civil division of *Alpes Penninæ*) and *Embrun* (*Alpes Maritimæ*), which take in the mountain region between Italy and Gaul, are of small size, though of course in the actual mountain lands the bishoprics are less thick on the ground. The Tarantasian province contained only three suffragan sees, *Sitten*, *Aosta*, and *Saint John of Maurienne*, three bishoprics which now belong to three distinct political powers. But in the southern part of the province of Embrun, which reaches to the sea, the bishops' sees are thick on the ground, just as they are in Italy. So they are in the small provinces

Tarantaise.

Embrun.

of *Aix* (*Narbonensis Secunda*) and *Arles*. But, as soon as we get out of Provence into those parts of Gaul which were less thoroughly romanized, and where cities, and consequently bishoprics, lay less close together, the phænomena of the ecclesiastical map begin to change. The Provençal provinces of Aix and Arles are bounded to the north and west by those of *Vienne* (which with Arles answers nearly to the civil *Viennensis*) and *Narbonne* (answering nearly to *Narbonensis Prima*). These provinces are of much greater size, and the suffragan sees are much further apart. To the west lies *Auch*, answering to the oldest Aquitaine or *Novempopulana*, and to the north of these, in the remainder of Gaul, the original provinces are of still greater size. Most of them answer very nearly to the older civil divisions. *Aquitania Prima* becomes the province of *Bourges*, *Aquitania Secunda* that of *Bourdeaux*. *Lugdunensis Prima*, *Secunda*, *Tertia*, and *Quarta*, answer to *Lyons*, *Rouen*, *Tours*, and *Sens*. Of these Lyons, as having been the temporal capital, became the seat of the Primate of all the Gauls. The province of Rouen too answers very nearly to the duchy of which that metropolis became the capital, and from which its archbishop took his metropolitan title.

Aix and Arles.

Vienne.

Narbonne.

Auch.

Bourges, Bourdeaux, Lyons, Rouen, Tours, and Sens.

These are the oldest ecclesiastical arrangements, closely following the civil divisions of the Empire. These divisions lived through the Teutonic conquests; and, though here and there a see was translated from one city to another, they were not seriously interfered with till the fourteenth century. Pope John the Twenty-second raised the see of *Toulouse* in the province of Narbonne and that of *Alby* in the province of Bourges to metropolitan rank, thus forming two new provinces. He also

Foundation of the provinces of Toulouse and Alby, 1322.

CHAP. VII.

founded new bishoprics in several towns in these two new provinces and in that of Narbonne. In the next century Sixtus the Fourth made the church of *Avignon* metropolitan. These changes help to give this whole district more of the special character of Italy and Provence than originally belonged to it. Lastly, in the seventeenth century the province of *Sens* was also divided, and the church of *Paris* became metropolitan. Some of these changes show how closely the ecclesiastical divisions followed the oldest civil divisions, and how slowly they were affected by changes in the civil divisions. When Gaul was first mapped out, Tolosa was of less account than Narbo; the Parisii and their city were of less account than the great nation of the *Senones*. Tolosa became the royal city of the Goth; but it did not rise to the highest ecclesiastical rank till ages after the Gothic kingdom had passed away. Paris, after having been several times a momentary seat of dominion, became the birthplace of the modern French kingdom. But it had been the continuous seat of kings for more than six hundred years before it became the seat of an archbishop.

Avignon, 1475.

Paris, 1622.

As we draw nearer to German ground, the ecclesiastical boundaries are found to have been somewhat more strongly affected by political changes. The ecclesiastical province of *Besançon* answers to *Maxima Sequanorum*; but it is not quite of the same extent; the boundary of the German and Burgundian kingdoms passed through the Roman province: its eastern part is therefore found in a German diocese. The province of *Rheims* answers nearly, but not quite, to *Belgica Secunda*: for the ecclesiastical province took in some terri-

Besançon.

Rheims.

tory to the east of the Scheld. Here again the boundary of the Eastern and Western kingdoms passed through the province. The metropolitan city lay within the region which became the kingdom of France, and it became the ecclesiastical head of the kingdom. Yet one of its suffragan sees, that of *Cambray*, was a city of the Empire. The province of *Trier* took in no part of the Western kingdom; but, besides the old province of *Belgica Prima*, it stretched away over the German lands even beyond the Rhine. When the old Gaulish bishopric of *Colonia Agrippina* became metropolitan under Charles the Great, its province took in nearly all the old Gaulish province of *Germania Secunda*; but it too came to stretch beyond the Rhine and beyond the Weser. These two metropolitan sees, Trier and Köln, were old Gaulish bishoprics of the frontier land. The see of *Mainz* has no certain historical being before Boniface in the eighth century. It too was founded on what was geographically Gaulish soil; but the greater part of its vast extent was strictly German. Three only of its suffragans, *Worms*, *Speyer*, and *Argentoratum* or *Strassburg*, were even geographically Gaulish. No province has had more fluctuating boundaries; the elevation of Köln to metropolitan rank cut it short to the west, while it grew indefinitely to the north, south, and east, as its boundaries were enlarged by conversion and conquest. To the east it was cut short in the fourteenth century, when the kingdom of Bohemia and its dependencies were formed into the ecclesiastical province of *Prag*. The famous bishopric of *Bamberg*, locally in the province of Mainz, was from the beginning immediately dependent on the see of Rome.

Trier, 785.

Köln, 785.

Mainz, 747.

Prag, 1344.

Bamberg (Babenberg), 1007.

CHAP. VII.

The three ecclesiastical Electors and Arch-chancellors.

These three great archbishoprics of the frontier land, all of whose sees were on the Gaulish side of the Rhine, remained distinguished by their temporal rank during the whole life of the German kingdom. All the German prelates became princes; but only these three were Electors. These ecclesiastical electors were also the Arch-chancellors of the three Imperial kingdoms, Mainz of Germany, Köln of Italy, Trier of Gaul. But, as the Frankish or German kingdom spread to the north-east, new ecclesiastical provinces were formed. The bishopric of *Salzburg* became metropolitan under Charles the Great, with a province stretching away to the east towards his conquests from the Avars. The bishopric of *Bremen*, another foundation of Charles the Great, was transferred under his son to *Hamburg*, as a metropolitan see which was designed to be a missionary centre for the Scandinavian nations. After some fluctuations, the see was finally settled at Bremen, as the metropolis of a province, which had now become in no way Scandinavian, but partly Old-Saxon, partly Wendish. Lastly, Otto the Great founded the metropolitan see of *Magdeburg* on the Slavonic march. Thus the German kingdom formed six ecclesiastical provinces, all of vast extent as compared with those of Southern Europe, and with their suffragan sees few and far apart. The difference is here clearly marked between the earlier sees which arose from the very beginning in the Roman cities, and the sees of later foundation which were gradually founded, as new lands were brought under the dominion of the Empire and the Church. Still the old tradition went on so far that each bishop had his see in a city, and took his name from that city. Though the German dioceses were of

Salzburg, 798.

Bremen or Hamburg, 788.

1223.

Magdeburg, 968.

large extent, yet none of the German bishoprics were in strictness territorial.

As regards more modern changes, the number of dioceses in France was greatly lessened by the concordat under the first Buonaparte. But the main ecclesiastical landmarks were to a great extent respected. Thus the Archbishop of Rouen keeps the old extent of his province and his title of *Primate of Normandy*, but, of the seven Norman dioceses, *Lisieux* has been joined to *Bayeux* and *Avranches* to *Coutances*, while the boundaries of *Rouen* and *Evreux* have been changed to adapt them to the modern departments. So, more lately, the great diocese of *Le Mans* has been divided into the two dioceses of Le Mans and *Laval*, answering to the modern departments of Sarthe and Mayenne. These are types of the kind of changes which have been made in other parts. The Archbishop of Lyons meanwhile keeps his title of Primate of all the Gauls, but both he and the Archbishop of Rheims now yield precedence to the modern metropolitan of Paris.

Modern ecclesiastical divisions of Germany and France.

In no part of Christendom have the ecclesiastical divisions been more completely upset in modern times than they have been in Germany. The country has been mapped out afresh to suit the boundaries of patched-up modern kingdoms. Mainz and Trier are no longer metropolitan sees, while the modern map shows such novelties as an Archbishop of *München* and an Archbishop of *Freiburg*. Long before, under Philip the Second of Spain, those parts of the German kingdom which had become practically detached under the Dukes of Burgundy underwent a complete change in their ecclesiastical divisions. *Cambray* and *Mechlin* in the province of Rheims, and *Utrecht* in the province

Changes of Philip the Second in the Netherlands.

Cambray, Mechlin, Utrecht.

CHAP. VII.

of Köln, became metropolitan sees. Later political changes have made these three cities members of three distinct political powers.

§ 4. *The Ecclesiastical Divisions of Spain.*

Peculiarities of Spanish ecclesiastical geography.

The ecclesiastical history of the Spanish peninsula presents phænomena of a different kind from those of Italy, Gaul, or Germany. In Italy and Gaul the ecclesiastical divisions go on uninterruptedly from the earliest days of Christianity. Western Germany must count for these purposes as part of Gaul. In eastern Germany the ecclesiastical divisions were formed in later times, as Christianity was spread over the country.

Old divisions lost, and mapped out afresh after the recovery from the Saracens.

In Spain the country must have been mapped out for ecclesiastical purposes quite as early as Gaul. But the Mahometan conquest of the greater part of the country, followed by the Christian reconquest, caused the old ecclesiastical lines to be wiped out, and new divisions had to be traced out afresh as the land was gradually won back.

Ecclesiastical divisions under the West-Goths.

The ecclesiastical divisions of Spain in the time of the Gothic kingdom simply reproduce the civil divisions of the period, as those civil divisions are only a slight modification of the Roman provinces. *Lusitania* and *Bœtica* survived, with a slight change of frontier, both as civil and as ecclesiastical divisions. *Tarraconensis* was for both purposes divided into three, *Tarraconensis*, *Carthagenensis*, and *Gallæcia*. As the land was won back, and as new ecclesiastical provinces were formed, the number was greatly increased, and some of them found their way to new sites. Thus the Tarraconensian

Tarragona, Zaragoza, Valencia.

province was again divided into three, those of *Tarragona*, *Zaragoza*, and *Valencia*, answering nearly to the kingdom of Aragon. New Carthage lost its metropolitan rank in favour of the great metropolis of *Toledo*, which numbered *Cordova* and *Valladolid* among its suffragans. Leaving out some anomalous districts, the rest of the peninsula formed the provinces of St. James of *Compostella*, *Burgos*, *Seville*, *Granada*, with *Braga*, *Evora*, and the later metropolis of *Lisbon*, the last three answering to the kingdom of Portugal. And it must be remembered that the Pyrenees did not form an eternal boundary in ecclesiastical, any more than in civil, geography. As the kingdom of Navarre stretched on both sides of the mountains, so did the diocese of *Pampeluna*; and to the west of it the Gaulish diocese of *Bayonne* took in ground which is now Spanish. All these are survivals of a time when, to use the phrase of a later day, there were no Pyrenees, or when at least the same rulers, first Gothic and then Saracen, reigned on both sides of them.

Toledo.

Compostella, Burgos, Seville, and Granada. Braga, Evora, Lisbon.

Dioceses of Pampeluna and Bayonne.

§ 5. *The Ecclesiastical Divisions of the British Islands.*

The historical phænomena of the British islands have points in common with more than one of the continental countries. In a very rough and general view of things, Britain has some analogies with Spain. It is not altogether without reason that in some legendary stories the names of Saxons and Saracens get confounded. In both cases a land which had been Christian was overrun by conquerors of another creed; in both a Christian people held their ground in a part of the country; in both the whole land was won back to Christianity, though by different and even opposite processes in the two cases. But there is no reason to believe that the Celtic churches in Britain and Ireland had anything like the same complete ecclesiastical organization as the Spanish

The British islands.

The Celtic episcopate.

CHAP. VII.

churches under the Goths. The Celtic episcopate was of an irregular and anomalous kind, and, in its most intelligible shape, it was, as was natural under the circumstances of the country, not a city episcopate, hardly a territorial episcopate, but one strictly tribal. This is nearly the only fact in the history of the early Celtic churches which is of any importance for our purpose. It might be too much to say that traces of this peculiarity were handed on from the Celtic to the English Church. The little likeness that there is between them is rather due to the fact that in Northern Europe generally, whether Celtic or Teutonic, a strictly city episcopate like that of Italy and Gaul was something which in the nature of things could not be.

Tribal episcopacy.

In truth the antiquities of the Celtic churches may fairly be left to be matter of local or of special ecclesiastical inquiry. Their effect on history is slight; their effect on historical geography is still slighter. For our purpose the ecclesiastical geography of Britain may be looked on as beginning with the mission of Augustine. The English Church was formed, and the Welsh, Scottish, and Irish Churches were reconstructed, partly under its authority, altogether after its model. In the original scheme of Gregory the Great, Britain was to be divided into two ecclesiastical provinces nearly equal in extent, the two metropolitan chairs being placed in the two greatest Roman cities of the island, London and York. The Celtic churches were to be brought under the same ecclesiastical obedience as the heathen English. As Wales was to form part of the lot of the southern metropolitan, so Scotland was to form part of the lot of the northern. This scheme was

Scheme of Gregory the Great.

Two equal provinces in Britain.

never fully carried out. The circumstances of the conversion caused the southern metropolis to be fixed at Canterbury instead of London, and the contemplated geographical partition of all Britain proved a failure. Wales was indeed brought into full submission to Canterbury; but Scotland was never brought into the same full submission to York. The allegiance of the Scottish sees to their Northumbrian metropolis was at all times very precarious, and it was in the end formally thrown off altogether. Of this came the singular disproportion in the territorial extent of the two English ecclesiastical provinces. Canterbury, since the English Church was thoroughly organized, has had a number of suffragans which would be unusual anywhere on the continent, while York has always had comparatively few, and for a considerable time had practically one only.

Relation of the Scottish Bishops to York.

Suffragan sees of Canterbury and York.

The actual provinces and dioceses of England were gradually formed, as the various English kingdoms embraced Christianity. As a rule, each kingdom or independent principality became a diocese. And, except in the case of a few sees fixed in cities which kept on something of old Roman memories, the bishops were more commonly called from the people who formed their flock, than from the cities which in some cases contained their chairs. For in many cases the *bishop-settle*, as our forefathers called it, was not placed in a city at all, but in some rural or even solitary spot. It was not till the time of the Norman Conquest that a movement began which systematically placed the ecclesiastical sees in the chief towns; from that time the civic title altogether displaces the territorial.

Foundation of the existing dioceses.

Territorial bishoprics.

As Kent was the first part of Teutonic Britain to accept Christianity, the metropolitan see of the south

CHAP. VII.

Canterbury.

was fixed at the East-Kentish capital of *Canterbury*. It was thus fixed in a city which has at no time held that temporal preeminence which has in different ages belonged to York, Winchester, and London. After

Rochester. London.

Canterbury the earliest formed sees were *Rochester* for the under-kingdom of West-Kent, and *London* for the East-Saxons. The independent conversion of the West-Saxons led to the foundation of the great diocese whose

Dorchester or Winchester. Sherborne, Wells, Ramsbury. Elmham.

see was first at *Dorchester* on the Thames and then at *Winchester*, and from which the sees of *Sherborne*, *Wells*, and *Ramsbury* were gradually parted off. The East-Angles formed a diocese with its see at *Elmham*; the Middle-Angles settled down, after some shiftings, into the vast diocese stretching from the Thames to the Humber, with its see, like that of the older West-Saxon

Dorchester or Lincoln. Worcester. Hereford. Lichfield.

diocese, at *Dorchester*. The West-Mercian lands formed the dioceses of the Hwiccas at *Worcester*, of the Magesætas at *Hereford*, and the great diocese of *Lichfield*, stretching northward to the Ribble. The South-Saxons, whose bishopric kept its tribal name down to the Norman Conquest, had their see at *Selsey*. Devonshire and Cornwall formed two dioceses, with their sees at *Crediton* and *Bodmin*. Considerable changes were made in the times immediately before and immediately after the Norman Conquest. The bishoprics of Cornwall and

Exeter, 1050.

Devonshire were united in the single diocese of *Exeter*. Those of Sherborne and Ramsbury formed the new

Salisbury, 1078.

diocese of *Salisbury*. By an opposite process, the huge diocese of Lincoln was dismembered by the foundation

Ely, 1109.

of an episcopal see at *Ely*. The sees of some other dioceses were also changed, commonly according to the continental practice of placing the bishop's chair in the chief city of the diocese. Then the see of the bishopric of Somerset was removed to *Bath*, that of Dorchester to *Lincoln*, that of Lichfield, first to *Chester* and then to *Coventry*, that of East-Angles first to *Thetford* and then to *Norwich*. The Conquest too brought about the more complete submission of the four Welsh sees, *Saint David's*, *Llandaff*, *Bangor*, and *Saint Asaph*, to the metropolis of Canterbury. Thus the province of Canterbury with its suffragan sees was gradually organized in the form which it kept from the reign of Henry the First to that of Henry the Eighth.

CHAP. VII.

The Welsh Sees.

Meanwhile in the northern province things never reached the same regular organization. York, after some changes, took the position of a metropolitan see, with one suffragan, first at *Lindisfarn* and then at *Durham*, and afterwards with another at *Carlisle*. As the Scottish dioceses broke off from York, they first acknowledged a kind of precedence in the Bishop of *Saint Andrews*; but it was not till a far later time that Scotland was divided into two regular ecclesiastical provinces with their sees at *Saint Andrews* and *Glasgow*. Several of the Scottish dioceses always kept their territorial titles; their sees were mostly fixed in small places; of the chief seats of Scottish royalty, Dunfermline and Stirling never attained episcopal rank at all, and *Edinburgh* only attained it in quite modern times. The endless and fluctuating bishoprics of Ireland were in the twelfth century gathered into the four provinces of *Armagh*, *Dublin*, *Cashel*, and *Tuam*, answering to the temporal divisions of *Ulster*, *Leinster*, *Munster*, and *Connaught*. It is to be noticed that, in marked contradiction to continental practice, the chief see in all the three British kingdoms has been placed in a city which has never held the first temporal rank. Canterbury,

York.

Lindisfarn or Durham.

Carlisle, 1133.

Saint Andrews. 1471.

Glasgow. 1492.

Edinburgh. 1634.

The four Irish provinces.

CHAP. VII.

Saint Andrews, Armagh, were never the temporal heads of England, Scotland, and Ireland. York, Dublin, Glasgow, though metropolitan sees, were of secondary rank, and London and Winchester were ordinary bishoprics.

§ 6. *The Ecclesiastical Divisions of Northern and Eastern Europe.*

Ecclesiastical division in the converted lands.

In the other parts of Europe which formed part of the communion of the Latin Church, the ecclesiastical divisions mark the steps by which Christianity was spread either by conversion or conquest. They continued the process of which the ecclesiastical organization of Eastern Germany was the beginning. As a rule, they strictly follow the political divisions of the age in which they were founded. As the Church in the Scandinavian kingdoms became more settled, its bishoprics parted off from their allegiance to Hamburg or Bremen, and each of the three kingdoms formed an ecclesiastical province, whose boundaries exactly answered to the earlier boundaries of the kingdom. Denmark had its metropolitan see at *Lund*, in that part of the Danish kingdom which geographically forms part of the greater Scandinavian peninsula, and which is now Swedish territory. Its boundary to the south was the Eider, the old frontier of Denmark and the Empire. The suffragan sees of this province, among which the specially royal bishopric of *Roeskild* is the most famous, naturally lie thicker on the ground than they do in the wilder regions of the two more northern kingdoms. But the Baltic conquests of Denmark also placed part of the isle of Rügen in the province of Lund and the diocese of Roeskild, and also gave the Danish

The Scandinavian provinces.

Lund, 1151.

metropolitan a far more distant suffragan in the Bishop of *Revel* on the Finnish gulf. The metropolitan see of Sweden was placed at *Upsala*, and the province was carried by Swedish conquest to the east of the Gulf of Bothnia, where the single bishopric of *Åbo* took in the whole of the Swedish territory in that region. In the like sort, the Norwegian province of *Nidaros* or *Trondhjem* stretched far over the Ocean to the distant colonies and dependencies of Norway in Iceland, Greenland, and Man.

Upsala.

Trondhjem.

The conversion of Poland and the conquest of Prussia and Livonia brought other lands within the pale of the Latin Church and her ecclesiastical organization. The original kingdom of Poland formed the province of *Gnezna*, a province whose boundaries were for some centuries very fluctuating, according as Poland or the Empire was stronger in the Slavonic lands on the Baltic. Each change of temporal dominion caused the ecclesiastical frontiers of Gnezna and Magdeburg to advance or fall back. The Silesian bishopric of *Breslau* always kept its old relation to the Polish metropolis, except so far as it was held to be placed under the immediate superiority of Rome. The later union of Lithuania with the Polish kingdom added a *Lithuanian* and a *Samogitian* bishopric to the original Polish province. The earlier Polish conquests from Russia formed a new province, the Latin province of *Leopol* or *Lemberg*, a province whose southern boundaries advanced and fell back along with the boundary of the kingdom of which it formed a part. The conquests of the Teutonic knights in Prussia and Livonia formed the ecclesiastical province of *Riga*, which was divided into two parts by the province of Gnezna in its greater extent.

Poland, &c.

Gnezna.

Leopol (Lvov).

Riga.

CHAP. VII.

It will be seen that some of the ecclesiastical divisions last mentioned belong to a later stage of European history than that which we have reached in our general narrative. But it seemed better to continue the survey over the whole of the Latin Church in Europe, as the later foundations are a mere carrying out of the same process which began in the earlier. The ecclesiastical divisions represent the political divisions of the time, whether those political divisions were Roman provinces or independent Teutonic or Slavonic kingdoms. But the ecclesiastical divisions, when once fixed, were more lasting than the temporal divisions, and many disputes have arisen out of political changes which transferred one part of a province or diocese from one political allegiance to another. Since the splitting-up of the Western Church, the old ecclesiastical organization has altogether vanished from some countries, and it has been greatly modified in others, in Germany most of all.

It seems hardly needful for the understanding of European history to carry our ecclesiastical survey beyond the limits of the Latin Church. One of the Polish provinces, that of Leopol, has carried us to the borderland of the Eastern and Western Churches, and, if we pass southwards into the Magyar and South-Slavonic lands, we find ourselves still more distinctly on an ecclesiastical march. The Kingdom of Hungary formed two Latin provinces, those of *Strigonium* or Gran, and of *Kolocza*; the latter had a very fluctuating boundary to the south. The Dalmatian coast, the borderland of all powers and of all religions, formed three Latin provinces. *Jadera* or *Zara*, on her peninsula, was the head of a small province chiefly made

Hungary.

Strigonium.

Kolocza.

Dalmatia.

Zara.

up of islands. Another metropolitan had his throne in the very mausoleum of Diocletian, and the province of *Spalato* stretched some way inland over the lands which have so often changed masters. To the south, the see of *Ragusa*, the furthest outpost of Latin Christendom properly so called, had, besides its own coasts and islands, an indefinite frontier inland. This marks the furthest extent to which it is needful to trace our ecclesiastical map. It is the furthest point at which Latin Christianity can be said to be in any sense at home. The ecclesiastical organization of the crusading and Venetian conquests further to the south and east has but little bearing on historical geography. But, within the bounds of Latin Christendom, the ecclesiastical divisions both of the provinces and dioceses within the older Empire and what we may call the missionary provinces beyond it, are of the highest importance, and they should always be kept in mind alongside of the political geography.

Spalato.

Ragusa.

CHAPTER VIII.

THE IMPERIAL KINGDOMS.

CHAP. VIII.

The Kingdom of the *East-Franks* or of *Germany*.

THE division of 887 parted off from the general mass of the Frankish dominions a distinct *Kingdom of the East-Franks*, the acknowledged head of the Frankish kingdoms, which, as being distinguished from its fellows as the *Regnum Teutonicum*, may be best spoken of as a *Kingdom of Germany*. But the lasting acquisition of the Italian and Imperial crowns by the German kings, and their later acquisition of the kingdom of Burgundy, gradually tended to obscure the notion of a distinct German kingdom. The idea of the Kingdom was merged in the idea of the Empire of which it formed a part. Later events too tended in the same direction.

Merging of the Kingdom in the Empire.

The Emperors lose Italy and Burgundy, but keep Germany.

The Italian kingdom gradually fell off from any practical allegiance to its nominal king the Emperor. So did the greater part of the Burgundian kingdom. In Germany meanwhile, though the powers of the German kings who were also Emperors were constantly lessening, their authority was never wholly thrown off till the present century. The Emperors in short lost their kingdoms of Italy and Burgundy, and kept their kingdom of Germany. In the fifteenth century the coronation of the Emperor at Rome had become a mere ceremony, carrying with it no real authority in Italy. In the sixteenth century the ceremony itself went out of use. The

Burgundian coronation at Arles became irregular at a very early time, and it is last heard of in the fourteenth century. But the election of the German kings at Frankfurt, their coronation, in earlier times at Aachen, afterwards at Frankfurt, went on regularly till the last years of the eighteenth century. So, while the national assemblies of Italy and Burgundy can hardly be said to have been regularly held at all, while they went altogether out of use at an early time, the national assembly of Germany, in one shape or another, never ceased as long as there was any one calling himself Emperor or German King. The tendency in all three kingdoms was to split up into separate principalities and commonwealths. But in Germany the principalities and commonwealths always kept up some show of connexion with one another, some show of allegiance to their Imperial head. In Italy and Burgundy they parted off altogether. Some became absolutely independent; some were incorporated with other kingdoms or became their distant dependencies; some were even held by the Emperors themselves in some other character, and not by virtue either of their Empire or of their local kingship. Thus, as the Empire became more and more nearly coextensive with the German Kingdom, the distinction between the two was gradually forgotten. The small parts of the other kingdoms which kept any trace of their Imperial allegiance came to be looked on as parts of Germany. In short, the Western Empire became a German kingdom; or rather it became a German Confederation with a royal head, a confederation which still kept up the forms and titles of the Empire. As no German king received an Imperial coronation after Charles the Fifth, it might in strictness be said

Charles the Fourth crowned at Arles, 1365.

1792.

Endurance of the German Diet.

Comparison of, Germany, Italy, and Burgundy.

The Empire identified with Germany.

The Empire becomes a Confederation.

1530.

CHAP. VIII.

1556.

that the Empire came to an end at his abdication. And in truth from that date the Empire practically became a purely German power. But, as the Imperial forms and titles still went on, the Western Empire must be looked on as surviving, in the form of a German kingdom or confederation, down to its final fall.

The German Kingdom represents the Empire.

The Kingdom of Germany then may be looked on as representing the Western Empire, as being what was left of the Western Empire after the other parts of it had fallen away. But the German kingdom itself underwent, though in a smaller degree, the same fate as the other two Imperial kingdoms. While all Italy and all Burgundy, with some very trifling exceptions, fell away from the Empire, the mass of Germany remained Imperial. Still large parts of Germany were lost to the Empire no less than Italy and Burgundy. A considerable territory on the western frontier of Germany gradually fell away. Part of this territory has grown into independent states; part has been incorporated with the French kingdom. The Swiss Confederation has grown up on lands partly German, partly Burgundian, partly Italian, but of which the oldest and greatest part belonged to the German kingdom. The Confederation of the United Provinces, represented by the modern kingdom of the Netherlands, lay wholly [1] within the old German kingdom: so did the greater part of the modern kingdom of Belgium. In our own day the same tendency has been shown in south-eastern as well as south-western Germany; several members of the ancient kingdom

Separation of parts of the Kingdom.

[1] Unless we except the small part of Flanders held by the Confederation.

Modern Austria.

have fallen away to form part of the new Austro-Hungarian monarchy. But on the northern and north-eastern frontier the tendency to extension, with some fluctuations, has gone on from the beginning of the kingdom to our own day. This tendency to lose territory to the west and south, and to gain territory to the east and north, had the effect of gradually cutting off the Western Empire, as represented by the German kingdom, from any close geographical connexion with the earlier Empire of which it was the historical continuation. The Holy Roman Empire, at the time of its final fall, contained but little territory which had formed part of the Empire of Trajan. It contained nothing which had formed part of the Empire of Justinian, save some small scraps of territory in the north-eastern corner of the old Italian kingdom.

Extension of Germany to the north-east.

Geographical contrast of the earlier and later Empire.

§ 1. *The Kingdom of Germany.*

Change in the geography and nomenclature of Germany.

In tracing out, for our present purpose, the geographical revolutions of Germany, it will be enough to look at them, as far as may be, mainly in their European aspect. Owing to the gradual way in which the various members of the Empire grew into practical sovereignty—owing to the constant division of principalities among many members of the same family—no country has undergone so many internal geographical changes as Germany has. In few countries also has the nomenclature shifted in a more singular way. To take two obvious examples, the modern kingdom of *Saxony* has nothing but its name in common with the Saxony which was brought under Frankish dominion by Charles the Great. The modern kingdom of *Bavaria* has a large territory in common with the

Ancient and modern Saxony and Bavaria.

CHAP. VIII.

ancient Bavaria; but it has gained so much at one end and lost so much at the other that the two cannot be said to be in any practical sense the same country. The name of *Austria* has shifted from the eastern part of the old *Francia* to the German mark against the Magyar, and it has lately wandered altogether beyond the modern German frontier. The name of *Burgundy* has borne endless meanings, both within the Empire and beyond it. Lastly, the ruling state of modern Germany, a state stretching across the whole land from east to west, strangely bears the name of the conquered and extinct *Prussian* race. Many of these changes affect the history of Europe as well as the history of Germany; but many of the endless changes among the smaller members of the Empire are matters of purely local interest, which belong to the historical geography of Germany only, and which claim no place in the historical geography of Europe. I shall endeavour therefore in the present section, first to trace carefully the shiftings of the German frontier as regards other powers, and then to bring out such, and such only, of the internal changes as have a bearing on the general history of Europe.

Uses of the name Austria.

Burgundy.

Prussia.

Extent of the Kingdom.

The extent of the German kingdom as it stood after the division of 887 has been roughly traced already. It will now be well to go over its frontiers somewhat more minutely, as they stood at the time of final separation between the Empire and the West-Frankish kingdom, the time of final union between the Empire and the East-Frankish kingdom. This marks the great age of the Saxon Ottos. The frontier towards the

Boundaries under the Ottos, 936–1002.

Western kingdom was now fairly ascertained, and it was subject to dispute only at a few points. It is hardly needful to insist again on the fact that all Lotharingia, in the sense of those days, taking in all the southern Netherlands except the French fief of Flanders, was now Imperial. It is along this line that the German border has in later times most largely fallen back. The advance of France has touched Burgundy more than Germany; but it has, first swallowed up, and afterwards partly restored, a considerable part of the German kingdom. The Netherlands had been practically cut off from Germany before the annexations of France in that quarter began; they will therefore be better spoken of in another section. The other points at which the frontier has fluctuated on a great scale have been the borderland of *Lorraine*—as distinguished from the Lower *Lotharingia* which has more to do with the history of the Netherlands—and the Swabian land of *Elsass*. The Duchy of *Bar*, the borderland of the borderland, fluctuated more than once. After its union with the Duchy of Lorraine, it followed the fortunes of that state. In the next century came the annexation of the three Lotharingian bishoprics of *Metz*, *Toul*, and *Verdun*, which gave France three outlying possessions within the geographical borders of the Lotharingian duchy. In the next century, as the result of the Thirty Years' War, France obtained by the Peace of Westfalia the formal cession of these conquests, and also the great advance of her frontier by the dismemberment of *Elsass*. The cession now made did not take in the whole of Elsass, but only the possessions and rights of the House of Austria in

Boundary towards the west.

Lotharingia.

Encroachments of France.

The Netherlands.

Lorraine and Elsass.

Fluctuations of Bar.

1470.

The Three Bishoprics 1552.

Loss of Austrian Elsass, 1648.

CHAP. VIII.

that country. This cession still left both Strassburg and various smaller towns and districts to the Empire; but it naturally opened the way to further French advances in a land where the frontier was so complicated and where difficulties were so easily raised as to treaty-rights. A series of annexations, *réunions* as they were called, gradually united nearly all Elsass to France. *Strassburg*, as all the world knows, was seized by Lewis the Fourteenth in time of peace. During the wars with the same prince, the duchy of Lorraine was seized and restored. In the next century it was separated from the Empire to become the life-possession of the Polish king Stanislaus, and on his death it was finally added to France just before a far greater series of French annexations began. The wars of the French Revolution, confirmed by the Peace of *Lunéville*, tore away from Germany and the Empire all that lay on the left bank of the Rhine. In other words, the Western *Francia*, the duchy of the lords of Paris, advanced itself to the utmost limits of the Gaul of Cæsar. This was the last annexation of France at the expense of the old German kingdom. It was indeed the main cause of the formal dissolution of the kingdom which happened a few years later. The utter transformation of Germany within and without which now followed must be spoken of at a later stage.

Gradual annexation of Elsass, 1679–1789.

Seizure of Strassburg, 1681.

Seizure of Lorraine, 1678–1697.

Its final annexation, 1766.

Loss of the left bank of the Rhine, 1801.

Dissolution of the Kingdom and Empire, 1806.

The frontier of Germany and Burgundy, while they still remained distinct kingdoms, fluctuated a good deal, especially in the lands which now form Switzerland. But this frontier ceased to be of any practical importance when the Burgundian kingdom was united with the Empire. The later history of Burgundy, consisting of the gradual incorporation by France of the

Frontier of Germany and Burgundy.

Union of Burgundy with the Empire, 1033.

greater part of the kingdom, and the growth of the remnant into the western cantons of the Swiss Confederation, will be told elsewhere.

Frontier of Germany and Italy.

Towards Italy again the frontier was sometimes doubtful. *Chiavenna*, for instance, sometimes appears in the tenth and eleventh centuries as German; so do the greater districts of *Trent*, *Aquileia*, *Istria*, and even *Verona*. All these formed a marchland, part of which in the end became definitely attached to Germany and part to Italy. But here again, as long as the German and Italian crowns were united, and as long as their common king kept any real authority in either kingdom, the frontier was of no great practical importance. So in later times, both before and after the dissolution of the German Kingdom, the question has practically been a question between Italy and the House of Austria rather than between Italy and Germany as such. These changes also will better come in another section.

The Marchland.

Union of the Crowns, 961–1530. 961–1250.

Eastern and Northern frontiers.

The case is quite different with regard to the eastern and northern frontiers, on which the really greatest changes took place, and where Germany, as Germany, made its greatest advances. Along this line the Roman Empire and the German Kingdom meant the same thing. On this side the frontier had to be marked, so far as it could be marked, against nations which had had nothing to do with the elder Empire. Here then for many ages the Roman Terminus advanced and fell back according to the accidents of a long warfare.

Advance of the Empire.

The whole frontier of the kingdom towards its northern and eastern neighbours was defended by a series of *marks* or border territories whose rulers were clothed with special powers for the defence and exten-

CHAP. VIII.

sion of the frontier.[1] They had to guard the realm against the Dane in the north, and against the Slave during the whole remaining length of the eastern frontier, except where, in the last years of the ninth century, the Magyar thrust himself in between the northern and southern Slaves. Here the frontier, as against Hungary and Croatia, was defended by the marks of *Krain* or *Carniola*, *Kärnthen* or *Carinthia*, and the *Eastern* or *Austrian* mark to the north of them. This frontier has changed least of all. It may, without any great breach of accuracy, be said to have remained the same from the days of the Saxon Emperors till now. The part where it was at all fluctuating was along the Austrian mark, rather than along the two marks to the south of it. The Emperors claimed, and sometimes enforced, a feudal superiority over the Hungarian kings. But this kind of precarious submission does not affect geography. Hungary always remained a separate kingdom; the Imperial supremacy was something purely external, and it was always thrown off on the first opportunity.

Hungarian frontier.

Mark of Austria.

Little change on this frontier.

Occasional homage of Hungary to the Emperors.

The same may be said of *Denmark*. For a short time a German mark was formed north of the Eider. But, when the Danish kingdom had grown into the Northern Empire of Cnut, the German frontier fell back here also, and the *Eider* remained the boundary of the Empire till its fall. As with Hungary, so with Denmark; more than one Danish king became the man of Cæsar; but here again the precarious acknowledgement of Imperial supremacy had no effect on geography.

Frontier towards Denmark.

The Danish Mark, 934–1027.

Boundary of the Eider, 1027–1806.

Occasional homage of the Danish Kings.

Slavonic frontier.

It is in the intermediate lands, along the vast

[1] On the marks, see Waitz, *Deutsche Verfassungsgeschichte*, vii. 62, et seq.

frontier where the Empire marched on the northern *Slavonic* lands, that the real historical geography of Germany lies for some ages. Here the boundary was ever fluctuating. At the time of the division of 887, the Slaves held all to the east of the Elbe and a good deal to the west. How far they had during the Wandering of the Nations stepped into the place of earlier Teutonic inhabitants is a question which belongs to another field of inquiry. We must here start from the geographical fact that, at the time when the modern states of Europe began to form themselves, the Slaves were actually in possession of the great north-eastern region of modern Germany. Their special mention will come in their special place; we must here mark that modern Germany has largely formed itself by the gradual conquest and colonization of lands which at the end of the ninth century were Slavonic. The German kingdom spread itself far to the north-east, and German settlements and German influences spread themselves far beyond the formal bounds of the German kingdom. Three special instruments worked together in bringing about this end. The Saxon Dukes came first. In after times came the great league of German cities, the famous *Hansa* which, like some other bodies originally commercial, became a political power, and which spread German influences over the whole of the shores of the Baltic. Along with them, from the thirteenth century onwards, worked the great military order of the Teutonic knights. Out of their conquests came the first beginnings of the Prussian state, and the extension of German rule and the German speech over much which in modern geography has become Russian. In a history of the German nation all these causes would have to be dealt

Fluctuation of territory.

Extent of Slavonic occupation.

German advance.

The Saxon dukes.

The *Hansa*.

The Teutonic Order.

CHAP. VIII.

with together as joint instruments towards the same end. In a purely geographical view the case is different. Some of these influences concern the formation of the actual German kingdom; others have geographically more to do with the group of powers more to the north-east, the Slavonic states of Poland and Russia, and their Lithuanian and Finnish neighbours. The growth and fall of the military orders will therefore most naturally come in another section. We have here to trace out those changes only which helped to give the German kingdom the definite geographical extent which it held for some centuries before its final fall.

Beginning at the north, in the lands where German, Slave, and Dane, came into close contact, in *Saxony beyond the Elbe*, the modern *Holstein*, the Slaves held the western coast, and the narrow *Saxon mark* fenced off the German land. The Saxon dukes of the house of Billung formed a German mark, which took in the lands reaching from the Elbe to the strait which divides the isle of Rügen from the mainland. But this possession was altogether precarious. It again became a Slavonic kingdom; then it was a possession of Denmark; it cannot be looked on as definitely becoming part of the German realm till the thirteenth century. The chief state in these lands which has lasted till later times is the duchy of *Mecklenburg*, the rulers of which, in its two modern divisions, are the only modern princes who directly represent an old Slavonic royal house. Meanwhile a way was opened for a vast extension of German influence through the whole North, by the growth of the city of *Lübeck*. Twice founded, the second time by Henry the Lion Duke of Saxony, it gradually became the leading member of the great

The Saxon Mark.

Mark of the Billungs, 960–1106.

Its fluctuations.

Slavonic princes continue in Mecklenburg.

Foundation of Lübeck, 1140–1158.

merchant League. To the south of these lands come CHAP. VIII.
those Slavonic lands which have grown into the mo-
dern kingdom of Saxony and the central parts of the The Hanse Towns.
modern kingdom of Prussia. These were specially
marchlands, a name which some of them have kept March-lands.
down to our own day. The mark of *Brandenburg* in
its various divisions, the mark of *Lausitz* or *Lusatia*, Branden-burg.
where a Slavonic population still lingers, and the mark Lausitz.
of *Meissen*, long preserved the memory of the times Meissen.
when these lands, which afterwards came to play so
great a part in the internal history of Germany, were
still outlying and precarious possessions of the German
realm.

To the south-east lay the *Bohemian* lands, whose
history has been somewhat different. The duchy, after-
wards kingdom, of *Bohemia* became, early in the tenth Bohemia a fief, 928.
century, a fief of the German kingdom. From that time Becomes a
ever afterwards, save during one moment of passing kingdom, 1198.
Polish annexation, it remained one of its principal mem- 1003.
bers, ruled, as long as the Empire lasted, by princes
holding electoral rank. The boundaries of the kingdom
itself have hardly varied at all. The dependent marchland of *Moravia* to the east, the remnant of the great Moravia.
Moravian kingdom whose history will come more fit- 1019.
tingly in another chapter, fluctuated for a long while
between Hungarian, Polish, and Bohemian supremacy.
But from the early part of the eleventh century it
remained under Bohemian rule, and therefore under
Imperial superiority. To the east of this nearer zone More
of Slavonic dependencies lay another range of Slavonic distant Slavonic
states, some of which were gradually incorporated states.
with the German kingdom, while others remained
distinct down to modern times. *Pomerania* on the Pomerania.

CHAP. VIII.

Baltic coast is a name which has often changed both its geographical extent and its political allegiance. Originally a province or dependency of Poland, in the end it took its place on the map in the form of two duchies, ruled, like Mecklenburg, by native princes under Imperial supremacy. South of Pomerania, the German march bordered on the more distinctively Polish land, and between Poland and Hungary lay the northern *Croatia* or *Chrobatia*. The German supremacy seems sometimes to have been extended as far as the Wartha, and, in the Chrobatian land, even beyond the Vistula. But this extension was quite momentary; Poland grew up, like Hungary, as a kingdom, some of whose dukes and kings admitted the Imperial supremacy, but which gradually became wholly independent. The border province of *Silesia*, after some fluctuations between Bohemia and Poland, became definitely Polish at the end of the tenth century. Afterwards it was divided into several principalities, whose dukes passed under Bohemian vassalage, and so became members of the Empire. Thus in the course of some ages, a boundary was drawn between Germany and Poland which lasted down to modern times.

Native princes go on.

Polish frontier.

Occasional homage of the Polish kings.

Silesia Polish, 999.

Bohemian, 1289–1327.

Extension of the Empire to the east.

The result of this survey is to show how great, and at the same time how gradual, was the extension of the German power eastward. A Roman Empire with a long Baltic coast was something that had never been dreamed of in earlier days. If the extension of the German name was but the recovery of long lost Teutonic lands, the extension to them of the Imperial name which had become identified with Germany was at least wholly new. In all the lands

The Slavonic lands germanized

now annexed, save in a few exceptional districts, German annexation meant German colonization, and the assimilation of the surviving inhabitants to the speech and manners of Germany. Colonists were brought, specially from the Frisian lands, by whose means the Low-Dutch tongue was spread along the whole southern coast of the Baltic. German cities were founded. The marchlands grew into powerful German states. At last one of these marchlands, united with a German conquest still further cut off from the heart of the old German realm, has grown into a state which in our own days has become the Imperial power of Germany.

Internal geography of Germany.

The internal geography of the German kingdom is the greatest difficulty of such a work as the present. To trace the boundaries of the kingdom as against other kingdoms is comparatively easy; but to trace out the endless shiftings, the unions and the divisions, of the countless small principalities and commonwealths which arose within the kingdom, would be a hopeless attempt. Still the growth of the dukes, counts, and other princes of Germany into independent sovereigns is the great feature of German history, as the consequent wiping out of old divisions, and shifting to and fro of old names, is the special feature of German historical geography. The dying out of the old names has an historical interest, and the growth of the new powers which have supplanted them has both an historical and a political interest. It is specially important to mark that the two powers which have stood at the head of Germany in modern times in no way represent any of the old divisions of the German name. They have

Growth of the principalities.

Changes in nomenclature.

CHAP. VIII.

Origin of Prussia and Austria.

grown out of the outlying *marks* planted against the Slave and the Magyar. The mark of *Brandenburg*, the mark against the Slave, has grown into the kingdom of *Prussia*, the Imperial state of Germany in its latest form. The *Eastern* mark, the mark against the Magyar, has grown into the archduchy which gave Germany so many kings, into the so-called Austrian 'empire,' into the Austro-Hungarian monarchy of our own day. The growth of Brandenburg or Prussia again affords an instructive comparison with the growth of Wessex in England, of France in Gaul, of Castile in Spain, we might even add, of Rome in her first advance to the headship of kindred Latium. In all these cases alike, it has been a marchland which has come to the front and has become the head of the united nation.

Analogies between Brandenburg and other marchlands.

The great Duchies under the Saxon and Frankish Kings, 919–1125.

Starting from the division of 887, we shall find several important landmarks in the history of the German kingdom which may help us in this most difficult part of our work. Under the Saxon and Frankish kings, while the kingdom is enlarged by Slavonic conquests to the east and by the definite adhesion of Lotharingia to the west, the great duchies still form the main internal divisions. The kingdom is still made up of the four duchies of the Eastern Francia, Saxony, Alemannia and Bavaria, together with the great borderland of Lotharingia. Under the Swabian kings we see the break-up of the great duchies. In the case of Saxony the process which was everywhere silently and gradually at work was formally carried out in the greatest case of all by Imperial and national authority. The *Gauverfassung*, the immemorial system of Teutonic communities, now finally changes into a system of territorial principalities, broken only by the many free cities

Decline of the Duchies under the Swabian Kings, 1137–1254.

End of the *Gauverfassung*. Growth of territorial Principalities.

and the few free districts which owned no lord but the King. In the twelfth century we see the beginnings of the powers which became chief at a later day, the powers of the eastern marchland. Here lay Saxony in the later sense, a power of no small moment in German and even in European history, but which has been altogether overshadowed by two other powers of the eastern frontier. The twelfth century is specially marked as the time when the two states which have had most to do with the making or unmaking of modern Germany begin to find their place in history. It is then that the two great marchlands of Brandenburg and Austria begin to take their place among the leading powers of the German kingdom. The time from the so-called *Interregnum* to the legislation under Maximilian is marked by the further growth of these powers. It is further marked by the beginning of that connexion of the Austrian duchy, and of the Imperial crown itself, with lands beyond the bounds of the Kingdom and the Empire which led in the end to the special and anomalous position of the House of Austria as an European power. During the same period comes the practical separation of *Switzerland* and the *Netherlands* from the German kingdom. In short, it was during this age that Germany in its later aspect was formed. The legislation of Maximilian's reign, the attempts which were then made to bring the kingdom to a greater degree of unity, have left their mark on geography in the division of Germany into *circles*. This division, though it was not thoroughly complete, though it did not reach to every corner of the kingdom, was strictly an administrative division of the kingdom itself as such; but the mapping out of the circles, the difference

Growth of the march powers. 1254–1512.

Growth of the House of Austria.

Separation of Switzerland, 1495–1648. Of the Netherlands, 1430–1648.

Legislation under Maximilian, 1495–1512.

Division into circles. 1500–1512.

CHAP VIII.

of which in point of size is remarkable, was itself affected by the geographical extent of the dominions of the princes who held lands within them. The circles were, in a faint way, a return to the ancient duchies, the names of which were to some extent kept on. The two *Saxon* circles, Upper and Lower, and the three circles of *Franconia*, *Swabia*, and *Bavaria*, all kept ancient names, and most of them kept some measure of geographical connexion with the ancient lands whose names they bore. The other circles, those of *Upper* and *Lower Rhine*, of *Westfalia*, *Austria*, and *Burgundy* —the last name being used in a sense altogether new— arose out of later changes.

Thirty Years' War, 1618–1648.

The seventeenth century is marked in German history by the results of the Thirty Years' War and of other changes. Its most important geographical result was to carry on the process which had begun with the Austrian House, the growth of powers holding lands both within and without the Empire. Thus, besides the union of the Hungarian kingdom with the Austrian archduchy, the King of Sweden now held lands as a prince of the Empire, and the same result was brought about in another way by the union of the Electorate of Brandenburg with the Duchy of Prussia. This, and other accessions of territory, now made Brandenburg as distinctly the first power of northern Germany as Austria was of southern Germany, and in the eighteenth century the rivalry of these two powers becomes the chief centre, not only of German but of European politics. The union of the Electorate of Hannover under the same sovereign with the kingdom of Great Britain further increased the number of princes ruling both within Germany and without it. Lastly, the wars of

Powers holding lands within and without Germany. Austria. Sweden.

Union of Brandenburg and Prussia.

Rivalry of Prussia and Austria.

Hannover and Great Britain, 1715.

the latter years of the eighteenth and the beginning of the nineteenth century led to the dissolution alike of the German kingdom and of the Roman Empire. Then, after a time of confusion and foreign occupation, comes the formation of a Confederation with boundaries nearly the same as the later boundaries of the kingdom. But the Confederation itself now appears as something quite subordinate to its two leading members. Germany, as such, no longer counts as a great European power, but Prussia and Austria, the two chief holders at once of German and of non-German lands, stand forth among the chief bearers of European rank. Lastly, the changes of our own day have given us an Imperial Germany with geographical boundaries altogether new, a Germany from which the south-eastern German lands are cut off, while the Polish and other non-German possessions of Prussia to the north-east have become an integral part of the new Empire. The task of the geographer is thereby greatly simplified. Down to the last changes, one of his greatest difficulties is to make his map show with any clearness what was the extent of the German Kingdom or Confederation, and at the same time what was the extent of the dominions of those princes who held lands both in Germany and out of it. By the last arrangements this difficulty at least is altogether taken away.

Dissolution of the Kingdom, 1806.

The German Confederation, 1815–1866.

Austria and Prussia greater than the Confederation.

The new Confederation and Empire, 1866–1870.

Under the Saxon and Frankish Kings, then, the old names, marking the great divisions of the German people, still keep their predominance. All smaller divisions are still subordinate to the great duchies. Among these, the kernel of the kingdom, the Eastern *Francia*, is the only one whose boundaries had little

Germany under the Saxon and Frankish Empire.

The great Duchies. Eastern Francia cut off

CHAP. VIII.

from extension.

Frontier position of Saxony, Bavaria, and Alemannia.

or no chance of being extended or lessened at the cost of foreign powers. It had the smallest possible frontier towards the Slave. On the other hand, *Saxony* has an ever fluctuating boundary against the Slave and the Dane; *Bavaria* marches upon the Slave, the Magyar, and the Kingdom of Italy, while *Alemannia* has a shifting frontier towards both Burgundy and Italy. Lotharingia, and Burgundy after its annexation, are the lands which lie exposed to aggression from the West. It is perhaps for this very reason that, of the four duchies which preserved the names of the four great divisions of the German nation, the Eastern Francia is the one which has most utterly vanished from the modern map and from modern memory. Another cause may have strengthened its tendency to vanish. The policy of the kings forbade that the Frankish duchy should become the abiding heritage of any princely family. The ducal title of the Eastern Francia was at two periods of its history borne by ecclesiastical princes in the persons of the Bishops of *Würzburg*; but it never gave its name, like Saxony and Bavaria, to any ruling house. The English student will notice the analogy by which, among all the ancient English kingdoms, Wessex, the cradle of the English monarchy, is the one whose name has most utterly vanished from modern memory.

Exposed position of Lotharingia and Burgundy.

Vanishing of Francia.

Its ecclesiastical Dukes.

Analogy with Wessex.

The only way to grasp the endless shiftings and divisions of the German principalities, so as to give anything like a clear general view, will be to take the great duchies, and to point out in a general way the steps by which they split asunder, and the chief states of any historical importance which rose out of their divisions. To begin with the greatest, the duchy of *Saxony* consisted of three main divisions, *Westfalia*, *Engern* or *Angria*, and *Eastfalia*. *Thuringia* to the south-east, and the *Frisian* lands to the north-west, may be looked on as in some sort appendages to the Saxon duchy.

Saxony; its three divisions, Westfalia, Angria, Eastfalia.

The duchy was capable of any amount of extension towards the east, and the lands gradually won from the Wends on this side were all looked on as additions made to the Saxon territory.

Growth of Saxony at the expense of the Slaves.

But the great Saxon duchy was broken up at the fall of Henry the Lion.

Break-up of the Duchy, 1182–1191.

The archiepiscopal Electors of *Köln* received the title of Dukes of *Westfalia* and *Engern*. But in the greater part of those districts the grant remained merely nominal, though the ducal title, with a small actual Westfalian duchy, remained to the electorate till the end.

Duchy of Westfalia.

The name of *Saxony*, as a geographical expression, now clave to the Eastfalian remnant of the old duchy, and to Thuringia and the Slavonic conquests to the east.

New use of the name *Saxony*.

In the later division of Germany these lands formed the two circles of *Upper* and *Lower Saxony*; and it was within their limits that the various states arose which have kept on the Saxon name to our own time.

The Saxon Circles.

From the descendants of Henry the Lion himself, and from the allodial lands which they kept, the Saxon name passed away, except so far as they became part of the Lower-Saxon circle. They held their place as princes of the Empire, no longer as Dukes of Saxony, but as Dukes of *Brunswick*, a house which gave Rome one Emperor and England a dynasty of kings.

Duchy of Brunswick.

After some of the usual divisions, two Brunswick principalities finally took their place on the map, those of *Lüneburg* and *Wolfenbüttel*, the latter having the town of

Its division, 1203.

Lüneburg and Wolfenbüttel

CHAP. VIII.

Lüneburg acquires the bishoprics of Bremen and Verden, 1715–1719. Electorate of Hannover or Brunswick Lüneburg, 1692.

Brunswick for its capital. The Lüneburg duchy grew. Late in the seventeenth century it was raised to the electoral rank, and early in the next century it was finally enlarged by the acquisition of the bishoprics of *Bremen* and *Verden*. Thus was formed the Electorate, and afterwards Kingdom, of *Hannover*, while the simple ducal title remained with the Brunswick princes of the other line.

The new Saxony.

The Saxon name itself altogether withdrew in the end from the old Saxony to the lands conquered from the Slave. On the fall of Henry the Lion, the duchy of Saxony, cut short by the grant to the archbishops of Köln, was granted to Bernhard of Ballensted, the founder of the Ascanian House. Of the older Saxon land his house kept only for a while the small district north of the Elbe which kept the name of *Sachsen-Lauenburg*, and which in the end became part of the Hannover electorate. But in Thuringia and the conquered Slavonic lands to the east of Thuringia a new Saxony arose, which kept on somewhat of the European position of the Saxon name down to modern times. The new Saxony, with Wittenberg for its capital, grew, through the addition of *Thuringia* and *Meissen*, into the Saxon electorate which played so great a part during the three last centuries of the existence of the German kingdom. But in Saxony too the usual divisions took place. Lauenburg parted off; so did the smaller duchies which still keep the Saxon name. The ducal and electoral dignities were divided, till the two, united under the famous Maurice, formed the Saxon electorate as it stood at the dissolution of the kingdom. It was in short a new state, one which had succeeded to the Saxon name, but which in no other

Bernhard duke of Saxony, 1180–1212.

Sachsen-Lauenburg.

1423. Divisions and unions. 1547.

way represented the Saxony whose conquest cost so many campaigns to Charles the Great.

CHAP. VIII.

The Mark of Brandenburg.

Another power which arose in the marchland of Saxon and Slave, to the north of Saxony in the later sense, was the land known specially as the *Mark*, the groundwork of the power which has in our own day risen to the head of Germany. The *North Mark* of Saxony became the *Mark of Brandenburg*. In the twelfth and thirteenth centuries, under Albert the Bear and his house, the Mark greatly extended itself at the expense of the Slaves. United for a time with the kingdom of Bohemia, it passed into the house of the Burggraves of *Nürnberg*, that House of Hohenzollern which has grown step by step till it has reached Imperial rank in our own day. The power thus formed presently acquired a special character by the acquisition of what may be called a German land out of Germany, a land which afterwards gave its princes a higher title, and which by its geographical position led irresistibly to a further increase of territory. Early in the seventeenth century the Electors of Brandenburg acquired by inheritance the *Duchy of Prussia*, that is Eastern Prussia, a fief, not of the Empire but of the crown of Poland, and which lay geographically apart from their strictly German dominions. The common sovereign of Brandenburg and Prussia was thus the man of two lords; but the Great Elector Frederick William became a wholly independent sovereign in his duchy, and his son Frederick took on himself the kingly title for the land which was thus freed from all homage. Both before and after the union with Prussia, the Electors of Brandenburg continued largely to increase their Ger-

Reign of Albert the Bear, 1134–1170.

Union with Bohemia, 1373–1415.

House of Hohenzollern, 1415.

Union of Brandenburg and Prussia, 1611–1618.

1656. Prussia independent of Poland, 1656; becomes kingdom, 1701.

CHAP. VIII. 1523–1623. man dominions. A temporary possession of the principality of *Jägerndorf* in Silesia, unimportant in itself, led to great events in later times. Westfalian possessions of Brandenburg, 1614–1666. 1702–1744. The acquisition, at various times in the seventeenth century, of *Cleve* and other outlying Westfalian lands, which were further increased in the next century, led in the same way to the modern dominion of Prussia in western Germany. Acquisitions in Pomerania, 1638–1648. But the most solid acquisition of Brandenburg in this age was that of *Eastern Pomerania*, to which a further increase of territory, including the town of Stettin, was added after the 1713–1719. wars of Charles the Twelfth of Sweden. The events of the Thirty Years' War also increased the dominions both of Brandenburg and Saxony at the expense of the neighbouring ecclesiastical princes. Later acquisitions of Prussia. The later acquisitions of the House of Hohenzollern, after the Electors of Brandenburg had taken the kingly title from their Prussian duchy, concern Prussia as an European power at least as much as they concern Brandenburg as a German power. Yet their proper place comes in the history of Germany. German character of the Prussian Monarchy. Unlike the other princes who held lands within and without the German kingdom, the Kings of Prussia and Electors of Brandenburg have remained essentially German princes. Their acquisitions of territory out of Germany have all been in fact enlargements, if not of the soil of Germany, at least of the sphere of German influence. And, at last, in marked contrast to the fate of the rival House of Austria, the whole Prussian dominions have been incorporated with the new German Empire, and form the immediate dominion of its Imperial head. Spread of the name of *Prussia*. The outward sign of this special position of Brandenburg, as compared with Holstein or Austria, is the strange extension of the Prussian name. Nothing of the same kind has taken place in the case of the dominions of the other princes who held both German and non-German lands. The Duke of Holstein was King of Denmark, but Holstein did not come to be called Denmark. The Archduke of Austria was King of Hungary, but Austria never came to be called Hungary; the change in that quarter was rather the other way. The Elector of Brandenburg was also King of Prussia, and the name of Prussia has gradually spread itself over Brandenburg and all his other dominions.

Conquest of Silesia, 1741.

Within Germany the greatest enlargement of the dominion of Prussia—as we may now begin to call it instead of Brandenburg—was the acquisition of by far the greater part of *Schlesien* or *Silesia*, hitherto part of the Bohemian lands, and then held by the House of Austria. This, it should be noted, was an acquisition which could hardly fail to lead to further acquisitions.

Geographical character of the Prussian dominions

The geographical characteristic of the Prussian dominions was the way in which they lay in detached pieces, and the enormous extent of frontier as compared with the area of the country. The kingdom itself lay detached, hemmed in and intersected by the territory of Poland. The electorate, with the Pomeranian territory, formed a somewhat more compact mass; but even this had a very large frontier compared with its area. The Westfalian possessions, the district of *Cottbus*, and other outlying dominions, lay quite apart. The addition of Silesia increased this characteristic yet further.

Position of Silesia.

The newly won duchy, barely joining the electorate, ran out as a kind of peninsula between Saxony, Bohemia, and Poland. Silesia, first as a Polish and then as a Bohemian fief, had formed part of a fairly compact geographical mass; as part of

CHAP. VIII.

the same dominion with Prussia and Brandenburg, it was an all but isolated land with an enormous frontier.

Acquisitions from Poland, 1772–1795.

The details of the Polish acquisitions of Prussia will be best given in our survey of Poland. But it should be

Their geographical character.

noted that each of the portions of territory which were added to Prussia by the several partitions has a geographical character of its own. The addition of *West-*

1772.

Prussia—that is the geographical union of the kingdom and the electorate—was something which in the nature of things could not fail to come sooner or later.

1793.

The second addition of *South-Prussia* might seem geographically needed in order to leave Silesia no longer peninsular. The last, and most short-lived addition of

1795.

New-East-Prussia had no such geographical necessity as the other two. Still it helped to give greater compactness to the kingdom, and to lessen its frontier in comparison with its area.

Another acquisition of the House of Hohenzollern during the eighteenth century, though temporary, deserves a passing notice. Among its Westfalian annexa-

East-Friesland, 1744.

tions was *East-Friesland*. The King of Prussia thus became, during the last half of the eighteenth century, an oceanic potentate, a character which he presently lost, and which, save for a moment in the days of confusion, he obtained again only in our own day.

Parts of Saxony held by foreign kings.

A large part of Saxony, both in the older and in the later sense, thus came to form part of a dominion containing both German and non-German lands, but in which the German character was in every way predominant. Other parts of Saxony in the same extended sense also came to form part of the dominions of princes who ruled both in and out of Germany, but in whom the non-German character was yet more predominant. The old *Saxony beyond the Elbe*, the modern *Holstein*, passed into the hands of the Danish Kings. Its shifting relations towards Denmark and Germany and towards the neighbouring land of *Sleswick*, as having become matter of international dispute between Denmark and Germany, will be best spoken of when we come to deal generally with the Baltic lands. The events of the Thirty Years' War also made the Swedish kings for a while considerable potentates in northern Germany. The Peace of Westfalia confirmed to them *Western Pomerania* and the town of *Wismar* on the Baltic, and the bishoprics of *Bremen* and *Verden* which gave them an oceanic coast. But these last lands were afterwards ceded to Hannover, and the Pomeranian possessions of Sweden were also cut short by cessions to Brandenburg. But the possession of Wismar and a part of Pomerania still gave the Swedish kings a position as German princes down to the dissolution of the Empire.

Holstein: its relation to Sleswick.

German territories of Sweden, 1648–1815.

1720.

These are the chief powers which rose to historical importance within the bounds of Saxony, in the widest sense of that word. To trace every division and union which created or extinguished any of the smaller principalities, or even to mark every minute change of frontier among the greater powers, would be impossible. But it must be further remembered that the Saxon circles were the seats of some of the greatest of the free cities of Germany, the leading members of the Hanseatic League. In the growth of German commerce the Rhenish lands took the lead, and, in the earliest days of the Hansa, *Köln* held the first place among its cities. The pre-eminence afterwards passed to havens nearer

Free cities of Saxony.

The Hanse Towns.

CHAP. VIII.

Lübeck, Bremen, Hamburg.

to the Ocean and the Baltic, where, among a crowd of others, the Imperial cities of *Lübeck* and *Bremen* stand out foremost, and with them *Hamburg*, a rival which has in later times outstripped them. And at this point it may be noticed that Lübeck and Bremen specially illustrate a law which extended to many other of the episcopal cities of Germany. The Bishop became a prince, and held a greater or smaller extent of territory in temporal sovereignty. But the city which contained his see remained independent of him in temporal things, and knew him only as its spiritual shepherd. Such were the archbishopric of Bremen and the bishopric of Lübeck, principalities which, after the change of religion, passed into secular hands. But the two cities always remained independent commonwealths, owning no superior but the Emperor.

The cities and the bishoprics.

Franconia.

The next among the great duchies, that of *Eastern Francia*, *Franken*, or *Franconia*, is of much less importance in European history than that of Saxony. Its ducal title lived on to the end; but it was borne only by ecclesiastical dukes, the Bishops of *Würzburg*. Ancient Francia cannot be said to be in any sense continued in any modern state. Its name gradually retreated, and the circle of *Franken* or *Franconia* took in only the most eastern part of the ancient duchy. The western and northern part of the duchy, together with a good deal of territory which was strictly Lotharingian, became part of the two Rhenish circles. Thus *Fulda*, the greatest of German abbeys, passed away from the Frankish name. In north-eastern Francia, the *Hessian* principalities grew up to the north-west. Within the Franconian circle lay *Würzburg*, the see of its

Bishops of Würzburg Dukes.

Extent of the Circle.

The Rhenish Circles.

episcopal dukes, as also the other great bishopric of *Bamberg*, together with the free city of *Nürnberg*, and various smaller principalities. In the Rhenish lands, both within and without the old Francia, one chief characteristic is the predominance of the ecclesiastical principalities, *Mainz*, *Köln*, *Worms*, *Speyer*, and *Strassburg*. The chief temporal power which arose in this region was the *Palatinate of the Rhine*, a power which, like others, went through many unions and divisions, and spread into four circles, those of Upper and Lower Rhine, Westfalia, and Bavaria. This last district, though united with the Palatine Electorate, was, from the early part of the fourteenth century, distinguished from the Palatinate of the Rhine as the *Oberpfalz* or *Upper Palatinate*. To the south of it lay the *Bavarian* principalities. These, united into a single duchy, formed the power which grew into the modern kingdom. But neither this duchy nor the whole Bavarian circle at all reached to the extent of the ancient Bavaria which bordered on Italy. The early stages of the Thirty Years' War gave the Rhenish Palatinate, with its electoral rights, to Bavaria; the Peace of Westfalia restored the Palatinate, leaving Bavaria as a new electorate. Late in the eighteenth century, Bavaria itself passed to the Elector Palatine, thus forming what may be called modern Bavaria with its outlying Rhenish lands. This acquisition was at the same time partly balanced by the cession to Austria of the lands east of the Inn, known as the *Innviertel*. The other chief state within the Bavarian circle was the great ecclesiastical principality of the archbishops of *Salzburg* in the extreme south-east.

Ecclesiastical States on the Rhine.

Bavaria.

Shiftings between Bavaria and the Palatinate, 1623.

Electorate of Bavaria, 1648.

Union of the two, 1777.

Cession to Austria, 1778.

Archbishopric of Salzburg.

The old *Lotharingian* divisions, as we see them in

CHAP. VIII.

Lotharingia.

Lower Lotharingia.

Duchy of Lothringen or Lorraine.

Elsass.

the time of the great duchies, utterly died out. The states which arose in the *Lower Lotharingia* are among those which silently fell off from the German Kingdom to take a special position under the name of the *Netherlands*. The special duchy of *Lothringen* or *Lorraine* was held to belong to the circle of Upper Rhine. *Elsass* also formed part of the same circle, the circle which was specially cut short by the encroachments of France.

Circle of Swabia.

The *Swabian* circle answered more nearly than most of the new divisions to the old Swabian duchy, as that duchy stood without counting the marchland of Elsass. No part of Germany was more cut up into small states than the old land of the Hohenstaufen. A crowd of principalities, secular and ecclesiastical—among them the lesser principalities of the Hohenzollern house—of free cities, and of outlying possessions of the houses of Austria, made up the main part of the circle.

Ecclesiastical powers of Swabia.

Part of Swabia becomes Switzerland.

Strassburg, *Augsburg*, *Constanz*, *St. Gallen*, *Chur*, *Zürich*, are among the great bishoprics and other ecclesiastical foundations of the old Swabia. But, as I shall show more fully in another section, large districts in the south-east, those which formed the *Old League of High Germany*, had practically fallen away from the kingdom before the new division was made, and were therefore never reckoned in any circle.

Baden.

Württemberg.

Two Swabian principalities, the mark of *Baden*, and *Württemberg*, first county and then duchy, came gradually to the first place in this region. As such they still remain, preserving in some sort a divided representation of the old Swabia.

Two important parts of the old kingdom, two circles of the division of Maximilian, still remain. These are the lands which form the circles of *Burgundy* and

CHAP. VIII.

Austria. These are lands which have, in earlier or later times, wholly fallen off from the German Kingdom. The *Austrian* circle was formed of the lands in southern Germany which gradually gathered in the hands of the second Austrian dynasty, the House of Habsburg. Starting from the original mark on the Hungarian frontier, those lands grew, first into a great German, and then into a great European, power, and the latest changes have made even their German lands politically non-German. The growth of the Austrian House will therefore be properly dealt with in a separate section. It is enough to say here that the Austrian dominion in Germany gradually took in, besides the original duchy, the south-eastern duchies of *Steiermark* or *Styria*, *Kärnthen* or *Carinthia*, and *Krain* or *Carniola*, with the Italian borderlands of *Görtz*, *Aquileia*, and part of *Istria*. Joined to these by a kind of geographical isthmus, like that which joins Silesia and Brandenburg, lay the western possessions of the house, the Bavarian county of *Tyrol* and various outlying strips and points of land in *Swabia* and *Elsass*. The growth of the Confederates cut short the Swabian possessions of Austria, as the later cession to France cut short its Alsatian possessions. Still a Swabian remnant remained down to the dissolution of the Kingdom. The kingdom of *Bohemia*, with the dependent lands of Moravia and *Silesia*, though held by the Archdukes of Austria and giving them electoral rank, was not included in any German circle. The Austrian circle moreover was not wholly made up of the dominions of the Austrian house; besides some smaller territories, it also took in the bishoprics of *Trent* and *Brixen* on the debateable frontier of Italy and old Bavaria.

Circle of *Austria*.

Growth of the House of Austria.

Extent of its German lands.

Tyrol.

Loss of Swabian lands.

Bohemia and its dependencies.

Trent and Brixen.

Circle of Burgundy. Dominion of the Valois Dukes within the Empire.

The *Burgundian* circle was the last and the strangest use of the Burgundian name. It consisted of those parts of the dominions of the Dukes of Burgundy of the House of Valois which remained to their descendants of the House of Austria at the time of the division into circles. These did not all lie strictly within the boundaries of the German kingdom. Within that kingdom indeed lay the Northern Netherlands, the Frisian lands of *Holland*, *Zealand*, and *West-Friesland*, as also *Brabant* and other Lotharingian lands. But the circle also took in the *County of Burgundy* or *Franche-Comté*, part of the old kingdom of Burgundy, and lastly *Flanders* and *Artois*, lands beyond the bounds of the Empire. These were fiefs of France which were released from their homage to that crown by the treaty between Charles the Fifth and Francis the First of France. The Burgundian circle thus took in all the Imperial fiefs of the Valois dukes, together with a small part of their French fiefs. As all, or nearly all, of these lands altogether fell away from the German kingdom, and as those parts of them which now form the two kingdoms of the Low Countries have a certain historical being of their own, it will be well to keep their more detailed mention also for a special section.

The Imperial Netherlands.

County of Burgundy.

Flanders and Artois released from homage to France, 1526.

§ 2. *The Confederation and Empire of Germany.*

Germany changed from a kingdom to a confederation.

Our survey in the last section has carried us down to the beginning of the changes which led to the break-up of the old German Kingdom. Germany is the only land in history which has changed from a kingdom to a confederation. The tie which bound the vassal princes to the king became so lax that it was at last thrown off altogether. In this process

Sketch of the process, 1806–1815.

foreign invasion largely helped. Between the two processes of foreign war and domestic disintegration, a chaotic time followed, in which boundaries were ever shifting and new states were ever rising and falling. In the end, nearly all the lands which had formed the old kingdom came together again, with new names and boundaries, as members of a lax Confederation. The latest events of all have driven the former chief of the Confederation beyond its boundaries; they have joined its other members together by a much closer tie; they have raised the second member of the former Confederation to the post of perpetual chief of the new Confederation, and they have further clothed him with the Imperial title. But it must be remembered that the modern Empire of Germany is still a Federal state. Its chief bears the title of Emperor; still the relation is federal and not feudal. The lesser members of the Empire are not vassals of the Emperor, as they were in the days of the old kingdom. They are states bound to him and to one another by a tie which is strictly federal. That the state whose prince holds Imperial rank far surpasses any of its other members in extent and power is an important political fact; but it does not touch the federal position of all the states of the Empire, great and small. Reuss-Schleiz is not a vassal state of Prussia; it is a member of a league in which the voice of Prussia naturally goes for more than the voice of Reuss-Schleiz. The dissolution of the German kingdom, and with it the wiping out of the last tradition of the Roman Empire, cannot be separated from the history of wars of the French Revolution which went before it, and which indeed led to it. For our purely geographical purpose, we must distinguish the changes which directly affected

The German *Bund*, 1815.

The new Confederation and Empire, 1866–1871.

The new Empire still federal.

Wars of the French Revolution, 1793–1814.

CHAP. VIII.

the German kingdom from those which affected the Austrian states, the Netherlands, and Switzerland, lands which have now a separate historic being from Germany.

War between France and the Empire, 1793–1801.

The left bank of the Rhine ceded by the Peace of Lunéville, 1801.

The last war which the Empire as such waged with France was the eight years' war which was ended by the Peace of Lunéville. By that peace, all Germany on the left bank of the Rhine was ceded to France. What a sacrifice this was we at once see, when we bear in mind that it took in the three metropolitan cities of Köln, Mainz, and Trier, the royal city of Aachen, and the famous bishoprics of Worms and Speyer. A number of princes thus lost all or part of their dominions, and it was presently agreed that they should compensate themselves within the lands which remained to the kingdom at the expense of the free cities and the ecclesiastical princes. The great German hierarchy of princely bishops and abbots now came to an end, with a solitary exception. As the ancient metropolis of Mainz had passed to France, the see of its archbishop was removed to *Regensburg*, where, under the title of *Prince-Primate*, he remained an Elector and Arch-Chancellor of the Empire. *Salzburg* became a secular electorate. The other ecclesiastical states were annexed by the neighbouring princes, and of the free cities six only were left. These were the Hanseatic towns of *Lübeck*, *Bremen*, and *Hamburg*, and the inland towns of *Frankfurt*, *Nürnberg*, and *Augsburg*. Besides Salzburg, three new Electorates arose, *Württemberg*, *Baden*, and *Hessen-Cassel*. None of these new Electors ever chose any King or Emperor. The next war led to the Peace of Pressburg, in which the Electors of Bavaria, Württemberg, and Baden, appear as allies of France, and by which those of Bavaria and Württemberg

The *Reichs-deputations-haupt-schluss*, 1803. End of the ecclesiastical principalities. The Prince-Primate of Regensburg. Salzburg a secular electorate. The Free Cities. New Electorates. Peace of Pressburg, 1805. Kingdoms of Württemberg and Bavaria.

are acknowledged as Kings. Austria was now wholly cut off from south-western Germany. Württemberg and Baden divided her Swabian possessions, while Tyrol, Trent, Brixen, together with the free city of Augsburg, fell to the lot of Bavaria. Austria received Salzburg, and the *Grand Duchy of Würzburg* was formed to compensate its Elector, himself an Austrian prince.

They divide the western lands of Austria.

Grand Duchy of Würzburg.

These were the last changes which took place while any shadow of the old Kingdom and Empire lasted. The reigning King of Germany and Emperor-elect, Francis King of Hungary and Bohemia and Archduke of Austria, had already begun to call himself '*Hereditary Emperor of Austria.*' In the treaty of Pressburg he is described by the strange title, unheard of before or after, of 'Emperor of Germany and Austria,' and the Empire itself is spoken of as a 'Germanic Confederation.' These formulæ were prophetic. The next year a crowd of princes renounced their allegiance, and formed themselves into the *Confederation of the Rhine* under the protectorate of France. The formal dissolution of the Empire followed at once. The succession which had gone on from Augustus ended; the work of Charles the Great was undone. Instead of the Frank ruling over Gaul, the Frenchman ruled over Germany. A time of confusion followed, in which boundaries were constantly shifting, states were constantly rising and falling, and new portions of German ground were being constantly added to France. At the time of the greatest extent of French dominion, the political state of Germany was on this wise. The dissolution of the Empire had released all its members from their allegiance, and the German possessions of the Kings of Denmark and

Title of 'Emperor of Austria,' 1804.

The Confederation of the Rhine, July 12, 1806.

Dissolution of the Empire, August 6, 1806.

Repeated changes, 1806–1811.

Germany in 1811–1813.

Territories of Denmark and Sweden.

CHAP. VIII.

Losses of Prussia and Austria.

Sweden had been incorporated with their several kingdoms. Hannover was wholly lost to its island sovereign; seized and lost again more than once by Prussia and by France, it passed at last wholly into the hands of the foreign power. Prussia had lost, not only its momentary possession of Hannover, but also everything west of the Elbe. Austria had yielded *Salzburg* to Bavaria, and part of her own south-western territory in Krain and Kärnthen had passed to France under the name of the

Annexations to France.

Illyrian Provinces. France too, beside all the lands west of the Rhine, had incorporated *East Friesland*, *Oldenburg*, part of *Hannover*, and the three *Hanseatic* cities. The remaining states of Germany formed the

Confederation of the Rhine.

Confederation of the Rhine. The chief among these were the four Kingdoms of *Bavaria*, *Württemberg*,

Kingdoms of Saxony and Westfalia.

Saxony, and *Westfalia*. Saxony had become a kingdom under its own Elector soon after the dissolution of the Empire: the new-made kingdom of Westfalia had a French king in Jerome Buonaparte. Besides *Mecklenburg*, *Baden*—now a Grand Duchy—*Berg*, *Nassau*, *Hessen*, and other smaller states, there were now among its members the Grand Duchy of *Würzburg*, and also a

Grand Duchy of Frankfurt.

Grand Duchy of *Frankfurt*, the possession of the Prince Primate, once of Mainz, afterwards of Regensburg.

Germany wiped out.

We may say with truth that during this time Germany had ceased to exist; its very name had vanished from the map of Europe.

Prussia was a power so thoroughly German that the fate even of its non-German possessions cannot well be separated from German geography. The same

The Kingdom of Prussia cut short, 1807.

blow which cut short the old electorate of Brandenburg no less cut short the kingdom of Prussia in its Polish acquisitions. *West-Prussia* only was left, and even here *Danzig* was cut off to form a separate republic. The other Polish territories of Prussia formed the *Duchy of Warsaw*, which was held by the new King of Saxony. Silesia thus fell back again on its half-isolated position, all the more so as it lay between the German and the Polish possessions of the Saxon king. The territory left to Prussia was now wholly continuous, without any outlying possessions; but the length of its frontier and the strange irregularity of its shape on the map were now more striking than ever.

Commonwealth of Danzig.

Duchy of Warsaw, 1806–1814.

Position of Silesia.

The liberation of Germany and the fall of Buonaparte brought with it a complete reconstruction of the German territory. Germany again rose, no longer as an Empire or Kingdom, but as a lax Confederation. Austria, the duchy whose princes had been so often chosen Emperors, became its presiding state. The boundaries of the new Confederation differed but slightly from those of the old Kingdom; but the internal divisions had greatly changed. Once more a number of princes held lands both in Germany and out of it. The so-called 'Emperor' of Austria, the Kings of Prussia, Denmark, and the Netherlands, became members of the Confederation for those parts of their dominions which had formerly been states of the Empire. In the like sort, the King of Great Britain and Ireland, having recovered his continental dominions, entered the Confederation by the title of *King of Hannover*. This new kingdom was made up of the former electorate with some additions, including *East-Friesland*. In other parts the Prussian territories were largely

The German Confederation, 1815.

Princes holding lands both within the Confederation and out of it.

Kingdom of Hannover, 1815–1866.

CHAP. VIII.

Increase of the Prussian territory. Dismemberment of Saxony.

increased. *Magdeburg* and *Halberstadt* were recovered. *Swedish Pomerania* was added to the rest of the ancient duchy; and, more important than this, a large part of the kingdom of *Saxony*, including the greater part of *Lausitz* and the formerly outlying land of *Cottbus*, was incorporated with Prussia. This change, which made the Saxon kingdom far smaller than the old electorate, altogether put an end to the peninsular position of Silesia, even as regarded the strictly German possessions of Prussia. The kingdom was at the same time rendered more compact by the recovery of part of its Polish possessions under the name of the Grand Duchy of

Posen.

Posen. In western Germany again Prussia now made

Rhenish and Westfalian territory.

great acquisitions. Its old outlying Rhenish and Westfalian possessions grew into a large and tolerably compact territory, though lying isolated from the great body of the monarchy. The greater part of the territory west of the Rhine which had been ceded to France now became Prussian. The Prussian dominions now took in the cities of *Köln*, no longer a metropolitan see, *Aachen*, *Trier*, *Münster*, and *Paderborn*. The main part of the Prussian possessions thus consisted of two detached masses, of very unequal size, but which seemed to crave for a closer geographical union. The

Neufchâtel.

Principality of *Neufchâtel*, which made the Prussian king a member of the Swiss Confederation, will be mentioned elsewhere.

Of the other powers which entered the Confederation for the German parts of their dominions, but which also had territories beyond the Confederation,

Territory recovered by Austria.

Austria recovered *Salzburg*, *Tyrol*, *Trent*, and *Brixen*, together with the south-eastern lands which had passed to France. Thus the territory of the Confederation, like that of the old Kingdom, again reached to the Hadriatic. *Denmark* entered the Confederation for *Holstein*, and for a new possession, that of *Lauenburg*, the duchy which in a manner represented ancient Saxony. The King of the *Netherlands* entered the Confederation for the Grand Duchy of *Luxemburg*, part of which however was cut off to be added to the Rhenish possessions of Prussia. Sweden, by the cession of its last remnant of *Pomerania*, ceased altogether to be a German power.

Possession of Denmark. Holstein and Lauenburg.

Luxemburg.

Sweden gives up Pomerania.

There were thus five powers whose dominions lay partly within the Confederation, partly out of it. In the case of one of these, that of Prussia, the division between German and non-German territory was purely formal. Prussia was practically a purely German power, and the greatest of purely German powers. Her rival Austria stood higher in formal rank in the Confederation, and her princes ruled over a much greater continuous territory; but here the distinction between German and non-German lands was really practical, as later events have shown. It has been found possible to shut out Austria from Germany. To shut out Prussia would have been to abolish Germany altogether. Hannover, though under a common sovereign with Great Britain, was so completely cut off from Great Britain, and had so little influence on British politics, that it was practically as much a purely German state before its separation from Great Britain as it was afterwards. In the cases of Denmark and the Netherlands, princes the greater part of whose territories lay out of Germany held adjoining territories in Germany. Here then were materials for political questions and difficulties; and in the case of Denmark, these questions and difficulties became of the highest importance.

Prussia the greatest German Power.

Austria.

Comparison of the position of Austria and Prussia.

Hannover.

Holstein and Luxemburg.

CHAP. VIII.

Kingdom of Bavaria.

Among those members of the Confederation whose territory lay wholly within Germany, the Kingdom of *Bavaria* stood first. Its newly acquired lands to the south were given back to Austria; but it made large acquisitions to the north-east. Modern Bavaria consists of a large mass of territory, Bavarian, Swabian, and Frankish, counting within its boundaries the once free cities of *Augsburg* and *Nürnberg* and the great bishoprics of *Bamberg* and *Würzburg*. Besides this, Bavaria recovered a considerable part of the ancient Palatinate west of the Rhine, which adds *Speyer* to the list of Bavarian cities. The other states which bore the kingly title, *Württemberg* and the remnant of *Saxony*, were of much smaller extent. Saxony however kept a position in many ways out of all proportion to the narrowed extent of its geographical limits. Württemberg, increased by various additions from the *Swabian* lands of *Austria* and from other smaller principalities, had, though the smallest of kingdoms, won for itself a much higher position than had been held by its former Counts and Dukes. Along with them might be ranked the Grand Duchy of *Baden*, with its strange irregular frontier, taking in Heidelberg and Constanz. Among a crowd of smaller states stand out the two Hessian principalities, the Grand Duchy of *Hessen-Darmstadt*, and *Hessen-Cassel*, whose prince still kept the title of Elector, and the Grand Duchy of *Nassau*. The Grand Duchy of *Oldenburg* nearly divided the Kingdom of Hannover into two parts. The principalities of *Anhalt* stretched into the Prussian territory between Halberstadt and the newly won Saxon lands. The Duchy of *Brunswick* helped to divide the two great masses of Prussian territory. In

[Margin notes: Her Rhenish territory. — Württemberg. — Saxony. — Baden. — Hessen. — Oldenburg. — Anhalt. — Brunswick.]

CHAP. VIII.

Mecklenburg.

the north *Mecklenburg* remained, as before, unequally divided between the Grand Dukes of *Schwerin* and *Strelitz*. Germany was thus thoroughly mapped out afresh. Some of the old names had vanished; some had got new meanings. The greater states, with the exception of Saxony, became greater. A crowd of insignificant principalities passed away. Another crowd of them remained, especially the smaller Saxon duchies in the land which had once been Thuringian. But, if we look to two of the most characteristic features of the old Empire, we shall find that one has passed away for ever, while the other was sadly weakened. No ecclesiastical principality revived in the new state of things. The territory of one of the old bishoprics, that of *Lüttich* or Liège, formerly absorbed by France, now passed wholly away from Germany, and became part of the new kingdom of Belgium. Of the free cities four did revive, but four only. The three *Hanse Towns*, no longer included in French departments, and Frankfurt, no longer a Grand Duchy, entered the Confederation as independent commonwealths. Germany, for a while utterly crushed, had come to life again; she had again reached a certain measure of national unity, which could hardly fail to become closer.[1]

No ecclesiastical principality.

Lüttich added to Belgium.

The four Free Cities.

Revival of German national life.

The Confederation thus formed lasted, with hardly any change that concerns geography, till the war of 1866. The Grand Duchy of *Luxemburg*, which had,

Division of Luxemburg, 1831.

[1] No influence was more powerful for this end than the *Zollverein* or customs union, which began in 1818 and gradually united most of the German states for certain purposes. But as it did not affect the boundaries or the governments of sovereign states, it hardly concerns geography. Neither do the strivings after more perfect union in 1848 and the following years.

by the arrangements of 1815, been held by the King of the Netherlands as a member of the German Confederation, was, on the separation of Belgium and the Netherlands, cut into two parts. Part was added to Belgium; another part, though quite detached from the kingdom of the Netherlands, was held by its king as a member of the Confederation. In 1839 he also entered it for the Duchy of Limburg. The internal movements which began in 1848, and the war in *Sleswick* and *Holstein* which began in the same time, led to no lasting geographical changes. In 1849 the Swabian principalities of *Hohenzollern* were joined to the Prussian crown. The last Danish war ended by the cession of Sleswick and Holstein, together with Lauenburg, to Prussia and Austria jointly, an arrangement in its own nature provisional. Austria ceded her right in Lauenburg to Prussia in the next year, and in the next year again came the Seven Weeks' War, and the great geographical changes which followed it. The German Confederation was abolished; Austria was shut out from all share in German affairs, and she ceded her joint right in Sleswick and Holstein to Prussia. The Northern states of Germany became a distinct Confederation under the presidency of Prussia, whose immediate dominion was increased by the annexation of the kingdom of *Hannover*, the duchy of *Nassau*, the electorate of *Hessen*, and the city of *Frankfurt*. The States south of the Main, Bavaria, Württemberg, Baden, and the southern part of Hessen-Darmstadt, remained for a while outside of the new League. The non-German dominions of Prussia, Prussia strictly so called with the Polish duchy of Posen and the newly acquired land of Sleswick, were now incorporated with the Confederation; on the other hand, all that Austria had held within

War in Sleswick and Holstein, 1848–1851.

Cession of the Duchies to Austria and Prussia, 1864.

Abolition of the Confederation. Exclusion of Austria. North-German Confederation. Cession of Sleswick and Holstein to Prussia, 1866. Prussian annexations.

All the Prussian lands admitted to the Confederation.

the Confederation was now shut out of it. *Luxemburg* also was not included in the new League, and, after some disputes, it was in the next year recognized as a neutral territory under its own duke the King of the Netherlands. The little principality of *Liechtenstein* was perhaps forgotten altogether; but, as not being included in the Confederation, nor yet incorporated with anything else, it must be looked on as becoming an absolutely independent state. Thus the geographical frontiers of Germany underwent, at a single blow, changes as great as they had undergone in the wars of the French Revolution. The geography of the presiding power of the new League was no less changed.

Settlement of Luxemburg, 1867.

Liechtenstein.

Great geographical changes, 1866.

That extraordinary extent of frontier which had hitherto been characteristic of Prussia was not wholly taken away by the new annexations, but it was greatly lessened. The kingdom, as a kingdom, is made far more compact, and the two great detached masses in which it formerly lay are now joined together. Moreover, the geographical character of Prussia becomes of much less political importance, now that her frontier marches to so great an extent on the smaller members of the League of which she is herself President. Next came the war with France, the first effect of which was the admission of the southern states of Germany into the new League, which presently took the name of an Empire, with the Prussian King as hereditary Emperor. Then by the peace with France, nearly the whole of *Elsass*, including *Strassburg*, and part of *Lotharingia*, including *Metz*, were restored to Germany. They have, under the name of *Elsass-Lothringen*, become an Imperial territory, forming part of the Empire and owning the sovereignty of the Emperor,

War with France, 1870–1871.

The German Empire. Incorporation of the Southern states.

Recovery of Elsass-Lothringen, 1871.

CHAP. VIII.

but not becoming part of the kingdom of Prussia or of any other German state. The assumption of the Imperial title could hardly be avoided in a confederation whose constitution was monarchic, and which numbered kings among its members. No name but that of Emperor could have been found to express the relation between the presiding chief and the lesser sovereigns.

The Imperial title.

The new Empire a revival of the German Kingdom, but not of the Roman Empire. Comparison of the old Kingdom and the new Empire.

Still it must be borne in mind that the new German Empire is in no sense a continuation or restoration of the Holy Roman Empire which fell sixty-four years before its creation. But it may be fairly looked on as a restoration of the old German Kingdom, the Kingdom of the East-Franks. Still, as far as geography is concerned, no change can be stranger than the change in the boundaries of Germany between the ninth century and the nineteenth. The new Empire, cut short to the north-west, south-west, and south-east, has grown somewhat to the north, and it has grown prodigiously to the north-east. Its ruling state, a state which contains such illustrious cities as Aachen, Köln, Trier, and Frankfurt, is content to call itself after an extinct heathen people whose name had most likely never reached the ears of Charles the Great. The capital of the new Empire, placed far away from any of the ancient seats of German kingship, stands in what in his day, and long after, was a Slavonic land. Germany, with its chief state bearing the name of *Prussia*, with the place of its national assemblies transferred from Frankfurt to Berlin, presents one of the strangest changes that historical geography can show us. But, strange as is the geographical change, it has come about gradually, by the natural working of historical causes. The Slavonic and Prussian lands have been germanized, while the

Name of *Prussia*.

Position of Berlin.

Formation of the new Empire.

western parts of the old kingdom which have fallen away have mostly lost their German character. Those German lands which have formed the kernel of the Swiss Confederation have risen to a higher political state than that of any kingdom or Empire. But the German lands which still remain so strangely united to the lands of the Magyar and the southern Slave await, at however distant a time, their natural and inevitable reunion. So does a Danish population in the extreme north await, with less hope, its no less natural separation from the German body. Posen, still mainly Slavonic, remains unnaturally united to a Teutonic body, but it is not likely to gain by a transfer to any other ruler. The reconstruction of the German realm in its present shape, a shape so novel to the eye, but preserving so much of ancient life and ancient history, has been the greatest historical and geographical change of our times.

§ 3. *The Kingdom of Italy.*

Small geographical importance of the kingdom as such.

We parted from the Italian kingdom at the moment of its separation from the Eastern and Western kingdoms of the Franks. Its history, as a kingdom, consists in little more than its reunion with the East-Frankish crown, and in the way in which the royal power gradually died out within its limits. There is but little to say as to any changes of frontier of the kingdom as such. As long as Germany, Italy, and Burgundy acknowledged a single king, any shiftings of the frontiers of his three kingdoms were of secondary importance. When the power of the Emperors in Italy had died out, the land became a system of independent commonwealths and principalities, which had hardly that degree of unity which could enable us to say that a certain

CHAP. VIII.

territory was added to Italy or taken from it. Even if a certain territory passed from an Italian to a German or Burgundian lord, the cession wrought a change in the frontier of this or that Italian state; it hardly wrought a change in the frontier of Italy itself. The shiftings of frontier along the whole Alpine border have been considerable; but it is only in our own day that we can say that Italy as such has become capable of extending or lessening her borders. When, in 1866, Venice and Verona were added to the Italian kingdom, that was a distinct change in the frontier of Italy. We can hardly give that name to endless earlier changes on the same marchland. In the fourteenth century, for instance, the town of *Trieste*, disputed between the patriarchs of Aquileia and the commonwealth of Venice, was acknowledged as an independent state, and it presently gave up its independence by commendation to the Duke of Austria. It is not likely that the question entered into any man's mind whether the frontiers of the German and Italian kingdoms were affected by such a change. Whether as a free city or as an Austrian lordship, Trieste remained under the superiority, formally undoubted but practically nominal, of the common sovereign of Germany and Italy, the Roman Emperor or King. Whether the nominal allegiance of the city was due to him in his German or in his Italian character most likely no one stopped to think. East and west, the Italian kingdom had no frontiers; the only question which could arise was as to the relation of the islands of Corsica and Sardinia to the kingdom itself or to any of the states which arose within it. To the south of the Imperial kingdom of Italy lay the independent Lombard duchies, and the possessions which at the time of

Changes on the Alpine frontier.

Case of Verona.

Case of Trieste, 1380.

No eastern or western frontiers.

the separation of the Empires still remained to the Eastern Cæsar. These southern lands, Lombard and Byzantine, changed in time into the Norman duchy of *Apulia* and kingdom of *Sicily*; but that kingdom, held as it was as a fief of the see of Rome, was never incorporated with the Italian kingdom of the Emperors, nor did its kings ever become the men of the Emperor. Particular Emperors in the twelfth and thirteenth centuries, in the sixteenth, and in the eighteenth, were also kings of one or both the Sicilian kingdoms; but at no time before our own day were Sicily and southern Italy incorporated with a Kingdom of Italy. When we remember that it was to the southern part of the peninsula that the name of Italy was first given, we see here a curiosity of nomenclature as remarkable as the shiftings of meaning in the names of Saxony and Burgundy.

The Norman kingdom of Sicily not an Imperial fief.

Naples and Sicily then, the Two Sicilies of later political nomenclature, lie outside our present subject. So does the commonwealth of *Venice*, except so far as Venice afterwards won a large subject territory on the Italian mainland. Both these states have to do with Italy as a geographical expression, but neither the Venetian commonwealth nor the Sicilian kingdom is Italian within the meaning of the present section. They formed no part of the Carolingian dominion. They were parts of the Eastern Empire, not of the Western. They remained attached to the New Rome after an Imperial throne had again been set up in the Old. They gradually fell away from their allegiance to the Eastern Empire, but they were never incorporated with the Empire of the West. I shall deal with them here only in their relations to the Imperial Kingdom of Italy, and treat of their special history

Venice no part of Italy.

Her Italian dominions.

Venice and the Sicilies part of the Eastern Empire.

CHAP. VIII.

elsewhere among the states which arose out of the break-up of the Eastern Empire. Again, on the north-western march of Italy a power gradually arose, partly Italian, but for a long time mainly Burgundian, which has in the end, by a strange fate, grown into a new Italian kingdom. This is the House of *Savoy*. The growth of the dominions of that house, the process by which it gradually lost territory in Burgundy and gained it in *Italy*, form another distinct subject. It will be dealt with here only in its relations to the kingdom of Italy.

The House of Savoy.

Its special history.

The Kingdom of Italy continues the Lombard kingdom.

The Italian Kingdom of the Karlings, the kingdom which was reunited to Germany under Otto the Great, was, as has been already said, a continuation of the old Lombard kingdom. It consisted of that kingdom, enlarged by the Italian lands which fell off from the Eastern Empire in the eighth century; that is by the *Exarchate* and the adjoining *Pentapolis*, and the immediate territory of *Rome* itself. The Lombard kingdom, in its full extent, took in the lands north of the Po, where we find, as elsewhere, an *Austria* to the east and a *Neustria* to the west. The Lombard Neustria stretches south of the Po, and takes in the western part of Æmilia, including the cities of Piacenza, Parma, Reggio, and Modena. The Lombard kingdom also took in *Tuscany*, a name which, as it no longer reaches to the Tiber, answers pretty nearly to its modern use. The Tuscan name has lived on; the Exarchate and Pentapolis, as having been the chief seat of the later Imperial power in Italy, got the name of *Romania*, *Romandiola*, or *Romagna*. This name also lives on; but the Lombard Neustria and Austria soon vanished from the map. Their disappearance was perhaps lucky,

Austria and Neustria. Æmilia. Tuscany.

Romagna.

as one knows not what arguments might otherwise have been built on the presence of an Austria south of the Alps. The Lombard Neustria, with the western part of Austria, taking in the cities of Bergamo and Brescia, got the special name of *Lombardy*. The rest of the Lombard Austria, after various shiftings of names taken from the principalities which rose and fell within it, came back in the end to its oldest name, *Venetia*. In the north-west corner *Iporedia* or *Ivrea* appears as a distinct march; but the Venetian march at the other corner, known at this stage as the duchy of *Friuli*, is of more importance. It takes in the county of *Trent*, the special march of *Friuli*, and the march of *Istria*. This is the corner in which the German and Italian frontier has so often fluctuated. We have seen that, after the union of the Italian and German crowns, even Verona itself was sometimes counted as German ground.

Lombardy proper.

Venetia.

Mark of Ivrea.

Duchy of Friuli.

Fluctuation of boundary at the north-west corner.

Under the German kings Italy came under the same influences as the other two Imperial kingdoms. Principalities grew up; free cities grew up; but, while in Germany the principalities were the rule and the cities the exception, in Italy it was the other way. The land gradually became a system of practically independent commonwealths. Feudal princes, ecclesiastical or temporal, flourished only in the north-western and north-eastern corners of the kingdom. But, if the range of the German cities was less wide, and their career less brilliant, than those of Italy, their freedom was more lasting. The Italian cities gradually fell under tyrants, and the tyrants gradually grew into acknowledged princes. The Bishops of Rome too, by a series of claims skilfully pressed at various times, contrived to form the greatest of ecclesiastical princi-

Comparison of Italy and Germany.

Growth of a system of commonwealths in Italy.

Tyrants grow into princes. Growth of the dominion of the Popes.

CHAP. VIII.

palities, one which stretched across the peninsula from sea to sea. The geographical history of Italy consists of four stages. In the first the kingdom fell asunder into principalities. In the second the principalities vanished before the growth of the free cities. In the third the cities were again massed into principalities, till in the fourth the principalities were at last merged in a kingdom of united Italy.

Four stages of Italian history.

Under the Saxon and Frankish Emperors the old Lombard names of Austria and Neustria pass away. Several small marches lie along the Burgundian frontier, as *Savona* on the coast, *Ivrea* among the mountains to the north-west, between them *Montferrat*, *Vasto*, and *Susa*, whose princes, as special guardians of the passage between the two kingdoms, bore the title of *Marquess in Italy*. It was in this region that the feudal princes were strongest, and that the system of free cities had the smallest developement. The Savoyard power was already beginning to grow up in the extreme north-west corner; but at this time a greater part in strictly Italian history is played by the Marquesses of Montferrat, who for many centuries kept their position as important feudal princes quite apart from the lords of the cities. In the north-east corner of the kingdom the place of the old Austria is taken by the border principalities where the Italian, the German, and the Slave all come in contact, and which fluctuated more than once between the Italian and the German crowns. We have here the great march of *Verona*, beyond it that of *Friuli*, *Trent*, the marchland of the marchland, between Verona and Bavaria, and the peninsula of *Istria* on the Slavonic side of the Hadriatic. Between the border districts on

The Marquesses of Montferrat, 938–1533.

either side lay the central land, Lombardy in the narrower sense, the chosen home of the free cities. Here, by the middle of the twelfth century, every city had practically become a separate commonwealth, owning only the most nominal superiority in the Emperor. Guelfic cities withstood the Emperor; Ghibelin cities welcomed him; but both were practically independent commonwealths. Hence came those long wars between the Swabian Emperors and the Italian cities which form the chief feature of Italian history in the second half of the twelfth century and the first half of the thirteenth. Round the younger and the elder capital, round Guelfic Milan and Ghibelin Pavia, gathered a crowd of famous names, *Como*, *Bergamo*, and *Brescia*, *Lodi*, *Crema*, and *Cremona*, *Tortona*, *Piacenza*, and *Parma*, and *Alessandria*, the trophy of republican and papal victory over Imperial power. The Veronese march was less rich in cities of the same historical importance; but both *Verona* itself and *Padua* played a great part, as the seats first of commonwealths, then of tyrants. Further north and east, the civic element was again weaker. *Trent* gradually parted off from Italy to become an ecclesiastical principality of the German kingdom; and the Patriarchs of *Aquileia* grew into powerful princes at the north-eastern corner of the Hadriatic. Within the Veronese or Trevisan march itself, the lords of *Romano* and the more important marquesses of *Este* also demand notice. Romano gave the Trevisan march its famous tyrant Eccelino in the days of Frederick the Second, and the Marquesses of Este, kinsmen of the great Saxon dukes, came in time to rank among the chief Italian princes. The extreme north-eastern march so completely fell off from Italy

Growth of the Lombard cities.

Wars of the Swabian Emperors.

Milan and Pavia.

The other Lombard cities. Alessandria, 1168.

Verona and Padua.

Trent.

Aquileia.

The lords of Romano and Este.

The north-eastern march falls off from Italy.

CHAP. VIII.

that it will be better treated in tracing the growth of the powers of Venice and Austria.

Tuscany, Romagna, and the March of Ancona.

In the more central lands of the kingdom, in the old exarchate, now known as *Romagna*, in the march variously called by the names of *Camerino*, *Fermo*, or *Ancona*, and above all in the march of *Tuscany* on the southern sea, the same developement of city life also took place, but somewhat later. North of the Apennines, along the Hadriatic coast, arose a crowd of small commonwealths which gradually changed into small tyrannies. Tuscany, on the other hand, was parted off into a few commonwealths of illustrious name. For a while one of these ran a course which stood rather apart from the common run of Italian history. *Pisa*, then one of the great maritime and commercial states of Europe, became, early in the eleventh century, a power which forestalled the crusades and won back lands from the Saracen. Though she was in every sense a city of the Italian kingdom, Pisa at this time held a position not unlike that which was afterwards held by Venice. Like her, she was a power which colonized and conquered beyond the seas, but which came only gradually to take a share in the main course of Italian affairs. Beyond the borders of Tuscany, the same position was held by *Genoa* on the Ligurian gulf. Pisa won *Sardinia* from the Saracen; Genoa, after long disputes with Pisa, obtained a more lasting possession of *Corsica*. Returning to Tuscany, three great commonwealths here grew up, which gradually divided the land between them. These were *Lucca* and *Siena*, and *Florence*, the last of Italian cities to rise to greatness, but the one which became in many ways the greatest among her fellows. In the

The Tuscan commonwealths.

Pisa; her wars with the Saracens, 1005–1115.

Genoa.

Occupation of the island of Sardinia by Pisa, and of Corsica by Genoa.

Lucca, Siena, Florence.

centre of Italy, within the bounds of old Etruria but not within those of modern Tuscany, *Perugia*, both as commonwealth and as tyranny, held a high place among Italian cities. Of Rome herself it is almost impossible to speak. She has much history, but she has little geography. Emperors were crowned there; Popes sometimes lived there; sometimes Rome appears once more as a single Latin city, waging war against Tusculum or some other of her earliest fellows. The claims of her Bishops to independent temporal power, founded on a succession of real or pretended Imperial and royal grants, lay still in the background; but they were ready to grow into reality as occasion served.

Perugia.

Rome.

Claims of the Popes.

The next stage of Italian political geography may be dated from the death of Frederick the Second, when the practical being of an Imperial kingdom in Italy may be said to have passed away. Presently begins the gradual change of the commonwealths into tyrannies, and the grouping together of many of them into larger states. We also see the beginning of more definite claims to temporal dominion on behalf of the Popes. In the course of the three hundred years between Frederick the Second and Charles the Fifth, these processes gradually changed the face of the Italian kingdom. It became in the end a collection of principalities, broken only by the survival of a few oligarchic commonwealths and by the anomalous dominion of Venice on the mainland. Between Frederick the Second and Charles the Fifth, we may look on the Empire as practically in abeyance in Italy. The coming of an Emperor always caused a great stir for the time, but it was only for the time. After the grant

Second stage, c. 1250–1530.

Growth of tyrannies.

Dominion of Spain, 1555–1701.

CHAP. VIII.

Grant of Rudolf, 1278.

Imperial and papal fiefs.

of Rudolf of Habsburg to the Popes, a distinction was drawn between Imperial and papal territory in Italy. While certain princes and commonwealths still acknowledged at least the nominal superiority of the Emperor, others were now held to stand in the same relation of vassalage to the Pope.

We must now trace out the growth of the chief states which were formed by these several processes. Beginning again in the north, it must be remembered that all this while the power of Savoy was advancing in those north-western lands where the influences which mainly ruled this period had less force than elsewhere. Montferrat too kept its old character of a feudal principality, a state whose rulers had in various ways a singular connexion with the East. As Marquesses of Montferrat had claimed the crown of Jerusalem and had worn the crown of Thessalonica, so, as if to keep even the balance between East and West, in return a branch of the Imperial house of Palaiologos came to reign at Montferrat. To the east of these more ancient principalities, two great powers of quite different kinds grew up in the old Neustria and Austria. These were the *Duchy of Milan* and the land power of *Venice*. Milan, like most other Italian cities, came under the influence of party leaders, who grew first into tyrants and then into acknowledged sovereigns. These at Milan, after the shorter domination of the Della Torre, were the more abiding house of the Visconti. Their dominion, after various fluctuations and revolutions, was finally established when the coming of the Emperor Henry the Seventh strengthened the rule of the lords of the cities throughout Italy. At the end of the fourteenth century their informal lordship was changed by a royal

Palaiologoi at Montferrat, 1306.

Duchy of Milan. Venice.

The Visconti at Milan, 1310–1447.

Grant of the Duchy by King Wenceslaus, 1395.

CHAP. VIII.

grant into an acknowledged duchy of the Empire. The dominion which they had gradually gained, and which was thus in a manner legalized, took in all the great cities of Lombardy, those especially which had formed the Lombard League against the Swabian Emperors. Pavia indeed, the ancient rival of Milan, kept a kind of separate being, and was formed into a distinct county. But the duchy granted by Wenceslaus to Gian-Galeazzo stretched far on both sides of the lake of Garda. *Belluno* at one end and *Vercelli* at the other formed part of it. It took in the mountain lands which afterwards passed to the two Alpine Confederations; it took in *Parma*, *Piacenza*, and *Reggio* south of the Po, and *Verona* and *Vicenza* in the old Austrian or Venetian land. Besides all this, *Padua*, *Bologna*, even *Genoa* and *Pisa*, passed at various times under the lordship of the Visconti. But this great power was not lasting. The Duchy of Milan, under various lords, native and foreign, lasted till the wars of the French Revolution; but, long before that time, it had been cut short on every side. The death of the first Duke was followed by a separation of the duchy of Milan and the county of Pavia between his sons, and the restored duchy never rose again to its former power. The eastern parts, Padua, Verona, Brescia, Bergamo, were gradually added to the dominion of Venice. By the middle of the fifteenth century, that republic had become the greatest power in northern Italy. In the duchy of Milan the house of Sforza succeeded that of Visconti; but the opposing claims of the Kings of France were one chief cause of the long wars which laid Italy waste in the latter years of the fifteenth century and the early years of the

County of Pavia.

Extent of the duchy.

Decrease on the death of Gian-Galeazzo, 1402.

The eastern cities won by Venice, 1406–1447.

House of Sforza, 1450–1535. Claims of the Kings of France, 1499–1525.

CHAP. VIII.

sixteenth. The duchy was tossed to and fro between the Emperor, the French King, and its own dukes. Meanwhile the dominion which was thus struggled for was cut short at the two ends. It was dismembered to the north in favour of the two Alpine Leagues, as will be hereafter shown more in detail. South of the Po, the Popes obtained *Parma* and *Piacenza*, which were afterwards granted as papal fiefs to form a duchy for the house of Farnese. Thus the Duchy of Milan which became in the end a possession of Charles the Fifth, and afterwards of his Spanish and Austrian successors, was but a remnant of the great dominion of the first Duke. The duchy underwent still further dismemberments in later times.

Cession to the Alpine Leagues, 1512–1513.

The Popes obtain Parma and Piacenza, 1515.

Duchy of Parma and Piacenza, 1545.

With Venice we have here to deal in her somewhat unnatural position as an Italian land power. This position she took on herself in the fifteenth century; in the sixteenth it led to the momentary overthrow and wonderful recovery of her dominion in the war of the League of Cambray. This land power of Venice stands quite distinct from the Venetian possessions east of the Hadriatic. With this last her possession of the coast of the *Istrian* peninsula must be reckoned, rather than with her Italian dominions. Between these lay Aquileia, Trieste, and the other lands in this quarter which gradually came under the power of Austria. The continuous Italian dominion of Venice, after her annexation of the lands of the patriarchate of Aquileia, took in *Udine* at one end and *Bergamo* at the other, besides *Crema*, and for a while *Ravenna*, as outlying possessions. Thus the Byzantine city which lay anchored off the shore of the Western Empire could for a season call the ancient seat of the Exarchate its own. But even

Land power of Venice only.

War of the League of Cambray, 1508–1517.

Istria.

Extent of Venetian dominion.

Ravenna, 1441–1530.

the continuous land territory of Venice lay in two portions. Brescia and Bergamo were almost cut off from Verona and the other possessions to the east by the Lake of Garda, the bishopric of Trent to the north, and the principality of *Mantua* to the south.

Two parts of the Venetian territory.

The mention of this last state leads us back again to the commonwealths which, like Milan, changed, first into tyrannies, and then into acknowledged principalities. It is impossible to mention all of them, and some of those which played for a while the most brilliant part in Italian history had no lasting effect on Italian geography. The rule of the house of Scala at Verona, the rule of the house of Carrara at Padua, left no lasting trace on the map. It was otherwise with the two states which bordered on the Venetian possessions to the south. The house of Gonzaga held sovereign power at *Mantua*, first as captains, then as marquesses, then as dukes, for nearly four hundred years. Of greater fame was the power that grew up in the house of *Este*, the Italian branch of the house of Welf. Their position is one specially instructive, as illustrating the various tenures by which dominion was held. The marquess of Este, feudal lords of that small principality, became, after some of the usual fluctuations, permanent lords of the cities of *Ferrara* and *Modena*. About the same time they lost their original holding of Este, which passed to Padua, and with Padua to Venice. Thus the nominal marquess of Este and real lord of Ferrara was not uncommonly spoken of as Marquess of Ferrara. In the fifteenth century these princes rose to ducal rank; but by that time the new doctrine of the temporal dominion of the Popes had made great advances. Modena, no man doubted, was a city of the

Rule of the Scala at Verona, 1260–1387; of the Carrara at Padua, 1318–1405; of the Gonzaga at Mantua, 1328–1708. Marquesses, 1433; Dukes, 1530. House of Este.

The lords of Ferrara and Modena, 1264–1288. Duchy of Modena, 1453. Duchy of Ferrara, 1471.

Duchy of Modena, 1453. Duchy of Ferrara, 1471.

Loss of Rovigo, 1484.

Empire; but Ferrara was now held to be under the supremacy of the Pope. The Marquess Borso had thus to seek his elevation to ducal rank from two separate lords. He was created Duke of Modena and Reggio by the Emperor, and afterwards Duke of Ferrara by the Pope. This difference of holding, as we shall presently see, led to the destruction of the power of the house of Este. In the times with which we are now concerned, their dominions lay in two masses. To the west lay the duchy of Modena and Reggio; apart from it to the east lay the duchy of Ferrara. Not long after its creation, this last duchy was cut short by the surrender of the border-district of *Rovigo* to Venice.

Cities of Romagna.

Bologna, Perugia, Rimini.

The Duchy of Urbino, 1478–1631.

Expansion of the papal dominions.

Between the two great duchies of the house of Este lay *Bologna*, in the land which gradually changed from *Romania* in one sense into *Romagna* in another. Like most other Italian cities, the commonwealths of the Exarchate and the Pentapolis changed into tyrannies, and their petty princes were one by one overthrown by the advancing power of the Popes. Every city had its dynasty; but it was only a few, like the houses of *Bentevoglio* at *Bologna*, of *Baglioni* at *Perugia*, and *Malatesta* at *Rimini*, that rose to any historical importance. One only combined historical importance with acknowledged princely rank. The house of *Montefeltro*, lords of *Urbino*, became acknowledged dukes by papal grants. From them the duchy passed to the house of La Rovere, and it flourished under five princes of the two dynasties. Gradually, by successive annexations, the papal dominions, before the middle of the sixteenth century, stretched from the Po to Tarracina. Ferrara and Urbino still remained distinct states, but states which were confessedly held as fiefs of the Holy See.

Creation of the Tuscan cities.

To the West, in Tuscany, the phænomena are somewhat different. The characteristic of this part of Italy was the grouping together of the smaller cities under the power of the larger. Nearly all the land came in the end under princely rule; but both acknowledged princely rule and the tyrannies out of which it sprang came into importance in Tuscany later than anywhere else. *Lucca* had in the fourteenth century a short time of greatness under her illustrious tyrant Castruccio; but, before and after his day, she plays, as a commonwealth, only a secondary part in Italy. Still she remained a commonwealth, though latterly an oligarchic one, through all changes down to the general crash of the French Revolution. *Pisa* kept for a while her maritime greatness, and her rivalry with the Ligurian commonwealth of *Genoa*. Genoa, less famous in the earliest times, proved a far more lasting power. She established her dominion over the coast on both sides of her, and kept her island of Corsica down to modern times. Physical causes caused the fall of the maritime power of Pisa; Sardinia passed from her to become a kingdom of the House of Aragon, and she herself passed under the dominion of *Florence*. This last illustrious city, the greatest of Tuscan and even of Italian commonwealths, begins to stand forth as the foremost of republican states about the time when her forerunner Milan came under the rule of tyrants. She extended her dominion over *Volterra*, *Arezzo*, and many smaller places, till she became mistress of all northern Tuscany. To the south the commonwealth of *Siena* also formed a large dominion. In Florence the rule of the Medici grew step by step into a hereditary tyranny; but it was an intermittent tyranny, one which was sup-

Lucca under Castruccio Castracani, 1320–1338.

Pisa.

Genoa.

Her rule in Corsica.

Sardinia ceded to Aragon, 1428.

Pisa subject to Florence, 1416.

Greatness of Florence.

Siena.

Rule of the Medici. 1434–1494. 1512–1527.

CHAP. VIII.

ported only by foreign force, and which was overturned whenever Florence had strength to act for herself. It was only after her last overthrow by the combined powers of Pope and Cæsar that she became, under Alexander, the first duke of the house of Medici, an acknowledged principality. Cosmo the First, the second duke, annexed Siena, and all the territory of that commonwealth, except the lands known as *Stati degli Presidi*, that is the isle of *Elba* and some points on the coast. These became parts of the kingdom of Naples; that is, at that time, parts of the dominion of Spain. The state thus formed by Cosmo was one of the most considerable in Italy, taking in the whole of Tuscany except the territory of Lucca and the lands which became Spanish. Its ruler presently exchanged by papal authority the title of Duke of Florence for that of Grand Duke of Tuscany.

Alexander, Duke of Florence, 1530.

Cosmo annexes Siena, 1557.

Elba, &c.

Cosmo Grand Duke of Tuscany, 1567.

§ 4. *The Later Geography of Italy.*

Abeyance of the kingdom of Italy, 1530–1805.

Under Charles the Fifth it might have seemed that both the Roman Empire and the kingdom of Italy had come to life again. A prince who wore both crowns was practically master of Italy. But though the power of the Emperor was restored, the power of the Empire was not. In truth we may look on all notion of a kingdom of Italy in the elder sense as having passed away with the coronation of Charles himself. The thing had passed away long before; after the pageant at Bologna the name was not heard for more than two centuries and a half. Italy became truly a 'geographical expression;' the land consisted of a number of principalities and a few commonwealths, all nominally independent, some more or less practically so, but the more part of which were under foreign influence, and

Italy a geographical expression.

Changes among the Italian states.

some of them were actually ruled by foreign princes. The states of Italy were united, divided, handed over from one ruler to another, according to the fluctuations of war and diplomacy, without any regard either to the will of the inhabitants or to the authority of any central power. A practically dominant power there was during the greater part of this period; but it was not the power of even a nominal King of Italy. For a long time that dominant power was held by the House of Austria in its two branches. The supremacy of Charles in Italy passed, not to his Imperial brother, but to his Spanish son. Then followed the long dominion of the Spanish branch of the Austrian house; then came the less thorough dominion of the German branch. This last was a dominion strictly of the House of Austria as such, not of the Empire or of either of the Imperial kingdoms. And now that the name of Italy means merely a certain surface on the map, we must take some notice, so far as they regard Italian history, at once of Savoy at one end and of the Sicilian kingdoms at the other. From this time both of them have a more direct bearing on Italian history.

Dominion of Spain, 1555–1701; of Austria, 1713–1793.

Massing of Italy into larger states.

By the time of the coronation of Charles the Fifth, or at least within the generation which could remember his coronation, the greater part of Italy had been massed into a few states, which, as compared with the earlier state of things, were of considerable size. A few smaller principalities and lordships still kept their place, of which one of the smallest, that of *Monaco* in the extreme south-west, has lived on to our own time. So has the small commonwealth of *San Marino*, surrounded first by the dominions of the Popes and now by the modern kingdom. But such states as these were mere

Monaco

San Marino.

CHAP. VIII.

Dominion of Venice on the mainland, 1406–1797.

survivals. In the north-east, Venice kept her power on the mainland untouched, from the recovery of her dominions after the league of Cambray down to her final fall. By the treaty of Bologna she lost *Ravenna*; she lost too *Otranto*, *Brindisi*, *Trani*, and other towns on that coast which she had gained during the wars of Naples; but her continuous dominion, both properly Venetian and Lombard, remained. The duchy of *Milan* to the west of her was held in succession by the two branches of the House of Austria, first the Spanish and then the German. But the duchy, as an Austrian possession, was constantly cut short towards the west by the growing power of Savoy. For a while the Milanese and Savoyard states were conterminous only during a small part of their frontier. The marquisate of *Montferrat*, as long as it remained a separate principality, lay between the southern parts of the two states. On the failure of the old line of marquesses, Montferrat was disputed between the Dukes of Savoy and Mantua. Adjudged to Mantua, and raised into a duchy by Imperial authority, it was still claimed, and partly conquered, by Savoy. At last, by one of the last exercises of Imperial authority in Italy, the duchy of Mantua itself was held to be forfeited to the Empire; that is, it became an Austrian possession. At the same time the Imperial authority confirmed Montferrat to Savoy. The Austrian dominions in Italy were thus extended to the south-east by the accession of the Mantuan territory; but the whole western frontier of the Milanese now lay open to Savoyard advance. The same treaties which confirmed Montferrat to Savoy and Milan to Austria also dismembered Milan in favour of Savoy. A corner of the duchy to the south-west,

She loses her outlying Italian possessions, 1530.

Duchy of Milan: Spanish, 1540–1706; Austrian, 1706–1796.

Advance of Savoy towards Milan.

Montferrat.

United to Mantua 1536, but claimed by Savoy, 1613–1631.

Mantua forfeited to the Empire, and Montferrat joined to Savoy, 1708–1713.

First dismemberment of Milan in favour of Savoy, 1713.

Alessandria and the neighbouring districts, were now given to Savoy; the Peace of Vienna further cut off *Novara* to the north and *Tortona* to the south. The next peace, that of Aix-la-Chapelle, gave up all west of the Ticino, which river became a permanent frontier.

Further cessions, 1738.

Among the other states, the duchy of *Parma* and *Piacenza* was, on the extinction of the house of Farnese, handed over to princes of the Spanish branch of the Bourbons. *Modena* and *Ferrara* remained united, till Ferrara was annexed as an escheated fief to the dominions of its spiritual overlord. But the house of Este still reigned over Modena with *Reggio* and *Mirandola*, while its dominions were extended to the sea by the addition of *Massa* and other small possessions between Lucca and Genoa. The duchy in the end passed by female succession to the House of Austria. *Genoa* and *Lucca* remained aristocratic commonwealths; but Genoa lost its island possession of *Corsica*, which passed to France. The Grand Duchy of *Tuscany* remained in the house of Medici, till it was assigned to Duke Francis of Lorraine, afterwards the Emperor Francis the First, and after that it remained in the House of Habsburg-Lorraine. The States of the Church, after the annexation of Ferrara, were in the next century further enlarged by the annexation of the duchy of Urbino.

Parma and Piacenza given to the Spanish Bourbons, 1731–1749.
Ferrara confiscated to the Popes, 1598.
1718.
1771–1803.
Corsica ceded to France, 1768.
Extinction of the Medici, 1737.
Francis of Lorraine Grand Duke of Tuscany.
Urbino annexed by the Popes, 1631.

Thus, except on the frontier of Piedmont and Milan, the whole time from Charles the Fifth to the French Revolution was, within the old kingdom of Italy, much less remarkable for changes in the geographical frontiers of the several states than for the way in which they are passed to and fro from one master to another. This is yet more remarkable, if we look to the southern part of the peninsula, and to the two great

1530–1797.
Comparatively little geographical change.

islands which in modern geography we have learned to look on as attached to Italy. The Norman kingdom which, by steps which will be told elsewhere, grew up to the south of the Imperial Kingdom of Italy, has hardly ever changed its boundaries, except by the various separations and unions of the insular and the continental kingdom. Even the outlying papal possession of *Benevento* went back after each war to its ecclesiastical master. But the shiftings, divisions, and reunions of the Two Sicilies and of the island of Sardinia have been endless. The Sicilian kingdom of the Norman and Swabian kings, containing both the island and the provinces on the mainland, passed unchanged to Charles of Anjou. The revolt of the island split the kingdom into two, one insular, one continental, each of which called itself the *Kingdom of Sicily*, though the continental realm was more commonly known as the *Kingdom of Naples.* The wars of the fourteenth and fifteenth centuries caused endless changes of dynasty in the continental kingdom, but no changes of frontier. Under the famous Alfonso in the fifteenth century, Aragon, Sardinia, and the continental Sicily, were three kingdoms under one sovereign, while the insular Sicily was ruled by another branch of the same house. Then continental Sicily passed to an illegitimate branch of the House of Aragon, while Sardinia and insular Sicily were held by the legitimate branch, which ruled in their Spanish kingdom. The French invasion under Charles the Eighth and the long wars that followed, the conquests, the restorations, the schemes of division, all ended in the union of both the Sicilian kingdoms, now known as the *Kingdom of the Two Sicilies*, along with Sardinia, as part of the great

The Norman kingdom of Sicily.

Benevento.

Charles of Anjou, 1265. Revolt of the island of Sicily, 1282. The two kingdoms.

Union of Aragon, Sardinia, and continental Sicily under Alfonso, 1442. Aragonese kings of the island, 1296–1442. 1458–1701. Wars beginning with Charles the Eighth, 1494–1528.

Kingdom of the Two Sicilies

Spanish monarchy. A momentary separation of the insular kingdom, in order to give the husband of Mary of England royal rank while his father yet reigned, is important only as the first formal use of the title of *King of Naples*. In the division of the Spanish monarchy, Sardinia and Naples fell to the lot of the Austrian House, while Sicily was given to the Duke of Savoy, who thus gained substantial kingly rank. Presently the kings of the two island kingdoms made an exchange; Sardinia passed to Savoy, and the Emperor Charles the Sixth ruled, like Frederick the Second and Charles the Fifth, over both Sicilies. Lastly, the joint kingdom was handed over from an Austrian to a new Spanish master, the first of the line of Neapolitan Bourbons. Thus, at the end of the last century, the Two Sicilies formed a distinct and united kingdom, while Sardinia formed the outlying realm of the Duke of Savoy and Prince of Piedmont. His kingdom was of far less value than his principality or his duchy. But, as Sardinia gave their common sovereign his highest title, the Sardinian name often came in common speech to be extended to the continental dominions of its king.

Spanish, 1556–1701. 1554–1555.

Sardinia and Naples Austrian. Duke of Savoy king of Sicily, 1713.

Exchange of Sicily and Sardinia, 1718.

The Spanish Bourbons, 1735–1806. 1817–1860.

Use of the name *Sardinia*.

This period, a period of change, but of comparatively slight geographical change, was followed by a time when, in Italy as in Germany, boundaries were changed, new names were invented or forgotten names revived, when old landmarks were rooted up, and thrones were set up and cast down, with a speed which baffles the chronicler. The first strictly geographical change which was wrought in Italy by the revolutionary wars was a characteristic one. A *Cispadane Republic*, the first of a number of momentary commonwealths bear-

Time of the Revolution, 1797–1814.

Cispadane Republic, 1796.

CHAP. VIII.

ing names dug up from the recesses of bygone times, took in the duchy of Modena and the Papal Legations of Romagna. Without exactly following the same boundaries, it answered roughly to the old Exarchate.

Transpadane Republic, 1797.

Then the French victories over Austria caused the Austrian duchies of Milan and Mantua to become a *Transpadane Republic.* Then Venice was wiped out at

Treaty of Campo Formio, 1797. Cisalpine Republic.

Campo Formio, and her Lombard possessions were joined together with the two newly made commonwealths, to form a *Cisalpine Republic.* But the same treaty wrought another change which was more distinctly geographical.

Venice surrendered to Austria.

Venice and the eastern part of her possessions on the mainland, the old Venetia, the Lombard *Austria*, was now handed over to the modern state which bore the latter name. This change may be looked on as distinctly cutting short the boundaries of Italy. The duchy of Milan in Austrian hands had been an outlying part of the Austrian dominions; but Venetia marches on the older territory of the Austrian house, and was thus more completely severed from Italy. The whole north of the Hadriatic coast thus became Austrian in the modern sense. One Italian commonwealth—for Venice had long counted as Italian—was thus handed over to a foreign king. But elsewhere, at this stage of revolutionary progress, the fashion ran in favour of the creation of local commonwealths. The

Ligurian Republic, 1797. Parthenopæan Republic.

dominions of Genoa became a *Ligurian Republic*; Naples became a *Parthenopæan Republic*; Rome herself exchanged for a moment the memories of kings, consuls, emperors, and pontiffs, to become the head of a

Tiberine Republic, 1798–1801.

Tiberine Republic. Piedmont was overwhelmed; the greater part was incorporated with France. Some small parts were added to the neighbouring republics, and the king of Sardinia withdrew to his island kingdom. Amid this crowd of new-fangled states and new-fangled names, ancient San Marino still lived on.

CHAP. VIII.

Piedmont joined to France, 1798–1800.

Thus far revolutionary Italy followed the example of revolutionary France, and the new states were all at least nominal commonwealths. In the next stage, when France came under the rule of a single man, above all when that single ruler took on him the Imperial title, the tide turned in favour of monarchy. In Rome and Naples it had already turned so in another way. By help of the Tzar and the Sultan, the new republics vanished, and the old rulers, Pope and King, came back again. And now France herself began to create kingdoms instead of commonwealths. Parma was annexed to France, and its Duke was sent to rule in Tuscany by the title of *King of Etruria*. Presently Italy herself gave her name to a kingdom. The Cisalpine republic, further enlarged by Venice and the other territory ceded to Austria at Campo Formio, enlarged also at one end by the *Valtellina*, the valley of the upper Adda, and the former bishopric of *Trent*, and at the other end by the march of *Ancona*, became the *Kingdom of Italy*. Its King, the first since Charles the Fifth who had worn the Italian crown, was no other than the new ruler of France, the self-styled 'Emperor.' But, in Buonaparte's later distributions of Italian territory, it was not his Italian kingdom, but his French 'empire,' whose frontiers were extended. The Ligurian Republic was annexed; so before long was the new kingdom of Etruria; *Lucca* meanwhile was made into a grand duchy for the conqueror's sister. Lastly, Rome itself, with what was left of the papal dominions, was incorporated with the French

Restoration of the Pope and the King of the Two Sicilies, 1801.

Kingdom of Etruria, 1801–1808.

Kingdom of Italy, 1805–1814.

Buonaparte king of Italy.

Annexation of Liguria, 1805; of Etruria, 1808.

Grand duchy of Lucca.

Incorporation of Rome

CHAP. VIII.

and France, 1809.

dominion. The work alike of Cæsar and of Charles was wiped out from the Eternal City. The Empire of the Gauls, which Civilis had dreamed of more than seventeen centuries before, had come at last.

Kingdoms of Naples and Sicily, 1806. 1809. *Stati degli Presidi.* Benevento.

The fate of the remainder of the peninsula had been already sealed before Rome became French. The kingdom of the Two Sicilies fell asunder. The Bourbon king kept his island, as the Savoyard king kept his. The continental kingdom passed, as a *Kingdom of Naples*, first to Joseph Buonaparte, and then to Joachim Murat. But the outlying Tuscan possessions of the Sicilian crown had already passed to France, and *Benevento*, the outlying papal possession in the heart of the kingdom, became a separate principality.

Italy under French dominion.

Part incorporated with France.

Extent of the kingdom of Italy.

Kingdom of Naples.

Revival of

Thus all Italy—unless we count the island kingdoms of Sardinia and Sicily as parts of Italy—was brought under French dominion in one form or another. But of that dominion there were three varieties. The whole western part of the land, from Ivrea to Tarracina—unless it is worth while to except the new Lucchese duchy—was formally incorporated with France. The north-eastern side, from Bozen to Ascoli, formed a Kingdom of Italy, distinct from France, but held by the same sovereign. And this Kingdom of Italy was further increased to the north by part of those Italian lands which had become Swiss and German. Southern Italy, the Kingdom of Naples, remained in form an independent kingdom; but it was held by princes who could not be looked on as anything but the humble vassals of their mighty kinsman. Never had Italy been brought more completely under foreign dominion. Still, in a part at least of the land, the name of Italy, and the shadow of a Kingdom of Italy, had been revived.

And, as names and shadows are not without influence in human affairs, the mere existence of an Italian state, called by the Italian name, did something. The creation of a sham Italy was no unimportant step towards the creation of a real one.

the Italian name. Its effects.

The settlement of Italy after the fall of Buonaparte was far more strictly a return to the old state of things than the contemporary settlement of Germany. Italy remained a geographical expression. Its states were, as before, independent of one another. They were practically dependent on a foreign power: but they were in no way bound together, even by the laxest federal tie. The main principle of settlement was that the princes who had lost their dominions should be restored, but that the commonwealths which had been overthrown should not be restored. Only harmless San Marino was allowed to live on. Venice, Lucca, and Genoa, remained possessions of princes. The sovereign of Hungary and Austria, now calling himself 'Emperor' of his archduchy, carved out for himself an Italian kingdom which bore the name of the *Kingdom of Lombardy and Venice.* On the strength of this, the Austrian, like his French predecessor, took upon him to wear the Italian crown. The new kingdom consisted of the older Italian possessions of Austria, that is the duchies of Milan and Mantua, enlarged by the former possessions of Venice, which had become Austrian at Campo Formio. The old boundary between Germany and Italy was restored. Trent, Aquileia, Trieste, were again severed from Italy. They remained possessions of the same prince as Milan and Venice, but they formed no part of his Lombardo-Venetian kingdom.

Settlement of, 1814–1815.

No tie between the Italian states.

The princes restored, but not the commonwealths.

Kingdom of Lombardy and Venice.

Its extent.

CHAP. VIII.

On another frontier, where restoration would have had to be made to a commonwealth, the arrangements were less conservative, and the *Valtellina* remained part of the new kingdom. The Ticino formed, as before, the boundary towards Piedmont. The King of Sardina came again into possession of this last country, enlarged by the former dominions of *Genoa*. This gave him the whole Ligurian seaboard, except where the little principality of *Monaco* still went on. *Parmà*, *Modena*, and *Tuscany* again became separate duchies. *Lucca* remained a duchy alongside of them. The family arrangements by which these states were handed about to this and that widow do not concern geography; all that need be marked is that, by virtue of one of these compacts, Lucca was in the end added to Tuscany. That grand-duchy was further increased by the addition of the former outlying possessions of the Sicilian crown, except the island of Elba, which for a moment became a new and narrower Empire for Buonaparte himself. On his second fall, the island was added to the Tuscan duchy. The Pope came back to all his old Italian possessions, outlying Benevento included. The Two Sicilies were again united by the restoration of the Kingdom of Naples to the Bourbon king. Thus was formed the Italy of 1815, an Italy which, save in the sweeping away of its commonwealths, and the consequent extension of Sardinian and Austrian territory, differed geographically but little from the Italy of 1748. But in 1815 there were hopes which had had no being in 1748. Italy was divided on the map; but she had made up her mind to be one.

Genoa annexed to Piedmont.

Monaco.

Tuscany, Parma, Modena, Lucca.

Lucca annexed to Tuscany.

The Papal states.

The Two Sicilies.

The union of Italy was at last to come from one of

The union

CHAP. VIII.

those corners which in earlier history we have looked on as being hardly Italian at all. It was not Milan or Florence or Rome which was to grow into the new Italy. That function was reserved for a princely house whose beginnings had been Burgundian rather than Italian, whose chief territories had long lain on the Burgundian side of the Alps, but which had gradually put on an Italian character, and which had now become the one national Italian dynasty. The Italian possessions of the Savoyard house, Piedmont, Genoa, and the island of Sardinia, now formed one of the chief Italian states, and the only one whose rule, if still despotic, was not foreign. Savoy, by ceasing to be Savoy, was to become Italy.

of Italy comes from Piedmont.

The movements of 1848 in Italy, like those in Germany, led to no lasting changes on the map: but they do so far affect geography that new states were actually founded, if only for a moment. Rome, Venice, Milan, were for a while republics, and the Two Sicilies were for a while separated. In the next year all came back as before. The next lasting change on the map was that which at last restored a real Kingdom of Italy.

Movements of 1848.

Momentary commonwealths.

The joint campaign of France and Sardinia won *Lombardy* for the Sardinian kingdom. Lombardy was now defined as that part of the Lombardo-Venetian kingdom which lay west of the Mincio, except that Mantua was left to Austria. A French scheme for an Italian confederation came to nothing. Tuscany, Modena, Parma, and Romagna voted their own annexation to Piedmont. The Two Sicilies were won by Garibaldi, and the kingly title of Sardinia was merged in that of the restored Kingdom of Italy. This new Italian kingdom was, by the addition of the Sicilies, extended over lands which had never been

Campaign of 1859.

Union of the smaller states, 1860.

CHAP. VIII.

Addition of the Sicilies.

Cession of Savoy and Nizza to France.

part of the elder Italian kingdom. But Venetia was still cut off; the Pope kept the lands on each side of Rome, the so-called *Patrimony* and the *Campagna*. France, too, annexed the lands, strictly Burgundian rather than Italian, of *Savoy* and *Nizza*. The Italian kingdom was thus again called into being; but it had not yet come to perfection. Italy had ceased to be a geographical expression; but the Italian frontier still presented some geographical anomalies.

Recovery of Venetia, 1866; of Rome, 1870.

Part of the old kingdom not yet recovered.

The war between Prussia and Austria gave Venetia to Italy; the war between Germany and France allowed Italy to recover Rome. The two great gaps in her frontier were thus made good; but, to say nothing of the annexations made by France, a large region, lying within the bounds of the old Italian kingdom, still remains outside its modern revival.[1] Trent, Aquileia, Trieste, Istria, are still parts, not of an Italian kingdom, not of a German kingdom, confederation, or empire, but of an Austro-Hungarian monarchy. Otherwise the Italian kingdom has formed itself, and it has taken its place among the great powers of Europe. Yet the whole peninsula does not form part of the Italian kingdom. Surrounded on every side by that kingdom, the commonwealth of *San Marino*, like Rhodes or Byzantium under the early Cæsars, still keeps its ancient freedom.

San Marino remains free.

§ 5. *The Kingdom of Burgundy.*

Union of Burgundy with Germany and Italy, 1032.

Dying out of the kingdom.

The Burgundian Kingdom, which was united with those of Germany and Italy after the death of its last separate king Rudolf the Third, has had a fate unlike that of any other part of Europe. Its memory, as a separate state, has gradually died out. The greater part

[1] Cp. *Historical Essays*, third series, p. 206.

of its territory has been swallowed up bit by bit by a neighbouring power, and the small part which has escaped that fate has long lost all trace of its original name or its original political relations. By a long series of annexations, spreading over more than five hundred years, the greater part of the kingdom has gradually been incorporated with France. Of what remains, a small corner forms part of the modern kingdom of Italy, while the rest still keeps its independence in the form of the commonwealths which make up the western cantons of Switzerland. These cantons, in fact, are the truest modern representatives of the Burgundian kingdom. And it is on the Confederation of which they form a part, interposed as it is between France, Italy, the new German Empire, and the modern Austrian monarchy, as a central state with a guaranteed neutrality, that some trace of the old function of Burgundy, as the middle kingdom, is thrown. This function it shares with the Lotharingian lands at the other end of the Empire, which now form part of the equally neutral kingdom of Belgium, lands which, oddly enough, themselves became Burgundian in another sense.

Chiefly annexed by France; part Italian; part Swiss. Burgundy represented by Switzerland. Neutrality of Switzerland and Belgium.

The Burgundian Kingdom, lying between the Alps, the Saône and the Rhone, and the Mediterranean, might be thought to have a fair natural boundary. And, while it kept any shadow of separate being, its boundaries did not greatly change. They were however somewhat fluctuating on the side of the Western kingdom, being sometimes bounded by the Rhone and sometimes reaching to the line of hills to the west of it. They were also, as we have seen, somewhat fluctuating on the side of Germany. At this end the kingdom took in some German-speaking districts; otherwise

Boundaries of the kingdom. Fluctuation of its frontier.

CHAP. VIII.

the language was Romance, including several dialects of the tongue of *Oc*.

Chiefly Romance-speaking. County Palatine. Lesser Burgundy.

The northern part of the kingdom, answering to the former *Regnum Jurense*, formed two chief states, the *County Palatine of Burgundy*—the modern *Franche-Comté*—and the *Lesser Burgundy*, roughly taking in western Switzerland and northern Savoy. On the Mediterranean lay the great county of *Provence*, with a number of smaller counties lying between it and the two northern principalities. But the great characteristic of the land was that, next to Italy, no part of Europe contained so many considerable cities lying near together. Many of these at different times strove more or less successfully after a republican independence, and a few have kept it to our own day.

Provence.

The Free Cities.

Little real unity in the kingdom.

But, though the Burgundian kingdom might be thought to have, on three sides at least, a good natural frontier, it had but little real unity. The northern part naturally clave to its connexion with the Empire much longer than the southern. The *County Palatine* of Burgundy often passed from one dynasty to another, and it is remarkable for the number of times that it was held as a separate state by several of the great princes of Europe. It was held by the Emperor Frederick Barbarossa in right of his wife; the marriage of one of his female descendants carried it to Philip the Fifth of France. Then it became united with the French duchy of Burgundy under the dukes of the House of Valois. Saving a momentary French occupation after the death of Charles the Bold, it remained with them and their Austrian and Spanish representatives. Among these it had a second Imperial Count in the person of Charles the Fifth. But,

The Burgundian Palatinate.

Held by the Emperor Frederick, 1156–1189; by Philip of France, 1315–1330. United with the French Duchy. 1477.

Held by the House of Austria. Charles the Fifth Count of Burgundy.

through all these changes of dynasty, it remained an acknowledged fief of the Empire, till its annexation to France under Lewis the Fourteenth. The capital of this county, it must be remembered, was *Dole*. The ecclesiastical metropolis of *Besançon*, though surrounded by the county, remained a free city of the Empire from the days of Frederick Barbarossa to those of Ferdinand the Third. It was then merged in the county, and along with the county it passed to France. And it should be noticed that a small Burgundian land in this quarter, the county of *Montbeliard* or *Mümpelgard*, first as a separate state, then in union with the duchy of Württemberg, kept its allegiance to the Empire till the wars of the French Revolution, when it was annexed to France and was never restored.

Annexed to France, 1674.

Dole the capital of the county.

Besançon a Free Imperial city. 1189–1651.

United to France.

Mont-beliard.

While the Burgundian Palatinate thus kept its being as an unit in European geography, the *Lesser Burgundy* to the south-west of it had a different history. The geography here gets somewhat confused through the fact that this Lesser Burgundy, which in the twelfth century passed under the power of the *Dukes of Zähringen* in Swabia as *Rectors*, took in some districts which were not parts of the Burgundian kingdom. The eastern part of the kingdom itself was of German speech, and its frontier towards the German duchy of Alemannia or Swabia was somewhat fluctuating. The Lesser Burgundy, as an administrative division, stretched much further to the east than the old kingdom. Thus *Basel*, as well as the foundations of the House of Zähringen at *Bern* and *Freiburg*, stood on strictly Burgundian ground, while the city of *Luzern* and the land of *Unterwalden* come under the head of the Lesser Burgundy, without forming part of the Burgundian kingdom. These lands

The Lesser Burgundy.

The eastern part German.

Cities of the Lesser Burgundy.

Dukes of Zähringen. End of their house, 1218. Break-up of the duchy. Savoyard territory.

Bishops, Counts, and Free Cities.

The Free Lands.

long kept up their connexion with the Empire, though the Lesser Burgundy did not long remain as a separate unit. When the House of Zähringen came to an end, the country began to split up into small principalities and free cities which gradually grew into independent commonwealths. The counts of Savoy, of whom more presently, acquired a large territory on both sides of the Lake of Geneva. Other considerable princes were the bishops of *Basel*, *Lausanne*, *Geneva*, and *Sitten*, the counts of *Geneva*, *Kyburg*, *Gruyères*, and *Neufchâtel*. *Basel*, *Solothurn*, and *Bern*, were Imperial cities. The complicated relations between the Bishops and the city of Geneva hindered that city from having a strict right to that title. In Unterwalden and in *Wallis*, notwithstanding the possessions and claims of various spiritual and temporal lords, the most marked feature was the retention of the old rural independence. Of the cities in this region, Luzern, Bern, Freiburg, Solothurn, and Basel, all gradually became members of the *Old League of High Germany*, the groundwork of the modern Swiss Confederation. The Savoyard lands north of the lake were conquered by Bern and Freiburg in the sixteenth century, a conquest which also secured the independence of Geneva. All these lands, after going through the intermediate stage of allies or subjects of some or other of the confederate cantons, have in modern times become independent cantons themselves. This process of annexation and liberation will be traced more fully when we come to the history of the Swiss Confederation.

The Old League of High Germany.

Conquests of Bern and Freiburg from Savoy, 1536.

The Burgundian cantons of Switzerland.

To the south of this group of states, and partly intermingled with them, lay another group, lying partly within the northern and partly within the southern

Burgundian kingdom, which gradually grew into a great power. These were the states which were united step by step under the Counts of *Maurienne*, afterwards Counts of *Savoy*. When their dominions were at their greatest extent, they held south of the Lake of Geneva, besides Maurienne and Savoy strictly so called, the districts of *Aosta*, *Tarantaise*, the *Genevois*, *Chablais*, and *Faucigny*, together with *Vaud* and *Gex* north of the lake. Thus grew up the power of Savoy, which has already been noticed in its purely Italian aspect, but which must receive fuller separate treatment in a section of its own.

Growth of Savoy.

Burgundian possessions of its counts.

The remainder of the Burgundian Kingdom consisted of a number of small states stretching from the southern boundary of the Burgundian county to the Mediterranean. North of the Rhone lay the districts of *Bresse* and *Bugey*, which passed at various times to the House of Savoy. Southwards on the Rhone lay a number of small states, among which the most important in history are the archbishopric, the county, and the free city of *Lyons*, the county or *Dauphiny* of *Vienne* and the city of *Vienne*, the county or principality of *Orange*, the city of *Avignon*, the county of *Venaissin*, the free city of *Arles*, the capital of the kingdom, the free city of *Massalia* or *Marseilles*, the county of *Nizza* or *Nice*, and the great county or marquisate of *Provence*. In this last power lay the first element of danger, especially to the republican independence of the free cities. After being held by separate princes of its own, as well as by the Aragonese kings, it passed by marriage into the hands of a French prince, Charles of Anjou, the conqueror of Sicily, and also the destroyer of the second freedom of Massalia. The possession of the greatest

States between the Palatinate and the Mediterranean.

Bresse and Bugey become Savoyard. Bugey, 1137–1344 Bresse, 1272–1402.

Lyons, Vienne, Orange, &c.

Provence.

Changes of dynasty.

The Angevins, 1246.

CHAP. VIII.

Growing French connexion.

member of the Burgundian kingdom by a French ruler, though it made no immediate change in the formal state of things, gave fresh strength to every tendency which tended to withdraw the Burgundian lands from their allegiance to the Empire and to bring them, first into connexion with France, and then into actual incorporation with the French kingdom.

Process of French annexation

Step by step, though by a process which was spread over many centuries, all the principalities and commonwealths of the Burgundian kingdom, save the lands which have become Swiss and the single valley which has become Italian, have come into the hands of France.

Avignon first seized, 1226.

The tendency shows itself early. *Avignon* was seized for a moment during the Albigensian wars; but the permanent process of French annexation began when

Annexation of Lyons, 1310.

Philip the Fair took advantage of the disputes between the archbishops and the citizens of *Lyons* to join that Imperial city to his dominions. The head of all the Gauls, the seat of the Primate of all the Gauls, thus passed into the hands of the new monarchy of Paris, the first-fruits of French aggrandizement at the cost of the Middle Kingdom. Later in the same century, the

Purchase of the Dauphiny of Vienne, 1343.

Dauphiny of *Vienne* was acquired by a bargain with its last independent prince. This land also passed, through the intermediate stage of an Imperial fief held by the heir-apparent of the French crown, into a mere province of France. But the acquisition of the Dauphiny did not

The city of Vienne annexed, 1448.

carry with it that of the city of *Vienne*, which escaped for more than a century. Between the acquisition of the Dauphiny and the acquisition of the city, the

Valence, 1446.

county of *Valence* was annexed to the Dauphiny. Later in the same century followed the great annexation of

Provence, 1481.

Provence itself. The rule of French princes in that

county for two centuries had doubtless paved the way for this annexation. And the acquisition of Provence carried with it the acquisition of the cities of *Arles* and *Marseilles*, which the counts of Provence had deprived of their freedom. But Provence, though practically incorporated with the French kingdom, kept, down to the French Revolution, somewhat more of separate being than the other lands which were annexed by France. At least within the county itself, the King of France still used the title of Count of Provence. By the annexation of this county the whole of the land between the Rhone and the sea had been swallowed up, save one state at the extreme south-east corner of the kingdom, and a group of small states which were now quite hemmed in by French territory. The first was the county of *Nizza* or Nice, which had passed away from Provence to Savoy before the French annexation of Provence. But by this time Savoy had become an Italian power, and Nizza was from henceforth looked on as Italian rather than Burgundian. Between Provence and the Dauphiny lay the city of *Avignon*, the county of *Venaissin*, and the principality of *Orange*. Avignon and Venaissin became papal possessions by purchase from the sovereign of Provence, Queen Joan of Naples; and, though they were at last quite surrounded by French territory, they remained papal possessions till they were annexed in the course of the great Revolution. These outlying possessions of the Popes perhaps did somewhat towards preserving the independence of a more interesting fragment of the ancient kingdom. This was the Principality of *Orange*, which the neighbourhood of the Pope hindered from being altogether surrounded by French territory. This little state, whose name has

Nizza passes to Savoy, 1388.

Avignon and Venaissin become Papal, 1348. Annexed to France, 1791.

Orange.

CHAP. VIII.

become so much more famous than itself, passed through several dynasties, and for a long time it was regularly seized by France in the course of every war. But it was as regularly restored to independence at every peace, and its final annexation did not happen till the eighteenth century. The acquisition of Orange, Avignon, and Venaissin, completed the process of French aggrandizement in the lands between the Rhone and the Var. The stages of the same process as applied to the Savoyard lands will be best told in another section.

Its annexation to France, 1714–1771.

Modern states which have split off from the three kingdoms.

We have thus traced the geographical history of the three Imperial kingdoms themselves. We have now to trace in the like sort the origin and growth of certain of the modern powers of Europe which have grown out of one or more of those kingdoms. Certain parts of the German, Italian, and Burgundian kingdoms have split off from these kingdoms, so as to form new political units, distinct from any of them. Five states of no small importance in later European history have thus been formed. Most of them partake more or less of the character of middle states, interposed between France and one or more of the Imperial kingdoms. First, there is the Confederation of *Switzerland*, which arose by certain German districts and cities forming so close an union among themselves that their common allegiance to the Empire gradually died out. The Confederation grew into its present form by the addition to these German districts of certain Italian and Burgundian districts. Secondly, there are, or rather were, the dominions of the Dukes of *Savoy*, formed by the union of various Italian and Burgun-

Their character as middle states.

Switzerland.

Savoy.

dian districts. This however, as a middle power, has ceased to exist; nearly all its Burgundian possessions have been joined to France, while its Italian possessions have grown into a new Italy. Thirdly, there were the dominions of the Dukes of *Burgundy*, forming a middle power between France and Germany, and made up by the union of French and Imperial fiefs. These are represented on the modern map by the kingdoms of the *Netherlands* and *Belgium*, the greater part of both of which belonged to the Burgundian dukes. Of these kingdoms much the greater part had split off from the old kingdom of Germany. Certain parts were once French fiefs, but had ceased to be so. The position of three out of these four states as middle powers, and their importance in that character, has been acknowledged even by modern diplomacy in the neutrality which is still guaranteed to Belgium and Switzerland, and which was formerly extended to certain districts of Savoy.

The Dukes of Burgundy. Represented by the kingdoms of the Low Countries.

Recognized neutrality of Belgium, Switzerland, and once of part of Savoy.

Of these four states, Switzerland, Savoy, and the duchy of Burgundy as represented by the two kingdoms of the Low Countries, some have been merged in other powers, and those which still remain count only among the secondary states of Europe. But a fifth power has also broken off from Germany which still ranks among the greatest in Europe. This is the power which, starting from a small German mark on the Danube, has, by the gradual union of various lands, German and non-German, grown into something distinct from Germany, first under the name of the *Austrian 'Empire'* and more latterly under that of the *Austro-Hungarian Monarchy*. This power differs from the other states of which we have been just speaking, not only in its vastly greater extent, but also in its position. It is

The Austrian dominions.

Position

CHAP. VIII.

of the Austrian dominion as a marchland.

a marchland, a middle kingdom, but in a different sense from Burgundy, Switzerland, Savoy, or Belgium. All these were marchlands between Christian states, between states all of which had formed part of the Carolingian Empire. All lie on the western side of the German and Italian kingdoms. Austria, on the other hand, as its name implies, arose on the eastern side of the German kingdom, as a mark against Turanian and heathen invaders. The first mission of Austria was to guard Germany against the Magyar. When the Magyar was admitted into the fellowship of Europe and Christendom—when, after a while, his realm was united under a single sovereign with Austria—the same duty was continued in another form. The power formed by the union of Hungary and Austria was one of the chief among those which had to guard Christendom against the Turk. Its history therefore forms one of the connecting links between Eastern and Western Europe. In this chapter it will be dealt with chiefly on its Western side, with regard to its relations towards Germany and Italy. The Eastern aspect of the Austro-Hungarian power has more to do with the states which arose out of the break-up of the Eastern Empire.

Comparison with the western marchlands.

Austria as the march against the Magyar.

Austria and Hungary the mark of Christendom against the Turk.

These states then, Switzerland, Savoy, the Duchy of Burgundy, the Netherlands, and the Austrian power, form a proper addition to the sections given to the three Imperial kingdoms. I will now go on to deal with them in order.

§ 6. *The Swiss Confederation.*

The original Confederation practically German,

I have just spoken of the Swiss Confederation as being in its origin purely German. This statement is practically correct, as all the original cantons were German in speech and feeling, and the formal style of their union was *the Old League of High Germany*. But in strict geographical accuracy there was, as we have seen in the last section, a small Burgundian element in the Confederation, if not from the beginning, at least from its aggrandizement in the thirteenth and fourteenth centuries. This is to say, part of the territory of the states which formed the old Confederation lay geographically within the kingdom of Burgundy, and a further part lay within the Lesser Burgundy of the Dukes of Zähringen. But, by the time when the history of the Confederation begins, the kingdom of Burgundy was pretty well forgotten, and the small German-speaking territory which it took in at its extreme north-east corner may be looked on as practically German ground. A more practical division than the old boundaries of the kingdoms is the boundary of the Teutonic and Romance speech; in this sense all the cantons of the old Confederation, except part of Freiburg, are German. The Romance cantons are those which were formed in modern times out of the allied and subject states. It is specially needful to bear in mind, first, that, till the last years of the thirteenth century, not even the germ of modern Switzerland had appeared on the map of Europe; secondly, that the Confederation did not formally become an independent power till the seventeenth century; lastly, that, though the *Swiss* name had been in common use for ages, it did not become the formal style of the Confederation till the nineteenth century. Nothing in the whole study of historical geography is more necessary than to root out the notion that there has always been a country of Switzerland, as there has always been a country of Germany, Gaul, or Italy. And it is no

though part of it geographically Burgundian.

All the old Cantons German in speech. The later Romance Cantons.

Many popular errors.

CHAP. VIII.

The Swiss do not represent the Helvetii.

less needful to root out the notion that the Swiss of the original cantons in any way represent the Helvetii of Cæsar. The points to be borne in mind are, that the Swiss Confederation is simply one of many German Leagues, which was more lasting and became more closely united than other German Leagues—that it gradually split off from the German Kingdom—that, in the course of this process, the League and its members obtained a large body of Italian and Burgundian allies and subjects—lastly, that these allies and subjects have in modern times been joined into one Federal body with the original German Confederates.

Summary of Swiss history. A German League, having become more united and independent than others, annexes Romance allies and subjects. The Three Lands on the boundary of the three kingdoms. First known document of union, 1291.

The three Swabian lands which formed the kernel of the Old League, the lands of *Uri*, *Schwyz*, and *Unterwalden*, lay at the point of union of the three Imperial kingdoms, parts of all of which were to become members of the Confederation in its later form. The first known document of confederation between the Three Lands dates from the last years of the thirteenth century. But that document is likely to have been rather the confirmation than the actual beginning of their union. They had for neighbours several ecclesiastical and temporal lords, some other Imperial lands and towns, and far greater than all, the Counts of the house of *Kyburg* and *Habsburg*, who had lately grown into the more dangerous character of Dukes of Austria. The Confederation grew for a while by the admission of neighbouring lands and cities as members of a free German Confederation, owning no superior but the Emperor. First of all, the city of *Luzern* joined the League. Then came the Imperial city of *Zürich*, which had already begun to form a little dominion in the adjoining lands. Then came

Growth of the League.

Luzern, 1332. Zürich, 1351.

the land of *Glarus* and the town of *Zug* with its small territory. And lastly came the great city of *Bern*, which had already won a dominion over a considerable body of detached and outlying allies and subjects. These confederate lands and towns formed the *Eight Ancient Cantons*. Their close alliance with each other helped the growth of each canton separately, as well as that of the League as a whole. Those cantons whose geographical position allowed them to do so, were thus able to extend their power, in the form of various shades of dominion and alliance, over the smaller lands and towns in their neighbourhood. These lesser changes and annexations cannot all be recorded here; but it must be carefully borne in mind that the process was constantly going on. Zürich, and yet more Bern, each formed, after the manner of an ancient Greek city, what in ancient Greece would have passed for an empire. In the fifteenth century, large conquests were made at the expense of the House of Austria, of which the earlier ones were made by direct Imperial sanction. The Confederation, or some or other of its members, had now extended its territory to the Rhine and the Lake of Constanz. The lands thus won, *Aargau*, *Thurgau*, and some other districts, were held as subject territories in the hands of some or other of the Confederate states.

Glarus and Zug, 1352. Bern, 1353.

The Eight Ancient Cantons

Their growth.

Dominion of Zürich and Bern.

Conquests from Austria, 1415–1460.

Aargau, Thurgau, &c.

It is a fact to be specially noticed in the history of the Confederation, that, for nearly a hundred and thirty years, though the territory and the power of the Confederation were constantly increasing, no new states were admitted to the rank of confederate cantons. Before the next group of cantons was admitted, the general state of the Confederation and its European position

No new canton formed for a long time.

CHAP. VIII.

Beginning of Italian dominions.

had greatly changed. It had ceased to be a purely German power. The first extension beyond the original German lands and those Burgundian lands which were practically German began in the direction of Italy. Uri had, by the annexation of Urseren, become the neighbour of the duchy of Milan, and in the middle of the fifteenth century, this canton acquired some rights in the *Val Levantina* on the Italian side of the Alps. This was the beginning of the extension of the Confederation on Italian ground. But far more important than this was the advance of the Confederates in the Burgundian lands to the west. The war with Charles of Burgundy enabled Bern to win several detached possessions in the Savoyard lands north and east of the lake, and even on the lower course of the Rhone. And, while Bern advanced, some points in the same direction were gained by her allies who are not yet members of the Confederation, by the city of *Freiburg* and the League of *Wallis*. This last confederation had grown up on the upper course of the Rhone, where the small free lands had gradually displaced the territorial lords. Soon after this came the next admission of two new cantons, those of the cities of *Freiburg* and *Solothurn*, each of them bringing with it its small following of allied and subject territory. Twenty years later, *Basel* and *Schaffhausen*, the latter being the only canton north of the Rhine, were admitted with their following of the like kind. Twelve years later, *Appenzell*, a little land which had set itself free from the rule of the abbots of *Saint Gallen*, after having long been in alliance with the Confederates, was admitted to the rank of a canton. Thus was made up the full number of Thirteen Cantons, which remained unchanged down to the wars of the French Revolution.

Uri obtains Val Levantina, 1441.

First Savoyard conquest of Bern. 1475.

Savoyard conquests of Freiburg and Wallis.

Growth of Wallis.

Freiburg and Solothurn become Cantons, 1481.

Basel and Schaffhausen, 1501.

Appenzell, 1513.

The Thirteen Cantons, 1513–1798.

Graubünden.

Their alliance with the Confederates.

1495–1567.

Italian dominion of the Confederation, 1512;

of the Grey Leagues, 1513.

Early Savoyard conquests of Bern, Freiburg, and Wallis, 1536. Vaud.

Lausanne.

Geneva in alliance with Bern and Freiburg.

But the time when the Confederation was finally settled as regards the number of cantons was also a time of great extension of territory on the part both of the Confederation and of several of its members. At the south-east corner of the Confederate territory, on the borders of the duchy of Milan and the county of Tyrol, the League of *Graubünden* or the *Grey Leagues* had gradually arisen. A number of communities, as in Wallis, had got rid of the neighbouring lords, and had formed themselves into three leagues, the *Grey League* proper, the *Gotteshausbund*, and the League of *Ten Jurisdictions*, which three were again united by a further federal tie. At the end of the fifteenth century, the Leagues so formed entered into an alliance with the Confederates. Then began a great accession of territory towards the south on the part both of the Confederates and of their new allies. The Confederates received a considerable territory within the duchy of Milan, including *Bellinzona*, *Locarno*, and *Lugano*, as the reward of services done to the House of Sforza. The next year their new allies of the Grey Leagues also won some Italian territory, the *Valtellina* and the districts of *Chiavenna* and *Bormio*. Next came the conquest of a large part of the Savoyard lands, of all north of the Lake and a good deal to the south, by the arms of Bern, Freiburg, and Wallis. Bern and Freiburg divided *Vaud* in very unequal proportions. Bern and Wallis divided *Chablais* on the south side of the lake, and Bern annexed the bishopric of *Lausanne* on the north. *Geneva*, the ally of Bern and Freiburg, with her little territory of detached scraps, was now surrounded by the dominion of her most powerful allies at Bern. But by a later treaty Bern and Wallis

CHAP. VIII.

Territory restored to Savoy, 1567.

gave back to Savoy all that they had won south of the Lake, with the territory of *Gex* to the west of it. Geneva thus again had Savoy for a neighbour, a neighbour at whose expense she even made some conquests —Gex among them—conquests which the French ally of the free city would not allow her to keep. Later changes gave her a neighbour yet more dangerous than Savoy in the shape of France itself. Before these changes, Bern and Freiburg divided the county of *Gruyères* between them, the last important instance of that kind of process.

Gruyères divided between Bern and Freiburg, 1554.

The Allies.

The Confederation was thus fully formed, with its Thirteen Cantons and their allied states. Of these the *Abbot of Saint Gallen*, the *town of Saint Gallen*, and the town of *Biel* or *Bienne*, were so closely allied with the Confederates as to have a place in their Diets. Besides relations of less close alliance which the Confederates had with various Alsatian cities, several other states had a connexion so close and lasting with the Confederation or with some of its members, as to form part of the same political system. Such were the Leagues of Wallis and Graubünden, the Bishop of *Basel*, the outlying town of *Mühlhausen* in Elsass, and for a while that of *Rottweil*. Bern too, and sometimes other cantons, had relations both with the town and with the princes of *Neufchâtel*, which, after passing through several dynasties, was at last inherited by the Kings of Prussia. *Constanz*, at the other end of the Confederate land, was refused admission as a canton, but for a while it was in alliance with some of the cantons. But this connexion was severed when Constanz, instead of a free Imperial city, became a possession of Austria. The power thus formed, a power in which a

Saint Gallen. Bienne.

Bischofbasel. Mühlhausen and Rottweil.

Neufchâtel passes to Prussia, 1707.

Constanz.

Passes to Austria, 1548.

body of German Confederates was surrounded by a body of allies and subjects, German, Italian, and Burgundian, all of them originally members of the Empire, was by the Peace of Westfalia formally released from all allegiance to the Empire and its chief. Their practical separation may be dated much earlier, from the time when the Confederates refused to accept the legislation of Maximilian.

The Confederation released from the allegiance to the Empire, 1658. Date of the practical separation, 1495.

The growth of the League into an independent power was doubtless greatly promoted by its geographical position, as occupying the natural citadel of Europe. But the piecemeal way in which it grew up was marked by the anomalous nature of its frontier on several points. On the north the Rhine would seem to be a natural boundary, but Schaffhausen beyond the Rhine formed part of the Confederation, while Constanz and other points within it did not. To the south the possession of territory on the Italian side of the Alps seems an anomaly, an anomaly which is brought out more strongly by a singularly irregular and arbitrary frontier. But looking on the Confederation as the middle state, arising at the point of junction of the three Imperial kingdoms, it was in a manner fitting that it should spread itself into all three.

Geographical position of the League.

Its anomalous frontier.

The Confederation as a middle state.

The form which the Confederation thus took in the sixteenth century remained untouched till the wars of the French Revolution. The beginning of change was when the Italian districts subject to the Grey Leagues were transferred to the newly formed *Cisalpine Republic*. In the next year the whole existing system was destroyed. The Federal system was abolished; instead of the Old League of High Germany, there

Wars of the French Revolution.

Dismemberment of the Grey Leagues, 1797.

Abolition of the Federal system, 1798.

CHAP. VIII.

The Helvetic Republic. Freedom of the subject districts. Freedom of Vaud. Annexation of *Bischofbasel* and Geneva to France. Act of Mediation, 1803. The nineteen cantons. Wallis incorporated with France. Neufchâtel. 1806. The Swiss Confederation of twenty-two cantons. 1815. *Bischofbasel* added to Bern.

arose, after the new fashion of nomenclature, a *Helvetic Republic*, in which the word *canton* meant no more than *department*. Yet even by such a revolution as this some good was done. The subject districts were freed from the yoke of their masters, whether those masters were the whole Confederation or one or more of its several cantons. Thus, above all, the Romance land of *Vaud* was freed from subjection to its German masters at Bern. Some of the allied districts, as the bishopric of Basel and the city of Geneva, were annexed to France. But the Leagues of Wallis and Graubünden were incorporated with the Helvetic Republic. In 1803 the Federal system was restored by Buonaparte's *Act of Mediation*, which formed a Federal republic of nineteen cantons. These were the original thirteen, with the addition of *Aargau*, *Graubünden*—this last shorn of its dependent Italian lands—*St. Gallen*, *Ticino*, *Thurgau*, and *Vaud*, which were formed out of the formerly allied and subject lands. *Wallis* was separated from the Confederation, and became, first a nominally distinct republic, and afterwards a French department. *Neufchâtel* was, in the course of Buonaparte's wars with Prussia, detached from that power, to form a principality under his General Berthier. At last, in 1815, the present *Swiss Confederation* was established, consisting of twenty-two cantons, the number being made up by the addition of *Neufchâtel*, *Wallis*, and *Geneva*. The bishopric of Basel was also again detached from France, and added to the canton of Bern, a canton differing in language and religion, and cut off by a mountain range. The great constitutional changes which have been made since that time have not affected geography, unless we count the division of the city and district of Basel, *Baselstadt* and *Baselland*, into distinct half-cantons. The separation of Neufchâtel from the Prussian dominions, and the later surrender of all rights over it by the Prussian king, was not strictly a geographical change; it was rather a change from a *quasi* monarchic to a purely republican government in that particular canton.

Neufchâtel separated from Prussia, 1848–1857.

§ 7. *The State of Savoy.*

Position and growth of Savoy.

The growth of the power of Savoy, the border state of Burgundy and Italy, has necessarily been spoken of more than once in earlier sections; but it seems needful to give a short connected account of its progress, and to mark the way in which a power originally Burgundian gradually lost on the side of Burgundy and grew on the side of Italy, till it has in the end itself grown into a new Italy. The lands which have at different times passed under the rule of the house of Savoy lie continuously, though with an irregular frontier, and though divided by the great barrier of the Alps. They fall however into three main geographical divisions, which at one time became also political divisions, being held by different branches of the Savoyard house. There are the Italian possessions of that house, which have grown into the modern Italian kingdom. There are the more strictly Savoyard lands south of the Lake of Geneva, and the other lands south of the Rhone after it issues from that lake, all of which have passed away under the power of France. And there are the lands north of the Lake and of the Rhone, part of which have also become French, while others have become part of the Swiss Confederation. Both these last lay within the kingdom of Burgundy, and stretched

Geographical position of the Savoyard lands.

Their three divisions.

Italian.

Burgundian south of the lake.

Burgundian north of the lake.

CHAP. VIII.

into both its divisions. In no part of our story is it more necessary to avoid language which forestalls the arrangements of later times. A wholly false impression is given by the use of language such as commonly is used. We often hear of the princes of Savoy holding lands 'in France' and 'in Switzerland.' They held lands which by virtue of later changes have severally become French and Swiss; but those lands became French and Swiss only by ceasing to be Savoyard. On the other hand, to speak of them from the beginning as holding lands in Italy is perfectly accurate. The Savoyard states were a large and fluctuating assemblage of lands on both sides of the Alps, lying partly within the Italian and partly within the Burgundian kingdom. These last have shared the fate of the other fiefs of that crown.

Popular confusions.

The Savoyard state originally Burgundian.

The cradle of the Savoyard power lay in the Burgundian lands immediately bordering upon Italy and stretching on both sides of the Alps. It was to their geographical position, as holding several great mountain passes, that the Savoyard princes owed their first importance, succeeding therein in some measure to the Burgundian kings themselves.[1] The early stages of the growth of the house are very obscure; and its power does not seem to have formed itself till after the union of Burgundy with the Empire. But it seems plain that, at the end of the eleventh century, the Counts of *Maurienne*, which was their earliest title, held rights of sovereignty in the Burgundian districts of *Maurienne*, *Savoy* strictly so called, *Tarantaise*, and *Aosta*. This last valley and city, though

Possessions of the Counts of Maurienne.

Aosta; its special position.

[1] Compare the mention of Rudolf in the letter of Cnut, on his Roman Pilgrimage, in Florence of Worcester, 1031. He is there 'Rodulphus rex, qui maxime ipsarum clausurarum dominatur.'

on the Italian side of the Alps, had hitherto been rather Burgundian than Italian.[1] Its allegiance had fluctuated several times between the two kingdoms; but, from the time that Savoy held lands in both, the question became of no practical importance. And, without entering into minute questions of tenure, it may be said that the early Savoyard possessions reached to the Lake of Geneva, and spread on both sides of the inland mouth of the Rhone. The power of the Savoyard princes in this region was largely due to their ecclesiastical position as advocates of the abbey of Saint Maurice. Thus their possessions had a most irregular outline, nearly surrounding the lands of *Genevois* and *Faucigny*. A state of this shape, like Prussia in a later age and on a greater scale, was, as it were, predestined to make further advances. But for some centuries those advances were made much more largely in Burgundy than in Italy. The original Italian possessions of the House bordered on their Burgundian counties of Maurienne and Aosta, taking in *Susa* and *Turin*. This small marchland gave its princes the sounding title of *Marquesses in Italy*. The endless shiftings of territory in this quarter could

Geographical character of the Burgundian territories.

Their early Italian possessions.

Marquesses in Italy.

[1] That Aosta was strictly Burgundian appears from the 'Divisio Imperii, 806' (Pertz, Leges, i. 141), where Italy is granted whole to Pippin, Burgundy is divided between Charles and Lewis; but it is provided that both Charles and Lewis shall have access to Italy, 'Karolus per vallem Augustanam quæ ad regnum ejus pertinet.' The Divisio Imperii of 839 is still plainer (Pertz, Leges, i. 373, Scriptores, i. 434). There the one share takes in 'Regnum Italiæ partemque Burgundiæ, id est, vallem Augustanam,' and certain other districts. So Einhard (Vita Karoli, 15) excludes Aosta from Italy. 'Italia tota, quæ ab Augusta Prætoria usque in Calabriam inferiorem, in qua Græcorum et Beneventanorum constat esse confinia, porrigitur.' As Calabria was not part of Italy in this sense, so neither was Aosta. So, in Eadmer's history, Anselm, a native of Aosta, is more than once spoken of as a stranger in Italy.

CHAP. VIII.

Fluctuations of dominion

be dealt with only at extreme length, and they are matters of purely local concern. In truth, they are not always fluctuations of territory in any strict sense at all, but rather fluctuations of rights between the feudal princes, the cities, and their bishops. In the

Their position in the twelfth and thirteenth centuries.

twelfth and thirteenth centuries, the princes of Savoy were still hemmed in in their own corner of Italy by princes of equal or greater power, at *Montferrat*, at *Saluzzo*, at *Ivrea*, and at *Biandrate*. And it must be remembered that their position as princes at once

Other princes at once Italian and Burgundian.

Burgundian and Italian was not peculiar to them. The Dauphins of the Viennois and the Counts of Provence both held at different times territories on the Italian side of the Alps. The Italian dominions of the family remained for a long while quite secondary to its Burgundian possessions, and the latter may therefore be traced out first.

Advance of Savoy in Burgundy. Faucigny and the Genevois.

The main object of Savoyard policy in this region was necessarily the acquisition of the lands of *Faucigny* and the *Genevois*. But the final incorporation of those lands did not take place till they were still more completely hemmed in by the Savoyard dominions through the extension of the Savoyard power to the north of the

First advance north of the Lake. Grant of Moudon. 1207. Romont the northern capital. Peter, Count of Savoy. 1263–1268.

Lake. This began early in the thirteenth century by a royal grant of *Moudon* to Count Thomas of Savoy. *Romont* was next won, and became the centre of the Savoyard power north of the Lake. Soon after, through the conquests of Peter of Savoy, who was known as the Little Charlemagne and who plays a part in English as well as in Burgundian history, these possessions grew into a large dominion, stretching along a great part of the shores of the Lake of Neufchâtel and reaching as

1239–1268.

far north as *Murten* or *Morat*. But it was a straggling,

and in some parts fragmentary, dominion, the continuity of which was broken by the scattered possessions of the Bishops of Lausanne and other ecclesiastical and temporal lords. This extension of dominion brought Peter into close connexion with the lands and cities which were afterwards to form the Old League of High Germany. Bern especially, the power to which his conquests were afterwards to be transferred, looked to him as a protector. This new dominion north of the Lake was, after Peter's reign, held for a short time by a separate branch of the Savoyard princes as *Barons of Vaud*; but in the middle of the fourteenth century, their barony came into the direct possession of the elder branch of the house. The lands of Faucigny and the Genevois were now altogether surrounded by the Savoyard territory. Faucigny had passed to the Dauphins of the Viennois, who were the constant rivals of the Savoyard counts, down to the time of the practical transfer of their dauphiny to France. Soon after that annexation, Savoy obtained *Faucigny*, with *Gex* and some other districts beyond the Rhone, in exchange for some small Savoyard possessions within the Dauphiny. The long struggle for the Genevois, the *county* of Geneva, was ended by its purchase in the beginning of the fifteenth century. This left the *city* of Geneva altogether surrounded by Savoyard territory, a position which before long altogether changed the relations between the Savoyard counts and the city. Hitherto, in the endless struggles between the Genevese counts, bishops, and citizens, the Savoyard counts, the enemies of the immediate enemy, had often been looked on by the citizens as friends and protectors. Now that they had become immediate neighbours of the city, they themselves began

His relations with Bern.

Barons of Vaud.

Union of Vaud with the elder branch. 1349.

Faucigny held by the Dauphins of the Viennois.

Savoy acquires Faucigny and Gex. 1355

The Genevois. 1401.

Changed relations to city of Geneva.

CHAP. VIII.

Amadeus the Eighth, Count 1391; Duke 1417; Antipope 1440; died 1451. Greatest extent of the dominions of Savoy in Burgundy.

before long to be its most dangerous enemies. The acquisition of the Genevois took place in the reign of the famous Amadeus the Eighth, the first Duke of Savoy, who received that rank by grant of King Siegmund, and who was afterwards the Antipope Felix. In his reign the dominions of Savoy, as a power ruling on both sides of the Alps, reached their greatest extent. But the Savoyard power was still pre-eminently Burgundian, and Chambéry was its capital. The continuous Burgundian dominion of the house now reached from the Alps to the Saône, surrounding the lake of Geneva and spreading on both sides of the lake of Neufchâtel. Besides this continuous Burgundian dominion, the house of Savoy had already become possessed of *Nizza*, by which their dominions reached to the sea. This last territory however, though technically Burgundian, had geographically more to do with the Italian possessions of the house. But this great extension of territory brought Savoy on its western side into closer connexion with the most dangerous of neighbours. Her frontier for a certain distance joined the actual kingdom of France. The rest joined the Dauphiny, which was now practically French, and the county of Provence, which was ruled by French princes and which before the end of the century became a French possession. To the north again, the change in the relations between the house of Savoy and the city of Geneva led in course of time to equally changed relations towards Bern and her Confederates. Through the working of these two causes, all that the house of Savoy now keeps of this great Burgundian territory is the single city and valley of Aosta. After the fifteenth century, the Burgundian history of that

Annexation of Nizza. 1388. Savoy brought into the neighbourhood of France.

New relations towards Bern and the Confederates.

Loss of the Burgundian dominion of Savoy.

house consists of the steps—steps spread over more than three hundred years—by which this great dominion was lost

The real importance of the house of Savoy in Italy dates from much the same time as the great extension of its power in Burgundy. During the eleventh and twelfth centuries, partly through the growth of the cities, partly through the enmity of the Emperor Henry the Sixth, the dominions of the Savoyard princes as marquesses of Susa had been cut short, so as hardly to reach beyond their immediate Alpine valleys. In the beginning of the thirteenth century, when Count Thomas obtained his first royal grant north of the lake, he also obtained grants of *Chieri* and other places in the neighbourhood of Turin. These grants were merely nominal; but they were none the less the beginning of the Italian advance of the house. In the same reign *Saluzzo* for the first time paid a precarious homage to Savoy. Later in the thirteenth century, Charles of Anjou, now Count of Provence and King of Sicily, made his way into Northern Italy also, and thus brought the house of Savoy into a dangerous neighbourhood with French princes on its Italian as well as on its Burgundian side. Through the thirteenth and fourteenth centuries the Savoyard border went on extending itself. But the Italian possessions of the house, like its possessions north of the lake, were separated from the main body of Savoyard territory to form a fief for one of the younger branches. This branch bore by marriage the empty title of Counts of *Achaia* and *Morea*—memories of Frank dominion within the Eastern Empire—while, as

Growth of Savoy in Italy.

The largest dominions cut short in the twelfth century.

Grants to Count Thomas. 1207.

First homage of Saluzzo. 1216.

Italian dominion of Charles of Anjou. 1259.

Counts of Achaia in Piedmont. 1301–1418.

CHAP. VIII.

if to keep matters straight, a branch of the house of Palaiologos reigned at Montferrat. During the fourteenth century, among many struggles with the marquesses of Montferrat and Saluzzo, the Angevin counts of Provence, and the lords of Milan, the Savoyard power in Italy generally increased. Under Amadeus the Eighth, the lands held by the princes of Achaia were united to the possessions of the head of the house. Before the end of the reign of Amadeus, the dominions of Savoy stretched as far as the Sesia, taking in *Biella*, *Santhia*, and *Vercelli*. Counting Nizza and Aosta as Italian, which they now practically were, the Italian dominions of the house reached from the Alps of Wallis to the sea. But they were nearly cut in two by the dominions of the Marquesses of *Montferrat*, from whom however the Dukes of Savoy now claimed homage. *Saluzzo*, lying between the old inheritance of Susa and the new possession of Nizza, also passed under Savoyard supremacy. But it lay open to a very dangerous French claim on the ground of a former homage done to the Viennese Dauphins. Amadeus, the first Duke of Savoy, took the title of *Count of Piedmont*, and afterwards that of *Prince*. His possessions were now fairly established as a middle state, Italian and Burgundian, in nearly equal proportions.

Advance in the fourteenth century.

Reunion of Piedmont. 1418.

Acquisition of Biella, &c. 1435.

Relations with Montferrat.

Claims on Saluzzo; its doubtful homage.

Establishment of Savoy as a middle state.

Effects of the Italian wars.

In the course of the next century and a half the Savoyard state altogether changed its character in many ways. The changes which affected all Europe, especially the great Italian wars, could not fail greatly to affect the border state of Italy and Gaul. And there is no part of our story which gives us more instructive lessons with regard to the proper limits of our subject. During this time the Savoyard power was brought

French influence and occupation.

under a number of influences, all of which deeply affected its history, but which did not all alike affect its geography. We have a period of French influence, a period of French occupation, and more than one formal change of the frontier. Mere influence does not concern us at all. Occupation concerns us only when it takes the form of permanent conquest. An occupation of nearly forty years comes very near to permanent conquest; still when, as in this case, it comes to an end without having effected any formal annexation, it is hardly to be looked on as actually working a change on the map. France occupied Piedmont for nearly as long a time as Bern occupied the lands south of the lake. Yet we look on the one occupation as simply part of the military history, while in the other we see a real, though only temporary, geographical change. But the result alike of influence, of occupation, and of actual change of boundaries, all tended the same way. They all tended to strengthen the Italian character of the house of Savoy, to cut short its Burgundian possessions, and, if not greatly to increase its Italian possessions, at least to put it in the way of greatly increasing them.

Occupation by France.

Increased Italian character of Savoy.

During the second half of the fifteenth century, the power of the house of Savoy greatly declined, partly through the growing influence of France, partly through the division, in the form of appanages, of the lands which had been so lately formed together into a compact state. Then came the Italian wars, in which the Savoyard dominions became the highway for the kings of France in their invasions of Italy. The strictly territorial changes of this period chiefly concern the marquisate of Saluzzo on the Italian side and the

Decline of Savoy.

The Italian wars.

CHAP. VIII.

First loss of lands north of the lake. 1475.

northern frontier on the Burgundian side. The first loss of territory on the northern frontier, the first sign that the Savoyard power in Burgundy was gradually to fall back, was the loss of part of the lands north of the lake in the war between Charles of Burgundy and the Confederates. *Granson* on the lake of Neufchâtel, *Murten* or *Morat* on its own lake, *Aigle* at the south-east end of the great lake, *Échallens* lying detached in the heart of Vaud, all passed away from Savoy and became for ever Confederate ground. Sixty years later, the affairs of Geneva led to the great intervention of Bern, Freiburg and Wallis, by which Savoy was for ever shorn of her possessions north of the lake. For a while indeed she was cut off from the lake altogether; Chablais passed away as well as Vaud. Geneva, with her detached scraps of territory, was now wholly surrounded by her own allies. Thirty years later, Bern restored all her conquests south of the lake, together with Gex to the west, leaving Geneva again surrounded by the dominions of Savoy. Wallis too gave up part of her share, keeping only the narrow strip on the left bank of the Rhone. The loss and the recovery mark the difference between the reigns of Duke Charles the Third, called the Good, and Duke Emmanuel Filibert with the Iron Head. The difference of the two reigns is equally marked with regard to France. Almost at the same moment as the conquests made by Bern, began that occupation, whole or partial, of Savoyard territory by the French arms which did not come wholly to an end for thirty-eight years. Savoy then appeared again as a power whose main strength lay in Italy, whose capital, instead of Burgundian Chambéry, was Italian

Loss of the lands on both sides of the lake. 1536.

Reunion of the lands south of the lake. 1567.

Charles the Good. 1504–1553. Emmanuel Filibert. 1553–1580.

Beginning of French occupation. 1536. Its end. 1574.

Turin. And all later changes of frontier tended in the same way to increase the Italian character of the Savoyard power, and to lessen its extent in the lands which we may distinguish as Transalpine, for the Burgundian name has now altogether passed away from them.

The first formal exchange of Burgundian for Italian ground happened under Emmanuel Filibert, shortly after the emancipation of his dominions. The small county of *Tenda* was acquired in exchange for the marquisate of *Villars* in Bresse. More important changes followed. The first of these was caused by the endless disputes which arose out of the disputed homage of Saluzzo. The Marquesses of Saluzzo preferred the French claimant of their homage to the Savoyard, a preference which led in the end to definite annexation by France. This was the first acquisition of Italian soil by France as such, as distinguished from the claims of French princes over Milan, Naples, and Asti. France thus threw a continuous piece of French territory into the heart of the states of Savoy. When the French occupation ceased, Saluzzo still remained to France. Presently it was conquered by Duke Charles Emmanuel. The reign of this prince marks the final change in the destiny of the house of Savoy. He himself had dreamed of wider conquests on the Gaulish side of the Alps than had ever come into the mind of any prince of his house. He was to be Count of Provence, King of Burgundy, perhaps King of France. The real results of his reign told in exactly the opposite way. By the treaty which ended his war with France, Saluzzo was ceded to Savoy in exchange for *Bresse*, *Bugey*, *Valromey*, and *Gex*. A powerful neighbour

Acquisition of Tenda.

Disputes about the homage of Saluzzo.

Annexation of Saluzzo by France. 1548.

Conquest of Saluzzo. 1588.

Reign of Charles Emmanuel. 1580–1630.

Bresse, &c. exchanged for Saluzzo. 1601.

CHAP. VIII.

was thus shut out from a possession which cut the Savoyard states in twain; but the price at which this advantage was gained amounted to a final surrender of the old possession of the Savoyard house beyond the Alps. The Rhone and not the Saône became the boundary, while the surrender of Gex brought France to the shores of the Lake. Geneva, her city and her scattered scraps of territory, had now, besides Bern, two other neighbours in France and Savoy. The two attempts of Charles Emmanuel to seize upon the city were fruitless. Savoy now became distinctly an Italian power, keeping indeed the lands between the Alps and the Lake, the proper Duchy of Savoy, but having her main possessions and her main interests in Italy. We may here therefore finish the history of the Transalpine possessions of the Savoyard House. The Duchy of Savoy remained in the hands of its own Dukes till their continental dominion was swept away in the storm of the French Revolution. It was restored after the first fall of Buonaparte, but with a narrowed frontier, which left its capital *Chambéry* to France. This was set right by the treaties of the next year. Lastly, as all the world knows, Savoy itself, including the guaranteed neutral lands on the Lake, passed, along with Nizza, to France. Savoy itself was so far favoured as to be allowed to keep its ancient name, and to form the departments of *Savoy* and *High Savoy*, instead of being condemned, as in the former temporary annexation, to bear the names of *Leman* and *Mont Blanc*. The Burgundian counts who have grown into Italian kings have thus lost the land under whose name their house grew famous. Aosta alone remains as the last relic of the times when the Savoyard Dukes, the greatest lords

Loss of position beyond the Alps.

Attempts on Geneva. 1602, 1609.

Later history of Savoy.

Annexed to France. 1792–1796. Restored. 1814–1815.

Savoy and Nizza annexed to France. 1860.

Aosta spared.

of the Middle Kingdom, still kept their place as the truest representatives of the Middle Kingdom itself.

CHAP. VIII.

Italian history of the House of Savoy. Its character.

We now turn to the purely Italian history of the house, a history which has been already sketched in dealing with the geography of Italy. Savoy now takes part in every European struggle, and, though its position led to constant foreign occupation, some addition of territory was commonly gained at every peace. Thus, before the reign of Charles Emmanuel was over, Piedmont was again overrun by French troops. Though the Savoyard possessions in Italy were presently increased by a part of the Duchy of *Montferrat*, this was a poor compensation for the French occupation of *Pinerolo* and other parts in the heart of Piedmont, which lasted till nearly the end of the century. The gradual acquisition of territory at the expense of the Milanese duchy, the acquisition and exchange of the two island kingdoms, the last annexation by France, the acquisition of the Genoese seaboard, the growth of the Kingdom of Sardinia into the Kingdom of Italy, have been already told. Our present business has been with Savoy as a middle power, a character which practically passed from it with the loss of Vaud and Bresse, and all traces of which are now sunk in the higher but less interesting character of one of the great powers of Europe. From Savoy in its character of a middle power, as one of the representatives of ancient Burgundy, we naturally pass to another middle power which prolonged the existence of the Burgundian name, and on part of which, though not on a part lying within its Burgundian possessions, some trace of the ancient functions of the Middle Kingdom is still laid by the needs of modern European policy.

French occupation. 1629.

Annexation of part of Montferrat. 1631.

French occupation of Pinerolo. 1630–1696.

Later Italian advance

CHAP. VIII.

§ 8. *The Duchy of Burgundy and the Low Countries.*

Position of the Valois Dukes of Burgundy.

Among all the powers which we have marked as having for their special characteristic that of being middle states, the one which came most nearly to an actual revival of the middle states of earlier days was the Duchy of Burgundy under the Valois Dukes. A great power was formed whose princes held no part of their dominions in wholly independent sovereignty. In practical power they were the peers of their Imperial and royal neighbours; but their formal character throughout every rood of their possessions was that of vassals of one or other of those neighbours. Such a twofold vassalage naturally suggested, even more strongly than vassalage to a single lord could have done, the thought of emancipation from all vassalage, and of the gathering together of endless separate fiefs into a single kingdom. The gradual acquisitions of earlier princes, especially those of Philip the Good, naturally led up to the design, avowed by his son Charles the Bold, of exchanging the title of Duke for that of King. The memories of the older Burgundian and Lotharingian kingdoms had no doubt a share in shaping the schemes of a prince who possessed so large a share of the provinces which had formed those kingdoms. The schemes of Charles, one can hardly doubt, looked to the formation of a realm like that of the first Lothar, a realm stretching from the Ocean to the Mediterranean. His actual possessions, at their greatest extent, formed a power to which Burgundy gave its name, but which was historically at least as much Lotharingian as Burgundian. And though this actual dominion was only momentary, no power

Their twofold vassalage.

Its effects.

Schemes for a Burgundian kingdom.

ever arose which fills a wider and more œcumenical place in history than the line of the Valois Dukes. Their power connects the earliest settlement of the European states with the latest. It spans a thousand years, and connects the division of Verdun with the last treaty that guaranteed the neutrality of Belgium. The growth of their power was directly influenced by memories of the early Carolingian partitions; and, even in its fall, it has itself influenced the geography and politics of Europe ever since. As a Burgundian power, it was as ephemeral as all other Burgundian powers have ever been. As a Lotharingian power, it abides still in its effects. The union of the greater part of the Low Countries under a single prince, and that a prince who was on the whole foreign to the Empire, strengthened that tendency to split off from the Empire which was already at work in some of those lands. Later events caused them to split off in two bodies instead of one. This last tendency became so strong that a modern attempt to unite them broke down, and their place in the modern polity of Europe is that of two distinct kingdoms. The existence of those two kingdoms is the final result of the growth of the Burgundian power in the fifteenth century. And by leading to the separation of the northern Netherlands from the Empire, it has led to one result which could never have been reckoned on, the preservation of one branch of the Low-Dutch tongue as the acknowledged literary speech of an independent nation. Its political results were the creation, in the shape of the northern Netherlands, of a power which once held a great place in the affairs of Europe and of the world, and the slower growth, in the shape of the southern Netherlands, of a state in which modern

Historical importance of the Burgundian Power.

1870.

History of the Low Countries.

Final result of the Burgundian dominion.

Its effect on language.

The Netherlands and Belgium.

CHAP. VIII.

European policy still acknowledges the character of a middle kingdom. As the neutral confederation of Switzerland represents the middle kingdom of Burgundy, so the neutral kingdom of Belgium represents the middle kingdom of Lotharingia.

Ducal Burgundy a fief of the Western Kingdom.

The Duchy of Burgundy which gave its name to the Burgundian power of the fifteenth century was that one among the many lands bearing the Burgundian name which lay wholly outside the Burgundian kingdom of the Emperors. This Burgundy, the only one which has kept the name to our own time, the duchy of which Dijon is the capital, never was a fief of the Eastern Kingdom; it never was a fief of the Empire after the final separation. It always acknowledged the supremacy of the kings of Laon and Paris. By these last the duchy was twice granted in fief to princes of their own house, once in the eleventh century and once in the fourteenth. This last grant was the beginning of the Dukes of the house of Valois, with the growth of whose power we have now to deal. Philip the Hardy, the first Duke of this line, obtained, by his marriage with Margaret of Flanders, the counties of *Flanders*, *Artois*, *Rhetel*, *Auxerre*, and *Nevers*, all fiefs of the crown of France, together with the *County Palatine of Burgundy* as a fief of the Empire. The peculiar position of the Dukes of Burgundy of this line was at once established by this marriage. Duke Philip held of two lords, and his dominions lay in two distinct masses. The two Burgundies, duchy and county, and the county of Nevers, lay geographically together; Flanders and Artois lay together at a great distance; the small possession of Rhetel lay again between the two. Any princes who held such a territory as

Two lines of Dukes. 1032. The Valois. 1363.

Union of Flanders and Burgundy. 1369.

The county of Burgundy.

Two masses of territory.

CHAP. VIII.

this could hardly fail to devote their main policy to the work of bringing about the geographical union of their scattered possessions. Nor was this all. The possession of the two Burgundies made their common sovereign a vassal at once of France and of the Empire. The possession of Flanders, Artois, and Rhetel further brought him into connexion with those borderlands of the Empire and of the French kingdom where the authority of either overlord was weakest, and which had long been tending to form themselves into a separate political system distinct alike from the Empire and from the Kingdom. The results of this complicated position, as worked out, whether by the prudence of Philip the Good or by the daring of Charles the Bold, form the history of the Dukes of Burgundy of the House of Valois.

Position of the Netherlands.

Imperial and French fiefs in the Netherlands.

The lands which we are accustomed to group together under the name of the *Netherlands* or *Low Countries* lay mostly within the bounds of the Empire; but the county of Flanders had always been a fief of France. Part however of the dominions of its counts, the north-eastern corner of their dominions, the lands of *Alost* and *Waas*, were held of the Empire. These lands, together with the neighbouring islands of *Zealand*, formed a ground of endless disputes between the Counts of Flanders and their northern neighbours the Counts of *Holland*. This last county gradually disentangles itself from the general mass of the Frisian lands which lie along the whole coast from the mouth of the Scheld to the mouth of the Weser. And those great inroads of the sea in the thirteenth century which gave the Zuyder-Zee its present extent helped to give the county a natural boundary, and to part it off from the Frisian lands to the north-east. Towards the end of the thir-

Fief of the Counts of Flanders within the Empire. Zealand.

County of Holland.

Inroads of the sea. 1219, 1282.

CHAP. VIII.

Disputes with the free Frisians.

Independence of West Friesland. 1417–1447.

County of East Friesland. 1454.

The Bishops of Utrecht.

teenth century Friesland west of the Zuyder-Zee had become part of the dominions of the Counts. The land immediately east of the gulf established its freedom, while *East Friesland* passed to a line of counts, under whom its fortunes parted off from those of the Netherlands. Part of its later history has been already given in the character of a more purely German state. Both the counts and the free Frisians had also dangerous neighbours in the Bishops of *Utrecht*, the great ecclesiastical princes of this region, who held a large temporal sovereignty lying apart from their city on the eastern side of the gulf. These disputes went on, as also disputes with the Dukes of Geldern, without any final settlement, almost to the time when all these lands began to be united under the Burgundian power. But before this time, the Counts of Holland had become closely connected with lands much further to the south. Among a number of states in this region, the most powerful was the Duchy of *Brabant*, which represented the Duchy of the Lower Lotharingia, and whose princes held the mark of *Antwerp* and the cities of *Brussels*, *Löwen* or *Louvain*, and *Mechlin*. To the south of them lay the county of *Hennegau* or *Hainault*. At the end of the thirteenth century, this county was joined by marriage with that of Holland. Holland and Hainault were thus detached possessions of a common prince, with Brabant lying between them. South of Brabant lay the small mark or county of *Namur*, which, without being united to Flanders, was held by a branch of the princes of that house.

Duchy of Brabant.

County of Hennegau or Hainault united with Holland. 1299.

Mark of Namur.

Common character of these states.

All these states, though their princes held of two separate overlords, had much in common, and were well fitted to be worked together into a single political system. They had much in common in the physical character of the country, and in the unusual number of great and flourishing cities which these countries contained. None of these cities reached the full position of free cities of the Empire; but their wealth, and the degree of practical independence which they possessed, form a main feature in the history of the Low Countries. In point of language, the northern part of these states spoke various dialects of Low-Dutch, from Flemish to Frisian; in the southern lands of Hainault, Artois, and Namur, the language, though not French, was not Teutonic, but an independent Romance speech, the Walloon. To the west of these states lay another group of small principalities connected with the former greater group in many ways, but not so closely as those which we have just gone through. The great ecclesiastical principality of *Lüttich* or *Liège*, lying in two detached parts, divided the lands of which we have been speaking from the counties, afterwards duchies, of *Lüzelburg* or *Luxemburg* and of *Limburg*. Of these the more distant Limburg passed in the fourteenth century to the Dukes of Brabant. Luxemburg is famous as having given a series of princes to the kingdom of Bohemia and to the Empire, and in their hands it rose to the rank of a duchy. Lastly, to the north of Lüttich, forming a connecting link between this group of states and the more purely Frisian powers, lay the duchy of *Geldern*, of whose quarters the most northern part stretched to the Zuyder-Zee. These eastern states, though not so closely connected with one another as those to the west, were easily led into the same political system. Without drawing any hard and fast line, we may say that all the states of this region formed, if not

Importance of the cities.

South-western group of states.

Bishopric of Lüttich.

Duchies of Luxemburg and Limburg.

Luxemburg a Duchy. 1358.

Geldern.

CHAP. VIII.

Middle position of all these states.

yet a middle state, yet a middle system, apart alike from France and from the Empire, though in various ways connected with both. Mainly Imperial, mainly Teutonic, they were not wholly so. Besides the homage lawfully due to France from Flanders and Artois, French influence in various ways, in politics, in manners, and in language, had made great inroads in the southern Netherlands. Brabant and Hainault had practically quite as much to do with France as with the Empire. And this French influence was of course helped by the fact that a considerable region in the south was, though not of French, yet not of Teutonic speech. Altogether, with much to unite them to the great powers on either side, with much to keep them apart from either of them, with much more to unite them to one another, the states of the Netherlands might almost seem to be designed by nature to be united as a separate power under a single head. Such a head was supplied by the princes who were at once Dukes of Burgundy and Counts of Flanders, by whom, in the course of the fifteenth and sixteenth centuries, nearly the whole of the Netherlands was united into a single power which was to be presently broken into two by the results of religious divisions.

French influence.

Walloon language.

Union of the Netherlands under the Dukes of Burgundy.

Leaving then for the present the growth and fall of the Burgundian power in the lands more to the south, we will go on to trace the steps by which the provinces of the Low Countries were united under the Valois Dukes and their Austrian descendants. The great increase of territory in this region was made during the long reign of Philip the Good. His first acquisition was the county of *Namur*, a small and outlying district,

Reign of Philip the Good. 1419–1467.

Namur. 1421–1429.

but one which, as small and outlying, would still more strongly suggest the rounding off of the scattered territory. A series of marriages and disputes next enabled Philip to make a much more important extension of his dominions. Brabant and Limburg had passed to a younger branch of the Burgundian house. John, Duke of Brabant, the cousin of Philip, by a marriage with Jacqueline, Countess of Holland and Hainault, united those states for a moment. The disputes and confusions which followed on her marriages and divorces led to the annexation of her territories by the Duke of Burgundy, a process which was finally concluded by the formal cession of her dominions by Jacqueline. Meanwhile Philip had succeeded to Brabant and Limburg, and the union of Flanders, Brabant, Hainault, Zealand, and Holland, together made a dominion which took in all the greatest Netherland states, and formed a compact mass of territory. On this presently followed a great acquisition of territory which was more strictly French than the fiefs which Philip already held of the French crown in Flanders and Artois. The Treaty of Arras, by which Philip, hitherto the ally of England against France, made peace with his western overlord, gave him, under the form of mortgage, the lands on the Somme. These lands, *Ponthieu*, *Vermandois*, *Amiens*, and *Boulogne*, had once been largely Teutonic, but they were by this time thoroughly French. Their acquisition advanced the Burgundian frontier to a dangerous neighbourhood to Paris on this side as well as on the side of the Burgundian duchy. It had the further effect of keeping the small continental possessions which England still held at Calais and Guînes apart from the French territory. During the

1429–1433.

1405.

1418.

Brabant and Limburg. 1430.

Holland and Hainault. 1433.

The towns on the Somme. 1435–1483.

CHAP. VIII.

reigns of Philip and Charles the Bold, the continental neighbour of England was not France but Burgundy. But this great southern dominion was not lasting. The towns on the Somme, redeemed and again recovered, passed on the fall of Charles the Bold once more into French hands. So did Artois itself, and, though Artois was won back, Amiens and the rest were not. Yet, if the towns on the Somme had stayed under the rule of the successive masters of the Low Countries, it might by this time have seemed as natural for Amiens to be Belgian as it now seems natural for Cambray and Valenciennes to be French. The Treaty of Madrid drew a definite boundary. France gave up the ancient claim to homage from Flanders and Artois, and Charles the Fifth, in his Burgundian, or rather in his Flemish, character, finally gave up all claim to the lands on the Somme.

Recovered by France.

France resigns the homage of Flanders and Artois. 1526.

The south-western frontier was thus fixed; but meanwhile the new state had advanced in other directions. Philip's last great acquisition was the duchy of *Luxemburg*. He now possessed the greater part of the Netherlands; but his dominions were still intersected by the bishoprics of Utrecht and Lüttich and the duchy of Geldern. The duchy of Geldern and county of Zutphen were added by Charles the Bold. But they formed a precarious possession, lost and won more than once, down to their final annexation under Charles the Fifth. Of the two great ecclesiastical principalities by which the Burgundian possessions in the Netherlands were cut asunder, the bishopric of *Lüttich*, though its history is much mixed up with that of the Burgundian Dukes, and though it came largely under their influence, was never formally annexed. But the temporal princi-

Luxemburg. 1443.

Geldern and Zutphen. 1472. Final annexation. 1543.

Bishopric of Lüttich never annexed.

pality of the Bishop of *Utrecht* was secularized under Charles the Fifth. *Friesland*, the Friesland immediately east of the Zuyder-Zee, had already been reincorporated with the dominions of the prince who represented the ancient counts of Holland. The whole Netherlands were thus brought together under the rule of Charles the Fifth. They were united with the far distant county of Burgundy, and with it they formed the Burgundian circle in the new division of the Empire. The bishopric of Lüttich, which intersected the whole southern part of the country, remained in the circle of Westfalia.

Annexation of the bishopric of Utrecht, 1531; and Friesland, 1515.

Dominions of Charles the Fifth.

Seventeen provinces, each keeping much of separate being, were united under a single prince, and, after the treaty of Madrid, they were free from any pretensions on the part of foreign powers. The Netherlands formed one of the most compact and important parts of the scattered dominions of the Emperor who was also lord of Burgundy, Castile, and Sicily.

The seventeen provinces.

But the final union of these lands under the direct dominion of an Emperor at once led to their practical separation from the Empire. They passed, with all the remaining possessions and claims of the Burgundian house, to Philip of Spain, and they were reckoned among the crowd of distant dependencies which had come under the rule of the crowns of Castile and Aragon. In Spanish hands they acted less as a middle state than as a power which helped to hem in France on both sides. Had the great revolt of the Netherlands ended in the final liberation of the whole seventeen provinces, the middle state would have been formed in its full strength.

Their separation from the Empire.

The possessions of Philip of Spain. 1555.

As it was, the work of the War of Independence was imperfect. The northern provinces won their freedom in the form of a federal commonwealth. The southern provinces re-

The War of Independence. 1568–1609.

mained dependencies of Spain, to become the chosen fighting ground of European armies, the chosen plaything of European diplomacy.

The end of the long war of independence waged by the northern provinces was the establishment of the

The Seven United Provinces. 1578.

famous federal commonwealth of the *Seven United Provinces*, *Holland*, *Zealand*, *Utrecht*, *Gelderland*, *Over-Yssel*, *Friesland*, and *Groningen*. These answered nearly to the dominions of the Counts of Holland and Bishops of Utrecht in earlier times. But besides

Gelderland.

these, part of the duchy of *Geldern* formed one of the United Provinces, while its southern part shared the fate of the southern provinces. But, besides the United Seven, the Confederation also kept parts of Brabant, Geldern, and Flanders as common possessions. The power thus formed, one which so long held an European importance quite disproportioned to

Formal independence of the Empire. 1648.

its geographical extent, had under Burgundian rule become practically independent of the Empire, but it was only by the Peace of Westfalia that its independence was formally acknowledged. The maritime strength of the Confederation made it more than an European power. It became a colonizing power in three parts of the world. In the course of the seventeenth and eighteenth centuries,

Colonies of the Netherlands.

the Seven Provinces extended their dominion over many points on the continent of India and over the neighbouring island of *Ceylon*, over the great equatorial islands of *Java*, *Sumatra*, and the *Moluccas*, over many points in *Guinea* and southern Africa, and over

New Netherland passes to England. 1664.

part of *Guiana* in South America. But the great North American settlement of *New Netherland* passed to England, and *New Amsterdam* became *New York*. Singularly enough, this great power never had any

CHAP. VIII.

No real name for the county.

Use of the name *Dutch*.

strict geographical name. *Netherlands* was too large, as it took in the whole of the Low Countries and not the emancipated provinces only. *Holland* was too small, as being the name of one province only, though the greatest. And, by one of the oddest cases of caprice of language, in common English usage the name of the whole Teutonic race settled down on this one small part of it, and the men of the Seven Provinces came to be exclusively spoken of as *Dutch*.

The Spanish Netherlands. 1578–1706.

Dunkirk held by England. 1658–1663.

Cession of parts of Artois and of Gravelines, 1659;

Dunkirk, 1663;

Philippeville, Marienburg, Thionville.

1668.

Meanwhile the southern provinces, the greater part of Brabant and Flanders, with Artois, Hennegau or Hainault, Namur, Limburg, Luxemburg, and the southern part of Geldern—a region taking in Antwerp at one end and Cambray at the other—remained under the sovereignty of the representatives of the Burgundian Dukes. That is, they remained an outlying dependency of the Spanish monarchy. But their southern frontier was open to constant aggressions on the part of France. *Dunkirk* indeed was for a moment held by England, as Calais and Boulogne had been in earlier times. By the Peace of the Pyrenees France obtained Arras and the greater part of Artois, leaving Saint Omer to Spain. France also began to work her way up along the coast of Flanders, taking *Gravelines* by virtue of the treaty, and presently adding Dunkirk by purchase from England. The treaty also added to France several points along the frontiers of Hainault, Liège, and Luxemburg, including the detached fortresses of *Philippeville* and *Marienburg*, and *Thionville* famous in far earlier days. During the endless wars of Lewis the Fourteenth's reign, the boundary fluctuated with each treaty. Acquisitions were made by France at the Treaty of Aix-la-Chapelle, some of which were surrendered, and

CHAP. VIII.

1677. others made, by the Peace of Nimwegen. At last the boundary was finally fixed by the Peace of Utrecht in the last days of Lewis. Part of Flanders and Hainault were finally confirmed to France, which thus kept *Lille*, *Cambray*, and *Valenciennes*. The provinces which had hitherto been Spanish now passed to the only surviving branch of the House of Austria, that which reigned in the archduchy and supplied the hereditary candidates for the Empire. The first wars of the French Revolution added the Austrian Netherlands to France, and with them the bishopric of Lüttich which still so oddly divided them. A later stage of the days of confusion changed the Seven United Provinces, enlarged by the addition of East Friesland, into a *Kingdom of Holland*, one of the states which the new conqueror carved out for the benefit of his kinsfolk. Presently the new kingdom was incorporated with the new 'Empire,' along with the German lands to the north-east of it. The Corsican had at last carried out the schemes of the kings of the house of Valois, and the whole Burgundian heritage formed for a moment part of France.

Boundary fixed by the Peace of Utrecht. 1713.

The Spanish Netherlands pass to Austria.

Annexed by France. 1792.

Kingdom of Holland. 1806–1810.

Holland annexed by France. 1810–1813.

At the general settlement of Europe, after the long wars with France, the restoration of the Low Countries as a middle state was a main object. This was brought about by the union of the whole Netherlands into a single kingdom bearing that name. The southern boundary did not differ greatly from that fixed by the Peace of Utrecht. As in the case of the Savoyard frontier, France kept a little more by the arrangements of 1814 than she finally kept by those of 1815. To the east, East-Friesland passed to Hannover, leaving the boundary

Kingdom of the Netherlands. 1814.

The boundaries.

of the new kingdom not very different from that of the two earlier powers which it represented, gaining only a small territory on the banks of the Maes. But

Incorporation of Lüttich.

the bishopric of Lüttich was incorporated with the lands which it had once parted asunder, and so ceased altogether to be German ground. The new king, as we have already seen, entered the German Confederation in his

Grand Duchy of Luxemburg.

character of Grand Duke of *Luxemburg*, the duchy being somewhat shortened to the east in favour of Prussia. Lastly, after fifteen years of union, the new kingdom again split asunder. It was now divided into the kingdom of the Netherlands, answering to the old United Provinces, and

Kingdom of Belgium. 1830–1831. Luxemburg divided.

the kingdom of Belgium, answering to the old Spanish or Austrian Netherlands. But part of Limburg remained to the northern kingdom, and its sovereign also kept part of Luxemburg, as a distinct state, forming part of the German Confederation; but this personal union with Holland came to an end on the death of William III., Luxemburg passing to the Duke of Nassau. The western part of the duchy formed part of the kingdom of Belgium. Later events, as has been already recorded, have severed the last tie between Germany and the Netherlands; they have wiped out the last survival of the days when the Counts of Holland and of Luxemburg were alike princes of the German kingdom.

1890. 1867.

Effects of Burgundian rule.

The above may pass as a sketch of the fluctuations along the borderland in their European aspect. It is needless to go through every small shifting of frontier, or to recount in detail the history of small border principalities like *Saint Pol* and *Bouillon*. The main historical aspect of these countries is their tendency, in all ages, to form somewhat of a middle system between

CHAP. VIII.

two greater powers on either side of them. The guaranteed neutrality of Belgium and the guaranteed neutrality of Switzerland are alike survivals or revivals —it is hard to say which they should be called—of the instinctive feeling which, in the ninth century, called the Lotharingian kingdom into being. The modern form of this thousand-year-old idea was made possible through the growth of the power of the Burgundian Dukes of the house of Valois.

Schemes of Charles the Bold.

The real historical work of those dukes was thus done in those parts of their dominions from which they did not take their name, but which took their name from them. The history of their other dominions may be told in a few words; indeed a great part of it has been told already. The schemes of Charles the Bold for uniting his scattered dominions by the conquest of the duchy of Lorraine, for extending the power thus formed to the seaboard of the royal Burgundy, for forming in short a middle kingdom stretching from the Ocean to the Mediterranean, acting as a barrier alike between France and Germany and between France and Italy, remained mere schemes. They are important only as showing how deeply the idea or the memory of a middle state was still fixed in men's minds. The conquests of Charles in Lorraine, his purchases in Elsass, were momentary possessions which hardly touch geography. But the fall of Charles, by causing the break-up of the southern dominion of his house, helped to give greater importance to its northern dominion. While the Netherlands grew together, the Burgundies split asunder. After the fall of Charles the fate of the two Burgundies was much the same as the fate of Flanders and Artois. Both were for a while seized by France; but the county, like Artois, was afterwards recovered for a season. The duchy of Burgundy was lost for ever; the county, along with the outlying county of Charolois, remained to those who by female succession represented the Burgundian Dukes, that is to Charles the Fifth and his Spanish son. The annexation of the Burgundian county, and with it of the city of Besançon, by Lewis the Fourteenth has been recorded in an earlier section.

§ 9. *The Power of Austria.*

We now come to one among these German states which have parted off from the kingdom of Germany whose course has been widely different from the rest, and whose modern European importance stands on a widely different level. As the Lotharingian and Frisian lands parted off on the north-west of the kingdom, as a large part of the Swabian lands parted off to the south-west of the kingdom, so the *Eastern Mark*, the mark of *Austria*, parted off no less, but with widely different consequences. The name of *Austria*, *Oesterreich*—*Ostrich* as our forefathers wrote it—is, naturally enough, a common name for the eastern part of any kingdom. The Frankish kingdom of the Merwings had its *Austria*; the Italian kingdom of the Lombards had its *Austria* also. In both of these cases *Austria*, the positive name of the eastern land, is balanced by *Neustria*, that is *Not-Austria*, the negative name of the western land. In short the division comes so naturally that we are half inclined to wonder that the name was never given in our own island either to Essex or to East-Anglia. But, while the other Austrias have passed away, the *Oesterreich*, the *Austria*, the

Origin of the name *Oesterreich*, *Austria*.

Other lands so called.

CHAP. VIII.

Eastern mark, of the German kingdom, its defence against the Magyar invader, has lived on to our own times. It has not only lived on, but it has become one of the chief European powers. Its small beginnings, as compared with the other bearers of the name, are shown by the fact that it never had a *Neustria* to balance it; but out of these small beginnings it has grown to a height which has caused all other bearers of the name to be forgotten. And it has grown by a process to which it would be hard to find a parallel. The Austrian duchy supplied Germany with so many Kings, and Rome with so many Emperors, that something of Imperial character came to cleave to the duchy itself. Its Dukes, in resigning, first, the crown of Germany, and then all connexion with Germany, have carried with them into their new position the titles and bearings of the German Cæsars. The power which began as a mark against the Magyar came to have a common sovereign with the Magyar kingdom; and the Austrian duchy and Magyar kingdom, each drawing with it a crowd of smaller states of endless nationalities, have figured together in the face of modern Europe as the *Austrian Empire* and the *Austro-Hungarian Monarchy*. It is not easy, in drawing a map, to find a place for the 'Empire' of Austria. The Archduchy is there, and its sovereign has not dropped his archiducal title. A crowd of kingdoms, duchies, counties, and lordships, all acknowledging the sovereignty of the same prince, are there also. But it is not easy to find the geographical place of an 'Empire' of Austria, as distinct from the Archduchy. It is not easy to understand on what principle an 'Empire' of Austria can be understood as taking in all the states which happen to own the Hungarian King

Special position of the Austrian power.

Union with Hungary.

The so-called 'Empire' of Austria.

and Austrian Archduke as their sovereign. Nor is it made any easier, when, as would seem to be the present official use of the name, the 'Empire of Austria' is taken to mean all the kingdoms, duchies, &c., held by the Archduke of Austria in some other character than that of King of Hungary.[1] The matter is made more difficult still when we remember that the title of 'Hereditary Emperor of Austria' was first taken while its bearer was still King of Germany and Roman Emperor-elect. But, putting questions like these aside, the gradual union of a great number of states, German and non-German, under the common rule of the archiducal house of Austria, by whatever name we call the power so formed, is a great fact both of history and of geography. A number of states, originally independent of one another, differing in origin and language and everything that makes states differ from one another, some of them members of the former Empire, some not, have, as a matter of fact, come together to form a power which fills a large space in modern history and on the modern map. But it is a power which is altogether lacking in national unity. It is a power which is not coextensive with any nation, but which takes in parts of many nations. It cannot even be said that there is a dominant nation surrounded by subject nations. The Magyar nation in its unity, and a fragment of the German nation, stand side by side on equal terms, while Italians, Roumans, and Slaves of almost every branch of the Slavonic race, are grouped around those two. There is no federal tie; it is a stretch of language to apply the federal name to the present relation between the

Union of separate states under the Austrian House.

Lack of national unity.

German, Magyar, and other races.

No strictly federal tie.

[1] For the lands thus negatively, and only negatively, defined, I once suggested, after the analogy of *Neustria*, the name of *Nungary*.

CHAP. VIII.

two chief powers of Hungary and Austria. Nor can any strictly federal tie be said to unite Croatia, Slavonia, and Transsilvania, Bohemia, Dalmatia, Trent, and Galicia, either with one another or with the Austrian archduchy. And yet these other members of the general body are not mere subject provinces, like the dominions of Old Rome. The same prince is sovereign of a crowd of separate states, two of which stand out prominently as centres among the rest. There is neither national unity, nor federation, nor mere subjection of one land or nation to another. All this has come by the gradual union by various means of many crowns upon the same brow. The result is an anomalous power which has nothing else exactly like it, past or present. Powers of the same kind have existed before. The dominion of the Angevins in Brittany and Gaul, the dominion of the Burgundian Dukes which we have just been describing, have much in common with the power of the House of Austria. But these powers lasted only for two or three reigns. The great anomaly of the Austrian dominion is that it has been enabled to maintain itself, in one shape or another, for some centuries. But the very anomaly makes the growth of such a power a more curious study.

Anomalous nature of the Austrian power.

The Eastern Mark.

The beginnings of the Austrian state are to be found in the small *Mark* on the Danube, lying between Bohemia, Moravia, and the Duchy of Kärnthen or Carinthia. It appears in its first form as an appendage to Bavaria.[1] This mark Frederick Barbarossa raised into a duchy, under its first duke Henry the Second, and it was enlarged to the westward at the expense of

[1] See Waitz, Deutsche Verfassungsgeschichte, vii. 75.

Bavaria by the addition of the lands above the Enns. Thus was formed the original *Duchy of Austria*, the duchy of the Dukes of the house of Babenberg. It had not long risen to ducal rank before it began to extend itself at the expense of states which had hitherto been of greater moment than itself. Itself primarily a mark against the Magyar, Austria had to the south of it the lands where the German Kingdom marched at once upon the Magyar, the Slave, and the Kingdom of Italy. Here lay the great Duchy of Carinthia, a land where the population was mainly Slavonic, though the Slaves on this frontier had been brought into much earlier and more thorough subjection to the German Kings than the Slaves on the north-eastern frontier. At the time of the foundation of the duchy of Austria, the Carinthian duchy had begun to split in pieces, and its northern part, hitherto the *Upper Carinthian Mark*, grew into the Duchy of *Steyermark* or *Styria*. Twelve years later, Leopold the Fifth of Austria inherited the duchy of Styria, a duchy greater than his own, by the will of its duke Ottokar. Carinthia itself went on as a separate duchy; but it now took in only a narrow territory in the south-western part of the old duchy, and that broken up by outlying possessions of the archbishops of Salzburg and other ecclesiastical lords. To the south, in the partially Slavonic land within the older Italian border, in the extreme north-eastern corner of what had been the Lombard Austria, a considerable power grew up in the hands of the counts of *Görz* or *Gorizia*. The possessions of these counts stretched, though not continuously, from Tyrol to Istria, and their influence was further enlarged by their position as advocates of the

Duchy of Austria, 1156.

Duchy of Carinthia, 976.

Duchy of Styria, 1180; united to Austria, 1192.

The county of Görz.

CHAP. VIII.

Ecclesiastical position of its Counts.

bishoprics of *Trent* and *Brixen* and of the more famous patriarchate of *Aquileia*. These are the lands, the marchlands of Germany towards its eastern and south-eastern neighbours, which came by gradual annexations to form the German possessions of the Austrian power. But the further growth of that power did not begin till the duchy itself had passed away to the hands of a wholly new line of princes.

Momentary union of Austria and Bohemia.

The first change was one which brought about for a moment from one side an union which was afterwards to be brought about in a more lasting shape from the other side. This was the annexation of Austria by the kingdom of *Bohemia*. That duchy had been raised to the rank of a kingdom, though of course without ceasing to be a fief of the Empire, a few years after the mark of Austria had become a duchy. The death of the last duke of Austria of the Babenberg line led to a disputed succession and a series of wars, in which the princes of Bavaria, Bohemia, and Hungary, all had their share. In the end, between marriage, conquest, and royal grant, Ottokar king of Bohemia obtained the duchies of Austria and Styria, and a few years later he further added Carinthia by the bequest of its Duke. Thus a new power was formed, by which several German states came into the power of a Slavonic king. The power of that king for a moment reached the Baltic as well as the Hadriatic; for Ottokar carried his arms into Prussia, and became the founder of *Königsberg*. But this great power was but momentary. Bohemia and Austria were again separated, and Austria, with its indefinite mission of extension over so many lands, including Bohemia itself, passed to a house sprung from a distant part of Germany.

Bohemia a kingdom, 1158.

Ottokar of Bohemia annexes Austria and Styria, 1252–1262. Carinthia, 1269.

Great power of Ottokar.

House of Habsburg.

We have now come to the European beginnings of the second House of Austria, the house whose name seems to have become inseparably connected with the name of Austria, though the spot from which that house drew its name has long ceased to be an Austrian possession. This is the house of the Counts of *Habsburg*. They took this name from their castle on the lower course of the Aar, in the north-west corner of the Aargau, in that southern Swabian land where the Old League of High Germany was presently to arise, and so greatly to extend itself at the cost of the power of Habsburg. By an union of the lands of Habsburg with those of the Counts of *Kyburg* and *Lenzburg*, a considerable, though straggling, dominion was formed. It stretched in and out among the mountains and lakes, taking in Luzern, and forming a dangerous neighbour to the free city of Zürich. Besides these lands, the same house also held *Upper Elsass* with the title of Landgrave, a dominion separated from the other Swabian lands of the house by the territory of the free city of Basel. The lord of this great Swabian dominion, the famous Rudolf, being chosen to the German crown, and having broken the power of Ottokar, bestowed the duchies of Austria and Styria on his son Albert, afterwards King. Carinthia at first formed part of the same grant; but it was presently granted to Meinhard Count of Görz and Tyrol. Görz passed to another branch of the house of its own Counts. Three powers were thus formed in these regions, the duchies of *Austria* and *Styria*, the duchy of *Carinthia* with the county of *Tyrol*, and the county of *Görz*.

Union of Habsburg, Kyburg, and Lenzburg.

Their possession in Elsass.

Rudolf king, 1273. His victories over Ottokar, 1276–1278. Albert of Habsburg Duke of Austria and Styria, 1282. Meinhard Duke of Carinthia and Count of Tyrol, 1286.

Thus under Albert the possessions of the house of Habsburg were large, but widely scattered. The two

Scattered territories of the

CHAP. VIII.

house of Habsburg.

newly acquired eastern duchies not only gave its princes their highest titles, but they formed a compact territory, well suited for extension northward and southward. But among the outlying Swabian territories, though some parts remained to the Austrian house down to the end of the German Kingdom, the tendency was to diminish and gradually to part off altogether from Germany. In the lands south of the Rhine this happened through union with the Confederates; in the Alsatian lands it happened at a later stage through French annexation.

Falling off of the Swabian lands.

Connexion of Austria with the Empire.

It is to be hoped that it is no longer needful to explain that the hereditary lands of the House of Habsburg or Austria had no inherent connexion with the German Kingdom and Roman Empire of which they were fiefs, beyond the fact that they were among its fiefs. They were further connected with it only by the accident that, from Rudolf onwards, many princes of that house were chosen Kings, and that, from the middle of the fifteenth century, onwards, all the Kings were chosen from that house and from the house into which it merged by female succession. It is to be hoped that there is no longer any need to explain that every Emperor was not Duke of Austria, and that every Duke of Austria was not Emperor. But it may be needful to explain that every Duke of Austria was not master of the whole dominions of the House of Austria. The divisions, the reunions, the joint reigns, which are common to the House of Austria with other German princely houses, become at once more important and more puzzling in the case of a house which gradually came to stand above all the others in European rank. The caution is specially needful in the case of the Swabian

Divisions of the Austrian dominions.

lands, as the history of the Confederates is liable to be greatly misunderstood, if every Duke of Austria who appears in it is taken for the sole sovereign of the Austrian dominions. It is needless here to go through all these shiftings between princes of the same house. Through all changes the unity of the house and its possessions was maintained, even while they were parted out or held in common by different members of the house. But it is important to bear in mind that some of the Dukes of Austria who figure in the history of Switzerland were rather Landgraves of Elsass or Counts of Tyrol than Dukes of Austria in any practical sense.

The fourteenth and fifteenth centuries may be defined as a time during which the Austrian house on the whole steadily advanced in the eastern part of its dominions and steadily fell back in the western. But in the course of the fourteenth century an acquisition was made which, without making them absolutely continuous, brought them into something more like geographical connexion with one another. This was the acquisition of the Duchy of Carinthia and County of *Tyrol*, the latter of which lands lay conveniently between the eastern and western dominions of the house. These now stretched continuously from the Bohemian frontier to Istria, and they threw out, in the form of Tyrol and the Swabian lands, a scattered, but nearly continuous, territory stretching to the borders of Lorraine and the county of Burgundy. The Austrian possessions now touched the eastern gulf of the Hadriatic and came into the neighbourhood of the Dalmatian Archipelago. Somewhat later they reached the main Hadriatic itself, when the city of *Trieste*,

Acquisition of Carinthia and Tyrol, 1335.

Extent of the Austrian territory.

CHAP. VIII.

Commendation of Trieste, 1382.

hitherto disputed between the commonwealth of Venice and the patriarchs of Aquileia, commended itself to the Austrian Duke Leopold as its lord. This is the same Leopold who four years later fell at Sempach. By this time the Swabian possessions of the house had been increased north of the Rhine, while south of the Rhine the Austrian dominion was steadily giving way. The Confederates and their several cantons advanced in every way, by purchase and conquest, till, after the loss of Thurgau, the House of Austria kept nothing south of the Rhine except the towns known as the *Waldstädte*.

Loss of Thurgau, 1460.

By this time the division of the estates of the house had taken a more lasting shape. One branch reigned in Austria, another in Carinthia and Styria, a third in Tyrol and the other western lands. At this time begins the unbroken series of Austrian elections to the German and Imperial crowns. The first of this line was Albert the Second, Duke of Austria. Then Frederick the Third, the first Emperor of the House, united the Austrian and Carinthian duchies, and raised Austria to the unique rank of an Archduchy. Meanwhile, Siegmund Count of Tyrol held the western lands, and appears as Duke of Austria in Confederate and Burgundian history. He there figures as the prince who lost Thurgau to the Confederates and who mortgaged his Alsatian lands to Charles the Bold. In Maximilian the whole possessions of the House of Austria were united. But by this time the affairs of the purely German lands which had hitherto formed the possessions of the Austrian house had begun to be mixed up with the succession to lands and kingdoms beyond the Empire, and with lands which, though technically within the Empire, had a distinct being of

Albert the Second, king, 1437–1440. Frederick the Third, king, 1440; Emperor, 1452. Archduke of Austria, 1453. Siegmund, Count of Tyrol, &c., 1429–1496.

Maximilian, King of the Romans, 1486; Archduke, 1493; Count of Tyrol, 1496; Emperor-elect, 1508. Beginning of union

their own. In the course of the fifteenth century the House of Austria, hitherto simply one of the chief German princely houses, put on two special characters. It became, as we have already seen, the house which exclusively supplied kings and Emperors to Germany and the Empire. And it became, by virtue of its hereditary possessions rather than of its Imperial position, one of the chief European powers. For a while the greatest of European powers, it has remained a great European power down to our own time.

with lands beyond the Empire.

Succession of Austrian Kings and Emperors.

The special feature in the history of the House of Austria from the fifteenth century onwards is its connexion—a connexion more than once broken, but still constantly recurring till in the end it becomes fully permanent—with the kingdom of Bohemia within the Empire and with the kingdom of Hungary beyond its bounds. These kingdoms, whose elective character only gradually passed away, stand distinguished from the earlier and more strictly German possessions of the house, which are distinctively known as the *Hereditary States*. The possession of these kingdoms has given the Austrian power its special character, that of a power formed by the union under one prince of several wholly distinct nations or parts of nations which have no tie beyond that union. The Austrian princes, originally purely German, equally in their Swabian and in their Austrian possessions, had already, by the extension of their power to the south, obtained some Slavonic and some Italian-speaking subjects. Still, as a power, they were purely German. But in the period which begins in the fifteenth and goes on into the nineteenth century, we shall see them gradually gathering together, sometimes gaining, sometimes losing—gaining and losing by

Union with Bohemia and Hungary.

Various acquisitions of Austria.

every process, warlike and peaceful, by which territory can be gained or lost—a crowd of kingdoms, duchies, and counties, scattered over all parts of Europe from Flanders to Transsilvania. But it is the acquisition of the two crowns of Bohemia and Hungary which, above all others, gave the House of Austria its special position as a middle power, a power belonging at once to the system of Western and to the system of Eastern Europe. Among the endless shiftings of the states which have been massed together under the rule of the house of Habsburg, that house has more than once been at the same moment the neighbour of the Gaul and the neighbour of the Turk ; and it has sometimes found Gaul and Turk arrayed together against it. Add to all this that, though the connexion between the house of Austria and the Empire was a purely personal one, renewed in each generation by a special election, still the fact that so many kings of Hungary and archdukes of Austria were chosen Emperors one after another, caused the house itself, after the Empire was abolished, to look in the eyes of many like a continuation of the power which had come to an end. The peculiar position of the Austrian house could hardly have been obtained by a mere union of Hungary, Austria, and the other states, under princes none of whom were raised to Imperial rank. Nor could it have been obtained by a series of mere dukes of Austria, even though they had been chosen Emperors from generation to generation. It was through the accidental union under one sovereign of a crowd of states which had no natural connexion with each other, and through the further accident that the Empire itself seemed to become a possession of the House, that the House of Habsburg, and its representative the

House of Lorraine, have won their unique position among European powers.

The first hints, so to speak, of a coming union between the Hungarian and Bohemian kingdoms and the Austrian duchy began, as we have seen, in the days of Ottokar. A Bohemian king had then held the Austrian duchy, while a Hungarian king had for a moment occupied part of Styria. So at a much later time, in the latter half of the fifteenth century, the Austrian duchy bowed for a moment to the victorious Hungarian king Matthias Corvinus. But the later form which the union was to take was not that of the Bohemian or the Hungarian reigning over Austria, but that of the Austrian reigning over Hungary and Bohemia. The duchy was not to be added to either of the kingdoms; but both kingdoms were in course of time to be added to the duchy. The growth of both Hungary and Bohemia as kingdoms will be spoken of elsewhere. We have now to deal only with their relations to the Austrian House. For a moment, early in the fourteenth century, an Austrian prince, son of the first Austrian King of Germany, was actually acknowledged as King of Bohemia. But this connexion was only momentary. The first beginnings of anything like a more permanent connexion begin a hundred and thirty years later. The second Austrian King of Germany wore both the Hungarian and the Bohemian crowns by virtue of his marriage with the daughter of Siegmund, Emperor and King. The steps towards the union of the various crowns are now beginning. Siegmund was the third King of Bohemia who had worn the crown of Germany, the second who had worn the crown of the Empire. Under his son-in-law, Hungary, Bohemia, and Austria,

Relations with Hungary and Bohemia.

Rudolf, son of Albert, King of Bohemia, 1306.

Albert the Second, King of Hungary and Bohemia, 1438.

Siegmund, King of Hungary, 1386; King of the Romans, 1414;

CHAP. VIII.

King of Bohemia, 1419; Emperor, 1433.

Wladislaus Postumus Duke of Austria, 1440–1457; King of Hungary and Bohemia, 1453–1457.

were for a moment united with the German crown; in the next reign, as we have seen, begins the lasting connexion between Austria and the Empire. But the Hungarian and Bohemian kingdoms parted again. One Austrian King, the son of Albert, reigned at least nominally over both kingdoms, as well as over the special Austrian duchy. But the final union did not come for another eighty years, a period diversified by what now seems a survival of a past state of things, the momentary dominion of Hungary over Austria. By this time the Turk was threatening and conquering on the Hungarian and Austrian borders. At Mohacz Lewis, king of Hungary and Bohemia, fell before the invaders. His Bohemian kingdom passed to Ferdinand of Austria, and from that day to this, unless we except the momentary choice of the Winter King, the Palatine Frederick, the Bohemian crown has always stayed in the House of Austria. And for many generations it has been worn by the actual sovereign of the Austrian archduchy.

Ferdinand, Archduke of Austria, 1519; King of Hungary and Bohemia, 1527; King of the Romans, 1531; Emperor-elect, 1556. Permanent union of Bohemia.

The acquisition of the crown of Hungary was of greater importance. It put the Austrian house into a wholly new position; it gave it its later character of a middle state between Eastern and Western Europe. The duchy had begun as a mark against the Turanian and heathen invaders of earlier times. Those Turanian and heathen invaders had now long settled down into a Christian kingdom; they had taken their place among the foremost champions of Christendom against the Turanian and Mahometan invaders who had seized the throne of the Eastern Cæsars. With the crown of Hungary, the main duty of the Hungarian crown, the defence of Christendom against the Ottoman, passed to the Archdukes and Emperors of the Austrian

Effects of the union with Hungary.

Mission against the Turk.

house. But for a long time Hungary was a most imperfect and precarious possession of its Austrian Kings. For more than a century and a half after the election of Ferdinand, his rule and that of his successors was disputed and partial. They had from the very beginning to strive against rival kings, while the greater part of the kingdom and of the lands attached to the crown was either held by the Turk himself or by princes who acknowledged the Turk as their superior lord. These strictly Hungarian affairs, as well as the changes on the frontier towards the Turk, will be spoken of elsewhere. It was not till the eighteenth century that the Austrian Kings were in full possession of the whole Hungarian kingdom and all its dependencies.

The Austrian kings in Hungary.

1526-1699.

Peace of Passarowitz, 1718.

Meanwhile the Austrian power had been making advances in other quarters. At the end of the fifteenth century the Austrian possessions at the north-east of the Hadriatic were greatly enlarged by the addition of the county of *Görz* or *Gorizia*, and the fallen city of Aquileia. The wars of the League of Cambray made no permanent addition to Austrian dominion in this quarter; but the master of Trieste, Gorizia, and Aquileia, whose territory cut off Venice from her Istrian possessions, was now an Italian sovereign, though his Italian dominions were, as Verona and other Italian lands had been in earlier days, now counted as part of Germany. The prince of the German Austria now counted part of the elder Lombard Austria among his many lordships. Under Charles the Fifth the Italian dominion of the House of Austria grew, as we have seen, to a vast extent. But after him that dominion passed away alike from the Empire and the German branch of the house,

Acquisition of Görz, 1500.

New position towards Italy.

Dominions of Charles the Fifth.

CHAP. VIII.

to become part of the heritage of the Austrian Kings of Spain. It was not, as we have already seen, till the beginning of the eighteenth century that either an Emperor or a reigning archduke again obtained any territory within what were now the acknowledged bounds of Italy. The fluctuations of Austrian rule in Italy, from the acquisition of the Duchy of Milan down to our own day, have been already told in the Italian section. Lombardy and western Venetia are now again Italian; but an Austrian sovereign still keeps the north-east corner of the great gulf. He still keeps Gorizia and Aquileia, Trieste and all Istria, to say nothing of the dangerous way which his frontier still stretches on Italian ground in the land of Trent and Roveredo.

Austrian rule in Italy.

These last-named possessions still abide as traces of the Austrian advance in these regions, and its fluctuations there have been among the most important facts of modern history. Another series of Austrian acquisitions in the West of Europe have altogether passed away. The great Burgundian inheritance passed to the House of Austria. But it was only for a short time, in the persons of Maximilian and his son Philip, that it was in any way united to the actual Austrian Archduchy. After Charles the Fifth the Burgundian possessions passed, like those in Italy, to the Spanish branch of the House, and, just as in Italy, it was not till the eighteenth century that actual Emperors or archdukes again reigned over a part of the Netherlands. Before this time the Alsatian dominion of the house had passed away to France, and the remnant of its Swabian possessions passed away, as we have seen, in the days of general confusion. The changes of Austrian territory in Germany during that period have been already spoken of. The

Burgundian possessions. Maximilian and Philip.

The Austrian Netherlands.

Loss of Elsass.

Austrian acquisitions in Eastern Europe will come more fully elsewhere; but a word must be given to them here. Looking at the House of Austria simply as a power, without reference to the German or non-German character of its dominions, the loss of *Silesia* may be looked on as counterbalanced by the territory gained from Poland at the first and third partitions. The first partition gave the Austrian house a territory of which the greater part was originally Russian rather than Polish, and in which the old Russian names of *Halicz* and *Vladimir* were strangely softened into a *Kingdom of Galicia and Lodomeria*. The third partition added *Cracow* and a considerable amount of strictly Polish territory. These last passed away, first to the Duchy of Warsaw, and then to the restored Kingdom of Poland. But Galicia has been kept, and it has been increased in our day by the seizure of the republic of Cracow. These lands lie to the north of the Hungarian kingdom. Parted from them by the whole extent of that kingdom, and adjoining that kingdom at its south-west corner, lie the coast lands of Austria on the Hadriatic. By the Peace of Campo Formio, Austria took *Dalmatia* strictly so called, and the other Venetian possessions as far south as Budua. These lands, lost in the wars with France, were won again at the Peace, with the addition of *Ragusa* and its territory.

Loss of Silesia, 1740.

Final partition of Poland, 1772.

Galicia and Lodomeria.

Third partition, 1795. New-Galicia.

Annexation of Cracow, 1846.

Dalmatia, 1797. Recovered, 1814.

Ragusa, 1814.

This account of the gains and losses of a power which has gained and lost in so many quarters is necessarily somewhat piecemeal. It may be well then to end this section with a picture of the Austrian power as it stood at several points of the history of the last century and a half, leaving the fluctuating frontier towards the Turk to be dealt with in our survey of the more strictly Eastern lands.

Reign of Maria Theresa, 1740–1780.

We will begin at a date when we come across a sovereign whose position is often strangely misunderstood, the Empress-Queen Maria Theresa—Queen in her own right of Hungary and Bohemia, Empress by the election of her husband to the Imperial Crown. The Pragmatic Sanction of her father Charles the Sixth made her heiress of his hereditary states, of his two kingdoms, and of his Burgundian and Italian dominions. That is, it made her heiress, within the Empire, of the kingdom of Bohemia with its dependencies of Moravia and Silesia—of the Archduchy of Austria with the duchies, counties, and lordships of Styria, Carinthia, Carniola, Tyrol, Gorizia, and Trieste—of Constanz and a few other outlying Swabian points—as also of Milan, Mantua, and the Austrian Netherlands, lands which it needs some stretch, whether of memory or of legal fiction, to look on as being then in any sense lands of the Empire. Beyond the Empire, in its widest sense, it gave her the Kingdom of Hungary with its dependent lands of Croatia, Slavonia, and Transsilvania or Siebenbürgen. These dominions, lessened by the loss of Silesia, increased by the addition of Galicia, she handed on to their later Kings and Archdukes. Her marriage transferring her dominions, indirectly transferred the Empire itself, to a new family, the House of Lorraine. The husband of Maria Theresa, Francis, who had exchanged his duchy of Lorraine for that of Tuscany, was in truth the first Lotharingian Emperor. After him came three Emperors of his house, under the third of whom the succession of Augustus and Charles came to an end.

Her hereditary dominions.

We may take another view of the Austrian territory

CHAP. VIII.

Austrian dominions in 1811.

at the moment when the French power in Germany was at its height. The Roman Empire and the German kingdom had now come to an end; but their last sovereign still, with whatever meaning, called himself Emperor of his archduchy, though without dropping his proper title of Archduke. From this time the word Austria has gradually come, by a common but inaccurate usage, to take in all the possessions of the House of Austria, an usage which disguises the real nature of the Austrian power, and suggests the notion that '*Austria*' is a nation in the same sense as Germany and Italy, and not simply the accumulation in the hands of a single man of territories which have no natural connexion. Still, as all the possessions of the House of Austria were now geographically continuous, it became more natural to speak of them by a single name than it had been when the dominions of that house in Italy and the Netherlands lay apart from the great mass of Austrian territory. And at this moment, when the Empire had come to an end and when the German Confederation had not yet been formed, there was no distinction between German and non-German lands. The 'Empire' of Francis the Second or First, as it stood at the time of Buonaparte's greatest power, had, as compared with the hereditary dominions of Maria Theresa, gone through these changes. Tyrol and the Swabian lands had passed to other German princes; Salzburg had been won and lost again. In Italy the Venetian possessions had been won and lost, and they, together with the older Italian possessions of Austria, had passed to the French kingdom of Italy. France in her own name had encroached on the Austrian dominions at two ends, on the Ocean and on the Hadriatic. She had absorbed the Austrian Netherlands

New use of the name *Austria*.

CHAP. VIII.

at one corner, the newly won Austrian territory in Dalmatia and Istria at another. These last first formed parts of the French kingdom of Italy; afterwards, together with parts of Carinthia and Carniola and of the Hungarian kingdom of Croatia, they were fully united with the French Empire under the name of the *Illyrian Provinces.* Illyrian they were in the widest and most purely geographical sense of that name. But this use of the Illyrian name was confusing and misleading, as tending to put out of sight that the true representatives of the old Illyrian race dwell to the south, not only of Carinthia and Carniola, but of Dalmatia itself. The loss of the Austrian possessions in this quarter brought back the new Austrian 'Empire' to the condition of the original Austrian duchy. It became a wholly inland dominion, without an inch of seacoast anywhere.

Austria at the peace. 1814–5.

We have already seen how Austria won back her lost Italian and Dalmatian territory, and so much of her lost German territory as was geographically continuous. Released from her inland prison, provided again with a great seaboard on both sides of the Hadriatic, she now refused to Ragusa the restoration of her freedom, and filched from Montenegro her hard-won haven of Cattaro. The recovered lands formed, in the new nomenclature of the Austrian possessions, the kingdoms of Lombardy and Venice, of Illyria, and of Dalmatia. The last was an ancient title of the Hungarian crown. The Kingdom of Illyria was a continuation of the affected nomenclature which had been bestowed on the lands which formed it under their French occupation. We have already traced the driving out of the Austrian power from Lombardy and Venetia,

Ragusa and Cattaro.

its momentary joint possession in Sleswick, Holstein, and Lauenburg. The only other actual change of frontier has been the annexation of the inland commonwealth of Cracow, to match the annexation of the sea-faring commonwealth of Ragusa. The movement of 1848 separated Hungary for a moment from the Austrian power. Won back, partly by Russian help, partly by the arms of her own Slavonic subjects, the Magyar kingdom remained crushed till Austria was shut out alike from Germany and from Italy. Then arose the present system, the so-called *dualism*, the theory of which is that the 'Austro-Hungarian Monarchy' consists of two states under a common sovereign. By an odd turning about of meanings, Austria, once really the *Oesterreich*, the Eastern land, of Germany, has become in truth the Western land, the *Neustria*, of the new arrangement. With the Hungarian kingdom are grouped the principality of Transsilvania and the kingdoms of Slavonia and Croatia. The Austrian state is made up of *Austria* itself—the archduchy with the addition of *Salzburg*—the duchy of *Styria*, the county of *Tyrol*, the kingdoms of *Bohemia*, *Galicia* and *Lodomeria*, *Illyria*, and *Dalmatia* with *Ragusa* and *Cattaro*. These last lands are not continuous. Thus two states are formed. In one the dominant German duchy has Slavonic lands on each side of it, and an Italian fringe on its coast. In the other state, the ruling Magyar holds also among the subjects of his crown the Slave, the Rouman, and the outlying Saxon of Siebenbürgen. Add to this that the latest arrangements of all have added to the Austrian dominions, under the diplomatic phrase of 'administration,' the Slavonic lands of *Herzegovina* and *Bosnia*, while the kingdom

Cracow, 1846.

Separation of Hungary, 1848.

Recovery of Hungary, 1849.

Austro-Hungarian Monarchy, 1867.

Modern Austria.

Modern Hungary.

CHAP. IX.

Herzegovina, Bosnia, and Spizza, 1878.

of Dalmatia is increased by the harbour of *Spizza*. A power like this, which rests on no national basis, is simply the estate of a particular family, patched together during a space of six hundred years by this and that grant, this and that marriage, this and that treaty, is surely an anachronism on the face of modern Europe. Germany and Italy are nations as well as powers. Austria, changed from the *Austria* of Germany into the *Neustria* of Hungary, is simply a name without a meaning.

We have thus gone through the geographical changes of the three Imperial kingdoms, and of the states and powers which were formed by parts of those kingdoms falling away, and in some cases uniting themselves with lands beyond the Empire. They have all to some extent kept a common history down to our own time. We have now to turn to another land which parted off from the Empire in like manner, but which parted off so early as to become a wholly separate and rival land, with an altogether independent history of its own.

CHAPTER IX.

THE KINGDOM OF FRANCE.

CHAP. IX.

Origin and growth of France.

THE process by which a great power grew up to the west of the Western Empire has something in common with the process by which the powers spoken of in the later sections of the last Chapter split off from the Western Empire. As in the case of Switzerland and the United Provinces, so in the case of France, a land which had formed part of the dominions of Charles the Great became independent of his successors. As in the case of Austria to the east, so in the case of France to the west, a duchy of the old Empire grew into a power distinct from the Empire, and tried to attach to itself the old Imperial titles and traditions. But there is more than one point of difference between the two cases. As a matter of geography, the power of the Austrian house has for some centuries largely rested on the possession of dominions beyond the boundaries of the Carolingian Empire, while it has been only for a moment, and that chiefly by the annexation of territory from Austria itself, that France has ever held any European possessions beyond the Carolingian frontier.[1] But the true difference lies in the date and circumstances of the separation. The Swabian, Lotharingian, Frisian, and Austrian lands which gradually

Comparison with Austria.

Different nature of the Austrian and the French territories.

Difference in the process of separation.

[1] Namely in the Illyrian Provinces and in the Ionian Islands. See above, p. 324.

The other powers split off after the Empire has become German.

split off from the Empire to form distinct states split off after the Empire had been finally annexed to the crown of Germany, indeed after Germany and the Empire had come to mean nearly the same thing. But France can hardly be said to have split off from the German kingdom or from the Empire itself. The first prince of the Western *Francia* who bore the kingly title was indeed the man of the King of the East-Franks.[1] But no lasting relation, such as afterwards bound the princes of the Empire to its head, sprang out of his homage. Again from 887 to 963 the Imperial dignity was not finally attached to any one kingdom. It fluctuated between Germany and Italy; it might have passed to Burgundy; it might have passed to Karolingia, as it had once already done in the person of Charles the Bald. The truer way of putting the matter is to say that in 887 the Empire split up into four kingdoms, of which three came together again, and formed the Empire in a new shape. The fourth kingdom remained separate; it can hardly be said to have split off from the Empire, but its separation hindered the full reconstruction of the Empire. It has had a distinct history, a history which made it the special rival of the Empire. This was *Karolingia*, the kingdom of the West-Franks, to which, through the results of the change of dynasty in 987, the name of *France* gradually came to be applied.

The Empire divided into four kingdoms, of which three are again united, while one remains distinct.

Karolingia receives the name of *France*.

France a nation as well as a power.

But there is yet another distinction of greater practical importance. France was so early detached from the rest of the elder Frankish dominions that it was able to form from the first a nation as well as a power. Its separation happened at the time when the

[1] See above, p. 139.

CHAP. IX.

European nations were forming. The other powers did not split off till long after those nations were formed, and they did not in any strict sense form nations. But France is a nation in the fullest sense. Its history is therefore different from the history of Austria, of Burgundy, of Switzerland, or even of Italy. As a state which had become wholly distinct from the Empire, which was commonly the rival and enemy of the Empire, which largely grew at the expense of the Empire, above all, as a state which won for itself a most distinct national being, France fully deserves a chapter, and not a mere section. Still that chapter is in some sort an appendage to that which deals with the Imperial kingdoms of the West. It naturally follows on our survey of those kingdoms, before we go on further to deal with the European powers which arose out of the dismemberment of the Empire of the East.

Extent of the royal domain at the accession of the Parisian house. 987.

We left Karolingia or the Western Kingdom at that point where the modern French state took its real beginning under the kings of the house of Paris. Their duchy of France had since its foundation been cut short by the great grant of Normandy, and by the practical independence which had been won by the counts of *Anjou*, *Maine*, and *Chartres*. By their election to the kingdom, the Dukes of the French added to their duchy the small territory which up to that time had still been in the immediate possession of the West-Frankish Kings at Laon. And, with the crown and the immediate territory of those kings, the French kings at Paris also inherited their claim to superiority over all the states which had arisen within the bounds of the Western Kingdom. But the name *France*, as it was

Definition

CHAP. IX.

of the word *France.*

Two forms of growth; annexation of fiefs of the French crown and of lands altogether beyond the kingdom.

used in the times with which we are dealing, means only the immediate territory of the King. The use of the name spreads with every increase of that territory, whether that increase was made by the incorporation of a fief or by the annexation of territory wholly foreign to the kingdom. And this constantly widening application of the name is as strictly accurate in the case of France as it is inaccurate in the case of Austria. Every land permanently annexed by the sovereigns of France has sooner or later really become French; but the lands annexed by the sovereigns of Austria show no tendency to become Austrian. But the two processes of incorporating fiefs of the French crown and of annexing lands with which the French crown had nothing to do must be carefully distinguished. Both went on side by side for some centuries; but the incorporation of the vassal states naturally began before the annexation of altogether foreign territory.

Various feudal gradations.

Among the fiefs which were gradually annexed a distinction must be drawn between the great princes who were really national chiefs owing an external homage to the French crown, and the lesser counts whose dominions had been cut off from the original duchy of France. And a distinction must be again drawn between these last and the immediate tenants of the Crown within its own domains, vassals of the Duke as well as of the King. To the first class belong the Dukes and Counts of *Burgundy*, *Aquitaine*, *Toulouse*, and *Flanders*; to the second the Counts of *Anjou*, *Chartres*, and *Champagne*. Historically, *Normandy* belongs to the second class, as the original grant to Rolf was undoubtedly cut off from the French duchy. But the whole circumstances of the Norman

The great vassals.

Special character of Normandy.

CHAP. IX.

duchy made it a truly national state, owing to the French crown the merest external homage. *Britanny*, yet more distinct in every way, was held to owe its immediate homage to the Duke of the Normans. The so-called Twelve Peers of France seem to have been devised by Philip Augustus out of the romances of Charlemagne; but the selection shows who were looked on as the greatest vassals of the crown in his day. The six lay peers were the Dukes of Burgundy, Normandy, and Aquitaine, the Counts of Flanders, Toulouse, and Champagne. This last was the only one of the six who could not be looked upon as a national sovereign. His dominions were *French* in a sense in which Normandy or Aquitaine could not be called French. The six ecclesiastical peers offer a marked contrast to the ecclesiastical electors of the Empire. The German bishops became princes, holding directly of the Empire. But the bishops within the dominions of the great vassals of the French crown were the subjects of their immediate sovereigns. The Archbishop of Rouen or the Archbishop of Bourdeaux stood in no relation to the King of the French. The ecclesiastical peerage of France consisted only of certain bishops who were immediate vassals of the King in his character of King, among whom was only one prelate of the first rank, the Archbishop and Duke of *Rheims*. The others were the Bishops and Dukes of *Langres* and *Laon*, and the Bishops and Counts of *Beauvais*, *Noyon*, and *Châlons*. As the bishops within the dominions of the great feudatories had no claim to rank as peers of the kingdom, neither had those prelates who were actually within the King's immediate territory, vassals therefore of the Duke of the French as well as of the King. Thus the

Britanny.

The Twelve Peers.

Champagne.

Different position of the bishops in the Eastern and Western kingdom.

CHAP. IX.

Bishop of Paris and his metropolitan the Archbishop of Sens had no place among the twelve peers.

§ 1. *Incorporation of the Vassal States.*

At the accession of the Parisian dynasty, the royal domain took in the greater part of the later *Isle of France*, the territory to which the old name specially clung, the greater part of the later government of *Orleans*, besides some outlying fiefs holding immediately of the King. Within this territory the counties of *Clermont*, *Dreux*, *Moulins*, *Valois*, and the *Gatinois*, are of the greatest historical importance. Two of the great rivers of Gaul, the Seine and the Loire, flowed through the royal dominions; but the King was wholly cut off from the sea by the great feudatories who commanded the lower course of the rivers. The coast of the Channel was held by the princes of Britanny, Normandy, and Flanders, and the smaller county of *Ponthieu*, which lay between Normandy and Flanders and fluctuated in its homage between the two. The ocean coast was held by the rulers of Britanny, of *Poitou* and *Aquitaine* united under a single sovereign, and of *Gascony* to the south of them. That part of the Mediterranean coast which nominally belonged to the Western Kingdom was held by the counts of *Toulouse* and *Barcelona*. Of these great feudatories, the princes of Flanders, Burgundy, Normandy, and Champagne, were all immediate neighbours of the King. To the west of the royal domain lay several states of the second rank which played a great part in the history of France and Normandy. These were the counties of *Chartres* and *Blois*, which were for a while united with *Champagne*. Beyond these, besides some

Chief vassals within the royal domain.

States on the Channel and on the Ocean; on the Mediterranean coast.

Neighbours of the royal domain.

Chartres and Blois. 1125–1152.

smaller counties, were *Anjou* and *Touraine*, and *Maine*, the borderland of Normandy and Anjou. Thus surrounded by their own vassals, the early Kings of the house of Paris had far less dealings with powers beyond their own kingdom than their Karolingian predecessors. They were thus able to make themselves the great power of Gaul before they stood forth on a wider field as one of the great powers of Europe.

Anjou and Touraine united. 1044.

Maine.

As regards their extent of territory, the Kings of the French at the beginning of the eleventh century had altogether fallen away from the commanding position which had been held by the Dukes of the French in the middle of the tenth. But this seeming loss of power was fully outweighed by the fact that they were now Kings and not merely Dukes, lords and no longer vassals. As feudal principles grew, opportunities were constantly found for annexing the lands of the vassal to the lands of his lord. Towards the end of the eleventh century the royal domain had already begun to increase by the acquisition of the *Gatinois* and of the viscounty of *Bourges*, a small part only of the later province of Berry, but an addition which made France and Aquitaine more clearly neighbours than before. Towards the end of the twelfth century began a more important advance to the north-east. The first aggrandizement of France at the expense of Flanders was the beginning of an important chain of events in European history. In the early years of Philip Augustus the counties of *Amiens* and *Vermandois* were united to the crown, as was the county of *Valois* two years later. So for a while was the more important land of *Artois*. Later in the reign of the same prince came an annexation on a far

The kingdom smaller than the old duchy.

Advantage of the kingly position.

First advances of the Kings.

Gatinois. 1068.

Viscounty of Bourges. 1100.

Amiens and Vermandois. 1183.

Valois. 1185.

Artois. 1180–1187.

CHAP. IX.

greater scale, which did not happen till the first years of the thirteenth century, but which was the result of causes which had been going on ever since the eleventh.

Growth of the House of Anjou.

In the course of the twelfth century a power grew up within the bounds of the Western Kingdom which in extent of territory threw the dominions of the French King into insignificance. The two great powers of northern and southern Gaul, Normandy and Aquitaine, each carrying with it a crowd of smaller states, were united in the hands of a single prince, and that a prince who was also the king of a powerful foreign kingdom. The Aquitanian duchy contained, besides the county of *Poitou*, a number of fiefs, of which the most important were those of *Périgueux*, *Limoges*, the dauphiny of *Auvergne*, and the county of *Marche* which gave kings to Jerusalem and Cyprus.

Union of Aquitaine and Gascony. 1052.

To these, in the eleventh century, the duchy of *Gascony*, with its subordinate fiefs, was added, and the dominions of the lord of Poitiers stretched to the Pyrenees. Meanwhile Duke William of Normandy, before his conquest of England, had increased his continental dominions, by acquiring the superiority of *Ponthieu* and the immediate dominion, first of the small district of *Domfront* and then of the whole of *Maine*. Maine was presently lost by his successor, and passed in the end to the house of Anjou. But the union of several lines in descent in the same person united England, Normandy, Anjou, and Maine in the person of Henry the Second.

Conquests of William of Normandy. Ponthieu. 1056. Domfront. 1049. Maine. 1063. Union of Maine and Anjou. 1110.

Dominions of Henry the Second.

For a moment it seemed as if, instead of the northern and southern powers being united in opposition to the crown, one of them was to be itself incorporated with the crown. The marriage of Lewis the Seventh with Eleanor of Aquitaine united his kingdom and her duchy. A king of Paris for the first time reigned on the Garonne and at the foot of the Pyrenees. But the divorce of Lewis and Eleanor and her immediate re-marriage with the Duke of Normandy and Count of Anjou again severed the southern duchy from the kingdom, and united the great powers of northern and southern Gaul. Then their common lord won a crown beyond the sea and became the first Angevin king of England. Another marriage brought Britanny, long the nominal fief of Normandy, under the practical dominion of its Duke. The House of Anjou thus suddenly rose to a dominion on Gaulish soil equal to that of the French king and his other vassals put together, a dominion which held the mouths of the three great rivers, and which was further strengthened by the possession of the English kingdom. But a favourable moment soon came which enabled the King to add to his own dominions the greater part of the estates of his dangerous vassal. On the death of Richard, first of England and fourth of Normandy, Normandy and England passed to his brother John, while in the other continental dominions of the Angevin princes the claims of his nephew Arthur, the heir of Britanny, were asserted. The success of Arthur would have given the geography of Gaul altogether a new shape. The Angevin possessions on the continent, instead of being held by a king of England, would have been held by a Duke of Britanny, the prince of a state which, though not geographically cut off like England, was even more foreign to France. On the fall of Arthur, Philip, by the help of a jurisprudence devised for the purpose, was able to declare

Momentary union of France and Aquitaine. 1137.

Their separation. 1152.

Union of Aquitaine, Normandy, and Anjou.

1152–1154.

Britanny. 1169.

Claims of Arthur of Britanny.

Possible effects of his success.

CHAP. IX.

all the fiefs which John held of the French crown to be forfeited to that crown, a sentence which did not

Annexation of Normandy, Anjou, &c. 1202–1205.

apply to the fiefs of his mother Eleanor. In the space of two years Philip was able to carry that sentence into effect everywhere on the mainland. Continental Normandy, Maine, Anjou, and Touraine, were joined to the dominions of the French crown, and

1258.

by a later treaty they were formally surrendered by John's son Henry. Poitou went with them, and all these lands may from this time be looked on as forming

Character and effects of the annexation.

part of France. Thus far the process of annexation was little more than the restoration of an earlier state of things. For all these lands, except Poitou, had

Territories kept by the English kings.

formed part of the old French duchy. The Kings of England still kept the duchy of Aquitaine[1] with Gascony.

The Norman Islands.

They kept also the insular Normandy, the Norman islands which have ever since remained distinct states

Aquitaine.

attached to the English crown. Aquitaine was now no longer part of the continental dominions of a prince who was equally at home on both sides of the Channel. It changed into a remote dependency of the insular kingdom, a dependency whose great cities clave to the English connexion, while its geographical position and the feelings of its feudal nobility tended to draw it towards France.

Sudden greatness of France.

The result of this great and sudden acquisition of territory was to make the King of the French incomparably greater on Gaulish ground than any of his own vassals. France had now a large seaboard on the Channel and a small seaboard on the Ocean. And now another chain of events incorporated a large terri-

[1] Aquitaine, the inheritance of Eleanor, did not come under the forfeiture of the fiefs actually held by John.

tory with which the crown had hitherto stood in no practical relation, and which gave the kingdom a third seaboard on the Mediterranean.

Fiefs of Aragon in Southern Gaul.

Counts of Toulouse.

The Albigensian War. 1207–1229.

Simon of Montfort at Toulouse.

Settlement of Meaux. Annexation of Narbonne, 1229; of Toulouse, 1270.

Roussillon and Barcelona released from homage. 1258.

While north-western and south-western Gaul were united in the hands of an insular king, the king of a peninsular kingdom became only less powerful in south-eastern Gaul. Hitherto the greatest princes in this region had been the counts of *Toulouse*, who, besides their fiefs of the French crown, had also possessions in the Burgundian kingdom beyond the Rhone. But during the latter part of the eleventh century and the beginning of the twelfth, the Counts of *Barcelona*, and the kings of Aragon who succeeded them, acquired by various means a number of Tolosan fiefs, both French and Imperial. *Carcassonne*, *Albi*, and *Nîmes* were all under the lordship of the Aragonese crown. The Albigensian war seemed at first likely to lead to the establishment of the house of Montfort as the chief power of southern Gaul. But the struggle ended in a vast increase of the power of the French crown, at the expense alike of the house of Toulouse and of the house of Aragon. The dominions of the Count of Toulouse were divided. A number of fiefs, *Béziers*, *Narbonne*, *Nîmes*, *Albi*, and some other districts, were at once annexed to the crown. The capital itself and its county passed to the crown fifty years later. By a settlement with Aragon, the domains of the French king were increased, while the French kingdom itself was nominally cut short. Two of the Aragonese fiefs, the counties of *Roussillon* and *Barcelona*, were relieved from even nominal homage. The name of Toulouse, except as the name of the city

CHAP. IX.

itself, now passed away, and the new acquisitions of France came in the end to be known by the name of the tongue which was common to them with Aquitaine and Imperial Burgundy. Under the name of *Languedoc* they became one of the greatest and most valuable provinces of the French kingdom.

Province of Languedoc.

The great growth of the crown during the reign of Saint Lewis was thus in the south; but he also extended his borders nearer home. He won back part of the old French duchy when he purchased the superiority of *Blois* and *Chartres*, to which *Perche* was afterwards added by escheat. Further off, he added *Macon* to the crown, a possession which afterwards passed away to the House of Burgundy.

Purchase of Blois and Chartres. 1234.

Escheat of Perche. 1257.

Annexation of Macon, 1239.

Southern advance of the Crown.

Thus, during the reigns of Philip Augustus and his grandson, the royal possessions had been enlarged by the annexations of two of the chief vassal states, two of the lay peerages, annexations which gave the French King a seaboard on two seas and which brought him into immediate connexion with the affairs of the Spanish peninsula. Later in the thirteenth century, the marriage of Philip the Fair with the heiress of *Champagne* not only extinguished another peerage, but made the French kings for a while actually Spanish sovereigns, and made France an immediate neighbour of the German kingdom. The county of *Champagne* had for two generations been united with the kingdom of Navarre. These dominions were held by three kings of France in right of their wives. Then Navarre, though it passed to a French prince, was wholly separated from France, while Champagne was incorporated with the kingdom. This last annexation gave

Marriage of Philip the Fair, 1284, with the heiress of Champagne and Navarre.

Separation of Navarre. 1328.

France a considerable frontier towards Germany, and especially brought the kingdom into the immediate neighbourhood of the Lotharingian bishoprics. These acquisitions, of Normandy and the states connected with it, of Toulouse and the rest of Languedoc, and now of Champagne, were the chief cases of incorporation of vassal states with the royal domain up to the middle of the fourteenth century. The mere grants and recoveries of appanages hardly concern geography. We now turn to two great struggles which, in the course of the fourteenth and fifteenth centuries, the Kings of France had to wage with two of their chief vassals who were also powerful foreign princes. In both cases, events which seemed likely to bring about the utter humiliation of France did in the end bring to it a large increase of territory.

Union of Champagne, 1335; incorporation, 1361.

Appanages.

The former of these struggles was the great war between England and France, called by French writers the *Hundred Years' War*. This war might be called either a war for the annexation of France to England or a war for the annexation of Aquitaine to France. By the peace between Henry the Third and Saint Lewis, Aquitaine became a land held by the king of England as a vassal of the French crown. From that time it was one main object of the French kings to change their feudal superiority over this great duchy into an actual possession. This object had once been obtained for a moment by the marriage of Eleanor and Lewis the Seventh. It was again obtained for a moment by the negotiations between Edward the First and Philip the Fair. The Hundred Years' War began through the attempts of Philip of Valois on the

The Hundred Years' War with England.

Designs of the French kings on Aquitaine.

Momentary occupation by Philip the Fair. 1294.

1337.

CHAP. IX. 1339.

Aquitanian dominions of Edward the Third. Then the King of England found it politic to assume the title of King of France. But the real nature of the controversy was shown by the first great settlement. At the Peace of *Bretigny* Edward gave up all claim to the crown of France, in exchange for the independent sovereignty of his old fiefs and of some of his recent conquests. *Aquitaine* and *Gascony*, including *Poitou* but not including *Auvergne*, together with the districts on the Channel, *Calais* with *Guînes* and the county of *Ponthieu*, were made over to the King of England without the reservation of any homage or superiority of any kind. These lands became a territory as foreign to the French kingdom as the territory of her German and Spanish neighbours. But in a few years the treaty was broken on the French side, and the actual possessions of England beyond the sea were cut down to Calais and Guînes, with some small parts of Aquitaine adjoining the cities of Bordeaux and Bayonne. Then the tide turned when the war was carried on with renewed vigour by Henry the Fifth. The Treaty of Troyes formally united the crowns of England and France. Aquitaine and Normandy were won back; Paris saw the crowning of an English king, and only the central part of the country obeyed the heir of the Parisian kingdom, no longer king of Paris but only of Bourges. But the final result of the war was the driving out of the English from all Aquitaine and France, except the single district of Calais. The geographical aspect of the change is that Aquitaine, which had been wholly cut off from the kingdom by the Peace of Bretigny, was finally incorporated with the kingdom. The French conquest of Aquitaine, the

Peace of Bretigny. 1360.

Renewal of the war. 1370–1374.

Losses of the English.

Conquests of Henry the Fifth.

Treaty of Troyes. 1420.

1431.

Conquest of Aquitaine. 1451–1453.

CHAP. IX.

result of the Hundred Years' War, was in form the conquest of a land which had ceased to stand in any relation to the French crown. Practically the result of the war was the incorporation with the French crown of its greatest fief, balanced by the loss of a small territory the value of which was certainly out of all proportion to its geographical extent. In its historical aspect the annexation of Aquitaine was something yet more. The first foreshadowing of the modern French kingdom was made by the addition of Aquitaine to Neustria, of southern to northern Gaul.[1] Now, after so many strivings, the two were united for ever. Aquitaine was merged in France. The grant to Charles the Bald took effect after six hundred years. France, in the sense which the word bears in modern use, may date its complete existence from the addition of Bourdeaux to the dominions of Charles the Seventh.

Final union of Aquitaine with France.

Beginning of the modern Kingdom of France.

Thus, in the course of somewhat less than four hundred years, the conquest of England by a vassal of France, followed by the union of a crowd of other French fiefs in the hands of a common sovereign of England and Normandy, had led to the union with France of all the continental possessions of the prince who thus reigned on both sides of the sea. Meanwhile, on the eastern side of the kingdom, the holder of another great French fief swelled into an European power, the special rival of his French overlord. The dukes of Burgundy rose to the same kind of position which had in the twelfth century been held by the dukes of Normandy and counts of Anjou. Their duchy, granted to a branch of the royal house in the earliest days of the

Growth of the Dukes of Burgundy.

Escheat of the duchy of Burgundy. 1361.

[1] See above, p. 135.

CHAP. IX.

Grant to Philip the Hardy. 1364.

Advance of the Valois Dukes.

Parisian kingdom, escheated to the crown in the fourteenth century, and was again granted out to a son of the reigning king. A series of marriages, purchases, conquests, transactions of every kind, gathered together, in the hands of the Burgundian dukes, a crowd of fiefs both of France and of the Empire.[1] The duchy of *Burgundy* with the county of *Charolois*, and the counties of *Flanders* and *Artois*, were joined under a common ruler with endless Imperial fiefs in the Low Countries and with the Imperial *County of Burgundy*. More than this, under Philip the Good and Charles the Bold, the Burgundian frontier was more than once advanced to the Somme, and *Amiens* was separated from the crown. The fall of Charles the Bold laid his dominions open to French annexation both on the Burgundian and on the Flemish frontier. In the first moments of his success, Lewis the Eleventh possessed himself of a large part of the Imperial as well as the French fiefs of the fallen Duke. But in the end Flanders and Artois remained French fiefs held by the House of Burgundy, which also kept the county of Burgundy and the isolated county of Charolois. But France not only finally recovered the towns on the Somme, but incorporated the Burgundian duchy, one of the greatest fiefs of the crown. This was the addition of a territory which the kings of France had never before ruled, and it marks an important stage in the advance of the French power towards the Imperial lands on its eastern border. By the marriage of Mary of Burgundy and Maximilian of Austria, the remains of the Burgundian dominions passed to the House of Austria, and thereby in the

Advance to the Somme.

Annexations at the death of Charles the Bold. 1479.

Momentary annexation of Artois and the County of Burgundy.

Treaty of Arras. 1435.

Incorporation of the duchy of Burgundy. 1479.

French advance to the east.

[1] See above, p. 292.

end to Spain. The result was that a French king had for a moment an Emperor for his vassal in his character of Count of Flanders and Artois. But by the treaty of Madrid Flanders and Artois were relieved from all homage to France, exactly as Aquitaine had been by the Peace of Bretigny, and Roussillon in the days of Saint Lewis. Flanders and Artois now became lands wholly foreign to France, and, as foreign lands, large parts of them were afterwards conquered by France, just as Aquitaine and Roussillon were. But the history of their acquisition belongs to the story of the advance of France at the expense of the Empire.

Flanders and Artois relieved from homage. 1525.

Thus, by the end of the reign of Lewis the Eleventh, all the fiefs of the French crown which could make any claim to the character of separate sovereignties had, with a single exception, been added to the dominions of the crown. The one which had escaped was that one which, more than any other, represented a nationality altogether distinct from that of France. *Britanny* still remained distinct under its own Dukes. The marriages of its Duchess Anne with two successive French kings, Charles the Eighth and Lewis the Twelfth, added Britanny to France, and so completed the work. The whole of the Western Kingdom, except those parts which had become foreign ground—that is to say, insular Normandy and Calais, Barcelona, Flanders, and Artois—was now united under the kings of Paris. Their duchy of *France* had spread its power and its name over the whole kingdom of *Karolingia*. We have now to see how it also spread itself over lands which had never formed part of that kingdom.

All the great fiefs annexed except Britanny.

1491–1499: incorporated 1532.

CHAP. IX.

§ 2. *Foreign Annexations of France.*

Foreign neighbours of Karolingia. Imperial and Spanish neighbours. England.

When the Western Kingdom finally parted off from the body of the Empire, its only immediate neighbours were the Imperial kingdoms to the east, and the Spanish kingdoms to the south. The union of Normandy and England in some sort made England and France immediate neighbours. And the long retention of Aquitaine by England, the English possession of Calais for more than two hundred years and of the insular Normandy down to our own day, have all tended to keep them so. But the acquisitions of France from England, and from Spain, in its character as Spain, have been comparatively small. Indeed the separation of the Spanish March and the insular Normandy may be thought to turn the balance the other way. From England France has won Aquitaine and Calais, territories which had once been under the homage of the French King. So in the sixteenth century *Boulogne* was lost to England and won back again; so in the seventeenth century *Dunkirk*, which had become an English possession, was made over to France. Since the final loss of Aquitaine, the wars between England and France have made most important changes in the English and French possessions in distant parts of the world, but they have had no effect on the geography of England, and very little on that of France.

Small acquisitions of France from England and Spain.

English conquest of Boulogne. 1544–1550.

1663.

Nearly the same may be said of the geographical relations between France and Spain. The long wars between those countries have added to France a large part of the outlying dominions of Spain; but they have not greatly affected the boundaries of the two countries themselves. The only important exception

Boundary of the Pyrenees.

CHAP. IX.

is the county of *Roussillon*, the land which Aragon kept on the north side of the mountain range. United to France by Lewis the Eleventh, given back by Charles the Eighth, it was finally annexed to France by the Peace of the Pyrenees. Towards the other end of the mountain frontier, a small portion of Spanish territory has been annexed to France, perhaps quite unconsciously. The old kingdom of *Navarre*, though it lay chiefly south of the Pyrenees, contained a small territory to the north. The accidents of female succession had given Navarre to more than one King of France, and in the person of Henry the Fourth the crown of France passed to a King of Navarre who held only that part of his kingdom which lay north of the Pyrenees. This little piece of Spain within the borders of Gaul was thus united with France. On the other hand, the Kings of France, as successors of the Counts of Foix, and the other rulers of France after them, have held, not any dominion but certain rights as advocates or protectors, over the small commonwealth of *Andorra* on the Spanish side of the mountains.

Roussillon, its shiftings.

Finally becomes French. 1659.

Navarre north of the Pyrenees.

Union of France and Navarre. 1589.

Protectorate of Andorra.

Of far greater importance is the steady acquisition of territory by France at the expense of the Imperial kingdoms, and of the modern states by which those kingdoms are represented. In the case of Burgundy, French annexation has taken the form of a gradual swallowing up of nearly the whole kingdom, a process which has been spread over more than five hundred years, from the annexation of Lyons by Philip the Fair to the last annexation of Savoy in our own day. The advance at the expense of the German kingdom did not begin till the greater part of the Burgundian

Advance at the expense of the Imperial kingdoms.

Burgundy.

1310–1860.

Annexations from Germany. 1552–1811.

CHAP. IX.

Late beginning of annexations from Germany.

kingdom was already swallowed up. The north-eastern frontier of the Western Kingdom changed but little from the accession of the Parisian house in the tenth century till the growth of the Dukes of Burgundy in the fifteenth. After Lotharingia finally became a part of the Eastern Kingdom, there was no doubt that the homage of Flanders was due to France, no doubt that the homage of the states which had formed the Lower Lotharingia was due to the Empire. The frontier towards the Upper Lotharingia and the Burgundian county also remained untouched. The Saône remained a boundary stream long after the Rhone had ceased to be one. It was on this latter river that the great Burgundian annexations of France began, annexations which gave France a wholly new European position.[1] The acquisition of the Dauphiny of Viennois made France the immediate neighbour of Italy; the acquisition of Provence at once strengthened this last position and more than doubled her Mediterranean coast. Add to this that, though France and the Confederate territory did not as yet actually touch, yet the Burgundian wars and many other events in the latter half of the fifteenth century enabled France to establish a close connexion with the power which had grown up north of Lake Leman. France had thus become a great Mediterranean and Alpine power, ready to threaten Italy in the next generation. Later acquisitions within the old border of the Burgundian kingdom had a somewhat different character. Annexations at the expense of Savoy, even when geographically Burgundian, were annexations at the cost of a power which was beginning to be Italian rather

Effect of the Burgundian acquisitions of France; of the Dauphiny; of Provence.

Relations with the Swiss.

Annexations at the expense of Savoy;

[1] See above, p. 264.

than Burgundian. The annexation of the County of Burgundy goes rather with the Alsatian annexations. It was territory won at the cost of the Empire and of the House of Austria. But the lands between the Rhone, the Alps, and the sea, had not, at the time when France first began to threaten them, wholly lost their middle character. They kept it at least negatively. They were lands which were neither German, French, nor Italian. The events of the fourteenth and fifteenth centuries ruled that this intermediate region should become French. And none of the acquisitions of France ever helped more towards the real growth of her power.

of the County of Burgundy.

Middle character of the Burgundian lands.

They become French.

It was while the later stages of this process were going on that the French kings added to their dominions the Aquitanian lands on one side and the Burgundian duchy on the other. The acquisition of Aquitaine has, besides its other characters, a third aspect which closely connects it with the annexations between the Rhone and the Alps. The strife between Northern and Southern Gaul, between the tongue of *oil* and the tongue of *oc*, now came to an end. Had the chief power in Gaul settled somewhere in Burgundy or Aquitaine, the tongue of *oil* might now pass for a *patois* of the tongue of *oc*. Had French dominion in Italy begun as soon and lasted as permanently as French dominion in Burgundy and Aquitaine, the tongue of *si*, as well as the tongue of *oc*, might now pass for a *patois* of the tongue of *oil*. But now it was settled that French, not Provençal, was to be the ruling speech of Gaul. Those lands of the Southern speech which escaped were almost wholly portions of the dominions of other powers. There was no longer any separate state wholly of that

Effect of French annexations on the *Langue d'oc*.

CHAP. IX.

speech, except the little principality of Orange. The work which the French kings had now ended amounted to little short of the extinction of an European nation.

Extinction of the Provençal speech and nation.

A tongue, once of at least equal dignity with the tongue of Paris and Tours, has sunk from the rank of a national language to the rank of a provincial dialect.

Italian conquests of France.

The next great conquests of France were made on Italian soil, but they are conquests which do not greatly concern geography. There is a marked difference between the relations of France towards Italy and her relations towards Burgundy. Down to the revolutionary wars, the Italian relations of France have comparatively little to do with geography. France has constantly interfered in Italian affairs; she has at various times held large Italian territories, and brought all Italy under French influence. But France has never permanently kept any large amount of Italian territory. The French possession of Naples and Milan was only temporary. And, if it had been lasting, the possession of these isolated territories by the French king could hardly have been looked on as an extension of the actual French frontier. Those lands could never have been incorporated with France in the same way in which other French conquests had been. Their retention would in truth have given the later history of France quite a different character, a character more like that which actually belonged to Spain. The long occupation of Savoyard territory on both sides of the Alps[1] would, if it had lasted, have been a real extension of the French kingdom. But down to our own day, while the lands won by France from the Burgundian kingdom form a

Not strictly extensions of France.

[1] See above, pp. 284, 285.

large proportion of the whole French territory, the lasting acquisitions of France from Italy hardly go beyond the island of Corsica and the insignificant district of *Mentone*.

Annexations at the expense of Germany.

The great annexations of France at the expense of the German kingdom and the lands more closely connected with it begin in the middle of the sixteenth century. The first great advance was the practical annexation of the three Lotharingian bishoprics, though their separation from the Empire was not formally acknowledged till the Peace of Westfalia. This kind of conquest can hardly fail to lead to other conquests. France now held certain patches of territory which lay detached from one another and from the main body of the kingdom. Yet the rounding off of the frontier was not the next step taken in this direction. The cause was most likely the close connexion which for some while existed between the ruling houses of France and Lorraine.

Annexation of Metz, Toul, and Verdun. 1552.

Effect of isolated conquests.

Before the next French advance on German ground, the frontier had been extended in other directions. Almost at the same time as the acquisition of the Three Bishoprics, *Calais* was won back from England—the short English possession of *Boulogne* had already come to an end. The first year of the sixteenth century saw the surrender of *Saluzzo*, in exchange for *Bresse*, *Bugey*, and *Gex*. Thirty years later came the renewed occupation of Italian territory at *Pinerolo* and other points in Piedmont, which lasted till nearly the end of the seventeenth century.

Recovery of Calais, 1558; of Boulogne, 1550.

Surrender of Saluzzo and annexation of Bresse, Bugey, and Gex.

Occupation of Pinerolo. 1630–1696.

The next great advance was the work of the Thirty Years' War and of the war with Spain which went on

CHAP. IX.

The Bishoprics surrendered by the Empire.

French acquisitions in Elsass. 1648.

for eleven years longer. Now came the legal cession of the Bishoprics and the further acquisition of the Alsatian dominions and rights of the House of Austria. The irregularities of the frontier, and the temptation to round off its angles, were increased tenfold. France received another and larger isolated territory lying to the east both of her earlier conquests and of the independent lands which surrounded them. A part of her dominion, itself sprinkled with isolated towns and districts which did not belong to her dominion, stretched out without any connexion into the middle of the Empire. The duchy of Lorraine, dotted over by the French lands of Metz, Toul, and Verdun, lay between the old French land of Champagne and the new French land of *Elsass* or *Alsace*. And while France was allowed,

Breisach.

by the possession of *Breisach*, to establish herself at one point on the right bank of the Rhine, her new territory on the left bank was broken up by the continued independence of *Strassburg* and the other Alsatian towns and districts which were still left to the Empire. Such

France reaches the Rhine.

a frontier could hardly be lasting; now that France had reached and even crossed the Rhine, the annexation of the outlying Imperial lands to the west of that river was sure to follow.

But, even after this further advance into the heart of Germany, the gap was not filled up at the next

Annexation of Bar. 1659.

stage of annexation. At the Peace of the Pyrenees, France obtained the scattered lands of the duchy of Bar, which made the greater part of the Three

Bar restored. 1661.

Bishoprics continuous with her older possessions. But Bar was presently restored, and, though Lorraine was constantly occupied by French armies, it was not incorporated with France for another century. Up to this last change the Three Bishoprics still remained isolated French possessions surrounded by lands of the Empire. But France advanced at the expense of the outlying possessions of Spain, lands only nominally Imperial, as well as of the Spanish lands on her own southern frontier. At the Peace of the Pyrenees *Roussillon* finally became French. No Spanish kingdom any longer stretched north of the great natural barrier of the peninsula. The same Treaty gave France her first acquisitions in *Flanders* and *Artois* since they had become wholly foreign ground, as well as her first acquisitions from *Hainault*, *Liège*, and *Luxemburg*, lands which had never owed her homage. Here again the frontier was of the same kind as the frontier towards Germany. Isolated points like *Philippeville* and *Marienburg* were held by France within Spanish or Imperial territory, and isolated points like *Aire* and *St. Omer* were still held by Spain in what had now become French territory. The furthest French advance that was recognized by any treaty was made by the earlier Peace of Aix-la-Chapelle, when, amongst other places, *Douay*, *Tournay*, *Lille*, *Oudenarde*, and *Courtray* became French. By the Peace of Nimwegen the French frontier again fell back in eastern Flanders, and Courtray and Oudenarde were restored to Spain. But in the districts more to the south France again advanced, gaining the outlying Spanish towns in Artois, *Cambray* and its district, and *Valenciennes* in Hainault. The Peace of Ryswick left the frontier as it had been fixed by the Peace of Nimwegen. Finally, the Treaty of Utrecht and the Barrier Treaty left France in possession of a considerable part of Flanders, and of much land which had been Imperial.

Annexation of Roussillon. 1659.

Annexation in the Netherlands. 1659.

Isolated points held by each power.

Further annexations. 1668.

Changes at the Peace of Nimwegen. 1678.

1697.

Treaty of Utrecht and Barrier Treaty. 1713–1715.

CHAP. IX.

The Barrier Towns.

The Netherlands, formerly Spanish and now Austrian, kept a frontier protected by the barrier towns of *Furnes*, *Ypres*, *Menin*, *Tournai*, *Mons*, *Charleroi*, *Namur*. The French frontier on the other side had its series of barrier towns stretching from *St. Omer* to *Charlemont* on the Maes. The arrangements then made have, with very slight changes, lasted ever since, except during the French annexation of the whole Netherlands during the revolutionary wars.

Franche-Comté conquered. 1668. Conquered again. 1674.

Freiburg.

Seizure of Strassburg. 1681.

Restoration of Freiburg and Breisach.

Peace of Rastadt. 1714.

Annexation of Orange. 1714.

The reign of Lewis the Fourteenth was also a time of at least equal advance on the part of France on her more strictly German frontier. The time was now come for serious attempts to consolidate the scattered possessions of France between Champagne and the Rhine. *Franche-Comté*, as the county of Burgundy was now more commonly called, with the city of *Besançon*, was twice seized by Lewis, and the second seizure was confirmed by the Peace of Nimwegen. By that peace also France kept *Freiburg-im-Breisgau* on the right bank of the Rhine. A number of small places in Elsass were annexed after the Peace of Nimwegen by the process known as *Réunion*. At last in 1681 *Strassburg* itself was seized in time of peace, and its possession was finally secured to France by the Peace of Ryswick. But Freiburg and Breisach were restored, and Lorraine, held by France, though not formally ceded, was given back to its own Duke. The arrangements of Ryswick were again confirmed by the Peace of Rastadt. In the same year the principality of *Orange* was annexed to France, leaving the Papal possessions of Avignon and Venaissin surrounded by French territory, the last relic of the Burgundian realm between the Rhone

Effects of the reign of Lewis the Fourteenth.

and the Alps. France had thus obtained a good physical boundary towards Spain and Italy, and a boundary clearly marked on the map towards the now Austrian Netherlands. Her eastern frontier was still broken in upon by the duchy of Lorraine, by the districts in Elsass which had still escaped, by the county of *Montbeliard*, and by the detached territories of the commonwealth of *Geneva*. But France could now in a certain part of her territory call the Rhine her frontier. It was an easy inference that the Rhine ought to be her frontier through its whole course.

The next reign, that of Lewis the Fifteenth, in a manner completed the work of Henry the Second and Lewis the Fourteenth. The gap which had so long yawned between Champagne and Elsass was now filled up. France obtained a reversionary right to the duchy of Lorraine, which was incorporated thirty-one years later. The lands of Metz, Toul, and Verdun, were no longer isolated. Elsass, which, by the acquisition of Franche-Comté, had ceased to be insular, now ceased to be even peninsular. Leaving out of sight a few spots of Imperial soil which were now wholly surrounded by France, the French territory now stretched as a solid and unbroken mass from the Ocean to the Rhine. And it must be remembered that all the lands which the monarchy of Paris had gradually brought under its power were in the strictest sense incorporated with the kingdom. There were no dependencies, no separate kingdoms or duchies. The geographical continuity of the French territory enabled France really to incorporate her conquests in a way in which Spain and Austria never could.

Arrangements as to Lorraine. 1735.

Its incorporation. 1766.

Thorough incorporation of French conquests.

Effect of geographical continuity.

Contrast

CHAP. IX.

with Spain and Austria.

And the process was further helped by the fact that each annexation by itself was small compared with the general bulk of the French monarchy. Except in the case of the fragment of Navarre which was held by its Bourbon king, France never annexed a kingdom or made any permanent addition to the royal style of her kings.

Purchase of Corsica. 1768.

The same reign saw another acquisition altogether unlike the rest in the form of the Italian island of *Corsica*. In itself the incorporation of this island with the French kingdom seems as unnatural as Spanish or Austrian dominion in Sicily or Sardinia. But the result has been different. Corsica has been far more thoroughly incorporated with France than such outlying possessions commonly are. The truth is that the strong continuity of the continental dominions of France made the incorporation of the island easier. There were no traditions or precedents which could suggest the holding of it as a dependency or as a separate state in any form. Corsica again was, in the end, more easily attached to France, because the man who did most to extend the dominion of France was a Frenchman only so far as Corsicans had become Frenchmen. Corsica has thus become French in a sense in which Sardinia and Sicily never became Spanish, partly because France had no other possession of the kind, partly because Napoleone Buonaparte was born at Ajaccio.

Its effects.

Birth of Buonaparte. 1769.

§ 3. *The Colonial Dominion of France.*

Early French colonization.

France, like all the European powers which have an oceanic coast, entered early on the field of colonization and distant dominion. At one time indeed it seemed as if France was destined to become the chief

European power both in India and in North America. French attempts at colonization in the latter country began early in the sixteenth century. Thus *Cape Breton* at the mouth of the Saint Lawrence was reached early in the sixteenth century, the colonization of *Canada* began a generation later, and French dominion in America was confirmed by the foundation of *Quebec*. The peninsula of *Acadie* or *Nova Scotia* was from this time a subject of dispute between France and Great Britain, till it was finally surrendered by France at the Peace of Utrecht. France now held or claimed, under the names of *New France*, or of *Canada* and *Louisiana*, a vast inland region stretching from the mouth of the Saint Lawrence to the mouth of the Mississippi, while the eastern coast was colonized by other powers. At the end of the seventeenth century the first colonization began at the mouth of the Mississippi; and the city of New Orleans was founded eighteen years later. France and England thus became distinctly rival powers in America as well as in Europe. The English settlers were pressing westward from the coast to the Ocean. The French strove to fix the Alleghany range as the eastern boundary of English advance. In every European war between the two powers the American colonies played an important part. Canada was wrested from France; and by the Treaty of Paris all the French possessions north of the present United States were finally surrendered to England, except a few small islands kept for fishing purposes. The Mississippi was now made the boundary of Louisiana, leaving nothing to France on its left bank except the city of New Orleans. These cessions ruled for ever that men of English blood, whether

CHAP. IX.

French colonies in North America 1506.

1540.

1603.

Acadia ceded to England. 1713.

Canada and Louisiana.

Colonization at the mouth of the Mississippi. 1699.

Foundation of New Orleans. 1717.

Rivalry of English and French settlements.

Share of the colonies in European wars.

English conquest of Canada. 1759.

1763.

The Mississippi boundary

CHAP. IX.

remaining subjects of the mother-country or forming independent states, should be the dominant power in the North American continent.

The West India islands.

Among the West India islands, France in the seventeenth century colonized several of the *Antilles*, some of which were afterwards lost to England. Later in the century she acquired part of the great island called variously *Hispaniola*, *Saint Domingo*, and *Hayti*. On the coast of South America lay the French settlements in *Guiana*, with *Cayenne* as their capital. This colony grew into more importance after the war of Canada.

St. Domingo. 1697.

French Guiana. 1624.

Cayenne. 1635.

The French in India.

Nearly the same course of things took place in the eastern world as in the western. In India neither English nor French colonized in any strict sense. But commercial settlements grew into dominion, or what seemed likely to become dominion: and in India, as in America, the temporary greatness of France came before the more lasting greatness of England. The French East India Company began later than the English; but its steps towards dominion were for a long time faster. Before this the French had occupied the *Isle of Bourbon*, an important point on the road to India. The first French factory on the mainland was at Surat. During the later years of the century various attempts at settlement were made; but no important or lasting acquisition was made, except that of *Pondicherry*. This has ever since remained a French possession, often lost in the course of warfare, but always restored at the next peace. A little later France obtained *Chandernagore* in Bengal. In the next century the island of *Mauritius*, abandoned by the Dutch, became a French colony under the name of the *Isle of France*. Under Labourdonnais and Dupleix France gained for a moment

1664.

Bourbon 1657.

Factory at Surat. 1668.

Pondicherry. 1672.

Chandernagore. 1676.

Isle of France. 1720.

a real Indian dominion. Madras was taken, and a large territory was obtained on the eastern coast of India in the Carnatic and the Circars. But all hope of French supremacy in India came to an end in the later years of the Seven Years' War. France was confined to a few points which have not seriously threatened the eastern dominion of England.

Taking of Madras. 1746.

Restored. 1748.

Effects of the Peace of Paris. 1763.

§ 4. *Acquisitions of France during the Revolutionary Wars.*

Thus the French monarchy grew from the original Parisian duchy into a kingdom which spread north, south, east, and west, taking in, with very small exceptions, all the fiefs of the West-Frankish kings, together with much which had belonged to the other kingdoms of the Empire. With the great French Revolution began a series of acquisitions of territory on the part of France which are altogether unparalleled. First of all, there were those small annexations of territory surrounded or nearly so by French territory, whose annexation was necessary if French territory was to be continuous. Such were Avignon, Venaissin, the county of *Montbeliard*, the few points in Elsass which had escaped the *réunions*, with the Confederate city of *Mühlhausen*. Avignon and Venaissin, and the surviving Alsatian fragments, were annexed to France before the time of warfare and conquest had begun. Mühlhausen, as Confederate ground, was respected as long as Confederate ground was respected. Montbeliard had been annexed already. And with these we might be inclined to place the annexations of Geneva and of the *Bishopric of Basel*, lands which lay hardly less temptingly when the work of annexation had

Acquisitions in the Revolutionary Wars.

Different classes of annexations.

Avignon.

Mühlhausen.

1796.

Geneva and *Bischofbasel.* 1801.

CHAP. IX.

Second zone; traditions of Gaul and the Rhine frontier.

once begun. And beyond these roundings off of the home estate lay a zone of territory which might easily be looked upon as being French soil wrongfully lost. When the Western *Francia* had made such great strides towards the dimensions of the Gaul of Cæsar, the inference was easily made that it ought to take in all that the Gaul of Cæsar had taken in. The conquest and incorporation of the Austrian Netherlands, of all Germany on the left bank of the Rhine, of Savoy and Nizza, thus became a matter of course. That the Gaul of Cæsar was not fully completed by the full incorporation of Switzerland, seems to have been owing to a personal tenderness for the Confederation on the part of Napoleon Buonaparte, who never incorporated with his dominions any part of the territory of the Thirteen Cantons. Otherwise, France under the Consulate might pass for a revival of the Transalpine Gaul of Roman geography. And there were other lands beyond the borders of Transalpine Gaul, which had formed part of Gaul in the earlier sense of the name, and whose annexation, when annexation had once begun, was hardly more wonderful than that of the lands within the Rhine and the Alps. The incorporation of Piedmont and Genoa was not wonderful after the incorporation of Savoy. In short, the annexations of republican France are at least intelligible. They have a meaning; we can follow their purpose and object. They stand distinct from the wild schemes of universal conquest which mark the period of the 'Empire.'

Buonaparte's feeling towards Switzerland.

Piedmont, &c.

Distinction between conquests under the Republic and under the 'Empire.'

Example of Corsica.

Still the example of such schemes was given during the days of the old monarchy. There was nothing to suggest a French annexation of Corsica, any more than a French annexation of Cerigo. Both were works of exactly the same kind, works quite different from incorporating isolated scraps of Elsass or of the old Burgundy, from rounding off the frontier by Montbeliard, or even from advancing to the left bank of the Rhine. The shiftings of the map which took place during the ten years of the first French Empire, the divisions and the unions, the different relations of the conquered states, seem like several centuries of the onward march of the old Roman commonwealth crowded into a single day. In both cases we mark the distinction between lands which are merely dependent and lands which are fully incorporated. And in both cases the dependent relation is commonly a step towards full incorporation. All past history and tradition, all national feelings, all distinctions of race and language, were despised in building up the vast fabric of French dominion. Such a power was sure to break in pieces, even without any foreign attack, before its parts could possibly have been fused together. As it was, Buonaparte never professed to incorporate either Spain or the whole of Italy and Germany with his Empire. He was satisfied with leaving large parts, either in the formally dependent relation, in the hands of puppet princes, or even in the hands of powers which he deemed too much weakened for further resistance. A large part of Germany was incorporated with France; another large part was under French protection or dependence; but a large part still remained in the hands of the native princes of Austria and Prussia. Much of Italy was incorporated, and the rest was held, partly by the conqueror himself under another title, partly by a prince of his own house. This last was the case with Spain. Till the final breach with Russia, the idea of

Character of Buonaparte's conquests.

Dependent and incorporated lands.

Buonaparte's treatment of Germany;

of Italy.

Division of Europe between France and Russia.

CHAP. IX.

Buonaparte's dominion seems to have been that of a twofold division of Europe between Russia and himself, a kind of revival on a vaster scale of the Eastern and Western Empires. The western potentate was careful to keep everywhere a dominant influence within his own world; but whether the territory should be incorporated, made dependent, or granted out to his kinsfolk and favourites, depended in each case on the conqueror's will.

Europe in 1811.

A glance at the map of Europe, as it stood at the beginning of 1811, will show how nearly this scheme was carried out. The kernel of the French Empire was France as it stood at the beginning of the Revolution, together with those conquests of the Republic which gave it the Rhine frontier from Basel to Nimwegen. Beyond these limits, the former United Provinces, with the whole oceanic coast of Germany as far as the Elbe, and the cities of Bremen, Hamburg, and Lübeck, were incorporated with France. France now stretched to the Baltic, and, as Holstein was now incorporated with Denmark, France and Denmark had a common frontier. The Confederation of the Rhine was a protected state, and the Kingdom of Prussia and the self-styled 'Empire' of Austria could practically hardly claim a higher place. Of the former Austrian possessions, those parts which had passed to Bavaria and to the kingdom of Italy formally stood in the dependent relation; the so-called Illyrian provinces were actually incorporated with France. So were the Ionian islands yet further on. Thus the new France, while at one end it marched upon the Dane, at the other end marched upon the Turk. In Italy, the whole western side of the ancient kingdom, with Rome itself, was incorporated with France. North-eastern Italy formed

CHAP. IX.

a separate kingdom held by the ruler of France. Naples, like Spain, was a dependent kingdom. In northern Europe, Denmark and Sweden, like Prussia and Austria, could practically claim no higher place. And the new duchy of Warsaw and the new republic of Danzig carried French influence beyond the ancient borders of Germany.

Arrangements of 1814–1815.

The first class of annexations retained by France, the rest restored.

Such was the extent of the French dominion when the power of Buonaparte was at its highest. At his fall all the great and distant conquests were given up. But those annexations which were necessary for the completion of France as she then stood were respected. The new Germanic body took back Köln, Trier, and Mainz, Worms and Speyer, but not Montbeliard or any part of Elsass. The new Swiss body received the Bishopric of Basel, Neufchâtel, Geneva, and Wallis. Savoy and Nizza went back to their own prince. But here a different frontier was drawn after the first and the second fall of Buonaparte. The earlier arrangement left Chambéry to France. The Pope again received Rome and his Italian dominions, but not his outlying Burgundian possession, the city of Avignon and county of Venaissin. The frontier of the new kingdom of the Netherlands, though traced at slightly different points by the two arrangements, differed in either case but little from the frontier of the Barrier Treaty. In short the France of the restored Bourbons was the France of the elder Bourbons, enlarged by those small isolated scraps of foreign soil which were needed to make it continuous.

Boundary of Savoy.

The geographical results of the rule of the second Buonaparte consist of the completion of the work which began under Philip the Fair, balanced by the utter undoing of the work of Richelieu, the partial undoing of the work of Henry the Second and Lewis the Four-

CHAP. IX.

Annexation of Savoy and Nizza. 1860.

Loss of Elsass and Lorraine. 1871.

teenth. *Savoy*, *Nizza*, and *Mentone* were added; but Germany recovered nearly all *Elsass* and a part of *Lorraine*. The Rhine now neither crosses nor waters a single rood of French ground. As it was in the first beginnings of Northern European history, so it is now; Germany lies on both sides of the German river.

Independence of Hayti, 1801.

Louisiana ceded to Spain, 1763; recovered, 1800; sold to United States, 1803.

Mauritius kept by England.

Pondicherry lost and restored.

The time of the greatest power of France in Europe was by no means equally favourable to her advance in other parts of the world. The greatest West India colony of France, Saint Domingo, now known as *Hayti*, became an independent negro state whose chiefs imitated home example by taking the title of Emperor. About the same time the last remnant of French dominion on the North American continent was voluntarily given up. Louisiana, ceded to Spain by the Peace of Paris and recovered under the Consulate, was sold to the United States. All the smaller French West India islands were conquered by England; but all were restored at the peace, except *Tobago* and *Saint Lucia*. The isles of *Bourbon* and *Mauritius* were also taken by England, and *Bourbon* alone was restored at the Peace. In India *Pondicherry* was twice taken and twice restored.

French conquest of Algeria, 1830; of Constantine, 1837.

Tunis. 1881.

But since France was thus wholly beaten back from her great schemes of dominion in distant parts of the world, she has led the way in a kind of conquest and colonization which has no exact parallel in modern times. On the northern coast of Africa she first annexed *Algeria* fifty years back, and she has, as one of the latest facts in historical geography, obtained an influence in *Tunis* which it is hard to distinguish from annexation. These French conquests in Africa are something different alike from political conquests in

Europe and from isolated conquests in distant parts of the world. It is conquest, not actually in Europe, but in a land on the shores of the great European sea, in a land which formed part of the Empire of Constantine, Justinian, and Heraclius. It is the winning back from Islam of a land which once was part of Latin-speaking Christendom, a conquest which, except in the necessary points of difference between continental and insular conquests, may be best paralleled with the Norman Conquest of Sicily. Sicily, as an island, could be wholly recovered for Europe and Christendom; but the African settlements of France can never be more than a mere fringe of Europe and its civilization on the edge of the barbaric continent. It is strictly the first colony of the kind. Portugal, Spain, England, had occupied this or that point on the northern coast of Africa; France was the first European power to spread her dominion over a long range of the southern Mediterranean shore, a land which in some sort answers alike to India and to Australia, but which lies within two days' sail of her own coast.

Character of African conquests.

We have thus finished our survey of the states which were formed out of the break-up of the later Western Empire. Our examination of the rest of Western Europe will come at a later stage, as neither the Spanish, the Scandinavian, nor the British kingdoms rose out of the break-up of the Empire of Charles the Great. In our next Chapter we must trace the historical geography of the states which arose out of the gradual dismemberment of the dominion of the Eastern Rome, a survey which will lead us to the most stirring events and to the latest geographical changes of our own day.

CHAPTER X.

THE EASTERN EMPIRE.

CHAP. X.

Contrast between the Eastern and Western Empires.

The Western Empire fell to pieces.

THE geographical, like the political, history of the Eastern Empire is wholly unlike that of the Western. The Western Empire, in the strictest sense, fell asunder. Some of its parts fell away formally, others practically. The tie that held the rest snapped at the first touch of a vigorous invader. But that invader was an European power whose territories had once formed part of the Empire itself. From the invasions of nations beyond the European pale the Western Empire, as such, suffered but little. The Western Empire again, long before its fall, had become, so far as it was a power at all, a national power, the *Roman Empire of the German nation.* Its fall was the half voluntary parting asunder of a nation as well as of an Empire The Western Emperors again had, as Emperors, practically ceased to be territorial princes. No lands of any account directly obeyed the Emperor, as such, as their immediate sovereign. When the Empire fell, the Emperor withdrew to his hereditary states, taking the Imperial title with him. In the Eastern Empire all is different. It did to some extent fall asunder from within, but its overthrow was mainly owing to its being broken in pieces from without. But, throughout its history, the Emperor remained the immediate sovereign

Position of the Western Emperors;

of the Eastern.

of all that still clave to the Empire, and, when the Empire fell, the Emperor fell with it. The overthrow of the Empire was mainly owing to foreign invasion in the strictest sense. It was weakened and dismembered by the Christian powers of Europe, and at last swallowed up by the barbarians of Asia. At the same time the tendency to break in pieces after the Western fashion did exist and must always be borne in mind. But it existed only in particular parts and under special conditions. It is found mainly in possessions of the Empire which had become isolated, in lands which had been lost and won again, and in lands which came under the influence of Western ideas. The importance of these tendencies is shown by the fact that three powers which had been cut off in various ways from the body of the Empire, Bulgaria, Venice, and Sicily, became three of its most dangerous enemies. But the actual destruction of the Empire came from those barbarian attacks from which the West suffered but little.

The Eastern Empire fell mainly through foreign invasion.

Tendencies to separation.

Speaking generally then, the Western Empire fell asunder from within; the Eastern Empire was broken in pieces from without. Of the many causes of this difference, perhaps only one concerns geography. At the time of the separation of the Empires, the Western Empire was really only another name for the dominions of the King of the Franks, whether within or without the elder Empire. The Eastern Empire, on the other hand, kept the political tradition of the elder Empire unbroken. No common geographical or national name took in the three Imperial kingdoms of the West and their inhabitants. But all the inhabitants of the Eastern Empire, down to the end, knew themselves by no national name but that of *Romans*, and the land gradu-

Closer connexion of the East with Roman political traditions.

Disuse of the Roman name in the West. Its retention in the East.

CHAP. X.

ally received the geographical name of *Romania*. But the Western Empire was not called *Romania*, nor were its people called *Romans*. The only *Romania* in the West, the Italian land so called, took its name from its long adhesion to the Eastern Empire.

Importance of distinctions of race in the East.

In the East again differences of race are far more important than they ever were in the West. In the West nations have been formed by a certain commingling of elements; in the East the elements remain apart. All the nations of the south-eastern peninsula, whether older than the Roman conquest or settlers of later times, are there still as distinct nations.

The original nations.

First among them come three nations whose settlement in the peninsula is older than the Roman conquest. One of these has kept its name and its language. One has kept its language, but has taken up its name afresh only in modern times. The third has for ages lost both its name and its language. The most unchanged people in the peninsula must be the *Albanians*, called by themselves *Skipetar*, the representatives of the old Illyrians. Next come the Greeks, who have always kept their language, but whose name of *Hellênes* went out of ordinary use till its revival in modern times. Lastly there are the *Vlachs*, representing those inhabitants of Thrace, Mœsia, and other parts of the peninsula, who, like the Western nations, exchanged their own speech for Latin. They must mainly represent the Thracian race in its widest sense. Both Greeks and Vlachs kept on the Roman name in different forms, and the Vlachs, the *Roumans* of our own day, keep it still. Of the invading races, the Goths passed through the Empire without making any lasting settlements in it. The last Aryan settlers, setting aside mere colonists in later times, were

Albanians. Greeks. Vlachs. Use of the Roman name. Slavonic settlers.

CHAP. X.

Turanian settlers.

the *Slaves*. Then came the Turanian settlers, Finnish, Turkish, or any other. Of these the first wave, the *Bulgarians*, were presently assimilated by the Slaves, and the Bulgarian power must be looked at historically as Slavonic. Then come Avars, Chazars, Magyars, Patzinaks, Cumans, all settling on or near the borders of the Empire. Of these the Magyars alone grew into a lasting European state, and alone established a lasting power over lands which had formed part of the Empire. All these invaders came by the way of the lands north of the Euxine. Lastly, there are the non-Aryan invaders who came by way of Asia Minor or of the Mediterranean sea. The Semitic Saracens, after their first conquests in Syria, Egypt, and Africa, made no lasting encroachments. They occupied for a while several of the great islands; but on the mainland of the Empire, European and Asiatic, they were mere plunderers. In their wake came the most terrible enemies of all, the Turks, first the Seljuk, then the Ottoman. Ethnologically they must be grouped with the nations which came in by the north of the Euxine. Historically, as Mahometans, coming in by the southern road, they rank with the Saracens, and they did the work which the Saracens tried to do. Most of these invading races have passed away from history; three still remain in three different stages. The Bulgarian is lost among the Aryan people who have taken his name. The Magyar abides, keeping his non-Aryan language, but adopted into the European commonwealth by his acceptance of Christianity. The Ottoman Turk still abides on European soil, unchanged because Mahometan, still an alien alike to the creed and to the tongues of Europe.

Turanian neighbours.

The Magyars.

The Saracens.

The Seljuk and Ottoman Turks.

Comparison of Bulgarians, Magyars and Ottomans.

The Eastern Empire becomes Greek.

Among all these nations one holds a special place

CHAP. X.

in the history of the Eastern Empire. The loss of the Oriental and Latin provinces of the Empire brought into practical working, though not into any formal notice, the fact that, as the Western Empire was fast becoming German, so the Eastern Empire was fast becoming Greek.

Loss of the Oriental provinces,

To a state which had both a Roman and a Greek side the loss of provinces which were neither Roman nor Greek was not a loss but a source of strength.

of the Latin provinces.

And if the loss of the Latin provinces was not a source of strength, it at least did much to bring the Greek element in the Empire into predominance.

Dying out of Roman ideas.

Meanwhile, within the lands which were left to the Empire, first the Latin language, and then Roman ideas and traditions generally, gradually died out. Before the end of the eleventh century, the Empire was far more Greek than anything else. Before the end of the twelfth century, it had become nearly co-extensive with the modern Greek nation, as defined by the combined use of the Greek language and profession of the Orthodox faith. The name *Roman*, in its Greek form, was coming to mean *Greek*. And, about the same time, the other primitive nations of the peninsula, hitherto merged in the common mass of Roman subjects, began to show themselves more distinctly alongside of the Greeks.

Appearance of Albanians and Vlachs.

We now first hear of *Albanians* and *Vlachs* by those names, and the importance of the nations which have thus come again to light increases as we go on.

The Latin Conquest, 1204.

Then the Greek remnant of the Empire was broken in pieces by the great Latin invasion, and, instead of a single power, Roman or Greek, we see a crowd of separate states, Greek and Frank. The reunion of some of these fragments formed the revived Empire of the Palaiologoi. But at no moment since the twelfth century has the whole Greek nation been united under a single power, native or foreign. And from the Ottoman conquest of Trebizond to the beginning of the Greek War of Independence, the whole of the Greek nation was under foreign masters.[1]

The revived Byzantine Empire.

1461–1821.

We have now first to trace out the steps by which the Empire was broken in pieces, and then to trace out severally the geographical history of the states which rose out of its fragments. And with these last we may class certain powers which do not strictly come under that definition, but which come within the same geographical range and which absorbed parts of the Imperial territory. Beginning in the West, the territory which the Empire at the final separation still held west of the Hadriatic, was gradually lost through the attacks, first of the Saracens, then of the Normans. These lands grew into the kingdom of *Sicily*, which has its proper place here as an offshoot from the Eastern Empire. At the other end of the Italian peninsula, *Venice* gradually detached itself from the Empire, to become foremost in its partition: here then comes the place of Venice as a maritime power. Then come the powers which arose on the north and north-west of the Empire, powers chiefly Slavonic, reckoning as Slavonic the great Bulgarian kingdom. Here too will come the kingdom of Hungary, which, as a non-Aryan power in the heart of Europe, has much both of likeness and of contrast with Bulgaria. The kingdom of Hungary itself lay beyond the bounds of the Empire, but a large part of its

Sicily.

Venice.

Slavonic powers.

Bulgaria.

Hungary.

[1] Unless we except the momentary existence of the first Septinsular Republic, to be spoken of below.

CHAP. X.

dependent territory had been Imperial soil. Here also we must speak of the states which arose out of the Albanians. Roumans. new developement of the Albanian and Rouman races, and of the states, Greek and Frank, which arose just before and at the time of the Latin Conquest. Asiatic powers. Then there are the powers, both Christian and Mahometan, which arose within the Imperial dominions in Asia. Here we have to speak alike of the states founded by the Crusaders and of the growth of the Ottoman Turks. Lastly, we come to the work of our own days, to the new European states which have been formed by the deliverance of old Imperial lands from Ottoman bondage.

We will therefore first trace the geographical
800–1204. changes in the frontier of the Empire itself down to the Latin Conquest. The Latin Empire of *Romania*,
1204–1453. the Greek Empire of *Nikaia*, the revived Greek Empire of Constantinople, will follow, as continuing, at least geographically, the true Eastern Roman Empire. Then will come the powers which have fallen off from the Empire or grown up within the Empire, from Sicily to free Bulgaria. But it must be remembered that it is not always easy to mark, either chronologically or on the map, when this or that territory was finally lost to the Empire. This is true both on the Slavonic border Distinction between conquest and settlement. and also in southern Italy. On the former above all it is often hard to distinguish between conquest at the cost of the Empire and settlement within the Empire. In either case the frontier within which the Emperors exercised direct authority was always falling back and advancing again. Beyond this there was a zone which could not be said to be under the Emperor's direct rule, but in which his overlordship was more or less

fully acknowledged, according to the relative strength of the Empire and of its real or nominal vassals.

§ 1. *Changes in the Frontier of the Empire.*

Power of revival in the Empire.

In tracing the fluctuations of the frontier of the Eastern Empire from the beginning of the ninth century, we are struck by the wonderful power of revival and reconquest which is shown throughout the whole history. Except the lands which were won by the first Saracens, hardly a province was finally lost till it had been once or twice won back. No one could have dreamed that the Empire of the seventh century, cut short by the Slavonic settlements to a mere fringe on its European coasts, could ever have become the Empire of the eleventh century, holding a solid mass of territory from Tainaros to the Danube. But before this great revival, the borders of the Empire had both advanced and fallen back in the further West. At the time of the separation of the Empires, the New Rome still held Sardinia, Sicily, and a small part of southern Italy. The heel and the toe of the boot still formed the themes of *Lombardy*[1] and *Calabria*, in the Byzantine sense of those names.[2] *Naples*, *Gaeta*, and *Amalfi*, were outlying Italian cities of the Empire; so was *Venice*, which can hardly be called an Italian

Sardinia, Sicily, Southern Italy.

[1] The longer form Λογγιβαρδία clave to this theme, while the Greeks learned to apply the contracted form Λαμπαρδοί to the Lombards of Northern Italy.

[2] [There were two steps in the curious translation of the name: (1) Calabria, Bruttii, and Apulia were united to constitute an official province called 'Calabria'; (2) Calabria and Apulia were lost to the Lombards, and the official name adhered to Bruttii, the only part of the province which remained to the Empire. This happened in the second half of the seventh century. See Schipa, in the *Archivio storico per le provinze napoletane*, 1895, pp. 23 sqq. and Bury's ed. of Gibbon's *Decline and Fall*, v. 24, editor's note.]

CHAP. X.

Loss of the islands. Advance on the continent. Loss of Sardinia. Loss of Sicily, 827–965. Loss of Agrigentum, 827; of Palermo, 831; Messina, 842; Malta, 869; Syracuse, 878.

city. In the course of the ninth century the power of the Empire was cut short in the islands, but advanced on the mainland. The history of Sardinia is utterly obscure; but it seems to have passed away from the Empire by the beginning of the ninth century. Sicily was now conquered bit by bit by the Saracens of Africa during a struggle of one hundred and forty years. *Agrigentum*, opposite to the African coast, fell first; *Palermo*, once the seat of Phœnician rule, became four years later the new Semitic capital. *Messina* on the strait soon followed; but the eastern side of the island, its most thoroughly Greek side, held out much longer. Before the conquest of this region, *Malta*, the natural appendage to Sicily, passed into Saracen hands. *Syracuse*, the Christian capital, did not fall till fifty years after the first invasion, and in the north-western corner of the island a remnant still held out for nearly ninety years.

Tauromenion, 902–963. Rametta, 965.

Tauromenion or *Taormina*, on its height, had to be twice taken in the course of the tenth century, and the single fort of *Rametta*, the last stronghold of the Eastern Empire in the island, held out longer still. By this time Eastern Christendom was fast advancing on Islam in Asia; but the greatest of Mediterranean islands passed from Christendom to Islam, from Europe to Africa, and a Greek-speaking people was cut off from the Empire which was fast becoming Greek. But

Partial recovery and final loss of Sicily. 1038–1042.

the complete and uninterrupted Mussulman dominion in Sicily was short. The Imperial claims were never forgotten, and in the eleventh century they were again enforced. By the arms of George Maniakês, Messina and Syracuse, with a part of the island which at the least took in the whole of its eastern side, was, if only for a few years, restored to the Imperial rule.

Advance of the Empire in Italy.

Taking of Bari, 871.

While Sicily was thus lost bit by bit, the power of the Empire was advancing in the neighbouring mainland of Italy. *Bari* was won back for Christendom from the Saracen by the combined powers of both Empires; but the lasting possession of the prize fell to the Cæsar of the East. At the end of the ninth century, the Eastern Empire claimed either the direct possession or the superiority of all southern Italy from Gaeta downwards. The extent of the Imperial dominion was always fluctuating; there was perhaps no moment when the power of the Emperors was really extended over this whole region; but there was perhaps no spot within it which did not at some time or other admit at least the Imperial overlordship. The eastern coast, with the heel and the toe in a wider sense than before, became a real and steady possession, while the allegiance of *Beneventum*, *Capua*, and *Salerno* was always very precarious. But *Naples*, *Gaeta*, and *Amalfi*, however nominal their allegiance might be, never formally cast it aside.

Fluctuations of the Imperial power in Italy.

Naples, Gaeta, and Amalfi.

Thus, at the beginning of the ninth century, the Eastern Emperors held all Sicily, with some patches of territory on the neighbouring mainland. At the beginning of the eleventh century, the island had been wholly lost, while the dominion on the mainland had been greatly enlarged. In the course of the eleventh century a new power, the Normans of Apulia, conquered the Italian possessions of the Empire, won Sicily from the Mussulman, and even made conquests from the Empire east of the Hadriatic. Thus arose the Sicilian kingdom, the growth of which will best be traced when we come to the powers which arose out of the breaking-up of the Empire.

The Normans in Italy and Sicily.

CHAP. X.

The great islands of the Eastern Mediterranean also fluctuated between Byzantine and Saracen dominion.

Loss of Crete, 823.

Crete was won by a band of Mussulman adventurers from Spain nearly at the time when the conquest of Sicily began.

Its recovery, 963.

It was won back in the great revival of the Imperial power one hundred and forty years later.

Cyprus lost, 708; recovered and lost again, c. 881–888; recovered again, 965.

Cyprus was lost sooner; but it went through many fluctuations and divisions, a recovery and a second loss, before its final recovery at the same time as the recovery of Crete and the complete loss of Sicily.

Loss and gain among the great islands.

Looking at the Empire simply as a power, there can be no doubt that the loss of Sicily was altogether overbalanced by the recovery of Crete and Cyprus. Geographically Sicily was an outlying Greek island; Crete and Cyprus lay close to the body of the Empire, essential parts of a Greek state. But Crete and Cyprus, as lands which had been lost and won back, were among the lands where the tendency to fall away from within showed itself earliest.

Separation of Cyprus, 1182–1185.

Crete never actually separated from the Empire. Cyprus fell away under a rebel Emperor, to be presently

Conquered by Richard of Poitou, 1191.

conquered by Richard, Count of Poitou and King of England, and to pass away from the Empire for ever.

Fluctuations in the possession of the great islands, 801.

We may thus sum up the fluctuations in the possession of the great islands. At the beginning of the ninth century, the Eastern Empire still took in Sardinia, Sicily, and Crete; Cyprus was in the hands

901.

of the Saracens. At the beginning of the tenth century, the Empire held nothing in any of the four

1001.

except the north-eastern corner of Sicily. At the beginning of the eleventh, Crete and Cyprus had been won

1101.

back; Sicily was wholly lost. At the beginning of the twelfth, Crete and Cyprus were still Imperial possessions; a great part of Sicily had been won and lost again. At the beginning of the thirteenth, Cyprus, like Sicily, had passed to a Western master; Crete was still held by the Empire, but only by a very feeble tie. Thus the great islands stood at the fall of the old Roman Empire of the East; of the revived Empire of the Palaiologoi none of them ever formed a part.

1201.

Relations of the Empire towards the Slavonic powers.

In the islands the enemies with whom the Empire had to strive were, first the Saracens, and then the Latins or Franks, the nations of Western Europe. On the mainland the part of the Saracen was taken by the Slave. During the four hundred years between the division of the Empires and the Frank conquest of the East, the geographical history of the Eastern Empire has mainly to deal with the shiftings of its frontier towards the Slavonic powers. These fall into three main groups. First, in the north-western corner of the Empire, are the Croatian and Servian settlements, whose history is closely connected with that of the kingdom of Hungary and the commonwealth of Venice. Secondly, there are the Slaves of Thrace, Macedonia, and Greece. Their presence in Greece at least has of late been disputed. It has been held that the alleged Slavonic settlements in Greece were in truth Albanian; but I see no ground to doubt the truth of the received view. Thirdly, between these southern Slavonic settlements and those in Servia and Croatia, comes the great Bulgarian kingdom. The two last ranges gradually merge into one; the first remains distinct throughout. Servia, Croatia, and Dalmatia, will be best treated of in another section, remembering that, amidst all fluctuations, the claims of the Empire over them were never denied or forgotten, and were from time to time

Three Slavonic groups.

Servia and Croatia.

Macedonia and Greece.

Bulgaria.

CHAP. X.

enforced. It was towards the Bulgarian kingdom that the greatest fluctuations of the Imperial frontier took place.

The Bulgarian kingdom.

The original Finnish Bulgarians were the vanguard of Turanian invasion in the lands with which we have to do. Earlier, it would seem, in their coming than the Avars, they were slower to settle down into actual occupation of European territory. But when they did settle, it was not on the outskirts of the Empire, but in one of its acknowledged provinces. Late in the seventh century, the first Bulgarian kingdom was established between Danube and Hæmus. It must be remembered that another migration in quite another direction founded another Bulgarian power on the Volga and the Kama. This settlement, *Great* or *Black Bulgaria*,[1] remained Turanian and became Mahometan; *Bulgaria* on the Danube became Christian and Slavonic. The modern Bulgarians bear the Bulgarian name only in the way in which the romanized Celts of Gaul bear the name of their Frankish masters from Germany, in the way in which the Slaves of Kief and Moscow bear the name of their Russian masters from Scandinavia. In all three cases, the power formed by the union of conquerors and conquered has taken the name of the conquerors and has kept the speech of the conquered. But though the Bulgarian power became essentially Slavonic, it took quite another character from the less fully organized Slavonic settlements to the west and south of it. Towards the Slaves of Thrace, Macedonia, and Greece, it cannot be said that the Empire

Settlement south of the Danube, 679.

Black Bulgaria.

Use of the Bulgarian name.

The Empire and the Macedonian Slaves.

[1] [For the name *Black* (not *White*, as in the former editions) *Bulgaria*, see Constantine Porphyrogennêtos, *De Administrando Imperio*, c. 12, and c. 42 (p. 180, ed. Bonn).]

CHAP. X.

had any definite frontier. Settled within the Empire, they were its tributaries or its enemies, according to the strength of the Empire at any particular moment. Up to the coming of the Bulgarians, we might, from different points of view, place the Imperial border either at the Danube or at no great distance from the Ægæan. But from the Bulgarian conquest onwards, there was on the Bulgarian side a real frontier, a frontier which often shifted, but which was often fixed by treaty, a frontier which, wherever it was fixed, marked off lands which were, for the time, wholly lost to the Empire. With the first Bulgarian settlement, the Imperial frontier definitely withdrew for three hundred years from the lower Danube to the line of Hæmus or Balkan. As the Bulgarian power pushed to the south and west, the two fields of warfare, against the Bulgarians to the north and against the half-independent Slaves to the west, gradually merged into one. But as long as the Isaurian Emperors reigned, the two fields were kept distinct. They kept the Balkan range against the Bulgarians, whose kingdom, stretching to the north-west over lands which are now Servian, had not, at the end of the eighth century, passed the mountain barrier of the Empire.

The Empire and the Bulgarian kingdom.

Loss of the Danubian frontier.

Bulgarians south of Hæmus.

Extent of Bulgaria in the eighth century.

Meanwhile, as a wholly distinct work, the Imperial power was restored over the Slaves of Thrace, Macedonia, and Greece. In the middle of the eighth century the inland parts of Greece were chiefly occupied by Slavonic immigrants, while the coast and the cities remained Greek. Before the end of the century, the Slaves of Macedonia were reduced to tribute, and early in the ninth, those of Greece wholly failed to recover their independence. The land was gradually settled afresh by Greek colonists, and by the middle of the

Recovery of the Slavonic settlements in Macedonia and Greece.

775–784.

807.

Recovery of Greece from the Slaves.

Slaves on Taygetos.

tenth, only two Slavonic tribes, *Melings* and *Ezerites* (*Melinci* and *Jezerci*), remained, distinct, though tributary, on the range of Taÿgetos or Pentedaktylos. From this time to the Frankish conquest, Greece, as a whole, was held by the Empire. But, as a recovered land, it was one of those parts of the Empire in which a tendency to separate began to show itself. And in the course of these changes, the name *Hellênes*, as a national name, quite died out. The names *Hellas* and *Hellên* might sometimes be brought in as a rhetorical flourish, as bygone names often are in all languages; but *Hellên* had long ceased to be the received name of a people, or *Hellas* to be the received name of any land beyond a small province. In ordinary use the name

Hellênes of Maina.

Hellên had long meant *pagan*, and it was confined to the people of *Maina*, who remained pagans till near the end of the ninth century. The Greeks, as a people, now knew no name but that of *Romans*. The local, perhaps contemptuous, name of the inhabitants of Hellas was *Helladikoi*.[1]

Thus, at the division of the Empires, Thrace, Macedonia, and Greece had been more or less thoroughly recovered by the Eastern Empire, while the lands between Hæmus and Danube were wholly lost. The Imperial dominion from the Hadriatic to the Euxine formed,

Romania.

together with the Asiatic provinces, *Romania*, the land

Dalmatia, Servia, and Croatia.

of the Romans of the East. The Emperors also kept the cities on the Dalmatian coast, and the precarious allegiance of the Servian and Croatian principalities.

[1] [There is no reason to suppose that there was anything contemptuous in the name *Helladikoi*. It was the official designation of the people of the *theme* of *Hellas*. See Bury, *English Historical Review*, vii. 80.]

CHAP. X.

Greatness of the first Bulgarian kingdom.

These lands were bound to the Empire by a common dread of the encroaching Bulgarian. The ninth century and the early years of the tenth was a great time of Bulgarian advance. The Bulgarians seem to have failed in establishing any lasting dominion to the north-west in Pannonia;[1] at the expense of the Empire they were more successful. At the end of the eighth century *Sardica*—afterwards called *Triaditza* and *Sofia*—and *Anchialos* were border cities of the Empire. The conquest of Sardica early in the ninth marks a stage of Bulgarian advance. At the end of the century, after the conversion of the nation to Christianity, comes the great æra of the first Bulgarian kingdom, the kingdom of *Peristhlava.* The Tzar Simeon established the Bulgarian supremacy over Servia, and carried his conquests deep into the lands of the Empire. In Macedonia and Epeiros the Empire kept only the sea-coast, Ægæan and Hadriatic; Sardica, Philippopolis,[2] Ochrida, were all cities of the Bulgarian realm. Hadrianople, a frontier city of the Empire, passed more than once into Bulgarian hands. Nowhere in Europe, save in old Hellas, did the Imperial dominion stretch from sea to sea.

Attempt on Pannonia, 818–829.

Advance against the Empire.

Conquests of Simeon, 923–934.

Revival of the Imperial power.

So stood matters in the middle of the tenth century. Then came that greatest of all revivals of the Imperial power which won back Crete and Cyprus, and which was no less successful on the mainland of Europe

[1] A temporary Bulgarian occupation seems clear from Einhard, Annals, 827, 828. But on the supposed existence of a Bulgarian duchy in the present Hungary see Roesler, *Romänische Studien*, 201. [But the Bulgarian realm at this time doubtless extended north of the Danube, including at least the present Walachia.]

[2] [The Slavs called and still call Philippopolis *Plovdiv*, which comes from Pulpudeva, the old native name of the place before the foundation of the Greek town. See Kalužniacki and Jireček in the *Archiv slav. Philologie*, xvi. 594 sqq.]

CHAP. X.

Conquest of Bulgaria. The Russians and Bulgarians. 968–971.

and Asia. Bulgaria was conquered and lost and conquered again. But the first time it was conquered, not from the Bulgarian but from the Russian. The Russians, long dangerous to Constantinople by sea, now suddenly appear as a land power. Their prince Sviatoslaf overthrew the first Bulgarian kingdom, and Philippopolis became for a moment a Russian outpost. But John Tzimiskês restored the power of the Empire over the whole Bulgarian dominions. The Danube was once more the frontier of the Eastern Rome.

The second Bulgarian kingdom.

It remained so for more than two hundred years during the lower part of its course. But in the inland regions the Imperial power fell back almost at once, to advance again further than ever. A large part of the conquered land soon revolted, and a second Bulgarian kingdom, Macedonian rather than Mœsian, arose. The kingdom of *Ochrida*, the kingdom of Samuel, left to the Empire the eastern part of the old Bulgaria between Danube and Hæmus, together with all Thrace and the Macedonian coast. But it took in all the inland region of Macedonia; it stretched down into Thessaly and Epeiros; and, while it nowhere touched the Euxine or the Ægæan, it had a small seaboard on the Hadriatic. Now came the great struggle between Romania and Bulgaria which fills the last years of the tenth century and the opening years of the eleventh.

Second conquest of Bulgaria, 1018. Croatia.

At last all Bulgaria, and with it for a while Servia, was restored to the Empire. Croatia continued in vassalage, and its princes were presently raised to royal rank by Imperial authority.

Thus the Eastern Empire again took in the whole south-eastern peninsula. Of its outlying European possessions, southern Italy was still untouched. At what moment Venice ceased to be a dependency of the Empire, it would be hard to say. Venetian dukes still received the Imperial investiture, and Venetian ships often joined the Imperial fleet. This state of things seems never to have been formally abolished, but rather to have dropped out of sight as Venice and Constantinople became practically hostile. In the other outlying city north of the Euxine the ninth and tenth centuries change places. Through all changes the Empire had kept its maritime province in the Tauric Chersonêsos. There the allied city of *Chersôn*, more formally annexed to the Empire in the ninth century, was taken by the Russian Vladimir in the interval between the two great Bulgarian wars.

Venice.

Chersôn annexed, 829–842; taken by Vladimir, 988.

In Asia the Imperial frontier had changed but little since the first Saracen conquests. The solid peninsula of Asia Minor was often plundered by the Mussulmans, but it was never conquered. Now, in Asia as in Europe, came a time of advance. For eighty years, with some fluctuations, the Empire grew on its eastern side. The Bagdad caliphate was now broken up, and the smaller emirates were more easily overcome. The wars of Nikêphoros Phôkas and John Tzimiskês restored *Kilikia* and *Syria* to the list of Roman provinces, *Tarsos*, *Antioch*, and *Edessa* to the list of Christian cities. Basil the Second extended the Imperial power over the *Iberian* and *Abasgian* lands east of the Euxine, and began a series of transactions by which, in the space of forty years, all *Armenia* was added to the Empire on the very eve of the downfall of the Imperial power in Asia.

The Empire in Asia.

Asiatic conquests of Nikêphoros and John, 963–976; of Basil the Second, 991–1022.

Beginning of the annexation of Armenia, 1021; Ani, 1045; of Kars, 1064.

For the great extension of the Empire laid it open to new enemies in both continents. In Asia it became the neighbour of the Seljuk *Turks*, in Europe of the

New enemies.

Turks.

CHAP. X. Magyars.

Magyars or Hungarians, who bear the name of *Turks* in the Byzantine writers of the tenth century. Hungary had now settled down into a Christian kingdom.

Revolt of Servia, 1040.
A Servian revolt presently placed a new independent state between Hungary and Romania, but Belgrade

Loss of Belgrade, 1064.
remained an Imperial possession till it passed under Magyar rule twenty-four years later.

Advance of the Turks.
By this time the Empire had begun to be cut short in a far more terrible way in Asia. The Seljuk Turks now reached

Loss of Ani, 1064.
the new Roman frontier. Plunder grew into conquest, and the first Turkish conquest, that of *Ani*, happened in the same year as the last Imperial acquisition of *Kars*. The Emperors tried to strengthen this dangerous frontier by the erection of vassal principalities. The very name of *Armenia* now changes its place. The

Lesser Armenia, 1080.
new or *Lesser Armenia* arose in the Kilikian mountains, and was ruled by princes of the old Armenian dynasty, whose allegiance to the Empire gradually died out. But before this time the Turkish power was fully established in the peninsula of Asia Minor. The plun-

1071.
derers had become conquerors. The battle of Manzikert

1074.
led to formal cessions and further advances. Throughout Asia Minor the Empire at most kept the coast;

The Sultans of *Roum*.
the mass of the inland country became Turkish. But the Roman name did not pass away; the invaders took

1081.
the name of Sultans of *Roum*. Their capital was at *Nikaia*, a threatening position indeed for Constantinople. But distant positions like Trebizond and Antioch

Loss of Antioch, 1081.
were still held as dependencies. Antioch was before long betrayed to the Turks.

By this time the Empire was attacked by a new

Normans in Corfu and
enemy in its European peninsula. The Norman conquerors of Apulia and Sicily crossed the Hadriatic, and

occupied various points, both insular and continental, especially *Dyrrhachion* or *Durazzo* and the island of *Korkyra*, now called by a new Greek name, *Koryphô* or *Corfu*. At every point of its frontier the Empire had, towards the end of the eleventh century, altogether fallen back from the splendid position which it held at its beginning. The geographical aspect of the Empire was now the exact opposite of what it had been in the eighth and ninth centuries. Then its main strength seemed to lie in Asia. Its European dominion had been cut down to the coasts and islands; but its Asiatic peninsula was firmly held, touched only by passing ravages. Now the Asiatic dominion was cut down to the coasts and islands, while the great European peninsula was, in the greater part of its extent, still firmly held. Never before had the main power of the Empire been so thoroughly European. No wonder that in Western eyes the Empire of Romania began to look like a kingdom of Greece.

Epeiros. 1081–1085.

Geographical aspect of the Empire.

The states founded by the crusaders will be dealt with elsewhere. The crusades concern us here only as helping towards the next revival of the Imperial power under the house of Komnênos. Alexios himself won back Nikaia and the other great cities of western Asia Minor. Some of these, as *Laodikeia*, were received rather as free cities of the Empire than as mere subjects. The conquering reigns of John and Manuel again extended the Empire in both continents. The Turk still ruled in the inland regions of Asia, but his capital was driven back from Nikaia to *Ikonion*. The superiority of the Empire was restored over Antioch and Kilikian Armenia at the one end, over Servia at the

Recovery of Asiatic territory, 1097.

Reigns of John and Manuel.

1097.

1137.

CHAP. X.

1148. other. Hungary itself had to yield *Zeugmin*, *Sirmium*, and all Dalmatia. For a moment the Empire again took in the whole eastern coast of the Hadriatic and

1163-1168. its islands; even on its western shore *Ancona* became something like a dependency of the Eastern Cæsar.

Falling of distant possessions.

The conquests of Manuel were clearly too great for the real strength of the Empire. Some lands fell away

Dalmatia, 1181.

at once. Dalmatia was left to be struggled for between Venice and Hungary. And the tendency to fall away within the Empire became strengthened by increased intercourse with the feudal ideas of the West. Cyprus, Trebizond, old Greece itself, came into the hands of rulers who were rather feudal vassals than Roman governors. We have seen how Cyprus fell away. Its Poitevin

Latin kingdom of Cyprus, 1192.

conqueror presently gave it to Guy of Lusignan. Thus, before the Latin conquest of Constantinople, a province had been torn from the Eastern Empire to become a Latin kingdom. The Greek-speaking lands were now beginning largely to pass under Latin rule. In Sicily the Frank might pass for a deliverer; in Corfu and Cyprus he was a mere foreign invader.

The third Bulgarian kingdom, 1187.

Meanwhile the Empire was again cut short to the north by a new Bulgarian revolt, which established a third Bulgarian kingdom, but a kingdom which seems to have been as much Vlach or Rouman as strictly Bulgarian. The new kingdom took in the old Bulgarian land between Danube and Hæmus, and it presently spread both to the west and to the south. The Bulgarian revolt was followed by other movements

Other Slavonic revolts.

among the Thracian and Macedonian Slaves, which did not lead to the foundation of any new states, but which had their share in the general break-up of the Imperial power. The work of Basil and Manuel was now un-

CHAP. X.

Increased Greek character of the Empire.

done; but its undoing had the effect of making the Empire more nearly a Greek state than ever. It did not wholly coincide with the Greek-speaking lands: the Empire had subjects who were not Greeks, and there were Greeks who were not subjects of the Empire. But the Greek speech and the new Greek nationality were dominant within the lands which were still left to the Empire. The Roman name was now merely a name: Roman and Greek meant the same thing. Whatever was not Greek in European Romania was mainly Albanian and Vlach. The dominion of the Empire in the peninsula was mainly confined to the primitive races of the peninsula. The great element of later times, the Slavonic settlers, had almost wholly separated themselves from the Empire, establishing their independence, but not their unity. They formed a group of independent powers which had simply fallen away from the Empire; it was by the powers of the West that the Empire itself was to be broken in pieces.

The Slavonic states.

Latin conquest of Constantinople, 1204.

The taking of Constantinople in the Fourth Crusade was the work of an alliance between the now independent commonwealth of Venice and a body of Western crusaders who, along with the states which they founded, may be indifferently called *Latins* or *Franks*. A regular act of partition was drawn out, by which the Empire was to be divided into three parts. One was to be assigned to a Latin *Emperor of Romania*, another to the pilgrims as his feudatories, a third to the commonwealth of Venice. But the partition was never carried out. A large part of the Empire was never conquered; another large part was not assigned by the act of partition. In fact the scheme of partition is hardly

Act of Partition.

CHAP. X.

a geographical fact at all. The real partition to which the Latin conquest led was one of quite another kind, a partition of the Empire among a crowd of powers, Greek, Frank, and Venetian, more than one of which had some claim to represent the Empire itself.

Latin Empire of Romania.

These were the Latin Empire of *Romania*, and the Greek Empire which maintained itself at *Nikaia*, and which, after nearly sixty years of banishment, won back the Imperial city. In the crusading scheme the Latin Emperor was to be the feudal superior of the lesser princes who were to establish themselves within the Empire. For his own Imperial domain he was to have the whole of the Imperial possessions in Asia, with a Thracian dominion stretching as far north as *Agathopolis*. Hadrianople, with a narrow strip of territory stretching down to the Propontis, was to be Venetian. The actual result was very different. The Latin Emperors never got any footing in Asia beyond parts of the themes bordering on the Propontis, reaching from Adramyttion to the mouth of the Sangarios. In Europe they held the eastern part of Thrace, with a fluctuating border towards Bulgaria on the north, and to the new Latin and Greek states which arose to the west. Their dominion also took in *Lêmnos*, *Lesbos*, *Chios*, and some others of the Ægæan islands.

Its extent.

But the Latin Empire of Romania was not the only Empire which arose out of the break-up of the old East-Roman power. Two, for a time three, Greek princes bore the Imperial title; there was also a Latin king. It will be convenient for a while to leave out of sight both Asia and southern Greece, and to look to the revolutions of Thrace, Macedonia, northern Greece, and the land which we may now begin to call *Albania*.

The immediate result of the Latin conquest was to divide these lands between three powers, two Latin and one Greek. Besides the Empire of Romania, there was the Latin kingdom of *Thessalonikê*, and the Greek *despotat*[1] of *Epeiros* held by the house of Angelos. Of these the Thessalonian kingdom was the most short-lived, and there can be little doubt that its creation was the ruin of the Latin Empire. It cut off the Emperor from his distant vassals in Greece, whose vassalage soon became nominal. It gave him, in successive reigns, a powerful neighbour who knew his own power, and a weak neighbour, who fell before the Greek advance sooner than himself. But the beginnings of the kingdom, under its first king Boniface, were promising. His power stretched over Thessaly—now, from the great extent of Rouman colonization within its borders, known as *Great Vlachia*—and he received the homage of the Frank princes further to the south. But within twenty years from its foundation, Frank rule had ceased in Macedonia. Thessalonikê was again a Greek and an Imperial city, and its recovery by the Greeks split the Latin Empire asunder.

Kingdom of Thessalonikê. 1204–1222 Despotat of Epeiros.

Thessalonikê again Greek.

The Epeirot despotat.

This blow came from the west. It was the Nicene Empire which did in the end win back the Imperial city; but, for some years after the Latin conquest, things looked as if the restoration of the Greek power in Europe was designed for Epeiros. The first despot Michael paid a nominal homage to all the neighbouring powers, Greek and Frank, in turn; but in truth he was the lord of an independent and growing state. His power began in the Epeirot land west of Pindos. For a 1208–1210.

[1] It must be remembered that δεσπότης was and is a common Byzantine title, with no worse meaning than *dominus* or any of the words which translate it.

CHAP. X.

1215. moment his power stretched into Peloponnêsos, where he held Corinth, Nauplia, and Argos. Durazzo and Corfu were won from Venice. The Epeirot power

1222. advanced also to the east. Thessalonikê was taken;

1225. its ruler took the Imperial title; Hadrianople followed, and the new Empire stretched across the peninsula from sea to sea, and took in Thessaly to the south. But the Thessalonian Empire was hardly more long-lived than the Thessalonian kingdom. It was first dismembered among the princes of the ruling house. The original Epeirot despotat, along with Corfu, parted away from the new Macedonian power, to survive it by many years. But by this time the championship of the Greek speech and faith against the Latin lords of Constantinople had passed to the foremost of the Greek powers which had grown up in Asia, to the Empire of Nikaia.

Separation of Epeiros and Thessalonia. 1237.

These Greek powers were two, which arose at the same time, but by different processes and with different destinies. The Empire of *Nikaia* was the truer continuation of the old East-Roman power; the Empire of *Trapezous* or *Trebizond* was fated to be the last independent fragment of Roman dominion and Greek culture. The Trapezuntine Empire was not in strictness one of the states which arose out of the Latin partition. One of the parts of the Empire which showed most disposition to fall away was independently seized by a rival Emperor, at the very moment of the Latin conquest. Alexios Komnênos occupied Trebizond, an occupation largely wrought by Iberian help, as if the Empire, already dismembered by the Christians of the West, was to be further dismembered by the Christians of the further East. The dominions of Alexios, enlarged by his brother David to the west, at first took in the

The Empire of Trebizond. 1204–1461.

Extent of the Komnenian dominion.

whole south coast of the Euxine from the Sangarios
eastward, broken by the city of *Amisos*, which contrived to make itself virtually independent, and by the
neighbouring Turkish settlement at *Samsoun*. But this
dominion was only momentary. The eastern part
alone survived to form the later Empire of Trebizond;
the western part, the government of David, soon passed
to the rising power of Nikaia.

The founder of that power was Theodore Laskaris, Empire of Nikaia,
in whom the succession of the Eastern Empire was held 1206–1261.
to be continued. Ten years after the taking of Con- 1214.
stantinople, a treaty fixed his border towards the small
Latin dominion in Asia. Six years after the Latins 1220.
kept only the lands north of the gulf of Nikomêdeia;
sixteen years later they held only the Asiatic coast of 1240.
the Bosporos. Seven years later Chios, Lêmnos, Samos, 1247.
Kôs, and other islands were won back by the growing The Nicene Empire in
Greek state. But, long before this, the Nicene Empire Europe.
had become an European power. The Thracian 1235.
Chersonêsos was first won, the work beginning at *Kallipolis*. Presently the Thessalonian Emperor sank to the 1242.
rank of a despot under him of Nikaia; four years later 1246.
Thessalonikê was incorporated with the Nicene dominions. A series of Bulgarian campaigns carried the 1245–1256.
Imperial frontier, first to the Hebros—already the Slavonic *Maritza*—and then to the foot of Hæmus. A 1254–1259.
series of Epeirot campaigns won a Hadriatic seaboard,
and made *Durazzo* for a while again a city of the
Empire. The Nicene power in these regions was con- 1259.
firmed by the victory of Pelagonia, won over the
combined forces of Epeiros, Achaia, and Sicily. The
next year *Selymbria* was won from the Latins, and the 1260.
Frank Empire was cut down to so much territory as

CHAP. X.

Recovery of Constantinople, 1261.

could be guarded from the walls of Constantinople. At last the recovery of Constantinople changed the Empire of Nikaia into the revived Byzantine Empire of the Palaiologoi.

Advance of the Empire in Europe.

That Empire still lasted a hundred and ninety years, and we must carefully distinguish between its European and its Asiatic history. The Asiatic border fell back almost as soon as the seat of rule was restored to Europe. In Europe the revived Empire kept the character of an advancing power till just before the entrance of the Ottoman into Europe, in some parts till just before the fall of Constantinople. Many events helped to weaken the real power of the Empire, which did not affect its geography. Such were the earlier Turkish inroads and the destroying visit of the Catalans.
1302. The land in which advance was most steady was Peloponnêsos, where, at the time of the recovery of

Advance in Peloponnêsos.

Constantinople, the Empire did not hold a foot of ground. *Misithra*, *Monembasia*, and *Maina*, were the fruits of
1262. the day of Pelagonia. For a while the Imperial frontier was stationary, but from the beginning of the fourteenth century it steadily advanced. It advanced perhaps all the more after Peloponnêsos became an Imperial dependency, or an appanage for princes of the Imperial house, rather than an immediate possession of the Empire.
1404. Early in the fifteenth century the greater part of the peninsula, including Corinth, was again in Greek hands.
1430. At last, twenty-three years only before the Turkish conquest of Constantinople, all Peloponnêsos, except the points held by Venice, was under the superiority of the Empire.

Advance in Macedonia and Epeiros.

In more northern parts the advance of the Empire, though chequered by more reverses, went on steadily till the growth of the Servian power in the middle of the fourteenth century. The frontier varied towards Servia, Bulgaria, Epeiros, and the Angevin power which established itself on the Hadriatic coast. Even under Andronikos the Second the Imperial dominion was extended over the greater part of Thessaly or *Great Vlachia*. Later still, all Epeiros, *Jôannina* and *Arta*—once *Ambrakia* —were won. At the moment of the great Servian advance, the Empire held the uninterrupted seaboard from the Euxine to the Pagasaian gulf, as well as its Hadriatic seaboard from the Ambrakian gulf northward. But the Frank principalities still cut off the main body of the Empire from its possessions in Peloponnêsos.

1308.

1318–1339.

Losses of the Empire in Asia.

In Asia there is another tale to tell. There the frontier of the Empire steadily went back after the recovery of Constantinople. A few points gained from or lost to European powers go for little. *Smyrna* passed for a while to Genoa. The Knights of Saint John won *Rhodes*, *Kôs*, and other islands, but they did not become a power on the mainland of Asia till the Empire had almost withdrawn from that continent. The Imperial power steadily crumbled away before the advance of the Turk, first the Seljuk and then the Ottoman. The small Turkish powers into which the Sultanate of Roum had now split up began to encroach on the Greek dominion in Asia as soon as its centre was transferred to Europe. By the end of the thirteenth century, the Imperial possessions in Asia had again shrunk up to a narrow strip on the Propontis, from the Ægæan to the Euxine. Losses followed more speedily when the Turkish power passed from the Seljuk to the Ottoman. *Brusa*, *Nikaia*, *Nikomêdeia*, were all lost within twelve years. By the middle of the fourteenth century, the Emperors

1260

The Knights of Saint John, 1309–1315.

Advance of the Turks.

1326–1338.

CHAP. X.

kept nothing in Asia, save a strip of land just opposite Constantinople, and the outlying cities of *Philadelphia* and *Phôkaia*, their allies rather than their subjects.

The Empire falls back towards Servia and Bulgaria.

The Ottoman was now all but ready to pass into
Europe, and the way was made easier for him by the
rise and fall of an European power which again cut
short the Empire in its western provinces. While the
1331. Imperial frontier was advancing in Epeiros and Thessaly,
it fell back towards Servia, and advanced towards
Bulgaria only to fall back again. *Philippopolis*, so often
lost and won, now passed away for ever. And now
came the great momentary advance of *Servia* under
Stephen Dushan, which wrested from the Empire a
large part of its Thracian, Macedonian, Albanian, and
Greek possessions. At the middle of the fourteenth
century, the Empire, all but banished from Asia, kept no
unbroken European dominion out of Thrace. Its other
possessions were isolated. It kept Thessalonikê and
Chalkidikê, with a small strip of Macedonia as far as
Berrhoia and *Vodena*. It kept a small Thessalian territory
about *Lamia* or *Zeitouni*. There was the Peloponnesian
province, fast growing into importance; there
1355. was *Lesbos*, and a few other islands. On Stephen's death
his dominion broke in pieces, but the Empire did not
win back its lost lands. For the Ottoman was already
in Europe, ready, in the space of the next hundred
years, to swallow up all that was left.

Loss of Philippopolis, 1344.

Conquests of Stephen Dushan.

Extent of the Empire.

As in the recovery of Romania by the Greeks of
Nikaia, so in the final conquest of Romania by the
Turks of Brusa, Constantinople itself was—with the
exception of the Peloponnesian appanage—the last
1356. point of the Empire to fall. The Turk, like the Greek,
made his way in by Kallipolis; like the Greek, he

hemmed in the Imperial city for years before it fell into CHAP. X.
his hands. In seven years from his first landing, Loss of
Hadrianople had become the European capital of the Hadrianople, 1361.
Turk ; the Empire was his tributary, keeping, besides
his outlying possessions, only the land just round the
city. The romantic expedition of Amadeo of Savoy 1366.
gave back to the Empire its Euxine coast as far as
Mesêmbria. Before the end of the century Philadelphia Loss of
was lost in Asia, and the Imperial dominion in Europe Philadelphia, 1374–1391.
hardly reached beyond the city itself and the Pelo-
ponnesian province. Thessalonikê and the Thessalian
province were both lost for a while. Bajazet was on
the point of doing the work of Mahomet, when the Effect of
Empire was saved for another half-century by the Timour's invasion,
invasion of Timur and the consequent break-up of 1401.
the Ottoman power. During the Ottoman civil wars, the
outlying points of the Empire were restored and seized
again more than once. At last the boundaries of the
Empire were fixed by treaty between Sultan Mahomet 1424.
and the Emperor Manuel, much as they had stood sixty
years before. The coast of the Propontis to Selymbria,
the coast of the Euxine to Mesêmbria, Thessalonikê and
Chalkidikê, the Peloponnesian province, the smaller
Thessalian province, the overlordship of Lesbos, Ainos,
and Thasos, was all that was left. Further losses soon
followed. Thessalonikê passed from the Empire within 1426.
two years. At last, as all the world knows, the Imperial 1453.
city itself fell, and the name of the Eastern Roman
Empire was blotted out of European geography. Constantinople became *Stambul.*[1] Six years later came the 1460.

[1] [Stambul or Istambol is derived from στὴν πόλι (*sti* passing into *sta* in Turkish). See Hesseling, *Revue des études grecques*, iii. 189 sqq. The colloquial name for Constantinople in the Middle Ages was regularly ἡ πόλις.]

CHAP. X.

conquest of Peloponnêsos, and the whole of European Greece passed into the hands of foreign masters.

States growing out of the Empire.

The Slavonic states.

Having thus sketched the changes in the extent of the Eastern Roman Empire during a period of six hundred and fifty years, we have now to trace the geography of the states which, within that time, grew up within its borders or upon its frontiers. These fall naturally into four groups. First come the national states which were formed by throwing off the dominion of the Empire. These are mainly the Slavonic powers to the north, Bulgaria, Servia, Croatia, and the later states which arose out of their divisions and combinations.

Hungary.

And with these, different as was their origin, we must, for our purposes, place both the *Hungarian* kingdom which annexed so many of the Slavonic lands, and the *Rouman* states, so closely connected with Hungarian history, which arose by migrations out of the Empire or out of lands which had been part of the Empire.

Rouman states.

The Greek states.

Another group consists of the Greek states which split off from the Empire before or at the Latin conquest, and which were not recovered by the Greek Emperors of Nikaia and Constantinople. Both these classes of states strictly belong to Eastern Christendom. The Catholic Magyar ruling over Orthodox Slaves forms a link between the East and the West; so do those Slaves who themselves belong to the Latin Church.

Latin states with the Empire.

Another link is supplied by a third group of states, namely those parts of the Empire which, either at or before the Latin conquest, came under Latin rule. This class is not confined to the Frank powers in Romania or to the Eastern settlements of Venice and Genoa.

Kingdom of Sicily.

From our point of view it takes in the Norman

kingdom of Sicily and the crusading kingdom of Jerusalem with its fiefs. In all these cases, territory which had formed part of the Eastern Empire came under Latin rule. And in all these cases, Latin masters bore rule over alien subjects, Greek, Slave, Syrian, or any other. None of the Latin powers were national states, like the Slavonic or even like the Greek powers. But the foreign masters of these lands were at least European and Christian. The last class consists of powers which lie beyond the range of European and Christian civilization. These are the Turkish dynasties which arose within the borders of the Empire. Of these only the last and greatest, the dynasty of *Othman*, became geographically European, and swallowed up nearly all the lands which had belonged to the Empire in Europe, together with much which lay beyond its bounds. Here we have, not only the absence of national being, but the rule of the Asiatic over the European, of the Mussulman over the Christian. Lastly, we come to the partial redressing of this wrong by the re-establishment of independent Greek and Slavonic states in our own century.

Kingdom of Jerusalem.

Turkish dynasties.

The Ottomans.

The New States.

These seem to make four natural groups, and it is needful to bear in mind their nature and relations to each other. But it will be more convenient to speak of the several states thus formed in an order approaching more nearly to the order of their separation from the Empire. And first comes a power which parted off so early, and which became so thoroughly a part of Western Europe, that it needs an effort to grasp the fact that its right place is among the powers which had their beginning in separation from the Imperial throne of Constantinople.

CHAP. X.

§ 2. *The Kingdom of Sicily.*

The Norman power in Italy and Sicily.

This is the power which, in the course of the eleventh century, was formed by the Norman adventurers in southern Italy and in Sicily. It was not wholly formed at the expense of the Eastern Empire. But all its insular, and the greater part of its continental, territory was either won from the Eastern Empire and its vassals, or else had once formed part of that Empire. Its kings also more than once established their power, for a longer or shorter time, in the Imperial lands east of the Hadriatic. With the Western Empire and the Kingdom of Italy the Sicilian kingdom had in its beginnings nothing to do, though it was afterwards somewhat enlarged at their expense.

Possessions of the Empire in Italy.

When the Norman conquests in Italy began, early in the eleventh century, the Eastern Empire still kept the coast of both seas from the further side of the peninsula of *Gargano* to the head of the gulf of *Policastro*. The Imperial duchies of Naples, Gaeta, and Amalfi, lying to the north of this point, were cut off by the duchies of *Benevento*, *Capua*, and *Salerno*, over which the Empire had at the most a very precarious superiority. Within a hundred years, all these lands, together with the island of Sicily, were brought under Norman rule. Thus grew up a new European power, sometimes forming one kingdom, sometimes two, sometimes held alone, sometimes together with other kingdoms. This power supplanted alike the Eastern Empire, the Saracen powers of Sicily, and the Lombard princes of southern Italy. It started from two points, two distinct Norman settlements, of which

Advance of the Normans.

CHAP. X.

the later outshone the earlier. The earliest Norman territorial settlement was the county of *Aversa*, held in vassalage of the Imperial duchy of Naples. Forty years later its counts became possessed of the principality of *Capua*, of which they received a papal confirmation which implied a denial of all dependence on either Empire. The more lasting duchy of *Apulia* began later under the adventurers of the house of Hauteville. Their first stage is marked by the foundation of the county of Apulia, with *Melfi* as its capital, under William of-the-Iron-arm. This took in the peninsula of Gargano and the lands immediately to the south of it. The next stage is when Leo the Ninth invested Count Humfrey, or rather the Normans as a body, with all that they could conquer in Apulia, Calabria, and Sicily. The first of several takings of *Tarentum*, and the assumption of the ducal title by Robert Wiscard, marks another stage. Less than twenty years later the Eastern Empire kept nothing but the duchy of Naples; *Benevento* had passed to the Popes. The rest of the lands both of the Empire and of the Lombard princes were now very unequally divided between two Norman lords, the Duke of Apulia and the Prince of Capua. The Byzantine power west of the Hadriatic being thus overthrown, Robert Wiscard for the first time pushed the Norman arms into the Eastern peninsula itself. For the last few years of his life he held the islands of Corfu and Kephallênia, with Durazzo and the coast to the south, and his power even stretched inland as far as *Kastoria* and *Trikkala*. His dominion was renewed for a moment by his son Behemund, and in the middle of the next century Corfu was again for a short time held by King Roger of Sicily.

County of Aversa, 1021.

Principality of Capua, 1062–1068.

County of Apulia, 1042.

Investiture by Pope Leo, 1053.

Robert Wiscard Duke, 1059. Completion of the Apulian duchy, 1077.

Robert Wiscard in Epeiros, 1081–1085.

1147–1150.

CHAP. X.

Norman Conquest of Sicily, 1060–1091.

For by that time the island of Sicily was a kingdom of Western Christendom. The second time of Mussulman rule over the whole island was short. In the space of thirty years Count Roger won the great island alike from Islam and from Eastern Christendom. Greek Messina was first won; after a while Saracen Palermo followed; Syracuse was won much later; the last Saracen post in the island to hold out was *Noto* in the south-eastern corner. *Malta*, the natural appendage of Sicily, was soon added. The first Norman capital was *Messina*. Duke Robert, as overlord of his brother Count Roger, kept Palermo and the surrounding district in his own hands. It was not till the next century that the Count of Sicily won full possession of the city. Palermo then became again, as it had been under the Saracens, the head of Sicily.

Taking of Messina, 1061; of Palermo, 1072; of Syracuse, 1086; of Noto, 1091; of Malta, 1091.

Palermo capital of Sicily.

The ruler of Sicily also became a potentate on the Italian mainland. First the half, then the whole, of Calabria formed part of his dominions. The third Great Count, the first King, of Sicily, Roger the Second, gradually won the whole possessions of his family on the mainland. To these he presently added the Norman principality of Capua, first as a dependent territory, then as fully incorporated with his dominions. He next won the last possession in the West which was still held by the Eastern Empire, the city of Naples. He then pressed beyond the bounds both of the Eastern Empire and of the early Norman conquests by the annexation of the *Abruzzi*. This was the only part of the Norman possessions in Italy which had belonged to the Kingdom of Italy held by the Western Emperors. At this point the Western Terminus must be held to have gone back. Roger next, as we have seen,

Roger the Second, 1105–1154.

King, 1130.

Capua, 1132–1136.

Naples, 1138.

The Abruzzi, 1140.

extended his power for a moment east of the Hadriatic. Meanwhile he was more successful against the common enemies of Eastern and Western Christendom. As Sicily had twice been conquered from Africa, Africa now began to be conquered from Sicily. Roger held a considerable dominion on the African coast, including *Mehadia*, *Bona*, and other points, which were lost under his son William.

Conquests in Africa, 1135–1137.

1160.

Thus was founded a kingdom which has, perhaps, oftener than any other European state, been divided and united and handed over from one dynasty of strangers to another. In the twelfth, in the sixteenth, in the eighteenth century, Sicily, the Two Sicilies, one of the Sicilies, found a king in the Western Emperor, but neither the whole nor either of its parts was ever incorporated with the Empire. And the boundaries, strictly so called, of the kingdom have hardly changed at all. For the only immediate neighbour of the Sicilian King was his ecclesiastical overlord. The question was whether the king of the mainland should be also king of the island. But the successive dynasties which reigned both over the whole kingdom and over its divided parts were for a long time eager to carry out the policy of their first founder, by conquests east of the Hadriatic. Before the Latin taking of Constantinople, William the Good began again to establish an Epeirot and insular dominion by the conquest of Durazzo, Corfu, Kephallênia, and Zakynthos. But these outlying dominions were granted in fief to the Sicilian Admiral Margarito,[1] who, himself bearing the

Epirot conquests of William the Good, 1185.

Kingdom of Margarito, 1186.

[1] On this very singular, but very obscure, little state see our own Benedict (ii. 199) and Roger of Howden (iii. 161, 269), and the Ghibeline Annals of Placentia, Pertz, xix. 468. See also Hopf, *Geschichte Griechenlands*, vi. 161.

CHAP. X. strange title of *King of the Epeirots*, founded a dynasty
which, with the title of Count Palatine, held *Kephallênia*,
Zakynthos, and *Ithakê* into the fourteenth century.
1338. Thus these lands, like Cyprus and Trebizond, were cut
off from the Empire just before its fall, and the revolutions of Sicily cut them off equally from the Sicilian
kingdom. A more lasting power in these regions
Epeirot dominion began under Manfred, who received, as his Greek wife's
of Manfred, 1258. dowry, Corfu, Durazzo, and a strip of the Albanian
coast, with the title of *Lord of Romania*. This
Of Charles of Anjou, dominion passed to his conqueror Charles of Anjou,
1266–69. who further established a feudal superiority over the
1272–1276. Epeirot despotat. But the plans of Charles were cut
1282. short by the revolution of the Vespers. The Two
Sicilies—to forestall the name—were now divided.
Both kingdoms had to do with the lands east of the
Hadriatic, but it was only the continental kingdom
History of Durazzo, which kept any actual dominion there. Durazzo was
1322. lost and won more than once; but it came back to the
Duchy of Durazzo, Angevin house, to become a separate Angevin duchy,
1333–1360. 1378. till it fell before the growth of the Albanian powers.
Another branch held *Lepanto*—once *Naupaktos*—which
1373–1386. lasted longer. Corfu and Butrinto became immediate
possessions of the Neapolitan crown till they found
more lasting masters at Venice.

This Eastern dominion of the Angevin lords of Naples, besides the influence of both Sicilian crowns in southern Greece, of which we shall have presently to speak, tends to keep up the connexion of the Sicilian kingdoms with the Empire out of which they sprang. But it can hardly be called a geographical enlargement of the kingdoms themselves. Still less can that name be given to the short occupation of *Acre* by Charles of

Acre occupied by Charles of Anjou.

Malta granted to the Knights, 1530.

Anjou in his character of one of the many Kings of Jerusalem. The Sicilian kingdoms themselves cannot be said to have gained or lost territory till Charles the Fifth granted Malta to the Knights of Saint John, till Philip the Second added the *Stati degli Presidi* to the Two Sicilies. The great revolution of all has taken place in our own day. The name of Sicily has for the first time been wiped from the European map. The island of Hierôn and Roger has sunk to form seven provinces of a prince who has not deigned to take the crown or the title of that illustrious realm.

§ 3. *The Crusading States.*

Comparison between Sicily and the crusading states.

The Sicilian kingdom has much in common with the states formed by the crusaders in Asia and Eastern Europe. Both grew out of lands won by Western conquerors, partly from the Eastern Empire itself, partly from Mussulman holders of lands which had belonged to the Eastern Empire. But the order of the two processes is different. The Sicilian Normans began by conquering lands of the Empire, and then went on to win the island which the Saracens had torn from the Empire. The successive crusades first founded Christian states in the lands which the Mussulmans had won from the Empire, and then partitioned the Empire itself. The first crusaders undertook to hold their conquest as fiefs of the Eastern Empire. This condition was only very partially carried out; but the mere theory marks a stage in the relations between the Eastern Empire and the Latin powers of Palestine which has nothing answering to it in the case of Sicily.

First among these powers came the *Kingdom of*

CHAP. X.

Kingdom of Jerusalem and Frank principalities in Syria. Cyprus.

Jerusalem and the other Frank principalities which arose out of the first crusade. The kingdom of *Cyprus*, which in some sort continued the kingdom of Jerusalem, forms a link between the true crusading states and those which arose out of the partition of the Empire in the fourth crusade. And closely connected

Armenia.

with this was the kingdom of *Kilikian Armenia* whose foundation we have already mentioned.[1] This last was an Eastern state which became to some extent latinized. But Cyprus, the Syrian states, and the Latin powers which arose out of the partition of the Empire, all agree in being colonies of Western Europe in Eastern lands, states where the Latin settlers appear as a dominant race over the natives, of whatever blood or creed.

The Crusaders cut off the Mussulmans from the sea.

The great geographical result of the first crusade was to cut off the Mussulman powers from the seas of Asia and Eastern Europe. In the first years of the twelfth century the Christian powers, Byzantine, Armenian, and Latin, held the whole coast of Asia

Extent of the Kingdom of Jerusalem.

Minor and Syria. The Kingdom of Jerusalem, at its greatest extent, stretched along the coast from *Berytos* to *Gaza*. To the east it reached some way beyond Jordan and the Dead Sea, with a strip of territory reaching southward to the eastern gulf of the Red Sea. To the north lay two Latin states which, in the days of Komnenian revival, acknowledged the superiority of the Eastern Emperor. These were the county of

Tripolis.

Tripolis, reaching northwards to the Syrian *Alexan-*

Antioch.

dretta, and the more famous principality of *Antioch*.

640.

That great city, lost to Christendom in the first days of Saracen conquest, won back to the Empire in the

968.

Macedonian revival, lost to the Turk, won back by the

[1] See above, p. 382.

Frank, remained a Christian principality long after the fall of Jerusalem, and did not pass again under Mussulman rule till late in the thirteenth century. North-east of Antioch lay the furthest of the Latin possessions, the inland county of *Edessa*. This was the first to be lost; it fell under the power of the Turkish Attabegs of Syria. They cut short the kingdom of Jerusalem, taking away the territory east of Jordan. On their ruin arose a mightier power of Saladin, lord alike of Egypt and Syria. He took Jerusalem, and the kingdom which still bore that name was cut down to the lands just round Tyre. The crusades which followed won back *Acre* and various points, and at last the diplomacy of Frederick the Second won back from the Egyptian Sultan Tyre, Sidon, and the Holy City itself. A strip of coast running inland at two points, so as to take in Tiberias and Nazareth at one end, Jerusalem and Bethlehem at the other, formed the Eastern realm of the lord of Rome and Sicily. Lost and won again by the Christians, Jerusalem was finally won for Islam by the invasion of the Chorasmians from the shores of the Caspian. But for nearly fifty years longer the points on the coast were lost and won, as the Mussulman powers or fresh crusaders from Europe had the upper hand. With the fall of *Acre*, the Latin dominion on the Syrian mainland came to an end. The land won by the Western Christians from the Mussulman went back to the disciples of the Prophet. The land won by the Western Christian from the Eastern, and the land where the Eastern Christian still maintained his independence, held out longer.

CHAP. X.

1081.

1098.

1268.

Edessa.

1128–1173.

Loss of the lands beyond Jordan.

Jerusalem taken by Saladin, 1187.

Jerusalem recovered by Frederick the Second, 1228.

1239–1243. Final loss of Jerusalem, 1244.

Fall of Acre, 1291.

These were the kingdoms of *Cyprus* and *Armenia*. The frontier of Cyprus hardly admitted of geographical

Cyprus.

CHAP. X.

change, unless it was when, for a part of the fourteenth and fifteenth centuries, the city and haven of *Famagosta*

Famagosta Genoese.

passed to Genoa. The kings of Cyprus however claimed

Connexion between Cyprus and Jerusalem.

the crown of Jerusalem, and sometimes, before the whole Syrian coast was lost, they really held this or that piece

Armenia acknowledges the Western Emperor, 1190.

of territory on the mainland. Meanwhile the Armenian kingdom in some sort entered the Western world, when its king, after receiving one confirmation from the Eastern Emperor, thought it wise to receive another from the Western Emperor also. The kingdom, though sadly

1342.

cut short by its Mussulman neighbours, lived on under native princes till the middle of the fourteenth century.

Connexion between Armenia and Cyprus, 1393.

Then the fragments of the kingdom passed, first to a branch of the Cypriot royal family, and then to the reigning king of Cyprus. But the first joint reign was

End of Armenia and Cyprus, 1489.

the last. The remnant of independent Armenia was swallowed up by the Mameluke lords of Syria, while Cyprus lingered on till Saint Mark and his commonwealth became the heirs of its last king.

The kingdom of Cyprus forms a link between the Latin states in Syria and those which arose in Romania after the crusading capture of Constantinople. And these

Frank principalities in Greece.

last again fall into two classes. There are the Frank principalities on the mainland of Greece, and there are the lands, chiefly insular, which fell to the lot of the

Possessions of the maritime commonwealths.

maritime commonwealths of the West and of their citizens. Among these the first place belongs to the great commonwealth which had now cast off all traces

Genoa.

of allegiance to the Empire. *Genoa*, which had no share in the original partition of the Empire, obtained several points of Imperial territory, both for the commonwealth itself and for particular Genoese citizens.

CHAP. X.

Venice.

But the part played by Genoa in the East is small beside the great and abiding dominion of Venice. No result of the partition was greater than the field which it gave to Venetian growth. The position of the two commonwealths is different. Genoa was a mere stranger in the East; Venice was in a manner at home. Once an outlying possession of the Empire, her really great historical position is due to her share in its overthrow.

Comparison between the two.

§ 4. *The Eastern Dominion of Venice and Genoa.*

We have already seen the origin of the Venetian state, and its position as an outlying member of the Eastern Empire which gradually became an independent power without any formal act of separation. The beginning of Venetian rule over the Slavonic coasts of the Hadriatic dates from the time when Venice was still undoubtedly a city of the Empire. Her first conquests 997. at the end of the tenth century, conquests which gave her chiefs the style of *Dukes of Venice and Dalmatia*, involved no casting aside of the Imperial superiority.[1] But the Eastern dominion of Venice had now begun, and the full developement of that dominion was inconsistent with the supremacy, or indeed with the existence, of the Empire. In a strictly geographical view, her Istrian and Dalmatian dominion cannot be separated from her Albanian and purely Greek dominion. Venice could not become a great European power till she passed from the Slavonic lands whose connexion with the Empire was nominal or precarious into the Albanian

Connexion of the Dalmatian and Greek dominion of Venice.

[1] See the Venetian Chronicle in Pertz, viii. 29, 32. After the Venetian conquest the Duke's name is placed after that of the Emperor in religious ceremonies.

CHAP. X.

Effect of the partition on Venice.

and Greek lands which were among its immediate possessions. Her greatness dates from that partition of the Empire which was the surest proof that she had wholly cast aside her Byzantine allegiance. From this point of view the history of Venice may be compared and contrasted with the history of Sicily. In each case, a part of the dominions of the Eastern Rome grew into a separate power; that power passed, so to speak, from Eastern Europe to Western, and, in its new Western character, it appeared as a conqueror in the Eastern lands. But, as Venice and Sicily parted from the Empire in different ways, so their later relations to the Empire were widely different. The Sicilian state began in actual conquests made by foreign invaders at the expense of the Empire. Venice was a dependency of the Empire which gradually drifted into independence. Thus Sicily became more thoroughly Western than Venice. The attempts of the kings, both of the whole Sicilian kingdom and of its divided parts, to establish an Eastern dominion were attacks from without, and were not really lasting. But Venice, whose princes were lords of one fourth and one eighth of the Empire of Romania,[1] took up in some sort the position of the Empire itself. If she destroyed one bulwark against the Mussulman, she set up another and a more lasting one.

Comparison between Venice and Sicily.

Venice inherits the position of the Empire.

The true scene of Venetian power was the East, and in the East her true sphere of enterprise was primarily the Hadriatic, and next to that, the coasts and islands of the Ægæan She remained both a Dalmatian and a

[1] It is well to see this familiar title in Greek. The Duke (δοὺξ Βενετίας) was δεσποτικῷ ἀξιώματι τιμηθεὶς, ἔχειν τε ἐξ ὅλου πρὸς τὸ ὅλον ὃ τὸ τῶν Φράγκων ἐκτήσατο γένος τὸ τέταρτον καὶ τοῦ τετάρτου τὸ ἥμισυ. George Akropolitês, 15. ed. Bonn.

CHAP. X.

Greek power down to the moment of her overthrow, and, at the moment of her overthrow, it was not eighty years since she had ceased to be a Peloponnesian and an Ægæan power. The Greek dominion of Venice was an enlargement of her Dalmatian dominion. The fourth crusade was the turning-point in her history. It is significant that Zara was taken—not for the first or the last time—on the way to the taking of Constantinople. Already mistress, or striving to be mistress, of the northern part of the eastern coast of the Hadriatic, the partition of the Empire opened to Venice the hope of becoming mistress of the southern part. Mistress of the whole coast she never was at any one moment; one point was gained and another lost. But extension in those lands was steadily aimed at for more than seven hundred years, and the greater part of the eastern Hadriatic coast has been, at one time or another, under Venetian rule.

Venetian power both Dalmatian and Greek.

Taking of Zara, 1202.

Hadriatic dominion of Venice.

This mission of Venice was fully recognized in the scheme of partition of the Eastern Empire. She was to be mistress of the Hadriatic and Ionian seas. To her were assigned, not only the islands off the west coast of the Empire, but the whole western coast itself, from the north of Albania to the southern point of Peloponnêsos. She was to have some points in the Ægæan, among them *Oreos* and *Karystos* at the two ends of Euboia. But she was also to have a large continental dominion. She was to have her quarter of the capital, with a Thracian and an Asiatic dominion, including, according to some versions, the strange allotment of *Lazia* at the east of the Euxine.[1] The actual possessions of Venice in the East

Territory assigned to Venice by the Act of Partition.

[1] If this is what is really meant by *Laza* or *Lacta* in the Act of Partition. Muratori, xii. 357.

CHAP. X.

Her actual possessions.

have a very different look. Much of the territory which was assigned to the republic never became hers, while she obtained large possessions which were not assigned to her. But the main point, the dominion of the

Her dominion primarily Hadriatic.

Hadriatic, was never forgotten, though some both of her earliest and of her latest conquests lay beyond its necessary range.

Possessions not assigned by the partition.

Crete. 1206–1669.

1645–1669.

Among those possessions of Venice which were not assigned to her in the act of partition was her greatest and most lasting possession of all, the island of *Crete*. This she won almost at the first moment of the conquest, and she kept it for more than four centuries and a half, till the war of *Candia* handed over all Crete, save two fortresses, to the Ottoman. Before this loss, Saint Mark had won and lost another great island which lay altogether beyond the scheme of the Latin conquerors of Constantinople. Late in the fifteenth century the

Acquisition of Cyprus, 1489.

republic succeeded the Latin kings in the possession of *Cyprus*. But this was held for less than a century. Cyprus, like Crete and Sicily, was a special scene of struggle between European and barbarian powers. But

Loss of Cyprus, 1571.

it shared the fate, not of Sicily but of Crete, and became the solid prize of the Ottoman, when Christendom won the barren laurels of Lepanto. Another possession

Occupation of Thessalonikê, 1426–1430.

which lay out of the usual course of Venetian dominion was the short occupation of *Thessalonikê*. Bought of a Greek despot, it was after four years taken by the Turk. Had Thessalonikê been kept, it might have passed as a late compensation to the republic for the early loss of Hadrianople and her other Thracian territory.

The short Venetian possession of Thessalonikê, the

longer possession of Cyprus, stand apart in time and place from that more nearly continuous Venetian dominion in the Hadriatic and the Ægean, of which Crete may be fairly looked on as the most distant point. The early stages of that dominion cannot be kept apart from the story of the Slavonic lands on the Hadriatic. The states of Servia and Croatia were from the beginning the inland neighbours of the Dalmatian coast cities. The river Tzettina may pass as the boundary between the Servian and Croatian states. *Pagania* on the Narenta, *Zachloumia* between the Narenta and Ragusa, *Terbounia*, represented by the modern *Trebinje*, the coast district of the *Canali*, *Dioklea*, taking in the modern Montenegro with the coast as far as the Drin—*Skodra* or *Scutari* on its lake, the harbours of *Spizza*, *Antivari*, and *Dulcigno*, were all originally Servian. The Dalmatian coast cities, *Dekatera* or *Cattaro*, *Raousion* or *Ragusa*, *Tragourion* or *Traü*, *Diadora*, *Jadera*, or *Zara*, formed a Roman fringe on what had become a Slavonic body. It was not even a continuous fringe, as the Slaves came down to the sea at more than one point. *Pagania* above all, the land of the heathen Narentines, cut Roman Dalmatia into two marked parts. It even took in most of the great islands, *Curzola*—once *Black Korkyra*—*Meleda*, *Lesina*—once *Pharos*—and others. At the separation of the two Empires the Croatian power was strongest in those lands. The wars of Charles the Great left the coast cities to the Eastern Empire, while inland Dalmatia and Croatia passed under Frankish rule. Presently Croatia won its independence of the Western Empire, while the coast cities were practically lost by the Eastern. Under Basil the Macedonian the Imperial authority was admitted, in

Servian districts on the coast.

The Dalmatian cities.

Pagania.

The Islands.

Croatia under Charles the Great, 806–810.

825–830.

Settlement under Basil the

CHAP. X.

Macedonian, 868–878.

First Venetian conquest, 995–997.

name at least, both by the cities and by the Croatian prince. More than a century later came the first Venetian conquest, which destroyed the pagan power on the Narenta and was looked on at Venice as a deliverance of the cities from Croatian rule. The pagan power on the Narenta was destroyed, and the Duke of Venice took the title of *Duke of Dalmatia*. But all this involved no formal separation from the Empire.[1] Such a separation may be held to have taken place in the middle of the next century, when the cities again passed under Croatian rule, and when the taking of the title of *King of Dalmatia* by the Croatian Kresimir may pass for an assertion of complete independence. But the kingdoms, first of Croatia, then of Dalmatia, were presently swallowed up by the growing power of the Magyar. Then comes a time in which this city and that passes to and fro between Venice and Hungary. Under Manuel Komnênos the whole of Croatia and Dalmatia was fully restored to the Empire; but ten years later the cities again passed to Hungary. This was their final separation from the Empire, and by this time Venice had thrown off all Byzantine allegiance.

The cities under Croatia, 1052.

Dalmatian Kingdom, 1062.

Magyar Kingdom of Croatia, 1091; of Dalmatia, 1102.

Croatia and Dalmatia restored to the Empire, 1171.

Dalmatia passes to Hungary.

Struggle for the dominion of Dalmatia.

From this time the history of Croatia forms part of the history of the Hungarian kingdom. The history of Dalmatia becomes part of the long struggle of Venice for Hadriatic dominion. For five hundred years the cities and islands of the whole Hadriatic coast were lost and won over and over again in the strifes of the powers

[1] But we see how slight was the real hold of the Empire on these distant dependencies, when we find that, on the submission of Croatia and Dalmatia to Basil the Macedonian, the tribute of the cities was assigned to the Croatian prince.

of the mainland. These were in Dalmatia the Hungarian and Bosnian Kings; more to the south they were the endless powers which rose and fell in Albania and northern Greece. In after times the Ottoman took the place of all. And many of the cities were able, amid the disputes of their stronger neighbours, to make themselves independent commonwealths for a longer or shorter time. *Ragusa*, above all, kept her independence during the whole time, modified in later times by a certain external dependence on the Turk. And the almost invisible inland commonwealth of *Polizza*—a Slavonic San Marino—kept its separate being into the present century.

Independence of Ragusa; of Polizza.

The crusading conquest of Zara, the first act of the conquest of Constantinople, was the beginning of this long struggle. The frontier between Venice and Hungary fluctuated during the whole of the thirteenth century; early in the fourteenth the whole coast was again Venetian. Meanwhile the republic was striving to make good her position further south. The Epeirot despotat long hindered her establishment either on the coasts or on the islands of northern Greece. *Durazzo*, the old Epidamnos, the central point between the older and the newer Venetian range, was won, along with *Corfu*, in the earliest days of the conquest; but both were presently lost, to come back again in after times. The famous island of Korkyra or Corfu has a special history of its own. No part of Greece has been so often cut off from the Greek body. Under Pyrrhos and Agathoklês, no less than under Michael Angelos and Roger, it obeyed an Epeirot or a Sicilian master. It was among the first parts of Greece to pass permanently under Roman dependence. At last, after yet another turn of

Fluctuations between Venice and Hungary, 1315.

First conquest of Durazzo and Corfu, 1206.

1216.

History of Corfu.

CHAP. X.

Second Venetian conquest of Corfu, 1386–1797.

Sicilian rule, it passed for four hundred years to the great commonwealth. In our own day Corfu was not added to free Greece till long after the deliverance of Attica and Peloponnêsos. But, under so many changes of foreign masters, the island has always remained part of Europe and of Christendom. Alone among the Greek lands, Corfu has never passed under barbarian
1716. rule. It has seen the Turk only, for one moment as
1800. an invader, for another moment as a nominal overlord.

Greek advance of Venice.

The second Venetian occupation of Corfu was the beginning of a great advance among the neighbouring islands. But, during the hundred and eighty years between the two occupations, the main fields of Venetian action lay more to the north and more to the south. The Greek acquisitions of the Republic at this time were in Peloponnêsos and the Ægæan islands. On the mainland she won, at the very beginning of Latin settlement in the East, the south-western peninsula of Peloponnêsos, with the towns of *Methônê* and *Korônê*—otherwise *Modon* and *Coron*—which she held for nearly three hundred years. Among the Ægæan islands Venice began very early to win an influence in the greatest of their number, that of *Euboia*, often disguised under the specially barbarous name of *Negropont.*[1] The history of that island, the endless shiftings between its Latin lords and the neighbouring powers of all kinds, is the most perplexed part of the perplexed Greek history of the time. Venice, mixed up

Modon and Coron, 1206.

History of Euboia.

[1] *Negroponte*—a wild corruption of *Euripos*—is strictly the name of one of the Latin baronies in Euboia, and has been carelessly transferred to the whole island, as Crete used often to be called *Candia.* [*Negro-ponte* was a 'popular etymology' from *ston Egripon*, suggested by the bridge at Chalcis.]

Complete occupation of Euboia, 1390. Turkish conquest of Euboia, 1470. Loss of the Ægæan islands, 1718.

in its affairs throughout, obtained in the end complete possession, but not till after the second occupation of Corfu. The island was kept till the Turkish conquest eighty years later. Several other islands were held by the Republic at different times. Of these *Tênos* and *Mykonos* were not finally lost till Venice was in the eighteenth century confined to the western seas.

Peace of Zara, 1358. Dalmatia Hungarian. New advance of Venice.

Between the first and the second occupation of Corfu, the Venetian power in Dalmatia had risen and fallen again. By the peace of Zara, Lewis the Great of Hungary shut out Venice altogether from the Dalmatian coasts, and, as Dalmatian King, he required the Venetian Duke to give up his Dalmatian title. Later in the century Venice again gained ground, and her Dalmatian, Albanian, and Greek possessions began to
draw near together, and to form one whole, though 1378–1455.
never a continuous whole. In the space of about eighty years, amid many fluctuations towards Hungary, Bosnia, and Genoa—a new claimant called into rivalry by the war of Chioggia—Venice again became mistress of the greater part of Dalmatia. Some districts however formed part of the duchy of *Saint Sava*, and Hungary kept part of the inland territory with the fortress of *Clissa*. The point where the Hadriatic coast turns nearly due south may be taken as the boundary of the lasting and nearly continuous dominion of the Republic; but for the present the Venetian power went on spreading far south of that point. On the second occupation of Corfu followed the acquisition of *Durazzo*, *Alessio*,

Recovery of Dalmatia. Advance in Albania and Greece, 1392.

and of the Albanian *Skodra* or *Scutari*. *Butrinto* and 1401.
the ever memorable *Parga* put themselves under Vene- 1407.
tian protection, and *Lepanto* was ceded by a Prince of
Achaia. In Peloponnêsos the Messenian towns were 1388.

CHAP. X.

still held, and to them were now added *Argos* and its port of *Nauplia*, known in Italian as *Napoli di Romania*.
1408–1413. *Patras* was held for a few years, *Monembasia* was won,
1419. 1423. and the isle of *Aigina*, which might almost pass for part of Peloponnêsos. On the other side of Greece, the possession of Corfu led to the acquisition of the other so-called Ionian Islands. The prince of *Kephallênia*, of *Zakynthos* or *Zante*, and of *Leukadia* or *Santa Maura*, found it to his interest, for fear of the advancing Ottoman, to put his dominions under the overlordship of Saint Mark.

The Western Islands. 1449.

Venice the champion against the Turk.

This marks an epoch in the history of Venice and of Europe. The championship of Christendom against the Turk now passes from the New Rome to the hardly less Byzantine city in the Lagoons. The short occupation of Thessalonikê may pass for the beginning of the struggle. Later in the fifteenth century, Venice and the Turk were meeting at every point. In Peloponnêsos, *Argos* was first lost to the Turk; at the same moment he appeared far to the north, and gradually occupied the Bosnian and Hungarian districts of Dalmatia.

Loss of Argos, 1463.

1505–1699. Throughout the sixteenth and seventeenth centuries the inland districts and the smaller towns were lost over and over again, but the Republic always kept the chief coast cities, *Zara*, *Sebenico*, and *Spalato*. Meanwhile, to the south of Dalmatia, the Venetian power went back everywhere, except in the western islands.

Losses of Venice.

1474–1478. On the mainland *Croja*, the city of Scanderbeg, was held for a while. But both Croja and Skodra were won by Mahomet the Conqueror, and the treaty which ended this war left to the Republic nothing on the coast of
1479. Albania and Northern Greece, save *Durazzo*, *Antivari*, and *Butrinto*. The treaty which followed the next war

took away *Durazzo*, *Butrinto*, and *Lepanto*. A series of revolutions in the islands of which the Republic already held the overlordship placed them under her immediate dominion, to be struggled for against the Turk. By the next peace *Zakynthos* was kept, on payment of a tribute to the Sultan; *Kephallênia* passed to the Turk, to be won back seventeen years later, and then to be permanently kept. *Leukadia* was at the same time won for a moment and lost again. In Peloponnêsos *Modon* and *Koron* were lost along with *Durazzo* and *Lepanto*, and the great naval war with Suleiman cost the Republic her last Peloponnesian possessions, *Nauplia* and *Monembasia*, together with all her Ægæan islands, except *Tênos* and *Mykonos*. The victory of Lepanto leaves its mark in geography only by the loss of the Greek island of Cyprus and the Albanian city of Antivari. The strictly Greek dominion of Venice was now for a hundred and forty years confined to the islands, and, after the loss of Cyprus and Crete, almost wholly to the western islands. But after the loss of Crete came a revival of the Venetian power, like one of the old revivals of the Empire. The great campaigns of Francesco Morosini, confirmed by the peace of Carlowitz, freed all Peloponnêsos from the Turk, and added it to the dominion of Saint Mark.

1500. The Western Islands, 1481–1483. 1485. 1502. 1502–1504. Loss of the Peloponnesian fortresses, 1502. 1540. Venetian conquest of Peloponnêsos, 1685–1699.

The same treaty confirmed Venice in the possession of the greater part of Dalmatia. The next war cost her the whole of Peloponnêsos, her two Cretan fortresses, and her two remaining Ægæan islands. She now withdrew wholly to the western side of Greece, where she had again won *Leukadia* and *Butrinto*, and had enlarged her dominion by the acquisition of *Prevesa*. During the last century the Venetian posses-

Loss of Peloponnêsos, 1715–1718.

CHAP. X.

Extent of Venetian dominion in Greece in the last century.

sions in Greece consisted of the seven so-called Ionian islands, with the continental posts of *Butrinto*, *Prevesa*, and *Parga*.

Venetian territory in Dalmatia.

The Dalmatian territory of the Republic during the same time consisted of a considerable inland district in the north-east, and of the whole coast down to *Budua*, except where the territory of independent Ragusa broke the continuity of her rule. Ragusa was so jealous of the mightier commonwealth that she preferred the Turk as a neighbour. At two points of the coast, at *Klek* at the bottom of the gulf formed by the long peninsula of Sabbioncello, and again at *Sutorina* on the *Bocche*, the Ottoman territory came down to the sea, so as to isolate the dominion of Ragusa from the Venetian possessions on either side. *Meleda* and the smaller islands near Ragusa were part of the Ragusan territory; the others, great and small, *Curzola*, once *Black Korkyra*, *Lesina*, once *Pharos*, and the rest, were Venetian. Such were the relations of the two Hadriatic commonwealths down to the days when, first Venice and then Ragusa, passed away.

Ragusan frontier.

Possessions of Venetian families.

Meanwhile, besides the direct possessions of the Venetian commonwealth, there were other lands within the former dominions of the Eastern Empire which were held by Venetian lords, as vassals either of the Republic or of the Empire of Romania. It would be endless to trace out the revolutions of every Ægæan island; but one among the few which claim our notice became the seat of a dynasty which proved, next to the Venetian commonwealth itself, the most long-lived Latin power in the Greek world. This is the duchy variously known as that of *Naxos*, of the *Dôdekannêsos*, and

The Duchy of Naxos.

of the *Archipelago*, the barbarous name given to the Ægæan or *White Sea*.[1] Founded in the early years of Latin settlement by the Venetian Marco Sanudo, the island duchy lived on as a Latin state, commonly as a vassal or tributary state of some greater power, till the last half of the sixteenth century. Shorn of many of its islands by its Ottoman overlord, granted afresh to a Jewish duke, it passed thirteen years later under the immediate dominion of the Sultan. Most of the *Kyklades* were either parts of this duchy or fiefs held of it by other Venetian families. All came into the hands of the Turk; but some of the very smallest remained merely tributary, and not fully annexed, into the seventeenth century.

1207. 1207. 1566. Annexed by the Turk, 1579. 1617.

The year which saw the Naxian duchy pass from Latin to Hebrew hands saw the fall of the most remarkable of the Genoese settlements in the Greek lands. These settlements, like those of Venice, formed two classes, those which were possessions of the Genoese commonwealth itself and those which came into the hands of Genoese citizens. Genoa had no share in the fourth crusade; she had therefore no share in the division of the Empire, though, after the restoration of Byzantine rule, her colony of *Galata* made her almost a sharer in the capital of the Empire. But the seat of direct Genoese dominion in the East was not the Ægæan but the Euxine. On the southern coast of that sea the republic held *Amastris* and *Amisos*, and in the Tauric Chersonêsos was her great colony of *Kaffa*. The Euxine dominion of Genoa came to an end during the

Settlements of Genoa and of Genoese citizens. 1304. Possessions of Genoa on the Euxine, 1461. 1475.

[1] Ἄσπρη θάλασσα, as distinguished from the Euxine, the μαύρη θάλασσα.

CHAP. X.

latter half of the fifteenth century; but it outlived the Empires both of Constantinople and of Trebizond.

The Ægæan dominion of the citizens of Genoa was longer lived than the Euxine dominion of Genoa her-
Lesbos. 1354–1462. self. The family of Gattilusio received *Lesbos* as an Imperial fief in the fourteenth century, and kept it till after the fall of Constantinople. But the most remarkable Genoese settlement in the Ægæan was that of
The Zaccaria at Chios. 1304–1346. *Chios*. First held by princes of the Genoese house of Zaccaria, the island, with some of its neighbours, passed into the hands of a Genoese commercial company or
The Maona. 1346–1566. *Maona*, a body somewhat like our own East India Company. *Samos*, *Kôs*, and *Phôkaia* on the mainland, came at different times under their power, and Chios did not fall under the Ottoman yoke till the same year
1566. as the duchy of Naxos.

One more insular dominion remains, chiefly famous as the possession, not indeed of a commonwealth, but of an order. In a few years of the thirteenth century
Revolutions of Rhodes. the island of *Rhodes* passed through all possible revolutions. In the first moment of the Latin conquest, it
1233. became an independent Greek principality, like Epeiros
1246. and Trebizond. Then it admitted the overlordship of
1249. the Nicene Emperors. Seized by Genoa, it was presently won back to the Empire, till seventy years later it was again seized by the Knights of Saint John.
Establishment of the Knights, 1310. From Rhodes as a centre, the order established its dominion over *Kôs* and some other islands, and on some
1315. points of the Asiatic coast, especially their famous fortress of *Halikarnassos*. They beat back Mahomet the
1480 Conqueror, but they yielded to Suleiman the Lawgiver
1522. forty years later. Driven from Rhodes, the order re-

ceived *Malta* from Charles the Fifth as a fief of his Sicilian kingdom. We are thus brought back to the island which had been lost to the Eastern Empire for seven hundred years. The knights in their new home beat back their former conqueror Suleiman, and kept their island till the times of confusion. Held by France, held by England, held, nominally at least, by its own Sicilian overlord, this fragment of the Empire of Leo and of the kingdom of Roger finally passed at the peace under the acknowledged rule of England.

Their removal to Malta, 1530.

1566.

Revolutions of Malta.

1814.

§ 5. *The Principalities of the Greek Mainland.*

The Greek possessions of Venice, of Genoa, and of the Knights of Saint John, consisted mainly of islands and detached points of coast. The Venetian conquest of Peloponnêsos was the only exception on a great scale. In this they are distinguished from the several powers, Greek and Frank, which arose on the Greek mainland. We have already heard, and we shall hear again, of the Greek despotat of Epeiros, which for a moment grew into an Empire of Thessalonikê. Among the Latin powers two rose to European importance. These are the *duchy of Athens* in central Greece—in *Hellas*, according to the Byzantine nomenclature—and the principality of *Achaia* or *Morea* in Peloponnêsos. This last name[1] has come to be a modern name of the

Duchy of Athens.

Principality of Achaia.

[1] [The origin of the name *Morea* (ἡ Μορέα or ὁ Μορέας) was for a long time a perplexing riddle, and several impossible derivations were proposed. Hatzidakis has shown (*Byzantinische Zeitschrift*, ii. 283 sqq.) that it meant mulberry-land. It originally designated Elis, where mulberries were cultivated for the silk industry, and afterwards received a wider signification, though it may be questioned whether (as is suggested in the text) it was used of the Principality, before it came to be used of the Peloponnêsos.]

CHAP. X.

Use of the name *Morea.*

peninsula itself. But the name of *Morea* seems strictly to belong to the domain lands of the principality, and never to go beyond the bounds of the principality, which at no time took in the whole of Peloponnêsos.

Both these powers were founded in the first days of the Latin conquest, and the Turk did not finally annex the territories of either till after the fall of Constantinople. But while the Athenian duchy lived on to become itself the prize of Mahomet the Conqueror, the lands of the Achaian principality had already gone back into Greek hands. The lordship of Athens, founded by Otho de la Roche, was first a fief of the kingdom of Thessalonikê, then of the Empire of Romania. But it was by the grant of Saint Lewis of France that the title of *Great Lord*[1] was exchanged for that of *Duke.* The duchy fell into the hands of the Catalan Great Company, who in central Greece grew from mere ravagers into territorial occupiers. They had already occupied the Thessalian land of *Neopatra*, and they transferred the nominal title of *Duke of Athens and Neopatra* to princes of the Sicilian branch of the House of Aragon. Thus the two claimants of the Sicilian crown were brought face to face on old Greek ground. The duchy next passed to the Florentine house of Acciauoli, which already held Corinth, Megara, Sikyôn, and the greater part of Argolis. But their Peloponnesian dominion passed to the Byzantine lords of the peninsula, and Neopatra fell into the hands of the Turk. The Athenian duchy itself, taking in Attica and Boiôtia, lived on, the vassal in turn of the Angevin king at Naples, of the

Lordship of Athens. 1204–1205.

The Duchy. 1260.

The Catalan conquest, 1311.

The Sicilian Dukes.

Dukes of the house of Acciauoli.

1390.

[1] *Grand Sire, Megaskyr,* = μέγας κύριος. See Nikêphoros Grêgoras, vii. 5, vol. i. p. 239.

Greek despot of Peloponnêsos, and of the Ottoman Sultan. Annexed at last to the Ottoman dominions, Athens remained in bondage till our own day, save only two momentary occupations by Venice, one soon after the first conquest, the other in the great war of Morosini.

CHAP. X.

Ottoman conquest. 1456–1460.

1466.

1687.

The smaller principalities of *Salôna* (the ancient Amphissa) and *Bodonitza* play their part in the history of the Athenian duchy; but we turn to the chief Latin power of Peloponnêsos, the principality of Achaia. The shiftings of its dynasties and feudal relations are endless; its geographical history is simpler. The peninsula was, at the time of the Latin conquest, already beginning to fall away from the Empire. King Boniface of Thessalonikê had to win the land from its Greek lord Leôn Sgouros. The princes of the house of Champlitte and Villehardouin were his vassals. They had to struggle with the Venetian settlement in Messênia, and with the Greek despot of Epeiros, who, oddly enough, held Corinth, Argos, and Nauplia. These last towns were won by the Latins, and became an Achaian fief in the hands of Otho of Athens. Before the end of half a century, the conquest of the whole peninsula, save the Venetian possessions, was completed by the taking of *Monembasia*. Things looked as if, now that the Latin power was waning at Constantinople, a stronger Latin power had arisen in Peloponnêsos. A crowd of Greek lands, Zakynthos, Naxos, Euboia, Athens, even Epeiros and Thessalonikê, acknowledged at one time or another the supremacy of Achaia. But Latin Achaia, like Latin Constantinople, had to yield to revived Greek energy.

Salôna and Bodonitza.

The Principality of Achaia.

1205.

1210–1212.

Its greatest extent. 1248.

CHAP. X.

Recovery of lands in Peloponnêsos by the Empire. 1262. 1263.

The Empire won back the three Lacedæmonian fortresses,[1] and presently made *Kalabryta* in northern Arkadia a Greek outpost. Here the Greek advance stopped for a while.

Angevin overlordship. 1278.

Before the end of the century the Frank principality lost its independence. It passed into vassalage to the Angevin crown, and was held, sometimes by the Neapolitan kings themselves, sometimes by princes of their house—some of them nominal Emperors of Romania—sometimes by princes of Savoy, who carried the Achaian name into Northern Italy.[2] In the

Dismemberment of the principality. 1337.

course of the fourteenth century the principality crumbled away. *Patras* became an ecclesiastical principality under the overlordship of the Pope of the

1356.

Old Rome. Argos and its port became a separate lordship. Both of these passed for a longer or a

1358.

shorter time under the power of Venice. Corinth and the north-east corner of the peninsula passed to the Acciauoli. Meantime the Byzantine province

Byzantine advance. 1343–1348.

grew. For some while, under despots of the house of Kantakouzênos, it might almost pass for an independent Greek state. Notwithstanding the inroads of the

1381.

Navarrese, the second Spanish invaders of Greece,

1387.

and the first appearance of the Ottoman, the Greek

1442.

power advanced, till it took in all Peloponnêsos save

Patras. 1430. Conquests of Constantine Palaiologos. 1458–1460.

the Venetian towns and included Patras. The last Constantine even appeared as a conqueror at Athens and in central Greece. Then came more Ottoman inroads, dismemberment, Albanian colonization, final

Successive Turkish conquests of Peloponnêsos.

annexation by the Turk. But the last conqueror has been twice driven to conquer Peloponnêsos afresh. The first revolt under Venetian support was crushed a

[1] See above, p. 390.

[2] See above, p. 283.

few years after the first conquest. Then the Turk CHAP. X.
gradually gathered in the Venetian ports, and the 1463–1540.
whole peninsula was his, save so far as *Maina* kept on 1670.
a kind of wild independence almost down to the last 1685.
Venetian conquest. The complete and unbroken possession of all Peloponnêsos by the Ottoman has never filled up the whole of any one century.

We have seen how the despotat of Epeiros parted Despotat of Epeiros.
away from the momentary Empire of Thessalonikê. The despots, like their neighbours, often found it convenient to acknowledge the overlordship of some other power, Venice, Nikaia, Sicily, or Achaia. The boundaries of their dominions were greatly cut short by the advance of the restored Empire and by the cessions to
Manfred of Sicily. A state was left which took in old Dismemberment of the despotat.
Epeiros, Akarnania, and Aitôlia, save the points on the coast which were held by other powers. *Arta*, the old
Ambrakia, was, as in the days of Pyrrhos, its head. 1271–1318.
Another branch reigned in *Great Vlachia* or Thessaly, 1309.
with its capital at *Neopatra*, a capital presently lost to the Catalan invaders. Next the greater part of Thessaly, 1318.
and then Epeiros itself, were recovered by the Empire, 1339.
and then all gradually passed under the Servian power. Servian conquest.
On the break-up of that power came a time of utter 1331–1355.
confusion and endless shiftings, which has however one
marked feature. The Albanian race now comes fully Advance of the Albanians.
to the front. Albanian settlers press into all the southern lands, and Albanian principalities stand forth on a level with those held by Greek and Latin lords.

The chief Albanian power which arose within the Kings of Albania of the house of Thopia,
bounds of the despotat was the house of *Thopia* in
northern Epeiros. They called themselves *Kings of* 1358–1392.

CHAP. X.

Albania; they won Durazzo from the Angevins, and
1366. their power lasted till that duchy passed to Venice. To
the south of them, in southern Epeiros, Akarnania,
Servian dynasty in Epeiros. 1359. and Aitôlia, reigned a Servian dynasty, a fragment of
the great Servian Empire of which we shall presently
have to speak; its prince Stephen Urosh, who bore an
1363. imperial style, added Thessaly to his dominions. His
western dominion passed from him. A Servian despot
ruled at *Jôannina*, and an Albanian despot at *Arta*. But
Kingdom of Thessaly. Thessaly went on as a kingdom, a kingdom which was
the first Hellenic land to pass under the power of the
Turkish conquest. Turk. It took in the greater part of the land
anciently so called, all except *Neopatra* which was
1393. attached to Athens, *Pteleon* which was held by Venice,
and *Zeitouni* which remained to the Empire. Neopatra
1396. and Salôna followed, and the Ottoman power stretched
to the Corinthian gulf, and parted asunder the still
independent states of Western Greece from Attica and
Peloponnêsos.

In Epeiros the Servian and Albanian despots had
both to yield to Italian princes. Northern Epeiros
Buondelmonti in Northern Epeiros. passed to the Florentine house of *Buondelmonte*. To
the south arose a dynasty of greater interest, the Bene-
The house of Tocco. 1357. ventan house of *Tocco*, the last independent princes in
Western Greece. They first, as counts palatine, held
Kephallênia and Zakynthos as a fief of the Latin Em-
1362. pire. Then they won Leukadia with the ducal title.
1394. They next began a continental dominion, first for a
moment in Peloponnêsos, then more lastingly in the lands
near their island duchy. Duke Charles of Leukadia
1405–1418. gradually won all Epeiros save the Venetian posts; and
he, his wife, and his heirs bore the titles of Despot of
Romania, King of Epeiros, and even Empress of the

Romans.[1] This dynasty, though not long-lived on the mainland, is of real and abiding importance in the history of the Greek nation. The advance of the Albanians was checked; their settlements were thrust further north and further south, while the Beneventan dominions became and remained purely Greek. Soon after the death of Duke Charles, the Turk won Jôannina and the greater part of Epeiros; but his son kept *Arta* and its neighbourhood for nineteen years as a vassal of Venice. Then the dominions of Duke *Charles* became the Turkish province of *Karlili*. The house of Tocco kept its island possessions for thirty years longer. Then they too passed to the Turk, to be recovered for a moment by their own Duke, and then to be struggled for between Turk and Venetian.

Its effects.

Venetian and Turkish occupation. 1430.

1449.

1449–1479.

1481–1483.

Meanwhile the strictly Albanian lands, from the Akrokeraunian point northwards, were subdued by the Turk, were freed, and subdued again. Early in the fifteenth century the Turk won all Albania, except the Venetian posts. Seventeen years later came a revolt and a successful defence of the country, whose later stages are ennobled by the name of George Kastriota of Croja, the famous Scanderbeg. His death gave his land back to the Ottoman, while Croja itself was for a while held by Venice. The whole Greek and Albanian mainland was now divided between Turk and Venetian.

Northern Albania.

1414.

Turkish conquest. 1431.

Revolt 1448.

Death of Scanderbeg. 1467.

Lastly, we must not forget that Greek state which outlived all the rest. Far away, on the furthest bounds of the elder Empire, the Empire of *Trebizond* had the

The Empire of Trebizond.

[1] 'Basilissa Romæorum' = Ῥωμαίων βασίλισσα. 'Romæi' is not uncommonly used for the Ῥωμαῖοι of the East, as distinguished from the 'Roma*n*orum Imperator' of the West.

CHAP. X.

honour of being the last remaining fragment of the Eastern Roman power. The rule of the Grand Komnênos survived the fall of Constantinople; it survived the conquest of Athens and Peloponnêsos.

Origin of the Empire. 1204.

We have seen the origin and early history of this power. After its western dominions passed to the Nicene Emperors and Sinôpê to the Turk, the Trapezuntine Empire was confined to the eastern part of the south coast of the Euxine, stretching over part of Iberia, and keeping the Imperial possessions in the Tauric Chersonêsos. Sometimes independent, sometimes tributary to Turks or Mongols, the power of Trebizond lived on for nearly eighty years as a distinct and rival Roman Empire. Then, when Constantinople was again in Greek hands, John Komnênos of Trebizond was content to acknowledge Michael Palaiologos as Emperor of the Romans, and to content himself with the style of 'Emperor of all the East, of Iberia, and of *Perateia*.' This last name means the *province beyond the sea*, in the Tauric Chersonêsos or *Crim*. We thus see that the style of 'Emperor of the East,' which it is sometimes convenient to give to him of Constantinople, strictly belongs to him of Trebizond. The new Empire of the East suffered many fluctuations of territory, chiefly at the hands of the neighbouring Turkomans. *Chalybia*, the land of iron, was lost; the coast-line was split asunder; the Empire bowed to Timour. But the capital and a large part of the coast bore up to the last, and did not pass under the Ottoman yoke till eight years after the fall of Constantinople. The outlying dependency of *Perateia* or *Gothia* was not conquered till eleven years later still. As the Tauric Chersonêsos had sheltered the last Greek commonwealth, it sheltered also the last Greek principality.

Agreement between Constantinople and Trebizond, 1281.

Turkish conquest of Trebizond, 1461; of Perateia, 1472.

§ 6. *The Slavonic States.*

The Greek and Frank states of which we have just been speaking arose, for the most part they directly arose, out of the Latin partition of the Empire. On the Slavonic powers the effect of that partition was only indirect. Servia and Bulgaria had begun their second career of independence before the partition. The partition touched them only so far as the splitting up of the Empire into a number of small states took away all fear of their being again brought under its obedience. In Croatia and Dalmatia all trace of the Imperial power passed away. The Magyar held the inland parts; the question was whether the Magyar or the Venetian should hold the coast.

Effects of the partition of the Empire on the Slavonic states.

The chief independent Slavonic powers were those of *Servia* and *Bulgaria*. Of these, Servia represents the unmixed Slave, as unmixed, that is, as any nation ever is; Bulgaria represents the Slave brought under some measure of Turanian influence and mixture. The history of the purer race is the longer and the more brilliant. The Servian people made a longer resistance to the Turk than the Bulgarian people; they were the first to throw off his yoke; one part of them never submitted to his yoke at all. The oldest Servia, as we have seen, stretched far beyond the bounds of the present principality, and had a considerable Hadriatic seaboard, though interrupted by the Roman cities. Among the Zupans or princes of the many Servian tribes, the chief were the northern Grand-Zupans of *Desnica* on the Drina, and the southern Grand-Zupans of *Dioklea* or *Rascia*, so called from their capital *Rassa*, the modern *Novi-Bazar*. This last principality was the

Servia and Bulgaria.

Extent of Servia.

CHAP. X.

Relations to the Empire.

germ of the historical kingdom of Servia. But till the fall of the old Empire, the Imperial claims over Servia were always asserted and were often enforced. Indeed common enmity to the Bulgarian, the momentary conqueror of Servia,[1] formed a tie between Servia and
1018. the Empire down to the complete incorporation of
1040. Servia by Basil the Second. The successful revolt of
Servia made room for more than one claimant of Servian
Conquest by Manuel Komnênos. 1148. dominion and kingship; but the Imperial claims remained, to be enforced again in their fulness by Manuel Komnênos. At last the Latin conquest relieved Servia from all danger on the part of Constantinople; it now stood forth as an independent power under the kings of the house of Nemanja.

Relations towards Hungary.

They had to struggle against more dangerous enemies to the north in the Kings of Hungary. Even before the last Imperial conquest, the Magyars had
Loss of Bosnia. cut away the western part of Servia, the land beyond the Drina, known as *Bosnia* or *Rama*. Under the last name it gave the Hungarian princes one of their royal
1286. titles. This land was more than once won back by
Servia; but its tendency was to separation and to growth at the cost of Servia. In the first half of the
1326. fourteenth century, Bosnia was enlarged by the Servian
lands bordering on the Dalmatian coast, the lands of *Zachloumia* and *Terbounia*, which were never permanently won back. So the lands on the Save, between the Drina and the Morava, taking in the modern capital of Belgrade, passed, in the endless shiftings of the frontier, at one time to Bulgaria and at another to
Servian advance eastward and southward. Hungary. Servia, thus cut short to the north and west, was driven to advance southward and eastward,

[1] See above, p. 379.

at the expense of Bulgaria and of the powers which had taken the place of the Empire on the lower Hadriatic coast. From the latter part of the thirteenth century onwards, Servia grew to be the greatest power in the south-eastern peninsula. Shorn of her old Hadriatic seaboard, she gained a new and longer one, stretching from the mouths of Cattaro to Durazzo. Durazzo itself twice fell into Servian hands; but at the time of the highest power of Servia that city remained an Angevin outpost on the Servian mainland. That highest power was reached in the reign of Stephen Dushan, who spread his dominions far indeed at the cost of Greeks and Franks, at the cost of his old Slavonic neighbours and of the rising powers of Albania. In the new Servian capital of *Skopia*, *Skoupi*, or *Skopje*, the Tzar Stephen took an Imperial crown as *Emperor of the Serbs and Greeks*. The new Empire stretched uninterruptedly from the Danube to the Corinthian gulf. At one end Bosnia was won back; at the other end the Servian rule was spread over Aitôlia and Thessaly, over Macedonia and Thrace as far as *Christopolis*. It only remained to give a head to this great body, and to make New Rome the seat of the Servian power.

Her seaboard. 1296. 1319–1322. Reign of Stephen Dushan, 1331–1355. 1346. The Servian Empire.

But the Servian tzardom broke in pieces at the death of the great Servian Tzar; and before he died, the Ottoman was already in Europe. In fact the historical result of the great advance of Servia was to split up the whole of the Greek and Slavonic lands, and to leave no power of either race able to keep out the barbarian. The titles of Stephen's Empire lived on for a generation in the Greek part of his dominions,[1]

Break-up of the Servian power, 1355.

[1] See above, p. 424.

where the younger Stephen, lord of Epeiros and Thessaly, still called himself Emperor of the Serbs and Greeks. In Macedonia and Thrace several small principalities sprang up, and a power arose at Skodra of which we shall have to speak again. To the north Bosnia fell away, and carried Zachloumia with it.

Later Kingdom of Servia.

Servia itself comes out of the chaos as a separate kingdom, a kingdom wholly cut off from the sea, but stretching southward as far as *Prisrend*, and again

Conquests and deliverances of Servia.

holding the lands between the Drina and the Morava.
The Turk first took *Nish*, and brought the kingdom
1375. under tribute. The overthrow at Kossovo made Servia
1389.
1403. wholly dependent. With the fall of Bajazet it again
1438. became free for a generation. Then the Turk won
1442. the whole land except Belgrade. Then the campaign
of Huniades restored Servia as a free kingdom; the
1444. event of Varna again brought her under tribute. At
1459. last Mahomet the Conqueror incorporated all Servia,
except Belgrade, with his dominions.

The Kingdom of Bosnia.

Its origin, 1376.

The history of *Bosnia*, as a really separate power, holding its own place in Europe, begins with the break-up of the momentary Servian Empire. The Ban Stephen Tvartko became the first king of the last Bosnian dynasty, under the nominal superiority of the Hungarian crown. Thus, at the very moment of the coming of the Turk, a kingdom of Latin creed and associations became the first power among the south-eastern Slaves. For a while it seemed as if Bosnia was going to take the place which had been held by Servia.

Greatest extent of Bosnia, 1382.

The Bosnian kingdom at its greatest extent took in all the present Bosnia and Herzegovina, with, it would seem, all Dalmatia except Zara, and the north-west corner of Servia stretching beyond the Drina. But the Bosnian power was broken at Kossovo as well as that of Servia. In the time of confusion which followed, *Jayce* in the north-west corner became a power connected with both Hungary and Bosnia, while the Turk established himself in the extreme south. The Turk was driven out for a while, but the kingdom was dismembered to form a new Latin power. The Lord of the old Zachloumia, a Bosnian vassal, transferred his homage to the Austrian King of the Romans, and became sovereign Duke of *Saint Sava*, perhaps rather of *Primorie*. Thus arose the state of *Herzegovina*, that is the *Duchy*, commemorating in its half-German name the relation of its prince to the Western Empire. But neither kingdom nor duchy was long-lived. Within ten years after the separation of Herzegovina the Turk held western Bosnia. Fourteen years later he subdued the whole kingdom. The next year the duchy became tributary, and twenty years after the conquest of Bosnia it was incorporated with the now Turkish province of Bosnia. But in the long struggle between Venice and the Turk various parts of its territory, especially the coast, came under the power of the Republic.

Loss of Jayce, 1391.

Duchy of Saint Sava or Herzegovina. 1440.

1449.

Turkish conquest of Bosnia, 1463; of Herzegovina, 1483.

Meanwhile one small Slavonic land, one surviving fragment of the great Servian dominion, maintained its independence through all changes. In the break-up of the Servian Empire, a small state, with Skodra for its capital, formed itself in the district of Zeta, reaching northwards as far as Cattaro. For a moment its princes of the house of *Balsa* spread their power over all northern Albania; but the new state was cut short

Dominion of the house of Balsa at Skodra

CHAP. X.

on all sides by Bosnia, Venice, and the Turk, and Skodra itself was sold to Venice. In the middle of the fifteenth century, the state took a more definite shape, though with a smaller territory, under a new dynasty, that of Tzernojevich. This independent remnant answered to the modern *Tzernagora* or *Montenegro*, with a greater extent to the east and with a small seaboard taking in Antivari. Its capital *Zabljak* was more than once lost and won from the Turk; at the end of the century it was found hopeless to defend the lower districts, and prince and people withdrew to the natural fortress of the Black Mountain with its newly founded capital of Tzetinje. The last prince of the dynasty resigned his power to the metropolitan bishop, and Montenegro remained an independent state under its Vladikas or hereditary prelates, till their dominion was in our own time again exchanged for that of temporal princes. During all this time the territory of Montenegro was simply so much of the mountain region as could maintain its practical independence against the ceaseless attacks of the Turk. The Christian state had no acknowledged frontier; it was often harried and sometimes for a moment occupied, but it never became either a province or a lasting dependency of the invader. Yet, while her existence was thus precarious, Montenegro, as the ally of England and Russia, bore her part in the great European struggle; she won for herself a haven and a capital at Cattaro, and received the free commendation of the men of the neighbouring *Bocche*. Her allies stood by while Cattaro and the *Bocche* were filched by the Austrian; and, more than forty years later, when a definite frontier was first traced, Western diplomacy so traced it as to give the Turk an

Loss of Skodra, 1394.

Beginning of Montenegro, 1456.

Establishment of Tzetinje, 1488.

The Vladikas, 1499.

Lay princes, 1851.

1813.

1858.

inlet on both sides to the unconquered Christian land. In the latest times the Montenegrin arms set free a large part of the kindred land of Herzegovina, and won back a considerable part of the lost territory to the east, including part of the old seaboard as far as *Dulcigno*. Then Western diplomacy drew another frontier, which forbade any large incorporation of the kindred Slavonic districts, while a small extension was allowed in that part of the lost ancient territory which had become Albanian. Of three havens won by Montenegro in the war, *Dulcigno* was given back to the Turk. Austria was allowed to filch *Spizza*, as she had before filched Ragusa and Cattaro. The third haven, that of *Antivari*, was left to those who had won it under insulting restrictions. Yet more lately the wrong has been partly redressed by English energy. In exchange for some small Albanian territory given back to the Turk, Montenegro has been again put into possession of her hard won prize of Dulcigno.

CHAP. X.

Montenegrin conquests, 1876–1877.

1878.

Spizza.

Dulcigno, 1878, 1881.

The continued independence of Montenegro enables the Servian branch of the Slavonic race to say that their nation has never been wholly enslaved. The case has been different with Bulgaria. We have seen the origin of the third Bulgarian, or rather *Vlacho-Bulgarian*, kingdom which won its independence of the Empire in the last years of the twelfth century. From that time to the Turkish conquest, one or more Bulgarian states always existed. And throughout the thirteenth century the Bulgarian kingdom, though its boundaries were ever shifting, was one of the chief powers of the south-eastern peninsula.

The third Bulgarian kingdom.

The oldest Bulgaria between Danube and Hæmus

CHAP. X.

Bulgarian advance. 1197–1207.

Dominion of John Asan. 1218–1241.

was the first to throw off the Byzantine dominion, and the last to come under the power of the Turk. The new Bulgarian power grew fast, and for a while called back the days of Simeon and Samuel. Under Joannice the frontier stretched far to the north-west, over lands which gradually passed to Servia, taking in Skupi, Nish, and even Belgrade. Under the Tzar John Asan the new Bulgaria, the kingdom of *Tirnovo*, reached its greatest extent. John claimed to rule over the Greek, the Servian, and the Albanian lands, from Hadrianople to Durazzo.[1] And certainly the greater part of Thrace, Philippopolis and the whole land of *Rhodopê* or *Achridos*, Hadrianople itself, Macedonia too stretching away to Samuel's Ochrida and to *Albanon* or Elbassan, were all under his rule. If his realm did not touch the Hadriatic or the Ægæan, it came very near to both; but Thessalonikê at least always remained to its Frank and Greek lords. But this great power, like so many other powers of its kind, did not survive its founder.

Decline of Bulgaria. 1246–1257.

Shiftings of the frontier.

Philippopolis finally Bulgarian. 1344–1366.

The revived Greek states, the Nicene Empire and the Epeirot despotat, cut the Bulgarian realm short. The disputes of an older and of a later time went on.[2] There was undisputed Bulgaria north of Hæmus, an ever-shifting frontier south of it. The inland Philippopolis, and the coast towns of *Anchialos* and *Mesêmbria*, passed backwards and forwards between Greek and Bulgarian. The last state of things, immediately before the common overthrow, gave Philippopolis to Bulgaria and the coast towns to the Empire.

[1] See Jireček, *Geschichte der Bulgaren*, p. 351.

[2] The history of George Akropolitês gives a narrative of these wars which is worth studying, if only for its close bearing on very recent events.

An attempt at extension to the north by an attack on the Hungarian Banat of *Severin*, the western part of modern Wallachia, led only to a Hungarian invasion, to a temporary loss of *Widdin*, and the assumption of a Bulgarian title by the Magyar king. Presently a new Turanian dynasty, this time of Cuman descent, reigned in Bulgaria, and soon after, the kingdom passed for the moment under a mightier overlord in the person of Nogai Khan. In the fourteenth century the kingdom broke up. The despot *Dobroditius*—his name has many spellings—formed a separate dominion on the seaboard, stretching from the Danube to the Imperial frontier, cutting off the King of Tirnovo from the sea. Part of his land preserves his memory in its modern name *Dobrutcha*. Presently we hear of three Bulgarias, the central state at Tirnovo, the sea-land of Dobroditius, and a north-western state at Widdin. By this time the Ottoman inroads had begun; Philippopolis was lost, and Bulgarian princes were blind enough to employ Turkish help in a second attack on Severin, which led only to a second temporary loss of Widdin. The Turk now pressed on; Sofia was taken; the whole land became a Turkish dependency. After Kossovo the land was wholly conquered, save only that the northern part of the land of Dobroditius passed to Wallachia. Bulgaria passed away from the list of European states both sooner and more utterly than Servia. Servia still had its alternations of freedom and bondage for sixty years. In after times large parts of it passed for a while to a rule which, if foreign, was at least European. In later days Servia was the first of the subject nations to win its freedom. But the bondage of Bulgaria was never disturbed from the days of Bajazet to our own time.

Wars with Hungary. 1260.

Cuman dynasty in Bulgaria. 1280.

Break-up of the kingdom. 1357.

Principality of Dobrutcha.

1362.

1365–1369.

1382.

1388.

Conquest by Bajazet, 1393.

CHAP. X.

§ 7. *The Kingdom of Hungary.*

The origin of the Hungarian kingdom, and the reasons for dealing with it along with the states which arose out of the break-up of the Eastern Empire, have already been spoken of.[1] The Finnish conquerors of the Slave, admitted within the pale of Western Christendom, founding a new Hungary on the Danube and the Theiss while they left behind them an older Hungary on the Kama, have points of contact at once with Asia and with both Eastern and Western Europe. But, as closely connected in its history with the nations of the south-eastern peninsula, as a sharer in the bondage and in the deliverance of Servia, Greece, and Bulgaria, the fitting place of the Hungarian kingdom in our geographical survey is one where it may be looked at strictly as part of the south-eastern world.

Character of the Hungarian kingdom.

Its position in south-eastern Europe.

It has been already noticed[2] that the main geographical work of the Magyar was to cut off that south-eastern world, the world where the Greek and the Slave, struggling for its supremacy, were both swallowed up by the Ottoman, from the Slavonic region between the Carpathians and the Baltic. At the moment of the Magyar inroad, the foundation of the *Great-Moravian* kingdom, the kingdom of Sviatopluk, made it more likely than it has ever been since that the Slaves of the two regions might be united into a single power. That kingdom, stretching to Sirmium, marched on the north-western dependencies of the Eastern Empire, while on the north it took in the Chrobatian land which was afterwards Little Poland. Such a power might have been dangerous to both Empires at

Effects of the Magyar invasion.

Great Moravia. 884–894.

[1] See above, p. 155. [2] See above, p. 156.

CHAP. X.

once; but the invaders whom the two Emperors called in proved far more dangerous than Great Moravia could ever have been. The Magyars, Ogres, or Hungarians, the Turks of the Imperial geographer,[1] were called in by his father Leo to check the Bulgarians, as they were called in by Arnulf in the West to check the new power of Moravia. They passed, from the north rather than from the east, into the land which was disputed between Moravian and Bulgarian. The Moravian power was overthrown, and the Magyars, 906.
stepping into its place, became constant invaders of both Empires and their dependent lands. But to the west, the victories of the Saxon kings put a check to their inroads, and, save some shiftings on the Austrian march, the frontier of Germany and Hungary has been singularly abiding.

Relations between Hungary and Germany.

The two Chrobatias separated by the Magyars.

While the Magyar settlement placed a barrier between the two chief regions of the Slavonic race as a whole, it specially placed a barrier between the two divisions of the *Croatian* or *Chrobatian* people, those on the Vistula and those on the Drave and Save. The northern *Chrobatia* still reached south of the Carpathians, and
it was not until the eleventh century that the Magyar 1025
kingdom, by the acquisition of its southern part, gained a natural frontier which, with some shiftings, served to part it off from the Slavonic powers to the north of it. To the south-east an uncultivated and wooded tract separated the Magyar territory from the lands between

[1] On the origin of the name, see Roesler, *Romänische Studien*, 159, 218, 260. There is something strange in Constantine [and Leo VI. in his *Tactics*] calling the Finnish Magyars Τοῦρκοι, in opposition to the really Turkish Patzinaks. His Τουρκία and Φραγγία are of course Hungary and Germany. De Adm. Imp. 13, 40. pp. 81, 173. ed. Bonn.

CHAP X.

Geographical position of the Magyars.

the Carpathians and the lower Danube which were still held by the Patzinaks. The oldest Magyar settlement thus occupied the central part of the modern kingdom, the lands on the Theiss and the middle Danube. There the Turanian invaders formed a ruling and central race, within a Slavonic fringe at each end. There were northern and southern Croats, *Slovaks* to the north, and *Ruthenians* to the north-east, towards the kindred land of *Halicz* or *Red Russia*.

Hungary a kingdom: its growth.

Hungary, ranking from the beginning of the eleventh century as a kingdom of Latin Christendom, presently grew in all directions. We have just seen its advance at the expense of the northern Chrobatian land. Its advance at the expense of the southern branch of that race, and of the other Slavonic lands which owed more or less of allegiance to the Eastern Empire, was still more marked. All these lands at one time or another gave royal titles to the King of Hungary, King also of Croatia, of Dalmatia, of Rama, even of Bulgaria. But in most of these lands the Hungarian kingship was temporary or nominal; in Croatia alone, though the frontier has often shifted, Hungarian rule has been abiding. Croatia has never formed an independent state since the first Hungarian conquest; it has never been fully wrested from Hungary since the days of Manuel Komnênos. In those days it was indeed a question whether Hungary itself had not an overlord in the Eastern Emperor. After the great Bulgarian revolt that question could never be raised again. But the Hungarian frontier was ever shifting towards the former lands of the Empire, Venetian, Servian, and Bulgarian. One part of the old Croatian kingdom, the land between Save and Drave, was cut off to form, first an appanage, then an annexed

Hungary and Croatia.

kingdom, by the special name of *Slavonia*, a name shared by it with lands on the Baltic, perhaps on the Ægæan.

CHAP. X.

Kingdom of Slavonia. 1492.

But, from the first days of its conversion, the Hungarian realm began to advance in other directions, in lands which had formed no part of the Empire since the days of Aurelian. Before their Chrobatian conquest, the Magyars passed the boundary which divided them from the Patzinaks, and won the land, which from its position took the name of *Transsilvania*.[1] Colonists were invited to settle in the thinly inhabited land. One chief settlement was of the Low-Dutch speech from Saxony and Flanders. Another element was formed by the Turanian *Szeklers*, whose Latin form of *Siculi* might easily mislead. Another migration brought back the name and speech of the Old Rome to the first land from which she had withdrawn her power.

Transsilvania or *Siebenbürgen*. 1004.

Various colonies

The unbroken life of the Roman name and speech in the lands north of the Danube, though it has been exaggerated, is not merely a legend. But there can be no reasonable doubt that the present principality of Roumania and the Rouman lands beyond its borders largely derived their present population and language from a settlement of the Rouman people further south.[2] South of the Danube, the Rouman or Vlach population, scattered among Greeks, Slaves, and Albanians, at many points from Pindos northwards, has kept its distinct

Origin of the Roumans.

[1] Also called *Siebenbürgen*, a corruption of the name of the fortress of *Cibin*, which has many spellings. [Transsilvania is the Latin equivalent of the Hungarian name *Erdély*.]

[2] Roesler's book, *Romänische Studien*, has shown this clearly. [But Roesler went too far. The greater part of the Roman population were certainly south of the Danube up to the twelfth century, but the evidence points to the conclusion that some Latin speaking people existed in the Carpathians.]

CHAP. X.

Their northern migration.

nationality, but it has never formed a political whole. But their migration beyond the Danube reinforced the scanty Rouman remnant which seems to have survived in the Dacian mountains since the days of Aurelian, and enabled the Roumans in course of time to found two distinct principalities, and to form a chief element in the population of a third. There is no sign of a considerable Rouman population north of the Danube before the thirteenth century. The events of that century opened a way for a reversal of the ordinary course of migration, for the settlement of lands beyond the Empire by former subjects of the Empire.

Rouman element in the third Bulgarian kingdom.

We have seen that the third Bulgarian kingdom, that which arose at the end of the twelfth century, was in its origin as much Rouman as Bulgarian. By this time the rule of the Patzinaks beyond the lower Danube had given way to that of the kindred *Cumans*. Then the storm of Mongolian invasion, which crushed Hungary itself for a moment, crushed the Cuman power for ever. But the remnant of the Cuman nation lived on within the Magyar realm, and gave its king yet another title, that of *King of Cumania*. The former Cuman land now lay open to new settlers, and the Rouman part of the inhabitants of the new Bulgaria began to cross the Danube into that land and the neighbouring districts. In the course of the thirteenth century they occupied the present Wallachia, and already formed an element in the mixed population of Transsilvania. A Rouman state thus began to be formed, which took the name by which the Roumans were known to their neighbours. The new *Vlachia, Wallachia*, stretched on both sides of the Aluta. To the west of that river, *Little Wallachia* formed, as the banat of *Severin*, an integral

Cumans in Dacia.

Mongolian invasion.

Rouman settlement in the Cuman land.

Little Wallachia.

part of the Hungarian kingdom. *Great Wallachia* to the east formed a separate principality, dependent on Hungary or independent, according to its strength from time to time.[1] And, towards the end of the fourteenth century, the land south of the Danube, called *Dobrutcha*, passed from Bulgaria to Wallachia. Another Rouman migration, passing from the land of *Marmaros* north of Transsilvania, founded the principality of *Moldavia* between the Carpathians and the Dniester. This too stood to the Hungarian crown in the same shifting relation as Great Wallachia, and sometimes transferred its vassalage to Lithuania and Poland.

CHAP X.

Great Wallachia.

Dobrutcha.

Moldavia. c. 1341.

The greatest extension of the Hungarian dominion was in the fourteenth century, under the Angevin King Lewis the Great. Before his time the Magyar frontier had advanced and fallen back. Hungary, having a Russian population within its borders, had for a while enlarged its Russian dominion by the annexation of the Red Russian land of *Halicz* or *Galicia*. It had also, for a shorter time, occupied the Bulgarian town of Widdin. Lewis renewed both these conquests, and made others. Halicz was not only won again, but was enlarged by the neighbouring principality of *Vladimir*. The great day of Hungary was contemporary with the great day of Servia, but it was a longer day, and Hungary profited greatly by the fall of Servia. While Lewis annexed Dalmatia, he also at various times established his supremacy over Bosnia and the Rouman principalities. That Lewis was king

Lewis the Great, 1342–1382.

First possession of Halicz, 1185–1220;

of Widdin, 1260–1264.

Conquests of Lewis. Halicz and Vladimir, 1342; Widdin, 1365–1369.

1356.

[1] [Distinguish from this Great and this Little Wallachia, the *Great Wallachia* in Thessaly, first mentioned by Anna Comnena, and the *Little Wallachia* in Aetolia and Acarnania. There were also the Black Wallachians (Mavro-vlachoi or Morlachs) of Dalmatia and Herzegovina.]

CHAP. X.

of Poland by a personal union did not affect Hungarian geography. But the separation of the crowns
Red Russia restored to Poland, 1390. at his death led presently to the restoration of the
Red Russian provinces to Poland. Somewhat later,
under Sigismund, a territory within the Hungarian
Pledging of Zips, 1412. border, part of the county of *Zips* or *Czepusz*, was
pledged to Poland, and continued to be held by that
power.

Meanwhile the Ottoman was on his march to overthrow Hungary as well as its neighbours, though the position of the Magyar kingdom made it the last to be devoured and the first to be delivered. The Turkish inroads as yet barely grazed the strictly Hungarian
First Turkish invasion. 1391. frontier. The first Turkish invasion of Hungary, the
first Turkish exaction of tribute from Wallachia, came
in the same year in which Sigismund established his
Battle of Nikopolis. 1396. supremacy over Bosnia. The defeat of Nikopolis confirmed the Turkish supremacy in Wallachia, a supre-
Campaign of Huniades. 1443. macy which was again won for Hungary in the great
campaign of Huniades, and was again lost at Varna.
Battle of Varna. 1444. Meanwhile the full possession of Dalmatia did not out-
live the reign of Lewis. Henceforth Hungary is merely
Disputes for Dalmatia. one competitor among others in the ceaseless shiftings
of the Dalmatian frontier.

Hungary under Matthias Corvinus. 1458–1490. Later in the fifteenth century came another day
of Hungarian greatness under the son of Huniades,
Matthias Corvinus. Its most distinguishing feature
1477. was the extension of the Magyar power to the west,
1485 over Bohemia and its dependencies, and even over the
1467. Austrian archduchy. In the south-eastern lands Wallachia and Moldavia again became Hungarian depen-
1463. dencies. *Jayce* was won back from the Turk, now lord

of Bosnia, and, Belgrade being now Hungarian, the frontier towards the Ottoman was fixed till the time of his great advance northwards.

Loss of Belgrade. 1521.

The first stage of Ottoman conquest in Hungary, as distinguished from mere ravage, was the taking of Belgrade. With the battle of Mohacz, five years later, the separate history of Hungary ends. That victory, followed by the disputes for the Hungarian crown between an Austrian archduke and a Transsilvanian palatine, enabled Suleiman to make himself master of the greater part of the kingdom, especially of the part which was most thoroughly Magyar. From the middle of the sixteenth century till the latter years of the seventeenth, the Austrian Kings of Hungary kept only a fragment of Croatia, including *Zagrab* or *Agram*, and a strip of north-western Hungary, including *Pressburg.* The whole central part of the kingdom passed under the immediate dominion of the Turk, and a Pasha ruled at Buda. Besides this great incorporation of Hungarian soil, the Turk held three vassal principalities within the dominions of Lewis the Great. One was *Transsilvania*, increased by a large part of north-eastern Hungary; the second was *Wallachia*; the third was *Moldavia*, which began to be tributary late in the fifteenth century. The Rouman lands became more and more closely dependent on the Turk, who took on him to name their princes. Indeed, one might for a while add the Austrian kingdom of Hungary itself as a fourth vassal state, for it paid tribute to the Turk even as late as the first years of the seventeenth century. 1606.

Battle of Mohacz. 1526.

Turkish occupation of the greater part of Hungary. 1552–1687.

Tributary principalities: Transsilvania, Wallachia, Moldavia. 1497.

The Rouman lands disputed between Poland and the Turk.

For the superiority of the Rouman principalities an endless struggle went on between Poland and the Turk. At last the same Slavonic power stepped in

CHAP. X.

Battle of Vienna. 1683.

to deliver Hungary and Austria also. With the overthrow of the Turk before Vienna began the reaction of Christendom against Islam which has gone on to our own day.

Recovery of Hungary from the Turk.

The wars which follow answer to the wars of independence in Servia and Greece in so far as the Turk was driven out of a Christian land. They differ in this, that the Turk was driven out of Greece and Servia to the profit of Greece and Servia themselves, while he was driven out of Hungary to the profit of the Austrian king. The first stage of the work, the war which was

Peace of Carlowitz. 1699.

ended by the Peace of Carlowitz, won back nearly all Croatia and Slavonia, and all Hungary proper, except the land of *Temeswar* between Danube, Theiss, and Maros. Transsilvania became a dependency of the

Incorporation of Transsilvania. 1713.

Hungarian kingdom, with which it was presently incorporated. Wallachia and Moldavia remained under Turkish supremacy. The next war, ended by the

Peace of Passarowitz. 1718.

Peace of Passarowitz, fully restored the Hungarian kingdom as part of Christendom. The Turk kept only a small part of Croatia. All Slavonia and the banat of Temeswar were won back; the frontier was even carried south of the Save, so as to take in a small strip of Bosnia and a great part of Servia, as also the Lesser Wallachia, the old banat of Severin. Thus, while the first stage delivered Buda, the second delivered Belgrade. But the next war, ended by the Peace of

Losses by the Peace of Belgrade. 1739.

Belgrade, largely undid the work. The frontier fell back to the point at which it stayed till our own day. From the mouth of the Unna to Orsova, the Save and the Danube became the frontier. Belgrade, and all the land south of those rivers, passed again to the Turk, and Little Wallachia became again part of a Turkish dependency. At a later stage of the century Belgrade was again delivered and again lost.

Final loss of Belgrade. 1789–1791.

Acquisitions from Poland.

The later acquisitions of the House of Austria were made in the character of Hungarian kings, but they did not lead to any enlargement of the Hungarian kingdom. Thus the claim to the Austrian acquisitions made at the first and third partitions of Poland, rested solely on the two Hungarian occupations of Red Russia. Under the softened forms of *Galicia* and *Lodomeria*, the Red Russian lands of *Halicz* and *Vladimir*, together with part of Poland itself, became a new kingdom of the House of Habsburg, as the greater part of the territory thus won still remains. Between the two partitions the new kingdom was increased by the addition of *Bukovina*, the north-western corner of Moldavia, which was claimed as an ancient part of the Transsilvanian principality. It was again only in its Hungarian character that the House of Habsburg could make any claim to Dalmatia. Certainly no Austrian duke had ever reigned over Dalmatia, Red Russia, or the Rouman principalities. Yet in the present dual arrangement of the Austro Hungarian monarchy the so-called *triple kingdom* of Croatia, Dalmatia, and Slavonia, is divided between the rule of Pest and the rule of Vienna. Galicia also counts to the Austrian, and not to the Hungarian, division of the monarchy. All this is perhaps in harmony with the generally anomalous character of the power of which they form part. The port of *Spizza* has been added to the Dalmatian kingdom. It is hard to say in which of his many characters the Hungarian King and Austrian Archduke holds the lands of *Bosnia* and *Herzegovina*, of which the Treaty of Berlin confers on

Galicia and Lodomeria.

Acquisition of Bukovina. 1776–1786.

Dalmatia.

Spizza. 1878.

Bosnia and Herzegovina. 1878.

CHAP. X.

him, not the sovereignty, but the administration. They might have been claimed by the Hungarian king in his ancient character of King of Rama. But the formal aspect of the transaction would seem rather to be that he has, like his predecessors in the sixteenth century, become the man of the Turk.

Later history of Roumania.

After the restoration of the Lesser Wallachia to the Turk and the addition of Bukovina to Galicia, the geographical history of the Rouman principalities parts off wholly from that of Hungary, and will be more fittingly treated in another section.

§ 8. *The Ottoman Power.*

The Ottoman Turks.

Last among the powers which among them supplanted the Eastern Empire, comes the greatest and most terrible of all, that which overthrew the Empire itself and most of the states which arose out of its ruins, and which stands distinguished from all the rest by its abiding possession of the Imperial city. This is the power of the *Ottoman Turks.* They stand distinguished from all the other invaders of the European mainland of the Empire by being Mahometan invaders. The examples of Bulgaria and Hungary show that Turanian invaders, as such, are not incapable of being received into European fellowship. This could not be in the case of a Mahometan power, bound by its religion to keep its Christian subjects in the condition of bondmen. The Ottomans could not, like the Bulgarians, be lost in the greater mass of those whom they conquered. But this very necessity helped in some measure to preserve the national being of the subject nations. Greeks, Servians, Bulgarians, have under Ottoman rule remained

Their special character as Mahometans.

Preservation of the subject nations

Greeks, Servians, and Bulgarians, ready to begin their national career afresh whenever the time for independence should come. The dominion of the Turk in Eastern Europe answers, as a Mahometan dominion, to the dominion of the Saracen in Western Europe. But in everything, save the mere reckoning of years, it has been far more abiding. The Mahometan dominion in southern Spain did indeed last two hundred years longer than Mahometan dominion has yet lasted in any part of Eastern Europe. But the Saracen power in the West began to fall back as soon as it was established, and its last two hundred years were a mere survival. The Ottomans underwent no considerable loss of territory till more than four centuries and a half after their first appearance in Asia, till more than three centuries after their passage into Europe. Constantinople has been Ottoman sixty years longer than Toledo was Saracen.

Comparison with the Saracen power in Spain.

Extent of the Ottoman dominion compared with the Eastern Empire.

The Ottoman, possessor of the Eastern Rome, does in a rough way represent the Eastern Roman in the extent of his dominion. The dominions and dependencies of the Sultans at the height of their power took in, in Eastern Europe, in Asia, and in Africa, nearly all that had formed part of the Empire of Justinian, with a large territory, both in Europe and Asia, which Justinian had not held. Justinian held nothing north of the Danube; Suleiman held, as sovereign or as overlord, a vast dominion from Buda to Azof. On the other hand, no part of the dominions of Justinian in Western Europe, save one Italian city for one moment, ever came under Ottoman rule. The Eastern Empire in the year 800 was smaller than even the present reduced dominion of the Turk. The Eastern Empire, at its height in the eleventh century, held in Europe a dominion far smaller than the dominion of the Turk in the sixteenth century, far larger than his dominion now. But in the essential feature of Byzantine geography, the possession of Constantinople and of the lands on each side of the Bosporos and Hellespont, the Ottoman Sultan took the place of the Eastern Emperor, and as yet he keeps it.

Effects of the Mongolian advance.

The history of the Eastern Empire, and that of the Ottomans in connexion with it, was largely affected by the movements of the Mongols in the further East. Mongolian pressure weakened the Seljuk Turks, and so allowed the growth of the Nicene Empire. Mongolian invasions also led indirectly to the growth of the Ottoman power, and at a later time they gave it its greatest check.

Origin of the Ottomans.

The Ottomans grew out of a Turkish band who served the Seljuk Sultan against the Mongols. As his vassals, they began to be a power in Asia and to harry the coasts of Europe. They passed into Europe, and won a great European dominion far more quickly than they had won their Asiatic dominion. This is the special characteristic of the Ottoman power. Asiatic in everything else, it is geographically European; most of its Asiatic and all its African dominion was won from an European centre.

Break-up and re-union of the Ottoman power.

Already a power in Europe, but not yet in possession of the Imperial city, the new Ottoman power was for a moment utterly broken in pieces by the second flood of Mongol invasion. That the shattered dominion came together again is an event without a parallel in Eastern history. The restored Ottoman power then won Constantinople, and from Constantinople, as representing the fallen Empire, it won back the lost dominion of the Empire.

Its permanence

The permanence of the Ottoman power, when Constantinople was once won, is in no way wonderful. Even the unreclaimed Asiatic, when he was once seated on the throne of the New Rome, inherited his share of Rome's eternity.

First settlements of the Ottomans.

The first settlements of the Ottoman Turks were made on the banks of the *Sangarios*, a position which gave them from the beginning a threatening aspect towards Europe. By the end of the thirteenth century 1299.
they were firmly established in that region. In the first half of the fourteenth they became the leading power in Western Asia. *Brusa*, their Asiatic capital, won in the last days of the Emir Othman, has a manifest eye towards Europe. *Nikaia* and *Nikomêdeia* followed, and the Ottoman stepped geographically into the same position towards the revived Greek Empire which the Nicene princes had held towards the Latin Empire. In the last days of the Emir Othman came their passage into Europe, and a few more years saw Amurath in his European capital of Hadrianople, completely hemming Constantinople in. The second half of the fourteenth century was a time of the most speedy Ottoman advance, and the amount of real advance is by no means represented by the change on the map. We have seen in the case of Servia, of Greece, and of Hungary, that the course of Turkish invasion commonly went through three stages. There was first the time of mere plunder. Then came the tributary stage, and lastly, the day of complete bondage. Under Bajazet, the first Ottoman prince who bore the title of Sultan, the immediate Ottoman dominion in Europe stretched from the Ægæan to the Danube. It took in all Bulgaria, all Macedonia, Thessaly, and Thrace, save only Chalkidikê and the

Conquest of Brusa, 1326–1330; of Nikaia and Nikomêdeia, 1330–1338.

Entry into Europe. 1354.

Conquest of Hadrianople. 1361.

Ottoman advance.

Bajazet first Sultan, 1389–1402.

CHAP. X.

district just round Constantinople. Servia and Wallachia were dependent states, as indeed was the Empire itself. Central and southern Greece, Bosnia, Hungary, even Styria, were lands open to plunder.

Battle of Angora. 1402.

Break-up of the Ottoman power.

This great dominion was broken in pieces by the victory of Timour at Angora. It seemed that the power of the Ottoman had passed away like the power of the Servian. The dominion of Bajazet was divided among his sons and the princes of the dispossessed Turkish dynasties. The Christian states had a breathing-time, and the sons of Bajazet were glad to give back to the Empire some important parts of its lost territories.

Reunited under Mahomet. 1413.

The Ottoman power came together again under Mahomet the First; but for nearly half a century its advance was slower than in the half-century before. The conquests of Mahomet and of Amurath the Second lay mainly in the Greek and Albanian lands. The Turk

Conquest of Thessalonikê. 1430.

now reached the Hadriatic, and the conquest of Thessalonikê gave him a firmer hold on the Ægæan. Towards Servia and Hungary he lost and he won again; he hardly

Mahomet the Conqueror. 1451–1481.

Conquest of Constantinople. 1453.

conquered. It was the thirty years of Mahomet the Conqueror which finally gave the Ottoman dominion its European position. From his first and greatest conquest of the New Rome, he gathered in what remained, Greek, Frank, and Slave. The conquest of the Greek mainland, of Albania and Bosnia, the final conquest of Servia, made him master of the whole south-eastern peninsula, save only the points held by Venice and the unconquered height of the Black Mountain. He began to gather in the Western islands, and he struck the first great blow to the Venetian power by the conquest of Euboia. Around the Euxine he won the Empire of Trebizond and the points held by Genoa. The great mass of the islands and the few Venetian points on the coast still escaped. Otherwise Mahomet the Conqueror held the whole European dominions of Basil the Second, with a greater dominion in Asia than that of Manuel Komnênos. From the Danube to the Tanais and beyond it, he held a vast overlordship, over lands which had obeyed no Emperor since Aurelian, over lands which had never obeyed any Emperor at all. At last the Mussulman lord of Constantinople seemed about to win back the Italian dominion of its Christian lords. In his last days, through the taking of Otranto, Mahomet ruled west of the Hadriatic.

Extent of his dominion.

Taking of Otranto, 1480.

It might have been deemed that the little cloud which now lighted on Otranto would grow as fast as the little cloud which a hundred and thirty years before had lighted on Kallipolis. But Bajazet the Second made no conquests save the points which were won from Venice. Selim the First, the greatest conqueror of his line against fellow Mahometans, had no leisure, while winning Syria and Egypt, to make any advance on Christian ground. But under Suleiman the Lawgiver, not only the overlordship but the immediate rule of Constantinople under its Turkish Sultans was spread over wide European lands which had never obeyed its Christian Emperors. Then too its Mussulman lords won back at least the nominal overlordship of that African seaboard which the first Mussulmans had rent away from the allegiance of Constantinople. The greatest conquest of Suleiman was made in Hungary; but he also made the Ægæan an Ottoman sea. The early years of his reign saw the driving of the Knights from Rhodes, and the winning of their fortress of Halikarnassos, the last European possession on Asiatic ground. His last

Conquest of Syria and Egypt. 1516–17.

Conquests of Suleiman. 1520–1566.

His African overlordship.

CHAP. X.

Algiers. 1519.

Tunis conquered by Charles the Fifth. 1531.

1535.

1574.

days saw the annexation of the Naxian duchy; at an intermediate stage Venice lost her Peloponnesian strongholds. In Africa the Turk received the commendation of *Algiers* and of *Tunis*. But Tunis, won for Christendom by the Imperial King of the Two Sicilies, was lost and won again, till it was finally won for Islam by the second Selim. *Tripolis*, granted to the Knights, also passed to Suleiman. Under Selim *Cyprus* was added; the fight of Lepanto could neither save nor recover it; but the advance of the Turk was stopped. The conquests of the seventeenth century were small compared with those of earlier days, and, before that century was out, the Ottoman Terminus had begun to go back.

Decline of the Ottoman power.

Greatest extent of the Ottoman power.

Conquest of Crete, 1641–1669; of Podolia, 1672–1676.

Yet it was in the last half of the seventeenth century that the Ottoman Empire reached its greatest geographical extent. *Crete* was now won; a few years later *Kamienetz* and all *Podolia* were ceded to the Turk by Poland. This was not absolutely his last European acquisition, but it was his last acquisition of a great province. The Ottoman dominion now covered a wider space on the map than it had done at any earlier moment. Suleiman in all his glory had not reigned over Cyprus, Crete, and Podolia. The tide now turned for ever. From that time the Ottoman has, like his Byzantine predecessor, had his periods of revival and recovery, but on the whole his frontier has steadily gone back.

The Ottoman frontier falls back.

Ottoman loss of Hungary. 1683–1699.

The first great blow to the integrity and independence of the Ottoman Empire was dealt in the war which was ended by the Peace of Carlowitz. We have seen how Hungary and Peloponnêsos were won back for Christendom; so was Podolia. We have seen too how at the next stage the Turk gained at one end and lost at the other, winning back Peloponnêsos, winning Mykonos and Tênos, but losing on the Save and the Danube. The next stage shows the Ottoman frontier again in advance; in our own day we have seen it again fall back. And the change which has given Bosnia and Herzegovina to the master of Dalmatia, Ragusa, and Cattaro, has, besides throwing back the frontier of the Turk, redressed a very old geographical wrong. Ever since the first Slavonic settlements, the inland region of northern Illyricum has been more or less thoroughly cut off from the coast cities which form its natural outlets. Whatever may be the fate of those lands, the body is again joined to the mouth, and the mouth to the body, and we can hardly fancy them again severed.

Union of inland and maritime Illyricum.

The same arrangements which transferred the 'administration' of Bosnia and Herzegovina to the King of Hungary and Dalmatia, have transferred another part of the Ottoman dominion to a more distant European power on terms which are still less easy to understand. The Greek island of *Cyprus* has passed to English rule; but it is after a fashion which may imply that the conquest of Richard of Poitou is held—not, it is to be hoped, by the Queen of Great Britain and Ireland, but possibly by the Empress of India—as a tributary of the Ottoman Sultan.

Cyprus. 1878.

During the former half of the eighteenth century the shiftings of the Ottoman territory to the north were all on the side of Austria or Hungary, whichever the

Relations of the Turk towards Russia.

CHAP. X.

Loss and recovery of Azof. 1696–1711.
Treaty of Kainardji. 1774.
Independence of Crim.
Russian annexation of Crim. 1783.
Of Jedisan. 1791.
Of Bessarabia. 1812.
Shiftings of the Moldavian frontier.
Treaty of Hadrianople. 1829.
Treaty of Paris, 1856; of Berlin, 1878.

northern neighbour of the Turk is to be called. But the Turk saw a new enemy appear towards the end of the seventeenth century, one who was, before the end of the eighteenth, to stand forth as his chief enemy. Under Peter the Great *Azof* was won by Russia and lost again. Sixty years later great geographical changes took place in the same region. By the Treaty of Kainardji, the dependent khanate of *Crim*—the old Tauric Chersonêsos and the neighbouring lands—was released from the superiority of the Sultan. This was a natural step towards its annexation by Russia, which thus again made her way to the Euxine. The Bug was now the frontier; presently, by the Russian annexation of *Oczakow* and the land of *Jedisan*, it fell back to the Dniester. By the Treaty of Bucharest the frontier alike of the dominion and of the overlordship of the Turk fell back to the Pruth and the lower Danube. Russia thus gained *Bessarabia* and the eastern part of *Moldavia*. By the Treaty of Hadrianople she further won the islands at the mouth of the Danube. The Treaty of Paris restored to Moldavia a small part of the lands ceded at Bucharest, so as to keep the Russian frontier away from the Danube. This last cession, with the exception of the islands, was recovered by Russia at the Treaty of Berlin. But changes of frontier in those regions no longer affect the dominion of the Turk.

§ 9. *The Liberated States.*

Lands liberated from the Ottoman.

The losses which the Ottoman power has undergone at the hands of its independent neighbours, Russia, Montenegro, and Austria or Hungary, must be distinguished from the liberation of certain lands from Turkish rule to form new or revived European states. We have seen that the kingdom of Hungary and its dependent lands might fairly come under this head, and we have seen in what the circumstances of their liberation differ from the liberation of Greece or Servia or Bulgaria. But it is important to bear in mind that the Turk had to be driven from Hungary, no less than from Greece, Servia, and Bulgaria. If the Turk has ruled at Belgrade, at Athens, and at Tirnovo, he has ruled at Buda no less. All stand in the same opposition to Tzetinje, where he has never ruled.[1]

As the Servian people was the only one among the south-eastern nations of which any part maintained its abiding independence, so the enslaved part of the Servian people was the first among the subject nations to throw off the yoke. But the first attempt to form anything like a free state in south-eastern Europe was made among a branch of the Greek nation, in the so-called *Ionian Islands*. But the form which the attempt took was no lessening of the Turkish dominion, but its increase. By the peace of Campoformio, the islands, with the few Venetian points on the mainland, were to pass to France. By the treaty of the next year between Russia and the Turk, the points on the mainland were to be handed over to the Turk, while the islands were to form a commonwealth, tributary to the Turk, but under the protection of Russia. Thus, besides an

The Ionian Islands.

Ceded to France. 1797.

Septinsular Republic under Ottoman overlordship. 1798.

[1] It is quite accurate to say that the Turk has never ruled at Tzetinje. It is perfectly true that the Turk has more than once harried Montenegro and Tzetinje itself; the Turk has professed to consider the land as included in a pashalik; but Montenegro has never been a regularly and avowedly tributary state, like Servia, Roumania, and Bulgaria.

CHAP. X.

The Venetian outposts given to the Turk.

advance of the Turk's immediate dominion on the mainland, his overlordship was to be extended over the islands, including Corfu, the one island which had never come under his power. The other points on the mainland passed, not so much to the Sultan as to his rebellious vassal Ali of Jôannina; but *Parga* kept its freedom till five years after the general peace. Then the Turk made his last encroachment on Christendom, and held for a moment the whole of the Greek and Albanian mainland. The islands meanwhile, tossed to and fro during the war between France and England, were at the peace again made into a nominal commonwealth, but under a form of British protection which it is not easy to distinguish from British sovereignty. Still a nominally free Greek state was again set up, and the possibility of Greek freedom on a larger scale was practically acknowledged.

Surrender of Parga. 1819.

All Albania and continental Greece under the Turk.

The Ionian Islands under English protection. 1815.

The Greek War of Independence. 1821.

Extent of the Greek nation.

It was only for a very short time that the Turk held complete possession of all Albania and continental Greece. Two years after the betrayal of Parga began the Greek War of Independence. The geographical disposition of the Greek nation has changed very little since the Latin conquest of Constantinople; it has changed very little since the later days of old Hellas. At all these stages some other people has held the solid mainland of south-eastern Europe and of western Asia, while the Greek has been the prevailing race on the coasts, the islands, the peninsular lands, of both continents, from Durazzo to Trebizond. Within this range the Greeks revolted at every point where they were strong enough to revolt at all. But it was only in the old Hellenic mainland, and in Crete and others of the Ægæan islands, that the Greeks were able to hold their

General Greek revolt.

Extent of the liberated territory.

ground. Of these lands some parts were allowed by Western diplomacy to keep their freedom. A *Kingdom of Greece* was formed, taking in Peloponnêsos, Euboia, the Kyklades, and a small part of central Greece, south of a line drawn from the gulf of Arta to the gulf of Volo. But the Turk was allowed to hold, not only the more distant Greek lands and islands, but Epeiros, Thessaly, and Crete. The kingdom was afterwards enlarged by the addition of the Ionian islands, whose nominal Septinsular Republic was merged in the kingdom. By the Treaty of Berlin, parts of Thessaly and Epeiros were ordered to be set free and to be added to the kingdom. Two years later the new frontier was again traced, so as to enforce the freedom of a great part of Epeiros, including Jôannina. Later still, the promises of Europe have been partly carried out. Thessaly, as a whole, is set free; so is a very small part of Epeiros. Arta and Larissa are restored to Christendom; Jôannina, a city as truly Greek as Athens, and Parga and Prevesa, points so lately torn away from Christendom, are left in bondage. Crete, which had twice arisen, was thrust back at Berlin into bondage; but it has since won practical independence, though it remains still, like Bulgaria, under the nominal suzerainty of the ruler of Turkey.

1829–1833. Kingdom of Greece.

Ionian islands added to Greece. 1864.

Treaty of Berlin. 1878.

Second Treaty of Berlin. 1880.

Liberation of Thessaly only, 1881.

Between the first and the second establishment of the Ionian commonwealth, Servia had been delivered and had been conquered again. The first revolt made Servia a tributary principality. It was then won back by the Turk and again delivered. Its freedom, modified by the payment of tribute and by the presence of Turkish garrisons in certain towns, was decreed by

First revolt and deliverance of Servia. 1805–1812.

Second revolt and deliverance. 1817–1829.

1826–1829.

CHAP. X.

Withdrawal of Turkish garrisons. 1867.

Servia independent with an enlarged territory. 1878.

Servian territory left to the Turk.

the peace of Akerman, and was carried out by the treaty of Hadrianople. Fifty years after the second establishment of the principality, its practical freedom was made good by the withdrawal of the Turkish garrisons. The last changes have made Servia, under a native dynasty, an independent state, released from all tribute or vassalage. The same changes have given Servia a slight increase of territory. But the boundary is so drawn as to leave part of the old Servian land to the Turk, and carefully to keep the frontiers of the Servian and Montenegrin principalities apart. That is to say, the Servian nation is split into four parts—Montenegro, free Servia, Turkish Servia, and those Servian lands which are, some under the 'administration,' some under the acknowledged rule, of the King of Hungary and Dalmatia.

The Rouman principalities.

Union of Wallachia and Moldavia. 1861.

Independence of Roumania. 1878.

Change of its frontier.

While Servia and Greece were under the immediate rule of the Turk, the Rouman lands of *Wallachia* and *Moldavia* always kept a certain measure of separate being. The Turk named and deposed their princes, but they never came under his direct rule. After the Treaty of Paris, the two principalities, being again allowed to choose for themselves, took the first step towards union by choosing the same prince. Then followed their complete union as the *Principality of Roumania*, paying tribute to the Turk, but otherwise free. The last changes have made Roumania, as well as Servia, an independent state. Its frontier towards Russia, enlarged at Paris, was cut short at Berlin. But this last treaty restored to it the land of *Dobrutcha* south of the Danube, thus giving the new state a certain Euxine seaboard. More lately still the emancipated principality has taken the rank of a kingdom. Thus the Roumans, the Romance-speaking people of Eastern Europe, still a scattered remnant in their older seats, have, in their great colony on the Danube, won for themselves a place among the nations of Europe.

Kingdom of Roumania, 1881.

Lastly, while Servia and Roumania have been wholly freed from the yoke, a part of *Bulgaria* has been raised to that position of practical independence which they formerly held. The Russian Treaty of San Stefano decreed a tributary principality of Bulgaria, whose boundaries came most nearly to those of the third Bulgarian kingdom at its greatest extent. But it was to have, what no Bulgarian state had had before, a considerable Ægæan seaboard. This would have had the effect of splitting the immediate dominion of the Turk in two. It would also have had the real fault of adding to Bulgaria some districts which ought rather to be added to free Greece. By the Treaty of Berlin the Turk was to keep the whole north coast of the Ægæan, while the Bulgarian nation was split into three parts, in three different political conditions. The oldest and latest Bulgarian land, the land between Danube and Balkan, forms, with the exception of the corner ceded to Roumania, the tributary *Principality of Bulgaria*. The land immediately south of the Danube, the southern Bulgaria of history—northern Roumelia, according to the compass—receives the diplomatic name of *Eastern Roumelia*, a name which would more naturally take in Constantinople. Its political condition is described as 'administrative autonomy,' a half-way house, it would seem, between bondage and freedom. Meanwhile in the old Macedonian land, the

The Bulgaria of San Stefano. 1878.

Treaty of Berlin. Division of Bulgaria.

Free.

Half-free.

CHAP. X.

Enslaved.

land for which Basil and Samuel strove so stoutly, the question between Greek and Bulgarian is held to be solved by handing over Greek and Bulgarian alike to the uncovenanted mercies of the Turk.

General Survey.

We may end our survey of the south-eastern lands by taking a general view of their geographical position at some of the most important points in their history. At the end of the eighth century we see the Eastern Empire still stretching from Tauros to Sardinia; but everywhere, save in its solid Asiatic peninsula, it has shrunk up into a dominion of coasts and islands. It still holds Sicily, Sardinia, and Crete, the heel and the toe of Italy, the outlying duchies of Campania, the outlying duchy at the head of the Hadriatic. In its great European peninsula it holds the whole of the Ægæan coast, a great part of the coasts of the Euxine and the Hadriatic. But the lord of the sea rules nowhere far from the sea; the inland regions are held, partly by the great Bulgarian power, partly by smaller Slavonic tribes fluctuating between independence and formal
900. submission. At the end of the next century the general character of the East-Roman dominion remains the same, but many points of detail have changed. Sardinia and Crete are lost; a corner is all that is left in Sicily; but the Imperial power is acknowledged along the whole eastern Hadriatic coast; the heel and the toe have grown into the dominion of all southern Italy; all Greece has been won back to the Empire. But the Empire has now new neighbours. The Turanian Magyar is seated on the Danube, and other kindred nations are pressing in his wake. Russians, Slaves, that is, under Scandinavian leadership, threaten

the Empire by sea. The last year of the tenth century
shows Sicily wholly lost, but Crete and Cyprus won back; 1000.
Kilikia and northern Syria are won again; Bulgaria is won and lost again; Russian establishment on the Danube is put off for eight hundred years; the great struggle is going on to decide whether the Slave or the Eastern Roman is to rule in the south-eastern peninsula. At one moment in the eleventh century we see the
dominion of the New Rome at its full height. Europe c. 1040.
south of the Danube and its great tributaries, Asia to Caucasus and almost to the Caspian, form a compact body of dominion, stretching from the Venetian isles to the old Phœnician cities. The Italian and insular dominion is untouched; it is enlarged for a moment
by Sicilian conquest. Another glance, half-a-century c. 1090.
later, shows the time when the Empire was most frightfully cut short by old enemies and new. The Servian wins back his own land; the Saracen wins back Sicily. The Norman in Italy cuts down the Imperial dominion to the nominal superiority of Naples, the last of Greek cities in the West, as Kymê was the first. For a moment he even plants himself east of Hadria, and rends away Corfu and Durazzo from the Eastern world, as Rome rent them away thirteen centuries before. The Turk swallows up the inland provinces of Asia; he plants his throne at Nikaia, and leaves to the Empire no Asiatic dominion beyond a strip of Euxine and
Ægæan coast. Towards the end of the twelfth century, c. 1180.
the Empire is restored to its full extent in Europe; Servia and Dalmatia are won back, Hungary itself looks like a vassal. In Asia the inland realm of the Turk is hemmed in by the strong Imperial grasp of the whole coast-line, Euxine, Ægæan, and Mediterranean.

CHAP. X. At the next moment comes the beginning of the final
c. 1200. overthrow; before the century is out, the distant
possessions of the Empire have either fallen away of
themselves, or have been rent away by other powers.
Bulgaria, Cyprus, Trebizond, Corfu, even Epeiros and
Hellas, have parted away, or are in the act of parting
away. Venice, its long nominal homage cast aside,
1204. joins with faithless crusaders to split the Empire in
pieces. The Flemish Emperor reigns at Constantinople;
the Lombard King reigns at Thessalonikê; Achaia,
Athens, Naxos, give their names to more abiding
dynasties; Venice plants herself firmly in Crete and
Peloponnêsos. Still the Empire is not dead. The
Frank, victorious in Europe, hardly wins a footing in
Asia. Nikaia and Trebizond keep on the Imperial succession, and a third Greek power, for a moment Imperial
also, holds it in Western Greece and the islands.
1250. Fifty years later, the Empire of Nikaia has become an
European power; it has already outlived the Latin
dominion at Thessalonikê; it has checked the revived
power of Bulgaria; it has cut short the Latin Empire
to the immediate neighbourhood of the Imperial city.
To the north Servia is strengthening herself; Bosnia is
coming into being; the Dalmatian cities are tossed to
and fro among their neighbours. Another glance at the
1300. end of the thirteenth century shows us the revived East-Roman Empire in its old Imperial seat, still in Europe
an advancing and conquering power, ruling on the
three seas of its own peninsula, established once more in
Peloponnêsos, a compact and seemingly powerful state,
as compared with the Epeirot, Achaian, and Athenian
principalities, or with the scattered possessions of Venice
in the Greek lands. But the power which seems so

firmly established in Europe has all but passed away in Asia. There the Turk has taken the place of the Greek, and the Greek the place of the Frank, as they stood a hundred years earlier. And behind the immediate Turkish enemies stands that younger and mightier Turkish power which is to swallow up all its neighbours, Mussulman and Christian. In the central years of the fourteenth century we see the Empire hemmed c. 1354.
in between two enemies, European and Asiatic, which have risen to unexpected power at the same time. Part of Thrace, Chalkidikê, part of Thessaly, a few scattered points in Asia, are left to the Empire; in Peloponnêsos alone is it an advancing power; everywhere else its frontiers have fallen back. The Servian Tzar rules from the Danube to the Gulf of Corinth. The Ottoman Emir has left but a few fragments to the Empire in Asia, and has already fixed his grasp on Europe. Before the century is ended, neither Constan- 1400.
tinople, nor Servia, nor any other Christian power, is dominant in the south-eastern peninsula. The Ottoman rules in their stead. The Empire is cut short to a corner of Thrace, with Thessalonikê, Chalkidikê, and the Peloponnesian province which now forms its greatest possession. Instead of the great power of Servia, we see a crowd of small principalities, Greek, Slavonic, and Albanian, falling for the most part under either Ottoman or Venetian supremacy. The Servian name is still borne by one of them; but its prince is a Turkish vassal; the true representative of Servian independence has already begun to show itself among the mountains which look down on the mouths of Cattaro and the lake of Skodra. Bulgaria has fallen lower still; the Turk's immediate power reaches to the

CHAP. X. Danube. Bosnia at one end, the Frank principalities at the other end, the Venetian islands in either sea, still hold out; but the Turk has begun, if not to rule over them, at least to harry them. Within the memory of men who could remember when the Empire of Servia was not yet, who could remember when the eagles of Constantinople still went forth to victory, the Ottoman had become the true master of the South-Eastern lands; whatever has as yet escaped his grasp remained simply as remnants ready for the gleaning.

1500. We will take our next glance in the later years of the fifteenth century, a few years after the death of the great conqueror. The momentary break-up of the power of the Ottoman has been followed by the greatest of his conquests. All now is over. The New Rome is the seat of barbarian power. Trebizond, Peloponnêsos, Athens, Euboia, the remnant of independent Epeiros, Servia, Bosnia, Albania, all are gathered in. The islands are still mostly untouched; but the whole mainland is conquered, save where Venice still holds her outposts, and where the warrior prelates of the Black Mountain, the one independent Christian power from the Save to Tainaros, have entered on their career of undying glory. With these small exceptions, the whole dominion of the Macedonian Emperors has passed into Ottoman hands, together with a vast tributary dominion beyond the Danube, much of which had never
1600. bowed to either Rome. At the end of another century, we see all Hungary, save a tributary remnant, a subject land of the Turk. We see Venice shorn of Cyprus and all her Peloponnesian possessions. The Dukes have gone from Naxos and the Knights from Rhodes, and the Mussulman lord of so many Christian lands has

spread his power over his fellow Mussulmans in Syria, Egypt, and Africa. Another century passes, and the tide is turned. The Turk can still conquer; he has won Crete for long and Podolia for a moment. But the crescent has passed away for ever from Buda and from the Western isles; it has passed away for a moment from Corinth and all Peloponnêsos. At the end of another century we see the Turk's immediate possession bounded by the Save and the Danube, and his overlordship bounded by the Dniester. His old rivals Poland and Venice are no more; but the power of Austria hems in his Slavonic provinces; France struggles for the islands off his western shore; Russia watches him from the peninsula so long held by the free Goth and the free Greek. Seventy-eight years more, and his shadow of overlordship ends at the Danube, his shadow of immediate dominion ends at the Balkan. Free Greece, free Servia, free Roumania—Thessaly set free, while Jôannina is denied the boon twice promised—Montenegro again reaching to her own sea—Bulgaria parted into three, but longing for reunion—Bosnia, Herzegovina, Cyprus, held in a mysterious way by neighbouring or distant European powers—all join to form, not so much a picture as a dissolving view. We see in them a transitional state of things, which, at each of its stages, diplomacy fondly believes to be an eternal settlement of an eternal question, but of which reason and history can say only that we know not what a day may bring forth.

1700. 1800. 1878. 1881.

CHAPTER XI.

THE BALTIC LANDS.

CHAP. XI.

Lands beyond the two Empires.

Our survey of the two Empires and of the powers which sprang out of them has still left out of sight a large part of Europe, including some lands which formed part of the elder Empire. It is only indirectly that we have spoken of the extreme north, the extreme east, or the extreme west, of Europe. In all these regions powers have risen and fallen which might pass for shadows of the two Empires of Rome. Thus in the north-west lie two great islands with a following of smaller ones, of which the elder Empire never held more than part of the greater island and those among the smaller ones which could not be separated from it. Britain passed for a world of its own, and the princes who rose to a *quasi*-Imperial position within that world took, by a kind of analogy, the titles of Empire.[1] In the extreme north are a larger and smaller peninsula, with their attendant islands, which lay wholly beyond the elder Empire, and of which the later Western Empire took in only a very small part for a short time. The momentary union of these two insular and peninsular systems, of Britain and Scandinavia, formed more truly a third Empire of the North, fully the fellow of those of the East and West.[1] In the south-west of

Quasi-Imperial position of certain powers.

The British islands.

Scandinavia.

Empire of Cnut.

[1] See above, p. 161.

Spain.

Europe again lies another peninsula, which was fully incorporated with the elder Empire, parts of which—at two opposite ends—belonged to the Empire of Justinian and to the Empire of Charles, but whose history, as a whole, stands apart from that of either the Eastern or the Western Roman power. And in Spain also, as being, like Britain, in some sort a world of its own, the leading power asserted an Imperial rank. As Wessex had its Emperors, so had Castile.

Castilian Emperors.

History of the lands beyond the Empires.

Britain, Scandinavia, and Spain, thus form three marked geographical wholes, three great divisions of that part of Europe which lay outside the bounds of either Empire at the time of the separation. But the geographical position of the three regions has led to marked differences in their history. Insular Britain is wholly oceanic. Peninsular Spain and Scandinavia have each an oceanic side; but each has also a side towards one of the great inland seas of Europe—Spain towards the Mediterranean, Scandinavia towards the northern Mediterranean, the Baltic. But the Baltic side of Scandinavia has been of far greater relative importance than the Mediterranean side of Spain. Of the three chief Spanish kingdoms Aragon alone has a Mediterranean history; the seaward course of Castile and Portugal was oceanic. Of the three Scandinavian kingdoms Norway alone is wholly oceanic. Denmark is more Baltic than oceanic; the whole historic life of Sweden lies on the Baltic coasts. The Mediterranean position of Aragon enabled her to win whole kingdoms as her dependencies. But they were not geographically continuous, and they never could be incorporated. Sweden, on the other hand, was able to establish a continuous dominion on both sides of the great northern

Geographical comparison of Scandinavia and Spain.

Position of Aragon in the Mediterranean.

Position of Sweden in the Baltic.

CHAP. XI.

gulfs, and to make at least a nearer approach to the incorporation of her conquests than Aragon could ever make. The history of Sweden mainly consists in the growth and the loss of her dominion in the Baltic lands out of her own peninsula. It is only in quite modern times that the union of the crowns, though not of the kingdoms, of Sweden and Norway has created a power wholly peninsular and equally Baltic and oceanic.

Growth and decline of Sweden.

Eastern and western aspects of Scandinavia.

This eastern aspect of Scandinavian history needs the more to be insisted on, because there is another side of it with which we are naturally more likely to be struck. Scandinavian inroads and conquests—inroads and conquests, that is, from Denmark and Norway—make up a large part of the early history of Gaul and Britain. When this phase of their history ends, the Scandinavian kingdoms are apt to pass out of our sight, till we are perhaps surprised at the great part which they suddenly play in Europe in the seventeenth century. But both Denmark and Sweden had meanwhile been running their course in the lands north, east, and south of the Baltic. And it is this Baltic side of their history which is of primary importance in our general European view.

The Baltic lands generally.

It follows then that, for the purposes of our present survey, while the British islands and the Spanish peninsula will each claim a distinct treatment, we cannot separate the Scandinavian peninsulas from the general mass of the Baltic lands. We must look at Scandinavia in close geographical connexion with the region which stretches from the centre to the extreme east of Europe, a region which, while by no means wholly Slavonic, is best marked as containing the seats of the northern branch of the Slavonic race. This region has a

The Northern Slavonic lands.

Germanized Slavonic lands.

constant connexion with both German and Scandinavian history. It takes in those wide lands, once Slavonic, which have at various times been more or less thoroughly incorporated with Germany, but which did not become German without vigorous efforts to make large parts of them Scandinavian. In another part of our survey we have watched them join on to the Teutonic body; we must now watch them drop off from the Slavonic body. And with them we must take another glimpse at those among the Northern Slaves who passed under the power of the Magyar, and of that composite dominion which claims the Magyar crown among many others. These North-Slavonic lands which have passed to non-Slavonic rulers form a region stretching from Holstein to the Austrian kingdom of Galicia and Lodomeria and to the Slovak and Ruthenian districts of Hungary. But above all, this North-Slavonic region takes in those two branches of the Slavonic race which have in turn lorded it over one another, neither of which passed permanently under the lordship of either Empire, but one of which owed its unity and national life to settlers from the Scandinavian North. That is to say, it is the land of the Pole and the Russian, the land of the two branches of the Slavonic race which passed severally under the spiritual dominion of the elder and the younger Rome without passing under the temporal dominion of either. And within the same region we have to deal with the remnant that is left of those ancient nations, Aryan and non-Aryan, which so long refused all obedience to either Church as well as to either Empire. The region at which we now look takes in the land of those elder brethren of the European family whose speech has changed less than any other

Northern Slaves under Hungary or Austria.

Characteristics of Poland and Russia.

The primitive nations.

Aryan nations; Prussians and Lithuanians.

CHAP. XI.

European tongue from the Aryan speech once common to all. Alongside of the Orthodox Russian, of the Catholic Pole, of the Swede first Catholic and then Lutheran, we have to look on the long abiding heathendom of the Lithuanian and the Prussian.[1] And at their side we have to look on older races still, on the præ-Aryan nations on either side of the Bothnian and Finnish gulfs. The history of the eastern coast of the Baltic is the history of the struggle for the rule or the destruction of these ancient nations at the hands of their Teutonic and Slavonic neighbours.

Non-Aryan Fins.

Central position of the North-Slavonic lands.

The whole North-Slavonic region, north-eastern rather than central with regard to Europe in general, has still a central character of its own. It is connected with the history of northern, of western, and of south-eastern Europe. The falling away of so many Slavonic lands to Germany is of itself no small part of German history. But besides this, the strictly Polish and Russian area marches at once on the Western Empire, on the lands which fringe the Eastern Empire, on the Scandinavian North, and on the barbarian lands to the north-east. This last feature is a characteristic both of the North-Slavonic region and of the Scandinavian peninsula. Norway, Sweden, Russia, are the only European powers whose land has always marched on the land of barbarian neighbours, and which have therefore been able to conquer and colonize in barbarian lands simply by extending their own frontiers. This was done by Norway and Sweden as far as their

Barbarian neighbours of Russia and Scandinavia.

[1] A common name for these closely allied nations is sometimes needed. *Lettic* is the most convenient; *Lett*, with the adjective *Lettish*, is the special name of one of the obscurer members of the family.

geographical position allowed them; but it has been done on a far greater scale by Russia. While other European nations have conquered and colonized by sea, Russia, the one European state of later times which has marched upon Asia, has found a boundless field for conquest and colonization by land. She has had her India, her Canada, and her Australia, her Mexico, her Brazil, her Java, and her Algeria, geographically continuous with her European territory. This fact is the key to much in the later history of Russia.

Russian conquest and colonization by land.

Relation of the Baltic lands to the two Empires.

With regard to the two Empires, the lands round the Baltic show us several relations. In Scandinavia, Norway stands alone in never having had anything to do with the Roman power in any of its forms. Sweden itself has always been equally independent; but in later times Swedish kings have held fiefs within the Western Empire. The position of Denmark has naturally caused it to have much more to do with its Roman or German neighbour. In earlier times some Danish kings became vassals of the Empire for the Danish crown; others made conquests within the lands of the Empire. In later times Danish kings have held fiefs within the German kingdom and have been members of the more modern Confederation. The western parts of the Slavonic region became formally part of the Western Empire. But this was after the Empire had put on the character of a German state; these lands were not drawn to it from its strictly Imperial side. Poland sometimes passed in early days for a fief of the German kingdom; in later days it was divided between the two chief powers which arose out of that kingdom. Russia, on the other hand, the pupil of the Eastern Empire, has never been the subject or the vassal of either Empire. When Russia

Norway always independent.

Relations of Sweden and Denmark to the Empire.

The Empire and the West-Slavonic lands.

Poland and the Empire.

Relations of Russia to the Eastern Church and Empire.

CHAP. XI.

had an external overlord, he was an Asiatic barbarian. The peculiar relation between Russia and Constantinople, spiritual submission combined with temporal independence, has led to the appearance in Russia of Imperial ideas and titles with a somewhat different meaning from that with which they were taken in Spain and in Britain. The Russian prince claims the Imperial style and bearings, not so much as holding an Imperial position in a world of his own, as because the most powerful prince of the Eastern Church in some sort inherits the position of the Eastern Emperor in the general world of Europe.

Imperial style of Russia.

§ 1. *The Scandinavian Lands after the Separation of the Empires.*

At the end of the eighth century the Scandinavian and Slavonic inhabitants of the Baltic lands as yet hardly touched one another. The most northern Scandinavians and the most northern Slaves were still far apart; if the two races anywhere marched on one another, it must have been at the extreme south-western corner of the Baltic coast. The greater part of that coast, all its northern and eastern parts, was still held by the earlier nations, Aryan and non-Aryan. But, within the two Scandinavian peninsulas, the three Scandinavian nations were fast forming. A number of kindred tribes were settling down into the kingdoms of Denmark, Norway, and Sweden,[1] which, sometimes separate, sometimes united, have existed ever since.

The Baltic still mainly held by the earlier races.

Formation of the Scandinavian kingdoms.

Of these three, Denmark, the only one which had a frontier towards the Empire, was naturally the first to

[1] See above, p. 131.

play a part in general European history. In the course of the tenth century, under the half-mythical Gorm and his successors Harold and Sven, the Danish kingdom itself, as distinguished from other lands held in after times by its kings, reached nearly its full historical extent in the two peninsulas and the islands between them. *Halland* and *Skåne* or *Scania*, it must always be remembered, are from the beginning at least as Danish as Zealand and Jutland. The Eider remained the frontier towards the Empire, save during part of the tenth and eleventh centuries, when the Danish frontier withdrew to the Dannewerk, and the land between the two boundaries formed the *Danish March* of the Empire. Under Cnut the old frontier was restored.

Formation of the Danish kingdom.

Denmark in the northern peninsula.

Frontier of the Eider.

The Danish March. 934–1027.

The name of *Northmen*,[1] which the Franks used in a laxer way for the Scandinavian nations generally, was confined to the people of *Norway*. These were formed into a single kingdom under Harold Harfagra late in the ninth century. The Norwegian realm of that day stretched far beyond the bounds of the later Norway, having an indefinite extension over tributary Finnish tribes as far as the White Sea. The central part of the eastern side of the northern peninsula, between Denmark to the south and the Finnish nations to the north, was held by two Scandinavian settlements which grew into the Swedish kingdom. These were

Formation of the kingdom of Norway.

[1] See Einhard, Annals A. 815, where we read, 'trans Ægidoram fluvium in terram Nordmannorum . . . perveniunt.' So Vita Karoli 12: 'Dani ac Sueones quos Nortmannos vocamus,' and 14, 'Nortmanni qui Dani vocantur.' But Adam of Bremen (ii. 3) speaks of 'mare novissimum, quod Nortmannos a Danis dirimit.' But the name includes the Swedes: as in i. 63 he says, 'Sueones et Gothi, vel, si ita melius dicuntur, Nortmanni,' and i. 16, 'Dani et ceteri qui trans Daniam sunt populi *ab historicis Francorum* omnes Nordmanni vocantur.'

CHAP. XI.

those of the Swedes strictly so called, and of the *Geátas* or *Gauts*.

The Swedes and *Gauts*.

This last name has naturally been confounded with that of the Goths, and has given the title of *King of the Goths* to the princes of Sweden. *Gothland*, east and west, lay on each side of Lake Wettern. *Swithiod* or *Svealand*, Sweden proper, lay on both sides of the great arm of the sea whose entrance is guarded by the modern capital. The union

The Swedish kingdom.

of Svealand and Gothland made up the kingdom of Sweden. Its early boundaries towards both Denmark

Fluctuations towards Norway and Denmark.

and Norway were fluctuating. *Wermeland*, immediately to the north of Lake Wenern, and *Jamteland* farther to the north, were long a debateable land. At the beginning of the twelfth century Wermeland passed finally

1111.

to Sweden, and Jamteland for several ages to Norway. *Bleking* again, at the south-east corner of the peninsula, was a debateable land between Sweden and Denmark which passed to Denmark. For a land thus bounded the natural course of extension by land lay to the

Growth to the north.

north, along the west coast of the gulf of Bothnia. In the course of the eleventh century at the latest, Sweden began to spread itself in that direction over *Helsingland*.

Sweden had thus a better opportunity than Denmark and Norway for extension of her own borders by land.

Western expeditions of the Danes and Northmen.

Meanwhile Denmark and Norway, looking to the west, had their great time of Oceanic conquest and colonization in the ninth and tenth centuries.[1] These two processes must be distinguished. Some lands, like the

Conquests.

Northumbrian and East-Anglian kingdoms in Britain and the duchy of Normandy in Gaul, received Scandinavian princes and a Scandinavian element in their population,

[1] See above, pp. 131, 158–9.

without the geographical area of Scandinavia being extended. But that area may be looked on as being extended by colonies like those of *Orkney*, *Shetland*, *Faroe*, the islands off the western coast of Scotland, *Man*, *Iceland*, *Greenland*. Some of these lands were actually discovered and settled for the first time by the Northmen. The settlements in the extreme north of Britain, in Caithness and Sutherland, and those on the coast of Ireland, Dublin, Waterford, Wexford, may also pass as outposts of Scandinavia on Celtic ground. Of these outlying Scandinavian lands, some of the islands, especially Iceland, have remained Scandinavian; the settlements on the mainland of Britain and Ireland, and on the islands nearest to them, have been merged in the British kingdoms or have become dependencies of the British crown.

Colonies.

Settlements in Ireland.

Against this vast range of Oceanic settlement there is as yet little to set in the form of Baltic conquest on the part of Norway and Denmark. Norway indeed hardly could become a Baltic power. But there was a Danish occupation of *Samland* in Prussia in the tenth century, which caused that land to be reckoned among the kingdoms which made up the Northern Empire of Cnut.[1] There is also the famous settlement of the *Jomsburg* Wikings at the mouth of the Oder. But the great eastern extension of Danish power came later. Nor did the lasting Swedish occupation of the lands east of the gulf of Bothnia begin till the twelfth century. But there is no doubt that, long before this, there were Swedish inroads and occasional Swedish conquests in other parts of the Baltic lands. Thus *Curland* is said to have been won for a while by Sweden, and to have

Expedition to the east.

Danes in Samland. 950.

Jomsburg. 935–1043.

Swedish conquest of Curland.

[1] See Adam of Bremen, iv. 16.

CHAP. XI.

been again won back by its own Lettic people.[1] The ninth century indeed saw a wonderful extension of Scandinavian dominion far to the east and far to the south. But it was neither ordinary conquest nor ordinary settlement. No new Scandinavian people was planted, as in Orkney and Iceland. Nor were Scandinavian outposts planted, as in Ireland. But Scandinavian princes, who in three generations lost all trace of their Scandinavian origin, created, under the name of *Russia*, the greatest of Slavonic powers. The vast results of their establishment have been results on the history and geography of the Slaves; on Scandinavian geography it had no direct effect at all. Still it forms a connecting link between the Scandinavian lands west and north of the Baltic and the Slavonic region to the east and south of that sea.

Scandinavians in Russia.

§ 2. *The Lands East and South of the Baltic at the Separation of the Empires.*

Slaves between Elbe and Dnieper.

At the beginning of the ninth century the inland region stretching from the Elbe to a line a little beyond the Dnieper was continuously held by various Slavonic nations. Their land marched on the German kingdom at one end, and on various Finnish and Turkish nations at the other. But their seaboard was comparatively small. Wholly cut off from the Euxine, from the northern Ocean, and from the great gulfs of the Baltic, their only coast was that which reaches from the modern haven of Kiel to the mouth of the Vistula. And this Slavonic coast was gradually brought under German influence and dominion, and has been in the end fully incorporated with the German state. It follows then

Their lack of seaboard.

[1] See Adam of Bremen, iv. 16.

that, in tracing the history of the chief Slavonic powers in this region, of Bohemia, Poland, and Russia, we are dealing with powers which are almost wholly inland. At the time of the separation of the Empires, there was no one great Slavonic power in these parts. One such, with Bohemia for its centre, had shown itself for a moment in the seventh century. This was the kingdom of Samo, which, if its founder was really of Frankish birth, forms an exact parallel to Bulgaria and Russia, also Slavonic powers created by foreign princes.[1] The next considerable power which arose nearly on the same ground was the Great-Moravian kingdom of Sviatopluk, which passed away before the advance of the Magyars. Before its fall the Russian power had already begun to form itself far to the north-east. Looking at the map just before the beginning of the momentary Moravian and the lasting Russian power, the North-Slavonic nations fall into four main historical groups. There are, first, the tribes to the north-west, whose lands, answering roughly to the modern Mecklenburg, Pomerania, Brandenburg, and Saxony, have been thoroughly germanized. Secondly, there are the tribes to the south-west in *Bohemia*, *Moravia*, and *Lusatia*, which were brought under German dominion or supremacy, but from which Slavonic nationality has not in the same sort passed away. *Silesia*, connected in different ways with both these groups, forms the link between them and the third group. This is formed by the central tribes of the whole

Bohemian kingdom of Samo. 623.

Great-Moravia. 884.

Four Slavonic groups.

North-western group; thoroughly german-ized.

South-western group under German supre-macy.

[1] The origin of Samo and the chief seat of his dominion, whether Bohemia or Carinthia, is discussed by Professor Fasching of Marburg (Austria) in the *Zweiter Jahresbericht der kk. Staats-Oberrealschule in Marburg*, 1872.

CHAP. XI.

Central group; Polish.

Eastern group; Russian.

region, lying between the Magyar to the south and the Prussian to the north, whose union made up the original Polish kingdom. Lastly, to the east lie the tribes which joined to form the original Russian state. Looking at these groups in our own time, we may say that from the first of them all signs of Slavonic nationality have passed away. The second and third, speaking roughly, keep nationality without political independence. The fourth group has grown into the one great modern power whose ruling nationality is Slavonic.

Polabic group.

Sorabi.

Leuticii.

Obotrites: their relation to the Empire.

With regard to the first group, we have now to trace from the Slavonic side the same changes of frontier which we have already slightly glanced at from the German side. In the land between the Elbe and the Oder, taking the upper course of those rivers as represented by their tributaries the Saale and the Bober, we find that division of the Slaves which their own historian marks off as *Polabic*.[1] These again fall under three groups. First, to the south, in the modern Saxony, are the *Sorabi*, the northern Serbs, cut off for ever from their southern brethren by the Magyar inroad. To the north of them lie the *Leuticii*, *Weleti*, *Weletabi*, or *Wiltsi*, and other tribes stretching to the Baltic in modern Mecklenburg and western Pomerania. In the north-west corner, in Mecklenburg and eastern Holstein, were the *Obotrites*, *Wagri*, and other tribes. Through the ninth, tenth, and eleventh centuries the relation between these lands and the Western Empire was not unlike the relation of the southern Slaves to the Eastern Empire during the same ages. Only

[1] See Schafarik, *Slawische Alterthümer*, ii. 503.

the Western Emperors never had such a rival on their immediate border as the Bulgaria of Simeon or Samuel. The Slavonic tribes on the north-eastern border of the Western Empire were tributary or independent, according as the Empire was strong or weak. Tributary under Charles the Great, tributary again under the great Saxon kings, they had an intermediate period of independence. The German dominion, which fell back in the latter part of the tenth century, was again asserted by the Saxon dukes and margraves in the eleventh and twelfth. Long before the end of the twelfth century the work was done. The German dominion, and with it the Christian religion, had been forced on the Slaves between Elbe and Oder.

Fluctuations of tribute and independence. 921–968.

Final conquest.

The Serbs between Elbe and Saale seem to have been the earliest and the most thoroughly conquered. They never won back their full independence after the victories of the first Saxon kings. The Serbs between Elbe and Bober, sometimes tributary to the Empire, were also sometimes independent, sometimes under the superiority of kindred powers like Poland or Bohemia. The lands included in the mark of *Meissen* were thoroughly germanized by the twelfth century. But in the lands included in the mark of Lausitz or *Lusatia* the Slavonic speech and nationality still keep a firm hold.

Conquest of the Sorabi.

Meissen.

Lusatia.

The Leutician land to the north was lost and won over and over again. *Branibor*, the German *Brandenburg*, was often taken and retaken during a space of two hundred years. Late in the tenth century the whole land won back its freedom. In the eleventh it came under the Polish power. At last, the reign of Albert the Bear finally added to Germany the land which

The Leuticians.

927–1157.

983.

1030–1101.

1134–1157.

CHAP. XI.

was to contain the latest German capital, and made Brandenburg a German *mark*.

In the land lying on that narrow part of the Baltic which bore the special name of the *Slavonic Gulf*, the alternations of revolt and submission, from the ninth century to the twelfth, were endless. Here we can trace out native dynasties, one of which has lasted to our own day. The mark of the Billungs[1]

Kingdom of Sclavinia.

alternates with the *kingdom of Sclavinia*, and the kingdom of Sclavinia alternates between heathen and

Przemyslaf. 1161.

Christian princes. At last, in the twelfth century, the last heathen King of the Wends became the first

House of Mecklenburg.

Christian Duke, the founder of the house of Mecklenburg. Part of this region, Western Pomerania and the island of *Rügen*, became, both in this and in later times, a special borderland of Germany and

Rügen under Denmark. 1168–1325.

Scandinavia. Rügen and the neighbouring coast became a Danish possession in the twelfth century, and so remained into the fourteenth. The kingdom of

1214–1223.

Sclavinia itself became Danish for a short season. A Scandinavian power appeared again in the same region in the seventeenth century. With these exceptions, the history of these lands from the twelfth century onward, is that of members of the German kingdom.

It was otherwise with the second group, with the Slaves who dwelled within the fence of the Giant Mountains, and with their neighbours to the north-east, on the upper course of the Oder as well as on the Wag and

Kingdom of Bohemia.

the northern Morava. Here a Slavonic kingdom has lived on to this day, though it early passed under German supremacy, and though it has been for ages ruled

[1] See above, p. 198.

by German kings. *Bohemia*, the land of the *Czechs*, tributary to Charles the Great, part of the kingdom of Sviatopluk, became definitely a German fief through 928. the wars of the Saxon kings. But this did not hinder Bohemia from becoming, later in the century, an advancing and conquering power, the seat of a short-lived dominion, like those of Samo and Sviatopluk. To the east of the Czechs of Bohemia lie the *Moravians* and *Slovaks*, that branch of the Slavonic race which formed the centre of the kingdom of Sviatopluk, and which bore the main brunt of the Magyar invasion. A large part of the Slaves of this region fell permanently under Magyar rule; so did Moravia itself for a season. Since then Bohemia and Moravia have usually had a common destiny. Later in the century the Czechish dominion reached to the Oder, and took in the Northern *Chrobatia* on the upper Vistula. This dominion passed away with the great growth of the Polish power. Bohemia itself for a moment, Moravia for a somewhat longer time, became Polish dependencies, and the Magyar won a further land between the Wag and the Olzava. Later events led to another growth of Bohemia, in more forms than one, but always as a member of the Roman Empire and the German kingdom.

Moravians and Slovaks.

Magyar conquest of Moravia. 906–955.

Advance of Bohemia. 973–999.

Bohemia and Moravia under Poland. 1003–1004.

1003–1029.

While our second group thus passed under German dominion without ceasing to be Slavonic, among the third group a great Slavonic power arose whose adhesion to the Western Church made it part of the general Western world, but which was never brought under the lasting supremacy of the Western Empire. Large parts of the old Polish lands have passed under German rule; some parts have been largely

The Polish kingdom.

Its relations to Germany.

CHAP. XI.

germanized. But Poland, as a whole, has never been either germanized or brought under lasting German rule. Holding the most central position of any European state, Poland has had to struggle against enemies from every quarter, against the Swede from the Baltic and the Turk from the Danube. But the distinguishing feature of its history has been its abiding rivalry with the Slavonic land to the east of it. The common history of Poland and Russia is a history of conquest and partition, wrought by whichever power was at the time the stronger.

Rivalry of Poland and Russia.

The Lechs or Poles.

Our first glimmerings of light in these parts show us a number of kindred tribes holding the land between Oder and Vistula, with the coast between the mouths of those rivers. East of the Vistula they are cut off from the sea by the Prussians; but in the inland region they stretch somewhat to the east of that river. To the west the Oder and Bober may be taken as their boundary. But the upper course of these rivers is the home of another kindred people, the northern branch of the Chrobatians or Croats, whose land of *White Chrobatia* stretched on both sides of the Carpathians. These Slaves of the central and lower Oder and Vistula would seem to be best distinguished as *Lechs*; *Poland* is the name of the land rather than of the people. *Mazovia*, *Cujavia*, *Silesia*—the German *Schlesien*—with the sea land, *Pomore*, *Pommern*, or *Pomerania*, mark different districts held by kindred tribes. In the tenth century a considerable power arose for the first time in these regions, having its centre between the Warta and the Vistula, at *Gniezno* or *Gnesen*, the abiding metropolitan city of Poland. The extent of the new power under the first Christian

White Chrobatia.

Polish tribes.

Beginning of the Polish kingdom at Gnesen. 931–992.

Conversion of Poland.

prince Mieczïslaf answered nearly to the later Great Poland, Mazovia, and Silesia. But the Polish duke became a vassal of the Empire for his lands west of Warta, and suffered some dismemberments to the advantage of Bohemia. Under his son Boleslaf, Poland rose to the same kind of momentary greatness to which Moravia and Bohemia had already risen. The dominions of Boleslaf took in, for longer or shorter times, Bohemia, Moravia, Lusatia, Silesia, Pomerania, Prussia, part of Russia, and part of that middle Slavonic land which became the mark of Brandenburg, the districts of *Barnim* and *Custrin*. Of this great dominion some parts fell away during the life of Boleslaf, and other parts at his death. But he none the less established Poland as a power, and some of his conquests were abiding Western Pomerania, Silesia, Barnim and Custrin, were kept for a longer or shorter time; and Chrobatia north of the Carpathians—the southern part fell to the Magyar at his death—remained, under the name of *Little Poland*, as long as Poland lasted at all. It supplied the land with its second capital, *Cracow*. From this time Poland ranked sometimes as a kingdom, sometimes as a duchy.[1] Constant divisions among members of the ruling house, occasional admissions of the outward supremacy of the Empire, did not destroy its national unity and independence. A Polish state always lived on. And from the end of the thirteenth century, it took its place as an important European kingdom, holding a distinctive position as the one Slavonic power

Tributary to the Empire. 963. 973.

Conquests of Boleslaf. 996–1025.

Effects of his reign.

Chrobatia becomes *Little Poland*.

Internal divisions.

The Polish state survives.

[1] The Poles claim Boleslaf the First as the first king. But Lambert (1067), who strongly insists on the tributary condition of Poland, makes Boleslaf the Second the first king. In any case the royal dignity was forfeited after the death of Boleslaf the Second.

CHAP. XI.

at once attached to the Western Church and independent of the Western Empire.

Relations of Russia to the Eastern Church.

Teutonic influence among eastern and western Slaves.

To the east of the Lechs and Chrobatians lay that great group of Slavonic tribes whose distinctive historical character is that they stood in the same relation to Eastern Christendom in which Poland stood to Western. Disciples of the Eastern Church, they were never vassals of the Eastern Empire. The Western Slaves were brought under Christian and under Teutonic influences by the same process, a process which implied submission, or attempted submission, to the Western Empire or to some of its princes. The Eastern Slaves were also brought under both Christian and Teutonic influences, but in wholly different shapes. The Teutonic influence came first. It did not take the form of submission to any existing Teutonic power; it was the creation of a new Slavonic power under Teutonic rulers. Christianity did not come till those Teutonic influences had died away, except in their results, and, coming from the Eastern centre of Christendom, it had the effect of keeping its disciples aloof from both the Christian and the Teutonic influences of the West. A group of Slavonic tribes, without losing their Slavonic character, grew up to national unity, and took a national name from Scandinavian settlers and rulers, the Warangians or *Russians* of the Swedish peninsula.[1]

Russia created by the Scandinavian settlement.

The name *Russian.*

[1] There can be no doubt that the Russian name strictly belongs to the Scandinavian rulers, and not to the Slavonic people. See Schafarik, i. 65; Historical Essays, iii. 386. The case is parallel to that of the Bulgarians and the Franks. Whether the name *Rus* is a real Scandinavian name or only a name applied to the Swedes by the Fins, in either case it was as the name of a Scandinavian people that it was first heard in the Slavonic lands.

CHAP. XI.

The Russian power began by the Scandinavian leaders obtaining, in the latter half of the ninth century, the dominion of the most northern members of the Slavonic race, the Slaves of *Novgorod* on the Ilmen. Thence they pushed their dominion southwards. East and north-east of the Lechs and Chrobatians lay a crowd of Slavonic tribes stretching beyond the Dnieper as far as the upper course of the Oka. Cut off from the Baltic by the Fins and Letts, they were cut off from the Euxine by various Turanian races in turn, first Magyars, then Patzinaks. To the south-east, from the Dnieper to the Caspian, lay the *Chazar* dominion, to which the Slaves east of Dnieper were tributary. To the north-east lay a crowd of Finnish tribes, among which is only one Finnish power of historic name, the kingdom of *Great* or *Black Bulgaria* on the Volga. Within this region, in the space of fifty years, the various Slavonic tribes joined in different degrees of unity to form the new power, called *Russian* from its Scandinavian leaders. The tribes who were tributary to the Chazars were set free, and the Russian power was spread over a certain Finnish area on the Upper Volga and its tributaries, nearly as far north as Lake Bielo. The centres of the new power were, first *Novgorod*, and then *Kief* on the Dnieper.

Origin of Russia. 862.

First seat at Novgorod.

Russian advance.

Extent of the eastern Slavonic lands.

Union of the eastern Slaves. 862–912.

Advance against Chazars and Fins.

Second centre at Kief.

How early the Scandinavian rulers of the new Slavonic power became themselves practically Slavonic is shown by the name of the prince Sviatoslaf, of whom we have already heard in the Danubian Bulgaria. Already had Russian enterprise taken the direction which it took in far later days. It was needful for the developement of the new Russian nation that it should have free access to the Euxine. From this they were cut off

The rulers of Russia become Slavonic. 957–972.

Russian enterprise.

Euxine.

CHAP. XI.

by a strange fate for nine hundred years. But from the very beginning more than one attempt was made on Constantinople, though the *Tzargrad*, the Imperial city, could be reached only by sailing down the Dnieper through an enemy's country. Sviatoslaf also appears as a conqueror in the lands by the Caucasus and the Caspian, and Vladimir, the first Christian prince, won his way to baptism by an attack on the Imperial city of Chersôn.

Conquests on the Caspian.

Vladimir takes Chersôn. 989.

Isolation of Russia.

The oldest Russia was thus, like the oldest Poland, emphatically an inland state; but Russia was far more isolated than Poland. Its ecclesiastical position kept it from sharing the history of the Western Slaves. Its geographical position kept it from sharing the history of the Servians and Bulgarians. And it must not be forgotten that the oldest Russia was formed mainly of lands which afterwards passed under the rule of Poland and Lithuania. *Little Russia*, *Black Russia*, *White Russia*, *Red Russia*, all came under foreign rule. The Dnieper, from which Russia was afterwards cut off, was the great central river of the elder Russia; of the Don and the Volga she held only the upper course. The northern frontier barely passed the great lakes of Ladoga and Onega, and the Gulf of Finland itself. It seems not to have reached what was to be the Gulf of Riga, but some of the Russian princes held a certain supremacy over the Finnish and Lettish tribes of that region.

Russian lands west of Dnieper.

Russian principalities. 1054.

Supremacy of Kief; of the Northern Vladimir, 1169.

In the course of the eleventh century, the Russian state, like that of Poland, was divided among princes of the reigning family, acknowledging the superiority of the great prince of *Kief*. In the next century the chief power passed from Kief to the northern *Vladimir* on the Kliasma. Thus the former Finnish land of *Susdal* on the upper tributaries of the Volga became the cradle of the second Russian power. *Novgorod the Great* meanwhile, under elective princes, claimed, like its neighbour *Pskof* (*Pleskau*), to rank among commonwealths. Its dominion was spread far over the Finnish tribes to the north and east; the White sea, and, far more precious, the Finnish gulf, had now a Russian seaboard. It was out of Vladimir and Novgorod that the Russia of the future was to grow. Meanwhile a crowd of principalities, *Polotsk*, *Smolensk*, the *Severian Novgorod*, *Tchernigof*, and others, grew up on the Duna and Dnieper. Far to the east arose the commonwealth of *Viatka*, and on the frontiers of Poland and Hungary lay the principality of *Halicz* or *Galicia*, which afterwards grew for a while into a powerful kingdom.

Susdal Russian. Commonwealths at Novgorod and Pskof.

The principalities.

Commonwealth of Viatka. 1174.

Halicz or Galicia. 1186.

Meanwhile in the lands on the Euxine the old enemies, Patzinaks and Chazars, gave way to the *Cumans*,[1] known in Russian history as *Polovtzi* and *Parthi*. They spread themselves from the Ural river to the borders of Servia and Danubian Bulgaria, cutting off Russia from the Caspian. In the next century Russians and Cumans—momentary allies—fell before the advance of the *Mongols*, commonly known in European history as *Tartars*. Known only as ravagers in the lands more to the west, over Russia they become overlords for two hundred and fifty years. All that escaped absorption by the Lithuanian became tributary to the Mongol. Still the relation was only a tributary one; Russia was never incorporated in the Mongol dominion, as Servia and Bulgaria were incorporated in the Ottoman dominion. But Kief was overthrown; Vladimir became dependent; Novgorod remained the

The Cumans. 1114.

1223.

Mongol invasion.

1238–40. Russia made tributary to the Mongols.

1240. Fall of Kief.

Russia represented by Novgorod.

[1] See above, pp. 367, 440.

CHAP. XI.

true representative of free Russia in the Baltic lands.

The earlier races on the Baltic.

But besides the Slaves of Poland and Russia, our survey takes in also the ancient races by which both Poland and Russia were so largely cut off from the Baltic. Down to the middle of the twelfth century, notwithstanding occasional Polish or Scandinavian occupations, those races still kept their hold of the whole Baltic north-eastwards from the mouth of the Vistula. The non-Aryan Fins, besides their seats to the north, still kept the coast of *Esthland* and *Livland*, in Latin shape *Esthonia* and *Livonia*, from the Finnish gulf to the Duna and slightly beyond, taking in a small strip of the opposite peninsula. The inland part of the later Livland was held by the *Letts*, the most northern branch of the ancient Aryan settlers in this region. Of this family were the tribes of *Curland* in their own peninsula, of *Samigola* or *Semigallia*, the *Samaites* of *Samogitia* to the south, the proper *Lithuanians* south of them, the *Jatwages*, *Jatvingi*—in many spellings—forming a Lithuanian wedge between the Slavonic lands of Mazovia and Black Russia. The Lithuanians, strictly so called, reached the coast just north of the Niemen; from the mouth of the Niemen to the mouth of the Vistula the coast was held by the *Prussians*. Of these nations, Aryan and non-Aryan, the Lithuanians alone founded a national dominion in historic times. The history of the rest is simply the history of their bondage, sometimes of their uprooting.

Fins in Livland and Esthland.

The Lettic nations.

Curland.

Samogitia.

Lithuania.

Prussia.

Survey in the twelfth century.

Taking a general survey of the lands round the Baltic about the middle of the twelfth century, we see the three Scandinavian kingdoms, the first fully formed states in these regions, all living and vigorous powers, but with fluctuating boundaries. Their western colonies are still Scandinavian. East and south of the Baltic they have not got beyond isolated and temporary enterprises. The Slavonic nations on the middle Elbe have fallen under German dominion; to the south, Bohemia and its dependencies keep their Slavonic nationality under German supremacy. Poland, often divided and no longer conquering, still keeps its frontier, and its position as the one independent Slavonic power belonging to the Western Church. Russia, the great Eastern Slavonic power, has risen to unity and greatness under Scandinavian masters, and has again broken up into states connected only by a feeble tie. The submission of Russia to barbarian invaders comes later than our immediate survey; but the weakening of the Russian power both by division and by submission is an essential element in the state of things which now begins. This is the spread in different ways of Teutonic dominion, German and Scandinavian, over the southern and eastern coasts of the Baltic, largely at the expense of the Slaves, still more largely at the expense of the primitive nations, Aryan and non-Aryan.

Teutonic advance, German and Scandinavian

§ 3. *The German Dominion on the Baltic.*

In the first half of the twelfth century, no Teutonic power, German or Scandinavian, had any lasting hold on any part of the eastern coast of the Baltic or its gulfs, nor had any such power made any great advances on the southern coast. Early in the fourteenth century

CHAP. XI.

Time of Teutonic conquest.

German influence stronger than Scandinavian

Extent of German dominion.

German influence abiding.

the whole of these coasts had been brought into different degrees of submission to several Teutonic powers, German and Scandinavian. Of the two influences the German has been the more abiding. Scandinavian dominion has now wholly passed away from these coasts, and it is only in the lands north of the Finnish gulf that it can be said to have ever been really lasting. But German influence has destroyed, assimilated, or brought to submission, the whole of the earlier inhabitants, from Wagria to Esthland. In our own day the whole coast, from the isle of Rügen to the head of the Gulf of Bothnia, is in the possession of two powers, one German, one Slavonic. But German influence abides beyond the bounds of German rule. Not only have Pomerania and Prussia become German in every sense, but Curland, Livland, and Esthland, under the dominion of Russia, are still spoken of as German provinces.

Beginning of Swedish conquest in Finland. 1155.

German conquest in Livland.

This great change was brought about by a singular union of mercantile, missionary, and military enterprise. The beginning came from Scandinavia, when the Swedish King Saint Eric undertook the conquest and conversion of the proper Finland, east of the Gulf of Bothnia. Here, in the space of about a century, a great province was added to the Swedish kingdom, a province whose eastern boundary greatly shifted, but the greater part of which remained Swedish down to the present century. To the south of the Gulf of Finland the changes of possession have been endless. The settled dominion of Sweden in those lands comes later; Danish occupation, though longer, was only temporary. Soon after the beginning of Swedish conquest in Finland began the work of German mercantile enterprise, followed fifty years later by German conquest and conversion, in Livland and the neighbouring lands. This hindered the growth of any native power on those coasts. Even Lithuania in the days of its greatness was cut off from the sea. Whatever tendencies towards Russian supremacy had arisen in those parts were hindered from growing into Russian dominion. The Knights of the Sword in Livland were followed by the Teutonic Knights in Prussia, and the two orders became one. Further west, the latter part of the twelfth and the beginning of the thirteenth century saw a great, but mostly short-lived, extension of Danish power over both German and Slavonic lands. While the coasts are thus changing hands, the relations of the Scandinavian kingdoms to one another are ever shifting. Poland is ever losing territory to the west, and, still more after the beginning of its connexion with Lithuania, ever gaining it to the east. And, alongside of princes and sovereign orders, this time is marked by the appearance of the first germs of the great German commercial league, which, without becoming a strictly territorial power, exercised the greatest influence on the disposal of power among all its neighbours.

Foundation of Riga. 1201.

Effect on Lithuania and Russia.

The Military Orders.

Danish advance.

The Scandinavian kingdoms.

Polish gains and losses.

The *Hansa*.

In Scandinavia itself the chief strictly geographical change was a temporary transfer to Sweden in the fourteenth century of the Danish lands within the northern peninsula. At the end of that century came the union of Calmar, the principle of which was that the three kingdoms, remaining separate states, should be joined under a common sovereign. But this union was never firmly established, and the arrangements of the three crowns were shifting throughout the fifteenth

Scania Swedish. 1332–1360.

Union of Calmar. 1397.

CHAP. XI.

Sweden separated, Denmark and Norway united. 1520.

century; a lasting state of things came only with the final breach of the union in the sixteenth century. From that time, Sweden, under the house of Vasa, forms one power; Denmark and Norway, under the house of Oldenburg, form another.

Loss of oceanic colonies.

With regard to the more distant relations of the three kingdoms, this period is marked by the gradual withdrawal of Scandinavian power from the oceanic lands. The union of Iceland and Greenland with Norway was the union of one Scandinavian land with another. But Greenland, the most distant Scandinavian land, vanishes from history about the time of the Calmar union. The Scandinavian settlements in and about the British Islands all passed away. The Ostmen of Ireland were lost in the mass of the Teutonic settlers who passed from England into Ireland. The Western Isles were sold to Scotland; Man passed under Scottish and English supremacy. Orkney and Shetland were pledged to the Scottish crown; and, though never formally ceded, they have become incorporated with the British kingdom.

Iceland and Greenland united to Norway. 1261–1262.

Ireland.

The Western Isles. Man. 1264.

Orkney pledged. 1468.

Swedish advance in Finland.

East of the Gulf of Bothnia Swedish rule advanced. Attempts at conquest both in Russia and in Esthland failed, but *Finland* and *Carelia* were fully subdued, and the Swedish power reached to Lake Ladoga. Denmark made a more lasting, but still short-lived, settlement in Esthland. The growth of Denmark at the other end of the Baltic lands began earlier and was checked sooner. But at the beginning of the thirteenth century things looked as if Denmark was about to become the chief power on all the Baltic coasts.

1248–1293.

Esthland Danish. 1238–1346.

Short-lived greatness of Denmark.

Holstein.

South of the boundary stream of the Eider the lands which make up the modern Holstein formed three settlements, two Teutonic and one Slavonic. To the west lay the free Frisian land of *Ditmarschen*. In the middle were the lands of the Saxons beyond the Elbe—the *Holtsætan*—with *Stormarn* immediately on the Elbe. On the Baltic side lay the Slavonic land of *Wagria*, which at the beginning of the twelfth century formed part of the kingdom of *Sclavinia*, a kingdom stretching from the haven of Kiel to the islands at the mouth of the Oder. In these lands began the eastern advance of Denmark in the latter half of the twelfth century. All Sclavinia was won, with at least a supremacy over the Pomeranian land as far as the Riddow. Thus far the Danish conquests, won mainly over Slaves, continue the chain of occasional Scandinavian occupation on those coasts, from the tenth century to the nineteenth. In another point of view, the Christian advance, the overthrow of the chief centre of Slavonic heathendom in Rügen, carries on the work of the Saxon Dukes. But in the first years of the next century began a Danish occupation of German ground. Holstein, and Lübeck itself, were won; a claim was set up to the free land of Ditmarschen; and all these conquests were confirmed by an Imperial grant.[1] The Danish kings took the title of *Kings of the Slaves*, afterwards of the *Vandals* or *Wends*. But this dominion was soon broken up by the captivity of the Danish king Waldemar. The Eider became again the boundary. Of her Slavonic dominion Denmark kept only an outlying fragment,

Ditmarschen.

Holstein.

Wagria.

Danish conquest of Sclavinia. 1168–1189.

Danish advance in Germany.

1214.

Fall of Danish power. 1223–1227

[1] This document, granted at Metz in 1214, will be found in Bréholles' *Historia Diplomatica Friderici Secundi*, i. 347. It reads like a complete surrender of all Imperial rights in both the German and the Slavonic conquests of Waldemar. But it may be that it seems to have that meaning only because the retreating of Terminus was deemed inconceivable.

CHAP. XI.

Denmark keeps Rügen, till ceded 1325, 1438.

the isle of Rügen and the neighbouring coast. This remained Danish for a hundred years longer, nominally for a hundred years longer still.

The next changes tended to draw the lands immediately on each side of the Eider into close connexion with one another. The southern part of the Danish peninsula, from the Eider to the Aa, became a distinct fief of the Danish crown, held by a Danish prince under the name of the duchy of *South-Jutland—Jutia* or *Sunder-Jutia*. In the next century this duchy and the county of Holstein are found in the hands of the same prince, and it is held that his grant of the Danish duchy contained a promise that it should never be united with the Danish crown. Henceforth South-Jutland begins to be spoken of as the *duchy of Sleswick*. But of the lands held together, Sleswick remained a fief of Denmark, while Holstein remained a fief of the Empire. The duchy was several times united to the crown and again granted out. At one moment of union the Roman King Sigismund expressly confirmed the union, and acknowledged Sleswick as a Danish land. At the next grant of the duchy, its perpetual separation from the crown is alleged to have been again confirmed by Christian the First. Yet Christian himself, already king of the three kingdoms, was afterwards elected Duke of Sleswick and Count of Holstein. The election was accompanied by a declaration that the two principalities, though the one was held of the Empire and the other of the Danish crown, should never be separated. In the same reign an Imperial grant raised the counties of Holstein and Stormarn with the land of Ditmarschen to the rank of a duchy. But the dominions of its duke were not a continuous territory stretching

Duchy of South-Jutland. 1232.

United with Holstein. 1325.

Duchy of Sleswick.

Fluctuations of Sleswick and Holstein.

1424.

1448.

1460.

Duchy of Holstein. 1474.

from sea to sea. To the west, *Ditmarschen*—notwithstanding a renewed Imperial grant—remained free; to the east, some districts of the old Wagria formed the *bishopric of Lübeck*. But now for the first time the same prince reigned in the threefold character of King of Denmark, Duke of the Danish fief of Sleswick, and Duke of the Imperial fief of Holstein. Endless shiftings, divisions, and reunions of various parts of the two duchies followed. In the partitions between the *royal* and *ducal* lines of the house of Oldenburg, the several portions of the Kings of Denmark and of the Dukes of Gottorp paid no regard to the boundary of the Eider, but each was made up of detached parts of both duchies. Meanwhile the freedom of Ditmarschen came to an end, and the old Frisian land became part of the royal share of the duchy of Holstein. And, as we began our story of Danish advance with the settlement in Esthland, we have to end it for the present with the acquisition of the islands of *Dago* and *Oesel* off the same coasts.

Freedom in Ditmarschen.

Bishopric of Lübeck.

Denmark, Sleswick, and Holstein under Christian.

Royal and ducal lines. 1580.

Conquest of Ditmarschen. 1559.

Acquisition of Dago and Oesel.

After the loss of Rügen, Denmark had little to do with the Slavonic lands, except so far as the possession of Holstein carried with it the possession of the old Slavonic land of Wagria. Still the advance of Denmark at the end of the twelfth century had a lasting effect on the Slavonic lands by altogether shaking the Polish dominion on the Baltic. But it shook it to the advantage, not of Scandinavia, but of Germany. Between the twelfth century and the fourteenth Poland lost all its western dominions. *Pomore*, *Pommern*, *Pomerania*, the seaboard of the Lechish Slaves, is strictly the land between the mouth of the Vistula and the mouth of the Oder; but the name had already spread further to the west.

Effect of the Danish advance on the Slavonic lands.

Pomerania falls away from Poland.

CHAP. XI.

Duchy of Slavia.

1298–1305. Loss of western territory by Poland.

1220–1260.

Silesia. 1289–1327.

After the fall of the Danish power on this coast, Pomerania west of the Riddow altogether fell away from Poland. As the duchy of *Slavia*, it became, like Mecklenburg, a land of the Empire, though ruled by Slavonic princes. But the eastern part of Pomerania, *Cassubia* and the mark of *Gdansk* or *Danzig*, remained under Polish superiority till the beginning of the fourteenth century. Then the greater part fell away, partly for ever, to the Pomeranian duchy of *Wolgast*, partly, for a season only, to the Teutonic Knights. To the south *Barnim* and *Custrin* passed, after some shiftings, to the mark of Brandenburg. Further to the south, Silesia, divided among princes of the house of Piast, gradually fell under Bohemian supremacy. Thus the whole western part of the Polish kingdom passed into the hands of princes of the Empire, and was included within the bounds of the German realm.

Bohemia under Ottocar. 1269–1278.

His German dominion.

The fate of Silesia brings us again to the history of the inland Slavonic land of the Czechs. *Bohemia* went on, as duchy and kingdom,[1] ruled by native princes as vassals of the Empire. Moravia was a fief of Bohemia. In the end Bohemia passed to German kings, but not till it had become again the centre of a dominion which recalls the fleeting powers of Samo and Sviatopluk. Ottocar the Second united the long-severed branches of the Slavonic race by annexing the German lands which lay between them. Lord of Bohemia, Moravia, Austria, Styria, Carinthia, and Car-

[1] Vratislaf, who reigned from 1061 to 1092, is called the first king of Bohemia, but his royal dignity was only personal. The succession of kings begins only with Ottocar the First, who reigned from 1197 to 1230.

niola, the Czech king reigned on the upper Oder and the middle Danube as far as the Hadriatic. The same lands were in after times to be again united, but from the opposite side.

The successors of Ottocar reigned only over Bohemia and Moravia. Early in the next century the Bohemian crown passed to the house of Luxemburg. Under them Bohemia became a powerful state, but a state becoming more and more German, less and less Slavonic. The gradual extension of Bohemian superiority over Silesia led to its formal incorporation. In the same century *Lusatia*, High and Low, was won from Brandenburg. The mark of Brandenburg itself became for a while a Bohemian possession, before it passed to the burggraves of Nürnberg. The Bohemian possession of the Upper Palatinate lies out of our Slavonic range. Among the revolutions of the fifteenth century, we find the Bohemian crown at one time held conjointly with that of Hungary, at another time held by a Polish prince. Later in the century the victories of Matthias Corvinus took away Moravia, Silesia, and Lusatia, from the Bohemian crown. But it was the fourfold dominion of Bohemia, Moravia, Silesia, and Lusatia, which finally passed to the House of Austria, to be shorn of its northern and eastern lands to the profit, first of Saxony, and then of Brandenburg or Prussia.

Luxemburg kings of Bohemia. 1308.

Silesia, 1355.

Lusatia. 1320–1370.

Brandenburg. 1373–1417.

1353.

Conquests of Matthias Corvinus. 1478–1490

Bohemia and Austria.

Its losses. 1635.

1740.

Thus far the Teutonic advance, both on the actual Baltic coast and on the inland Slavonic region, had been made to the profit, partly of the Scandinavian kingdoms, partly of the princes of the Empire. But there were two other forms of Teutonic influence and dominion, which fell to the share, not of princes, but of

German corporations.

CHAP. XI.

The Hansa.

Second foundation of Lübeck. 1158.

corporate bodies, mercantile and military or religious. The Hanseatic League was a power indeed in these regions, but it hardly has a place on the map. Even before the second foundation of Lübeck by Henry the Lion, German mercantile settlements had begun at Novgorod, in Gotland, and in London. Gradually, in the course of the thirteenth and fourteenth centuries, the League into which the union of the merchant towns of Germany grew spread itself over the Baltic, the Westfalian, and the Netherlandish lands. A specially close tie bound together the five *Wendish* towns, *Lübeck*, *Rostock*, *Wismar*, *Stralsund*, and *Greifswald*. But the union of a town with the Hansa did not necessarily affect its political position. It might, at least in the later stages of the League, be a free city of the Empire, a town subject to some prince of the Empire, or a town subject to a prince beyond its bounds. Not only the Pomeranian and Prussian cities under the rule of the Knights, but Revel in Esthland under Danish rule, formed part of the League. The League waged wars, made peace, overthrew and set up kings, as suited its interests; but territorial dominion, strictly so called, was not its object. Still in some cases privileges grew into something like dominion; in others military occupation might pass for temporary dominion. Thus in the isle of *Gotland* the Hansa had an ascendency which was overthrown by the conquest of the island by the Danish king Waldemar, a conquest avenged by a temporary Hanseatic occupation of Scania. In fact the nature of the League, the relations of the cities to one another, geographical as well as political, hindered the Hansa from ever becoming a territorial power like Switzerland

Extent of the League.

Nature of the union.

The Hansa not a territorial power.

The Hansa in Gotland and Scania.

1361.

1368–1385.

and the United Provinces. In the history of the Baltic lands it takes for some ages a position at least equal to that of any kingdom. But it is only casually and occasionally that its triumphs can be marked on the map.

The other great German corporation was not commercial, but military and religious. The conquests of the Order of Christ and of the Order of Saint Mary—better known as the *Sword-brothers* and the *Teutonic Order*—were essentially territorial. These orders became masters of a great part of the Baltic coast, and wherever they spread their dominion, Christianity and German national life were, by whatever means, established. As both the chiefs of the Order and the Livonian prelates ranked as princes of the Empire, the conquests of the Knights were in some sort an extension of the bounds of the Empire. Yet we can hardly look on Livonia and Prussia as coming geographically within the Empire in the same sense as Pomerania and Silesia.[1] But whether strictly an extension of the Western Empire or not, the conquests of the Knights were an extension of the Western Church, the Western world, and the German nation, as against both heathendom and Eastern Christianity, as against all the other Baltic nationalities, non-Aryan and Aryan.

The Sword-bearers and the Teutonic Order.

Their connexion with the Empire.

Effects of their rule.

The first settlement began in *Livland*. In the beginning of the thirteenth century, the Knights of the Order of Christ were called in as temporal helpers by Bishop Albert of Riga, and they gradually won the dominion of the lands on the gulf called from his city. For a while they had a partner in the Danish crown, which held part of *Esthland*. But the rest of Esthland,

The Sword-bearers in Livland. 1201.

Foundation of Riga. 1201.

The Danes in Esthland.

[1] [Livonia may be described as a transmarine colony of the Empire.]

Livland in the narrower sense, Curland, Semigola, the special Lettish land, and the Russian territory on the
Extent of their dominion. Duna, made up this Livonian dominion, which was
Dago and Oesel. afterwards enlarged by the isles of Dago and Oesel and by the Danish portion of Esthland. *Riga* and *Revel*
Esthland. 1346. became great commercial cities, and Riga became an ecclesiastical metropolis under a prince-archbishop. The natives were reduced to bondage, and the Russian powers of Novgorod and Polotsk were effectually kept away from the gulf.

The Teutonic Order in Prussia. 1226. The dominion of the Knights of Saint Mary, the Teutonic Order, in Prussia and in a small part of Lithuania, began a little later than that of the Sword-brothers in Livland. Invited by a Polish prince, Conrad of Mazovia, they received from him their first
Union of the Orders. 1237. Polish possession, the palatinate of *Culm*. Eleven years later the Prussian and Livonian orders were united.
Purchase of Pomerelia. 1311. Their dominion grew. Their acquisition of *Pomerelia*, the eastern part of the old *Pomore*, immediately west
Conquest of Samogitia. 1384. of the lower Vistula, cut off Poland from the sea. Later in the century, Lithuania was equally cut off by
Occupation of Gotland. 1398–1408. the cession of *Samogitia*. The isle of *Gotland* was held for a while; the *New Mark* of Brandenburg was pledged
The New Mark pledged to the Order. 1402. by King Sigismund. The whole coast from Narva on the Finnish gulf to the point where the Pomeranian
Their coast line. coast trends south-west formed the unbroken seaboard of the Order.

Losses of the Prussian Knights. Of the two seats of the Order the northern one proved the stronger and more lasting. Livland remained untouched long after Poland had won back her
Samogitia restored to Lithuania. 1410. lost ground from the Prussian Knights. The battle of Tannenberg won back Samogitia for Lithuania, and again parted the Livonian and Prussian lands of the

Order. By the peace of Thorn its Prussian dominion was altogether cut short. *Culm* and *Pomerelia*, with the cities of *Danzig* and *Thorn*, went back to Poland. And a large part of Prussia itself, the bishopric of *Ermeland*, a district running deep into the land still left to the knights, was added to Poland. The rest of Prussia was left to the Order as a Polish fief.

Peace of Thorn. 1646.

Cessions of the Order to Poland.

Vassalage of the Order.

The thirteenth century was the special time when Teutonic dominion spread itself over the Baltic lands. It was also the time when heathendom gave way to Christianity at nearly every point of those lands where it still held out. But, while the old creeds and the old races were giving way, a single one among them stood forth for a while as an independent and conquering state, the last heathen power in Europe. While all their kinsfolk and neighbours were passing under the yoke, the *Lithuanians*, strictly so called, showed themselves the mightiest of conquerors in all lands from the Baltic to the Euxine. From their own land on the Niemen they began, under their prince Mendog, to advance at the expense of the Russian lands to the south. Mendog embraced Christianity, and was crowned King of Lithuania, a realm which now stretched from the Duna beyond the Priepetz. But heathendom again won the upper hand, and the next century saw the great advance of the Lithuanian power, the momentary rule of old Aryan heathendom alike over Christendom and over Islam. Under two conquering princes, Gedymin and Olgierd, further conquests were made from the surrounding Russian lands. The Lithuanian dominion was extended at the expense of Novgorod and Smolensk; the Lithuanian frontier

Advance of Christianity.

Lithuania the last heathen power.

Advance of Lithuania. c. 1220.

Mendog king. 1252.

Conquests from Russia. 1315–1340. 1345–1377. 1315–1360.

CHAP. XI.

stretched far beyond both the Duna and the Dnieper; Kief was a Lithuanian possession. The kingdom of Galicia lost *Volhynia* and *Podolia*, which became a land disputed between Lithuania and Poland. These last conquests carried the Lithuanian frontier to the Dniester, and opened a wholly new set of relations among the powers on the Euxine. By the conquest of the Tartar dominion of *Perekop*, Lithuania, cut off from the Baltic, reached to the Euxine.

Volhynia and Podolia.

Perekop. 1363.

Consolidation of Poland. 1295–1320.

Meanwhile Poland, from a collection of duchies under a nominal head, had again grown into a consolidated and powerful kingdom. The western frontier had been cut short by various German powers, and the Teutonic Order shut off the kingdom from the sea. Mazovia and Cujavia remained separate duchies; but Great and Little Poland remained firmly united, and were ready to enlarge their borders to the eastward. Casimir the Great added *Podlachia*, the land of the *Jatvingi*, and in the break-up of the Galician kingdom, he incorporated *Red Russia* as being a former possession of Poland. But, as it had also been a former possession of Hungary,[1] Lewis the Great, the common sovereign of Hungary and Poland, annexed it to his southern kingdom.

Conquests of Casimir the Great. 1333–1370.

Red Russia. 1340. Annexed to Hungary. 1377.

Union of Poland and Lithuania.

1386.

The two powers which had thus grown up were now to be gradually fused into one. Jagiello, the heathen prince of Lithuania, became, by conversion and marriage, a Christian King of Poland. He enlarged the kingdom at the expense of the duchy, by incorporating *Podolia* and *Volhynia* with Poland, making Poland as well as Lithuania the possessor of a large extent of Russian soil. The older Russian territory of Poland, Red Russia, was won back from Hungary; *Moldavia*

Volhynia and Podolia added to Poland.

Recovery of Red Russia. 1392.

[1] See above, p. 442.

began to transfer its fleeting allegiance from Hungary to Poland; within Hungary itself part of the county of *Zips* was pledged to the Polish crown. The Polish duchies now began to fall back to the kingdom. *Cujavia* came in early in the fifteenth century, and parts of *Mazovia* in its course. Of the relation of the kingdom to the Teutonic order we have already spoken. Lithuania meanwhile, as part of Western Christendom, remained, under its separate grand-dukes of the now royal house, the rival both of Islam and of Eastern Christendom. Under Witold the advance on Russian ground was greater than ever. *Smolensk* and all *Severia* became Lithuanian; Kief lay in the heart of the grand duchy; Moscow did not seem far from its borders. Lithuania was presently cut short further to the south by the loss of its Euxine dominion. At the beginning of the sixteenth century Poland and Lithuania were united as distinct states under a common sovereign. But by that time a new state of things had begun in the lands on the Duna and the Dnieper.

Moldavia. Pledge of Zips. 1412. Recovery of the Polish duchies. 1401. 1463–1476. Conquests of Witold. 1392–1430. Loss of Perekop, 1474. Closer union of Poland and Lithuania. 1501.

While the military orders had thus established themselves on the Baltic coast, and had already largely given way to the combined Polish and Lithuanian power behind them, a new *Russia* was growing up behind them all. Cut off from all dealings with Western Europe, save with its immediate western neighbours, cut off from its own ecclesiastical centre by the advance of Mussulman dominion, the new power of *Moscow* was schooling itself to take in course of time a greater place than had ever been held by the elder power of Kief. The Mongol conquest had placed the Russian principalities in much the same position

Revival of Russia. Power of Moscow.

CHAP. XI.

The Russian princes dependent on the Golden Horde.

as that through which most of the south-eastern lands passed before they were finally swallowed up by the Ottoman. The princes of Russia were dependent on the Tartar dominion of *Kiptchak*, which stretched from the Dniester north-eastwards over boundless barbarian lands as far as the lower course of the Jenisei. Its capital, the centre of the *Golden Horde*, was at *Sarai* on the lower course of the Volga.

Homage of Novgorod. 1252–1263.

Even Novgorod, under its great prince Alexander Nevsky, did homage to the Khan. But this dependent relation did not, like the Lithuanian conquests to the west, affect the geographical frontiers of Russia. The Russian centre at the time of the Mongol conquest was the northern Vladimir. Towards the end of the

Moscow the new centre. c. 1328.

thirteenth century, *Moskva*, on the river of that name, grew into importance, and early in the next century it became the centre of Russian life.

Name of *Muscovy*.

From *Moskva* or *Moscow* comes the old name of *Muscovy*, a name which historically describes the growth of the second Russian power. Muscovy was to Russia what France in the older sense was to the whole land which came to bear that name. Moscow was to Russia all, and more than all, that Paris was to France. It was to Moscow as the centre that the separate Russian principalities fell in; it was from Moscow as the centre that the lost Russian lands were won back.

Other Russian states.

Besides Novgorod, there still were the separate states of *Viatka*, *Pskof*, *Tver*, and *Riazan*. Disunion and dependence lasted till

Decline of the Mongol power.

late in the fifteenth century. But the Tartar power had already begun to grow weaker before the end of the fourteenth, and the invasion of Timour, while making Russia for a moment more completely subject, led to the dissolution of the dominion of the older Khans.

In the course of the fifteenth century the great power of the Golden Horde broke up into a number of smaller khanats. The khanat of *Crim*—the old Tauric Chersonêsos—stretched from its peninsula inwards along the greater part of the course of the Don. The khanat of *Kazan* on the Volga supplanted the old kingdom of Black Bulgaria. Far to the east, on the lower course of the Obi, was the khanat of *Siberia*. The Golden Horde itself was represented by the khanat of *Astrakhan* on the lower Volga, with its capital at the mouth of that river. Of these Crim and Kazan were immediate neighbours of the Muscovite state. The yoke was at last broken by Ivan the Great. Seven years later he placed a tributary prince on the throne of Kazan, and himself took the title of *Prince of Bulgaria*. By this time the khans of Crim had become dependents of the Ottoman Sultans, the beginning of the long strife between Russia and the Turk in Europe.

Break-up of the Mongol power. Khanat of Crim; of Kazan, 1438; of Siberia of Astrakhan. Deliverance of Russia. 1480. 1487. Crim dependent on the Ottoman.

But before Muscovy thus became an independent power, it had taken the greatest of steps towards growing into Russia. Novgorod the Great, the only Russian rival of Moscow, first lost its northern territory, and then itself became part of the Muscovite dominion. The commonwealth of *Viatka*, the principality of *Tver*, and some small appanages of the house of Moscow followed. The annexation of what remained, as *Pskof* and *Riazan*, was only a question of time, and it came in the next reign. Of the three works which were needful for the full growth of the new Russia, two were accomplished. The Russian state was one, and it was independent. And the third work, that of winning back the lost Russian lands, had already begun.

Advance of Moscow in Russia. Annexation of Novgorod. 1471–8; of Viatka, 1489; of Tver, 1485. Reign of Basil Ivanovitch, 1505–1533. Annexation of Pskof, 1510; and Riazan, 1521. Russia united and

CHAP. XI.

independent.

Survey at the end of the fifteenth century.

Thus, at the end of the fifteenth century, five powers held the Baltic coast. Sweden held the west coast from the Danish frontier northward, with both sides of the gulf of Bothnia and both sides of the gulf of Finland. Denmark held the extreme western coast and the isle of Gotland. Poland and Lithuania had a small seaboard indeed compared to their inland extent. Poland had only the Pomeranian and Prussian coast which she had just won from the Knights. Lithuania barely touched the sea between Prussia and Curland. To the west of the Polish coast lay the now germanized lands of Pomerania and Mecklenburg. To the northwest lay the coast of the German military Order, under Polish vassalage in Prussia, independent in its northern possessions. Thus almost the whole Baltic coast was held by Teutonic powers; the Slavonic powers still lie mainly inland. The Polish frontier towards the Empire has been cut down to the limit which it kept till the end. Pomerania, Silesia, a great part of the mark of Brandenburg, have fallen away from the Polish realm. On the other hand, that realm and its confederate Lithuania have grown wonderfully to the east at the cost of divided and dependent Russia, and have begun to fall back again before Russia one and independent. Bohemia, enlarged by Silesia and Lusatia, has entered so thoroughly into the German world as almost to pass out of our sight.

§ 4. *The Growth of Russia and Sweden.*

Changes of the last four centuries.

The work of the last four centuries on the Baltic coast has been to drive back the Scandinavian powers, after a vast momentary advance, wholly to the west of the Baltic—to give nearly the whole eastern coast to Russia—to make the whole southern coast German. These changes involve the wiping out, first of the German military Order, and then of Poland and Lithuania. This last change involves the growth of Russia, and the creation of Prussia in the modern sense, a sense so strangely different from its earlier meaning. These two, Russia and Prussia, have been the powers by which Sweden and Denmark have been cut short, by which Poland and Lithuania have been swallowed up. In this last work they indeed had a third confederate. Still the share of the Austrian in the overthrow of Poland was in a manner incidental. But the existence of such a Polish and Lithuanian state as stood at the end of the fifteenth, or even of the seventeenth, century was inconsistent with the existence of either Russia or Prussia as great European powers.

Growth of Russia and creation of Prussia.

The period with which we have now to deal takes in only the former stage of this process. Russia advances; Prussia in the modern sense comes into being. But Sweden is still the most advancing power of all; and, if Denmark falls back, it is before the power of Sweden. The Hansa too and the Knights pass away; Sweden is the ruling power of the Baltic.

Greatness of Sweden.

The sixteenth century saw the fall of both branches of the Teutonic Order. Out of the fall of one of them came the beginnings of modern *Prussia*. The two branches of the Order were separated; the Livonian lands had an independent Master. Before long the Prussian Grand Master, Albert of Brandenburg, changed from the head of a Catholic religious order into a Lutheran temporal prince, holding the hereditary *duchy of Prussia* as a Polish fief. That

Separation of the Prussian and Livonian knights. 1515.

Beginning of the Duchy of Prussia. 1525.

CHAP. XI.

Geographical position of Prussia

Union of Prussia and Brandenburg. 1611.

duchy had so strange a frontier towards the kingdom that it could not fail sooner or later either to be swallowed up by the kingdom which hemmed it in, or else to make its way out of its geographical bonds. When the Prussian duchy and the mark of Brandenburg came into the hands of one prince, when the dominions of that prince were enlarged by the union of Brandenburg and Pomerania, the second of these solutions became only a question of time. The first formal step towards it was the release of the duchy from all dependence on Poland. Prussia became a distinct state, a state now essentially German, but lying beyond the bounds of the Empire.

Prussia independent of Poland. 1647.

As the rights of the Empire had been formally cut short when Prussia passed under Polish vassalage, they were also formally cut short by the dissolution of the northern branch of the Teutonic order. The rule of the Livonian Knights survived the secularization of the Prussian duchy by forty years; their dominion then fell asunder. As in the case of Prussia, part of their territory, *Curland* and *Semigola*, was kept by the Livonian Master Godhard Kettler, as an hereditary duchy under Polish vassalage. The rest of the lands of the order were parted out among the chief powers of the Baltic. A Livonian kingdom under the Danish prince Magnus was but for a moment. Denmark in the end received the islands of *Dago* and *Oesel*, her last conquests east of the Baltic. Sweden advanced south of the Finnish gulf, taking the greater part of Esthland. Northern Livland fell to Russia, the southern part to Poland. Twenty years later all Livland became a Polish possession.

Fall of the Livonian Order. 1558–1561.

Duchy of Curland.

Momentary kingdom of Livonia.

Denmark takes Dago and Oesel.

Sweden takes Esthland.

Livland goes to Poland and Russia.

All Livland Polish. 1582.

This acquisition of Livland and of the superiority

Greatest Baltic

over Prussia and Curland raised the united power of Poland and Lithuania to its greatest extent on the Baltic coast. Meanwhile the union of *Lublin* joined the kingdom and the grand duchy yet more closely together. But, long before this time, the eastern frontier of Lithuania had begun to fall back. The central advance of Russia to the west had begun. A revived state, such as Russia was at the end of the fifteenth century, must advance, unless it be artificially hindered; and the new Russian state was driven to advance if it was to exist at all. It had no seaboard, except on the White Sea; it did not hold the mouth of any one of its great rivers, except the Northern Dvina, a stream thoroughly cut off from European life. The dominions of Sweden, Lithuania, and the Knights cut Russia off from the Baltic and from central Europe. To the south and east she was cut off from the Euxine and the Caspian, from the mouths of the Don and the Volga, by the powers which represented her old barbarian masters. Russia was thus not only driven to advance, but driven to advance in various directions. She had to win back her lost lands; she had, if she was really to become an European power, to win her way to the Baltic and to the Euxine. Her position made it almost equally needful to win her way to the Caspian, and made it unavoidable that she should spread her power over the barbarian lands to the north-east. Of these several fields of advance the path to the Euxine was the longest barred. First, at the end of the fifteenth century, began the recovery of the lost lands, a work spread over the sixteenth, seventeenth, and eighteenth centuries. Then, in the sixteenth, came the eastern extension at the cost of the now weakened Mongol

extent of Poland and Lithuania.

Union of Lublin, 1569.

Russian advance.

Its causes.

Advance to the north-east.

Order of Russian advances.

CHAP. XI.

The Euxine reached last.

enemy. Strictly Baltic extension was in the sixteenth century merely momentary; it did not become lasting till the beginning of the eighteenth. But Russia had been established on the Caspian for more than two centuries, she had become a Baltic power for more than two generations, before she made her way to the oldest scene of her seafaring enterprise.

Recovery of the lands conquered by Lithuania.

1514.

1563.

The recovery of the lands which had been lost to Lithuania began before the end of the fifteenth century. Ivan the Great won back *Severia*, with *Tchernigof* and the Severian *Novgorod* and part of the territory of *Smolensk*. Under Basil Smolensk itself followed; under Ivan the Terrible Polotsk again became Russian. Then the tide turned for a season. Russia first lost her newly-won territory in Livland. The recovery of Smolensk by Poland was followed by the momentary Polish conquest of independent Russia, and the occupation of the throne of Moscow by a Polish prince. The Muscovite state came again to life; but it was shorn of a large part of the national territory, which had to be won again by a second advance. Smolensk, Tchernigof, and the greater part of the Lithuanian conquests beyond the Dnieper, were again surrendered to the united Polish and Lithuanian state. In the middle of the century came the renewed Russian advance. The Treaty of Andraszovo gave back to Russia most of the lands which had been surrendered fifty years before. By the last advance in the seventeenth century Russia won back a small territory west of the Dnieper, including her ancient capital of Kief At the same time Poland finally gave up to Russia the superiority over the Cossacks of Ukraine, between the Bug and the Lower Dnieper. But, with this exception, Poland and Lithuania still

Recovery of Smolensk by Poland. 1582.

Polish conquest of Russia, 1606.

Second revival of Russia, and second advance.

Cessions to Poland.

Lands recovered by the Peace of Andraszovo, 1667.

Recovery of Kief. 1686.

Superiority over the Ukraine Cossacks.

kept all the Russian lands south of Duna and west of Dnieper, with some districts beyond those rivers. Nor was Russia the only power to which Poland had to give way on her south-eastern frontier. In this quarter the Ottoman for the last time won a new province from a Christian state by the acquisition of *Kamienetz* and all *Podolia*.[1]

Russian lands still kept by Poland.

Podolia lost to the Turk.

But Poland had during this period to give way at other points also. This was the time of the great growth of the Swedish power. The contrast between the growth of Sweden and the contemporary growth of Russia is instructive. The revived power of Moscow was partly winning back its own lost lands, partly advancing in directions which were needful for national growth, almost for national being. The growth of Sweden in so many directions was almost wholly a growth beyond her own borders. Hence doubtless it came that the advance of Russia has been lasting, while the advance of Sweden was only for a season. Sweden has lost by far the greater part of her conquests; she has kept only those parts of them which went to complete her position in her own peninsula.

Growth of Sweden and Russia compared.

Russian advance lasting.

Swedish advance temporary.

On the Swedish conquest of Esthland followed a series of shiftings of the frontiers of Sweden and Russia which lasted into the nineteenth century. During the reign of Gustavus Adolphus, and the period which we might almost call the continuation of his reign after his death, Sweden advanced both in her own peninsula and east of the Baltic, while she also gained a wholly new footing on German ground, both on the Baltic and on the Ocean. A long period of alternate war and peace,

Advance under and after Gustavus Adolphus. 1611–1660.

[1] See above, p. 452.

CHAP. XI.

Wars between Sweden and Russia. 1576–1617.

Peace of Stolbova.

Sweden gains Ingermanland.

Wars between Sweden and Poland. 1619–1660.

Sweden's conquest of Livland, 1621–1625; of Dago and Oesel, 1645.

Advance of Sweden against Denmark and Norway.

Conquest of Gotland and Bornholm. 1645.

Of Jämteland.

Of Trondhjemlän. 1658.

Of Bohuslän, and Scania, &c.

Trondhjem restored to Norway. 1660.

a time in which Novgorod the Great passed for a moment into Swedish hands, was ended, as far as Sweden and Russia were concerned, by the peace of Stolbova. The Swedish frontier thus fixed took in all *Carelia* and *Ingermanland*, and wholly cut off Russia from the Baltic and its gulfs. Such an advance could not fail to lead to further advance, though at the expense of another enemy. The long war between Sweden and Poland gave to Sweden Riga and the greater part of Livland. Her conquests in this region were completed by winning the islands of Dago and Oesel from Denmark.

This last acquisition, geographically connected with the Swedish conquests from Russia and Poland, was politically part of an equally great advance which Sweden was making at the cost of the rival Scandinavian power, the united realms of Denmark and Norway. Along with the two eastern islands, Denmark lost the isle of *Gotland* for ever and that of *Bornholm* for a moment,[1] and the Norwegian provinces east of the mountains, *Jämteland* and *Herjedalen*. The treaty of Roskild yet further enlarged Sweden at the expense of Norway. By the cession of *Trondhjemlän* the Norwegian kingdom was split asunder; the ancient metropolis was lost, and Sweden reached to the Ocean. With Trondhjem Sweden also received *Bohuslän*, the southern province of Norway, and, more than all, the ancient possessions of Denmark in the northern peninsula, with her old metropolis of *Lund*. Here comes in the application of the rule. In annexing Trondhjem Sweden had overshot her mark; it was restored within two years. It was

[1] Conquered by Sweden 1643, restored to Denmark 1645. Ceded to Sweden 1658, but recovered the same year.

otherwise with Bohuslän, Scania, and her other conquests within what might seem to be her natural borders; they have remained Swedish to this day.

Lands held by Sweden in Germany, Pomerania and Rügen, Bremen and Verden. 1648.

The Swedish acquisition of the eastern lands of Denmark was made more necessary by the position which Sweden had now taken on the central mainland. The peace of Westfalia had confirmed her in the possession of *Rügen* and *Western Pomerania* on the Baltic, and of the bishoprics of *Bremen* and *Verden* which made her a power on the Ocean. These lands were not strictly an addition to the Swedish realm; they were fiefs of the Empire held by the Swedish king. Here again comes in the geographical law. The Swedish possession of the German lands on the Ocean was short; part of the German lands on the Baltic was kept into the nineteenth century.

Denmark gives up the sovereignty of the Gottorp lands. 1658.

The peace of Roskild, which cut short the kingdoms of Denmark and Norway in the northern peninsula, also marks an epoch in the controverted history of the duchies of Sleswick and Holstein. The Danish king gave up the *sovereignty* of the Gottorp districts of the duchies. Even if that cession implied the surrender of his own feudal superiority over the Gottorp districts of Sleswick, he could not alienate any part of the Imperial rights over Holstein. This sovereignty, in whatever it consisted, was lost and won several times between king and Duke before the end of the century. Meanwhile the Danish crown became possessed of the outlying duchies of *Oldenburg* and *Delmenhorst*, which in some sort balanced the Swedish possession of Bremen and Verden.

Fluctuations in the duchies. 1675–1700.

Danish possession of Oldenburg. 1678.

The wars and treaties which were ended by the

CHAP. XI.

Sweden after the peace of Oliva.

peace of Oliva fixed the boundaries of the Baltic lands for a season. They fixed the home extent of Sweden down to the present century. They cut off Denmark, save its one outpost of *Bornholm*, from the Baltic itself, as distinguished from the narrow seas which lead to it. They fixed the extent of Poland down to the partitions. What they failed to do for any length of time was to cut off Russia from the Baltic, and to establish Sweden on the Ocean. But for the present we leave Sweden ruling over the whole western and the greater part of the eastern coast of the Northern Mediterranean, and holding smaller possessions both on its southern coast and on the Ocean. The rest of the eastern and southern coast of the Baltic is divided between the Polish fief of Curland, the dominions of the common ruler of Pomerania and Prussia,—now an independent prince in his eastern duchy,—and the small piece of recovered Polish territory placed invitingly between the two parts of his dominions. In her own peninsula Sweden has reached her natural frontier, and has given back what she won for a moment beyond it. While Sweden has this vast extent of coast with comparatively little extent inland, the vast inland region of Poland and Lithuania has hardly any seaboard, and the still vaster inland region of Russia has none at all in Europe, except on the White Sea. Thus the most striking feature of this period is the advance of Sweden; but we have seen that it was also a time of great advance on the part of Russia. It was a time of yet greater advance on that side of her dominion where Russia had no European rivals.

In the case of Russia, the only European power which could conquer and colonize by land in barbarian regions,[1] her earlier barbarian conquests were absolutely necessary to her existence. No hard line can be drawn between her earliest and her latest conquests, between the first advance of Novgorod and the last conquests in Turkestan. But the advance which immediately followed the deliverance from the Tartar yoke marks a great epoch. The smaller khanats into which the dominion of the Golden Horde had been broken up still kept Russia from the Euxine and the Caspian. The two khanats on the Volga, *Kazan* and *Astrakhan*, were subdued by Ivan the Terrible. The coast of the Caspian was now reached. But the khans of *Crim* remained, unsubdued and dangerous enemies, still cutting off Russia from the Euxine. Yet, even in this direction an advance was made when the Russian supremacy was acknowledged by the Cossacks of the Don. The conquest of the Siberian khanat, with its capital *Tobolsk*, next followed, and thence, in the course of the next century, the boundless extent of northern Asia was added to the Russian dominion.

Eastern advance of Russia.

Conquest of Kazan and Astrakhan. 1552–1554.

Superiority over the Don Cossacks. 1577.

Beginning of Siberian conquest. 1581. 1592–1706.

§ 5. *The Decline of Sweden and Poland.*

In the last section we traced out the greatest advance of Sweden and a large advance of Russia, both made at the cost of Poland, that of Sweden also at the cost of Denmark. We saw also the beginnings of a power which we still called *Brandenburg* rather than *Prussia*. In the present section, describing the work of the eighteenth century, we have to trace the growth of this last power, which now definitely takes the

Growth of Prussia.

[1] See above, p. 471.

CHAP. XI.

Decline of Sweden. Extinction of Poland. Kingdom of Prussia. 1701. Empire of Russia. 1721.

Prussian name, and which we have to look at in its Prussian character. The period is marked by the decline of Sweden and the utter wiping out of Poland and Lithuania, Russia and Prussia in different degrees being chief actors in both cases. At the beginning of the period Prussia becomes a kingdom—a sign of advance, though not accompanied by any immediate increase of territory. A little later the ruler of Russia, already Imperial in his own tongue,[1] more definitely takes the Imperial style as *Emperor of all the Russias.* This might pass as a challenge of the Russian lands, Black, White, and Red, which were still held by Poland.

Russia on the Baltic. Wars of Charles and Peter. 1700–1721. Foundation of Saint Petersburg. 1703. Cession of Livland, &c., by Sweden. Further advance of Russia. 1741–1743.

But more pressing than the recovery of these lands was the breaking down of the barrier by which Sweden kept Russia away from the Baltic. To a very slight extent this was a recovery of old Russian territory; but the position now won by Russia was wholly new. The war with Charles the Twelfth made Russia a great Baltic power, and Peter the Great, early in the struggle, set up the great trophy of his victory in the foundation of his new capital of Saint Petersburg on ground won from Sweden. The peace of Nystad confirmed Russia in the possession of Swedish Livland, Esthland, Ingermanland, part of Carelia, and a small part of Finland itself. Another war, ended by the Peace of Åbo, gave Russia another small extension in Finland.

Sweden loses Bremen,

At the same time Sweden was cut short in her other

[1] There is no doubt that the title of *Czar*, or rather *Tzar*, borne by the Russian princes, as by those of Servia and Bulgaria in earlier times, is simply a contraction of *Cæsar*. In the Treaty of Carlowitz Peter the Great appears as Tzar of endless countries, but he is not called *Imperator*, though the Sultan is.

outlying possessions. Of her German fiefs, the duchies of Bremen and Verden passed, first to Denmark, then to Hannover. But her Baltic possessions were only partly lost, to the profit of Brandenburg. The frontier of Swedish Pomerania fell back to the north-west, losing Stettin, but keeping Stralsund, Wolgast, and Rügen. Denmark meanwhile advanced in the debateable land on her southern frontier. The Danish occupation of Bremen and Verden was only momentary; but the Gottorp share of Sleswick and Holstein was conquered, and the possession of all Sleswick was guaranteed to Denmark by England and France. But the Gottorp share of Holstein, as an Imperial fief, was given back to its Duke. Lastly, when the house of Gottorp had mounted the throne of Russia, the Gottorp portion of Holstein was ceded to Denmark in exchange for Oldenburg and Delmenhorst, which were at once given to another branch of the family.

Verden, and part of Pomerania.

Danish conquest of the Gottorp lands. 1713–1715.

The Gottorp lands in Holstein restored.

They pass to Denmark in exchange for Oldenburg. 1767–1773.

In the latter part of the eighteenth century the three partitions of Poland brought about the all but complete recovery of the lands which the Lithuanian dukes had won from Russia. The first partition gave Russia Polish Livland, and all the lands which Poland still kept beyond Duna and Dnieper. The greater part of *White Russia* was thus won back. At the same time the house of Hohenzollern gained its great territorial need, the geographical union of the kingdom of Prussia with the lands of Brandenburg and Pomerania, now increased by nearly all Silesia. This union was made by Poland giving up *West-Prussia* —Danzig remaining an outlying city of Poland—and part of *Great Poland* and *Cujavia* known as the *Netz*

First partition of Poland. 1772.

Russian share.

Prussian share.

Brandenburg and Prussia geographically united.

CHAP. XI.

Austrian share.

Kingdom of Galicia and Lodomeria.

Russian territory held by Austria.

District.[1] The Austrian share, the new kingdom of *Galicia and Lodomeria*, was a kind of commemoration of the conquests of Lewis the Great:[2] but, while it did not take in all *Red Russia*, it took in part of *Podolia* and of *Little Poland* south of the Vistula, making Cracow a frontier city. Austria thus became possessed of a part of the old Russian territory, most of which she has kept ever since.

Second partition. 1793.

The Polish state was thus maimed on all sides; but it still kept a considerable territorial extent. The second partition, the work of Russia and Prussia only, could only be a preparation for the final death-blow.

Russian share.

It gave to Russia the rest of *Podolia* and *Ukraine*, and part of *Volhynia* and *Podlasia*. *Little Russia* and *White Russia* were thus wholly won back, and the Russian frontier was advanced within the old Lithuanian duchy.

Prussian share.

Prussia took nearly all that was left of the oldest Polish state, the rest of *Great Poland* and *Cujavia*, and part of *Mazovia*, forming the *South Prussia* of the new nomenclature. Gnesen, the oldest Polish capital, the metropolis of the Polish Church, now passed away from Poland.

The remnant that was left to Poland took in the greater part of *Little Poland*, part of *Mazovia*, the greater part of the old *Lithuania* with the fragment still left of its Russian territory, *Samogitia* and the fief of *Curland*.

Third partition. 1795.

The final division was delayed only two years. This time all three partners joined.

Russian share.

Russia took all *Lithuania* east of the Niemen, with its capital *Vilna*, also *Curland* and *Samogitia* to the north, and the old Russian remnant to the south.

Austrian share.

Austria took *Cracow*, with nearly all the rest of *Little*

[1] See above, p. 212.

[2] See above, pp. 321, 441.

Prussian share.

Poland, as also part of *Mazovia*, by the name of *New Galicia*. Prussia took *Danzig* and *Thorn*, as also a small piece of *Little Poland* to improve the frontiers of South Prussia and Silesia, perhaps without thinking that this last process was an advance of the Roman Terminus. The capital *Warsaw*, with the remnant of *Mazovia* and the strip of *Lithuania* west of the Niemen, also fell to Prussia. The names of Poland and Lithuania now passed away from the map.

No original Polish territory gained by Russia in the partitions.

It is important to remember that the three partitions gave no part of the original Polish realm to Russia. Russia took back the Russian territory which had been long before won by Lithuania, and added the greater part of Lithuania itself, with the lands immediately to the north. The ancient kingdom of Poland was divided between Prussia and Austria, and the oldest Poland of all fell to the lot of Prussia. Great Poland, Silesia, Pomerania, the Polish lands which had passed to the mark of Brandenburg, once united under Polish rule, were again united under the power to which they had gradually fallen away. Austria or Hungary meanwhile took the rest of the northern Chrobatia, seven hundred years after the acquisition of the former part, and also the Russian land which had been twice before added to the Magyar kingdom.

The old Poland divided between Prussia and Austria.

Poland passes to Prussia,

Chrobatia to Austria.

Advance to the Euxine.

Meanwhile Russia made advances in other quarters of nearly equal extent. As the remnant of the Saracen at Granada cut off the Castilian from his southern coast on the Mediterranean, for more than two hundred years, so did the remnant of the Tartar in *Crim* cut off the Russian for as long a time from his southern coast on the Euxine. Peter the Great first made his way, if not

CHAP. XI.

Occupation of Azof. 1696–1711.

Independence of Crim. 1774.

Annexation of Crim. 1783.

to the Euxine, at least to its inland gulf, by the taking of *Azof*. But the new conquest was only temporary. After seventy years more the work was done. First came the nominal independence of the Crimean khanat, then its incorporation with Russia. The work at which Megarian and Genoese colonists had laboured was now done; the northern coast of the Euxine was won for Europe.[1] The road through which so many Turanian invaders had pressed into the Aryan continent was blocked for ever. The next advance, the limit of Russian advance made strictly at the expense of the barbarian as distinguished from his Christian vassals, carried the Russian frontier from the Bug to the Dniester.

Conquest of Jedisan. 1791.

Russian conquests from Persia. 1727–1734.

The chief Asiatic acquisition of Russia in the eighteenth century took a strange form. It was conquest beyond the sea, though only beyond the inland Caspian. Turk and Russian joined to dismember Persia, and for some years Russia held the south coast of that great lake, the lands of *Daghestan*, *Ghilan*, and *Mazanderan*. Later in the century the ancient Christian kingdom of *Georgia* passed under Russian superiority, the earnest of much Russian conquest on both sides of Caucasus. And nearly at the same time as the first steps towards the acquisition of Crim, the Russian dominion was spread over the *Kirghis* hordes west of the river Ural, winning a coast on the eastern Caspian, the sea of Aral, and the Baltash lake.

Superiority over Georgia. 1783.

Superiority over the Kirghis. 1773.

Thus, by the end of the eighteenth century, the

[1] It is however to be regretted that, in bringing back the old names into these regions, they have been so often applied to wrong places. Thus the new *Sebastopol* answers to the old *Cherson*, while the new *Cherson* is elsewhere. The new *Odessa* has nothing to do with the old *Odêssos*, and so in other cases.

Survey at the end of the eighteenth century.

Swedish power has fallen back. Its territory east of the Baltic is less than it was at the beginning of the sixteenth century. Denmark, on the other hand, has grown by an advance in the debateable southern duchies. All Sleswick is added to the Danish crown; all Holstein is held by the Danish king. Poland has vanished. The anomalous power on the middle Danube, the power for which it is so hard to find a name which is not misleading, the power whose princes, it must be remembered, still wore the crown of the Empire, has thrust itself into the very heart of the old Polish land. But the power which has gained most by the extinction of Poland has been the new kingdom of Prussia. If part of her annexations lasted only a few years, she made her Baltic coast continuous for ever. But Prussia and Austria alike, by joining to wipe out the central state of the whole region, have given themselves a mighty neighbour. Russia has wholly cast aside her character as a mere inland power, intermediate between Europe and Asia. She has won her way, after so many ages, to her old position and much more. She has a Baltic and an Euxine seaboard. Her recovery of her old lands on the Duna and the Dnieper, her conquest of new lands on the Niemen, have brought her into the heart of Europe. And she has opened the path which was also to lead her into the heart of Asia, and to establish her in the intermediate mountain land between the Euxine and the Caspian.

§ 6. *The Modern Geography of the Baltic Lands.*

The French revolutionary wa

The territorial arrangements of Northern and Eastern Europe were not affected by the French revolutionary wars till after the fall of the Western Empire. At that moment the frontier of Germany and Denmark was still what it had been under Charles the Great; 'Eidora Romani terminus Imperii.' Only now the Danish king ruled to the south of the boundary stream in the character of a prince of the Empire. The fall of the Empire put an end to this relation, and the duchy of Holstein was incorporated with the Danish realm. In the like sort, the Swedish kingdom was extended to the central mainland of Europe, by the incorporation of the Pomeranian dominions of the Swedish king. Before long, the last war between Sweden and Russia was ended by the peace of Frideriks-hamn, when Sweden gave up all her territory east of the gulf as far as the river Tornea, together with the isles of *Åland*. These lands passed to the Russian Emperor as a separate and privileged dominion, the *Grand Duchy of Finland*. Thus Sweden withdrew to her own side of the Baltic, while Russia at last became mistress of the whole eastern coast from the Prussian border northward. The general peace left this arrangement untouched, but decreed the separation of Norway from Denmark and its union with Sweden. This was carried out so far as to effect the union of Sweden and Norway as independent kingdoms under a single king. Denmark got in compensation, as diplomacy calls it, a scrap of its old Slavonic realm, Rügen and Swedish Pomerania. These detached lands were presently exchanged with Prussia for a land adjoining Holstein, the duchy of *Lauenburg*, the representative of ancient Saxony.[1] Denmark kept Iceland, but the Frisian island of *Heligoland* off the coast of Sleswick

Holstein incorporated with Denmark, and Swedish Pomerania with Sweden. 1806.

Russian conquest of Finland, 1809.

Grand Duchy of Finland.

Union of Sweden and Norway. 1814–1815.

Swedish Pomerania passes to Denmark. Exchanged with Prussia for Lauenburg. Heligoland passes to England.

[1] See above, p. 208.

passed to England. Thus the common king of Sweden and Norway reigns over the whole of the northern peninsula and over nothing out of it. No such great change had affected the Scandinavian kingdoms since the union of Calmar.

Holstein and Lauenburg join the German Confederation.

Meanwhile the king of Denmark, remaining the independent sovereign of Denmark, Iceland, and Sleswick, entered the German Confederation for his duchies of Holstein and Lauenburg. Disputes and wars made no geographical change till the war which followed the accession of the present king. The changes which then followed have been told elsewhere.[1] They amount to the transfer to Prussia of Lauenburg, Holstein, and Sleswick, with a slight change of frontier and a redistribution of the smaller islands. A conditional engagement for the restoration of northern Sleswick to Denmark was not fulfilled, and has been formally annulled. Heligoland, the island which naturally belongs to Sleswick, has also passed from England to Germany, in exchange for Zanzibar.

Disputes and wars in the Duchies.

Transfer of Sleswick and Holstein, with Lauenburg, to Prussia. 1864–1866.

Heligoland passes to Germany, 1890.

Losses of Prussia. 1806.

In the lands which had been Poland and Lithuania, the immediate result of the French wars was the creation of a new Polish state; their final result was a great extension of the dominion of Russia. Prussia had to surrender its whole Polish territory, save West-Prussia.[2] A small Lithuanian territory, the district of *Bialystok*, was given to Russia; *Danzig* became a separate commonwealth. The rest of the Prussian share of Poland formed the new *Duchy of Warsaw*. This state was really no bad representative of the oldest Poland of all. Silesia was gone; but the new

Bialystok added to Russia.

Danzig a commonwealth.

Duchy of Warsaw.

[1] See above, p. 228.

[2] See also p. 223.

CHAP. XI.

Enlarged by part of Austrian Poland. 1810.

duchy took in Great Poland and Cujavia, with parts of Little Poland, Mazovia, and Lithuania. It took in the oldest capital at Gnesen and the newest at Warsaw. The new state was presently enlarged by the addition of the territory added to Austria by the last partition. Cracow, with the greater part of Little Poland, was

Extent of the Duchy.

again joined to Great Poland. Speaking roughly, the duchy took in nearly the whole of the old Polish kingdom, without Silesia, but with some small Lithuanian and Russian territory added.

Arrangements of 1815.

It was the Poland thus formed, a state which answered much more nearly to the Poland of the fourteenth than to the Poland of the eighteenth century, which, by the arrangements of the Vienna Congress, first received a Russian sovereign. Prussia now again rounded off her *West-Prussian* province by the recovery

Danzig and Posen restored to Prussia.

of Danzig and Thorn, and she rounded off her southern frontier by the recovery of Posen and Gnesen, which had been part of her *South-Prussian* province. The *Grand Duchy of Posen* became again part of the

Cracow a commonwealth. Annexed by Austria. 1846.

Prussian state. *Cracow* became a republic, to be annexed by Austria thirty years later. The remainder of the Duchy of Warsaw, under the style of the

Kingdom of Poland united to Russia. 1831–1863.

Kingdom of Poland, became a separate kingdom, but with the Russian Emperor as its king. Later events have destroyed, first its constitution, then its separate being; and now all ancient Poland, except the part of

Russia takes old Polish territory for the first time.

Great Poland kept by Prussia and the part of Little Poland kept by Austria, is merged in the Russian Empire. Thus the Russian acquisition of strictly Polish, as distinguished from old-Russian and Lithuanian territory, dates, not from the partitions, but from the Congress of Vienna. It was to the behoof of

Prussia and Austria, not of Russia, that the old kingdom of the Piasts was broken in pieces.

Fluctuation of the Russian frontier towards Moldavia. 1812–1878.

The changes of the nineteenth century with regard to the lands on the European coasts of the Euxine have been told elsewhere.[1] They amount, as far as the geographical boundaries of Russia are concerned, to her advance to the Pruth and the Danube, her partial withdrawal, her second partial advance. Meanwhile the Russian advance in the nineteenth century on the Asiatic shores of the Euxine and in the lands on and beyond the Caspian has been far greater than her advance during the eighteenth. It is in the nineteenth century that Russia has taken up her commanding position between the Euxine and the Caspian seas, a position which in some sort amounts to an enlargement of Europe at the expense of Asia. The old frontier on the Caspian, which had hardly changed since the conquest of Astrakhan, reached to the *Terek*. The annexation of Crim made the *Kuban* the boundary on the side of the Euxine. The incorporation of the *Georgian* kingdom gave Russia an outlying territory south of the Caucasus on the upper course of the *Kur*. Next came the acquisition of the Caspian coast from the mouth of the Terek to the mouth of the Kur, the land of *Daghestan* and *Shirwan*, including part of the territory which had been held for a few years in the eighteenth century. The Persian and Turkish wars gave Russia the Armenian land of *Erivan* as far as the *Araxes*, *Mingrelia*, and *Immeretia*, and the nominal cession of the Euxine coast between them and the older frontier. But it was thirty years before the mountain region of *Circassia* was fully subdued. The

Advance in the Caucasus.

Incorporation of Georgia. 1800.

Advance on the Caspian. 1802.

Advance in Armenia and Circassia. 1829.

1859.

[1] See above, pp. 453–4.

CHAP. XI.

1878.

last changes have extended the Trans-Caucasian frontier of Russia to the south by the addition of *Batoum* and *Kars*.

Advance in Turkestan. 1853–1868.

In the lands east of the Caspian the new province of Turkestan gradually grew up in the lands on the Jaxartes, reaching southward to Samarkand. *Khokand* to the south-east followed, while *Khiva* and *Bokhara*, the lands on the Oxus, have passed under Russian suzerainty. *Samarcand* and *Ferganah* have become part of Russian dominion in the fullest sense. The Turcoman tribes immediately east of the Caspian have also been annexed. The Caspian has thus nearly become a Russian lake. Hardly anything remains to Persia except the extreme southern coast which was once for a moment Russian.

Khiva, 1872. Bokhara, 1873.

Advance in Eastern Asia. 1858.

Kwang-Tung, 1898.

Far again to the east, Russia has added a large territory on the Chinese border on the river Amoor, and now the territory adjoining the Korea on the west is a province administered by Russia, under the Chinese name *Kwang-Tung*, held under lease from China. All these conquests form the greatest continuous extent of territory by land which the world has ever seen, unless during the transient dominion of the old Mongols. No other European power in any age has, or could have had, such a continuous dominion, because no other European power ever had the unknown barbarian world lying in the same way at its side. Nowhere again has any European power held a dominion so physically unbroken as that which stretches from the gulf of Riga to the gulf of Okhotsk. The greater part of the Asiatic dominion of Russia belongs to that part of Asia which has least likeness to Europe. It is only on the Frozen Ocean that we find a kind of mockery of inland seas,

Extent and character of the Russian dominion.

islands, and peninsulas. Massive unbroken extent by land is its leading character. And as this character extends to a large part of European Russia also, Russia is the only European land where there can be any doubt where Europe ends. The barbarian dominion of other European states, a dominion beyond the sea, has been a dominion of choice. The barbarian dominion of Russia in lands adjoining her European territory is a dominion forced on her by geographical necessity. The annexation of Kamtschatka became a question of time when the first successors of Ruric made their earliest advance towards the Finnish north.

Russian America.

Alongside of this continuous dominion in Europe and Asia, the Russian occupation of territory in a third continent, an occupation made by sea after the manner of other European powers, has not been lasting. The Russian territory in the north-west corner of America, the only part of the world where Russia and England marched on one another, has been sold to the United States.

Final Survey.

To return to Europe, the events of the nineteenth century have, in the lands with which we are dealing, carried on the work of the eighteenth by the further aggrandizement of Russia and Prussia. The Scandinavian powers have withdrawn into the two Scandinavian peninsulas and the adjoining islands, and in the southern peninsula the power of Denmark has been cut short to the gain of Prussia. The Prussian power meanwhile, formed in the eighteenth century by the union of the detached lands of Prussia and Brandenburg, has in the nineteenth grown into the Imperial power of Germany, and has, even as a local kingdom, become, by the acquisition of Swedish Pomerania, Holstein, and Sleswick, the dominant power on the southern Baltic. The acquisition of the duchies too, not only of Sleswick and Holstein, but of Bremen and Verden also, as parts of the annexed kingdom of Hannover, have given her a part of the former oceanic position both of Denmark and Sweden. Russia has acquired the same position on the gulfs of the Baltic which Prussia has on the south coast of the Baltic itself. The acquisition of the new Poland has brought her frontier into the very midst of Europe; it has made her a neighbour, not merely of Prussia as such, but of Germany. The third sharer in the partition has drawn back from her northern advance, but she has increased her scrap of Russia, her scrap of Little Poland, her scrap of Moldavia,[1] by the suppression of a free city. The southern advance of Russia on European ground has been during this century an advance not so much of territory as of influence. The frontier of 1878 is the restored frontier of 1812. It is in the lands out of Europe that Russia has in the meanwhile advanced by strides which look startling on the map, but which in truth spring naturally from the geographical position of the one modern European power which cannot help being Asiatic as well.

[1] See above, p. 446.

CHAPTER XII.

THE SPANISH PENINSULA AND ITS COLONIES.

CHAP. XII.

Analogy between Spain and Scandinavia.

Slight relations with the Empire.

Break between earlier and later history.

THE great peninsula of the West has much in common with the great peninsula of the North. Save Sweden and Norway, no part of Western Europe had so little to do with the later Empire as Spain. And in no land that formed part of the earlier Empire, save our own island, is the later history so completely cut off from the earlier history. The modern kingdoms of Spain have still less claim to represent the West-Gothic kingdom than the modern kingdom of France had to represent the Frankish kingdom. The history of Spain, as an element in the European system, begins with the Saracen invasion. For a hundred years before that time all trace of dependence on the elder Empire had passed away. With the later Western Empire Spain had nothing to do after the days of Charles the Great and his immediate successors. Their claims over a small part of the country passed away from the Empire to the kings of Karolingia.

Modern Spanish history begins with the Saracen conquest.

Analogy between Spain and South-eastern Europe

Comparison of the effects of conquest

With the Eastern Empire and the states which grew out of it Spain has the closest connexion in the way of analogy. Each was a Christian land conquered by the Mussulman. Each has been wholly or partially won back from him. But the deliverance of south-western Europe was mainly the work of its own people, and its

and deliverance in each. deliverance was nearly ended when the bondage of south-eastern Europe was only beginning. Again, in south-eastern Europe the nations were fully formed before the Mussulman conquest, and they have lived through it. *The Spanish nation formed by the war with the Mussulmans.* In Spain the Mussulman conquest cut short the West-Gothic power just as it was growing into a new Romance nation; the actual Romance nation of Spain was formed by the work of withstanding the invaders. *Analogy between Spain and Russia.* The closest analogy of all is between Spain and Russia. Each was delivered by its own people. In each case, long after the main deliverance had been wrought, long after the liberated nation had begun again to take its place in Europe, the ransomed land was still cut off, by a fragment of its old enemies, from the coasts of its own southern sea.

Extent of the West-Gothic and the Saracen dominions. The Saracen dominion in the West, as established by the first conquerors, answered very nearly to the West-Gothic kingdom, as it then stood; but it did not exactly answer to *Spain*, either in the geographical or in the later Roman sense.[1] When the Saracen came, the Empire, not the Goth, still held the Balearic Isles, and the fortresses of *Tangier* and *Ceuta* on the Mauretanian side of the strait. On the other hand, the Goth did not hold quite the whole of the peninsula, while his dominion took in the Gaulish land of *Septimania*. Strictly speaking, the Saracen conquest was a conquest, not of Spain geographically, but of the West-Gothic dominions in and out of Spain, and of the outlying Imperial possessions in their neighbourhood. *Two centres of deliverance.* It was from the lands which hindered both the West-Gothic and the Saracen dominion from exactly answering to

[1] See above, p. 154.

geographical Spain that deliverance came, and it came in two forms. From the land to the north-west, which had held out against both Goth and Saracen, came that form of deliverance which was strictly native. At the other end, the Frank first won back for Christendom the Saracen province in Gaul, and then carried his arms into the neighbouring corner of Spain. Thus we get two centres of deliverance, two groups of states which did the work. There are the north-western lands, whose history is purely Spanish, which simply withstood the Saracen, and the north-eastern lands, which were first won from the Saracen by the Frank, and which gradually freed themselves from their deliverer. The former class are represented in later Spanish history by the kingdoms of Castile and Portugal, the latter by the kingdom of Aragon. Navarre lies between the two, and shares in the history of both. The former start geographically from the mountain region washed by the Ocean. The latter start geographically from the mountains which divide Gaul and Spain, and which stretch eastward to the Mediterranean. The geographical position of the regions foreshadows their later history. It was Aragon, looking to the East, which first played a great part in European affairs, and which carried Spanish influence and dominion into Gaul, Sicily, Italy, and Greece. It was Portugal and Castile, looking to the West, which established an Iberian dominion beyond the bounds of Europe. And of these it was Castile which was fated to play the same part which was played by Wessex in England, to become the leading power of the peninsula and for a moment to incorporate the whole peninsula under the rule of her kings. The lasting union of

The independent lands.

The Frankish dominion. 752–759.

778.

Represented severally by Castile and Portugal, and by Aragon.

Later history of Aragon.

Of Castile and Portugal.

Castile and Aragon, the momentary union of Castile, Portugal, and Aragon was to form that great Spanish monarchy which became the terror of Europe. The more lasting of these annexations has led to a change in ordinary geographical language. The fact that a Queen of Castile in the fifteenth century married a King of Aragon and not a King of Portugal has led us to speak of the peninsular kingdoms as '*Spain* and *Portugal*.'[1] For some ages 'Spain and Aragon' would have been a more natural division. But the very difference in the fields of action of Castile and Aragon hindered any such strong opposition. Between Castile and Portugal, on the other hand, a marked rivalry arose in the field which was common to both.

The more strictly native centre foremost in the work of deliverance.

Of these two centres, one purely Spanish, the other brought for a long time under a greater or less degree of foreign influence, the more strictly native region was foremost in the work of national deliverance. How far western Spain stood in advance of eastern Spain is shown by the speaking fact that Toledo, so much further to the south, was won by Castile a generation before Zaragoza was won by Aragon.

Relations of Castile and Aragon towards Navarre.

But both Castile and Aragon, as powers, grew out of the break-up of a momentary dominion in the land which lay between them, and whose later history is much less illustrious than theirs. In the second quarter of the eleventh century the kingdom of *Pampeluna* or *Navarre* had, by the energy of a single man, the Sviatopluk or Stephen Dushan of his little realm, risen to the first place among the Christian powers of Spain. Castile and Aragon do not appear with kingly rank till both had passed under the

[1] See above, p. 154.

momentary rule of a neighbour which in after times seemed so small beside either of them. And the name of *Castile*, whether as county, kingdom, or empire, marks a comparatively late stage of Christian advance. We must here go back for a moment to the early days of the long crusade of eight hundred years.

§ 1. *The Foundation of the Spanish Kingdoms.*

We have seen how the union of the small independent lands of the north, *Asturia* and *Cantabria*, grew into the first Christian kingdom of reviving Spain. This was the kingdom which bore the name, first of *Oviedo* and then of *Leon*. *Gallicia*, on the one side, representing in some sort the old Suevian kingdom, *Bardulia* or the oldest *Castile*, the land of Burgos, on the other side, were lands of this kingdom which were early inclined to fall away. The growth of the Christian powers on this side was favoured by internal events among the Mussulmans, by famines and revolts which left a desert border between the hostile powers. The Ommiad emirate, afterwards caliphate, was established almost at the moment of the Saracen loss of Septimania. Then came the *Spanish March* of Charles the Great, which brought part of northern Spain once more within the bounds of the new Western Empire, as the conquests of Justinian had brought back part of southern Spain within the bounds of the undivided Empire. This march, at its greatest extent, took in Pampeluna at one end and Barcelona at the other, with the intermediate lands of *Aragon*, *Ripacurcia*, and *Sobrarbe*. But the Frankish dominion soon passed away from Aragon, and still sooner from Pampeluna. The eastern part of

Founding of the kingdom of Leon. 753. 916.

Christian advance.

The Ommiad emirate. 755.

The Spanish March. 778–801.

Its extent.

Its division.

the march, which still acknowledged the superiority of the Kings of Karolingia, split up into a number of practically independent counties, which made hardly any advance against the common enemy.

Navarre under Sancho the Great. 1000–1035.

Meanwhile the land of Pampeluna became, at the beginning of the eleventh century, an independent and powerful kingdom. The Navarre of Sancho the Great stretched some way beyond the Ebro; to the west it took in the ocean lands of *Biscay* and *Guipuzcoa*, with the original Castile; to the east it took in *Aragon*, *Ripacurcia*, and *Sobrarbe.* The two Christian kingdoms of Navarre and Leon took in all north-eastern Spain. The Douro was reached and crossed; the Tagus itself was not far from the Christian boundary; but the states which owned the superiority of the power which we may now call *France* were still far from the lower Ebro.

Break-up of the kingdom of Navarre (1035), and of the Ommiad caliphate (1028).

Small Mussulman states.

At the death of Sancho the Great his momentary dominion broke up. Seven years earlier the dominion of the Ommiad caliphs had broken up also. These two events, so near together, form the turning-point in the history of the peninsula. Instead of the one Ommiad caliphate, there arose a crowd of separate Mussulman kingdoms, at Cordova, Seville, Lisbon, Zaragoza, Toledo, Valencia, and elsewhere. Weaker each one by itself than their Christian neighbours, they had to call for help to their Mussulman brethren in Africa. This led to what was really a new African conquest of Mussulman Spain. The new deliverers or conquerors spread their dominion over all the Mussulman powers, save only Zaragoza. This settlement, with other later ones of the same kind, gives a specially African look to the later history of Mahometan Spain, and it has doubtless helped to give the Spanish Mussulmans the common

Invasion of the Almoravides. 1086–1110.

name of *Moors*. But their language and culture remained Arabic, and the revolution caused by the African settlers among the ruins of the Western caliphate was far from being so great as the revolution caused by the Turkish settlers among the ruins of the Eastern caliphate.

Use of the name *Moors*.

Out of the break-up of the dominion of Sancho came the separate kingdom of Navarre, and the new kingdoms of *Castile*, *Aragon*, and *Sobrarbe*. Of these the two last were presently united, thus beginning the advance of Aragon. Thus we come to four of the five historic kingdoms of Spain—Navarre, Castile, Aragon, and Leon, whose unions and divisions are endless. The first king Ferdinand of Castile united Castile and Leon; Castile, Leon, and Gallicia were again for a moment separated under his son. Aragon and Navarre were united for nearly sixty years. Presently Spain has an Emperor in Alfonso of Castile, Leon, and Gallicia. But Empire and kingdom were split asunder. Leon and Castile became separate kingdoms under the sons of Alfonso, and they remained separate for more than sixty years. Their final union created the great Christian power of Spain.

New kingdoms, Castile, Aragon, and Sobrarbe. 1035.

Union of Aragon and Sobrarbe. 1040.

Shiftings of Castile and Leon. 1037.

1065–1073.

1076–1134.

The Emperor Alfonso. 1135.

1157.

Final union of Castile and Leon. 1230.

Navarre meanwhile, cut short by the advance of Castile, shorn of its lands on the Ocean and beyond the Ebro, lost all hope of any commanding position in the peninsula. It passed to a succession of French kings, and for a long time it had no share in the geographical history of Spain. But the power of Aragon grew, partly by conquests from the Mussulmans, partly by union with the French fiefs to the east. The first union between the crown of Aragon and the county of *Barcelona* led to the great growth of the power of

Decline of Navarre.

1234.

Growth of Aragon.

Union with Barcelona. 1131.

CHAP. XII.

1213. Aragon on both sides of the Pyrenees and even beyond the Rhone.[1] This power was broken by the overthrow of King Pedro at Muret. But by the final arrangement which freed *Barcelona*, *Roussillon*, and *Cerdagne*, from all homage to France, all trace of foreign superiority passed away from Christian Spain. The independent kingdom of Aragon stretched on both sides of the Pyrenees, a faint reminder of the days of the West-Gothic kings.

Settlement with France. 1258.

County of Portugal. 1094.

On the other side of the peninsula the lands between Douro and Minho began to form a separate state, a state which was to hold no mean place in the history of Europe, which was first to extend her borders at the cost of the common enemy and then to become the pioneer of European enterprise in distant lands. The county of *Portugal* was held by princes of the royal house of France, as a fief of the crown of Castile and Leon. The county became a kingdom, and its growth cut off Leon, as distinguished from Castile, from any advance against the Mussulmans. Navarre was already cut off from such advance. But the three kingdoms of Castile, Aragon, and Portugal were all ready for the work. A restored Western Christendom was growing up to balance the falling away in the East. The first great advance of the Christians in Spain began about the time of the Seljuk conquests from the Eastern Empire. The work of deliverance was not ended till the Ottoman had been for forty years established in the New Rome.

Kingdom, 1139.

Beginning of the great Christian advance.

The Christian powers however were disunited, while the Mussulmans had again gained, though at a

[1] See above, p. 337.

heavy price, the advantage of union. Alfonso the Sixth, commanding the powers of Castile and Leon, pressed far to the south, and won the old Gothic capital of *Toledo*. But his further advance was checked by the African invaders at the battle of Zalacca. The Almoravide power was too strong for any present hope of conquests on the part of Castile; but the one independent Mussulman state at *Zaragoza* lay open to the Christians of the north-east. Zaragoza itself was taken by the king of Aragon, and *Tarragona* by the Count of Barcelona. Both these powers advanced, and the conquest of *Tortosa* made the Ebro the Christian boundary. As the power of the Almoravides weakened, Castile and Portugal again advanced on their side. The latter kingdom made the great acquisition of its future capital *Lisbon*, and a generation later, it reached the southern coast by the conquest of *Silvas* in Algarve. Castile meanwhile pressed to the Guadiana and beyond, counting *Calatrava* and *Badajoz* among its cities. The line of struggle had advanced in about a century from the land between Douro and Tagus to the land between Guadiana and Guadalquivir.

Conquest of Toledo. 1085.

Battle of Zalacca. 1086.

Advance of the Almoravides.

Advance of Aragon.

Conquest of Zaragoza. 1118.

Of Tarragona.

Of Tortosa. 1148.

Advance of Portugal.

Conquest of Lisbon. 1147.

Of Silvas. 1191.

Advance of Castile. 1147–1166.

This second great Christian advance in the twelfth century was again checked in the same way in which the advance in the eleventh century had been. A new settlement of African conquerors, the *Almohades*, won back a large territory from both Castile and Portugal. The battle of Alarcos broke for a while the power of Castile, and the Almohade dominion stretched beyond the lower Tagus. To the east, the lands south of Ebro remained an independent Mussulman state. But, as the Almohades were of doubtful Mahometan orthodoxy, their hold on Spain was weaker

Invasion of the Almohades. 1146.

Battle of Alarcos. 1196.

Decline of the Almohades.

CHAP. XII.

Battle of Navas de Tolosa. 1211.

than that of any other Mahometan conquerors. Their power broke up, and the battle of Navas de Tolosa ruled that Spain should be a Christian land. All three kingdoms advanced, and within forty years the Mussulman power in the peninsula was cut down to a mere survival.

Conquest of the Balearic Isles. 1228–1236.

Of Valencia. 1237–1305.

Of Murcia. 1243–1253.

Advance of Portugal. 1217–1256.

Kingdom of Algarve.

Aragon won the *Balearic Isles* and formed her kingdom of *Valencia.* But as Castile, by the incorporation of *Murcia*, reached to the Mediterranean, any further advance in the peninsula was forbidden to Aragon. On the eastern side Portugal won back her lost lands, reached her southern coast, kept all the land west of the lower Guadiana and some points to the east of it. To the kingdom of Portugal was added the kingdom of *Algarve.*

Conquest of Castile under Saint Ferdinand.

Conquest of Cordova. 1236.

Of Jaen. 1246.

Of Seville. 1248.

Of Nibla. 1257.

Of Tarifa. 1285.

But the central power of Castile pressed on faster still. Under Saint Ferdinand began the recovery of the great cities along the Guadalquivir. *Cordova*, the city of the caliphs, was won; *Jaen* followed; then more famous *Seville*; and *Cadiz*, eldest of Western cities, passed again, as when she first entered the Roman world, from Semitic into Aryan hands. The conquest of *Nibla* and *Tarifa* at last made the completion of the work only a question of time.

Kingdom of Granada. 1238.

Reconquered from Castile. 1298.

Recovery by Castile. 1316.

1430.

Gibraltar lost and won. 1309.

No one in the middle of the twelfth century could have dreamed that a Mussulman power would live on in Spain till the last years of the fifteenth. This was the kingdom of *Granada*, which began, amid the conquests of Saint Ferdinand, as a vassal state of Castile. Yet, sixty years later, it was able to win back a considerable territory from its overlord. Part of the land now gained was soon lost again; but part, with the city of *Huascar*, was kept by the Mussulmans far into the fifteenth century. Meanwhile, on the strait between the Ocean and the Mediterranean, *Gibraltar* was won by Castile, lost, and won again.

CHAP. XII.

1333. 1344.

Geographical position of the four kingdoms.

Thus, in the latter part of the thirteenth century, the peninsula of Spain was very unequally divided between one Mussulman and four Christian states. Aragon on the one side, Portugal on the other, were kingdoms with a coast line out of all proportion to their extent inwards. Aragon had become a triangle, Portugal a long parallelogram, cut off on each side from the great trapezium formed by the whole peninsula. Between these two lay the central power of Castile, with Christian Navarre still separate at one corner and Mussulman Granada still separate at another. Of these five kingdoms, Navarre and Aragon alone marched to any considerable extent on any state beyond the peninsula. Castile barely touched the Aquitanian dominions of England, while Navarre and Aragon, both stretching north of the Pyrenees, had together a considerable frontier towards Aquitaine and France. Navarre and Aragon again marched on one another, while Portugal and Granada marched only on Castile, the common neighbour of all. The destiny of all was written on the map. Navarre at one end, Granada at the other, were to be swallowed up by the great central power. Aragon, after gaining a high European position, was to be united with Castile under a single sovereign. Portugal alone was to become distinctly a rival of Castile, but wholly in lands beyond the bounds of Europe.

Title of 'King of Spain.'

Of the five Spanish powers Castile so far outtopped the rest that its sovereign was often spoken of in other lands as *King of Spain.* But Spain contained more

The lesser kingdoms.

kingdoms than it contained kings. Castile, Aragon, and Portugal were all formed by a succession of unions and conquests, each of which commonly gave their kings a new title. The central power was still the power of *Castile and Leon*, not of Castile only. *Leon* was made up of the kingdoms of *Leon* and *Gallicia*. Castile took in Castile proper or *Old Castile*, with the principality of the *Asturias*, and the free lands of *Biscay*, *Guipuzcoa*, and *Alava*. To the south it took in the kingdoms—each marking a stage of advance—of *Toledo* or *New Castile*, of *Cordova*, *Jaen*, *Seville*, and *Murcia*. The sovereign of Portugal held his two kingdoms of *Portugal* and *Algarve*. The sovereign of Aragon, besides his enlarged kingdom of *Aragon* and his counties of *Catalonia*, *Roussillon*, and *Cerdagne*, held his kingdom of *Valencia* on the mainland, while
1262. the Balearic Isles formed the kingdom of *Majorca*.
This last, first granted as a vassal kingdom to a branch
1349. of the royal house, was afterwards incorporated with
the Aragonese state.

§ 2. *Growth and Partition of the Great Spanish Monarchy.*

Little geographical change after the thirteenth century.

After the thirteenth century the strictly geographical changes within the Spanish peninsula were but few. The boundaries of the kingdoms changed but little towards one another, and not much towards France, their only neighbour from the fifteenth century onwards. But the five kingdoms were gradually grouped under two kings, for a while under one only. The external geography, so to speak, forms a longer story. We have to trace out the acquisition of territory within

Europe, first by Aragon and then by Castile, and the acquisition of territory out of Europe, first by Portugal and then by Castile. The permanent union of the dominions of Castile and Aragon, the temporary union of the dominions of Castile, Aragon, and Portugal, formed that great *Spanish Monarchy* which in the sixteenth century was the wonder and terror of Europe, which lost important possessions in the sixteenth and in the seventeenth century, and which was finally partitioned in the beginning of the eighteenth.

Territories beyond the peninsula.

The great Spanish Monarchy.

Within the peninsula we have seen Castile, in the first half of the fifteenth century, win back the lands which had been lost to Granada at the end of the fourteenth. The last decade of the fifteenth saw the ending of the struggle. Men fondly deemed that the recovery of Granada balanced the loss of Constantinople. But the last Moorish prince still kept for a moment a small tributary dominion in the Alpujarras, and it was the purchase of this last remnant which finally put an end to the long rule of the Mussulman in Spain.

1410–1430.

Conquest of Granada. 1492.

End of Mussulman rule in Spain.

The conquest of Granada was the joint work of a queen of Castile and a king of Aragon. But the marriage of Ferdinand and Isabel did not at once unite their crowns. That union may be dated from the beginning of Ferdinand's second reign in Castile. Meanwhile *Roussillon* and *Cerdagne* had been, after thirty years' French occupation, won back by Aragon. Then came the conquest of *Navarre* south of the Pyrenees, which left only the small part on the Gaulish side to pass to the French kings of the house of Bourbon. Portugal was now the only separate kingdom in the peninsula,

1469.

Union of Castile and Aragon. 1506.

Loss and recovery of Roussillon. 1462–1493.

Conquest of Navarre. 1513.

CHAP. XII.

and the tendency to look on the peninsula as made up of *Spain* and *Portugal* was of course strengthened.

Annexation and separation of Portugal. 1581–1640.

But later in the century Portugal itself was for sixty years united with Castile and Aragon. Portugal won back its independence; and the Spanish dominion was further cut short by the final loss of *Roussillon*. The Pyrenees were now the boundary of France and Spain, except so far as the line may be held to be broken by the French right of patronage over *Andorra*.[1] Since the Peace of the Pyrenees, the peninsula itself has seen hardly any strictly geographical change. *Gibraltar* has been for nearly two hundred years occupied by England. The fortress of *Olivença* has been yielded by Portugal to Spain. And during the eighteenth century *Minorca* passed to and fro between Spain and England more times than it is easy to remember.[2]

Final loss of Roussillon. 1659.

Gibraltar lost to England, 1704–1713.

Olivença. 1801.

Minorca.

Advance of Aragon beyond the peninsula.

The acquisition of territory beyond the peninsula naturally began with Aragon. The acquisition of the Balearic isles may pass as the enlargement of a peninsular kingdom; but before that happened, Aragon had won and lost what was practically a great dominion north of the Pyrenees. But this dominion was continuous with its Spanish territory. The real beginning of Aragonese dominion beyond the sea was when the war of the Vespers for a moment united the crowns of Aragon and the insular Sicily. Then the island crown was held by independent Aragonese princes, and lastly was again united to the Aragonese crown. The continental Sicily had, during the reign of Alfonso the

Union of Aragon and Sicily. 1282–1285.

Second union of Aragon and Sicily. 1409.

Union of Aragon and continental

[1] See above, p. 345.

[2] Conquered by England 1708. Ceded 1713. Recovered 1756. Ceded to England 1763. Recovered 1782. Conquered by England 1798. Recovered 1802.

Magnanimous, a common king with Aragon and the island. Then the continental kingdom was—save during the momentary French occupations—held by Aragonese princes till the final union of the crowns of Aragon and the Two Sicilies. Meanwhile a war of more than a hundred years gave to Aragon the island of *Sardinia* as a new kingdom. Thus, at the final union of Castile and Aragon, Aragon brought with it the outlying crowns of the Two Sicilies and of Sardinia. The insular Sicilian kingdom was slightly lessened by the grant of *Malta* and *Gozo* to the Knights of Saint John. The continental kingdom was increased by the addition of a small Tuscan territory.

Sicily. 1442–1458. Continental Sicily under Aragonese princes. Final union of Aragon and the Sicilies. 1503. War of Sardinia. 1309–1428. 1530. 1557.

The outlying possessions of Aragon were thus strictly acquisitions made by the Kings of Aragon on behalf of the crown of Aragon. But the extension of Castilian dominion over distant parts of Europe was due only to the fact that the crown of Castile passed to an Austrian prince who had inherited the greater part of the dominions of the Dukes of Burgundy. But thereby the *Netherlands* and the counties of *Burgundy* and *Charolois* became appendages to Castile, and went to swell the great Spanish Monarchy. The duchy of *Milan* too, in whatever character the Emperor Charles held it, became a Spanish dependency when it passed to his son Philip.

Difference between the outlying possessions of Aragon and those of Castile. The Burgundian inheritance. 1504. Duchy of Milan. 1535. 1555.

The European possessions of the Spanish Monarchy thus took in, at the time of their greatest extent, the whole peninsula, the Netherlands and the other Burgundian lands of the Austrian house, Roussillon, the Sicilies, Sardinia, and Milan. But this whole dominion was never held at once, unless for form's sake we count the United Netherlands as Spanish territory till the Twelve Years'

Extent of the Spanish Monarchy. Loss of the United Netherlands.

CHAP. XII. 1578–1609. Truce. Holland and its fellows had become practically independent before Portugal was won. But it was not till after the loss of Portugal that Spain suffered her great losses on the side of France, when the conquests of Lewis the Fourteenth cost her Roussillon, Cerdagne, Charolois, the County of Burgundy, Artois, and other parts of the Netherlands. The remainder of the Netherlands, with Milan and the three outlying Aragonese kingdoms, were kept till the partitions in the beginning of the eighteenth century. The final result of so much fighting and treaty-making was to take away all the outlying possessions of both Aragon and Castile, and to confine the Spanish kingdom to the peninsula and the Balearic isles, less Portugal and Gibraltar for ever, and less Minorca for a season. Since then Spain has never won back any part of the lost possessions of Castile; but she has more than once won back the lost possessions of Aragon, insular Sicily twice, continental Sicily once. And if the Sicilies were not kept as part of the Spanish dominions, they passed to a branch of the Spanish royal house, as the duchies of *Parma* and *Piacenza* passed to another.

Lands lost to France. 1659–1677.

Partition of the Spanish Monarchy. 1713.

Recovery of Sicily. 1718, 1735.

Spanish kings of the Two Sicilies. 1735–1860.

Duchy of Parma. 1731–1860.

§ 3. *The Colonial Dominion of Spain and Portugal.*

The distinction between Spain and Portugal is most strikingly marked in the dominion of the two powers beyond the bounds of Europe. Portugal led the way among European states to conquest and colonization out of Europe. She had a geographical and historical call so to do. Her dominion out of Europe was not indeed a matter of necessity like that of Russia, but it stood on a different ground from that of England,

Character of the Portuguese dominion out of Europe.

CHAP. XII.

France, or Holland. It was not actually continuous with her own European territory, but it began near to it, and it was a natural consequence and extension of her European advance. The Asiatic and American dominion of Portugal grew out of her African dominion, and her African dominion was the continuation of her growth in her own peninsula.

Portugal fully formed in the thirteenth century.

When the Moor was driven out of Spain, it was natural to follow him across the narrow seas into a land which lay so near to Spain, and which in earlier geography had passed as a Spanish land. But as far as Castile was concerned, the Moor was not driven out till late in the fifteenth century; as far as Portugal was concerned, he was driven out in the thirteenth. Portugal had then reached her full extent in the peninsula, and she could no longer advance against the misbelievers by land. One is tempted to wonder that her advance beyond sea did not begin sooner. It came in the fifteenth century, when fifty years of conquest gave to Portugal her kingdom of *Algarve beyond the Sea*, an African dominion older than the Castilian conquest of Granada. The king of *Portugal and the Algarves* thus held the southern pillar of Hercules, while Castile held the northern. The greater part of this African kingdom was lost after the fall of Sebastian. *Ceuta* remained a Spanish possession after the dominion of Portugal, so that Spain now holds the southern pillar and England the northern. *Tangier* too once passed from Portugal to England as a marriage gift, and was presently forsaken as useless.

Her African conquests, 1415–1471.

The Algarves.

Loss of African dominion, 1578.

Ceuta Spanish.

Tangier English, 1662–1683.

Advance in Africa and the islands.

But before the kingdom of Algarve beyond the sea had passed away, its establishment had led to the discovery of the whole coast of the African continent, and

CHAP. XII

Madeira, 1419. Azores and Cape Verde Islands. 1448–1454. to the growth of a vast Portuguese dominion in various parts of the world. *Madeira* was the first insular possession, followed by the *Azores* and *Cape Verde Islands*. Gradually, under the care of Don Henry, the Portuguese power spread along the north-west coast of Africa. Cape of Good Hope, 1497. The work went on: Vasco de Gama made his great discovery of the Cape of Good Hope; the road to India Dominion o Arabia and India. was opened; dominion on the coasts of Arabia and India, and even in the islands of the Indian Archipelago, was added to dominion on the coast of Africa. This dominion perished through the annexation of Portugal by Spain. Since the restoration of Portuguese independence, only fragments of this great African and Indian dominion have been kept. Modern extent of Portuguese dominion abroad. But Portugal still holds the Atlantic islands, various points and coasts in Africa, and a small territory in India and the Eastern islands.

But Portuguese enterprise led also to a more lasting work, to the creation of a new European nation beyond the Ocean, the single European monarchy which has taken root in the New World. *Brazil* was Discovery of Brazil, 1500. discovered by Portuguese sailors at the end of the 1531. fifteenth century; it was settled as a Portuguese possession early in the sixteenth. During the union of 1624–1654. Portugal with Spain the Dutch won for a while a large part of the country, but the whole was won back by independent Portugal. The peculiar position of Portugal, ever threatened by a more powerful neighbour, gave her great Transatlantic dominion a special importance. It was looked to as a possible place for shelter, which it actually became during the French 1807. invasion of Portugal. The Portuguese dominions took Kingdom of Portugal and Brazil, 1813. the style of 'the United Kingdom of Portugal, Brazil, and Algarve.' Nine years later these kingdoms were separated, and Brazil became an independent state. But it remains a monarchy with the title of Empire, and it is still ruled by the direct representative of the Portuguese royal house, while Portugal itself has passed away from the native line by the accidents of female succession.

Empire of Brazil, 1822

In the sixteenth century Brazil held a wholly exceptional position. It was the only settlement of Portugal, it was the only considerable settlement of any European power, in a region which Spain claimed as her exclusive dominion. By Papal authority Spain was to have all the newly found lands that lay to the west, and Portugal all that lay to the east, of a line on the map, drawn at 370 leagues west of the Cape Verde Islands. Spain thus held the whole South American continent, with the exception of Brazil, together with that part of the North American continent which is most closely connected with the southern. While the non-European dominion of Portugal was primarily African and Indian, the non-European dominion of Spain was primarily American. It did not in the same way spring out of the European history of the country; it was rather suggested by rivalry of Portugal. In Africa the Spanish dominion hardly went beyond the possession of *Oran* and the more lasting possession of *Ceuta*. The conquest of *Tunis* by Charles the Fifth[1] was made rather in his Sicilian than in his Castilian character. Within the range of Portuguese dominion the settlements of Spain were exceptional. But they took in the *Canaries* off the Atlantic coast of Africa, and the *Philippine Islands* in the extreme eastern Archi-

Division of the Indies between Spain and Portugal 1494.

Oran, 1516–1708. 1732–1791.

Tunis, 1531.

Insular possessions of Spain

[1] See above, p. 451.

CHAP. XII.

pelago. The Canaries Spain still keeps; the Philippines have passed to the United States of America.

1898.

Spanish dominion in America.

Meanwhile the great Spanish dominion in the New World, in both Americas and in the adjoining islands of the West Indies, had risen and fallen. It began with the first conquest of Columbus, *Hispaniola* or *Saint Domingo*. Thus the dominion of Castile beyond the Ocean began at the very moment when she reached the full extent of her own Mediterranean coast. Then followed the great continental dominion in *Mexico*, *Peru*, and the other lands on or south of the isthmus which joins the two western continents. But into the body of the North American continent, the land which was to be disputed between France and England, Spain never spread. *New Mexico*, *California*, *Florida*, barely stretched along its western and southern coasts. The whole of this continental dominion passed away in a series of revolutions within our own century. While Portugal and England have really founded new European nations beyond the Ocean, the result of Spanish rule in America has been to create a number of states of ever shifting extent and constitution, keeping the Spanish language, but some of which are as much native American as Spanish. Of these *Mexico* is the one which has had most to do with the general history of Europe and European America. It has twice taken the name of Empire, once under a native, once under a foreign, adventurer. And vast provinces, once under its nominal rule, have passed to the United States. The loss of *Texas*, *New Mexico*, and *Upper California*, has cut down the present Mexico nearly to the extent of the first Spanish conquests.

Hispaniola, 1492.

1519.

1532.

Revolutions of the Spanish colonies.

Mexico.

Two Mexican Empires, 1822–1823. 1866–1867.

Cessions to the United States.

Spanish West India

Of the Spanish West India islands, some, like

Jamaica and *Trinidad*, have passed to other European powers. The oldest possession of all, the Spanish part of Hispaniola, has become a state distinct from that of Hayti in the same island. The largest possession of all, *Cuba*, has likewise gained its independence, and in consequence of the same war which won for Cuba her liberty, *Puerto Rico* passed from Spain to the United States. In short, the dominion of Spain out of Europe has followed its European dominion out of Spain. The eighteenth century destroyed the one; the nineteenth century has cut down the other to mere fragments.

islands.

Jamaica, 1655.

Saint Domingo, 1864.

Cuba, 1898.

Puerto Rico, 1898.

CHAPTER XIII.

THE BRITISH ISLANDS AND COLONIES.

CHAP. XIII.

WE have now gone, first through that great mass of European lands which formed part either of the Eastern or of the Western Empire, and then through those more distant, and mainly peninsular, lands which so largely escaped the Imperial dominion. We end by leaving the mainland of Europe, by leaving the world of either Empire, for that great island, or rather group of islands, which for ages was looked on as forming a world of its own. In Western Europe Britain was the last land to be won, and the first to be lost, in the days of the elder Empire. And, after all, Britain itself was only partly won, while the conquest of Ireland was never tried at all. After the English Conquest, Britain had less to do with the revived Western Empire than any Western land except Norway. The momentary dealings of Charles the Great with the Northumbrians and Scots, the doubtful and precarious homage done by Richard the First to Henry the Sixth, are the only exceptions, even in form, to the complete independence of the continental Empire which was maintained by every part of the British islands. The doctrine was that Britain, the other world, formed an Empire of its own. That Empire, being an island, was secured against the constant fluctuations of its external boundary to which continental states lie open. For several

The British islands.

Late Roman conquest and early loss of Britain.

Independence of Britain in the later Empire.

Britain another world and another Empire.

Changes within Britain.

centuries the boundaries, both of the Celtic and Teutonic occupants of Britain and of the Teutonic kingdoms among themselves, were always changing. But these changes hardly affect European history, which is concerned only with the broad general results—with the establishment of the Teutonic settlers in the island—with the union of those settlers in one kingdom under the West-Saxon house—with the extension of the imperial power of the West-Saxon kings over the whole island of Britain. And, from the eleventh century onwards, there has been singularly little change of boundaries within the island. The boundaries of England towards Scotland and Wales changed much less than might have been looked for during ages of such endless warfare. Even the lesser divisions within the English kingdom have been singularly lasting. The land, as a whole, has not been mapped out afresh since the tenth century. While a map of France or Germany in the eleventh century, or even in the eighteenth, is useless for immediate practical objects, a map of England in the days of Domesday practically differs not at all from a map of England now. The only changes of any moment, and they are neither many nor great, are in the shires on the Welsh and Scottish borders.

Slight change in the internal divisions of England.

Thus the historical geography of the isle of Britain comes to little more than a record of these border changes, down to the incorporation of England, Scotland, and Wales into a single kingdom. In the other great island of Ireland there is little to do except to trace how the boundary of English conquest advanced and fell back, a matter after all of no great European concern. The history of the smaller outlying islands,

CHAP. XIII.

from Scandinavian Shetland to the insular Normandy, has really more to do with the general geography of Europe than of either Britain or Ireland. The dominion of the English kings on the continent is of the highest European moment, but, from its geographical side, it is Gaul and not Britain which it affects. The really great geographical phænomenon of English history is that which it shares with Spain and Portugal, and in which it surpasses both. This is the vast extent of outlying English dominion and settlement, partly in Europe, but far more largely in the distant lands of Asia, Africa, America, and Australia. But it is not merely that England has become a great power in all quarters of the world: England has been, like Portugal, but on a far greater scale, a planter of nations. One group of her settlements has grown into one of the great powers of the world, into a third England beyond the Ocean, as far surpassing our insular England in geographical extent as our insular England surpasses the first England of all in the marchland of Germany and Denmark. The mere barbaric dominion of England concerns our present survey but little; but the historical geography of Europe is deeply concerned in the extension of England and of Europe in lands beyond the Western and the Southern Ocean.

English settlements beyond sea.

English nations.

In tracing out the little that we have to say of the geography of Britain itself, it will be well to begin with that northern part of the island where changes have been both more numerous and more important than they have been in England.

§ 1. *The Kingdom of Scotland.*

Historical position of Scotland.

In Northern Britain, as in some other parts of Europe, we see a land which has taken its name from a people to which it does not owe its historic importance. *Scotland* has won for itself a position in Britain and in Europe altogether out of proportion to its size and population. But it has not done this by virtue of its strictly Scottish element. The Irish settlers who first brought the Scottish name into Britain could never have made Scotland what it really became. What founded the greatness of the Scottish kingdom was the fact that part of England gradually took the name of Scotland and its inhabitants took the name of Scots. The case is as when the Duke of Savoy and Genoa and Prince of Piedmont took his highest title from that Sardinian kingdom which was the least valuable part of his dominions. It is as when the ruler of a mighty German realm calls himself king of the small duchy of Prussia and its extinct people. The truth is that, for more than five hundred years, there were two English kingdoms in Britain, each of which had a troublesome Celtic background which formed its chief difficulty. One English king reigned at Winchester or London, and had his difficulties in Wales and afterwards in Ireland. Another English king reigned at Dunfermline or Stirling, and had his difficulties in the true Scotland. But the southern kingdom, ruled by kings of native English or of foreign descent, but never by kings of British or Irish descent,[1] always

Greatness of Scotland due to its English element.

Two English kingdoms in Britain

[1] The Tudor kings were doubtless of British descent; but they did not reign by virtue of that descent, and they did not come in till ages after the English kingdom was completely formed.

CHAP. XIII.

kept the English name, while the northern kingdom, ruled by kings of Scottish descent, adopted the Scottish name. The English subjects of the King of Scots gradually took the Scottish name to themselves. As the present Swiss nation is made up of parts of the German, Burgundian, and Italian nations which have detached themselves from their several main bodies, so the present Scottish nation is made up of parts of the English, Irish, and British nations which have detached themselves from their several main bodies. But in both cases it is the Teutonic element which forms the life and strength of the nation, the kernel to which the other elements have attached themselves. We cannot read the mediæval history of Britain aright, unless we remember that the King of Scots was in truth the English king of Teutonic Lothian and teutonized Fife. The people from whom he took his title were at most his unwilling subjects; they were often his open enemies, the allies of his southern rival.

Extension of the Scottish name. Analogy of Switzerland. Threefold elements in the later Scotland. True position of the King of Scots. Enmity of the true Scots.

Lothian, Strathclyde, and Scotland.

The modern kingdom of Scotland was made up of English *Lothian*, British *Strathclyde*, and Irish *Scotland*. The oldest Scotland is Ireland, whence the Scottish name, long since forgotten in Ireland itself, came into Britain and there spread itself These three elements stand out plainly. But the Scottish or Irish element swallowed up another, that of the *Picts*, of whom there can be no doubt that they were Celts, like the Scots and Britons, but about whom it may be doubted whether their kindred was nearer to the Scots or to the Britons. For our purpose the question is of little moment. The Picts, as far as geography is concerned, either vanished or became Scots.

The Picts.

Early in the ninth century the land north of the firths of Clyde and Forth was still mainly Pictish. The second Scotland (the first Scotland in Britain) had not spread far beyond the original Irish settlement in the south-west. The union of Picts and Scots under a Scottish dynasty created the larger Scotland, the true Celtic Scotland, taking in all the land north of the firths, except where Scandinavian settlers occupied the extreme north. South of the firths, English *Bernicia*, sometimes a separate kingdom, sometimes part of *Northhumberland*, stretched to the firth of Forth, with *Edinburgh* as a border fortress. To the west of Bernicia, south and east of the firth of Clyde, lay the British kingdom of *Cumberland* or *Strathclyde*, with *Alcluyd* or *Dumbarton* as its border fortress. To the south-west again lay the outlying Pictish land of *Galloway*, which long kept up a separate being. Parts of Bernicia, parts of Strathclyde, were one day to join with the true Scotland to make up the later Scottish kingdom. As yet the true Scotland was a foreign and hostile land alike to Bernicia and to Strathclyde.

Position of the Picts and Scots in the ninth century.

Union of Picts and Scots, 843.

The Celtic Scotland.

Bernicia.

Strathclyde or Cumberland.

Galloway.

In the next century we see the Scottish power cut short to the north and west, but advancing towards the south and east. The Northmen have settled in the northern and western islands, in those parts of the mainland to which they gave the names of *Caithness* and *Sutherland*, and even in the first Scottish land in the west. Scotland itself has also admitted the external supremacy of the English overlord. On the other hand, the Scots have pressed within the English border, and have occupied Edinburgh, the border fortress of England. Later in the same century or early in the next, the Kings of Scots received Northern Bernicia,

Settlements of the Northmen.

Caithness.

Scotland acknowledges the English supremacy, 924.

Taking of Edinburgh, c. 954

Cession of Lothian, 966 or 1018.

CHAP. XIII.

the land of *Lothian*, as an English earldom. On the other side, *Strathclyde* or *Cumberland*—its southern boundary is very uncertain—had become in a manner united to England and Scotland at once. An English conquest, it was granted in fief to the King of Scots, and was commonly held as an appanage by Scottish princes.[1] Thus the King of Scots held three dominions on three different tenures. Scotland was a kingdom under a merely external English supremacy; Cumberland was a territorial fief of England; Lothian was an earldom within the English kingdom. In after times these distinctions were forgotten, and the question now was whether the dominions of the King of Scots, as a whole, were or were not a fief of England. When the question took this shape, the English king claimed more than his ancient rights over Scotland, less than his ancient rights over Lothian.

Grant of Cumberland, 945.

Different tenures of the dominion of the King of Scots.

The distinctions forgotten in later controversies.

Effects of the grant of Lothian.

The acquisition of Lothian made the Scottish kingdom English. Lothian remained English; Cumberland and the eastern side of Scotland itself, the Lowlands north of the firth of Forth, became practically English also. The Scottish kings became English princes, whose strength lay in the English part of their dominions. But late in the eleventh century it would seem that the southern part of Cumberland had become a separate principality ruled by a refugee Northumbrian prince under Scottish supremacy. This territory, the city of *Carlisle* and its immediate district, the old diocese of Carlisle, was added to England by William Rufus. On the other hand, in the troubles of Stephen's reign, the king of Scots received two English earldoms, Cumberland—in a somewhat wider

Fate of southern Cumberland.

Carlisle and its district added to England by William Rufus, 1092.

Cumberland and Northumberland granted to David, 1136

[1] See Norman Conquest, vol. i. p. 580.

sense—and *Northumberland* in the modern sense, the land from the Tweed to the Tyne. Had these earldoms been kept by the Scottish kings, they would doubtless have become Scottish lands in the same sense in which Lothian did; that is, they would have become parts of the northern English kingdom. But Northumberland and Cumberland were won back by Henry the Second; and the boundary has since remained as it was then fixed, save that the town of *Berwick* fluctuated according to the accidents of war between one kingdom and the other.

Recovered by England, 1157.

The boundary permanent, except as to Berwick.

Relations between England and Scotland.

But though the boundaries of the kingdoms were fixed, their relations were not. Scotland in the modern sense—that is, Scotland in the older sense, Lothian, and Strathclyde—was for a moment held strictly as a fief of England. It was then for another moment 1292.
incorporated with England. It was then acknowledged 1296.
as an independent kingdom. It again fell under 1327.
vassalage for a moment, and again won its independ- 1333.
ence. Then, at the beginning of the seventeenth 1603.
century, England and Scotland, as distinct, independent, and equal kingdoms, passed under a common king. They were separated again for a moment when Scotland 1649.
acknowledged a king whom England rejected. For another moment Scotland was incorporated with an 1652.
English commonwealth. Again Scotland and England became independent kingdoms under a common king, 1660.
till the two kingdoms were, by common consent, joined 1707.
in the one kingdom of *Great Britain*.

Struggle with the Northmen. Scandinavian advance, 1014–1064.

Meanwhile the Scottish kings had, like those of England somewhat earlier, to struggle against Scandinavian invaders. The settlements of the Northmen

CHAP. XIII.

advanced, and for some years in the eleventh century they took in *Moray* at one end and *Galloway* at the other. But it was only in the extreme north and in the northern islands that the land really became Scandinavian. In the *Sudereys* or *Hebrides*—the southern islands as distinguished from Orkney and Shetland—and in *Man*, the Celtic speech has survived. *Caithness* was brought under Scottish supremacy early in the thirteenth century. *Galloway* was incorporated. Later again, after the battle of Largs, the Sudereys and Man passed under Scottish supremacy. But the authority of the Scottish crown in the islands was for a long time very precarious. Man, the most central of the British isles, lying at a nearly equal distance from England, Scotland, Ireland, and Wales, remained a separate kingdom, sometimes under Scottish, sometimes under English, superiority. Granted to English subjects, the kingdom sank to a lordship. The lordship was united to the crown of Great Britain, and Man, like the Norman islands, remains a distinct possession, forming no part of the United Kingdom. The earldom of Orkney meanwhile remained a Norwegian dependency till it was pledged to the Scottish crown. Since then it has silently become part, first of the kingdom of Scotland, and then of the kingdom of Great Britain.

The Sudereys, and Man. *Caithness submits, 1203.* *Galloway incorporated, 1235.* *Sudereys and Man submit, 1263–1266.* *History of Man.* *1764–1826.* *Orkney, 1469.*

§ 2. *The Kingdom of England.*

Harold's conquests from Wales, 1063. *Enlargement of the border shires.*

The changes of boundary between England and *Wales* begin, as far as we are concerned with them, with the great Welsh campaign of Harold. All the border shires, Cheshire, Shropshire, Herefordshire, Gloucestershire, seem now to have been enlarged; the

English border stretched to the *Conwy* in the north, and to the *Usk* in the south. But part of this territory seems to have been recovered by the Welsh princes, while part passed into the great *march* district of England and Wales, ruled by the Lords Marchers. The gradual conquest of South Wales began under the Conqueror and went on under his sons; but it was more largely the work of private adventurers than of the kings themselves. The lands of *Morganwg*, *Breheiniog*, *Dyfed*, and *Ceredigion*, answering nearly to the modern South Wales, were gradually subdued. In some districts, especially in the southern part of the present Pembrokeshire, the Britons were actually driven out, and the land was settled by Flemish colonists, the latest of the Teutonic settlements in Britain. Elsewhere Norman lords, with a Norman, English, and Flemish following, held the towns and the more level country, while the Welsh kept on a half independence in the mountains. Meanwhile in North Wales native princes—*Princes of Aberffraw* and *Lords of Snowdon*—still ruled, as vassals of the English king, till the war of Edward the First. In the first stage the vassal prince was compelled again to cede to his overlord the territory east of the Conwy. Six years later followed the complete conquest. But complete incorporation with England did not at once follow. Wales, North and South, remained a separate dominion, giving the princely title to the eldest son of the English king. Some shires were formed; some new towns were founded; the border districts remained under the anomalous jurisdiction of the Marchers. The full incorporation of the principality and its marches dates from Henry the Eighth. Thirteen new counties were

The Marches.

Conquest of South Wales, 1070–1121.

Flemish settlement in Pembrokeshire, 1111.

Character of the conquest of South Wales.

Princes of North Wales.

Cessions to England, 1277.

Conquest of North Wales, 1282.

The Principality of Wales.

Full incorporation. 1535.

formed, and some districts were added or restored to the border shires of England. One of the new counties, *Monmouthshire*, was, under Charles the Second, added to an English circuit, and it has since been reckoned as an English county.

The Domesday shires.

Setting aside these new creations, all the existing shires of England were in being at the time of the Norman Conquest, save those of *Lancaster*, *Cumberland*, *Westmoreland*, and *Rutland*. The boundaries were not always exactly the same as at present; but the differences are commonly slight and of mere local interest.

Two classes of shires.

Ancient kingdoms and principalities.

The shires, as they stood at the Conquest, were of two classes. Some were old kingdoms or principalities, which still kept their names and boundaries as shires. Such were the kingdoms of *Kent*, *Sussex*, and *Essex*, and the East-Anglian, West-Saxon, and Northumbrian shires. Most of these keep old local or tribal names; a few only are called from a town.

Mercian shires mapped out in the tenth century.

In Mercia on the other hand, the shires seem to have been mapped out afresh when the land was won back from the Danes. They are called after towns, and the town which gives the name commonly lies central to the district, and remains the chief town of the shire, except when it has been outstripped by some other in modern times.[1] Both classes of shires survived the Conquest, and both have gone on till now with very slight changes.

On the Welsh border, all the shires, for reasons already given, stretch further west in Domesday than they do now.

Cumberland and Westmoreland.

On the Scottish border *Cumberland* and *Westmoreland* were made out of the Cumbrian conquest of William Rufus, enlarged by districts which

[1] See Norman Conquest, vol. i. p. 48; and Macmillan's Magazine, April, 1880.

in Domesday appear as part of Yorkshire. *Lancashire* was made up of lands taken from Yorkshire and Cheshire, the Ribble forming the older boundary of those shires. The older divisions are marked by the boundaries of the dioceses of *York*, *Carlisle*, and *Lichfield* or *Chester*, as they stood down to the changes under Henry the Eighth. In central England the only change is the formation of the small shire of *Rutland* out of the Domesday district of Rutland (which, oddly enough, appears as an appendage to *Nottinghamshire*), enlarged by a small part of what was then *Northamptonshire*.

CHAP. XIII.

Lancashire.

Rutland.

§ 3. *Ireland.*

The second great island of the British group, *Ireland*, the original *Scotia*, has had less to do with the general history of the world than any other part of Western Europe. Its ancient divisions have lived on from the earliest times. The names of its five great provinces, *Ulster*, *Meath*, *Leinster*, *Munster*, and *Connaught*, are all in familiar use, though *Meath* has sunk from its old rank alongside of the other four. The Celtic inhabitants of the island remained independent of foreign powers till the days of Scandinavian settlement. Just like the English kingdoms in Britain, the great divisions of Ireland were sometimes independent, sometimes united under the supremacy of a head king. Gradually the Northmen, called in Ireland *Ostmen*, formed settlements on the coast, and held some of the chief ports, as *Dublin*, *Waterford*, *Wexford*, two of which names bear witness to Teutonic occupation.[1] The great Irish victory

Ireland the first Scotland.

The five provinces

Settlement of the Ostmen.

Irish victory at Clontarf. 1012.

[1] [It may be noticed that the terminations of the names of the three provinces, *Mun-ster*, *Lein-ster*, and *Ul-ster*, are Scandinavian additions to the native names, *Mumu*, *Laigin*, and *Ulaid*.]

CHAP. XIII.

Increasing connexion with England.

at Clontarf weakened, but did not destroy, the Scandinavian power. And, from the latter half of the tenth century onward, the eastern coast of Ireland shows a growing connexion with England. Whether any actual English supremacy ever existed is extremely doubtful; but both commercial and ecclesiastical ties became closer during the eleventh and twelfth centuries.

The English conquest, 1169–1652.

This connexion led to the actual English conquest of
Ireland, begun under Henry the Second, but really
finished only by Cromwell. All Ireland admitted for a
1171. moment the supremacy of Henry; but, till the sixteenth
Fluctuations of the Pale. century, the actual English dominion, called the *Pale*,
with Dublin for its centre, was always fluctuating, and
for a while it fell back rather than advanced.

Kingdom and Lordship of Ireland.

In the early days of the conquest Ireland is spoken
of as a kingdom; but the title soon went out of use.
The original plan seems to have been that Ireland, like
Wales afterwards, should form an appanage for a son
of the English King. It became instead, so far as it
was an English possession at all, a simple dependency
of England, from which the King took the title of *Lord*
1542. *of Ireland*. Henry the Eighth took the title of *King*
Relations of Ireland to England. *of Ireland*; but the kingdom remained a mere dependency, attached to the crown, first of England and then
of Great Britain. This state of things was diversified
1652. by a short time of complete incorporation under the
1689. Commonwealth, and a short time of independence
under James the Second. But for the last eighteen
1782–1800. years of the eighteenth century, Ireland was formally
acknowledged as an independent kingdom, connected
1801. with Great Britain only by the tie of a common king.
Since that time it has formed an integral part of the
United Kingdom of Great Britain and Ireland.

§ 4. *Outlying European Possessions of England.*

Ireland, the sister island of Britain, has thus been united with Britain into a single kingdom. Man, lying between the two, remains a distinct dependency. This last is also still the position of that part of the Norman duchy which clave to its own dukes, which never became French, but always remained Norman. It might be a question what was the exact position of *Guernsey*, *Jersey*, *Alderney*, *Sark*, and their smaller neighbours, when the English kings took the titles of the French kingdom and actually held the Norman duchy. Practically the islands have, during all changes, remained attached to the English crown; but they have never been incorporated with the kingdom. Other more distant European lands have been, some still are, in the same position. Such were *Aquitaine*, *Ponthieu*, and *Calais*, as fixed by the Peace of Bretigny. Since the loss of Aquitaine, England has had no considerable continental dominion in Europe, but she has from time to time held several islands and detached points. Such are *Calais*, *Boulogne*, *Dunkirk*, *Gibraltar*, *Minorca*, *Malta*, *Heligoland*, all of which have been spoken of in their natural geographical places. To these we may add *Tangier*, which has more in common with the possession of Gibraltar and Minorca than with the English settlements in the further parts of Africa. Of these points, Gibraltar, and Malta, are still held by England. The virtual English possession of the *Ionian Islands* made England for a while a sharer in the fragments of the Eastern Roman Empire. And later still she has again put on the same character by

The Norman Islands. 1805.

Other European dependencies, Aquitaine, &c.

Outposts and islands.

Greek possessions, Ionian Islands, 1814–1864.

Cyprus, 1878.

CHAP. XIII.

the occupation, on whatever terms, of another Greek and Imperial land, the island of *Cyprus*.

§ 5. *The American Colonies of England.*

Colonies of England.

England, like France and Holland, became a colonizing power by choice. Extension over barbarian lands was not a necessity, as in the case of Russia, nor did it spring naturally out of earlier circumstances, as in the case of Portugal. But the colonizing enterprise of England has done a greater work than the colonizing enterprise of any other European power. The greatest colony of England—for in a worthier use of language the word *colony* would imply independence rather than dependence[1]—is that great Confederation which is to us what Syracuse was to Corinth, what Milêtos was to Athens, what Gades and Carthage were to the cities of the older Canaan. The *United States of America*, a vaster England beyond the Ocean, an European power, on a level with the greatest European powers, planted beyond the bounds of Europe, form the great work of English and European enterprise in non-European lands.

The United States.

First English settlements in North America, 1497.

The settlements which grew into the United States were not the first English possessions in North America, but they were the first which really deserved to be called colonies. The first discoveries of all led only to the establishment of the *Newfoundland* fisheries. Raleigh's attempts at real colonization ninety years later only pointed the way to something more lasting. In the seventeenth century began the planting of the

Attempts of Raleigh, 1585–1587.

The Thirteen Colonies.

[1] The Latin *colonia* certainly does not imply independence; but the word *colony*, in our use of it, rather answers to the Greek ἀποικία, which does.

thirteen settlements which won their independence.
Of these the earliest and the latest, the most southern
and the most northern, began through English coloniza-
tion in the strictest sense. First came *Virginia*. Then Virginia, 1607.
followed the Puritan colonization much further to the
north which founded the *New England* states. The The New England States, 1620–1638.
shiftings among these settlements, from *Plymouth* to
Maine, the unions, the divisions, the colonies of colonies
—the Epidamnos and the Sinôpê of the New World—
the various and varying relations between the different
settlements, read like a piece of old Greek or of Swiss
history.[1] By the end of the seventeenth century they 1629–1692.
had arranged themselves into four separate colonies.
These were *Massachusetts*, formed by the union of *Mas-sachusetts* and *Plymouth*, with its northern dependency
of *Maine*, which became a separate State long after the 1820.
Revolution; *New Hampshire*, annexed by Massachusetts
and after a while separated from it; *Connecticut*, formed
by the union of *Connecticut* and *Newhaven*; *Rhode Island*,
formed by the union of *Rhode Island* and *Providence*.
These New England States form a distinct geographical
group, with a marked political and religious character
of their own. Meanwhile, at some distance to the The Southern Colonies.
south, around Virginia as their centre, grew up another

[1] It may be well to give the dates in order:—

Plymouth	1620	Rhode Island and Providence united	1644
Massachusetts	1628	Connecticut and Newhaven united	1664
New Hampshire	1629	New Hampshire separated from Massachusetts	1671
Connecticut	1635	Maine purchased by Massachusetts	1677
Newhaven	1638	Plymouth and Massachusetts united	1691
Providence	1644		
Rhode Island	1634		
Maine	1638		
New Hampshire annexed by Massachusetts	1641		

CHAP. XIII.

Maryland. 1634. Carolina, 1650–1663. Divided, 1720.

group of colonies, with a history and character in many ways unlike those of New England. To the north of Virginia arose the proprietary colony of *Maryland*; to the south arose *Carolina*, afterwards divided into *North* and *South*. South Carolina for a long while marked the end of English settlement to the south, as Maine did to the north.

Intermediate space occupied by the United Provinces and Sweden.

But between these two groups of English colonies in the strictest sense lay a region in which English settlement took the form of conquest from another European power. Earlier than any English settlement except Virginia, the great colony of the United Provinces had arisen on Long Island and the neighbouring mainland. It bore the name of *New Netherlands*, with its capital of *New Amsterdam*. To the south, on the shores of Delaware Bay, the other great power of the seventeenth century founded the colony of *New Sweden*. Three European nations, closely allied in race, speech, and creed, were thus for a while established side by side on the eastern coasts of America. But the three settlements were fated to merge together, and that by force of arms. A local war added New Sweden to New Netherlands; a war between England and the United Provinces gave New Netherlands to England. New Amsterdam became *New York*, and gave its name to the colony which was to become the greatest State of the Union. Ten years later, in the next war between the two colonizing powers, the new English possession was lost and won again.

New Netherlands, 1614. New Sweden, 1658. Union of New Sweden with New Netherlands, 1655. English conquest of New Netherlands, 1664. New York. 1674.

The Jerseys. 1665.

Meanwhile the gap which was still left began to be filled up by other English settlements. *East* and *West Jersey* began as two distinct colonies, which were afterwards united into one. The great colony of *Pennsyl-*

1702.

CHAP. XIII.

vania next arose, from which the small one of *Delaware* was parted off twenty years later. Pennsylvania was thus the last of the original settlements of the seventeenth century, which in the space of nearly eighty years had been formed fast after one another. Fifty years after the work of the benevolent Penn came the work of the no less benevolent Oglethorpe; *Georgia*, to the south of all, now filled up the tale of the famous Thirteen, the fitting number, it would seem, for a Federal power, whether in the Old World or in the New.

Pennsylvania, 1682. Delaware, 1703. Georgia, 1733.

By the Peace of Paris the Thirteen Colonies were acknowledged as independent States. The great work of English settlement on foreign soil was brought to perfection. The new and free English land beyond the Ocean took in the whole temperate region of the North American coast, all between the peninsula of *Acadia* to the north and the other peninsula of *Florida* to the south. Both of these last lands were English possessions at the time of the War of Independence, but neither of them had any share in the work. Acadia, under the name of *Nova Scotia*, had been ceded by France in the interval between the settlement of Pennsylvania and the settlement of Georgia. Next came the conquest of *Canada*, in which the men of the colonies played their part. Hitherto the English colonies had been shut in to the west by the French claim to the line of the Alleghany mountains. The Treaty of Paris took away this bugbear, and left the whole land as far as the Mississippi open to the enterprise of the English colonists. Thus, when the Thirteen States started on their independent career, the whole land between the great lakes, the Ocean, and the Mississippi, was open to them. Florida

Independence of the United States, 1783.

Nova Scotia, 1713.

Conquest of Canada, 1759–1763.

The French barrier at Alleghany.

Florida

CHAP. XIII.

indeed, first as an English, then again as a Spanish possession, cut them off from the Gulf of Mexico. The city of *New Orleans* remained, first a Spanish, then a French, outpost east of the Mississippi, and the possessions still held by England kept them from the mouth of the Saint Lawrence. But within these limits, such of the old States as were allowed by their geographical position might extend themselves to the west, and new States might be formed. Both processes went on, and two of the barriers formed by European powers were removed. The purchase of *Louisiana* from France, the acquisition of *Florida* from Spain, gave the States the seaboard of the Gulf of Mexico, and allowed their extension to the Pacific. The details of that extension, partly by natural growth, partly at the expense of the Spanish element in North America, it is hardly needful to go through here. But, out of the English settlements on the North-American coast, a new English nation has arisen, none the less English, in a true view of history, because it no longer owes allegiance to the crown of Great Britain. But the power thus formed, exactly like earlier confederations in Europe, lacks a name. The *United States of America* is hardly a geographical or a national name, any more than the names of the *Confederates* and the *United Provinces*. In the two European cases common usage gave the name of a single member of the Union to the whole, and in the case of Switzerland the popular name at last became the formal name. In the American case, on the other hand, popular usage speaks of the Confederation by the name of the whole continent of which its territory forms part. For several purposes, the words *America* and *American* are always understood as shutting out Canada and Mexico, to say

again Spanish, 1781–1821.

Extension to the West.

Louisiana, 1803.

Florida, 1821.

A new English nation.

Lack of a name.

Use of the word *America*.

nothing of the southern American continent. For some other purposes, those names still take in the whole American continent, north and south. But it is easier to see the awkwardness of the usual nomenclature than to suggest any improvement on it.

Second English nation in North America.

While one set of events in the eighteenth century created an independent English nation on North American soil, another set of events in the same century, earlier in date but later in their results, has led to the formation in its immediate neighbourhood of another English nation which still keeps its allegiance to the English crown. A confederation of states, practically independent in their internal affairs, but remaining subjects of a distant sovereign, is a novelty in political science. Such is the *Confederation of British North America*. But this dependent Confederation did not arise out of colonization in the same sense as the independent Confederation to the south of it. The central land which gives it its character is the conquered land of *Canada*. Along with Canada came the possession of the smaller districts which received the names of *New Brunswick* and *Prince Edward's Island*, districts which were at first joined to Nova Scotia, but which afterwards became distinct colonies. Now they are joined with the *Dominion of Canada*, which, like the United States, grows by the incorporation of new states and territories. The addition of *British Columbia* has carried the Confederation to the Pacific; that of *Rupertsland* carries it indefinitely northward towards the pole. This second English-speaking power in North America stretches, like the elder one, from Ocean to Ocean. *Newfoundland* alone, a possession

Dependent confederacy.

British North America.

New Brunswick, &c.

The Dominion, 1867.

British Columbia, 1871. Rupertsland.

Newfoundland, 1713.

CHAP. XIII.

secured to England after many debates at the same time as Nova Scotia, remains distinct.

The West Indies. Barbadoes, 1605. Jamaica, 1655. Smaller settlements.

Of the British possessions in the *West Indies* a few only, among them *Barbadoes*, the earliest of all, were colonies in the same sense as Virginia and Massachusetts. The greater number, *Jamaica* at their head, were won by conquest from other European powers. No new English nation, like the American and the Canadian, has grown up in them. Still less is there any need to dwell on the *Bahamas*, the *Falkland Islands*, or the South-American possession of *British Guiana*.

§ 6. *Other Colonies and Possessions of England.*

Colonies in the southern hemisphere. Australia. South Africa.

The story of the North-American colonies may be both compared and contrasted with the story of two great groups of colonies in the southern hemisphere. In Australia and the other great southern islands, a body of English colonies have arisen, the germs at least of yet another English nation, but which have not as yet reached independence, though the Australian colonies including Tasmania have formed a federal state within the British Empire. In South Africa, another group of possessions and colonies, beginning, like Canada, in conquest from another European power, may likewise feel their way towards confederation.

New South Wales, 1787.

The beginning of English settlement in the greatest of islands began in the years which immediately followed the establishment of American independence. First came *New South Wales*, on the eastern coast, designed originally as a penal settlement. It outgrew this stage, and another penal settlement was founded in *Western Australia*. Then colonization spread into the intermediate region of *Southern Australia* (which however stretches right through the island to its northern coast) into the district called *Victoria*, south-west of the original settlement, and lastly, into *Queensland* to the north-east. Since the middle of the nineteenth century all these colonies have gradually established constitutions which give them full internal independence. South of the great island lies one smaller, but still vast, that of *Van Diemen's Land*, now *Tasmania*, which was settled earlier than any Australian settlement except New South Wales. And to the east lie the two great islands of *New Zealand*, where six English colonies founded at different times have been united into one.

Western Australia, 1829. South Australia, 1836. Victoria, 1837. Queensland, 1859. Colonies' Act, 1850. Tasmania, 1804. 1839. Six colonies, 1852. United, 1875.

While the Australian settlements were colonies in the strictest sense, the English possessions in South Africa began, like New York, in a settlement first planted by the United Provinces. The *Cape Colony*, after some shiftings during the French revolutionary wars, was conquered by England, and its possession by England was confirmed at the general peace. Migration northward, both of the English and Dutch inhabitants, has produced new settlements, as the *Eastern Colony* and *Natal*. British dominion gradually pushed north-eastward from Cape Colony to join Natal, a process which was completed by the annexation of *Pondoland*. All this territory was incorporated in Cape Colony, to which were also added on the west Walfish Bay and a number of islets off the coast of the barren territory which Germany has made into a *South-west African Protectorate*. On the other side Natal has been enlarged by the acquisition of Zululand and Tongaland. Meanwhile independent Dutch states had arisen, as the

South Africa. Conquest of the Cape, 1806. 1815. Eastern Colony and Natal, 1820–1836. Pondoland, 1894. German Protectorate, 1894. (1897.)

CHAP. XIII.

Orange River State, 1847–1856. Transvaal, 1861–1877. South African Republic, 1884–1900. Orange River Colony and Transvaal Colony, 1900.

Orange River Republic, annexed by England, then set free, then dismembered and the *Transvaal* annexed after sixteen years of independence, and then established under British suzerainty as the *South African Republic*. Sixteen years later the free Dutch state known as the *Orange Free State*, the remnant of the Orange River Republic, was annexed under the name of the *Orange River Colony*, and the semi-dependent South African Republic (which had meanwhile extended its border on the side of Zululand by annexing a region known as the New Republic) was reduced to the condition of a colony under its old name of the *Transvaal*. The annexation of *British Bechuanaland* to the north of Cape Colony, and the establishment of a protectorate beyond it, were followed by the acquisition (by the British South Africa Company) of the large territory known as *Rhodesia* to the north of the Transvaal. Thus all the African continent south of the Zambesi is British, with the exceptions of the German Protectorate in the west and the Portuguese colony of Delagoa in the east.

British Bechuanaland, 1894. Rhodesia, 1899.

Europe extended by colonization.

In all these cases of real colonization, of real extension of the English or any other European nation, it is hardly a figure to say that the bounds of Europe have been enlarged. All that makes Europe Europe, all that parts off Europe from Africa and Asia, has been carried into America and Australia and Africa itself. The growth of this new Europe, no less than the changes of the old, is an essential part of European geography. It is otherwise with territories, great or small, which have been occupied by England and other European powers merely for military or

Barbarian dominion.

commercial purposes. Forts, factories, or empires, on barbarian soil, where no new European nation is likely ever to grow up, are not cases of true colonization; they are no extension of the bounds of Europe. The climax of this kind of barbarian dominion is found in those vast Indian possessions in which England has supplanted Portugal, France, and the heirs of Timour. Of that dominion the scientific frontier has yet to be traced; yet it has come to give an Imperial title to the sovereign of Great Britain and Ireland, while those two European islands, as perhaps befits their inferiority in physical size, remain content with the lowlier style of the United Kingdom. Whether the loftier pretensions of Asia do, or do not, imply any vassalage on the part of Europe, it is certain that the Asiatic Empire of the sovereign of the British kingdom is no extension of England, no extension of Europe, no creation of a new English or European nation. The Empire of India stands outside the European world, outside the political system which has gathered round the Old and the New Rome. But a place amongst the foremost members of that system belongs to the great European nation on American soil, where the tongue of England is kept, and the constitution of old Achaia is born again, in a confederation stretching from the Western to the Eastern Ocean.

English dominion in India.

Empire of India, 1876.

We have thus traced the geography, and in tracing the geography we have in a slighter way traced the history, of the various states and powers of Europe, and of the lands beyond the Ocean which have been planted from Europe. We have throughout kept steadily before our eyes the centre, afterwards the

Summary.

CHAP. XIII.

two centres, of European life. We have seen how the older states of Europe gradually lose themselves in the dominion of Rome, how the younger states gradually spring out of the dominion of Rome. We have followed, as our central subjects, the fates of those powers in the East and West which continued the Roman name and Roman traditions. We have traced out the states which were directly formed by splitting off from those powers, and the states which arose beyond the range of Roman power, but not beyond the range of Roman influence. We have seen the Western Empire first pass to a German prince, then gradually shrink into a German kingdom, to be finally dissolved into a German confederation. We have watched the states which split off at various dates from its body, the power of France on one side, the power of Austria on another, the powers of Italy on a third, the free states of Switzerland at one end, the free states of the Netherlands at the other. We have beheld the long tragedy of the Eastern Rome; we have told the tale of the states which split off from it and arose around it. We have seen its territorial position pass to a barbarian invader, and something like its position in men's minds pass to the mightiest of its spiritual disciples. And we have seen, painted on the map of our own age, the beginning of the great work which is giving back the lands of the Eastern Rome to their own people. We have then traced the shiftings of the powers which lay wholly or partly beyond the bounds of either Empire, the great Slavonic mainland, the Scandinavian and the Iberian peninsulas, ending with that which is geographically the most isolated land of all, the other world of Britain. We have seen too how Europe may be said to have spread herself beyond her geographical limits in the foundation of new European states beyond the Ocean. We have contrasted the different positions and destinies of the colonizing European powers—where, as in the days of Old Rome, a continuous territory has been extended over neighbouring barbarian lands—where growth beyond the sea was the natural outcome of growth at home—where European powers have colonized and conquered simply of their own free will. In thus tracing the historical geography of Europe, we have made the round of the world. But we have never lost sight of Europe; we have never lost sight of Rome. Wherever we have gone, we have carried Europe with us; wherever we have gone, we have never got beyond the power of the two influences which, mingling into one, have made Europe all that it has been. The whole of European history is embodied in the formula which couples together the 'rule of Christ and Cæsar;' and that joint rule still goes on, in the shape of moral influence, wherever the tongues and the culture of Europe win new realms for themselves in the continents of the western or in the islands of the southern Ocean.

INDEX